CENSUS OF INDIA 1921

Census of India 1871-1951, 9 Sets In 384 Bindings (9788121258876) Rs. 700000

Census of India 1921, 25 Vols. In 44 Bindings (9788121271257) Rs. 71000

1. India - Report (9788121277198) Rs. 1875 (Vol. I, Pt. 1)
2. India - Tables (9788121277174) Rs. 1790 (Vol. I, Pt. 2)
3. The Andaman And Nicobar Islands - Report & Tables (9788121277150) Rs. 500 (Vol. II, Pt. 1 & 2)
4. Assam - Report (9788121277136) Rs. 1200 (Vol. III, Pt. 1)
5. Assam - Tables and Administrative Report (9788121277112) Rs. 2070 (Vol. III, Pt. 2)
6. Baluchistan - Report & Tables (9788121277099) Rs. 1425 (Vol. IV, Pt. 1 & 2)
7. Bengal - Report (9788121277075) Rs. 2300 (Vol. V, Pt. 1)
8. Bengal - Tables and Administrative (9788121277051) Rs. 2800 (Vol. V, Pt. 2 & 3)
9. City of Calcutta - Report (9788121277013) Rs. 690 (Vol. VI, Pt. 1)
10. City of Calcutta - Tables (9788121276993) Rs. 825 (Vol. VI, Pt. 2)
11. Bihar And Orissa - Report (9788121276979) Rs. 1600 (Vol. VII, Pt.1)
12. Bihar And Orissa - Tables (9788121276955) Rs. 1425 (Vol. VII, Pt.2)
13. Bombay Presidency - General Report (9788121276931) Rs. 2500 (Vol. VIII, Pt. 1)
14. Bombay Presidency - Tables (Imperial And Provincial) and Report And Tables - Aden (9788121276917) Rs. 2580 (Vol. VIII, Pt. 2 & 3)
15. Bombay Presidency - Administrative Report (9788121276870) Rs. 540 (Vol. VIII, Pt. 4)
16. Cities of The Bombay Presidency - Report (9788121276856) Rs. 775 (Vol. IX, Pt. 1)
17. Cities of The Bombay Presidency - Tables (9788121276832) Rs. 1625 (Vol. IX, Pt. 2)
18. Burma - Report (9788121276818) Rs. 1650 (Vol. X, Pt. 1)
19. Burma - Tables and Administrative (9788121276795) Rs. 3070 (Vol. X, Pt. 2 & 3)
20. Central Provinces And Berar - Report (9788121276757) Rs. 1100 (Vol. XI, Pt. 1)
21. Central Provinces And Berar - Tables (9788121276733) Rs. 2200 (Vol. XI, Pt. 2)
22. Coorg - Report & Tables and Madras - Report (9788121276696) Rs. 1950 (Vol. Vol. XIII, Pt. 1)
23. Madras - Imperial And Provincial Tables and Provincial Tables and Administrative Report (9788121276672) Rs. 2900 (Vol. XIII, Pt. 2 & 3 & 4)
24. North - West Frontier Province - Report & Tables (9788121276610) Rs. 2800 (Vol. XIV, Pt. 1 & 2)
25. Punjab And Delhi - Report (9788121276597) Rs. 2360 (Vol. XV, Pt. 1)
26. Punjab And Delhi - Tables (9788121276573) Rs. 2275 (Vol. XV, Pt. 2)
27. Punjab And Delhi - Administrtive (9788121276559) Rs. 500 (Vol. XV, Pt. 4)
28. United Provinces of Agra & Oudh - Report (9788121276535) Rs. 1300 (Vol. XVI, Pt. 1)
29. United Provinces of Agra & Oudh - Imperial Tables & Administrative Report (9788121276511) Rs. 2490 (Vol. XVI, Pt. 2 & 3)
30. Baroda State - Report (9788121276498) Rs. 2300 (Vol. XVII, Pt. 1)
31. Baroda State - Imperial Tables (9788121276474) Rs. 740 (Vol. XVII-A, Pt. 2)
32. Baroda State - State Tables (9788121276450) Rs. 780 (Vol. XVII-B, Pt. 3)
33. Census India Agency - Report & Tables & Administrative Report (9788121276436) Rs. 1610 (Vol. XVIII, Pt. 1 & 2 & 3)
34. Cochin - Report & Imperial Tables (9788121276412) Rs. 1460 (Vol. XIX, Pt. 1 & 2)
35. Gwalior - Report & Tables (9788121276399) Rs. 1725 (Vol. XX)
36. Hyderabad State - Report (9788121276375) Rs. 1740 (Vol. XXI, Pt. 1)
37. Hyderabad State - Imperial Tables (9788121276351) Rs. 1400 (Vol. XXI, Pt. 2)
38. Kashmir - Report (9788121276337) Rs. 1190 (Vol. XXII, Pt. 1)
39. Kashmir - Tables and Final Report (9788121276313) Rs. 1370 (Vol. XXII, Pt. 2 & 3)
40. Mysore - Report (9788121276290) Rs. 900 (Vol. XXIII, Pt. 1)
41. Mysore - Tables and Administrative Report (9788121276276) Rs. 1820 (Vol. XXIII, Pt. 2 & 3)
42. Rajputana And Ajmer-merwara - Report (9788121276238) Rs. 1600 (Vol. XXIV, Pt. 1)
43. Rajputana And Ajmer-merwara - Tables (9788121276214) Rs. 1840 (Vol. XXIV, Pt. 2)
44. Travancore - Report & Imperial Tables and Administrative Report (9788121276191) Rs. 1750 (Vol. XXV, Pt. 1 & 2 & 5)

Owing to the antiquity and rarity of this book, certain pages are regrettably absent, and readability is compromised due to the blurring of the original text. If you possess any insights regarding the availability of these missing sections, kindly inform us. Your assistance is crucial in ensuring the completion of this significant work for the benefit of future generations.

CENSUS OF INDIA, 1921

VOLUME - XXII

KASHMIR

PART II - TABLES
PART III - FINAL REPORT

KHAN BAHADUR CHAUDHRI KHUSHI MOHAMMED

GYAN

Published by

Gyan Publishing House
5, Ansari Road
Daryaganj, New Delhi-110002
Phone: 011-47034999, 9811692060
E-mail: books@gyanbooks.com

Distribution Network
gyanbooks.com
India, USA, Canada, UK, Australia

ISBN: 978-81-212-7125-7 (Set) 25 Vols. In 44 Bindings

ISBN: 978-81-212-7631-3 (PB) Vol. XXII, Pt. II, III

First Published, 1923

2nd Impression 2024

Printed at: Gyan Press, Delhi.

CENSUS OF INDIA 1921

CENSUS OF INDIA 1921.

VOLUME XXII

KASHMIR

PART II
TABLES

BY

KHAN BAHADUR CHAUDHRI KHUSHI MOHAMMED, B. A.

DIRECTOR OF CENSUS OPERATIONS, JAMMU AND KASHMIR STATE.

LAHORE

PRINTED AT MUFID-I-'AM PRESS.

1923.

TABLE OF CONTENTS.

NOTE.—Imperial Table XIX showing certain mixed occupations and Table XX showing occupations by religion, being optional have not been compiled for this State.

CORRIGENDA.

TABLE I.

Page	Item		Against		For		Read
Page 2, I.	Col. 15 Urban	.. against	Jammu Province	.. for	..	read	35, 670
,, ,, II	,, 2 Towns	.. ,,	Kashmir Province	.. ,,	..	,,	13
,, ,, ,,	,, 6 ,,	.. ,,	,, ,,	.. ,,	..	,,	34, 522

TABLE IV.

Page	Item		Against		For		Read
,, 7, Para. 1	Line 2 Title page	..		.. ,,	Raduced	,,	Reduced
,, 8, No. 3	Col. 8 (1911-1921)	.. against	Islamabad (Anantnag)	.. ,,	+445	,,	+355

TABLE VII.

Page	Item		Against		For		Read
,, 20,	Hindu Col. 8	.. against	0·1	.. ,,	9,782	,,	9,789
,, 22,	Religion ,, 1	.. ,,	,,	.. ,,	Budh	,,	Buddhists
,, ,,	Musalman ,, 5	.. ,,	45-50	.. ,,	68,039	,,	30,039
,, 25	Religion ,, 1	.. ,,	,,	.. ,,	Budh	,,	Buddhists
,, 28	,, ,,	.. ,,	,,	.. ,,	,,	,,	,,
,, 31	,, ,,	.. ,,	,,	.. ,,	,,	,,	,,
,, 34	,, ,,	.. ,,	,,	.. ,,	Age	,,	Religion
,, ,,	,, ,, ,,	.. ,,	,,	.. ,,	Religion	,,	Age.
,, ,,	,, ,, ,,	.. ,,	,,	.. ,,	Budh	,,	Buddhists
,, 40	,, ,, ,,	.. ,,	,,	.. ,,	,,	,,	,,

TABLE VIII.

Page	Item		Against		For		Read
,, 46	All Religion Col. 2 Persons	.. against	0-10	.. ,,	969,285	,,	969,283
,, ,,	,, ,, ,, 4 Females	.. ,,	,,	.. ,,	470,967	,,	470,965
,, ,,	,, ,, ,, 8 Persons	.. ,,	,,	.. ,,	967,210	,,	976,208
,, ,,	,, ,, ,, 10 Females	.. ,,	,,	.. ,,	470,655	,,	470,653
,, ,,	,, ,, ,, 2 Persons	.. ,,	20 and over	.. ,,	1,640,366	,,	1,640,368
,, ,,	,, ,, ,, 4 Females	.. ,,	,,	.. ,,	766,321	,,	736,323
,, ,,	,, ,, ,, 8 Persons	.. ,,	,,	.. ,,	1,584,869	,,	1,584,871
,, ,,	,, ,, ,, 10 Females	.. ,,	,,	.. ,,	763,704	,,	763,706
,, ,,	Hindu ,, ,, 2 Persons	.. ,,	0-10	.. ,,	170,117	,,	170,115
,, ,,	,, ,, ,, 4 Females	.. ,,	,,	.. ,,	84,001	,,	83,999
,, ,,	,, ,, ,, 8 Persons	.. ,,	,,	.. ,,	168,960	,,	168,958
,, ,,	,, ,, ,, 10 Females	.. ,,	,,	.. ,,	83,852	,,	83,850
,, ,,	,, ,, ,, 2 Persons	.. ,,	20 and over	.. ,,	372,301	,,	372,303
,, ,,	,, ,, ,, 4 Females	.. ,,	,,	.. ,,	169,944	,,	169,646
,, ,,	,, ,, ,, 8 Persons	.. ,,	,,	.. ,,	340,805	,,	340,807
,, ,,	,, ,, ,, 10 Females	.. ,,	,,	.. ,,	169,033	,,	169,035

TABLE X.

Page	Item		Against		For		Read
,, 78	I Col. 14	.. ,,	Jammu Province	.. ,,	422	,,	447
,, ,,	,, ,, 15	.. ,,	,,	.. ,,	223	,,	228
,, 102	Part I Col. 6 Males	.. ,,	25-30	.. ,,	86	,,	82
,, ,,	,, II ,, 3 Males	.. ,,	Kashmir State	.. ,,	6,988	,,	6,989
,, ,,	,, ,, ,, 6 ,,	.. ,,	,,	.. ,,	374	,,	874

TABLE XVII.

Page	Item		Against		For		Read
,, 129	Col. 26	.. against	Muzaffarabad District	.. ,,	203, 291	,,	23,291
,, 131	,, 62	.. ,,	Jammu District	.. ,,	..	,,	278
,, 158	,, 543	.. ,,	Jammu	.. ,,	7	,,	*nil*
,, ,,	,, ,,	.. ,,	Srinagar	.. ,,	*nil*	,,	7
,, 165	Under District Jagir, etc.		State for Kashmir State	..			
,, ,,	,, ,, ,, ,,		Cities below serial No. 12 Gilgit District.				
,, 169	Col. 754	.. Against	II Kashmir Province	.. ,,	1,487	,,	1,407
,, 170	,, 764	.. ,,	Jammu District	.. ,,	74	,,	474
,, 859	,, 859	.. ,,	Kashmir South	.. ,,	162	,,	163
,, 177	,, 889	.. ,,	Kashmir North	.. ,,	38	,,	32
,, 200	,, 1,298	.. ,,	,, State	.. ,,	1,337	,,	3,574

TABLE I.

AREA, HOUSES AND POPULATION.

Jammu and Kashmir State Census 1921.

1. The present area figures have been revised on the basis of information obtained from the Survey Department of the Government of India The resultant decrease at this Census is $174\frac{1}{6}$ square miles.

2. The total number of villages is exclusive of 176 uninhabited villages besides 29 inhabited villages which constitute the City of Srinagar and the towns of Kathua, Parol, Pampur and Skardu. The city and the towns so constituted have been included as separate units in the total of column 3.

3. The enumeration of Political *Ilaqas* comprising the Gilgit Agency and known collectively as Frontier *Ilaqas* (for details see Provincial Table I at the end of this volume) has again been conducted on special lines and the schedules prescribed for these *Ilaqas* do not contain information as to the age, civil condition, birthplace, mother-tongue, literacy and infirmities. Information regarding religion and occupations also differs in detail from that available from the general schedules. The Frontier *Ilaqas* will, therefore, not appear in some of the Imperial Tables.

4. Population figures for Tahsils and smaller units, including Political units composing the Frontier *Ilaqas*, will be found in Provincial Table I at the end of this volume.

5. Scattered villages of the private *jagirs* of His Highness the Maharaja Sahib Bahadur and General Raja Sir Hari Singh are included in the totals of the Districts in which they are situated.

The population (2,111 persons) of the 3 villages constituting the Karlup *jagir* of the Raja of Punch has been included in the population of the Jammu District in which they lie, and not in the "Punch *Ilaqa*" as was done at the last Census.

1 Area, Houses and Population.

TABLE I.

Area, Houses and Population.

Jammu and Kashmir State Census 1921.

District, *Ilaqa* or *Jagir*.	Area in square miles.	Towns.	Villages.	Occupied Houses.			Population.								
							Persons.			Males.			Females.		
				Total.	In towns.	In villages.	Total.	Urban.	Rural.	Total.	Urban.	Rural.	Total.	Urban.	Rural.
1	2	3	4	5	6	7	8	9	10	11	12	13	14	15	16
Kashmir State ..	**84,258**	**37**	**8,915**	**599,287**	**57,849**	**541,438**	**3,320,518**	**291,693**	**3,028,825**	**1,757,122**	**161,919**	**1,595,203**	**1,563,396**	**129,774**	**1,433,622**
I.—Jammu Province (including *Jagirs*).	**12,165**	**20**	**4,549**	**329,116**	**21,022**	**308,094**	**1,640,259**	**84,768**	**1,555,491**	**859,619**	**49,098**	**810,521**	**780,640**	**35,670**	**744,970**
1. Jammu District (including City).	1,147	6	1,163	74,531	11,111	63,420	334,834	43,161	291,673	182,681	26,300	156,381	152,153	16,861	135,292
2. Kathua	1,023	3	570	32,810	2,222	30,588	154,209	9,144	145,065	82,467	5,136	77,331	71,742	4,008	67,734
3. Udampur (including Chaneni).	4,399	3	660	41,151	1,752	39,399	218,261	6,913	211,348	115,135	3,830	111,305	103,126	3,083	100,043
4. Riasi	1,833	2	657	40,606	988	39,618	224,589	4,193	220,396	118,575	2,287	116,288	106,014	1,906	104,108
5. Mirpur	1,583	4	709	74,047	2,991	71,056	318,971	11,728	307,243	160,186	6,073	154,113	158,785	5,655	153,130
6. Bhadarwah *Jagir* ...	553	1	308	6,913	606	6,307	37,614	2,603	35,011	19,227	1,369	17,858	18,387	1,234	17,153
7. Punch *Ilaqa* ..	1,627	1	482	59,058	1,352	57,706	351,781	7,026	344,755	181,848	4,103	177,245	170,433	2,923	167,510
II.—Kashmir Province (including *Jagirs*).	**8,533**	**13**	**3,595**	**221,941**	**34,522**	**187,419**	**1,407,086**	**195,892**	**1,211,194**	**757,824**	**106,433**	**651,391**	**649,262**	**89,459**	**559,803**
Kashmir valley ...	*6,131*	*12*	*2,778*	*189,020*	*33,793*	*155,227*	*1,190,977*	*192,313*	*998,664*	*642,144*	*104,302*	*537,842*	*548,833*	*88,011*	*460,822*
8. Kashmir North (including Langet *Jagir*).	3,317	4	1,382	78,353	3,683	74,670	502,490	20,853	481,637	269,685	11,431	258,254	232,805	9,422	223,383
9. Kashmir South (including City).	2,814	8	1,396	110,667	39,110	80,557	689,487	171,460	517,027	372,459	92,871	279,588	316,028	78,589	237,439
10. Muzaffarabad ..	2,402	1	817	32,921	729	32,192	216,109	3,579	212,530	115,680	2,131	113,549	100,429	1,448	98,981
III.—Frontier Districts ..	**63,560**	**4**	**771**	**48,230**	**2,305**	**45,925**	**273,173**	**11,033**	**262,140**	**139,679**	**6,388**	**133,291**	**133,494**	**4,645**	**128,849**
11. Ladakh (including Mansar).	45,762	2	468	34,692	1,238	33,454	183,476	4,683	178,793	91,258	2,428	88,830	92,218	2,255	89,963
12. Gilgit	3,118	1	82	4,353	711	3,642	28,706	4,393	24,313	15,880	2,947	12,933	12,826	1,446	11,380
13. Frontier *Ilaqas* ..	14,680	1	221	9,185	356	8,829	60,991	1,957	59,034	32,541	1,013	31,528	28,450	944	27,506

TABLE II.

VARIATION IN POPULATION SINCE 1891.

Jammu and Kashmir State Census 1921.

1. The first two regular Indian Censuses of 1871 and 1881 were not extended to this State, and the columns of population and variation relating to these two Censuses have, therefore, been excluded.

2. The population of 1891 has been adopted at 2,543,952 as shown in the India Table II of 1911, instead of 2,598,387 appearing in Kashmir Table II of 1911, as the latter represents the adjusted population of 1891, by adding the population of Frontier Ilaqas ascertained for the first time in 1911.

The total population of Frontier Districts for 1891 has also been revised accordingly.

3. The abolition of Tahsil Astore in Gilgit District and the re-distribution of Ilaqa Punch into 4 Tehsils—Haveli, Mahendar, Bagh and Sadhnoti,—have left the internal District totals unaffected.

II Variation in Population.

TABLE II.

VARIATION IN POPULATION SINCE 1891.

Jammu and Kashmir State Census 1921.

District, *Ilaqa* or *Jagir*.	PERSONS.				VARIATION. Increase (+) Decrease (—).			Net Variation in period 1891—1921 Increase (+) Decrease (—)	MALES.				FEMALES.			
	1921.	1911.	1901.	1891.	1911 to 1921.	1901 to 1911.	1891 to 1901.		1921.	1911.	1901.	1891.	1921.	1911.	1901.	1891.
1	2	3	4	5	6	7	8	9	10	11	12	13	14	15	16	17
Kashmir State ..	**3,320,518**	**3,158,126**	**2,905,878**	**2,543,952**	**+162,392**	**+252,548**	**+361,626**	+776,566	**1,757,122**	**1,674,367**	**1,542,057**	**1,353,229**	**1,563,396**	**1,483,759**	**1,363,521**	**1,190,723**
I.—Jammu Province (including *Jagirs*).	**1,640,259**	**1,597,865**	**1,516,450**	**1,434,686**	**+42,394**	**+81,415**	**+81,764**	**+205,573**	**859,619**	**846,790**	**805,415**	**767,864**	**780,640**	**751,075**	**711,035**	**666,822**
1. Jammu Distr (including City).	334,834	326,691	..	..	+8,143	..	..	..	182,681	180,691	..	—	152,153	146,000	..	..
2. Kathua	154,209	151,802	154,213	151,518	+2,407	+2,411	+2,695	+2,691	82,467	81,375	82,391	81,434	71,742	70,427	71,822	70,084
3. Udhampur (including Chaneni).	218,261	215,725	..	..	+2,536	..	..	..	115,135	113,877	..	..	103,126	101,848	..	..
4. Riasi	224,589	206,809	..	..	+17,780	..	..	..	118,575	109,026	..	..	106,014	97,783	..	..
5. Mirpur	318,971	324,933	..	..	—5,962	..	..	..	160,186	169,276	..	..	158,785	155,657	..	..
6. Bhadarwah *Jagir* ..	37,614	37,512	34,311	32,433	+102	+3,201	+1,878	+5,181	19,227	18,975	17,500	16,775	18,387	18,537	16,811	15,658
7. Punch *Ilaqa*	351,781	334,393	304,488	268,608	+17,388	+29,905	+35,880	+83,173	181,348	173,570	160,679	141,945	170,433	160,823	143,809	126,663
II.—Kashmir Province (including *Jagirs*).	**1,407,086**	**1,295,201**	**1,157,394**	**949,041**	**+111,885**	**+137,807**	**+208,353**	**+458,045**	**757,824**	**691,780**	**616,887**	**502,345**	**649,262**	**603,421**	**540,507**	**446,696**
Kashmir Valley ..	*1,190,977*	*1,099,996*	*989,196*	*814,241*	*+90,981*	*+110,800*	*+174,955*	*+376,736*	*642,144*	*587,472*	*526,158*	*229,464*	*548,833*	*512,524*	*643,038*	*884,777*
8. Kashmir North (including Langet *Jagir*).	502,490	460,786	..	..	+41,704	..	..	..	269,685	244,637	..	..	232,805	216,149	..	..
9. Kashmir South (including City).	688,487	639,210	..	..	+49,2 7	..	..	..	372,459	342,835	..	..	316,028	296,375	..	..
10. Muzaffarabad	216,109	195,205	168,198	134,800	+20,904	+27,007	+33,398	+81,309	115,680	104,308	90,729	72;881	100,429	90,897	77,469	61,919
III.—Frontier Districts	**273,173**	**265,060**	**231,734**	**160,225**	**+8,113**	**+33,326**	**+71,509**	**+112,948**	**139,679**	**135,797**	**119,755**	**83,020**	**133,494**	**129,263**	**111,979**	**77,205**
11. Ladakh (including Mansar)	183,476	186,656	..	..	—3,180	..	..	..	91,258	93,220	..	..	92,218	93,436	..	..
12. Gilgit	28,706	23,969	60,888	—	+4,737	+17,519	..	..	15,880	13,299	33,778	..	12,826	10,670	27,107	..
13. Frontier *Ilaqas*	60,991	54,436			+6,556				32,541	29,276			28,450	25,187		

TABLE III.

TOWNS AND VILLAGES CLASSIFIED BY POPULATION.

JAMMU AND KASHMIR STATE CENSUS 1921.

1. Each town, which is composed of more than one inhabited village, has been treated as a single unit in column 2, and its aggregate population exhibited in the proper column after deducting the unclassed population, if any, which is shown separately in column 22.

2. The unclassed population in column 22 is made up as follows :—

(1)	Railway (Jammu District)	316
(2)	Labour employed on Lachhman Pattan Motor Road in Punch Jagir	1,570
(3)	Water-borne population in Kashmir Valley ...	12,265
	Total ...	14,151

III Towns and Villages Classified.

TABLE III.

Towns and Villages classified by Population.

Jammu and Kashmir State Census 1921.

District *Ilaqa* or *Jagir*.	Total number of inhabited Towns and Villages.	Population.	Under 500.		500—1,000.		1,000—2,000.		2,000—5,000.		5,000—10,000.		10,000—20,000		20,000—50,000.		50,000-100,000		100,000 & over.		Encampments, boat and Railway Population unclassed.
			Number.	Population.	Number.	Population.	Number.	Population.	Number.	Population.	Number.	Population.	Number.	Population.	Number.	Population.	Number.	Population.	Number.	Population.	
1	2	3	4	5	6	7	8	9	10	11	12	13	14	15	16	17	18	19	20	21	22
Kashmir State ..	**8,952**	**3,320,518**	**7,130**	**1,366,560**	**1,289**	**887,661**	**423**	**568,891**	**99**	**254,479**	**9**	**59,937**	..	..	**1**	**31,506**	..	..	**1**	**137,333**	**14,151**
I. Jammu Province (including *Jagirs*).	**4,569**	**1,640,259**	**3,644**	**689,508**	**617**	**428,745**	**243**	**328,171**	**60**	**156,019**	**4**	**24,424**	..	..	**1**	**31,506**	..	..	..	..	**1,836**
1. Jammu District (including City).	1,169	334,834	1,038	179,580	93	63,450	28	37,861	9	22,121	..	..	..	..	1	31,506	..	..	..	..	316
2. Kathua District ..	573	154,209	485	81,870	74	50,099	12	15,010	1	2,158	1	5,072	..	..	..	..	..	..	..	..	..
3. Udhampur District (including Chaneni).	663	218,261	542	112,901	93	63,707	25	34,480	3	7,173	..	..	..	..	..	..	..	..	..	..	..
4. Riasi District ..	659	224,589	511	94,328	112	76,631	33	44,789	3	8,841	..	..	..	..	..	..	..	..	..	..	..
5. Mirpur District ..	713	318,971	520	101,349	119	84,442	55	75,116	17	45,738	2	12,326	..	..	..	..	..	..	..	..	..
6. Bhadarwah *Jagir* ..	309	37,614	306	33,702	2	1,309	..	..	1	2,603	..	..	..	..	..	..	..	..	..	..	..
7. Punch *Ilaqa* ..	483	351,781	242	65,778	124	89,107	90	120,915	26	67,385	1	7,026	..	..	..	..	..	..	..	..	1,570
II.—Kashmir Province (including *Jagirs*).	**3,608**	**1,407,086**	**2,871**	**569,949**	**550**	**376,972**	**152**	**201,770**	**29**	**73,284**	**5**	**35,513**	..	..	..	..	..	..	**1**	**137,333**	**12,265**
Kashmir Valley ..	*2,790*	1,190,977	*2,168*	448,084	454	313,718	137	181,023	25	63,046	5	35,513	..	..	..	..	..	..	1	137,333	12,265
8. Kashmir North (including Langet *Jagir*).	1,386	502,490	1,093	220,798	211	144,181	70	92,870	9	22,560	3	20,121	..	..	..	..	..	..	..	..	1,960
9. Kashmir South (including City).	1,404	688,487	1,075	227,286	243	169,532	67	88,153	16	40,486	2	15,392	..	..	..	..	..	..	1	137,333	10,305
10. Muzaffarabad District ..	818	216,109	703	121,865	96	63,259	15	20,747	4	10,238	..	..	..	..	..	..	..	..	..	..	..
III.—Frontier Districts ..	**775**	**273,173**	**615**	**127,103**	**122**	**81,944**	**28**	**38,950**	**10**	**25,176**	..	..	..	..	..	..	..	..	..	..	..
11. Ladakh District (including Mansar).	470	183,476	359	79,153	80	53,513	23	32,091	8	18,719	..	..	..	..	..	..	..	..	..	..	..
12. Gilgit District ..	83	28,706	67	13,774	15	10,539	..	..	1	4,393	..	..	..	..	..	..	..	..	..	..	..
13. Frontier *Ilaqas* ..	222	60,991	189	34,176	27	17,892	5	6,859	1	2,064	..	..	..	..	..	..	..	..	..	..	..

TABLE IV.

TOWNS CLASSIFIED BY POPULATION WITH VARIATION SINCE 1891.

Jammu and Kashmir State Census 1921.

1. Besides the two cities, Srinagar and Jammu, the number of places treated as towns at the last Census has been raduced from 59 to 35, as a large number of these places not only failed to respond to the prescribed numerical test, but were nothing better than overgrown villages and devoid of characteristics usually associated with urban life.

2. Srinagar City falls in Class I with population exceeding 100,000, Jammu City in Class III and of the remaining 35 towns, only 7 belong to Class V with population ranging between 5,000 and 10,000. There are no towns of Classes II and IV.

3. The total population of towns in column 4 is the aggregate population in 1911 of the 35 places treated as towns alike in 1911 and 1921 and not the total population of the 59 towns of 1911.

4. The increase of 15,391 persons (males 8,226, females 7,165) in Srinagar is due partly to the transfer of two Villages, Zadibal and Buchhiwara to the City from the Revenue Tehsil after the Census of 1911. The adjusted population of 1911, so as to eliminate the effect of subsequent transfer of area, works out at 130,201 (males 70,419, females 59,782).

The only other town reporting change in area is Gilgit, but the net result is a decrease of only six houses, and, therefore, too unimportant for serious notice.

IV Towns classified by Population.

TABLE IV.

Towns classified by Population with Variation since 1891.

Jammu and Kashmir State Census 1921.

Towns.	District, Ilaqa or Jagir.	Municipality, Suburbs, Cantonments, etc.	Population. 1921.	Population. 1911.	Population. 1901.	Population. 1891.	Variation Increase (+) Decrease (—). 1911 to 1921.	Variation Increase (+) Decrease (—). 1901 to 1911.	Variation Increase (+) Decrease (—). 1891 to 1901.	Variation in period 1891 to 1921 Increase (+) Decrease (—).	Males. 1921.	Males. 1911.	Males. 1901.	Females. 1921.	Females. 1911.	Females. 1901.
1	2	3	4	5	6	7	8	9	10	11	12	13	14	15	16	17
Total Urban Population ..	..	..	**291,693**	**271,185**	**158,290**	**192,079**	+14,508	+118,895	—33,789	+98,614	161,919	154,034	87,414	129,774	123,151	70,876
Total Cities	..	..	**173,241**	**158,070**	**158,290**	**153,044**	+15,171	—220	+5,246	+20,197	95,725	87,740	87,414	77,516	70,330	70,876
							Class I.—100,000 and over.									
1. Srinagar	Kashmir South ..	**Total** ..	**141,735**	**126,344**	**122,618**	**118,960**	+15,391	+3,726	+3,658	+22,775	76,604	68,378	65,542	65,131	57,966	57,076
		Municipality ..	139,520	124,240	122,618	118,960	+15,280	+1,622	+3,658	+20,560	75,152	66,994	65,542	64,368	57,246	57,076
		Cantonment ..	2,215	2,104	..	..	+111	+2,104	..	..	1,452	1,384	..	763	720	..
							Class III.—20,000 to 50,000.									
2. Jammu	Jammu ..	**Total** ..	**31,506**	**31,726**	**35,672**	**34,084**	—220	—3,946	+1,588	—2,578	19,121	19,362	21,872	12,385	12,364	13,800
		Municipality ..	30,009	29,857	34,421	34,084	+152	—4,564	+337	—4,075	17,793	17,712	20,730	12,216	12,145	13,691
		Cantonment ..	1,497	1,869	1,251	..	—372	+618	+1,251	..	1,328	1,660	1,142	169	219	109
Total Towns	..	..	**118,452**	**119,115**	...	**39,035**	—663	..	..	+79,417	66,194	66,294	..	52,258	52,821	..
							Class V.—5,000 to 10,000.									
3. Islamabad (Anantnag) ..	Kashmir South ..	..	9,464	9,109	...	10,22	+445	..	..	—763	5,303	4,937	..	4,161	4,082	..
4. Sopur	Do North ..	..	8,524	8,514	...	8,410	+10	..	..	+114	4,610	4,465	..	3,914	4,049	..
5. Punch	Punch *Ilaqa* ..	..	7,026	7,564	...	7,489	—538	..	..	—463	4,103	4,662	..	2,923	2,902	..
6. Baramula	Kashmir North ..	..	6,744	6,599	...	5,656	+145	...	..	+1,088	3,691	3,586	..	3,053	3,013	..
7. Mirpur	Mirpur ...	..	6,490	6,640	...	7,253	—150	..	..	—763	3,251	3,441	..	3,239	3,199	..
8. Zunimar	Kashmir South ..	Suburbs of Srinagar.	5,928	8,095	..	..	—2,167	...	..	..	3,228	4,369	..	2,705	3,720	..
9. Kathua	Kathua ..	..	5,072	5,240	..	..	—168	..	..	...	2,948	3,008	...	2,124	2,282	..
							Class VI.—Under 5,000.									
10. Gilgit	Gilgit ..	..	4,393	3,562	...	...	+831	..	...	..	2,947	2,301	..	1,446	1,261	..
11. Bijbihara	Kashmir South ...	..	4,270	4,424	...	..	—154	..	..	..	2,311	2,360	..	1,959	2,064	..
12. Muzaffarabad ..	Muzaffarabad ..	..	3,579	3,462	...	...	+117	..	...	...	2,131	2,015	..	1,448	1,447	..
13. Pampur	Kashmir South ..	..	3,494	3,348	...	...	+146	...	...	..	1,941	1,851	..	1,553	1,497	..
14. Cherar-Sharif ..	Do. North ..	..	3,342	3,380	..	..	—38	..	..	..	1,894	1,853	..	1,448	1,527	..
15. Satwari Cantonment ..	Jammu ..	Cantonment ..	2,969	3,201	..	..	—232	..	..	..	2,567	2,847	..	402	354	..
16. Akhnur	Do. ..	..	2,905	3,033	...	..	—128	..	..	..	1,496	1,550	..	1,409	1,483	..
17. Bhadarwah, (Nagar Khas)	Bhadarwah *Jagir*	..	2,603	2,563	...	..	+40	..	..	..	1,369	1,348	..	1,234	1,215	..
18. Kishtwar	Udhampur ..	..	2,546	2,378	..	...	+168	...	..	..	1,396	1,277	..	1,150	1,101	..
19. Samba	Jammu ..	..	2,418	2,307	..	..	+111	..	..	..	1,263	1,210	..	1,155	1,097	..
20. Leh	Ladakh ..	..	2,401	2,895	..	..	—494	...	..	..	1,182	1,464	..	1,219	1,431	..
21. Udhampur	Udhampur ..	..	2,390	2,360	..	...	+30	..	..	...	1,373	1,311	..	1,017	1,049	..
22. Skardu	Ladakh ..	..	2,282	2,197	..	..	+85	..	..	..	1,246	1,137	..	1,036	1,060	..
23. Rampur Rajouri ..	Riasi ..	..	2,253	2,192	..	..	+61	..	..	..	1,214	1,203	..	1,039	989	..
24. Pattan	Kashmir North ..	..	2,243	1,903	..	..	+340	..	..	..	1,236	1,018	..	1,007	885	..
25. Shopian (Hiragam) ..	Kashmir South ..	..	2,236	2,114	..	...	+122	..	..	..	1,223	1,161	..	1,013	958	..
26. Doru	Do. ..	..	2,177	2,202	...	...	—25	..	..	...	1,163	1,157	..	1,014	1,045	..
27. Parol	Kathua ..	..	2,158	1,678	...	...	+480	..	..	..	1,209	917	..	949	761	..
28. Verinag	Kashmir South ..	..	2,156	2,095	...	..	+61	..	..	..	1,103	1,063	..	1,053	1,032	..
29. Ramnagar	Udhampur ..	..	1,977	2,073	..	...	—96	..	..	..	1,061	1,107	..	916	966	..
30. Manawar	Mirpur ..	..	1,966	2,057	...	...	—91	..	..	..	1,078	1,142	..	888	915	..
31. Hunza (Baltit) ..	Frontier *Ilaqas* ..	..	1,957	1,971	..	..	—14	..	...	..	1,013	1,082	..	944	889	..
32. Riasi	Riasi ..	..	1,940	1,905	..	..	+35	..	..	..	1,078	1,062	..	867	843	..
33. Basohli	Kathua ..	..	1,914	1,954	..	...	—40	..	..	..	979	1,003	..	935	951	..
34. Hamirpur (Sidhar) ..	Jammu ..	..	1,752	1,832	...	..	—80	..	..	..	963	1,024	..	789	808	..
35. Bhimbar	Mirpur ..	..	1,709	1,438	...	..	+271	..	..	..	931	777	..	778	661	..
36. Sri Ranbir Singhpura ..	Jammu ..	..	1,611	1,336	...	...	+275	..	.	..	890	761	..	721	575	..
37. Kotli	Mirpur ..	..	1,563	1,584	..	..	—21	..	...	..	813	825	..	750	759	..

TABLE V.

TOWNS ARRANGED TERRITORIALLY WITH POPULATION: BY RELIGION.

Jammu and Kashmir State Census 1921.

(1). The term "Others" in this Table consists of 12 Sansis in the town of Ranbir Singhpura of the Jammu District.

(2). In the term "Hindu" Aryas and Brahmos are also included.

TABLE V

Towns arranged territorially

Jammu and Kashmir

Towns arranged territorially and by religion.

District, *Ilaqa* or *Jagir*.	Town, Municipality, Suburbs, Cantonments, etc.	Total Population.			Hindu.			Sikh.			Jain.		
		Persons.	Males.	Females.	Persons.	Males.	Females.	Persons.	Males.	Females.	Persons.	Males.	Females.
1	2	3	4	5	6	7	8	9	10	11	12	13	14
Kashmir State ..	..	**291,693**	**161,919**	**129.774**	**85,600**	**49,262**	**36,338**	**3,285**	**1,852**	**1,433**	**526**	**292**	**234**
I.—Jammu Province ..	..	**84,768**	**49,098**	**35,670**	**49,402**	**28,919**	**20,483**	**2,182**	**1,157**	**1,025**	**526**	**292**	**234**
Jammu District ..	..	**43,161**	**26,300**	**16,861**	**27,901**	**17,254**	**10,647**	**802**	**450**	**352**	**520**	**289**	**231**
1. Jammu City ..	Municipality ..	30,009	17,793	12,216	19,821	11,848	7,973	703	398	305	520	289	231
Do. ..	Cantonment ..	1,497	1,328	169	974	858	116	5	2	3	..	..	..
	Total ..	31,506	19,121	12,385	20,795	12,706	8,089	708	400	308	520	289	231
2. Satwari ..	Cantonment ..	2,969	2,567	402	2,253	1,970	283	..	..	..	..	..	..
3. Akhnur ..	Town ..	2,905	1,496	1,409	1,462	748	714	50	26	24	..	..	—
4. Samba ..	,,	2,418	1,263	1,155	1,398	718	680	31	15	16	..	..	..
5. Hamirpur Sidhar	,,	1,752	963	789	1,299	724	575	..	..	..	..	..	..
6. Sri Ranbir Singhpura.	,,	1,611	890	721	694	388	306	13	9	4	..	..	..
Kathua District ..	..	**9,144**	**5,136**	**4,008**	**5,811**	**3,210**	**2,601**	**40**	**22**	**18**	..	..	..
7. Kathua ..	,,	5,072	2,948	2,124	2,982	1,731	1,251	34	19	15	..	..	..
8. Parol ..	,,	2,158	1,209	949	1,365	748	617	1	1	..	..	..	..
9. Basohli ..	,,	1,914	979	935	1,464	731	733	5	2	3	..	..	..
Udhampur District ..	..	**6,913**	**3,830**	**3,083**	**4,509**	**2,480**	**2.029**	**35**	**20**	**15**	..	..	..
10. Kishtwar ..	,,	2,546	1,396	1.150	797	454	343	1	1	..	..	..	..
11. Udhampur ..	,,	2,390	1,373	1,017	2,026	1,145	881	22	13	9	..	..	..
12. Ram Nagar ..	,,	1,977	1,061	916	1,686	881	805	12	6	6	..	..	..
Risai District ..	..	**4,193**	**2,287**	**1,906**	**2,102**	**1,121**	**981**	**27**	**15**	**12**	..	..	..
13. Rampur Rajouri.	,,	2,253	1,214	1,039	786	402	384	22	12	10	..	..	..
14. Riasi ..	,,	1,940	1,073	867	1,316	719	597	5	3	2	..	..	..
Mirpur District ..	..	**11,728**	**6,073**	**5,655**	**6,180**	**3,195**	**2,985**	**915**	**464**	**451**	**5**	**2**	**3**
15 Mirpur ..	,,	6.490	3,251	3,239	3,243	1,657	1,586	618	299	319	5	2	3
16. Manawar ..	,,	1,966	1,078	888	799	418	381	248	135	113	..	..	..
17. Bhimbar ..	,,	1,709	931	778	841	445	396	35	20	15	..	..	..
18. Kotli ..	,,	1,563	813	750	1,297	675	622	14	10	4	..	..	..
Jagirs ..	..	**9.629**	**5,472**	**4,157**	**2,899**	**1,659**	**1,240**	**363**	**186**	**177**	**1**	**1**	..
19. Punch ..	,,	7,026	4,103	2,923	1,952	1,138	814	357	183	174	1	1	..
20. Bhadarwah ..	,,	2,603	1,369	1,234	947	521	426	6	3	3	..	..	..
II.—Kashmir Province ..	..	**195 892**	**106,433**	**89,459**	**35,528**	**19.748**	**15,780**	**1,028**	**648**	**380**	..	..	..
Kashmir Valley .	..	**192.313**	**104,302**	**88 011**	**34,644**	**19,244**	**15,400**	**725**	**477**	**248**	..	..	..
Kashmir North	..	**20,853**	**11,431**	**9,422**	**2.055**	**1,203**	**852**	**119**	**79**	**40**	..	..	..
21. Sopur ..	,,	8,524	4,610	3,914	814	445	369	20	16	4	..	..	..
22. Baramula ..	,,	6,744	3,691	3,053	1,209	733	476	48	31	17	..	..	..
23. Cherar Sharif ..	,,	3,342	1,894	1,448	..	..	..	..	..	..	..	..	..
24. Patan ..	,,	2,243	1,236	1,007	32	25	7	51	32	19	..	..	..

V

WITH POPULATION BY RELIGION.

State Census 1921.

V

Towns arranged territorially and by religion.

Buddhist.			Musalman.			Zoroastrian.			Christian.			Others.		
Persons.	Males.	Females.	Persons.	Males.	Females.	Persons.	Males.	Females.	Persons.	Males.	Females.	Persons	Males.	Females.
15	16	17	18	19	20	21	22	23	24	25	26	27	28	29
1,306	**669**	**637**	**200,057**	**109,341**	**90,716**	**2**	**2**	...	**904**	**494**	**410**	**13**	**7**	**6**
4	**4**	..	**32,035**	**18,392**	**13,643**	...	...	...	**607**	**327**	**280**	**12**	**7**	**5**
4	**4**	..	**13,407**	**8,014**	**5,393**	...	...	...	**515**	**282**	**233**	**12**	**7**	**5**
4	4	..	8,483	4,995	3,488	...	...	...	478	259	219	...	...	...
...	...	...	518	468	50	...	...	...	...	...	...	...	...	...
4	4	..	9,001	5,463	3,538	...	...	...	478	259	219	...	...	...
...	...	...	713	595	118	...	...	...	3	2	1	...	...	...
...	...	...	1,393	722	671	...	...	...	...	...	...	...	...	...
...	...	...	989	530	459	...	...	...	...	...	...	...	...	...
...	...	...	453	239	214	...	...	.	...	...	...	...	...	..
...	...	...	858	465	393	...	...	...	34	21	13	12	7	5
...	...	...	**3,211**	**1,863**	**1,348**	...	...	...	**82**	**41**	**41**	...	...	...
...	...	...	1,974	1,157	817	...	...	...	82	41	41	...	..	...
...	...	...	792	460	332	...	...	...	...	...	...	...	...	...
...	...	...	445	246	199	...	..	...	...	...	...	...	...	...
.	...	...	**2,368**	**1,329**	**1,039**	...	...	...	**1**	**1**	...	...	...	...
...	...	...	1,748	941	807	...	...	...	...	...	...	...	...	...
...	...	...	341	214	127	...	...	...	1	1	...	..	...	...
...	...	...	279	174	105	...	...	...	...	...	...	...	...	...
...	...	...	**2,064**	**1,151**	**913**	...	...	...	...	...	...	...	...	...
...	...	...	1,445	800	645	..	...	...	...	...	...	..	...	...
...	...	...	619	351	268	...	...	...	...	...	...	...	...	...
...	...	...	**4,628**	**2,412**	**2,216**	...	...	...	...	...	...	...	...	...
...	...	...	2,624	1,293	1,331	...	...	...	...	...	...	..	...	...
...	...	...	919	525	394	...	...	...	...	...	...	...	..	...
...	...	...	833	466	367		...	...	...	...	...	...	...	...
...	...	...	252	128	124	...	...	...	...	...	...	...	...	...
...	...	...	**6,357**	**3,623**	**2,734**	...	...	...	9	3	6	...	..	...
...	...	...	4,708	2,779	1,929	...	...	..	8	2	6	...	...	...
...	..	...	1,649	844	805	...	..	...	1	1	...	...	...	...
1	**1**	...	**159,094**	**85,901**	**73,193**	**2**	**2**	...	**238**	**133**	**105**	**1**	...	**1**
1	**1**	...	**156,702**	**84,445**	**72,257**	**2**	**2**	..	**238**	**133**	**105**	**1**	...	**1**
...	...	...	**18,679**	**10,149**	**8,530**	...	...	...	...	...	...	...	..	...
...	...	...	7,690	4,149	3,541	...	...	...	...	...	...	...	...	...
...	...	...	5,487	2,927	2,560	...	...	...	...	...	...	...	...	...
...	...	...	3,342	1,894	1,448	...	...	...	..	...	...	...	...	...
...	...	...	2,160	1,179	981	...	...	...	...	...	...	...	...	...

V

Towns arranged territorially and by religion.

TABL

TOWNS ARRANGED TERRITORIALL

Jammu and Kashmi

District, *Ilaqa* or *Jagir*.	Town, Municipality, Suburbs, Cantonments, etc.	TOTAL POPULATION.			HINDU.			SIKH.			JAIN.		
		Persons.	Males.	Females.	Persons.	Males.	Females.	Persons.	Males.	Females.	Persons.	Males.	Females.
1	2	3	4	5	6	7	8	9	10	11	12	13	14
Kashmir South ..	..	**171,460**	**92,871**	**78,589**	**32,589**	**18,041**	**14,548**	**606**	**398**	**208**	..	..	..
25. Srinagar City ..	Municipality ..	139,520	75,152	64,368	29,319	15,986	13,333	468	317	151	..	..	..
	Cantonment ..	2,215	1,452	763	698	542	156	73	44	29	..	..	..
	Total ..	1,41,735	76,604	65,131	30,017	16,528	13,489	541	361	180	..	..	..
26. Islamabad ..	Town ..	9,464	5,303	4,161	1,279	777	502	45	26	19	..	..	..
27. Zunimar ..	„	5,928	3,223	2,705	345	188	157	..	..	..	..	..	..
28. Bijbihari ..	„	4,270	2,311	1,959	413	238	175	6	3	3	..	..	..
29. Pampur ..	„	3,494	1,941	1,553	107	57	50	3	3	..	..	..	..
30. Shopian ..	„	2,236	1,223	1,013	41	34	7	5	1	4	..	..	..
31. Doru ..	„	2,177	1,163	1,014	37	29	8	6	4	2	..	..	..
32. Verinag ..	„	2,156	1,103	1,053	350	190	160	..	..	...	..	..	..
Muzaffarabad District ..	..	**3,579**	**2,131**	**1,448**	**884**	**504**	**380**	**303**	**171**	**132**	..	..	..
33. Muzaffarabad ..	Town ..	3,579	2,131	1,448	884	504	380	303	171	132	..	..	..
II.—Frontier Districts ..	..	**11,033**	**6,388**	**4,645**	**670**	**595**	**75**	**75**	**47**	**28**	..	..	..
Ladakh District ..	..	**4,683**	**2,428**	**2,255**	**177**	**128**	**49**	**22**	**15**	**7**	..	..	..
34. Leh ..	Town ..	2,401	1,182	1,219	47	34	13	1	1	..	..	..	..
35. Skardu ..	„	2,282	1,246	1,036	130	94	36	21	14	7	..	..	..
Gilgit District ..	..	**4,393**	**2,947**	**1,446**	**493**	**467**	**26**	**36**	**25**	**11**	..	..	..
36. Gilgit ..	Town ..	4,393	2,947	1,446	493	467	26	36	25	11	..	..	..
Frontier Ilaqas ..	..	**1,957**	**1,013**	**944**	..	..	..	**17**	**7**	**10**	..	..	..
37. Hunza ..	Town ..	1,957	1,013	944	..	...	..	17	7	10	..	..	..

V.

WITH POPULATION BY RELIGION.

State Census 1921.

V

Towns arranged territorially and by religion.

Buddhist.			Musalman.			Zoroastrian.			Christian.			Others.		
Persons.	Males.	Females.	Persons.	Males.	Females.	Persons.	Males.	Females	Persons.	Males.	Females.	Persons.	Males.	Females.
15	16	17	18	19	20	21	22	23	24	25	26	27	28	29
1	**1**	..	**138,023**	**74,296**	**63,727**	**2**	**2**	..	**238**	**133**	**105**	**1**	..	**1**
1	1	..	109,496	58,716	50,780	2	2	..	233	130	103	1	..	1
..	..	..	1,439	863	576	..	..	..	5	3	2	..	..	..
1	1	..	110,935	59,579	51,356	2	2	..	238	133	105	1	..	1
..	..	..	8,140	4,500	3,640	..	..	..	..	..	..	..	..	..
..	..	..	5,583	3,035	2,548	..	..	..	..	..	..	..	..	..
..	..	..	3,851	2,070	1,781	..	..	..	..	..	..	..	..	..
..	..	..	3,384	1,881	1,503	..	..	..	..	..	..	..	..	..
..	..	..	2,190	1,188	1,002	..	..	..	..	..	..	..	..	..
..	..	..	2,134	1,130	1,004	..	..	..	..	..	..	..	..	..
..	..	..	1,806	913	893	..	..	..	..	..	..	..	..	..
..	..	..	**2,392**	**1,456**	**936**	...	...	..	..	..	..	..	..	..
..	..	..	2,392	1,456	936	..	...	...	..	..	..	..	..	..
1,301	**664**	**637**	**8,928**	**5,048**	**3,880**	..	...	...	**59**	**34**	**25**	..	..	..
1,301	**664**	**637**	**3,127**	**1,590**	**1,537**	..	..	..	**56**	**31**	**25**	..	..	..
1,260	623	637	1,037	493	544	..	..	..	56	31	25	..	..	..
41	41	..	2,090	1,097	993	..	..	..	..	..	..	..	..	..
..	..	...	**3,861**	**2,452**	**1,409**	..	..	..	**3**	**3**	...	...	...	...
..	..	..	3,861	2,452	1,409	..	..	..	3	3	..	..	..	..
..	..	..	**1,940**	**1,006**	**934**	..	..	..	..	..	..	..	..	..
..	..	..	1,940	1,006	934	..	..	..	..	..	..	..	..	..

TABLE VI.

POPULATION BY RELIGION.

Jammu & Kashmir State Census 1921.

In this Table 302 Sansis (162 males, 140 females) have been included in the head Hindu "Brahmanic", and 22 Sapiadas (11 males, 11 females) in the head "Musalman".

TABLE VI.

POPULATION BY RELIGION.

Jammu and Kashmir State Census 1921.

District, *Ilaqa* or *Jagir*.	Total Population.			I.—Indo Aryan.											
				Hindu.									Sikh.		
				Brahmanic.			*Arya.*			*Brahmo.*					
	Persons.	Males.	Females.	Persons.	Males.	Females.	Persons.	Males.	Females.	Persons.	Males.	Females.	Persons.	Males.	Females.
1	2	3	4	5	6	7	8	9	10	11	12	13	14	15	16
Kashmir State	**3,320,518**	**1,757,122**	**1,563,396**	**669,510**	**357,738**	**311,772**	**23,116**	**12,608**	**10,508**	**15**	**7**	**8**	**39,507**	**20,786**	**18,721**
I.—Jammu Province (including *Jagirs*) ..	**1,640,259**	**859,619**	**780,640**	**603,746**	**320,033**	**283,713**	**23,045**	**12,560**	**10,485**	**15**	**7**	**8**	**21,627**	**11,381**	**10,246**
1. Jammu District (including city) ..	334,834	182,681	152,153	191,979	104,658	87,321	5,595	3,242	2,353	15	7	8	4,932	2,651	2,281
2. Kathua	154,209	82,467	71,742	109,572	57,696	51,876	7,930	4,444	3,486	..	..	...	257	148	109
3. Udhampur (including Chaneni) ..	218,261	115,135	103,126	132,214	68,935	63,279	21	10	11	...	..	...	332	175	157
4. Riasi	224,589	118,575	106,014	74,065	39,122	34,943	5,515	2,672	2,843	...	...	...	814	401	413
5. Mirpur	318,971	160,186	158,785	52,591	27,319	25,272	3,930	2,159	1,771	...	...	...	4,698	2,481	2,217
6. Bhadarwah *Jagir*	37,614	19,227	18,387	22,561	11,384	11,177	3	1	2	...	..	...	9	5	4
7. Punch *Ilaqa*	351,781	181,348	170,433	20,764	10,919	9,845	51	32	19	...	...	...	10,585	5,520	5,065
II.—Kashmir Province (including *Jagirs*) ..	**1,407,086**	**757,824**	**649,262**	**64,565**	**38,639**	**27,926**	**29**	**21**	**8**	...	...	...	**17,742**	**9,316**	**8,426**
Kashmir Valley	*1,190,977*	*642,144*	*548,833*	*60,168*	*33,937*	*26,231*	*29*	*21*	*8*	...	...	...	*8,534*	*4,557*	*3,977*
8. Kashmir North (including Langet *Jagir*)	502,490	269,685	232,805	10,444	6,278	4,166	...	...	...	..	...	...	5,332	2,779	2,553
9. Kashmir South (including city) ..	688,487	372,459	316,028	49,724	27,659	22,065	29	21	8	...	...	...	3,202	1,778	1,424
10. Muzaffarabad	216,109	115,680	100,429	4,397	2,702	1,695	...	..	...	...	...	...	9,208	4,759	4,449
III.—Frontier Districts	**273,173**	**139,679**	**133,494**	**1,199**	**1,066**	**133**	**42**	**27**	**15**	...	...	...	**138**	**89**	**49**
11. Ladakh (including Mansar)	183,476	91,258	92,218	268	185	83	25	16	9	...	...	...	48	30	18
12. Gilgit	28,706	15,880	12,826	711	665	46	17	11	6	...	...	...	69	46	23
13. Frontier *Ilaqas*	60,991	32,541	28,450	220	216	4	..	..	..	...	...	...	21	13	8

VI
Religion.

TABLE VI.

POPULATION BY RELIGION.

Jammu & Kashmir State Census 1921.

District, *Ilaqa* or *Jagir*.	I—INDO-ARYAN.						II—IRANIAN.			III—SEMITIC.								
	JAIN.			BUDDHIST.			ZOROASTRIAN.			MUSALMAN.			CHRISTIAN.			OTHERS.		
	Persons.	Males.	Females.	Persons.	Males.	Females.	Persons.	Males.	Females.	Persons.	Males.	Females.	Persons.	Males.	Females.	Persons.	Males.	Females.
	17	18	19	20	21	22	23	24	25	26	27	28	29	30	31	32	33	34
Kashmir State	**529**	**295**	**234**	**37,685**	**18,833**	**18,847**	**7**	**5**	**2**	**2,548,514**	**1,345,957**	**1,202,557**	**1,634**	**888**	**746**	**1**	..	**1**
I.—Jammu Province (including *Jagirs*) ..	**523**	**294**	**234**	**442**	**226**	**216**	**5**	**3**	**2**	**989,644**	**514,453**	**475,191**	**1,207**	**662**	**545**	..	..	..
1. Jammu District (including city) ..	521	290	231	4	4	...	5	3	2	130,743	71,253	59,490	1,040	573	467	..	..	..
2. Kathua	1	1	..	...	...	...	..	..	..	36,303	20,099	16,204	146	79	67	..	..	..
3. Udhampur (including Chaneni) ..	..	..	..	438	222	216	..	..	..	85,254	45,792	39,462	2	1	1	..	..	..
4. Riasi	..	..	..	...	...	...	..	..	..	144,195	76,380	67,815	...	...	...	..	..	..
5. Mirpur	5	2	3	...	...	...	..	..	..	257,741	128,222	129,519	6	3	3	..	..	..
6. Bahadarwah *Jagir*	..	..	..	...	..	...	..	..	..	15,040	7,836	7,204	1	1	...	..	..	..
7. Punch *Ilaqa*	1	1	..	...	...	...	..	..	..	320,368	164,871	155,497	12	5	7	..	..	..
II.—Kashmir Province (including *Jagirs*) ..	**1**	**1**	..	**2**	**2**	...	**2**	**2**	..	**1,324,403**	**711,664**	**612,739**	**341**	**179**	**162**	**1**	..	**1**
Kashmir Valley	*1*	*1*	..	*2*	*2*	...	*2*	*2*	..	*1,121,905*	*603,449*	*518,456*	*335*	*175*	*160*	*1*	..	*1*
8. Kashmir North (including Langet *Jagir*)	1	1	..	...	...	...	..	..	..	486,680	260,608	226,072	33	19	14	..	..	..
9. Kashmir South (including city) ..	..	..	..	2	2	...	2	2	..	635,225	342,841	292,384	302	156	146	1	..	1
10. Muzaffarabad	..	..	..	...	...	...	..	..	..	202,498	108,215	94,283	6	4	2	..	..	..
III.—Frontier Districts	..	..	..	**37,241**	**18,610**	**18,631**	..	..	..	**234,467**	**119,840**	**114,627**	**86**	**47**	**39**	..	..	..
11. Ladakh (including Mansar)	..	..	..	37,241	18,610	18,631	..	..	..	145,824	72,380	73,444	70	37	33	..	..	..
12. Gilgit	..	..	..	...	...	...	..	..	..	27,894	15,149	12,745	15	9	6	..	..	..
13. Frontier *Ilaqas*	..	..	..	...	...	...	..	..	..	60,749	32,311	28,438	1	1	...	..	..	..

TABLE VII.

AGE, SEX AND CIVIL CONDITION (BY RELIGION).

Jammu and Kashmir State Census 1921.

The Frontier *Ilaqas* having been enumerated on special lines without detail of age and civil condition, do not find a place in this table.

The details by religion of the population (males 32,541, females 28,450) of these *Ilaqas* will be found in Provincial Table II.

325 persons (173 males, 152 females) classed as "others" though not shown as a separate religion are included in the total population of the State in the column for "All Religions."

VII.
Age, Sex
and Civil.
Condition.

TABLE VII.

AGE, SEX AND CIVIL CONDITION BY RELIGION.

Jammu and Kashmir State Census 1921,

Part I—Provincial Tables.

Religion.	Age.	Population. Persons.	Population. Males.	Population. Females.	Unmarried. Persons.	Unmarried. Males.	Unmarried. Females.	Married. Persons.	Married. Males.	Married. Females.	Widowed. Persons.	Widowed. Males.	Widowed. Females.
1	2	3	4	5	6	7	8	9	10	11	12	13	14
							(i) ENTIRE STATE.						
All Religions.	**Total**	**3,259,527**	**1,724,581**	**1,534,946**	**1,516,150**	**911,886**	**604,264**	**1,450,716**	**706,736**	**743,980**	**292,661**	**105,959**	**186,702**
	0—1	104,549	52,983	51,566	104,523	52,978	51,545	24	5	19	2	...	2
	1—2	64,418	32,656	31,762	64,391	32,646	31,745	24	10	14	3	..	3
	2—3	89,842	44,890	44,952	89,707	44,856	44,851	127	33	94	8	1	7
	3—4	112,417	56,701	55,716	111,964	56,557	55,407	426	134	292	27	10	17
	4—5	102,145	51,847	50,298	101,455	51,598	49,857	591	173	418	99	76	23
	Total 0—5	**473,371**	**239,077**	**234,294**	**472,040**	**238,635**	**233,405**	**1,192**	**355**	**837**	**139**	**87**	**52**
	5—10	495,912	259,241	236,671	479,663	255,590	224,073	15,349	3,455	11,894	900	196	704
	10—15	373,886	208,565	165,321	299,224	190,880	108,344	72501	17,000	55,501	2,161	685	1,476
	15—20	275,990	143,653	132,337	123,387	101,901	21,486	147,716	40,269	107,447	4,887	1,483	3,404
	20—25	266,897	127,531	139,366	59,399	52,524	6,875	197,506	71,288	126,218	9,992	3,719	6,273
	25—30	272,122	137,026	135,096	32,979	30,515	2,464	224,023	99,521	124,502	15,120	6,990	8,130
	30—35	266,201	143,519	122,682	16,744	14,816	1,928	226,713	118,728	107,985	22,744	9,975	12,769
	35—40	175,598	98,594	770,04	8,371	6,499	1,872	147,898	84,041	63,857	19,329	8,054	11,275
	40—45	181,807	95,869	85,938	7,899	6,386	1,513	140,630	78,495	62,135	33,278	10,988	22,290
	45—50	97,810	55,594	42,216	4,072	3,327	745	72,193	44,951	27,242	21,545	7,316	14,229
	50—55	134,701	75,074	59,627	4,559	3,988	571	86,806	57,521	29,285	43,336	13,565	29,771
	55—60	41,776	25,721	16,055	1,651	1,389	262	26,170	18,894	7,276	13,955	5,438	8,517
	60—65	103,134	58,138	44,996	3,123	2,824	299	52,462	40,004	12,458	47,549	15,310	32,239
	65—70	19,779	12,079	7,700	708	588	120	9,893	7,939	1,954	9,178	3,552	5,626
	70 & over	80,543	44,900	35,643	2,331	2,024	307	29,664	24,275	5,389	48,548	18,601	29,947
Hindu.	**Total**	**668,988**	**357,360**	**311,628**	**284,073**	**186,581**	**97,492**	**290,175**	**141,809**	**148,366**	**94,740**	**28,970**	**65,770**
	0—1	19,871	10,082	9,789	19,871	10,082	9,782	..	...	...	...	...	...
	1—2	11,236	5,884	5,352	11,235	5,883	5,352	1	1	..	...	...	...
	2—3	15,066	7,567	7,499	15,041	7,564	7,477	20	3	17	5	..	5
	3—4	17,876	8,710	9,166	17,736	8,697	9,039	131	12	119	9	1	8
	4—5	16,933	8,566	8,367	16,812	8,547	8,265	105	16	89	16	3	13
	Total 0—5	**80,982**	**40,809**	**40,173**	**80,695**	**40,773**	**39,922**	**257**	**32**	**225**	**30**	**4**	**26**
	5—10	89,133	45,307	43,826	83,815	44,685	39,130	4,900	582	4,318	418	40	378
	10—15	70,988	39,914	31,074	52,488	36,908	15,580	17,711	2,885	14,826	789	121	668
	15—20	55,582	28,973	26,609	23,221	21,494	1,727	30,729	7,178	23,551	1,632	301	1,331
	20—25	51,352	25,818	25,534	13,393	13,070	323	34,693	12,064	22,629	3,266	684	2,582
	25—30	58,976	31,334	27,642	10,382	10,143	239	43,306	19,468	23,848	5,288	1,728	3,560
	30—35	55,662	30,009	25,653	6,250	6,065	185	41,741	21,528	20,213	7,671	2,416	5,255
	35—40	38,610	21,826	16,784	3,156	3,056	100	28,312	16,395	11,917	7,142	2,375	4,767
	40—45	42,402	22,441	19,961	3,067	2,973	94	27,898	16,249	11,649	11,437	3,219	8,218
	45—50	25,249	14,944	10,305	1,855	1,783	72	15,525	10,723	4,802	7,869	2,438	5,431
	50—55	34,295	18,801	15,494	2,087	2,053	34	18,533	12,797	5,736	13,675	3,951	9,724
	55—60	12,962	8,105	4,857	938	917	21	6,683	5,248	1,435	5,341	1,940	3,401
	60—65	26,126	14,585	11,541	1,421	1,389	32	10,928	8,927	2,001	13,777	4,269	9,508
	65—70	5,868	3,478	2,390	362	353	9	2,364	2,015	349	3,142	1,110	2,032
	70 & over	20,801	11,016	9,785	943	919	24	6,595	5,723	872	13,263	4,374	8,889
Arya.	**Total**	**23,116**	**12,608**	**10,508**	**9,283**	**5,928**	**3,361**	**11,091**	**5,579**	**5,512**	**2,736**	**1,101**	**1,635**
	0—1	723	366	357	723	366	357	..	..	..	..	..	..
	1—2	418	222	196	418	222	196	..	..	..	..	...	..
	2—3	628	345	283	628	345	283	..	..	..	..	..	..
	3—4	701	352	349	698	352	346	3	..	3	...	..	..
	4—5	624	322	302	619	322	297	5	..	5	...	..	..
	Total 0—5	**3,094**	**1,607**	**1,487**	**3,086**	**1,607**	**1,479**	**8**	..	**8**	..	...	..
	5—10	3,248	1,720	1,528	2,961	1,682	1,279	268	31	237	19	7	12
	10—15	2,609	1,459	1,150	1,801	1,295	506	778	159	619	30	8	22
	15—20	1,846	972	874	642	590	52	1,159	363	796	46	19	27
	20—25	1,809	931	878	314	310	4	1,401	585	816	94	36	58
	25—30	2,083	1,089	994	198	193	5	1,705	840	865	180	56	124
	30—35	2,004	1,087	917	110	103	7	1,645	889	756	249	95	154
	35—40	1,262	729	533	65	42	23	1,029	605	424	168	82	86
	40—45	1,361	740	621	40	39	1	984	577	407	337	124	213
	45—50	807	444	363	21	21	..	526	328	198	260	95	165
	50—55	952	570	382	18	18	..	606	428	178	328	124	204
	55—60	335	215	120	3	3	..	199	150	49	133	62	71
	60—65	827	512	315	21	21	..	432	335	97	374	156	218
	65—70	164	95	69	..	..	..	62	50	12	102	45	57
	70 & over	715	438	277	9	7	2	290	239	51	416	192	224

TABLE VII.

Age, Sex and Civil Condition by Religion.

Jammu and Kashmir State Census 1921.

Part I—Provincial Tables.

Religion.	Age.	Population.			Unmarried.			Married.			Widowed.		
		Persons.	Males.	Females.	Persons.	Males.	Females.	Persons.	Males.	Females.	Persons.	Males.	Females.
1	2	3	4	5	6	7	8	9	10	11	12	13	14
Brahmo.	**Total**	**15**	**7**	**8**	**6**	**3**	**3**	**6**	**3**	**3**	**3**	**1**	**2**
	0—1	1	1	..	1	1	..	..	..	..	..	..	..
	1—2	..	..	..	..	..	..	..	..	..	..	..	..
	2—3	..	..	..	..	..	..	..	..	..	..	..	..
	3—4	..	..	..	..	..	..	..	..	..	..	..	..
	4—5	1	..	1	1	..	1	..	..	..	..	..	..
	Total 0—5	**2**	**1**	**1**	**2**	**1**	**1**	..	..	..	..	..	..
	5—10	2	2	..	2	2	..	..	..	..	..	..	..
	10—15	2	..	2	2	..	2	..	..	..	..	..	..
	15—20	..	..	..	..	..	..	..	..	..	..	..	..
	20—25	..	..	..	..	..	..	..	..	..	..	..	..
	25—30	2	..	2	..	..	..	2	..	2	..	..	..
	30—35	2	1	1	..	..	..	2	1	1	..	..	..
	35—40	1	1	..	..	..	..	1	1	..	..	..	..
	40—45	..	..	..	..	..	..	..	..	..	..	..	..
	45—50	..	..	..	..	..	..	..	..	..	..	..	..
	50—55	2	1	1	..	..	..	1	1	..	1	..	1
	55—60	..	..	..	..	..	..	..	..	..	..	..	..
	60—65	2	1	1	..	..	..	..	..	..	2	1	1
	65—70	..	..	..	..	..	..	..	..	..	..	..	..
	70 & over	..	..	..	..	..	..	..	..	..	..	..	..
Sikh.	**Total**	**39,486**	**20,773**	**18,713**	**19,189**	**11,464**	**7,725**	**17,056**	**8,183**	**8,873**	**3,241**	**1,126**	**2,115**
	0—1	1,368	714	654	1,366	714	652	2	..	2	..	..	..
	1—2	973	505	468	973	505	468	..	..	..	..	..	..
	2—3	1,154	609	545	1,153	609	544	1	..	1	..	..	..
	3—4	1,334	650	684	1,331	649	682	3	1	2	..	..	..
	4—5	1,415	672	743	1,414	672	742	1	..	1	..	..	..
	Total 0—5	**6,244**	**3,150**	**3,094**	**6,237**	**3,149**	**3,088**	**7**	**1**	**6**	..	..	..
	5—10	6,512	3,406	3,106	6,360	3,393	2,967	147	12	135	5	1	4
	10—15	4,621	2,579	2,042	3,779	2,432	1,347	827	143	684	15	4	11
	15—20	3,218	1,487	1,731	1,251	1,110	141	1,924	361	1,563	43	16	27
	20—25	2,927	1,443	1,484	588	541	47	2,269	880	1,389	70	22	48
	25—30	3,262	1,697	1,565	426	396	30	2,685	1,232	1,453	151	69	82
	30—35	2,945	1,513	1,432	133	122	11	2,556	1,294	1,262	256	97	159
	35—40	2,111	1,245	866	158	147	11	1,740	1,006	734	213	92	121
	40—45	2,046	986	1,060	70	55	15	1,584	834	750	392	97	295
	45—50	1,304	796	508	27	21	6	1,007	687	320	270	88	182
	50—55	1,508	816	692	51	31	20	972	646	326	485	139	346
	55—60	524	328	196	40	21	19	304	236	68	180	71	109
	60—65	1,081	639	442	32	20	12	576	472	104	473	147	326
	65—70	269	158	111	11	6	5	125	95	30	133	57	76
	70 & over	914	530	384	26	20	6	333	284	49	555	226	329
Jain.	**Total**	**529**	**295**	**234**	**271**	**158**	**113**	**203**	**113**	**90**	**55**	**24**	**31**
	0—1	25	11	14	25	11	14	..	..	..	..	..	..
	1—2	11	4	7	11	4	7	..	..	..	..	..	..
	2—3	8	6	2	8	6	2	..	..	..	..	..	..
	3—4	19	6	13	19	6	13	..	..	..	1	..	1
	4—5	17	5	12	16	5	11	..	..	..	..	..	..
	Total 0—5	**80**	**32**	**48**	**79**	**32**	**47**	..	..	..	**1**	..	**1**
	5—10	62	30	32	62	30	32	..	..	..	..	..	..
	10—15	70	42	28	68	42	26	2	..	2	..	..	..
	15—20	39	24	15	24	17	7	15	7	8	..	..	..
	20—25	57	29	28	12	12	..	43	15	28	2	2	..
	25—30	42	28	14	14	13	1	26	14	12	2	1	1
	30—35	42	26	16	5	5	..	30	19	11	7	2	5
	35—40	27	17	10	3	3	..	20	11	9	4	3	1
	40—45	33	21	12	2	2	..	25	17	8	6	2	4
	45—50	20	13	7	2	2	..	10	8	2	8	3	5
	50—55	24	13	11	..	..	..	15	10	5	9	3	6
	55—60	7	6	1	..	..	..	5	4	1	2	2	..
	60—65	17	8	9	..	..	..	7	4	3	10	4	6
	65—70	5	2	3	..	..	..	3	2	1	2	..	2
	70 & over	4	4	..	..	..	..	2	2	..	2	2	..

VII Age, Sex and Civil Condition.

TABLE VII.

Age, Sex and Civil Condition by Religion.

Jammu and Kashmir Census 1921.

Part I—Provincial Tables.

Religion.	Age.	Population.			Unmarried.			Married.			Widowed.		
		Persons.	Males.	Females.	Persons.	Males.	Females.	Persons.	Males.	Females.	Persons.	Males.	Females.
1	2	3	4	5	6	7	8	9	10	11	12	13	14
Budh.	**Total**	**37,685**	**18,838**	**18,847**	**17,100**	**8,368**	**8,732**	**16,249**	**9,329**	**6,920**	**4,336**	**1,141**	**3,**
	0—1	781	382	399	781	382	399	..	..	..	..	..	..
	1—2	670	328	342	670	328	342	..	..	..	...	..	..
	2—3	561	267	294	561	267	294	..	..	..	..	..	..
	3—4	920	454	466	918	454	464	2	0	2	..	..	..
	4—5	713	326	387	712	326	386	1	0	1	..	..	..
	Total 0—5	**3,645**	**1,757**	**1,888**	**3,642**	**1,757**	**1,885**	**3**	**0**	**3**	..	..	..
	5—10	3,668	1,789	1,879	3,646	1,773	1,873	20	16	4	2	0	
	10—15	3,444	1,723	1,721	3,204	1,562	1,642	237	158	79	3	3	
	15—20	3,633	1,991	1,642	2,608	1,316	1,292	1,001	665	336	24	10	
	20—25	3,102	1,526	1,576	1,093	463	630	1,924	1,028	896	85	35	
	25—30	2,813	1,310	1,503	556	226	330	2,132	1,038	1,094	125	46	
	30—35	2,162	1,593	569	609	431	178	1,384	1,105	279	169	57	
	35—40	2,750	1,340	1,410	479	169	310	2,130	1,115	1,015	141	56	
	40—45	2,550	1,347	1,203	228	184	44	2,016	1,065	951	306	98	
	45—50	1,798	838	960	260	93	167	1,338	686	652	200	59	
	50—55	2,090	1,042	1,048	184	120	64	1,558	838	720	348	84	
	55—60	1,311	626	685	219	75	144	815	471	344	277	80	
	60—65	1,415	807	608	136	82	54	711	537	174	568	188	
	65—70	791	415	376	77	44	33	446	274	172	268	97	
	70 & over	2,513	734	1,779	159	73	86	534	333	201	1,820	328	1,
Zoroastrian.	**Total**	**7**	**5**	**2**	**2**	**1**	**1**	**5**	**4**	**1**	..	..	..
	0—1	..	..	..	..	..	..	..	..	..	..	..	..
	1—2	..	..	..	..	..	..	..	..	..	...	..	..
	2—3	..	..	..	..	..	..	..	..	..	..	..	..
	3—4	..	..	..	..	..	..	..	..	..	..	..	..
	4—5	..	..	..	..	..	..	..	..	..	..	..	..
	Total 0—5	..	..	..	..	..	..	..	..	..	..	..	..
	5—10	..	..	..	..	..	..	..	..	..	..	..	..
	10—15	..	..	..	..	..	..	..	..	..	..	..	..
	15—20	2	1	1	1	..	1	1	1	..	..	..	..
	20—25	..	..	..	..	..	..	..	..	..	..	..	..
	25—30	..	..	..	..	..	..	..	..	..	..	..	..
	30—35	1	..	1	..	..	..	1	..	1	..	..	..
	35—40	3	3	..	1	1	..	2	2	..	..	..	..
	40—45	..	..	..	..	..	..	..	..	..	..	..	..
	45—50	1	1	..	..	..	..	1	1	..	..	..	..
	50—55	..	..	..	..	..	..	..	..	..	..	..	..
	55—60	..	..	..	..	..	..	..	..	..	..	..	..
	60—65	..	..	..	..	..	..	..	..	..	..	..	..
	65—70	..	..	..	..	..	..	..	..	..	..	..	..
	70 & over	..	..	..	..	..	..	..	..	..	..	..	..
Musalman.	**Total**	**2,487,743**	**1,313,635**	**1,174,108**	**1,185,302**	**698,858**	**486,444**	**1,115,102**	**541,280**	**573,822**	**187,339**	**73,497**	**113,**
	0—1	81,693	41,380	40,313	81,669	41,375	40,294	22	5	17	2	..	
	1—2	51,081	25,705	25,376	51,055	25,696	25,359	23	9	14	3	..	
	2—3	72,388	36,078	36,310	72,280	36,047	36,233	105	30	75	3	1	
	3—4	91,501	46,487	45,014	91,198	46,357	44,841	285	121	164	18	9	
	4—5	82,383	41,930	40,453	81,824	41,701	40,123	478	157	321	81	72	
	Total 0—5	**379,046**	**191,580**	**187,466**	**378,026**	**191,176**	**186,850**	**913**	**322**	**591**	**107**	**82**	
	5—10	393,052	206,868	186,184	382,587	203,909	178,678	10,009	2,811	7,198	456	148	
	10—15	291,955	162,747	129,208	237,714	148,552	89,162	52,921	13,649	39,272	1,320	546	
	15—20	211,511	110,118	101,393	95,556	77,312	18,244	112,820	31,674	81,146	3,135	1,132	2,
	20—25	207,498	97,693	109,805	43,940	38,086	5,854	157,085	56,669	100,416	6,473	2,938	3,
	25—30	204,770	101,463	103,307	21,362	19,507	1,855	174,052	76,877	97,175	9,356	5,077	4,
	30—35	203,213	109,199	94,014	9,617	8,073	1,544	179,218	93,828	85,390	14,378	7,298	7,
	35—40	130,718	73,372	57,346	4,493	3,071	1,422	114,576	64,863	49,713	11,649	5,438	6,
	40—45	133,282	70,265	63,017	4,486	3,131	1,355	108,031	59,696	48,335	20,765	7,438	13,
	45—50	68,551	38,512	30,039	1,899	1,402	497	53,732	32,483	21,249	12,920	4,627	8,
	50—55	95,755	53,794	41,961	2,218	1,766	452	65,062	42,768	22,294	28,475	9,260	19,
	55—60	26,584	16,415	10,169	446	373	73	18,135	12,765	5,370	8,003	3,277	4,
	60—65	73,603	41,543	32,060	1,513	1,312	201	39,775	29,702	10,073	32,315	10,529	21,
	65—70	12,656	7,912	4,744	255	182	73	6,878	5,491	1,387	5,523	2,239	3,
	70 & over	55,549	32,154	23,395	1,190	1,004	186	21,895	17,682	4,213	32,464	13,468	18,

TABLE VII.

VII Age, Sex and Civil Condition.

Age, Sex and Civil Condition by Religion.

Jammu and Kashmir State Census 1921.

Part I.—Provincial Tables.

Religion.	Age.	Population. Persons.	Population. Males.	Population. Females.	Unmarried. Persons.	Unmarried. Males.	Unmarried. Females.	Married. Persons.	Married. Males.	Married. Females.	Widowed. Persons.	Widowed. Males.	Widowed. Females.
1	2	3	4	5	6	7	8	9	10	11	12	13	14
Christian.	**Total**	**1,633**	**887**	**746**	**744**	**419**	**325**	**712**	**387**	**325**	**177**	**81**	**96**
	0—1	56	24	32	56	24	32	..	..	..	..	..	..
	1—2	20	4	16	20	4	16	..	..	..	..	..	..
	2—3	33	16	17	32	16	16	1	..	1	..	..	..
	3—4	48	27	21	46	27	19	2	..	2	..	..	..
	4—5	51	24	27	50	24	26	1	..	1	..	..	..
	Total 0—5	**208**	**95**	**113**	**204**	**95**	**109**	**4**	..	**4**	..	..	..
	5—10	187	92	95	185	92	93	2	..	2	..	..	..
	10—15	152	77	75	130	73	57	21	4	17	1	..	1
	15—20	137	74	63	73	53	20	61	19	42	8	2	1
	20—25	136	81	55	55	39	16	80	41	39	1	1	..
	25—30	149	92	57	36	30	6	97	51	46	16	11	5
	30—35	145	83	62	19	16	3	113	57	56	13	10	3
	35—40	96	54	42	16	10	6	71	36	35	9	8	1
	40—45	118	63	55	6	2	4	79	51	28	33	10	23
	45—50	74	40	28	7	5	2	50	35	15	17	6	11
	50—55	70	37	33	1	..	1	56	33	23	13	4	9
	55—60	47	23	24	5	..	5	24	18	6	18	5	13
	60—65	55	38	17	..	..	..	31	25	6	24	13	11
	65—70	19	13	6	3	3	..	10	7	3	6	3	3
	70 & over	40	19	21	4	1	3	13	10	3	23	8	15
						(ii) JAMMU PROVINCE.							
All Religions.	**Total**	**1,640,259**	**859,619**	**780,640**	**743,870**	**457,283**	**286,587**	**719,332**	**343,094**	**376,238**	**177,087**	**59,242**	**117,8 5**
	0—1	55,044	27,697	27,347	55,026	27,693	27,333	17	4	13	1	..	1
	1—2	30,265	15,491	14,774	30,244	15,485	14,759	19	6	13	2	..	2
	2—3	42,427	21,312	21,115	42,307	21,282	21,025	113	30	80	7	..	7
	3—4	50,964	25 574	25,390	50,559	25,456	25,103	381	110	271	24	8	16
	4—5	50,335	25,571	24,764	49,746	25,399	24,347	548	151	397	41	21	20
	Total 0—5	**229,035**	**115,645**	**113,390**	**227,882**	**115,315**	**112,567**	**1,078**	**301**	**777**	**75**	**29**	**46**
	5—10	248,317	129,346	118,971	235,837	127,103	108,734	11,676	2,075	9,601	804	168	636
	10—15	188,521	104,629	83,892	145,397	95,583	49,814	41,479	8,482	32,997	1,645	564	1,081
	15—20	135,251	68,573	66,678	59,779	49,848	9,931	72,595	17,928	54,667	2,877	797	2,080
	20—25	118,675	55,737	62,938	26,872	24.941	1,931	86.113	29,017	57,096	5,690	1,779	3,91
	25—30	134,541	66,869	67,672	18.494	17,502	992	106,754	45,543	61,211	9,293	3,824	5,469
	30—35	132,395	68 801	63,594	10,101	9,384	717	108,219	54,073	54,146	14,075	5,344	8,731
	35—40	87,305	48,614	38,691	5 153	4.241	912	70,149	39,765	30,384	12,003	4,608	7,395
	40—45	95,533	49,706	45,827	4,354	4,044	310	71,061	39,638	31,423	20,118	6,024	14,094
	45—50	51,993	29 691	22,302	2,311	2,125	186	36,369	23,149	13,220	13,313	4,417	8,896
	50—55	72,167	38.894	33,273	2,664	2,509	155	44,640	29,073	15,567	24,863	7,312	17,551
	55—60	25,278	15,376	9,902	1,037	986	51	15,029	11,045	8,984	9,212	3,345	5,867
	60—65	58,980	33.061	25,929	1,895	1,762	133	29,224	22,569	6,655	27,861	8,720	19,141
	65—70	12,032	7,087	4,945	453	430	23	5,844	4,612	1,232	5,735	2,045	3,690
	70 & over	50,236	27,600	22,636	1,641	1,510	131	19,102	15,824	3,278	29,493	10,266	19,227
Hindu.	**Total**	**603,549**	**319,928**	**283,621**	**252,885**	**165,624**	**87,261**	**263,721**	**128,114**	**135,607**	**86,943**	**26,190**	**60,753**
	0—1	18,252	9,232	9,020	18,252	9.232	9,020	..	..	..	..	..	..
	1—2	10,655	5,519	5,136	10,654	5,518	5,136	1	1	..	..	..	..
	2—3	13,685	6,814	6,871	13.660	6,811	6,849	20	3	17	5	..	5
	3—4	16,218	7,926	8,292	16,078	7,913	8,165	131	12	119	9	1	8
	4—5	15,367	7 728	7,639	15,246	7,709	7,537	105	16	89	16	3	13
	Total 0—5	**74,177**	**37,219**	**36,958**	**73,890**	**37,183**	**36,707**	**257**	**32**	**225**	**30**	**4**	**26**
	5—10	80,4[illegible]	41,140	39,343	75,33[illegible]	40,6[illegible]3	34,711	4,734	477	4,257	415	40	375
	10—15	[illegible]3,52[illegible]	35,547	27,9[illegible]	45,95[illegible]	32,6[illegible]3	13,268	16,854	2,750	14,104	721	114	607
	15—20	49,[illegible]	25,446	24,461	20,267	18.769	1,49[illegible]	28,140	6,437	21,703	1,500	240	1.260
	20—25	41,01[illegible]	22,0[illegible]9	22,908	11,139	10,847	29[illegible]	30,678	10,542	20,136	3,100	620	2,180
	25—30	52,820	27,697	25,12[illegible]	9,007	8,777	230	38,999	17 324	21,675	4,814	1,596	3,218
	30—35	49,023	26,621	23,202	5,439	5,267	172	37,358	19,148	18,210	7,026	2,206	4,820
	35—40	34,70[illegible]	19,525	15,184	2,721	2,621	100	25,551	14,825	10,726	6,437	2,079	4,358
	40—45	38,387	20,171	18,216	2,550	2,459	91	25,402	14,826	10,576	10,435	2,886	7,549
	45—50	22,430	13,086	9,344	1,546	1,474	72	13,809	9,437	4,372	7,075	2,175	4, 00
	50—55	31,092	16,893	14,199	1,819	1,785	34	16,934	11,636	5,298	12,339	3,472	8,867
	55—60	11,529	7,265	4,264	815	794	21	5,983	4,756	1,227	4,731	1,715	3,016
	60—65	24,360	13,569	10,791	1,242	1,210	32	10,390	8,473	1,917	12,728	3,886	8,842
	65—70	5,323	3,158	2,165	306	297	9	2,223	1,888	335	2,794	973	1,821
	70 & over	20,066	10,582	9,484	859	835	24	6,409	5,563	846	12,798	4,184	8,614

VII
Age, Sex
nd Civil
Condition.

TABLE VII.

Age, Sex and Civil Condition by Religion.

Jammu and Kashmir State Census 1921.

Part I—Provincial Tables.

Religion.	Age.	Population.			Unmarried.			Married.			Widowed.		
		Persons.	Males.	Females.	Persons.	Males.	Females.	Persons.	Males.	Females.	Persons.	Males.	Females.
1	2	3	4	5	6	7	8	9	10	11	12	13	14
Arya.	**Total**	**23,045**	**12,560**	**10,485**	**9,240**	**5,891**	**3,349**	**11,069**	**5,568**	**5,501**	**2,736**	**1,101**	**1,6[illegible]**
	0—1	720	364	356	720	364	356	..	..	..	..	..	..
	1—2	416	220	196	416	220	196	..	..	..	..	..	..
	2—3	624	342	282	624	342	282	..	..	..	..	..	..
	3—4	699	350	349	696	350	346	3	..	3	..	..	..
	4—5	621	320	301	616	320	296	5	..	5	..	..	..
	Total 0—5	**3,080**	**1,596**	**1,484**	**3,072**	**1,596**	**1,476**	**8**	..	**8**	..	..	..
	5—10	3,233	1,713	1,520	2,946	1,675	1,271	268	31	237	19	7	1
	10—15	2,601	1,452	1,149	1,793	1,285	508	778	159	619	30	8	2
	15—20	1,844	970	874	640	588	52	1,158	363	795	46	19	2
	20—25	1,801	927	874	311	307	4	1,396	584	812	94	36	5
	25—30	2,077	1,086	991	196	191	5	1,701	839	862	180	56	12
	30—35	1,996	1,081	915	108	101	7	1,639	885	754	249	95	15
	35—40	1,258	726	532	64	41	23	1,026	603	423	168	82	8
	40—45	1,356	735	621	38	37	1	981	574	407	337	124	21
	45—50	807	444	363	21	21	..	526	328	198	260	95	16
	50—55	952	570	382	18	18	..	606	428	178	328	124	20
	55—60	335	215	120	3	3	..	199	150	49	133	62	7
	60—65	826	512	314	21	21	..	431	335	96	374	156	21
	65—70	164	95	69	..	..	..	62	50	12	102	45	57
	70 & over	715	438	277	9	7	2	290	239	51	416	192	224
Brahmo.	**Total**	**15**	**7**	**8**	**6**	**3**	**3**	**6**	**3**	**3**	**3**	**1**	**1**
	0—1	1	1	..	1	1	..	..	..	..	..	..	..
	1—2	..	..	..	..	..	..	..	..	..	..	..	..
	2—3	..	..	..	..	..	..	..	..	..	..	..	..
	3—4	..	..	..	..	..	..	..	..	..	..	..	..
	4—5	1	..	1	1	..	1	..	..	..	..	..	..
	Total 0—5	**2**	**1**	**1**	**2**	**1**	**1**	..	..	..	..	..	..
	5—10	2	2	..	2	2	..	..	..	..	..	..	..
	10—15	2	..	2	2	..	2	..	..	..	..	..	..
	15—20	..	..	..	..	..	..	..	..	..	..	..	..
	20—25	..	..	..	..	..	..	..	..	..	..	..	..
	25—30	2	..	2	..	..	..	2	..	2	..	..	..
	30—35	2	1	1	..	..	..	2	1	1	..	..	..
	35—40	1	1	..	..	..	..	1	1	—	..	..	..
	40—45	..	..	..	..	..	..	..	..	..	..	..	..
	45—50	..	..	..	..	..	..	..	..	..	..	..	..
	50—55	2	1	1	..	..	..	1	1	..	1	..	1
	55—60	..	..	..	..	..	..	..	..	..	..	..	..
	60—65	2	1	1	..	..	..	..	..	..	2	1	1
	65—70	..	..	..	..	..	..	..	..	..	..	..	..
	70 & over	..	..	..	..	..	..	..	..	..	..	..	..
Sikh.	**Total**	**21,627**	**11,381**	**10,246**	**10,238**	**6,269**	**3,969**	**9,332**	**4,416**	**4,916**	**2,057**	**696**	**1,[illegible]**
	0—1	806	414	392	804	414	390	2	..	2	..	..	..
	1—2	389	191	198	389	191	198	..	..	..	..	..	..
	2—3	601	320	281	600	320	280	1	..	1	..	..	..
	3—4	691	360	331	688	359	329	3	1	2	..	..	..
	4—5	702	359	343	701	359	342	1	..	1	..	..	..
	Total 0—5	**3,189**	**1,644**	**1,545**	**3,182**	**1,643**	**1,539**	**7**	**1**	**6**	..	..	..
	5—10	3,441	1,763	1,678	3,308	1,757	1,551	132	6	126	1	..	1
	10—15	2,652	1,482	1,170	2,126	1,381	745	517	97	420	9	4	5
	15—20	1,871	931	940	805	708	97	1,038	211	827	28	12	16
	20—25	1,469	727	742	330	320	10	1,097	390	707	42	17	25
	25—30	1,701	824	877	208	202	6	1,404	587	817	89	35	54
	30—35	1,624	829	795	90	85	5	1,359	672	687	175	72	103
	35—40	1,201	701	500	53	50	3	1,024	603	421	124	48	76
	40—45	1,075	507	568	40	37	3	801	417	384	234	53	181
	45—50	826	535	291	19	18	1	623	449	174	184	68	116
	50—55	869	453	416	31	26	5	524	346	178	314	81	233
	55—60	333	203	130	16	15	1	199	144	55	118	44	74
	60—65	663	386	277	12	12	...	329	265	64	322	109	213
	65—70	176	93	83	4	4	...	81	61	20	91	28	63
	70 & over	537	303	234	14	11	3	197	167	30	326	125	201

TABLE VII.

VII
Age, Sex
and Civil
Condition.

Age, Sex and Civil Condition by Religion,

Jammu and Kashmir State Census 1921.

Part I.—Provincial Tables.

Religion.	Age.	Population.			Unmarried.			Married.			Widowed.		
		Persons.	Males.	Females.	Persons.	Males.	Females.	Persons.	Males.	Females.	Persons.	Males.	Females.
1	2	3	4	5	6	7	8	9	10	11	12	12	14
Jain.	**Total**	**528**	**294**	**234**	**271**	**158**	**113**	**202**	**112**	**90**	**55**	**24**	**31**
	0—1	25	11	14	25	11	14	..	..	..	..	..	..
	1—2	11	4	7	11	4	7	..	..	..	..	..	..
	2—3	8	6	2	8	6	2	..	..	..	..	..	..
	3—4	19	6	13	19	6	13	..	..	..	..	..	..
	4—5	17	5	12	16	5	11	..	..	..	1	..	1
	Total 0—5	**80**	**32**	**48**	**79**	**32**	**47**	...	..	..	**1**	...	**1**
	5—10	62	30	32	62	30	32	..	..	..	..	..	..
	10—15	70	42	28	68	42	26	2	...	2	..	..	..
	15—20	39	24	15	24	17	7	15	7	8	..	..	..
	20—25	57	29	28	12	12	..	43	15	28	2	2	..
	25—30	41	27	14	14	13	1	25	13	12	2	1	1
	30—35	42	26	16	5	5	..	30	19	11	7	2	5
	35—40	27	17	10	3	2	...	20	11	9	4	3	1
	40—45	33	21	12	2	2	..	25	17	8	6	2	4
	45—50	20	13	7	2	2	..	10	8	2	8	3	5
	50—55	24	13	11	..	..	...	15	10	5	9	3	6
	55—60	7	6	1	..	..	..	5	4	1	2	2	..
	60—65	17	8	9	..	..	..	7	4	3	10	4	6
	65—70	5	2	3	..	..	...	3	2	1	2	...	2
	70 & over	4	4	..	..	..	..	2	2	..	2	2	..
Budh.	**Total**	**442**	**226**	**216**	**165**	**94**	**71**	**235**	**119**	**116**	**42**	**13**	**29**
	0—1	7	5	2	7	5	2	..	..	..	..	..	..
	1—2	6	4	2	6	4	2	..	...	..	..	..	...
	2—3	5	1	4	5	1	4	...	..	..	..	..	..
	3—4	10	5	5	10	5	5	...	..	..	..	..	..
	4—5	6	3	3	6	3	3	...	...	..	..	..	..
	Total 0—5	**34**	**18**	**16**	**34**	**18**	**16**	..	..	..	..	..	..
	5—10	48	25	23	48	25	23	..	..	..	..	..	..
	10—15	34	18	16	31	16	15	3	2	1	..	..	..
	15—20	52	26	26	32	18	14	20	8	12	..	..	..
	20—25	39	23	16	7	7	..	31	15	16	1	1	...
	25—30	36	15	21	3	2	1	31	13	18	2	...	2
	30—35	39	17	22	4	2	2	31	13	18	4	2	2
	35—40	27	16	11	1	1	..	24	14	10	2	1	1
	40—45	41	17	24	1	1	..	31	14	17	9	2	7
	45—50	19	9	10	1	1	...	16	8	8	2	...	2
	50—55	31	17	14	3	3	...	19	12	7	9	2	7
	55—60	7	4	3	..	..	..	6	4	2	1	..	1
	60—65	19	11	8	..	..	..	11	8	3	8	3	5
	65—70	1	1	..	..	..	..	1	1	...	...	...	...
	70 & over	15	9	6	..	...	..	11	7	4	4	2	2
Zoroastrian.	**Total**	**5**	**3**	**2**	**2**	**1**	**1**	**3**	**2**	**1**	..	..	..
	0—1	..	..	..	..	..	..	...	...	...	...	...	..
	1—2	..	..	..	..	..	..	...	...	...	...	...	...
	2—3	..	..	..	..	..	..	...	...	...	...	...	...
	3—4	..	..	..	..	..	..	...	...	...	...	...	...
	4—5	..	..	..	..	..	..	...	...	...	...	...	...
	Total 0—5	..	..	..	..	..	..	...	...	...	...	...	...
	5—10	..	..	..	..	..	..	...	...	...	...	...	...
	10—15	..	..	..	..	..	..	...	...	...	...	...	...
	15—20	1	..	1	1	..	1	...	...	...	...	...	...
	20—25	..	..	..	..	..	..	...	...	...	...	...	...
	25—30	..	..	..	..	..	..	...	...	...	...	...	...
	30—35	1	...	1	...	..	..	1	...	1	...	...	...
	35—40	3	3	..	1	1	..	2	2	...	...	...	...
	40—45	..	..	..	..	..	...	..	..	..	..	..	..
	45—50	..	..	..	..	..	...	..	..	..	..	..	..
	50—55	..	..	..	..	..	..	..	..	..	..	..	..
	55—60	..	..	..	..	..	..	..	..	..	..	..	..
	60—65	..	..	..	..	..	..	..	..	..	..	..	..
	65—70	..	..	..	..	..	...	..	..	..	..	..	..
	70 & over	..	..	..	..	..	..	..	..	..	..	..	..

VII
Age, Sex and Civil Condition.

TABLE VII.

Age, Sex and Civil Condition by Religion.

Jammu and Kashmir State Census 1921.

Part I.—Provincial Tables.

Religion.	Age.	Population: Persons.	Population: Males.	Population: Females.	Unmarried: Persons.	Unmarried: Males.	Unmarried: Females.	Married: Persons.	Married: Males.	Married: Females.	Widowed: Persons.	Widowed: Males.	Widowed: Females.
1	2	3	4	5	6	7	8	9	10	11	12	13	14
Musalman.	**Total**	**989,622**	**514,442**	**475,180**	**470,379**	**278,845**	**191,534**	**434,182**	**204,459**	**229,723**	**85,061**	**31,138**	**50 485**
	0—1	35,156	17,628	17,528	35,140	17,624	17,516	15	4	11	1	..	1
	1—2	18,764	9,546	9,218	18,744	9,541	9,203	18	5	13	2	..	1
	2—3	27,475	13 815	13,660	27,382	13 788	13,591	91	27	64	2	..	..
	3—4	33,279	16,894	16,385	33,022	16,790	16,232	242	97	145	15	7	1
	4—5	33,571	17,136	16,435	33,112	16,984	16,128	436	135	301	23	17	3
	Total 0—5	**148,245**	**75,019**	**73,226**	**147,400**	**74,727**	**72,673**	**802**	**268**	**534**	**43**	**24**	**6**
	5—10	160862	34,579	76,283	153,956	82,900	71,056	6,537	1,558	4,979	369	121	53
	10—15	119,468	66,001	53,467	95.286	60,097	35,189	23,300	5,468	17,832	882	436	252
	15—20	81,401	41,103	40,298	37,943	29,698	8,245	42,159	10,882	31,277	1,299	523	1,103
	20—25	70,288	31,957	38,331	15,039	13,420	1,619	52,799	17,435	35,364	2,450	1,102	1,669
	25—30	77,742	37,143	40,599	9,047	8,299	748	64,503	26,717	37,786	4,192	2,127	2,030
	30—35	78,753	40,171	38,582	4,446	3,915	531	67,705	33,297	34 408	6,602	2,959	3,112
	35—40	50,006	27,586	22,420	2,306	1,521	785	42,444	23,678	18,766	5,256	2,387	2,483
	40—45	54,551	28,206	26,345	1,721	1,506	215	43,763	23,753	20,010	9,067	2,947	6,701
	45—50	27,842	15 578	12,264	720	607	113	21,352	12,900	8,453	5 769	2,071	2,947
	50—55	39,157	20,925	18,232	793	677	116	26,510	16,621	9,889	11,854	3,627	10,311
	55 60	13,040	7,667	5,373	203	174	29	8,622	5,976	2,646	4,215	1,517	1,832
	60—65	33,053	18,534	14,519	620	519	101	18,037	13,466	4,571	14,396	4,549	9,799
	65—70	6,347	3,724	2,623	142	128	14	3,464	2,601	863	2,741	995	1,242
	70& over	28,867	16,249	12,618	757	657	100	12,184	9,839	2,345	15,926	5,753	6.815
Christian.	**Total**	**1,207**	**662**	**545**	**558**	**318**	**240**	**511**	**275**	**236**	**138**	**69**	**25**
	0—1	48	20	28	48	20	28	...	...	...	..	..	..
	1—2	18	4	14	18	4	14	...	...	..	..	..	..
	2—3	29	14	15	28	14	14	1	..	1	..	..	...
	3—4	32	18	14	30	18	12	2	...	2	..	..	..
	4—5	43	19	24	42	19	23	1	..	1	..	..	..
	Total 0—5	**170**	**75**	**95**	**166**	**75**	**91**	**4**	..	**4**	..	..	...
	5—10	154	76	78	152	76	76	2	..	2	..	..	..
	10—15	138	71	67	116	67	49	21	4	17	1	..	...
	15—20	119	62	57	56	41	15	60	19	41	3	2	...
	20—25	101	64	37	33	28	5	67	35	32	1	1	...
	25—30	110	69	41	16	15	1	81	46	35	13	8	..
	30—35	101	54	47	8	8	..	82	38	44	11	8	...
	35—40	56	33	23	4	3	1	43	22	21	9	8	..
	40—45	82	48	34	2	2	..	52	36	16	28	10	..
	45—50	44	26	18	2	2	..	28	19	9	14	5	1
	50—55	37	22	15	..	..	..	29	19	10	8	3	3
	55—60	22	14	8	..	..	..	11	10	1	11	4	6
	60—65	36	29	7	..	..	..	19	18	1	17	11	5
	65—70	10	8	2	1	1	..	5	4	1	4	3	2
	70& over	27	11	16	2	..	2	7	5	2	18	6	3
						(iii) KASHMIR PROVINCE.							
All Religions.	**Total**	**1,407,086**	**757,824**	**649,262**	**673,408**	**400,743**	**272,665**	**635,652**	**315,331**	**320,321**	**98,026**	**41.750**	**12,011**
	0—1	42,931	22,057	20,874	42,923	22,056	20,267	7	1	6	1	..	..
	1—2	29,135	14,747	14,388	29,129	14,743	14,386	5	4	1	1	..	..
	2—3	41,723	20,780	20,943	41,709	20,777	20,932	13	2	11	1	1	..
	3—4	54,388	27,630	26,758	54,343	27,605	26,738	42	23	19	3	2	..
	4—5	46,082	23,465	22,617	45,984	23,390	22,594	40	20	20	58	55	..
	Total 0—5	**214,259**	**108,679**	**105,580**	**214,088**	**108,571**	**105,517**	**107**	**50**	**57**	**64**	**58**	..
	5—10	220,287	115,915	104,372	216,889	114,620	102,269	3,318	1,274	2,044	80	21	9
	10—15	162,443	91,956	70,487	133,438	84,137	49,301	28,553	7,726	20,827	452	93	36
	15—20	121,212	64 391	56,821	52,610	44,935	7,675	66,837	18,875	47,962	1,765	581	149
	20—25	124,115	60,523	63,592	27,564	24,104	3,460	93,257	34,918	58.339	3,294	1,501	569
	25—30	128,902	65,539	63,363	13,159	12,112	1,047	110,350	50,463	59,887	5,393	2,964	232
	30—35	121,872	68,112	53,760	5,599	4,696	903	108,355	59,101	49,254	7,918	4,315	435
	35—40	69,521	41,226	28,295	2,243	1,787	456	61,318	36,415	24,903	5,960	3,024	943
	40—45	76,646	40,783	35,863	3,043	1,927	1,116	61,444	34,246	27,198	12,159	4,610	647
	45—50	33,326	19,975	13,351	1,381	1,043	338	25,937	16,467	9,470	6,008	2,465	1,710
	50—55	55,934	32,520	23,414	1,562	1,230	332	37,173	25,376	11,797	17,199	5,914	935
	55—60	13,826	8,880	4,946	385	321	64	9,269	6,644	2,625	4,172	1,915	393
	60—65	35,675	20,921	14,754	836	743	93	18,417	14,339	4,078	18,422	5,839	2,515
	65—70	5,795	3,904	1,891	148	107	41	2,929	2,548	381	2,718	1,249	467
	70& over	23,273	14,500	8,773	463	410	53	8,388	6,889	1,499	14,422	7,201	3.499

TABLE VII.

Age, Sex and Civil Condition by Religion.

Jammu and Kashmir State Census 1921.

Part I—Provincial Tables.

Religion.	Age.	Population.			Unmarried.			Married.			Widowed.		
		Persons.	Males.	Females.	Persons.	Males.	Females.	Persons.	Males.	Females.	Persons.	Males.	Females.
1	2	3	4	5	6	7	8	9	10	11	12	13	14
Hindu.	**Total**	**64,460**	**36,582**	**27,878**	**30,779**	**20,607**	**10,172**	**25,929**	**13,234**	**12,695**	**7,752**	**2,741**	**5,011**
	0—1	1,598	840	758	1,598	840	758	..	..	..	..	..	..
	1—2	576	363	213	576	363	213	..	..	..	..	..	..
	2—3	1,373	750	623	1,373	750	623	..	..	..	..	..	..
	3—4	1,649	780	869	1,649	780	869	..	..	..	..	..	..
	4—5	1,557	834	723	1,557	834	723	..	..	..	..	..	..
	Total 0—5	**6,753**	**3,567**	**3,186**	**6,753**	**3,567**	**3,186**	..	..	..	..	..	..
	5—10	8,600	4,139	4,461	8,432	4,034	4,398	165	105	60	3	..	3
	10—15	7,442	4,353	3,089	6,517	4,211	2 306	857	135	722	68	7	61
	15—20	5,581	3,445	2,136	2,889	2,662	227	2,561	722	1,839	131	61	70
	20—25	6,242	3,632	2,610	2,141	2,110	31	3,937	1,460	2,477	164	62	102
	25—30	5,978	3,471	2,507	1,303	1,294	9	4,212	2,055	2,157	463	122	341
	30—35	5,729	3,289	2,440	790	777	13	4,299	2,307	1,992	640	205	435
	35—40	3,843	2,254	1,589	430	430	..	2,714	1,533	1,181	699	291	408
	40—45	3,961	2,221	1,740	512	510	2	2,456	1,387	1,069	993	324	669
	45—50	2,767	1,807	960	308	308	..	1,669	1,239	430	790	260	530
	50—55	3,097	1,804	1,293	265	265	..	1,408	1,062	430	1,304	477	857
	55—60	1,428	836	592	121	121	..	699	491	208	608	224	384
	60—65	1,762	1,012	750	179	179	..	535	451	84	1,048	382	666
	65—70	543	318	225	55	55	..	141	127	14	347	136	211
	70 & over	734	434	300	84	84	..	186	160	26	464	190	274
Arya.	**Total**	**29**	**21**	**8**	**21**	**18**	**3**	**8**	**3**	**5**	..	..	...
	0—1	1	1	..	1	1	..	..	..	..	..	..	..
	1—2	1	1	..	1	1	..	..	..	..	..	..	...
	2—3	3	2	1	3	2	1	..	..	..	..	..	..
	3—4	..	..	..	..	..	..	..	..	..	..	..	..
	4—5	2	1	1	2	1	1	..	..	..	..	..	...
	Total 0—5	**7**	**5**	**2**	**7**	**5**	**2**	..	..	..	..	..	..
	5—10	4	4	..	4	4	..	..	..	..	..	..	..
	10—15	4	3	1	4	3	1	..	..	..	..	..	...
	15—20	1	1	..	1	1	..	..	..	..	...	...	...
	20—25	5	2	3	1	1	..	4	1	3	...	...	..
	25—30	1	..	1	...	...	...	1	..	1	...	..	...
	30—35	3	3	..	1	1	...	2	2	..	..	..	..
	35—40	1	1	..	1	1	...	...	..	..	..	..	..
	40—45	2	2	..	2	2	...	..	..	...	...	...	..
	45—50	..	..	..	..	..	...	..	..	..	...	..	..
	50—55	..	..	..	..	..	...	..	..	..	..	..	..
	55—60	..	..	..	..	..	...	..	..	...	..	..	..
	60—65	1	..	1	..	..	..	1	..	1	..	..	...
	65—70	..	..	..	..	..	..	..	..	...	..	..	..
	70 & over	..	..	..	..	..	..	..	..	..	..	...	..
Sikh.	**Total**	**17,742**	**9,316**	**8,426**	**8,897**	**5,165**	**3,732**	**7,666**	**3,723**	**3,943**	**1,179**	**428**	**751**
	0—1	560	299	261	560	299	261	..	..	..	..	..	..
	1—2	580	313	267	580	313	267	..	..	..	..	..	..
	2—3	550	289	261	550	289	261	..	..	..	..	..	..
	3—4	63	287	352	639	287	352	..	..	..	..	..	..
	4—5	7 [illegible]	312	398	710	312	398	..	...	..	..	..	..
	Total 0—5	**3 03[illegible]**	**1,500**	**1,539**	**3,039**	**1,500**	**1,539**	..	..	..	..	..	..
	5—10	3,062	1,642	1,420	3,043	1,635	1,408	15	6	9	4	1	3
	10—15	1,954	1,086	868	1,639	1,041	598	309	45	264	6	..	6
	15—20	1,335	550	785	440	397	43	881	149	732	14	4	10
	20—25	1,437	698	739	251	215	36	1,160	479	681	26	4	22
	25—30	1,555	869	686	218	194	24	1,275	641	634	62	34	28
	30—35	1,307	674	633	42	36	6	1,184	613	571	81	25	56
	35—40	901	537	364	105	97	8	707	396	311	89	44	45
	40—45	963	472	491	29	17	12	776	411	365	158	44	114
	45—50	474	258	216	8	3	5	382	236	146	84	19	65
	50—55	637	361	276	20	5	15	446	298	148	171	58	113
	55—60	190	124	66	24	6	18	104	91	13	62	27	35
	60—65	418	253	165	20	8	12	247	207	40	151	38	113
	65—70	93	65	28	7	2	5	44	34	10	42	29	13
	70 & over	377	227	150	12	9	3	136	117	19	229	101	128

VII
Age, Sex and Civil Condition.

TABLE VII.

AGE, SEX AND CIVIL CONDITION BY RELIGION.

Jammu and Kashmir State Census 1921.

Part I—Provincial Tables.

Religion.	Age.	Population.			Unmarried.			Married.			Widowed.		
		Persons.	Males.	Females.	Persons.	Males.	Females.	Persons.	Males.	Females.	Persons.	Males.	Females.
1	2	3	4	5	6	7	8	9	10	11	12	13	14
Jain.	Total	1	1	..	..	..	..	1	1	..	..	..	..
	0—1	..	..	..	..	..	..	..	..	..	..	..	..
	1—2	..	..	..	..	..	..	..	..	..	..	..	..
	2—3	..	..	..	..	..	..	..	..	..	..	..	..
	3—4	..	..	..	..	..	..	..	..	..	..	..	..
	4—5	..	..	..	..	..	..	..	..	..	..	..	..
	Total 0—5	..	..	..	..	..	..	..	..	..	..	..	..
	5—10	..	..	..	..	..	..	..	..	..	..	..	..
	10—15	..	..	..	..	..	..	..	..	..	..	..	..
	15—20	..	..	..	..	..	..	..	..	..	..	..	..
	20—25	..	..	..	..	..	..	..	..	..	..	..	..
	25—30	1	1	..	..	..	..	1	1	..	..	..	..
	30—35	..	..	..	..	..	..	..	..	..	..	..	..
	35—40	..	..	..	..	..	..	..	..	..	..	..	..
	40—45	..	..	..	..	..	..	..	..	..	..	..	..
	45—50	..	..	..	..	..	..	..	..	..	..	..	..
	50—55	..	..	..	..	..	..	..	..	..	..	..	..
	55—60	..	..	..	..	..	..	..	..	..	..	..	..
	60—65	..	..	..	..	..	..	..	..	..	..	..	..
	65—70	..	..	..	..	..	..	..	..	..	..	..	..
	70 & over	..	..	..	..	..	..	..	..	..	..	..	..
Budh.	Total	2	2	..	..	..	..	2	2	..	..	..	..
	0—1	..	..	..	..	..	..	..	..	..	..	..	..
	1—2	..	..	..	..	..	..	..	..	..	..	..	..
	2—3	..	..	..	..	..	..	..	..	..	..	..	..
	3—4	..	..	..	..	..	..	..	..	..	..	..	..
	4—5	..	..	..	..	..	..	..	..	..	..	..	..
	Total 0—5	..	..	..	..	..	..	..	..	..	..	..	..
	5—10	..	..	..	..	..	..	..	..	..	..	..	..
	10—15	..	..	..	..	..	..	..	..	..	..	..	..
	15—20	..	..	..	..	..	..	..	..	..	..	..	..
	20—25	..	..	..	..	..	..	..	..	..	..	..	..
	25—30	1	1	..	..	..	..	1	1	..	..	..	..
	30—35	..	..	..	..	..	..	..	..	..	..	..	..
	35—40	..	..	..	..	..	..	..	..	..	..	..	..
	40—45	..	..	..	..	..	..	..	..	..	..	..	..
	45—50	..	..	..	..	..	..	..	..	..	..	..	..
	50—55	1	1	..	..	..	..	1	1	..	..	..	..
	55—60	..	..	..	..	..	..	..	..	..	..	..	..
	60—65	..	..	..	..	..	..	..	..	..	..	..	..
	65—70	..	..	..	..	..	..	..	..	..	..	..	..
	70 & over	..	..	..	..	..	..	..	..	..	..	..	..
Zoroastrian.	Total	2	2	..	..	..	..	2	2	..	..	..	..
	0—1	..	..	..	..	..	..	..	..	..	..	..	..
	1—2	..	..	..	..	..	..	..	..	..	..	..	..
	2—3	..	..	..	..	..	..	..	..	..	..	..	..
	3—4	..	..	..	..	..	..	..	..	..	..	..	..
	4—5	..	..	..	..	..	..	..	..	..	..	..	..
	Total 0—5	..	..	..	..	..	..	..	..	..	..	..	..
	5—10	..	..	..	..	..	..	..	..	..	..	..	..
	10—15	..	..	..	..	..	..	..	..	..	..	..	..
	15—20	1	1	..	..	..	..	1	1	..	..	..	..
	20—25	..	..	..	..	..	..	..	..	..	..	..	..
	25—30	..	..	..	..	..	..	..	..	..	..	..	..
	30—35	..	..	..	..	..	..	..	..	..	..	..	..
	35—40	..	..	..	..	..	..	..	..	..	..	..	..
	40—45	..	..	..	..	..	..	..	..	..	..	..	..
	45—50	1	1	..	..	..	..	1	1	..	..	..	..
	50—55	..	..	..	..	..	..	..	..	..	..	..	..
	55—60	..	..	..	..	..	..	..	..	..	..	..	..
	60—65	..	..	..	..	..	..	..	..	..	..	..	..
	65—70	..	..	..	..	..	..	..	..	..	..	..	..
	70 & over	..	..	..	..	..	..	..	..	..	..	..	..

TABLE VII.

AGE, SEX AND CIVIL CONDITION BY RELIGION.

Jammu and Kashmir State Census 1921.

Part I—Provincial Tables.

Religion.	Age.	Population. Persons.	Population. Males.	Population. Females.	Unmarried. Persons.	Unmarried. Males.	Unmarried. Females.	Married. Persons.	Married. Males.	Married. Females.	Widowed. Persons.	Widowed. Males.	Widowed. Females.
1	2	3	4	5	6	7	8	9	10	11	12	13	14
Musalman.	**Total**	**1,324,403**	**711,664**	**612,739**	**633,523**	**374,847**	**258,676**	**601,831**	**298,253**	**303,578**	**89,049**	**38,564**	**50,485**
	0—1	40,764	20,912	19,852	40,756	20,911	19,845	7	1	6	1	..	1
	1—2	27,974	14,069	13,905	27,968	14,065	13,903	5	4	1	1	..	1
	2—3	39,792	19,737	20,055	39,778	19,734	20,044	13	2	11	1	1	..
	3—4	52,087	26,555	25,532	52,042	26,530	25,512	42	23	19	3	2	1
	4—5	43,805	22,313	21,492	43,707	22,238	21,469	40	20	20	58	55	3
	Total 0—5	**204,422**	**103,586**	**100,836**	**204,251**	**103,478**	**100,773**	**107**	**50**	**57**	**64**	**58**	**6**
	5—10	208,582	110,111	98,471	205,371	108,928	96,443	3,138	1,163	1,975	73	20	53
	10—15	153,022	86,503	66,519	125,258	78,872	46,386	27,387	7,546	19,841	377	85	292
	15—20	114,276	60,382	53,894	49,267	41,865	7,402	63,392	18,003	45,389	1,617	514	1,103
	20—25	116,391	56,168	60,223	25,149	21,764	3,385	88,139	32,970	55,16	3,103	1,434	1,669
	25—30	121,319	61,171	60,148	11,618	10,608	1,010	104,836	47,758	57,078	4,865	2,805	2,060
	30—35	114,787	64,117	50,670	4,758	3,876	882	102,833	56,157	46,676	7,196	4,084	3,112
	35—40	64,742	38,417	26,325	1,697	1,254	443	57,873	34,474	23,399	5,172	2,689	2,483
	40—45	71,685	38,073	33,612	2,497	1,398	1,099	58,185	32,433	25,752	11,003	4,242	6,761
	45—50	30,057	17,892	12,165	1,060	730	330	23,865	14,977	8,88	5,132	2,185	2,947
	50—55	52,168	30,342	21,826	1,276	960	316	35,203	24,004	11,199	15,689	5,378	10,311
	55—60	12,184	7,912	4,272	235	194	41	8,454	6,055	2,399	3,495	1,663	1,832
	60—65	33,471	19,643	13,828	637	556	81	17,620	13,672	3,948	15,214	5,415	9,799
	65—70	5,149	3,516	1,633	84	48	36	2,739	2,384	358	2,826	1,084	1,242
	70 & over	22,148	13,831	8,317	365	316	49	8,060	6,607	1,453	13,723	6,908	6,815
Christian.	**Total**	**341**	**179**	**162**	**140**	**80**	**60**	**167**	**90**	**77**	**34**	**9**	**25**
	0—1	6	4	2	6	4	2	..	..	..	..	..	..
	1—2	1	..	1	1	..	1	..	..	..	..	..	..
	2—3	1	..	1	1	..	1	..	..	..	..	..	...
	3—4	11	8	3	11	8	3	..	..	..	..	..	..
	4—5	7	4	3	7	4	3	..	..	..	..	..	..
	Total 0—5	**26**	**16**	**10**	**26**	**16**	**10**	...	..	..	..	..	...
	5—10	23	10	13	23	10	13	..	...	..	..	..	...
	10—15	6	3	3	6	3	3	...	..	..	...	..	...
	15—20	13	10	3	13	10	3	...	...	..	..	..	...
	20—25	27	14	13	19	11	8	8	3	5	..	..	..
	25—30	34	21	13	18	14	4	14	5	9	2	2	...
	30—35	35	22	13	8	6	2	26	15	11	1	1	...
	35—40	31	16	15	10	5	5	21	11	10	..	...	..
	40—45	28	10	18	3	..	3	20	10	10	5	...	5
	45—50	26	17	9	4	2	2	20	14	6	2	1	1
	50—55	29	12	17	1	..	1	24	11	13	4	1	3
	55—60	23	7	16	5	...	5	11	6	5	7	1	6
	60—65	19	9	10	..	...	...	12	7	5	7	2	5
	65—70	9	5	4	2	2	...	5	3	2	2	—	2
	70 & over	12	7	5	2	1	1	6	5	1	4	1	3
						(iv) FRONTIER DISTRICTS.							
All Religions.	**Total**	**212,182**	**107,138**	**105,044**	**98,872**	**53,860**	**45,012**	**95,732**	**48,311**	**47,421**	**17,578**	**4,967**	**12,611**
	0—1	6,574	3,229	3,345	6,574	3,229	3,345	...	...	...	..	..	...
	1—2	5,018	2,418	2,600	5,018	2,418	2,600	...	...	..	..	..	..
	2—3	5,692	2,798	2,894	5,691	2,797	2,894	1	1	..	..	...	..
	3—4	7,065	3,497	3,568	7,062	3,496	3,566	3	1	2	..	..	..
	4—5	5,728	2,811	2,917	5,725	2,809	2,916	3	2	1	..	..	..
	Total 0—5	**30,077**	**14,753**	**15,324**	**30,070**	**14,749**	**15,321**	**7**	**4**	**3**	..	..	..
	5—10	27,308	13,980	13,328	26,937	13,867	13,070	355	106	249	16	7	9
	10—15	22,922	11,980	10,942	20,389	11,160	9,229	2,469	792	1,677	64	28	36
	15—20	19,527	10,689	8,838	10,99	7,118	3,880	8,284	3,466	4,818	245	105	140
	20—25	24,107	11,271	12,836	4,963	3,479	1,484	18,136	7,353	10,783	1,008	439	569
	25—30	8,679	4,618	4,061	1,326	901	425	6,919	3,515	3,404	434	202	232
	30—35	11,934	6,606	5,328	1,044	736	308	10,139	5,554	4,585	751	316	435
	35—40	18,772	8,754	10,018	975	471	504	16,431	7,861	8,570	1,366	422	945
	40—45	9,628	5,380	4,248	502	415	87	8,125	4,611	3,514	1,001	354	647
	45—50	12,491	5,928	6,563	380	159	221	9,887	5,335	4,552	2,224	434	1,790
	50—55	6,600	3,660	2,940	333	249	84	4,993	3,072	1,921	1,274	339	935
	55—60	2,672	1,465	1,207	229	82	147	1,872	1,205	667	571	178	393
	60—65	8,479	4,166	4,313	392	319	73	4,821	3,096	1,725	3,266	751	2,515
	65—70	1,95	1,08	864	107	51	56	1,120	779	341	725	258	467
	70 & over	7,034	2,800	4,234	227	104	123	2,174	1,562	612	4,633	1,134	3,499

VII Age, Sex and Civil Condition.

TABLE VII.

AGE, SEX AND CIVIL CONDITION BY RELIGION.

Jammu and Kashmir State Census 1921.

Part I—Provincial Tables.

Religion.	Age.	*Population.*			*Unmarried.*			*Married.*			*Widowed.*		
		Persons.	Males.	Females.	Persons.	Males.	Females.	Persons.	Males.	Females.	Persons.	Males.	Females
1	2	3	4	5	6	7	8	9	10	11	12	13	14
Hindu.	**Total**	**979**	**850**	**129**	**409**	**350**	**59**	**525**	**461**	**64**	**45**	**39**	
	0—1	21	10	11	21	10	11	..	..	..	..	..	..
	1—2	5	2	3	5	2	3	..	..	..	..	..	..
	2—3	8	3	5	8	3	5	..	..	..	..	..	..
	3—4	9	4	5	9	4	5	..	..	..	..	..	..
	4—5	9	4	5	9	4	5	..	..	..	..	..	..
	Total 0—5	**52**	**23**	**29**	**52**	**23**	**29**	..	..	..		..	..
	5—10	50	28	22	49	28	21	1	..	1	..	..	..
	10—15	20	14	6	20	14	6	..	..	..	..	..	..
	15—20	94	82	12	65	63	2	28	19	9	1	..	
	20—25	193	177	16	113	113	..	78	62	16	2	2	..
	25—30	178	166	12	72	72	..	95	84	11	11	10	
	30—35	110	99	11	21	21	..	84	73	11	5	5	..
	35—40	58	47	11	5	5	..	47	37	10	6	5	
	40—45	54	49	5	5	4	1	40	36	4	9	9	..
	45—50	52	51	1	1	1	..	47	47	—	4	3	
	50—55	106	104	2	3	3	..	101	99	2	2	2	..
	55—60	5	4	1	2	2	..	1	1	..	2	1	..
	60—65	4	4	...	...	..	..	3	3	..	1	1	..
	65—70	2	2	...	1	1	..	..	..	..	1	1	..
	70& over	1	..	1	..	..	...	..	..	..	1	..	
Arya.	**Total**	**42**	**27**	**15**	**28**	**19**	**9**	**14**	**8**	**6**	..	..	..
	0—1	2	1	1	2	1	1	..	..	..	..	..	..
	1—2	1	1	..	1	1	..	..	..	..	..	..	..
	2—3	1	1	..	1	1	..	..	..	..	..	..	..
	3—4	2	2	..	2	2	..	..	..	..	..	..	..
	4—5	1	1	..	1	1	..	..	..	..	..	..	..
	Total 0—5	**7**	**6**	**1**	**7**	**6**	**1**	..	..	..	..	..	..
	5—10	11	3	8	11	3	8	..	..	..	..	..	..
	10—15	4	4	..	4	4	..	...	..	..	..	..	..
	15—20	1	1	..	1	1	..	..	...	..	..	..	..
	20—25	3	2	1	2	2	..	1	..	1	..	...	..
	25—30	5	3	2	2	2	..	3	1	2	..	..	...
	30—35	5	3	2	1	1	..	4	2	2	..	..	..
	35—40	3	2	1	..	..	..	3	2	1	...	..	..
	40—45	3	3	..	..	..	..	3	3	...	..	..	..
	45—50	..	..	..	..	..	..	..	...	..	..	...	..
	50—55	..	..	..	..	..	..	...	..	...	..	..	..
	55—60	..	..	..	..	..	..	..	..	..	...	...	...
	60—65	..	..	..	..	..	..	..	...	..	..	..	..
	65—70	..	..	..	..	..	..	..	..	..	...	..	...
	70& over	..	..	..	..	..	..	..	..	...	..	..	...
Sikh.	**Total**	**117**	**76**	**41**	**54**	**30**	**24**	**58**	**44**	**14**	**5**	**2**	
	0—1	2	1	1	2	1	1	..	..	..	...	..	..
	1—2	4	1	3	4	1	3	..	..	..	..	..	..
	2—3	3	...	3	3	...	3	..	..	..	..	..	..
	3—4	4	3	1	4	3	1	..	..	..	..	..	..
	4—5	3	1	2	3	1	2	..	..	..	..	..	..
	Total 0—5	**16**	**6**	**10**	**16**	**6**	**10**	..	..	..	..	..	..
	5—10	9	1	8	9	1	8			..	..	..	..
	10—15	15	11	4	14	10	4	1	1			..	
	15—20	12	6	6	6	5	1	5	1	4	1	..	
	20—25	21	18	3	7	6	1	12	11	1	2	1	
	25—30	6	4	2	...	..	..	6	4	2	—	..	...
	30—35	14	10	4	1	1	..	13	9	4	..	..	..
	35—40	9	7	2	...	..	...	9	7	2	..	..	..
	40—45	8	7	1	1	1	..	7	6	1	..	..	..
	45—50	4	3	1	...	..	...	2	2	..	2	1	
	50—55	2	2	...	..	..	..	2	2	..	..	..	..
	55—60	1	1	...	..	..	..	1	1	..	..	..	..
	60—65	..	..	..	..	..	..	..	..	..	..	..	...
	65—70	...	..	..	...	..	..	..	..	..	..	...	..
	70& over	...	..	...	...	..	..	..	..	..	...	..	..

TABLE VII.

Age, Sex and Civil Condition by Religion.

Jammu and Kashmir State Census 1921.

Part I Provincial Tables.

Religion.	Age.	Population. Persons.	Population. Males.	Population. Females.	Unmarried. Persons.	Unmarried. Males.	Unmarried. Females.	Married. Persons.	Married. Males.	Married. Females.	Widowed. Persons.	Widowed. Males.	Widowed. Females.
1	2	3	4	5	6	7	8	9	10	11	12	13	14
Budh.	**Total**	**37,241**	**18,610**	**18,631**	**16,935**	**8 274**	**8,661**	**16,012**	**9,208**	**6,804**	**4,294**	**1,128**	**3,166**
	0—1	774	377	397	774	377	397	..	..	..	..	..	..
	1—2	664	324	340	664	324	340	..	..	..	..	..	..
	2—3	556	266	290	556	266	290	...	..	..	..	..	..
	3—4	910	449	461	908	449	459	2	..	2	...	..	..
	4—5	707	323	384	706	323	383	1	..	1	..	..	...
	Total 0—5	**3,611**	**1,739**	**1,872**	**3,608**	**1,739**	**1,869**	**3**	..	**3**	..	..	..
	5—10	3,620	1,764	1,856	3,598	1,748	1,850	20	16	4	2	..	2
	10—15	3,410	1,705	1,705	3,173	1,546	1,627	234	156	78	3	3	..
	15—20	3,581	1,965	1,616	2 576	1,298	1,278	981	657	324	24	10	14
	20—25	3,063	1,503	1,560	1,086	456	630	1,893	1,013	880	84	34	50
	25—30	2,776	1,294	1,482	553	224	329	2,100	1,024	1,076	123	46	77
	30—35	2,123	1,576	547	605	429	176	1,353	1,092	261	165	55	110
	35—40	2,723	1,324	1,399	478	168	310	2,106	1,101	1,005	139	55	84
	40—45	2,509	1,330	1,179	227	183	44	1,985	1,051	934	297	96	201
	45—50	1,779	829	950	259	92	167	1,322	678	644	198	59	139
	50—55	2,058	1,024	1,034	181	117	64	1,538	825	713	339	82	257
	55—60	1,304	622	682	219	75	144	809	467	342	276	80	196
	60—65	1,396	796	600	136	82	54	700	529	171	560	185	375
	65—70	790	414	376	77	44	33	445	273	172	268	97	171
	70& over	2,498	725	1,773	159	73	86	523	326	197	1,816	326	1,490
Musalman	**Total**	**173,718**	**87,529**	**86,189**	**81,400**	**45,166**	**36,234**	**79,089**	**38,568**	**40,521**	**13,229**	**3,795**	**9,434**
	0—1	5,773	2,840	2,933	5,773	2,840	2,933	..	..	..	..	..	..
	1—2	4,343	2,090	2,253	4,343	2,090	2,253	..	..	..	..	..	..
	2—3	5,121	2,526	2,595	5,120	2,525	2,595	1	1	..	..	..	..
	3—4	6,135	3,038	3,097	6,134	3,037	3,097	1	1	..	..	..	..
	4—5	5,007	2,481	2,526	5,005	2,479	2,526	2	2	..	..	..	..
	Total 0—5	**26,379**	**12,975**	**13,404**	**26,375**	**12,971**	**13,404**	**4**	**4**	..	..	..	..
	5—10	23,608	12,178	11,430	23,260	12,081	11,179	334	90	244	14	7	7
	10—15	19,465	10,243	9,222	17,170	9 583	7,587	2,234	635	1,599	61	25	36
	15—20	15,834	8,633	7,201	8,346	5,749	2,597	7,269	2,789	4,480	219	95	124
	20—25	20,819	9,568	11,251	3,752	2,902	850	16,147	6,264	9,883	920	402	518
	25—30	5,709	3,149	2,560	697	602	95	4,713	2,402	2,311	299	145	154
	30—35	9,673	4,911	4,762	413	282	131	8,680	4,374	4,306	580	255	325
	35—40	15,970	7,369	8,601	490	296	194	14,259	6,711	7,548	1,221	362	859
	40—45	7,046	3,986	3,060	268	227	41	6,083	3,510	2,573	695	249	446
	45—50	10,652	5 042	5,610	119	65	54	8,514	4,606	3,908	2,019	371	1,648
	50—55	4,430	2,527	1,903	149	129	20	3,349	2,143	1,206	932	255	677
	55—60	1,360	836	524	8	5	3	1,059	734	325	293	97	196
	60—65	7,079	3,366	3,713	256	237	19	4,118	2,564	1,554	2,705	565	2,140
	65—70	1,160	672	488	29	6	23	675	506	169	456	160	296
	70& over	4,534	2,074	2,460	68	31	37	1,651	1,236	415	2,815	807	2,008
Christian.	**Total**	**85**	**46**	**39**	**46**	**21**	**25**	**34**	**22**	**12**	**5**	**3**	**2**
	0—1	2	..	2	2	..	2	..	..	..	..	..	..
	1—2	1	..	1	1	..	1	..	..	..	..	..	..
	2—3	3	2	1	3	2	1	..	..	..	..	..	..
	3—4	5	1	4	5	1	4	..	..	..	..	..	..
	4—5	1	1	..	1	1	..	..	..	..	..	..	..
	Total 0—5	**12**	**4**	**8**	**12**	**4**	**8**	..	..	..	..	..	..
	5—10	10	6	4	10	6	4	..	..	..	..	..	..
	10—15	8	3	5	8	3	5	..	..	..	..	..	..
	15—20	5	2	3	4	2	2	1	..	1	..	..	..
	20—25	8	3	5	3	..	3	5	3	2	..	..	..
	25—30	5	2	3	2	1	1	2	..	2	1	1	..
	30—35	9	7	2	3	2	1	5	4	1	1	1	..
	35—40	9	5	4	2	2	..	7	3	4	..	..	..
	40—45	8	5	3	1	..	1	7	5	2	..	..	..
	45—50	4	3	1	1	1	..	2	2	..	1	..	1
	50—55	4	3	1	..	..	..	3	3	..	1	..	1
	55—60	2	2	..	..	..	..	2	2	..	..	..	..
	60—65	..	..	..	..	..	..	..	..	..	..	..	..
	65—70	..	..	..	..	..	..	..	..	..	..	..	..
	70& over	1	1	..	..	..	..	..	..	..	1	1	..

TABLE VII.

AGE, SEX AND CIVIL CONDITION BY RELIGION.

Jammu and Kashmir State Census 1921.

Part II—District Tables.

Religion	Age.	Population.			Unmarried.			Married.			Widowed.		
		Persons.	Males.	Females.	Persons.	Males.	Females.	Persons.	Males.	Females.	Persons.	Males.	Females.
1	2	3	4	5	6	7	8	9	10	11	12	13	14
						(1) JAMMU.							
All Religions.	**Total**	**334,834**	**182,681**	**152,153**	**145,269**	**92,726**	**52,543**	**148,641**	**74,397**	**74,244**	**40,924**	**15,558**	**25,366**
	0—1	10,582	5,394	5,188	10,581	5,394	5,187	1	..	1	..	..	..
	1—5	33,289	16,647	16,592	32,997	16,604	16,393	211	36	175	31	7	24
	5—10	47,636	24,848	22,788	44,576	24,401	20,175	2,697	379	2,318	363	68	295
	10—15	38,593	21,773	16,820	28,141	19,251	8,890	9,906	2,231	7,675	546	291	255
	15—20	27,320	14,586	12,734	11,487	10,386	1,101	15,101	3,988	11,213	632	212	420
	20—30	53,911	29,416	24,495	10,692	10,366	326	39,722	17,570	22,152	3,497	1,480	2,017
	30—40	45,220	25,344	19,876	3,576	3,321	255	35,663	19,385	16,278	5,981	2,638	3,343
	40—50	32,607	18,220	14,387	1,643	1,524	119	22,563	13,720	8,843	8,401	2,976	5,425
	50—60	22,455	12,961	9,494	794	762	32	12,937	9,157	3,780	8,724	3,042	5,682
	60 & over	23,271	13,492	9,779	782	717	65	9,740	7,931	1,809	12,749	4,844	7,905
Hindu.	**Total**	**191,782**	**104,553**	**87,229**	**81,964**	**53,813**	**28,151**	**83,824**	**42,078**	**41,746**	**25,994**	**8,662**	**17,332**
	0—1	5,827	2,970	2,857	5,827	2,970	2,857	..	..	..	..	..	..
	1—5	18,059	9,128	8,931	17,951	9,127	8,824	87	1	86	21	..	21
	5—10	25,752	13,390	12,362	24,203	13,216	10,987	1,259	161	1,098	290	13	277
	10—15	20,824	11,820	9,004	15,391	10,832	4,559	5,224	936	4,288	209	52	157
	15—20	15,661	8,330	7,331	6,657	6,212	445	8,586	2,022	6,564	418	96	322
	20—30	31,785	17,415	14,370	7,141	6,950	191	22,297	9,692	12,605	2,347	773	1,574
	30—40	27,099	15,020	12,079	2,463	2,319	144	20,607	11,147	9,460	4,029	1,554	2,475
	40—50	19,568	10,947	8,621	1,207	1,113	94	12,788	8,084	4,704	5,573	1,750	3,823
	50—60	13,291	7,537	5,754	588	568	20	7,255	5,279	1,976	5,448	1,690	3,758
	60 & over	13,916	7,996	5,920	536	506	30	5,721	4,756	965	7,659	2,734	4,925
Arya.	**Total**	**5,595**	**3,242**	**2,353**	**2,447**	**1,590**	**857**	**2,577**	**1,356**	**1,221**	**571**	**296**	**275**
	0—1	200	113	87	200	113	87	..	..	..	..	..	..
	1—5	609	343	266	609	343	266	..	..	..	..	..	..
	5—10	846	480	366	795	470	325	48	7	41	3	3	..
	10—15	668	391	277	499	351	148	166	38	128	3	2	1
	15—20	465	273	192	195	173	22	264	94	170	6	6	..
	20—30	917	517	400	111	109	2	755	379	376	51	29	22
	30—40	737	420	317	22	18	4	628	358	270	87	44	43
	40—50	509	304	205	10	9	1	382	232	150	117	63	54
	50—60	316	198	118	3	3	..	186	139	47	127	56	71
	60 & over	328	203	125	3	1	2	148	109	39	177	93	84
Sikh.	**Total**	**4,932**	**2,651**	**2,281**	**2,323**	**1,436**	**887**	**2,095**	**1,000**	**1,095**	**514**	**215**	**299**
	0—1	207	113	94	206	113	93	1	..	1	..	..	..
	1—5	504	255	249	500	254	246	4	1	3	..	..	..
	5—10	763	383	380	709	382	327	53	1	52	1	..	1
	10—15	652	362	290	522	341	181	226	19	107	4	2	2
	15—20	397	219	178	181	159	22	204	53	151	12	7	5
	20—30	678	333	345	129	125	4	523	201	322	26	7	19
	30—40	589	320	269	34	29	5	493	261	232	62	30	32
	40—50	499	289	210	21	19	2	372	219	153	106	51	55
	50—60	322	187	135	12	7	5	186	136	50	124	44	80
	60 & over	321	190	131	9	7	2	133	109	24	179	74	105
Jain.	**Total**	**521**	**290**	**231**	**267**	**156**	**111**	**199**	**110**	**89**	**55**	**24**	**31**
	0—1	25	11	14	25	11	14	..	..	..	..	..	..
	1—5	54	21	33	53	21	32	..	..	..	1	..	1
	5—10	61	29	32	61	29	32	..	..	..	..	..	..
	10—15	70	42	28	68	42	26	2	..	2	..	..	..
	15—20	38	24	14	23	17	6	15	7	8	..	..	..
	20—30	95	54	41	25	24	1	66	27	39	4	3	1
	30—40	69	43	26	8	8	..	50	30	20	11	5	6
	40—50	53	34	19	4	4	..	35	25	10	14	5	9
	50—60	30	18	12	..	..	..	19	13	6	11	5	6
	60 & over	26	14	12	..	..	..	12	8	4	14	6	8
Musalman.	**Total**	**130,721**	**71,242**	**59,479**	**57,656**	**35,371**	**22,285**	**59,423**	**29,584**	**29,839**	**13,642**	**6,287**	**7,355**
	0—1	4,250	2,144	2,106	4,250	2,144	2,106	..	..	..	..	..	..
	1—5	13,877	6,832	7,045	13,753	6,792	6,961	116	34	82	8	6	2
	5—10	20,049	10,481	9,568	18,648	10,222	8,426	1,332	207	1,125	69	52	17
	10—15	16,227	9,082	7,145	11,536	7,617	3,919	4,364	1,232	3,132	327	233	94
	15—20	10,638	5,674	4,964	4,370	3,779	591	6,076	1,795	4,281	192	100	92
	20—30	20,236	10,974	9,262	3,243	3,121	122	15,938	7,194	8,744	1,055	659	396
	30—40	16,552	9,452	7,100	1,037	935	102	13,743	7,525	6,218	1,772	992	780
	40—50	11,864	6,587	5,277	397	375	22	8,916	5,118	3,798	2,551	1,094	1,457
	50—60	8,433	4,985	3,448	191	184	7	5,248	3,562	1,686	2,994	1,239	1,755
	60 & over	8,595	5,031	3,564	231	202	29	3,690	2,917	773	4,674	1,912	2,762

TABLE VII.

Age, Sex and Civil Condition by Religion.

Jammu and Kashmir State Census 1921.

Part II – District Tables.

Religion.	Age.	Population.			Unmarried.			Married.			Widowed		
		Persons.	Males.	Females.	Persons.	Males.	Females.	Persons.	Males.	Females.	Persons.	Males.	Females.
1	2	3	4	5	6	7	8	9	10	11	12	13	14
Hindu.	**Total**	**10,371**	**6,242**	**4,129**	**5 064**	**3,488**	**1,576**	**4,179**	**2,333**	**1,846**	**1,128**	**421**	**707**
	0—1	267	137	130	267	137	130	..	..	..	..	..	..
	1—5	826	424	402	826	424	402	..	..	..	..	..	..
	5—10	1,378	711	667	1,347	710	637	30	1	29	1	..	1
	10—15	1,112	637	475	989	627	362	118	9	109	5	1	4
	15—20	807	486	321	450	421	29	351	64	287	6	1	5
	20—30	2,028	1,266	762	669	655	14	1,283	588	695	76	23	53
	30—40	1,622	1,066	556	198	196	2	1,243	802	441	181	68	113
	40—50	1,073	697	376	129	129	..	671	476	195	273	92	181
	50—60	713	476	237	102	102	..	341	273	68	270	101	169
	60&over	545	342	203	87	87	..	142	120	22	316	135	181
Sikh.	**Total**	**5,332**	**2,779**	**2,553**	**2 535**	**1,447**	**1,088**	**2,480**	**1,226**	**1,254**	**317**	**106**	**211**
	0—1	215	111	104	215	111	104	..	..	..	..	..	..
	1—5	659	331	328	659	331	328	..	..	..	..	..	..
	5—10	904	498	406	896	491	405	7	6	1	1	1	..
	10—15	546	283	263	450	267	183	94	16	78	2	..	2
	15—20	441	212	229	160	140	20	277	71	206	4	1	3
	20—30	881	397	484	102	76	20	749	312	437	30	9	21
	30—40	800	474	326	25	19	6	727	432	295	48	23	26
	40—50	430	197	233	19	5	14	342	180	162	69	12	57
	50—60	234	134	100	3	1	2	170	112	58	61	21	40
	60&over	222	142	80	6	6	..	114	97	17	102	39	63
Musalman.	**Total**	**486,680**	**260,608**	**226,072**	**229,490**	**135,305**	**94,185**	**227,106**	**112,089**	**115,017**	**30,084**	**13,214**	**16,870**
	0—1	16,695	8,592	8,103	16,695	8,592	8,103	..	..	..	..	..	..
	1—5	60,483	30,302	30,181	60,451	30,281	30,170	29	20	9	3	1	2
	5—10	77,188	40,973	36,215	76,246	40,732	35,514	918	228	690	24	13	11
	10—15	56,059	31,285	24,774	45,626	28,539	17,087	10,302	2,707	7,595	131	39	92
	15—20	42,038	22,400	19,638	16,937	14,615	2,322	24,463	7,542	16,921	638	243	395
	20—30	89,232	44,047	45,185	10,732	10,084	648	75,611	32,359	43,252	2,889	1,604	1,285
	30—40	64,707	36,668	28,039	1,495	1,299	196	58,953	33,034	25,919	4,259	2,335	1,924
	40—50	35,509	19,088	16,421	654	595	59	29,817	16,748	13,069	5,038	1,745	3,293
	50—60	22,437	13,150	9,287	260	213	47	16,064	10,696	5,368	6,113	2,241	3,872
	60&over	22,332	14,103	8,229	394	355	39	10,949	8,755	2,194	10,989	4,993	5,996
						(9) KASHMIR SOUTH.							
All Religions.	**Total**	**688,487**	**372,459**	**316,028**	**324,587**	**196,425**	**128,162**	**311,368**	**153,455**	**157,913**	**52,532**	**22,579**	**29,953**
	0—1	21,607	11,122	10,485	21,600	11,121	10,479	6	1	5	1	..	1
	1—5	80,183	40,937	39,246	80,067	40,855	39,212	57	25	32	59	57	2
	5—10	105,403	54,823	50,580	104,042	54,502	49,540	1,319	318	1,001	42	3	39
	10—15	80,459	45,499	34,960	65,741	41,498	24,243	14,471	3,956	10,515	247	45	202
	15—20	58,483	31,558	26,925	24,668	22,098	2,570	32,947	9,228	23,719	868	232	636
	20—30	125,414	62,746	62,668	20,352	19,056	1,296	100,499	41,424	59,075	4,563	2,266	2,297
	30—40	95,402	55,281	40,121	4,138	3,819	319	83,737	47,437	36,300	7,527	4,025	3,502
	40—50	57,051	31,716	25,335	2,129	1,858	271	43,999	25,305	18,694	10,923	4,553	6,370
	50—60	36,609	22,151	14,458	1,212	1,036	176	22,879	16,427	6,452	12,518	4,688	7,830
	60& over	27,876	16,626	11,250	638	582	56	11,454	9,334	2,120	15,784	6,710	9,074
	Total	**49,692**	**27,638**	**22,054**	**23,738**	**15,799**	**7,939**	**19,750**	**9,712**	**10,038**	**6,204**	**2,127**	**4,077**
	0—1	1,261	663	598	1,261	663	598	..	..	..	..	..	..
	1—5	3,891	2,085	1,806	3,891	2,085	1,806	..	..	..	..	..	..
	5—10	6,740	3,211	3,529	6,611	3,107	3,504	127	104	23	2	..	2
	10—15	5,893	3,472	2,421	5,175	3,359	1,816	658	107	551	60	6	54
	15—20	4,335	2,669	1,666	2,248	2,066	182	2,012	588	1,424	75	15	60
	20—30	9,267	5,193	4,074	2,516	2,492	24	6,239	2,554	3,685	512	147	365
	30—40	7,332	4,021	3,311	946	939	7	5,287	2,680	2,607	1,099	402	697
	40—50	5,247	3,032	2,215	598	596	2	3,207	1,977	1,230	1,442	459	983
	50—60	3,450	1,996	1,454	273	273	..	1,590	1,160	430	1,587	563	1,024
	60& over	2,276	1,296	980	219	219	..	630	542	88	1,427	535	892
Sikh.	**Total**	**3,202**	**1778**	**1,424**	**1,567**	**919**	**648**	**1,458**	**795**	**663**	**177**	**64**	**113**
	0—1	114	55	59	114	55	59	..	..	..	..	—	..
	1—5	483	200	283	483	200	283	..	..	..	..	..	..
	5—10	496	298	198	496	298	198	..	..	..	..	..	..
	10—15	356	210	146	303	204	99	52	6	46	1	..	1
	15—20		140	133	112	103	9	158	34	124	3	3	—
	20—30		296	211	46	46	..	444	242	202	17	8	9
	30—40		245	180	8	8	..	394	231	163	23	6	17
	40—50		162	115	1	1	..	242	151	91	34	10	24
		141	88	53	—	—	..	101	75	26	40	13	27
	60& over	130	84	46	4	4	..	67	56	11	59	24	35

VII Age, Sex and Civil Condition.

TABLE VII.

Age, Sex and Civil Condition by Religion.

Jammu and Kashmir State Census 1921.

Part II—District Tables.

Age.	Religion.	Population.			Unmarried.			Married.			Widowed.		
		Persons.	Males.	Females.	Persons.	Males.	Females.	Persons.	Males.	Females.	Persons.	Males.	Females.
1	2	3	4	5	6	7	8	9	10	11	12	13	14
Christian.	**Total**	**146**	**79**	**67**	**68**	**38**	**30**	**63**	**35**	**28**	**15**	**6**	
	0—1	6	..	6	6	..	6	..	..	..	..	..	..
	1—5	13	5	8	13	5	8	..	..	..	..	..	..
	5—10	20	10	10	20	10	10	..	..	..	..	..	..
	10—15	17	11	6	16	11	5	1	..	1	..	..	..
	15—20	14	7	7	5	4	1	9	3	6	..	..	..
	20—30	25	17	8	7	7	..	17	9	8	1	1	..
	30—40	20	12	8	1	1	..	15	8	7	4	3	
	40—50	21	13	8	..		..	16	11	5	5	2	
	50—60	5	2	3	..	..	..	3	2	1	2	..	
	60 & over	5	2	3	..	..	..	2	2	..	3	..	
							(3) UDHAMPUR.						
All Religions.	**Total**	**218,261**	**115,135**	**103,126**	**93,163**	**58,789**	**34,374**	**98,476**	**48,181**	**50,295**	**26,622**	**8,165**	**18,**
	0—1	7,036	3,572	3,464	7,036	3,572	3,464	..	..	..	...	..	..
	1—5	21,510	10,889	10,621	21,397	10,839	10,558	112	50	62	1	..	
	5—10	30,338	15,411	14,927	28,538	15,201	13,337	1,759	203	1,556	41	7	
	10—15	22,654	12,285	10,369	16,477	11,112	5,365	5,938	1,141	4,797	239	32	
	15—20	18,519	9,441	9,078	7,642	6,670	972	10,320	2,681	7,639	557	90	
	20—30	35,550	17,598	17,952	6,622	6,149	473	26,545	10,702	15,843	2,383	747	1,
	30—40	30,578	16,900	13,678	2,586	2,469	117	24,021	13,077	10,944	3,971	1,354	2,
	40—50	20,664	11,303	9,361	1,167	1,133	34	14,360	8,588	5,772	5,137	1,582	3,
	50—60	14,257	8,378	5,879	876	857	19	8,444	6,018	2,426	4,937	1,503	3,
	60 & over	17,155	9,358	7,797	822	787	35	6,977	5,721	1,256	9,356	2,850	6,
Hindu.	**Total**	**132,214**	**68,935**	**63,279**	**53,169**	**34,866**	**18,303**	**59,192**	**28,615**	**30,577**	**19,853**	**5,454**	**14,**
	0—1	3,916	1,983	1,933	3,916	1,983	1,933	..	..	..	..	..	..
	1—5	11,889	5,873	6,016	11,848	5,869	5,979	40	4	36	1	..	
	5—10	16,933	8,409	8,524	15,704	8,321	7,383	1,195	84	1,111	34	4	
	10—15	12,848	6,971	5,877	8,778	6,320	2,458	3,881	630	3,251	189	21	
	15—20	10,980	5,470	5,510	4,214	3,868	346	6,347	1,564	4,783	419	38	
	20—30	21,611	10,619	10,992	4,235	4,132	103	15,551	6,022	9,529	1,825	465	1,
	30—40	18,930	10,380	8,550	2,010	1,960	50	13,913	7,584	6,329	3,007	836	2,
	40—50	13,382	7,065	6,317	963	945	18	8,422	5,003	3,419	3,997	1,117	2,
	50—60	9,852	5,749	4,103	784	771	13	5,404	3,943	1,461	3,664	1,035	2,
	60 & over	11,873	6,416	5,457	717	697	20	4,439	3,781	658	6,717	1,938	4,
Sikh.	**Total**	**332**	**175**	**157**	**141**	**82**	**59**	**154**	**79**	**75**	**37**	**14**	
	0—1	7	3	4	7	3	4	..	..	..	..	...	..
	1—5	37	17	20	37	17	20	...	..	...	..	...	..
	5—10	40	18	22	40	18	22	..	..	..	..	...	..
	10—15	36	20	16	27	17	10	9	3	6	..	...	..
	15—20	27	12	15	10	8	2	17	4	13	...	..	..
	20—30	58	35	23	13	12	1	43	22	21	2	1	
	30—40	44	27	17	5	5	..	32	17	15	7	5	
	40—50	32	15	17	..	...	..	27	13	14	5	2	
	50—60	26	15	11	1	1	..	17	12	5	8	2	
	60 & over	25	13	12	1	1	..	9	8	1	15	4	
Budh.	**Total**	**438**	**222**	**216**	**164**	**93**	**71**	**232**	**116**	**116**	**42**	**13**	
	0—1	7	5	2	7	5	2	...	..	..	..	..	..
	1—5	27	13	14	27	13	14	..	..	..	..	..	..
	5—10	48	25	23	48	25	23	..	..	..	..	..	..
	10—15	34	18	16	31	16	15	3	2	1	..	..	..
	15—20	52	26	26	32	18	14	20	8	12	..	..	..
	20—30	74	37	37	9	8	1	62	28	34	3	1	...
	30—40	63	30	33	5	3	2	52	24	28	6	3	
	40—50	60	26	34	2	2	..	47	22	25	11	2	
	50—60	38	21	17	3	3	...	25	16	9	10	2	
	60 & over	35	21	14	..	..	..	23	16	7	12	5	
Musalman.	**Total**	**85,254**	**45,792**	**39,462**	**39,675**	**23,740**	**15,935**	**38,890**	**19,369**	**9,521**	**6,689**	**2,683**	**4,0**
	0—1	3,105	1,580	1,525	3,105	1,580	1,525	..	...	...	..	..	..
	1—5	9,553	4,985	4,568	9,481	4,939	4,542	72	46	26	..	..	..
	5—10	13,315	6,958	6,357	12,744	6,836	5,908	564	119	445	7	3	
	10—15	9,733	5,275	4,458	7,639	4,758	2,881	2,044	506	1,538	50	11	
	15—20	7,459	3,932	3,527	3,385	2,775	610	3,936	1,105	2,831	138	52	
	20—30	13,803	6 906	6,897	2,364	1,996	368	10,886	4,630	6,256	553	280	
	30—40	11,535	6,460	5,075	564	500	64	10,021	5,451	4,570	950	509	
	40—50	7,188	4,195	2,993	201	185	16	5,863	3,549	2,314	1,324	461	
	50—60	4,341	2,593	1,748	88	82	6	2,998	2,047	951	1,255	464	
	60 & over	5,222	2,908	2,314	104	89	15	2,500	1,916	590	2,612	903	1

TABLE VII.

VII Age, Sex and Civil Condition.

Age, Sex and Civil Condition by Religion.

Jammu and Kashmir State Census 1921.

Part II—District Tables.

Religion.	Age.	Population.			Unmarried.			Married.			Widowed.		
		Persons.	Males.	Females.	Persons.	Males.	Females.	Persons.	Males.	Females.	Persons.	Males.	Females.
1	2	3	4	5	6	7	8	9	10	11	12	13	14
						(4) RIASI.							
All Religions.	**Total**	**224,589**	**118,575**	**106,014**	**101,103**	**62,998**	**38,107**	**99,639**	**47,891**	**51,748**	**23,847**	**7,688**	**16,159**
	0—1	7,175	3,648	3,527	7,168	3,644	3 524	7	4	3	..	..	
	1—5	24,550	12,581	11,969	24,286	12,445	11,841	248	124	124	16	12	4
	5—10	33,562	17,215	16,347	31,468	16,724	14,744	1,976	452	1,524	118	39	79
	10—15	25,861	14,224	11,637	19,136	12,813	6,323	6,437	1,338	5,099	288	73	215
	15—20	18,516	9,370	9,146	7,722	6,702	1,020	10,330	2,555	7,775	464	113	351
	20—30	34,554	16,577	17,977	6,522	6,103	419	25,963	9,793	16,170	2,069	681	1,388
	30—40	30,002	16,358	13,644	2,318	2,202	116	24,100	12,907	11,193	3,584	1,249	2,335
	40—50	19,722	11,036	8,686	1,164	1,096	68	14,475	8,674	5,801	4,083	1,266	2,817
	50—60	12,409	7,036	5,373	610	575	35	7,581	5,155	2,426	4,218	1,306	2,912
	60&over	18,238	10,530	7,708	709	692	17	8,522	6,889	1,633	9,007	2,949	6,058
Hindu.	**Total**	**74,065**	**39,122**	**34,943**	**28,680**	**19,625**	**9,055**	**32,927**	**16,067**	**16,860**	**12,458**	**3,430**	**9,028**
	0—1	1,765	844	921	1,765	844	921	..	..	..	..	..	
	1—5	6,361	3,209	3,152	6,279	3,186	3,093	79	20	59	3	3	
	5—10	8,986	4,502	4,484	8,069	4,376	3,693	866	111	755	51	15	36
	10—15	7,285	4,029	3,256	4,787	3,672	1,115	2,370	339	2,031	128	18	110
	15—20	5,747	2,914	2,833	2,258	2,155	103	3,266	742	2,524	223	17	206
	20—30	11,906	5,889	6,017	2,452	2,382	70	8,396	3,285	5,111	1,058	222	836
	30—40	10,748	5,892	4,856	1,292	1,261	31	7,492	4,118	3,374	1,964	513	1,451
	40—50	8,120	4,499	3,621	803	785	18	4,965	3,089	1,876	2,352	625	1,727
	50—60	5,629	3,274	2,355	464	456	8	2,874	21,37	737	2,291	681	1,610
	60&over	7,518	4,070	3,448	511	508	3	2,619	2,226	393	4,388	1,336	3,052
Arya.	**Total**	**5,515**	**2,672**	**2,843**	**1,944**	**1,202**	**742**	**2,747**	**1,255**	**1,492**	**824**	**215**	**609**
	0—1	144	76	68	144	76	68	..	..	..	..	..	
	1—5	470	221	249	470	221	249	..	..	..	..	..	
	5—10	674	316	358	595	307	288	67	9	58	12	..	12
	10—15	526	250	276	335	223	112	182	27	155	9	..	9
	15—20	447	183	264	133	118	15	303	63	240	11	2	9
	20—30	946	429	517	136	131	5	714	283	431	96	15	81
	30—40	818	415	403	64	59	5	627	320	307	127	36	91
	40—50	577	288	289	33	33	..	394	214	180	150	41	109
	50—60	374	194	180	15	15	..	210	145	65	149	34	115
	60&over	539	300	239	19	19	..	250	194	56	270	87	183
Sikh.	**Total**	**814**	**401**	**413**	**336**	**199**	**137**	**373**	**175**	**198**	**105**	**27**	**78**
	0—1	33	17	16	33	17	16	..	..	..	..	..	
	1—5	73	30	43	73	30	43	..	..	..	..	..	
	5—10	117	58	59	108	57	51	9	1	8	..	..	
	10—15	76	34	42	55	32	23	20	2	18	1	..	1
	15—20	77	30	47	25	23	2	48	7	41	4	..	4
	20—30	141	57	84	24	22	2	106	34	72	11	1	10
	30—40	103	56	47	9	9	..	81	46	35	13	1	12
	40—50	81	53	28	6	6	..	58	42	16	17	5	12
	50—60	37	23	14	2	2	..	20	15	5	15	6	9
	60&over	76	43	33	1	1	..	31	28	3	44	14	30
Musalman.	**Total**	**144,195**	**76,380**	**67,815**	**70,143**	**41,970**	**28,173**	**63,592**	**30,394**	**33,198**	**10,460**	**4,016**	**6,444**
	0—1	5,233	2,711	2,522	5,226	2,707	2,519	7	4	3	..	..	
	1—5	17,646	9,121	8,525	17,464	9,008	8,456	169	104	65	13	9	4
	5—10	23,785	12,339	11,446	22,696	11,984	10,712	1,034	331	703	55	24	31
	10—15	17,974	9,911	8,063	3,959	8,886	5,073	3,865	970	2,895	150	55	95
	15—20	12,245	6,243	6,002	5,306	4,406	900	6,713	1,743	4,970	226	94	132
	20—30	21,561	10,202	11,359	3,910	3,568	342	16,747	6,191	10,556	904	443	461
	30—40	18,333	9,995	8,338	953	873	80	15,900	8,423	7,477	1,480	699	781
	40—50	10,944	6,196	4,748	322	272	50	9,058	5,329	3,729	1,564	595	969
	50—60	6,369	3,545	2,824	129	102	27	4,477	2,858	1,619	1,763	585	1,178
	60&over	10,105	6,117	3,988	178	164	14	5,622	4,441	1,181	4,305	1,512	2,793
						(5) MIRPUR.							
All Religions.	**Total**	**318,971**	**160,186**	**158,785**	**152,794**	**89,700**	**63,094**	**132,539**	**59,416**	**73,123**	**33,638**	**11,070**	**22,568**
	0—1	10,790	5,516	5,274	10,788	5,516	5,272	1	..	1	1	..	1
	1—5	35,680	18,125	17,555	35,516	18,095	17,421	151	28	123	13	2	11
	5—10	51,099	27,007	24,092	49,941	26,767	23,174	1,107	221	886	51	19	32
	10—15	37,274	20,449	16,825	31,495	19,420	12,075	5,666	999	4,667	113	30	83
	15—20	23,768	11,251	12,517	11,996	8,634	3,362	11,418	2,508	8,910	354	109	245
	20—30	45,263	19,401	25,862	7,797	7,104	693	35,094	11,367	23,727	2,372	930	1,442
	30—40	41,699	20,510	21,189	3,116	2,275	841	33,936	16,421	17,515	4,647	1,814	2,833
	40—50	29,051	14,292	14,759	1,098	955	143	21,856	11,570	10,286	6,097	1,767	4,330
	50—60	19,271	10,075	9,196	513	462	51	12,118	7,679	4,439	6,640	1,934	4,706
	60& over	25,076	13,560	11,516	534	472	62	11,192	8,623	2,569	13,350	4,465	8,885

TABLE VII.

Age, Sex and Civil Condition by Religion.

Jammu and Kashmir Census 1921.

Part II—District Tables.

Religion.	Age.	Population. Persons.	Population. Males.	Population. Females.	Unmarried. Persons.	Unmarried. Males.	Unmarried. Females.	Married. Persons.	Married. Males.	Married. Females.	Widowed. Persons.	Widowed. Males.	Widowed. Females.
1	2	3	4	5	6	7	8	9	10	11	12	13	14
Hindu.	**Total**	**52,591**	**27,319**	**25,272**	**24,411**	**15,391**	**9,020**	**21,981**	**10,105**	**11,876**	**6,199**	**1,823**	**4,37**
	0—1	1,903	964	939	1,903	964	939	..	..	..	..	..	..
	1—5	5,282	2,650	2,632	5,274	2,645	2,629	8	5	3	..	..	..
	5—10	8,047	4,315	3,732	7,915	4,311	3,604	128	4	124	4	..	
	10—15	5,932	3,301	2,631	4,705	3,143	1,562	1,198	154	1,044	29	4	2
	15—20	4,234	2,234	2,000	1,848	1,632	216	2,320	589	1,731	66	13	5
	20—30	7,437	3,438	3,999	1,574	1,529	45	5,347	1,739	3,608	516	170	34
	30—40	6,790	3,442	3,348	612	607	5	5,281	2,538	2,743	897	297	60
	40—50	5,068	2,769	2,299	257	240	17	3,684	2,204	1,480	1,127	325	80
	50—60	3,518	1,904	1,614	179	177	2	2,060	1,330	730	1,279	397	88
	60 & over	4,380	2,302	2,078	144	143	1	1,955	1,542	413	2,281	617	1,66
Arya.	**Total**	**3,930**	**2,159**	**1,771**	**1,448**	**893**	**555**	**1,958**	**984**	**974**	**524**	**282**	**24**
	0—1	114	50	64	114	50	64	..	..	..	..	..	..
	1—5	373	202	171	373	202	171	..	..	..	..	..	..
	5—10	443	213	230	425	213	212	18	..	18	..	..	..
	10—15	341	195	146	268	183	85	71	12	59	2	..	[illegible]
	15—20	321	146	175	118	111	7	193	35	158	10	..	1
	20—30	663	324	339	98	96	2	528	217	311	37	11	2
	30—40	597	347	250	40	26	14	495	276	219	62	45	1
	40—50	403	221	182	8	8	..	288	166	122	107	47	6
	50—60	248	168	80	2	2	..	166	121	45	80	45	3
	60 & over	427	293	134	2	2	..	199	157	42	226	134	9
Sikh.	**Total**	**4,698**	**2,481**	**2,217**	**2,189**	**1,370**	**819**	**2,063**	**978**	**1,085**	**446**	**133**	**313**
	0—1	168	101	67	167	101	66	1	..	1	..	..	..
	1—5	518	292	226	518	292	226	..	..	..	..	..	..
	5—10	680	363	317	674	362	312	6	1	5	..	..	..
	10—15	567	313	254	473	290	183	93	23	70	1	..	1
	15—20	374	169	205	149	124	25	223	44	179	2	1	1
	20—30	716	343	373	109	106	3	578	229	349	29	8	21
	30—40	630	327	303	47	45	2	524	259	265	59	23	36
	40—50	404	220	184	16	16	..	310	189	121	78	15	63
	50—60	300	161	139	23	22	1	182	113	69	95	26	69
	60 & over	341	192	149	13	12	1	146	120	26	182	60	122
Musalman.	**Total**	**257,741**	**128,222**	**129,519**	**124,739**	**72,043**	**52,696**	**106,533**	**47,347**	**59,186**	**26,469**	**8,832**	**17,637**
	0—1	8,605	4,401	4,204	8,604	4,401	4,203	..	..	..	1	..	1
	1—5	29,505	14,980	14,525	29,349	14,955	14,394	143	23	120	13	2	11
	5—10	41,927	22,115	19,812	40,925	21,880	19,045	955	216	739	47	19	28
	10—15	30,434	16,640	13,794	26,049	15,804	10,245	4,304	810	3,494	81	26	55
	15—20	18,838	8,702	10,136	9,880	6,767	3,113	8,682	1,840	6,842	276	95	181
	20—30	36,443	15,294	21,149	6,014	5,372	642	28,639	9,181	19,458	1,790	741	1,049
	30—40	33,681	16,394	17,287	2,417	1,597	820	27,635	13,348	14,287	3,629	1,449	2,180
	40—50	23,[illegible]75	11,081	12,094	817	691	126	17,573	9,010	8,563	4,785	1,380	3,405
	50—60	15,205	7,842	7,363	309	261	48	9,710	6,115	3,595	5,186	1,466	3,720
	60 & over	19,928	10,773	9,155	375	315	60	8,892	6,804	2,088	10,661	3,654	7,007
					(6) BHA	DARWAH							
All Religions.	**Total**	**37,614**	**19,227**	**18,387**	**17,024**	**10,362**	**6,662**	**16,137**	**7,511**	**8,626**	**4,453**	**1,354**	**3,099**
	0—1	1,167	591	576	1,167	591	576	..	..	..	..	..	..
	1—5	3,718	1,893	1,825	3,718	1,893	1,825	..	..	..	..	..	..
	5—10	5,215	2,634	2,581	5,185	2,634	2,551	30	..	30	..	..	..
	10—15	4,282	2,393	1,889	3,612	2,307	1,305	670	86	584	..	..	..
	15—20	3,457	1,511	1,946	1,383	1,127	256	1,984	367	1,617	90	17	73
	20—30	6,484	3,110	3,374	1,142	1,063	79	4,879	1,901	2,978	463	146	317
	30—40	5,216	2,742	2,474	452	409	43	4,108	2,155	1,953	656	178	478
	40—50	3,447	1,780	1,667	191	180	11	2,373	1,355	1,018	883	245	638
	50—60	2,129	1,168	961	81	74	7	1,168	852	316	880	242	638
	60 & over	2,499	1,405	1,094	93	84	9	925	795	130	1,481	526	955
Hindu.	**Total**	**22,561**	**11,384**	**11,177**	**9,664**	**5,974**	**3,690**	**9,776**	**4,527**	**5,249**	**3,121**	**883**	**2,238**
	0—1	651	321	330	651	321	330	..	..	..	..	..	..
	1—5	1,984	1,014	970	1,984	1,014	970	..	..	..	..	..	..
	5—10	2,893	1,471	1,422	2,893	1,471	1,422	..	..	..	..	..	..
	10—15	2,459	1,385	1,074	2,039	1,325	714	420	60	860	..	..	..
	15—20	2,035	810	1,225	752	603	149	1,215	198	1,017	68	9	59
	20—30	3,911	1,856	2,055	736	678	58	2,849	1,087	1,762	326	91	235
	30—40	3,266	1,670	1,596	338	309	29	2,504	1,281	1,223	424	80	344
	40—50	2,249	1,143	1,106	142	133	9	1,509	855	654	598	155	443
	50—60	1,377	742	635	61	57	4	705	529	176	611	156	455
	60 & over	1,736	972	764	68	63	5	574	517	57	1,094	392	762

TABLE VII.

Age, Sex and Civil Condition by Religion.

Jammu and Kashmir Census 1921.

Part II—District Tables.

Religion.	Age.	Population. Persons.	Population. Males.	Population. Females.	Unmarried. Persons.	Unmarried. Males.	Unmarried. Females.	Married. Persons.	Married. Males.	Married. Females.	Widowed. Persons.	Widowed. Males.	Widowed. Females.
1	2	3	4	5	6	7	8	9	10	11	12	13	14
Musalman.	**Total**	**15,040**	**7,836**	**7,204**	**7,354**	**4,385**	**2,969**	**6,354**	**2,980**	**3,374**	**1,332**	**471**	**861**
	0—1	516	270	246	516	270	246	..	..	..	..	..	..
	1—5	1,732	879	853	1,732	879	853	..	..	..	..	..	..
	5—10	2,321	1,162	1,159	2,291	1,162	1,129	30	..	30	..	..	..
	10—15	1,821	1,007	814	1,571	981	590	250	26	224	..	..	..
	15—20	1,422	701	721	631	524	107	769	169	600	22	8	14
	20—30	2,571	1,253	1,318	405	384	21	2,029	814	1,215	137	55	82
	30—40	1,947	1,070	877	114	100	14	1,601	872	729	232	98	134
	40—50	1,197	637	560	49	47	2	863	500	363	285	90	195
	50—60	759	424	326	20	17	3	461	321	140	269	86	183
	60 & over	763	433	330	25	21	4	351	278	73	387	134	253
							(7) PUNCH.						
All Religions.	**Total**	**351,781**	**181,348**	**170,433**	**170,744**	**101,109**	**69,635**	**154,656**	**71,835**	**82,821**	**26,381**	**8,404**	**17,977**
	0—1	13,216	6,438	6,778	13,208	6,438	6,770	8	..	8	..	..	..
	1—5	40,328	20,245	20,083	40,047	20,194	19,853	273	45	228	8	6	2
	5—10	58,782	31,139	27,643	56,537	30,584	25,953	2,058	539	1,519	187	16	171
	10—15	42,686	23,722	18,964	34,956	22,200	12,756	7,498	1,442	6,056	232	80	152
	15—20	30,131	15,335	14,796	14,586	11,581	3,005	15,130	3,612	11,518	415	142	273
	20—30	51,761	23,461	28,300	8,178	7,389	789	41,416	15,108	26,308	2,167	964	1,203
	30—40	46,695	24,126	22,569	1,708	1,465	243	41,128	21,113	20,015	3,859	1,548	2,311
	40—50	27,922	14,900	13,022	659	541	118	22,684	13,061	9,623	4,579	1,298	3,281
	50—60	16,876	9,019	7,857	278	222	56	12,033	7,562	4,471	4,565	1,235	3,330
	60 & over	23,384	12,963	10,421	587	495	92	12,428	9,353	3,075	10,369	3,115	7,254
Hindu.	**Total**	**20,764**	**10,919**	**9,845**	**10,024**	**6,190**	**3,834**	**8,461**	**3,961**	**4,500**	**2,279**	**768**	**1,511**
	0—1	678	374	304	678	374	304	..	..	..	..	..	..
	1—5	2,241	1,093	1,148	2,222	1,090	1,132	17	2	15	2	1	1
	5—10	3,347	1,806	1,541	3,206	1,772	1,434	132	31	101	9	3	6
	10—15	2,484	1,411	1,073	2,133	1,362	771	347	49	298	4	..	4
	15—20	1,662	840	822	850	714	136	775	121	654	37	5	32
	20—30	3,104	1,460	1,644	585	547	38	2,313	846	1,467	206	67	139
	30—40	2,818	1,501	1,317	185	177	8	2,229	1,181	1,048	404	143	261
	40—50	1,837	977	860	82	77	5	1,329	796	533	426	104	322
	50—60	1,201	688	513	57	54	3	718	482	236	426	152	274
	60 & over	1,392	769	623	26	23	3	601	453	148	765	293	472
Sikh.	**Total**	**10,585**	**5,520**	**5,065**	**5,125**	**3,103**	**2,022**	**4,527**	**2,116**	**2,411**	**933**	**301**	**632**
	0—1	381	176	205	381	176	205	..	..	..	..	..	..
	1—5	1,225	623	602	1,224	623	601	1	..	1	..	..	..
	5—10	1,803	919	884	1,739	916	823	64	3	61	..	..	..
	10—15	1,293	736	557	1,025	685	340	265	49	216	3	2	1
	15—20	970	485	485	422	378	44	539	103	436	9	4	5
	20—30	1,535	762	773	259	253	6	1,214	474	740	62	35	7
	30—40	1,421	772	649	48	47	1	1,218	665	553	155	60	5
	40—50	863	454	409	16	14	2	641	398	245	206	44	1 2
	50—60	495	258	237	7	7	..	305	205	100	183	46	137
	60 & over	599	335	264	4	4	..	280	221	59	315	110	205
Musalman.	**Total**	**320,368**	**164,871**	**155,497**	**155,566**	**91,796**	**63,770**	**141,636**	**65,741**	**75,895**	**23,166**	**7,334**	**15,832**
	0—1	12,157	5,888	6,269	12,149	5,888	6,261	8	..	8	..	..	..
	1—5	36,855	18,524	18,331	36,594	18,476	18,118	255	43	212	6	5	1
	5—10	53,625	28,411	25,214	51,585	27,893	23,692	1,862	505	1,357	178	13	165
	10—15	38,903	21,570	17,333	31,792	20,148	11,644	6,886	1,344	5,542	225	78	147
	15—20	27,490	14,008	13,482	13,310	10,487	2,823	13,811	3,388	10,423	369	133	236
	20—30	47,108	21,229	25,879	7,329	6,584	745	37,880	13,783	24,097	1,899	862	1,037
	30—40	42,445	21,846	20,599	1,475	1,241	234	37,671	19,260	18,411	3,299	1,345	1,954
	40—50	25,216	13,466	11,750	561	450	111	20,708	11,866	8,842	3,947	1,150	2,797
	50—60	15,178	8,071	7,107	214	161	53	11,008	6,873	4,135	3,956	1,037	2,919
	60 & over	21,391	11,858	9,533	557	468	89	11,547	8,679	2,868	9,287	2,711	6,576
							(8) KASHMIR NORTH.						
All Religions.	**Total**	**502,490**	**269,685**	**232,805**	**237,132**	**140,260**	**96,872**	**233,818**	**115,677**	**118,141**	**31,540**	**13,748**	**17,792**
	0—1	17,180	8,842	8,338	17,180	8,842	8,338	—	..	..	..	..	..
	1—5	61,977	31,058	30,919	61,945	31,037	30,908	29	20	9	3	1	2
	5—10	79,474	42,186	37,288	78,493	41,937	36,556	955	235	720	26	14	12
	10—15	57,730	32,212	25,518	47,078	29,440	17,638	10,514	2,732	7,782	138	40	98
	15—20	43,297	23,100	20,197	17,554	15,176	2,378	25,092	7,677	17,415	651	247	404
	20—30	92,163	45,722	46,441	11,508	10,819	689	77,659	33,266	44,393	2,996	1,637	1,359
	30—40	67,148	38,219	28,929	1,720	1,516	204	60,940	34,277	26,663	4,488	2,426	2,062
	40—50	37,025	19,990	17,035	802	729	73	30,842	17,411	13,431	5,381	1,850	3,531
	50—60	23,386	13,761	9,625	365	316	49	16,577	11,082	5,495	6,444	2,363	4,081
	60 & over	23,110	14,595	8,515	487	448	39	11,210	8,977	2,233	11,413	5,170	6,243

VII
Age, Sex and Civil Condition.

TABLE VII.

AGE, SEX AND CIVIL CONDITION BY RELIGION.

Jammu and Kashmir State Census 1921.

Part II - District Tables.

Religion.	Age.	Population. Persons.	Population. Males.	Population. Females.	Unmarried. Persons.	Unmarried. Males.	Unmarried. Females.	Married. Persons.	Married. Males.	Married. Females.	Widowed. Persons.	Widowed. Males.	Widowed. Females.
1	2	3	4	5	6	7	8	9	10	11	12	13	14
Hindu.	**Total**	**10,371**	**6,242**	**4,129**	**5,064**	**3,488**	**1,576**	**4,179**	**2,333**	**1,846**	**1,128**	**421**	**707**
	0—1	267	137	130	267	137	130	..	..	..	..	..	..
	1—5	826	424	402	826	424	402	..	..	..	..	..	..
	5—10	1,378	711	667	1,347	710	637	30	1	29	1	..	1
	10—15	1,112	637	475	989	627	362	118	9	109	5	1	4
	15—20	807	486	321	450	421	29	351	64	287	6	1	5
	20—30	2,028	1,266	762	669	655	14	1,283	588	695	76	23	53
	30—40	1,622	1,066	556	198	196	2	1,243	802	441	181	68	113
	40—50	1,073	697	376	129	129	..	671	476	195	273	92	181
	50—60	713	476	237	102	102	..	341	273	68	270	101	169
	60&over	545	342	203	87	87	..	142	120	22	316	135	181
Sikh.	**Total**	**5,332**	**2,779**	**2,553**	**2,535**	**1,447**	**1,088**	**2,480**	**1,228**	**1,254**	**317**	**106**	**211**
	0—1	215	111	104	215	111	104	..	..	..	..	..	..
	1—5	659	331	328	659	331	328	..	..	..	..	..	..
	5—10	904	498	406	896	491	405	7	6	1	1	1	..
	10—15	546	283	263	450	267	183	94	16	78	2	..	2
	15—20	441	212	229	160	140	20	277	71	206	4	1	3
	20—30	881	397	484	102	76	26	749	312	437	30	9	21
	30—40	800	474	326	25	19	6	727	432	295	48	23	25
	40—50	430	197	233	19	5	14	342	180	162	69	12	57
	50—60	234	134	100	3	1	2	170	112	58	61	21	40
	60&over	222	142	80	6	6	..	114	97	17	102	39	63
Musalman.	**Total**	**486,680**	**260,608**	**226,072**	**229,490**	**135,305**	**94,185**	**227,106**	**112,089**	**115,017**	**30,084**	**13,214**	**16,876**
	0—1	16,695	8,592	8,103	16,695	8,592	8,103	..	..	..	..	..	..
	1—5	60,483	30,302	30,181	60,451	30,281	30,170	29	20	9	3	1	2
	5—10	77,188	40,973	36,215	76,246	40,732	35,514	918	228	690	24	13	11
	10—15	56,059	31,285	24,774	45,626	28,539	17,087	10,302	2,707	7,595	131	39	92
	15—20	42,038	22,400	19,638	16,937	14,615	2,322	24,463	7,542	16,921	638	243	395
	20—30	89,232	44,047	45,185	10,732	10,084	648	75,611	32,359	43,252	2,889	1,604	1,285
	30—40	64,707	36,668	28,039	1,495	1,299	196	58,953	33,034	25,919	4,259	2,335	1,924
	40—50	35,509	19,088	16,421	654	595	59	29,817	16,748	13,069	5,038	1,745	3,293
	50—60	22,437	13,150	9,287	260	213	47	16,064	10,696	5,368	6,113	2,241	3,872
	60&over	22,332	14,103	8,229	394	355	39	10,949	8,755	2,194	10,989	4,993	5,996
						(9) KASHMIR SOUTH.							
All Religions.	**Total**	**688,487**	**372,459**	**316,028**	**324,587**	**196,425**	**128,162**	**311,368**	**153,455**	**157,913**	**52,532**	**22,579**	**29,953**
	0—1	21,607	11,122	10,485	21,600	11,121	10,479	6	1	5	1	..	1
	1—5	80,183	40,937	39,246	80,067	40,855	39,212	57	25	32	59	57	2
	5—10	105,403	54,823	50,580	104,042	54,502	49,540	1,319	318	1,001	42	3	39
	10—15	80,459	45,499	34,960	65,741	41,498	24,243	14,471	3,956	10,515	247	45	202
	15—20	58,483	31,558	26,925	24,668	22,098	2,570	32,947	9,228	23,719	868	232	636
	20—30	125,414	62,746	62,668	20,352	19,056	1,296	100,499	41,424	59,075	4,563	2,266	2,297
	30—40	95,402	55,281	40,121	4,138	3,819	319	83,737	47,437	36,300	7,527	4,025	3,502
	40—50	57,051	31,716	25,335	2,129	1,858	271	43,999	25,305	18,694	10,923	4,553	6,370
	50—60	36,609	22,151	14,458	1,212	1,036	176	22,879	16,427	6,452	12,518	4,688	7,830
	60& over	27,876	16,626	11,250	638	582	56	11,454	9,334	2,120	15,784	6,710	9,074
	Total	**49,692**	**27,638**	**22,054**	**23,736**	**15,799**	**7,939**	**19,750**	**9,712**	**10,038**	**6,204**	**2,127**	**4,077**
	0—1	1,261	663	598	1,261	663	598	..	..	..	..	..	--
	1—5	3,891	2,085	1,806	3,891	2,085	1,806	..	..	..	..	..	--
	5—10	6,740	3,211	3,529	6,611	3,107	3,504	127	104	23	2	..	2
	10—15	5,893	3,472	2,421	5,175	3,359	1,816	658	107	551	60	6	54
	15—20	4,335	2,669	1,666	2,248	2,066	182	2,012	588	1,424	75	15	60
	20—30	9,267	5,193	4,074	2,516	2,492	24	6,239	2,554	3,685	512	147	365
	30—40	7,332	4,021	3,311	940	939	7	5,287	2,680	2,607	1,099	402	697
	40—50	5,247	3,032	2,215	598	596	2	3,207	1,977	1,230	1,442	459	983
	50—60	3,450	1,996	1,454	273	273	..	1,590	1,160	430	1,587	563	1,024
	60& over	2,276	1,296	980	219	219	..	630	542	88	1,427	535	892
Sikh.	**Total**	**3,202**	**1778**	**1,424**	**1,567**	**919**	**648**	**1,458**	**795**	**663**	**177**	**64**	**113**
	0—1	114	55	59	114	55	59	..	..	..	..	--	..
	1—5	483	200	283	483	200	283	..	..	..	..	..	..
	5—10	496	298	198	496	298	198	..	..	..	..	..	--
	10—15	356	210	146	303	204	99	52	6	46	1	..	1
	15—20		140	133	112	103	9	158	34	124	3	3	--
	20—30		296	211	46	46	..	444	242	202	17	8	9
	30—40		245	180	8	8	..	394	231	163	23	6	17
	40—50		162	115	1	1	--	242	151	91	34	10	24
		141	88	53	--	--	..	101	75	26	40	13	27
	60& over	130	84	46	4	4	--	67	56	11	59	24	35

TABLE VII.

VII Age, Sex and Civil Condition.

Age, Sex and Civil Condition by Religion.

Jammu and Kashmir State Census 1921.

Part II—District Tables.

Religion.	Age.	Population.			Unmarried.			Married.			Widowed.		
		Persons.	Males.	Females.	Persons.	Males.	Females.	Persons.	Males.	Females.	Persons.	Males.	Females.
1	2	3	4	5	6	7	8	9	10	11	12	13	14
Musalman.	**Total**	**635,225**	**342,841**	**292,384**	**299,118**	**179,605**	**119,513**	**289,990**	**142,858**	**147,132**	**46,117**	**20,378**	**25,739**
	0—1	20,226	10,400	9,826	20,219	10,399	9,820	6	1	5	1	..	1
	1—5	75,782	38,633	37,149	75,666	38,551	37,115	57	25	32	59	57	2
	5—10	98,133	51,295	46,838	96,901	51,078	45,823	1,192	214	978	40	3	37
	10—15	74,200	41,810	32,390	60,254	37,929	22,325	13,761	3,843	9,918	185	38	147
	15—20	53,859	28,737	25,122	22,294	19,918	2,376	30,775	8,605	22,170	790	214	576
	20—30	115,571	57,218	58,353	17,754	16,493	1,261	93,786	38,617	55,169	4,031	2,108	1,923
	30—40	87,580	50,977	36,603	3,166	2,861	305	78,010	44,500	33,510	6,404	3,616	2,788
	40—50	51,476	28,496	22,980	1,520	1,257	263	40,515	23,155	17,360	9,441	4,084	5,357
	50—60	32,965	20,047	12,918	933	763	170	21,152	15,174	5,978	10,880	4,110	6,770
	60& over	25,433	15,228	10,205	411	356	55	10,736	8,724	2,012	14,286	6,148	8,138
Christian.	**Total**	**302**	**156**	**146**	**127**	**71**	**56**	**144**	**77**	**67**	**31**	**8**	**23**
	0—1	5	3	2	5	3	2	..	..	..	..	..	..
	1—5	17	11	6	17	11	6	..	..	..	..	..	..
	5—10	22	9	13	22	9	13	..	..	..	..	..	..
	10—15	4	2	2	4	2	2	..	..	..	..	..	..
	15—20	13	10	3	13	10	3	..	..	..	..	..	..
	20—30	55	31	24	33	22	11	20	7	13	2	2	..
	30—40	56	32	24	16	9	7	39	22	17	1	1	..
	40—50	45	22	23	7	2	5	32	20	12	6	..	6
	50—60	49	18	31	6	..	6	33	16	17	10	2	8
	60 &over	36	18	18	4	3	1	20	12	8	12	3	9
					(10) MUZ	ZAFFARA	BAD						
All Religions.	**Total**	**216,109**	**115,680**	**100,429**	**111,689**	**64,058**	**47,631**	**90,466**	**46,199**	**44,267**	**13,954**	**5,423**	**8,531**
	0—1	4,144	2,093	2,051	4,143	2,093	2,050	1	..	1	..	..	..
	1—5	29,168	14,627	14,541	29,153	14,623	14,530	14	4	10	1	..	1
	5—10	35,405	18,906	16,499	34,349	18,181	16,168	1,044	721	323	12	4	8
	10—15	24,252	14,245	10,007	20,617	13,199	7,418	3,568	1,038	2,530	67	8	59
	15—20	19,439	9,733	9,706	10,395	7,661	2,734	8,798	1,970	6,828	246	102	144
	20—30	35,439	17,594	17,845	8,863	6,341	2,522	25,448	10,691	14,757	1,128	562	566
	30—40	28,844	15,838	13,006	1,984	1,148	836	24,997	13,802	11,195	1,863	888	975
	40—50	15,896	9,052	6,844	1,493	383	1,110	12,540	7,997	4,543	1,863	672	1,191
	50—60	9,765	5,488	4,277	370	199	171	6,986	4,511	2,475	2,409	778	1,631
	60 &over	13,757	8,104	5,653	322	230	92	7,070	5,465	1,605	6,365	2,409	3,956
Hindu.	**Total**	**4,397**	**2,702**	**1,695**	**1,977**	**1,320**	**657**	**2,000**	**1,189**	**811**	**420**	**193**	**227**
	0—1	70	40	30	70	40	30	..	..	..	..	..	..
	1—5	438	218	220	438	218	220	..	..	..	..	..	..
	5—10	482	217	265	474	217	257	8	..	8	..	..	..
	10—15	437	244	193	353	225	128	81	19	62	3	..	3
	15—20	439	290	149	191	175	16	198	70	128	50	45	5
	20—30	925	644	281	259	257	2	627	373	254	39	14	25
	30—40	618	456	162	76	72	4	483	358	125	59	26	33
	40—50	408	299	109	93	93	..	247	173	74	68	33	35
	50—70	362	168	194	11	11	..	266	120	146	85	37	48
	60 &over	218	126	92	12	12	..	90	76	14	116	38	78
Sikh.	**Total**	**9,208**	**4,759**	**4,449**	**4,795**	**2,799**	**1,996**	**3,728**	**1,702**	**2,026**	**685**	**258**	**427**
	0—1	231	133	98	231	133	98	..	..	..	..	..	..
	1—5	1,337	670	667	1,337	670	667	..	..	..	..	..	..
	5—10	1,662	846	816	1,651	846	805	8	..	8	3	..	3
	10—15	1,052	593	459	886	570	316	163	23	140	3	..	3
	15—20	621	198	423	168	154	14	446	44	402	7	..	7
	20—30	1,604	874	730	321	287	34	1,242	566	676	41	21	20
	30—40	983	492	491	114	106	8	770	346	424	99	40	59
	40—50	730	371	359	17	14	3	574	316	258	139	41	98
	50—60	452	263	189	41	10	31	279	202	77	132	51	81
	60& over	536	319	217	29	9	20	246	205	41	261	105	156
Musalman.	**Total**	**202,498**	**108,215**	**94,283**	**104,915**	**59,937**	**44,978**	**84,735**	**43,306**	**41,429**	**12,848**	**4,972**	**7,876**
	0—1	3,843	1,920	1,923	3,842	1,920	1,922	1	..	1	..	..	..
	1—5	27,393	13,739	13,654	27,378	13,735	13,643	14	4	10	1	..	1
	5—10	33,261	17,843	15,418	32,224	17,118	15,106	1,028	721	307	9	4	5
	10—15	22,763	13,408	9,355	19,378	12,404	6,974	3,324	996	2,328	61	8	53
	15—20	18,379	9,245	9,134	10,036	7,332	2,704	8,154	1,856	6,298	189	57	132
	20—30	32,907	16,074	16,833	8,281	5,795	2,486	23,578	9,752	13,826	1,048	527	521
	30—40	27,242	14,889	12,353	1,794	970	824	23,743	13,097	10,646	1,705	822	883
	40—50	14,757	8,381	6,376	1,383	276	1,107	11,718	7,507	4,211	1,656	598	1,058
	50—60	8,950	5,057	3,893	318	178	140	6,441	4,189	2,252	2,191	690	1,501
	60& over	13,003	7,659	5,344	281	209	72	6,734	5,184	1,550	5,988	2,266	3,722

VII
Age, Sex and Civil Condition.

TABLE VII.

Age, Sex and Condition by Religion.

Jammu and Kashmir State Census 1921.

Part II.—District Tables.

Religion.	Age.	Population. Persons.	Population. Males.	Population. Females.	Unmarried. Persons.	Unmarried. Males.	Unmarried. Females.	Married. Persons.	Married. Males.	Married. Females.	Widowed. Persons.	Widowed. Males.	Widowed. Females.
1	2	3	4	5	6	7	8	9	10	11	12	13	14
						(11) LADAKH.							
All Religions	**Total**	**183,476**	**91,258**	**92,218**	**83,585**	**44,802**	**38,783**	**83,938**	**42,129**	**41,809**	**15,953**	**4,327**	**11,6**
	0—1	5,860	2,862	2,998	5,860	2,862	2,998	..	..	..	..	..	..
	1—5	19,761	9,719	10,042	19,754	9,715	10,039	7	4	3	..	..	..
	5—10	22,466	11,583	10,883	22,152	11,473	10,679	301	106	195	13	4	
	10—15	19,972	10,454	9,518	17,705	9,637	8,068	2,210	791	1,419	57	26	[illegible]
	15—20	17,038	9,120	7,918	9,503	5,849	3,654	7,318	3,174	4,144	217	97	1
	20—30	27,864	13,003	14,861	4,982	3,159	1,823	21,618	9,297	12,321	1,264	547	7
	30—40	26,616	13,030	13,586	1,850	1,095	755	22,942	11,359	11,583	1,824	576	1,2
	40—50	19,848	9,948	9,900	730	431	299	16,178	8,830	7,348	2,940	687	2,2
	50—60	7,946	4,296	3,650	446	22[illegible]	223	3,918	3,631	2,287	1,582	442	1,1
	60 & over	16,105	7,243	8,862	603	35[illegible]	245	7,446	4,937	2,509	8,056	1,948	6,1
Budh.	**Total**	**37,241**	**18,610**	**18,631**	**16,935**	**8,274**	**8,661**	**16,012**	**9,208**	**6,804**	**4,294**	**1,128**	**3,16**
	0—1	774	377	397	774	377	397	..	..	..	..	..	..
	1—5	2,837	1,362	1,475	2,834	1,362	1,472	3	..	3	..	..	..
	5—10	3,620	1,764	1,856	3,598	1,748	1,850	20	16	4	2	..	
	10—15	3,410	1,705	1,705	3,173	1,546	1,627	234	156	78	3	3	..
	15—20	3,581	1,965	1,616	2,576	1,298	1,278	981	657	324	24	10	1
	20—30	5,839	2,797	3,042	1,639	680	959	3,993	2,037	1,956	207	80	12
	30—40	4,846	2,900	1,946	1,083	597	486	3,459	2,193	1,266	304	110	19
	40—50	4,288	2,159	2,129	486	275	211	3,307	1,729	1,578	495	155	34
	50—60	3,362	1,646	1,716	400	192	208	2,347	1,292	1,055	615	162	45
	60 & over	4,684	1,935	2,749	372	199	173	1,668	1,128	540	2,644	608	2,03
Musalman.	**Total**	**145,824**	**72,380**	**73,444**	**66,450**	**36,404**	**30,046**	**67,734**	**32,791**	**34,943**	**11,640**	**3,185**	**8,4**
	0—1	5,068	2,479	2,589	5,068	2,479	2,589	..	..	..	..	..	..
	1—5	16,889	8,341	8,548	16,885	8,337	8,548	4	4	..	..	..	..
	5—10	18,796	9,795	9,001	18,504	9,701	8,803	281	90	191	11	4	
	10—15	16,541	8,735	7,806	14,511	8,077	6,434	1,976	635	1,341	54	23	3
	15—20	13,425	7,138	6,287	6,909	4,538	2,371	6,323	2,513	3,810	193	87	1
	20—30	21,924	10,132	11,792	3,302	2,443	859	17,568	7,225	10,343	1,054	464	5
	30—40	21,691	10,075	11,616	761	492	269	19,413	9,120	10,293	1,517	463	1,0
	40—50	15,512	7,750	7,762	239	153	86	12,834	7,069	5,765	2,439	528	1,9
	50—60	4,564	2,633	1,931	41	26	15	3,560	2,329	1,231	963	278	6
	60 & over	11,414	5,302	6,112	230	158	72	5,773	3,806	1,969	5,409	1,338	4,0
Christian.	**Total**	**70**	**37**	**33**	**38**	**16**	**22**	**28**	**19**	**9**	**4**	**2**	
	0—1	2	..	2	2	..	2	..	..	..	..	..	—
	1—5	8	4	4	8	4	4	..	..	..	..	..	—
	5—10	10	6	4	10	6	4	..	..	..	..	..	—
	10—15	8	3	5	8	3	5	..	..	..	..	..	—
	15—20	5	2	3	4	2	2	1	..	1	..	..	—
	20—30	11	5	6	5	1	4	5	3	2	1	1	..
	30—40	9	5	4	..	..	..	9	5	4	..	..	..
	40—50	10	6	4	1	..	1	8	6	2	1	..	
	50—60	6	5	1	..	..	..	5	5	..	1	..	
	60 & over	1	1	..	..	..	..	..	..	..	1	1	..
						(12) GILGIT.							
All Religions.	**Total**	**28,706**	**15,880**	**12,826**	**15,287**	**9,058**	**6,229**	**11,794**	**6,182**	**5,612**	**1,625**	**640**	**98**
	0—1	714	367	347	714	367	347	..	..	..	..	..	—
	1—5	3,742	1,805	1,937	3,742	1,805	1,937	..	..	..	..	..	—
	5—10	4,842	2,397	2,445	4,785	2,394	2,391	54	..	54	3	3	..
	10—15	2,950	1,526	1,424	2,684	1,523	1,161	259	1	258	7	2	
	15—20	2,489	1,569	920	1,495	1,269	226	966	292	674	28	8	2
	20—30	4,922	2,886	2,036	1,307	1,221	86	3,437	1,571	1,866	178	94	8
	30—40	4,090	2,330	1,760	169	112	57	3,628	2,056	1,572	293	162	13
	40—50	2,271	1,360	911	152	143	9	1,834	1,116	718	285	101	18
	50—60	1,326	829	497	116	108	8	947	646	301	263	75	18
	60 & over	1,360	811	549	123	116	7	669	500	169	568	195	37

TABLE VII.

Age, Sex and Condition by Religion.

Jammu and Kashmir State Census 1921.

Part II—District Tables.

Religion.	Age.	Population. Persons.	Population. Males.	Population. Females.	Unmarried. Persons.	Unmarried. Males.	Unmarried. Females.	Married. Persons.	Married. Males.	Married. Females.	Widowed. Persons.	Widowed. Males.	Widowed. Females.
1	2	3	4	5	6	7	8	9	10	11	12	13	14
Hindu.	**Total**	**711**	**665**	**46**	**284**	**264**	**20**	**396**	**374**	**22**	**31**	**27**	**4**
	0—1	8	5	3	8	5	3	..	..	..	..	..	..
	1—5	11	5	6	11	5	6	..	..	..	..	..	..
	5—10	21	14	7	20	14	6	1	..	1	..	..	..
	10—15	12	7	5	12	7	5	..	..	..	..	..	..
	15—20	76	72	4	56	56	..	19	16	3	1	..	1
	20—30	293	282	11	153	153	..	129	119	10	11	10	1
	30—40	118	112	6	22	22	..	88	83	5	8	7	1
	40—50	73	70	3	2	2	..	62	60	2	9	8	1
	50—60	98	97	1	..	..	..	97	96	1	1	1	..
	60 & over	1	1	..	..	—	..	..	..	..	1	1	..
Musalman.	**Total..**	**27,894**	**15,149**	**12,745**	**14,950**	**8,762**	**6,188**	**11,355**	**5,777**	**5,578**	**1,589**	**610**	**979**
	0—1	705	361	344	707	361	344	..	..	..	..	..	..
	1—5	3,717	1,794	1,923	3,716	1,794	1,923	..	..	..	—	..	..
	5—10	4,812	2,383	2,429	4,759	2,380	2,376	53	..	53	3	3	..
	10—15	2,924	1,508	1,416	2,657	1,506	1,153	258	..	258	7	2	5
	15—20	2,409	1,495	914	1,437	1,211	226	946	276	670	26	8	18
	20—30	4,604	2,585	2,019	1,142	1,061	86	3,292	1,441	1,851	165	83	82
	30—40	3,952	2,205	1,747	145	86	56	3,526	1,965	1,561	284	154	130
	40—50	2,186	1,278	908	148	139	9	1,763	1,047	716	275	92	183
	50—60	1,226	730	496	116	108	8	848	548	300	262	74	188
	60 & over	1,359	810	549	123	116	7	669	500	169	567	194	373

VII. Age, Sex and Civil Condition.

TABLE VII.

Age, Sex and Civil Condition by Religion.

Jammu and Kashmir State Census 1921.

Part III—City Tables.

Religion	Age	Population: Persons	Population: Males	Population: Females	Unmarried: Persons	Unmarried: Males	Unmarried: Females	Married: Persons	Married: Males	Married: Females	Widowed: Persons	Widowed: Males	Widowed: Females
1	2	3	4	5	6	7	8	9	10	11	12	13	14
							(1) JAMMU.						
All Religions.	**Total**	**31,506**	**19,121**	**12,385**	**13,037**	**8,984**	**4,053**	**14,440**	**8,475**	**5,965**	**4,029**	**1,662**	**2,367**
	0—1	772	410	362	772	410	362	..	..	..	..	..	..
	1—5	2,000	967	1,033	1,983	963	1,020	16	4	12	1	..	1
	5—10	3,061	1,587	1,474	3,005	1,571	1,434	56	16	40	..	..	..
	10—15	2,928	1,750	1,178	2,532	1,670	862	384	76	308	12	4	8
	15—20	3,219	1,986	1,233	1,854	1,651	203	1,321	316	1,005	44	19	25
	20—30	6,678	4,291	2,387	1,861	1,803	58	4,403	2,284	2,119	414	204	210
	30—40	5,399	3,492	1,907	689	588	101	3,979	2,570	1,409	731	334	397
	40—50	3,535	2,221	1,314	185	179	6	2,370	1,655	715	980	387	593
	50—60	2,220	1,391	829	91	89	2	1,229	979	250	900	323	577
	60 & over	1,694	1,026	668	65	60	5	682	575	107	947	391	556
Hindu.	**Total**	**20,220**	**12,380**	**7,840**	**8,058**	**5,737**	**2,321**	**9,401**	**5,579**	**3,822**	**2,761**	**1,064**	**1,697**
	0—1	468	240	228	468	240	228	..	..	..	..	..	..
	1—5	1,114	525	589	1,114	525	589	..	..	..	..	..	..
	5—10	1,804	931	873	1,774	924	850	30	7	23	..	..	..
	10—15	1,799	1,116	683	1,518	1,060	458	273	55	218	8	1	7
	15—20	2,095	1,307	788	1,174	1,097	77	890	199	691	31	11	20
	20—30	4,373	2,838	1,535	1,231	1,202	29	2,833	1,507	1,326	309	129	180
	30—40	3,665	2,349	1,316	532	445	87	2,613	1,697	916	520	207	313
	40—50	2,332	1,491	841	131	128	3	1,534	1,106	428	667	257	410
	50—60	1,484	924	560	67	67	..	798	640	158	619	217	402
	60 & over	1,086	659	427	49	49	..	430	368	62	607	242	365
Arya.	**Total**	**560**	**319**	**241**	**251**	**150**	**101**	**271**	**148**	**123**	**38**	**21**	**17**
	0—1	15	6	9	15	6	9	..	..	..	..	..	..
	1—5	59	33	26	59	33	26	..	..	..	..	..	..
	5—10	66	36	30	62	35	27	4	1	3	..	..	..
	10—15	51	23	28	49	23	26	2	..	2	..	..	..
	15—20	75	48	27	51	41	10	24	7	17	..	..	..
	20—30	108	58	50	11	9	2	94	48	46	3	1	2
	30—40	85	55	30	2	1	1	75	48	27	8	6	2
	40—50	51	34	17	..	..	..	46	31	15	5	3	2
	50—60	31	16	15	2	2	..	19	10	9	10	4	6
	60 & over	19	10	9	..	..	..	7	3	4	12	7	5
Brahman.	**Total**	**15**	**7**	**8**	**6**	**3**	**3**	**6**	**3**	**3**	**3**	**1**	**2**
	0—1	1	1	..	1	1	..	..	..	..	..	..	..
	1—5	1	..	1	1	..	1	..	..	..	..	..	..
	5—10	2	2	..	2	2	..	..	..	..	..	..	..
	10—15	2	..	2	2	..	2	..	..	..	..	..	..
	15—20	..	..	..	..	..	..	..	..	..	..	..	..
	20—30	2	..	2	..	..	..	2	..	2	..	..	..
	30—40	3	2	1	..	..	..	3	2	1	..	..	..
	40—50	..	..	..	..	..	..	..	..	..	..	..	..
	50—60	2	1	1	..	..	..	1	1	..	1	..	1
	60 & over	2	1	1	..	..	..	..	..	..	2	1	1
Sikh.	**Total**	**708**	**400**	**308**	**335**	**200**	**135**	**307**	**170**	**137**	**66**	**30**	**36**
	0—1	21	14	7	21	14	7	..	..	..	..	..	..
	1—5	68	32	36	68	32	36	..	..	..	..	..	..
	5—10	103	52	51	103	52	51	..	..	..	..	..	..
	10—15	75	41	34	71	41	30	4	..	4	..	..	..
	15—20	51	30	21	32	25	7	18	4	14	1	1	..
	20—30	130	66	64	25	23	2	102	41	61	3	2	1
	30—40	92	60	32	3	3	..	82	53	29	7	4	3
	40—50	73	45	28	7	6	1	54	33	21	12	6	6
	50—60	46	33	13	4	3	1	27	24	3	15	6	9
	60 & over	49	27	22	1	1	..	20	15	5	28	11	17
Jain.	**Total**	**520**	**289**	**231**	**267**	**156**	**111**	**198**	**109**	**89**	**55**	**24**	**31**
	0—1	25	11	14	25	11	14	..	..	..	..	..	..
	1—5	54	21	33	53	21	32	..	..	..	1	..	1
	5—10	61	29	32	61	29	32	..	..	..	..	..	..
	10—15	70	42	28	68	42	26	2	..	2	..	..	..
	15—20	38	24	14	23	17	6	15	7	8	..	..	..
	20—30	94	53	41	25	24	1	65	26	39	4	3	1
	30—40	69	43	26	8	8	..	50	30	20	11	5	6
	40—50	53	34	19	4	4	..	35	25	10	14	5	9
	50—60	30	18	12	..	..	..	19	13	6	11	5	6
	60 & over	26	14	12	..	..	..	12	8	4	14	6	8

TABLE VII.

VII. Age, Sex and Civil Condition.

Age, Sex and Civil Condition by Religion.

Jammu and Kashmir State Census 1921.

Part III.—City Tables.

Religion.	Age.	Population.			Unmarried.			Married.			Widowed.		
		Persons.	Males.	Females.	Persons.	Males.	Females.	Persons.	Males.	Females.	Persons.	Males.	Females.
1	2	3	4	5	6	7	8	9	10	11	12	13	14
Musalman.	**Total**	**9,001**	**5,463**	**3,538**	**3,900**	**2,606**	**1,294**	**4,045**	**2,360**	**1,685**	**1,056**	**497**	**559**
	0—1	226	127	99	226	127	99	..	..	..	..	..	..
	1—5	664	338	326	650	334	316	14	4	10	..	..	..
	5—10	961	503	458	939	495	444	22	8	14	..	..	..
	10—15	878	502	376	777	478	299	97	21	76	4	3	1
	15—20	901	544	357	546	450	96	346	89	257	9	5	4
	20—30	1,897	1,236	661	552	531	21	1,254	638	616	91	67	24
	30—40	1,405	939	466	138	125	13	1.092	711	381	175	103	72
	40—50	984	595	389	41	39	2	676	444	232	267	11	155
	50—60	599	383	216	18	17	1	344	277	67	237	8	148
	60 & over	486	296	190	13	10	3	200	168	32	273	11	155
Christian.	**Total**	**478**	**259**	**219**	**219**	**131**	**88**	**209**	**103**	**106**	**50**	**25**	**25**
	0—1	16	11	5	16	11	5	..	..	..	..	..	..
	1—5	40	18	22	38	18	20	2	..	2	..	..	..
	5—10	64	34	30	64	34	30	..	..	..	..	..	..
	10—15	53	26	27	47	26	21	6	..	6	..	..	..
	15—20	59	33	26	28	21	7	28	10	18	3	2	1
	20—30	73	39	34	16	13	3	53	24	29	4	2	2
	30—40	77	41	36	6	6	..	61	26	35	10	9	1
	40—50	42	22	20	2	2	..	25	16	9	15	4	11
	50—60	28	16	12	..	..	..	21	14	7	7	2	5
	60 & over	26	19	7	2	..	2	13	13	..	11	6	5
						(2) SRINAGAR.							
All Religions.	**Total**	**141,735**	**76,604**	**65,131**	**67,057**	**41,053**	**26,004**	**60,855**	**30,029**	**30,826**	**13.823**	**5,522**	**8 301**
	0—1	2,655	1,321	1,334	2,654	1,321	1,333	1	..	1	..	..	..
	1—5	13,534	6,819	6,715	13,532	6,819	6,713	2	..	2	..	..	..
	5—10	20,638	9,934	10,704	20,490	9,819	10,671	148	115	33	..	..	..
	10—15	17,804	10,384	7,480	15,730	9,601	6,129	2,049	770	1,279	85	13	72
	15—20	12,492	6,895	5,597	6,454	5,652	802	5,827	1,198	4,629	211	45	166
	20—30	26,163	13,710	12,453	5,700	5,507	193	19,264	7,720	11,544	1,199	483	716
	30—40	21,034	11,926	9,108	671	632	39	17,536	9,678	7,858	2,039	885	1,154
	40—50	13,600	7,622	5,978	1,459	1,363	96	9,416	5,482	3,934	3,513	1,508	2,005
	50—60	8,311	4,848	3,463	203	181	22	4,835	3,564	1,271	3,273	1,103	2,170
	60 & over	5,444	3,145	2,299	164	158	6	1,777	1,502	275	3,503	1,485	2,018
Hindu.	**Total**	**30,004**	**16,515**	**13,489**	**13,876**	**9,201**	**4,675**	**12,396**	**6,068**	**6,328**	**3,732**	**1,246**	**2,486**
	0—1	620	313	307	620	313	307	..	..	..	..	..	..
	1—5	2,221	1,214	1,007	2,221	1,214	1,007	..	..	..	..	..	..
	5—10	4,064	1,864	2,200	3,964	1,764	2,200	100	100	..	..	..	..
	10—15	3,500	2,154	1,346	3,071	2,071	1,000	378	78	300	51	5	46
	15—20	2,850	1,769	1,081	1,483	1,342	141	1,323	416	907	44	11	33
	20—30	5,764	3,217	2,547	1,403	1,390	13	4,067	1,733	2,334	294	94	200
	30—40	4,466	2,354	2,112	531	524	7	3,327	1,639	1,688	608	191	417
	40—50	3,203	1,792	1,411	367	367	..	1,924	1,124	800	912	301	611
	50—60	2,052	1,153	899	121	121	..	946	679	267	985	353	632
	60 & over	1,264	685	579	95	95	..	331	299	32	838	291	547
Arya.	**Total**	**13**	**13**	..	**13**	**13**	..	..	..	..	..	..	..
	0—1	1	1	..	1	1	..	..	..	..	..	..	..
	1—5	3	3	..	3	3	..	..	..	..	..	..	..
	5—10	2	2	..	2	2	..	..	..	..	..	..	..
	10—15	2	2	..	2	2	..	..	..	..	..	..	..
	15—20	1	1	..	1	1	..	..	..	..	..	..	..
	20—30	1	1	..	1	1	..	..	..	..	..	..	..
	30—40	1	1	..	1	1	..	..	..	..	..	..	..
	40—50	2	2	..	2	2	..	..	..	..	..	..	..
	50—60	..	..	..	..	..	..	..	..	..	..	..	..
	60 & over	..	..	..	..	..	..	..	..	..	..	..	..
Sikh.	**Total**	**541**	**361**	**180**	**202**	**135**	**67**	**331**	**226**	**105**	**8**	..	**8**
	0—1	13	4	9	13	4	9	..	..	..	..	..	..
	1—5	40	22	18	40	22	18	..	..	..	..	..	..
	5—10	54	28	26	54	28	26	..	..	..	..	..	..
	10—15	61	45	16	56	42	14	5	3	2	..	..	..
	15—20	54	27	27	27	27	..	27	..	27	..	..	..
	20—30	110	83	27	12	12	..	96	71	25	2	..	2
	30—40	77	57	20	..	..	..	77	57	20	..	..	..
	40—50	70	48	22	..	..	..	70	48	22	..	..	..
	50—60	36	26	10	..	..	..	30	26	4	6	..	6
	60 & over	26	21	5	..	..	..	26	21	5	..	..	..

VII.
Age, Sex and Civil Condition.

TABLE VII.

Age, Sex and Civil Condition Religion.

Jammu and Kashmir State Census 1921.

Part III—City Tables.

Religion.	Age.	Population.			Unmarried.			Married.			Widowed.		
		Persons.	Males.	Females.	Persons.	Males.	Females.	Persons.	Males.	Females.	Persons.	Males.	Females.
1	2	3	4	5	6	7	8	9	10	11	12	13	14
Musalman.	**Total**	**110,935**	**59,579**	**51,356**	**52,869**	**31,642**	**21,227**	**48,000**	**23,664**	**24,336**	**10,066**	**4,273**	**5,793**
	0—1	2,017	1,001	1,016	2,016	1,001	1,015	1	..	1	..	..	..
	1—5	11,258	5,572	5,686	11,256	5,572	5,684	2	..	2	..	..	..
	5—10	16,503	8,032	8,471	16,455	8,017	8,438	48	15	33	..	..	..
	10—15	14,298	8,181	6,117	12,598	7,484	5,114	1,666	689	977	34	8	26
	15—20	9,576	5,088	4,488	4,933	4,273	660	4,476	781	3,695	167	34	133
	20—30	20,241	10,380	9,861	4,256	4,083	173	15,083	5,909	9,174	902	388	514
	30—40	16,440	9,483	6,957	915	829	86	14,095	7,961	6,134	1,430	693	737
	40—50	10,289	5,761	4,528	296	261	35	7,394	4,293	3,101	2,599	1,207	1,392
	50—60	6,185	3,654	2,531	77	60	17	3,833	2,845	988	2,275	749	1,526
	60 & over	4,128	2,427	1,701	67	62	5	1,402	1,171	231	2,659	1,194	1,465
Christian.	**Total**	**238**	**133**	**105**	**96**	**62**	**34**	**125**	**68**	**57**	**17**	**3**	**14**
	0—1	4	2	2	4	2	2	..	..	..	..	..	..
	1—5	12	8	4	12	8	4	..	..	..	..	..	..
	5—10	15	8	7	15	8	7	..	..	..	..	..	..
	10—15	3	2	1	3	2	1	..	..	..	..	..	..
	15—20	10	9	1	10	9	1	..	..	..	..	..	..
	20—30	47	29	18	28	21	7	18	7	11	1	1	..
	30—40	50	31	19	12	9	3	37	21	16	1	1	—
	40—50	34	18	16	5	2	3	27	16	11	2	..	
	50—60	37	14	23	5	—	5	25	13	12	7	1	6
	60 & over	26	12	14	2	1	1	18	11	7	6	..	6

TABLE VIII.

EDUCATION BY RELIGION AND AGE.

Jammu and Kashmir State Census 1921.

1. The general arrangement of this table follows that of Table VII and shows literacy by various territorial sub-divisions and religions.

2. One European female falling under the category of " Indefinite Beliefs " and 302 Sansis (162 males, 140 females) and 22 Sapiadas (11 males, 11 females) who could not be assigned to any prevailing religion, have been grouped under the head " Others. "

3. The " Frontier Ilaqas " are excluded from this Table, as the special Schedule adopted for these Ilaqas did not provide for record of literacy.

4. Details for minor written languages are included in the head " Others."

5. Figures for Hindi are inclusive of those for Sanskrit.

6. The total literacy of Christians is distributed as follows between Indian Christians and the rest.

Christians.	TOTAL.			0—10.			10—15.			15—20.			20 and over.		
	Persons.	Males.	Females.	Persons.	Males.	Females.	Persons.	Males.	Females.	Persons.	Males.	Females.	Persons.	Males.	Females.
Total literate.															
Europeans and Anglo-Indians.	303	153	150	13	2	11	2	1	1	8	4	4	280	146	134
Indian Christians	96	65	31	32	18	14	18	12	6	23	14	9	23	21	2
Literate in English.															
Europeans and Anglo-Indians.	303	153	150	13	2	11	2	1	1	8	4	4	280	146	134
Indian Christians	43	31	12	11	7	4	9	5	4	15	11	4	8	8	..

TABLE

EDUCATION BY

Jammu and Kashmir

Part I—Pro

Age.	POPULATION.									Liter					
	Total.			Literate.			Illiterate.			Urdu.			Persian.		
	Persons.	Males.	Females.	Persons.	Males.	Females.	Persons.	Males.	Females.	Persons.	Males.	Females.	Persons.	Males.	Females.
1	2	3	4	5	6	7	8	9	10	11	12	13	14	15	16
														(i) ENTIRE	
All Religions	**3,259,527**	**1,724,581**	**1,534,946**	**72,228**	**68,221**	**4,007**	**3,187,299**	**1,656,360**	**1,530,939**	**28,202**	**27,464**	**738**	**9,616**	**9,488**	**128**
0—10 ..	969,285	498,318	470,967	2,075	1,763	312	967,210	496,555	470,655	1,406	1,325	81	63	54	9
10—15 ..	373,886	208,565	165,321	6,435	5,918	517	367,451	202,647	164,804	3,856	3,756	100	225	218	7
15—20 ..	275,990	143,653	132,337	8,221	7,660	561	267,769	135,993	131,776	3,902	3,799	103	515	503	12
20 & over ..	1,640,366	874,045	766,321	55,497	52,880	2,617	1,584,869	821,165	763,704	19,038	18,584	454	8,813	8,713	100
Hindu ...	**668,988**	**357,360**	**311,628**	**41,324**	**39,737**	**1,587**	**627,664**	**317,623**	**310,041**	**14,870**	**14,601**	**269**	**3,580**	**3,550**	**30**
0—10 ..	170,117	86,116	84,001	1,157	1,008	149	168,960	85,108	83,852	785	759	26	24	20	4
10—15 ..	70,988	39,914	31,074	3,819	3,558	261	67,169	36,356	30,813	2,246	2,208	38	48	48	..
15—20 ..	55,582	28,973	26,609	4,852	4,586	266	50,730	24,387	26,343	2,173	2,136	37	100	99	1
20 & over ..	372,301	202,357	169,944	31,496	30,585	911	340,805	171,772	169,033	9,666	9,498	168	3,408	3,383	25
Arya ...	**23,116**	**12,608**	**10,508**	**904**	**730**	**174**	**22,212**	**11,878**	**10,334**	**318**	**293**	**25**	..	..	..
0—10 ..	6,342	3,327	3,015	50	26	24	6,292	3,301	2,991	25	23	2	..	..	..
10—15 ..	2,609	1,459	1,150	103	69	34	2,506	1,390	1,116	45	39	6	..	..	..
15—20 ..	1,846	972	874	115	91	24	1,731	881	850	39	37	2	..	..	..
20 & over ..	12,319	6,850	5,469	636	544	92	11,683	6,306	5,377	209	194	15	..	..	..
Brahmo ...	**15**	**7**	**8**	**6**	**3**	**3**	**9**	**4**	**5**	**1**	**1**	..	..	..	..
0—10 ..	4	3	1	1	..	1	3	3	..	..	..	..	..	..	..
10—15 ..	2	—	2	..	..	..	2	..	2	..	..	..	..	..	..
15—20 ..	—	—	..	..	—	—	..	—	..	..	..	..	..	—	..
20 & over ..	9	4	5	5	3	2	4	1	3	1	1	..	..	..	..
Sikh ...	**39,488**	**20,773**	**18,713**	**3,868**	**3,333**	**535**	**35,618**	**17,440**	**18,178**	**971**	**936**	**35**	**12**	**11**	**1**
0—10 ..	12,756	6,556	6,200	131	92	39	12,625	6,464	6,161	49	46	3	..	..	..
10—15 ..	4,621	2,579	2,042	401	336	65	4,220	2,243	1,977	178	175	3	..	..	..
15—20 ..	3,218	1,487	1,731	375	303	72	2,843	1,184	1,659	142	137	5	..	..	..
20 & over ..	18,891	10,151	8,740	2,961	2,602	359	15,930	7,549	8,381	602	578	24	12	11	1
Jain ...	**529**	**295**	**234**	**185**	**161**	**24**	**344**	**134**	**210**	**28**	**26**	**2**	..	..	..
0—10 ..	142	62	80	3	2	1	139	60	79	1	1	..	..	..	..
10—15 ..	70	42	28	22	16	6	48	26	22	10	9	1	..	..	..
15—20 ..	39	24	15	25	17	8	14	7	7	5	4	1	..	..	..
20 & over ..	278	167	111	135	126	9	143	41	102	12	12	..	..	..	..
Buddhist ...	**37,685**	**18,838**	**18,847**	**1,203**	**1,169**	**34**	**36,482**	**17,669**	**18,813**	**14**	**13**	**1**	**5**	**5**	..
0—10 ..	7,313	3,546	3,767	2	2	..	7,311	3,544	3,767	..	—	..	..	..	..
10—15 ..	3,444	1,723	1,721	35	35	..	3,409	1,688	1,721	1	1	..	..	—	..
15—20 ..	3,633	1,991	1,642	54	51	3	3,579	1,940	1,639	3	3	..	..	..	..
20 & over ..	23,295	11,578	11,717	1,112	1,081	31	22,183	10,497	11,686	10	9	1	5	5	..
Zoroastrian ...	**7**	**5**	**2**	**7**	**5**	**2**	..	..	..	..	..	..	..	..	..
0—10 ..	..	..	..	..	..	..	..	..	..	..	..	..	..	..	..
10—15 ..	..	..	..	..	—	..	..	..	..	..	..	..	..	..	..
15—20 ..	2	1	1	2	1	1	..	..	..	..	..	..	..	..	..
20 & over ..	5	4	1	5	4	1	..	..	..	..	..	..	..	..	..
Musalman ..	**2,487,743**	**1,313,635**	**1,174,108**	**24,328**	**22,863**	**1,465**	**2,463,415**	**1,290,772**	**1,172,643**	**11,964**	**11,569**	**395**	**6,017**	**5,920**	**97**
0—10 ..	772,098	398,448	373,650	685	613	72	771,413	397,835	373,578	529	486	43	38	33	5
10—15 ..	291,955	162,747	129,208	2,035	1,891	144	289,920	160,856	129,064	1,369	1,318	51	176	169	7
15—20 ..	211,511	110,118	101,393	2,767	2,593	174	208,744	107,525	101,219	1,534	1,479	55	415	404	11
20 & over ..	1,212,179	642,322	569,857	18,841	17,766	1,075	1,193,338	624,556	568,782	8,532	8,286	246	5,388	5,314	74
Christian ..	**1,633**	**887**	**746**	**399**	**218**	**181**	**1,234**	**669**	**565**	**36**	**25**	**11**	**2**	**2**	..
0—10 ..	395	187	208	45	20	25	350	167	183	17	10	7	1	1	..
10—15 ..	152	77	75	20	13	7	132	64	68	7	6	1	1	1	..
15—20 ..	137	74	63	31	18	13	106	56	50	6	3	3	..	..	..
20 & over ..	949	549	400	303	167	136	646	382	264	6	6	..	..		..
Others ...	**325**	**173**	**152**	**4**	**2**	**2**	**321**	**171**	**150**	..	..	..	—	..	..
0—10 ..	118	73	45	1	..	1	117	73	44	..	..	..	..	..	..
10—15 ..	45	24	21	..	..	..	45	24	21	..	..	..	..	—	—
15—20 ..	22	13	9	..	..	..	22	13	9	..	..	..	..	—	—
20 & over ..	140	63	77	3	2	1	137	61	76	—	..	..	..	..	—

VIII.

/III Education.

RELIGION AND AGE.

State Census 1921.

incial Tables.

ATE IN.

Arabic.			Dogri.			Hindi.			Bodhi.			Gurmukhi.			Others.			English.		
Persons.	Males.	Females.	Persons.	Males.	Females.	Persons.	Males.	Females.	Persons.	Males	Females.	Persons.	Males.	Females.	Persons.	Males.	Females.	Persons.	Males.	Females.
17	18	19	20	21	22	23	24	25	26	27	28	29	30	31	32	33	34	35	36	37
STATE.																				
3,796	**3,371**	**425**	**5,821**	**5,600**	**221**	**8,316**	**6,904**	**1,412**	**1,248**	**1,219**	**29**	**2,983**	**2,331**	**652**	**1,749**	**1,679**	**70**	**10,497**	**10,165**	**332**
82	58	24	29	24	5	200	97	103	2	2	..	108	53	55	16	9	7	169	141	28
285	209	76	141	134	7	440	225	215	32	31	1	198	120	78	110	99	11	1,148	1,126	22
340	268	72	292	280	12	577	358	219	54	50	4	224	130	94	112	105	7	2,205	2,167	38
3,089	2,836	253	5,359	5,162	197	7,099	6,224	875	1,160	1,136	24	2,453	2,028	425	1,511	1,466	45	6,975	6,731	244
..	..	..	**5,423**	**5,353**	**70**	**7,058**	**6,215**	**843**	**2**	**2**	..	**822**	**603**	**219**	**1,685**	**1,639**	**46**	**7,884**	**7,774**	**110**
..	..	..	26	22	4	160	82	78	..	..	..	31	12	19	15	9	6	116	104	12
..	..	..	135	131	4	355	193	162	..	..	..	42	9	33	107	98	11	886	873	13
..	..	..	280	277	3	479	314	165	1	1	..	72	32	40	109	105	4	1,638	1,622	16
..	..	..	4,982	4,923	59	6,064	5,626	438	1	1	..	677	550	127	1,454	1,429	25	5,244	5,175	69
..	..	..	**51**	**51**	..	**234**	**109**	**125**	**1**	**1**	..	**34**	**21**	**13**	**1**	**1**	..	**265**	**254**	**11**
..	..	..	..	..	..	23	2	21	..	..	..	1	..	1	..	..	..	1	1	..
..	..	..	..	..	..	34	7	27	..	..	..	1	1	..	..	..	..	23	22	1
..	..	..	..	..	..	24	6	18	..	..	..	3	1	2	..	..	..	49	47	2
..	..	..	51	51	..	153	94	59	1	1	..	29	19	10	1	1	..	192	184	8
..	..	..	..	..	..	**3**	..	**3**	..	..	..	..	..	..	..	..	..	**2**	**2**	..
..	..	..	..	..	..	1	..	1	..	..	..	..	..	..	..	..	..	..	..	..
..	..	..	..	..	..	..	..	..	..	..	..	..	..	..	..	..	..	..	..	..
..	..	..	..	..	..	..	..	..	..	..	..	..	..	..	..	..	..	..	..	..
..	..	..	..	..	..	2	..	2	..	..	..	..	..	..	..	..	..	2	2	..
..	..	..	**21**	**20**	**1**	**461**	**383**	**78**	..	..	..	**2,088**	**1,684**	**404**	**30**	**27**	**3**	**285**	**272**	**13**
..	..	..	1	1	..	9	7	2	..	..	..	68	35	33	..	..	..	4	3	1
..	..	..	..	..	..	35	16	19	..	..	..	153	110	43	2	2	..	33	33	..
..	..	..	1	1	..	37	24	13	..	..	..	146	95	51	2	..	2	47	46	1
..	..	..	19	18	1	380	336	44	..	..	..	1,721	1,444	277	26	25	1	201	190	11
..	..	..	—	—	..	**127**	**108**	**19**	..	..	..	**2**	..	**2**	..	..	..	**28**	**27**	**1**
..	..	..	..	..	..	2	1	1	..	..	..	..	..	..	..	..	..	..	..	..
..	..	..	..	..	..	9	6	3	..	..	..	2	..	2	..	..	..	1	1	..
..	..	..	..	..	..	16	10	6	..	..	..	..	..	..	..	..	..	4	3	1
..	..	..	..	..	..	100	91	9	..	..	..	..	..	..	..	..	..	23	23	..
..	..	..	**1**	**1**	..	..	..	..	**1,165**	**1,142**	**23**	..	..	..	**13**	**3**	**10**	**5**	**5**	—
..	..	..	..	..	..	..	..	..	2	2	..	..	..	..	..	..	..	..	..	..
..	..	..	..	..	..	..	..	..	31	31	..	..	..	..	..	..	..	3	3	..
..	..	..	..	..	..	..	..	..	49	47	2	..	..	..	1	..	1	1	1	..
..	..	..	1	1	..	..	..	..	1,083	1,062	21	..	..	..	12	3	9	1	1	..
..		..	..	..	..	..	..	..	..	..	..	..	..	..	..	..	..	**7**	**5**	**2**
..		..	..	..	..	..	..	..	..	..	..	..	..	..	..	..	..	..	..	..
..	—	..	..	..	..	..	..	..	..	..	..	..	..	..	..	..	..	..	..	..
..	..	..	..	..	..	..	..	..	..	..	..	..	..	..	..	..	..	2	1	1
..	..	..	..	..	..	..	..	..	..	..	..	..	..	..	..	..	..	5	4	1
3,796	**3,371**	**425**	**324**	**175**	**149**	**433**	**89**	**344**	**67**	**66**	**1**	35	**23**	**12**	**19**	**9**	**10**	**1,673**	**1,641**	**32**
82	58	24	1	1	..	5	5	..	..	..	..	6	6	..	..	..	..	24	24	..
285	209	76	6	3	3	7	3	4	..	..	..	..	..	..	1	1	..	191	188	3
340	268	72	11	2	9	21	4	17	2	2	..	3	2	1	..	..	..	441	432	9
3,089	2,836	253	306	169	137	400	77	323	65	64	1	26	15	11	18	8	10	1,017	997	20
..	..	..	**1**	..	**1**	..	..	..	**12**	**7**	**5**	**2**	..	**2**	..	..	..	**346**	**184**	**162**
..	..	..	1	..	1	..	..	..	..	..	..	2	..	2	..	..	..	24	9	15
..	..	..	..	..	..	..	..	..	1	..	1	..	..	..	..	..	..	11	6	5
..	..	..	..	..	..	..	..	..	2	..	2	..	..	..	..	..	..	23	15	8
..	..	..	..	..	..	..	..	..	9	7	2	..	..	..	..	..	..	288	154	134
..	..	..	..	..	..	..	..	..	**1**	**1**	..	..	..	..	**1**	..	**1**	**2**	**1**	**1**
..	..	..	..	..	..	..	..	..	..	..	..	..	..	..	1	..	1	..	..	..
..	..	..	..	..	..	..	..	..	..	..	..	..	..	..	..	..	..	..	..	..
..	..	..	..	..	..	..	..	..	..	..	..	..	..	..	..	..	..	..	..	..
..	..	..	..	..	..	..	..	..	1	1	..	..	..	..	..	..	..	2	1	1

TABLE

EDUCATION BY

Jammu and Kashmir

Part I—Prov

Age.	POPULATION. Total. Persons.	Total. Males.	Total. Females.	Literate. Persons.	Literate. Males.	Literate. Females.	Illiterate. Persons.	Illiterate. Males.	Illiterate. Females.	LITER Urdu. Persons.	Urdu. Males.	Urdu. Females.	Persian. Persons.	Persian. Males.	Persian. Females.
1	2	3	4	5	6	7	8	9	10	11	12	13	14	15	16
														(ii) JAMMU	
All Religions.	**1,640,259**	**859,619**	**780,640**	**37,461**	**34,756**	**2,705**	**1,602,798**	**824,863**	**777,935**	**17,306**	**16,860**	**446**	**494**	**476**	**18**
0—10 ..	477,354	244.991	232,363	1,310	1,104	206	476,044	243,887	232,157	956	902	54	8	6	2
10—15 ..	188,521	104.629	83.892	3,532	3,168	364	184,989	101,461	83,528	2,463	2,404	59	17	14	3
15—20 ..	135,251	68,573	66.678	4,404	3,999	405	130,847	64,574	66,273	2,549	2,481	68	43	39	4
20 & over ..	839,133	441,426	397,707	28,215	26,485	1,730	810,918	414,941	395,977	11,338	11,073	265	426	417	9
Hindu ..	**603,549**	**319,928**	**283,621**	**23,831**	**22,636**	**1,195**	**579,718**	**297,292**	**282,426**	**8,889**	**8,748**	**141**	**201**	**200**	**1**
0—10 ..	154,662	78,359	76,303	745	653	92	153,917	77,706	76,211	535	526	9	1	1	..
10—15 ..	63,526	35,547	27,979	2 142	1,944	198	61,384	33,603	27,781	1,440	1,420	20	6	6	..
15—20 ..	49,907	25,446	24,461	2,778	2,561	217	47,129	22,885	24,244	1,509	1,489	20	15	15	..
20 & over ..	335,454	180,576	154,878	18,166	17,478	688	317,288	163,098	154,190	5,405	5,313	92	179	178	1
Arya ..	**23,045**	**12,560**	**10,485**	**869**	**701**	**168**	**22,176**	**11,859**	**10,317**	**303**	**281**	**22**	..	..	..
0—10 ..	6,313	3,309	3,004	42	20	22	6,271	3,289	2,982	17	17	..	..	..	..
10—15 ..	2,601	1,452	1,149	99	65	34	2,502	1,387	1,115	42	36	6	..	..	..
15—20 ..	1,844	970	874	114	90	24	1,730	880	850	39	37	2	..	..	..
20 & over ..	12,287	6,829	5,458	614	526	88	11,673	6,303	5,370	205	191	14	..	..	..
Brahmo ..	**15**	**7**	**8**	**6**	**3**	**3**	**9**	**4**	**5**	**1**	**1**	..	..	..	..
0—10 ..	4	3	1	1	..	1	3	3	—				..	..	..
10—15 ..	2	..	2	..	..	..	2	..	2	..	..	..	..	..	..
15—20 ..	..	..	..	..	..	..	..	..	..	..	..	..	..	..	..
20 & over ..	9	4	5	5	3	2	4	1	3	1	1	..	..	..	..
Sikh ..	**21,627**	**11,381**	**10,246**	**2,036**	**1,726**	**310**	**19,591**	**9,655**	**9,936**	**653**	**635**	**18**	..	..	..
0—10 ..	6,630	3,407	3,223	73	46	27	6,557	3,361	3.196	29	27	2	..	..	..
10—15 ..	2,652	1,482	1,170	228	179	49	2,424	1,303	1,121	132	130	2	..	..	..
15—20 ..	1,871	931	940	236	187	48	1.636	744	892	95	94	1	..	..	..
20 & over ..	10,474	5,561	4,913	1,500	1,314	186	8,974	4,247	4,727	397	384	13	..	..	..
Jain ..	**528**	**294**	**234**	**184**	**160**	**24**	**344**	**134**	**210**	**28**	**26**	**2**	..	..	..
0—10 ..	142	62	80	3	2	1	139	60	79	1	1	..	..	..	..
10—15 ..	70	42	28	22	16	6	48	26	22	10	9	1	..	..	..
15—20 ..	39	24	15	25	17	8	14	7	7	5	4	1	..	..	..
20 & over ..	277	166	111	134	125	9	143	41	102	12	12	..	..	..	..
Buddhist ..	**442**	**226**	**216**	**8**	**8**	..	**434**	**218**	**216**	..	..	..	..	..	..
0—10 ..	82	43	39	..	..	..	82	43	39	..	..	..	..	..	..
10—15 ..	34	18	16	..	..	..	34	18	16	..	..	..	..	..	..
15—20 ..	52	26	26	..	..	..	52	26	26	..	..	..	..	..	..
20 & over ..	274	139	135	8	8	..	266	131	135	..	..	..	..	..	..
Zoroastrian ..	**5**	**3**	**2**	**5**	**3**	**2**	..	..	..	..	..	..	..	..	..
0—10 ..	..	..	..	..	..	..	..	..	..	..	..	..	..	..	..
10—15 ..	..	..	..	..	..	..	..	..	..	..	..	..	..	..	..
15—20 ..	1	..	1	1	..	1	..	..	..	..	..	..	..	..	..
20 & over ..	4	3	1	4	3	1	..	..	..	..	..	..	..	..	..
Musalman ..	**989,622**	**514,442**	**475,180**	**10,442**	**9,472**	**970**	**979,180**	**504,970**	**474,210**	**7,401**	**7,149**	**252**	**293**	**276**	**17**
0—10 ..	309,107	159,598	149,509	416	367	49	308,691	159,231	149,460	359	323	36	7	5	2
10—15 ..	119,468	66,001	53,467	1,028	956	72	118,440	65,045	53,395	833	804	29	11	8	3
15—20 ..	81,401	41,103	40,298	1,237	1,138	99	80,164	39,965	40,199	896	855	41	28	24	4
20 & over ..	479,646	247,740	231,906	7,761	7,011	750	471,885	240,729	231,156	5,313	5,167	146	247	239	8
Christian ..	**1,207**	**662**	**545**	**80**	**47**	**33**	**1,127**	**615**	**512**	**31**	**20**	**11**	..	..	..
0—10 ..	324	151	173	30	16	14	294	135	159	15	8	7	..	..	..
10—15 ..	138	71	67	13	8	5	125	63	62	6	5	1	..	..	..
15—20 ..	119	62	57	14	6	8	105	56	49	5	2	3	..	..	..
20 & over ..	626	378	248	23	17	6	6o3	361	242	5	5	..	..	..	..
Others ..	**219**	**116**	**103**	..	..	..	**219**	**116**	**103**	..	..	..	..	..	—
0—10 ..	90	59	31	..	..	..	90	59	31	..	..	..	..	..	—
10—15 ..	30	16	14	..	..	..	30	16	14	..	..	..	..	..	—
15—20 ..	17	11	6	..	..	..	17	11	6	..	..	..	..	..	—
20 & over ..	82	30	52	..	—	..	82	30	52	..	..	..	..	..	—

VIII.

VIII Education.

RELIGION AND AGE

State Census 1921.

incial Tables.

ATE IN.

Arabic.			Dogri.			Hindi.			Bodhi.			Gurmukhi.			Others.			English.		
Persons.	Males.	Females.	Persons.	Males.	Females.	Persons.	Males.	Females.	Persons.	Males.	Females.	Persons.	Males.	Females.	Persons.	Males.	Persons.	Persons.	Males.	Females.
17	18	19	20	21	22	23	24	25	26	27	28	29	30	31	32	33	34	35	36	37
PROV	INCE.																			
1,351	**1,177**	**174**	**5,672**	**5,460**	**212**	**7,564**	**6,237**	**1,327**	**5**	**5**	..	**1,592**	**1,174**	**418**	**100**	**89**	**11**	**3,377**	**3,278**	**99**
31	20	11	28	23	5	176	88	88	..	..	..	60	23	37	1	..	1	50	42	8
111	80	31	139	132	7	391	200	191	..	..	..	89	29	60	4	4	..	318	305	13
120	96	24	289	277	12	520	310	210	..	..	..	141	76	65	6	4	2	736	716	20
1,089	981	108	5,216	5,028	188	6,477	5,639	838	5	5	..	1,302	1,046	256	89	81	8	2,273	2,215	58
..	..	..	**5,287**	**5,225**	**62**	**6,397**	**5,629**	**768**	..	..	..	**699**	**526**	**173**	**72**	**69**	**3**	**2,286**	**2,239**	**47**
..	..	..	25	21	4	138	75	63	..	..	..	17	6	11	1	..	1	28	24	4
..	..	..	133	129	4	314	175	139	..	..	..	32	3	29	2	2	..	215	209	6
..	..	..	278	275	3	496	270	156	..	..	..	56	26	30	6	4	2	488	482	6
..	..	..	4,851	4,800	51	5,519	5,109	410	..	..	..	594	491	103	63	63	..	1,555	1,524	31
..	..	..	**51**	**51**	..	**230**	**107**	**123**	**1**	**1**	..	**34**	**21**	**13**	**1**	**1**	..	**249**	**239**	**10**
..	..	..	..	..	..	23	2	21	..	..	..	1	..	1	..	..	..	1	1	..
..	..	..	..	..	..	34	7	27	..	..	..	1	1	..	..	..	..	22	21	1
..	..	..	..	..	..	24	6	18	..	..	..	3	1	2	..	..	..	48	46	2
..	..	..	51	51	..	149	92	57	1	1	..	29	19	10	1	1	..	178	171	7
..	..	..	..	..	..	**3**	..	**3**	..	..	..	..	..	..	..	..	..	**2**	**2**	..
..	..	..	..	..	..	1	..	1	..	..	..	..	..	..	..	..	..	..	..	
..	..	..	..	..	..	..	..	..	..	..	..	..	..	..	..	..	..	..	..	
..	..	..	..	..	..	..	..	..	..	..	..	..	..	..	..	..	..	..	..	
..	..	..	..	..	..	2	..	2	..	..	..	..	..	..	..	..	..	2	2	..
..	..	..	**15**	**15**	..	**379**	**308**	**71**	..	..	..	**829**	**612**	**217**	**10**	**10**	..	**150**	**146**	**4**
..	..	..	1	1	..	7	5	2	..	..	..	35	12	23	..	..	..	1	1	..
..	..	..	..	..	..	27	9	18	..	..	..	54	25	29	2	2	..	13	13	..
..	..	..	..	..	..	33	20	13	..	..	..	80	47	33	..	..	..	27	26	1
..	..	..	14	14	..	312	274	38	..	..	..	660	528	132	8	8	..	109	106	3
..	..	..	..	..	..	**127**	**108**	**19**	..	..	..	**2**	..	**2**	..	..	..	**27**	**26**	**1**
..	..	..	..	..	..	2	1	1	..	..	..	..	..	..	..	..	..	..	..	..
..	..	..	..	..	..	9	6	3	..	..	..	2	..	2	..	..	..	1	1	..
..	..	..	..	..	..	16	10	6	..	..	..	..	..	..	..	..	..	4	3	1
..	..	..	..	..	..	100	91	9	..	..	..	..	..	..	..	..	..	2[illegible]	22	..
..	..	..	**1**	**1**	..	..	..	..	**4**	**4**	..	..	..	..	**3**	**3**	..	..	..	..
..	..	..	..	..	..	..	..	..	..	..	..	..	..	..	..	..	..	..	..	..
..	..	..	..	..	..	..	..	..	..	..	..	..	..	..	..	..	..	..	..	..
..	..	..	..	..	..	..	..	..	..	..	..	..	..	..	..	..	..	..	..	..
..	..	..	1	1	..	..	..	..	4	4	..	..	..	..	3	3	..	..	..	..
..	..	..	..	..	..	..	..	..	..	..	..	..	..	..	..	..	..	**5**	**3**	**2**
..	..	..	..	..	..	..	..	..	..	..	..	..	..	..	..	..	..	..	..	..
..	..	..	..	..	..	..	..	..	..	..	..	..	..	..	..	..	..	..	..	..
..	..	..	..	..	..	..	..	..	..	..	..	..	..	..	..	..	..	1	..	1
..	..	..	..	..	..	..	..	..	..	..	..	..	..	..	..	..	..	4	3	1
1,351	**1,177**	**174**	**317**	**168**	**149**	**428**	**85**	**343**	..	..	..	**26**	**15**	**11**	**14**	**6**	**8**	**612**	**596**	**16**
31	20	11	1	1	..	5	5	..	..	..	..	5	5	..	..	..	..	8	8	..
111	80	31	6	3	3	7	3	4	..	..	..	..	..	..	..	..	..	60	58	2
120	96	24	11	2	9	21	4	17	..	..	..	2	2	..	..	..	..	159	155	4
1,089	981	108	299	162	137	395	73	322	..	..	..	19	8	11	14	6	8	385	375	10
..	..	..	**1**	..	**1**	..	..	..	..	..	..	**2**	..	**2**	..	..	..	**46**	**27**	**19**
..	..	..	1	..	1	..	..	..	..	..	..	2	..	2	..	..	..	12	8	4
..	..	..	..	..	..	..	..	..	..	..	..	..	..	..	..	..	..	7	3	4
..	..	..	..	..	..	..	..	..	..	..	..	..	..	..	..	..	..	9	4	5
..	..	..	..	..	..	..	..	..	..	..	..	..	..	..	..	..	..	18	12	6
..	..	..	..	..	..	..	..	..	..	..	..	..	..	..	..	..	..	..	..	..
..	..	..	..	..	..	..	..	..	..	..	..	..	..	..	..	..	..	..	..	..
..	..	..	..	..	..	..	..	..	..	..	..	..	..	..	..	..	..	..	..	..
..	..	..	..	..	..	..	..	..	..	..	..	..	..	..	..	..	..	..	..	..
..	..	..	..	..	..	..	..	..	..	..	..	..	..	..	..	..	..	..	..	..

VIII
Education.

TABLE

EDUCATION BY

Jammu and Kashmir

Part I—Prov

Age.	POPULATION. Total. Persons.	Males.	Females.	Literate. Persons.	Males.	Females.	Illiterate. Persons.	Males.	Females.	LITER... Urdu. Persons.	Males.	Females.	Persian. Persons.	Males.	Females.
1	2	3	4	5	6	7	8	9	10	11	12	13	14	15	16
													(iii)	KASHMIR	
All Religions	**1,407,086**	**757,824**	**649,262**	**31,347**	**30,172**	**1,175**	**1,375,739**	**727,652**	**648,087**	**10,027**	**9,756**	**271**	**8,445**	**8,349**	**96**
0—10 ..	434,543	224,594	209,952	740	638	101	433,806	223,955	209,851	4[illegible]9	405	24	55	48	7
10—15 ..	162,443	91,956	70,4[illegible]	2,761	2,618	143	159,682	89,338	70,344	1,322	1,283	39	200	196	4
15—20 ..	121,212	64,391	56,821	3,532	3,394	138	117,680	60,997	56,683	1,227	1,194	33	439	431	8
20 & over ..	688,885	376,883	312,002	24,314	23,521	793	664,571	353,362	311,209	7,049	6,874	175	7,751	7,674	77
Hindu ..	**64,460**	**36,582**	**27,878**	**17,060**	**16,692**	**368**	**47,400**	**19,890**	**27,510**	**5,841**	**5,726**	**115**	**3,378**	**3,349**	**29**
0—10 ..	15,[illegible]53	7,706	7,64[illegible]	398	344	54	14,955	7,362	7,593	238	222	16	23	19	4
10—15 ..	7,442	4,3[illegible]3	3,089	1,663	1,605	58	5,779	2,748	3,031	798	782	16	42	42	..
15—20 ..	5,581	3,445	2,13[illegible]	2,027	1,980	47	3,554	1,465	2,089	644	629	15	85	84	1
20 & over ..	36,084	21,078	15,006	12,972	12,763	209	28,112	8,315	14,797	4,161	4,093	68	3,228	3,204	24
Arya ..	**29**	**21**	**8**	**13**	**12**	**1**	**16**	**9**	**7**	**6**	**6**	..	..	..	..
0—10 ..	11	9	2	5	5	..	6	4	2	5	5	..	..	..	..
10—15 ...	4	3	1	1	1	..	3	2	1	1	1	..	..	..	..
15—20	1	1	..	..	..	..	1	1	..	..	..	..	..	..	..
20 & over ..	13	8	5	7	6	1	6	2	4	..	..	..	..	..	..
Sikh ..	**17,742**	**9,316**	**8,426**	**1,763**	**1,555**	**208**	**15,979**	**7,761**	**8,218**	**299**	**284**	**15**	**12**	**11**	**1**
0—10 ...	6,101	3,142	2,959	53	46	12	6,043	3,09[illegible]	2,947	20	19	1	..	..	..
10—15 ..	1,954	1,086	869	16[illegible]	150	15	1,789	93[illegible]	853	40	39	1	..	..	..
15—20 ..	1,3[illegible]5	550	78[illegible]	13[illegible]	112	18	1,205	438	767	43	39	4	..	..	..
20 & over ..	8,352	4,538	3,814	1,410	1,247	163	6,942	3,291	3,651	196	187	9	12	11	1
Jain ..	**1**	**1**	..	**1**	**1**	..	..	..	..	..	..	..	..	..	..
0—10 ..	..	..	..	..	..	..	..	..	..	..	..	..	..	..	..
10—15 ..	..	..	..	..	..	..	..	..	..	..	..	..	..	..	..
15—20 ..	..	..	..	..	..	..	..	..	..	..	..	..	..	..	..
20 & over ...	1	1	..	1	1	..	..	..	..	..	..	..	..	..	..
Buddhist ..	**2**	**2**	..	**2**	**2**	..	..	..	..	..	..	..	..	..	..
0—10 ..	..	..	..	..	..	..	..	..	..	..	..	..	..	..	..
10—15 ..	..	..	..	..	..	..	..	..	..	..	..	..	..	..	..
15—20 ..	..	..	..	..	..	..	..	..	..	..	..	..	..	..	..
20 & over ..	2	2	..	2	2	..	..	..	..	..	..	..	..	..	..
Zoroastrian ..	**2**	**2**	..	**2**	**2**	..	..	..	..	..	..	..	..	..	..
0—10 ..	..	..	..	..	..	..	..	..	..	..	..	..	..	..	..
10—15 ..	..	..	..	..	..	..	..	..	..	..	..	..	..	..	..
15—20 ..	1	1	..	1	1	..	..	..	..	..	..	..	..	..	..
20 & over ...	1	1	..	1	1	..	..	..	..	..	..	..	..	..	..
Musalman ..	**1,324,403**	**711,664**	**612,739**	**12,228**	**11,765**	**463**	**1,312,175**	**699,899**	**612,276**	**3,879**	**3,738**	**141**	**5,053**	**4,987**	**66**
0—10 ..	413,004	213,697	199,307	264	241	23	412,740	213,456	199,284	165	158	7	31	28	3
10—15 ..	153,022	86,503	66,519	920	860	69	152,093	85,643	66,450	483	461	22	157	153	4
15—20 ..	114,276	60,382	53,894	1,361	1,291	70	112,915	59,091	53,824	540	526	14	354	347	7
20 & over ..	644,101	351,082	293,019	9,674	9,373	301	634,427	341,709	292,718	2,691	2,593	98	4,511	4,459	52
Christian ..	**341**	**179**	**162**	**274**	**141**	**133**	**67**	**38**	**29**	**2**	**2**	..	**2**	**2**	..
0—10 ..	49	26	23	14	3	11	35	23	12	1	1	..	1	1	..
10—15 ..	6	3	3	[illegible]	2	1	3	1	2	..	..	..	1	1	..
15—20 ..	13	10	3	1[illegible]	10	[illegible]	..	..	..	..	..	..	..	..	..
20 & over ...	273	140	133	244	12[illegible]	11[illegible]	29	14	15	1	1	..	..	..	..
Others ..	**106**	**57**	**49**	**4**	**2**	**2**	**102**	**55**	**47**	..	..	..	..	..	..
0—10 ..	28	14	14	1	..	1	27	14	13	..	..	..	..	..	..
10—15 ..	15	8	7	..	..	..	15	8	7	..	..	..	..	..	..
15—20 ..	5	2	3	..	..	..	5	2	3	..	..	..	..	..	..
20 & over ..	58	33	25	3	2	1	55	31	24	..	..	..	..	..	..

VIII.

Religion and Age.

State Census 1921.

incial Tables.

ATE IN.

Arabic. Persons.	Arabic. Males.	Arabic. Females.	Dogri. Persons.	Dogri. Males.	Dogri. Females.	Hindi. Persons.	Hindi. Males.	Hindi. Females.	Bodhi. Persons.	Bodhi. Males.	Bodhi. Females.	Gurmukhi. Persons.	Gurmukhi. Males.	Gurmukhi. Females.	Others. Persons.	Others. Males.	Others. Females.	English. Persons.	English. Males.	English. Females.
17	18	19	20	21	22	23	24	25	26	27	28	29	30	31	32	33	34	35	36	37
PROV	INCE																			
2,300	**2,064**	**236**	**119**	**110**	**9**	**717**	**639**	**78**	**5**	**5**	..	**1,345**	**1,125**	**220**	**1,531**	**1,485**	**46**	**6,858**	**6,639**	**219**
51	38	13	1	1	..	23	9	14	..	..	..	48	30	18	15	9	6	118	90	19
171	129	42	1	1	..	46	24	22	..	..	..	107	90	17	106	95	11	808	800	8
204	161	43	3	3	..	56	47	9	2	2	..	78	53	25	94	92	2	1,429	1,411	18
1,874	1,736	138	114	105	9	592	559	33	3	3	..	1,112	952	160	1,316	1,289	27	4,503	4,329	174
..	..	..	**109**	**101**	**8**	**630**	**560**	**70**	**2**	**2**	..	**115**	**72**	**43**	**1,509**	**1,466**	**43**	**5,476**	**5,416**	**69**
..	..	..	1	1	..	21	7	14	..	..	..	14	6	8	14	9	5	87	80	7
..	..	..	1	1	..	39	18	21	..	..	..	9	5	4	105	94	11	669	663	6
..	..	..	2	2	..	52	43	9	1	1	..	15	5	10	94	92	2	1,134	1,124	10
..	..	..	105	97	8	518	492	26	1	1	..	77	56	21	1,296	1,271	25	3,536	3,549	37
..	..	..	..	..	..	**2**	**1**	**1**	..	..	..	..	..	..	..	..	..	**5**	**5**	..
..	..	..	..	..	..	..	..	..	..	..	..	..	..	..	..	..	..	..	..	..
..	..	..	..	..	..	..	..	..	..	..	..	..	..	..	..	..	..	..	..	..
..	..	..	..	..	..	..	..	..	..	..	..	..	..	..	..	..	..	..	..	..
..	..	..	..	..	..	2	1	1	..	..	..	..	..	..	..	..	..	5	5	..
..	..	..	**6**	**5**	**1**	**80**	**74**	**6**	..	..	..	**1,222**	**1,046**	**176**	**17**	**17**	..	**127**	**118**	**9**
..	..	..	..	..	..	2	2	..	..	..	..	33	23	10	..	..	..	3	2	1
..	..	..	..	..	..	7	6	1	..	..	..	98	85	13	..	..	..	20	20	..
..	..	..	1	1	..	4	4	..	..	..	..	62	48	14	..	..	..	20	20	..
..	..	..	5	4	1	67	62	5	..	..	..	1,029	890	139	17	17	..	84	75	8
..	..	..	..	..	..	..	..	..	..	..	..	..	..	..	..	..	..	**1**	**1**	..
..	..	..	..	..	..	..	..	..	..	..	..	..	..	..	..	..	..	..	..	..
..	..	..	..	..	..	..	..	..	..	..	..	..	..	..	..	..	..	..	..	..
..	..	..	..	..	..	..	..	..	..	..	..	..	..	..	..	..	..	..	..	..
..	..	..	..	..	..	..	..	..	..	..	..	..	..	..	..	..	..	1	1	..
..	..	..	..	..	..	..	..	..	**1**	**1**	..	..	..	..	..	..	..	**1**	**1**	..
..	..	..	..	..	..	..	..	..	..	..	..	..	..	..	..	..	..	..	..	..
..	..	..	..	..	..	..	..	..	..	..	..	..	..	..	..	..	..	..	..	..
..	..	..	..	..	..	..	..	..	..	..	..	..	..	..	..	..	..	..	..	..
..	..	..	..	..	..	..	..	..	1	1	..	..	..	..	..	..	..	1	1	..
..	..	..	..	..	..	..	..	..	..	..	..	..	..	..	..	..	..	**2**	**2**	..
..	..	..	..	..	..	..	..	..	..	..	..	..	..	..	..	..	..	..	..	..
..	..	..	..	..	..	..	..	..	..	..	..	..	..	..	..	..	..	..	..	..
..	..	..	..	..	..	..	..	..	..	..	..	..	..	..	..	..	..	1	1	..
..	..	..	..	..	..	..	..	..	..	..	..	..	..	..	..	..	..	1	1	..
2,300	**2,064**	**236**	**4**	**4**	..	**5**	**4**	**1**	**1**	**1**	..	**8**	**7**	**1**	**4**	**2**	**2**	**974**	**958**	**16**
51	38	13	..	..	..	..	..	..	..	..	..	1	1	..	..	..	..	16	16	..
171	129	42	..	..	..	..	..	..	..	..	..	..	..	..	1	1	..	117	116	1
204	161	43	..	..	..	..	..	..	1	1	..	1	..	1	..	..	..	261	256	5
1,874	1,736	138	4	4	..	5	4	1	..	..	..	6	6	..	3	1	2	580	570	10
..	..	..	..	..	..	..	..	..	..	..	..	..	..	..	..	..	..	**270**	**137**	**133**
..	..	..	..	..	..	..	..	..	..	..	..	..	..	..	..	..	..	12	1	11
..	..	..	..	..	..	..	..	..	..	..	..	..	..	..	..	..	..	2	1	1
..	..	..	..	..	..	..	..	..	..	..	..	..	..	..	..	..	..	13	10	3
..	..	..	..	..	..	..	..	..	..	..	..	..	..	..	..	..	..	243	125	118
..	..	..	..	..	..	..	..	..	**1**	**1**	..	..	..	..	**1**	..	**1**	**2**	**1**	**1**
..	..	..	..	..	..	..	..	..	..	..	..	..	..	..	1	..	1	..	..	..
..	..	..	..	..	..	..	..	..	..	..	..	..	..	..	..	..	..	..	..	..
..	..	..	..	..	..	..	..	..	..	..	..	..	..	..	..	..	..	..	..	..
..	..	..	..	..	..	..	..	..	1	1	..	..	..	..	..	..	..	2	1	1

TABLE

EDUCATION BY

Jammu and Kashmir

Part I—Prov

Age.	POPULATION.									LITER					
	Total.			*Literate.*			*Illiterate.*			*Urdu.*			*Persian.*		
	Persons.	Males.	Females.	Persons.	Males.	Females.	Persons.	Males.	Females	Persons.	Males.	Females.	Persons.	Males.	Females.
1	2	3	4	5	6	7	8	9	10	11	12	13	14	15	16
													(iv) FRONTIER		
All Religions	**212,182**	**107,138**	**105,044**	**3,420**	**3,293**	**127**	**208,762**	**103,845**	**104,917**	**869**	**848**	**21**	**677**	**663**	**14**
0—10 ..	57,385	28,733	28,652	25	20	5	57,360	28,713	28,647	21	18	3	..	..	..
10—15 ..	22,922	11,980	10,942	142	132	10	22,780	11,848	10,932	71	69	2	8	8	..
15—20 ..	19,527	10,689	8,838	285	267	18	19,242	10,422	8,820	126	124	2	33	33	..
20 & over ..	112,348	55,736	56,612	2,968	2,874	94	109,380	52,862	56,518	651	637	14	636	622	14
Hindu ..	**979**	**850**	**129**	**433**	**409**	**24**	**546**	**441**	**105**	**140**	**127**	**13**	**1**	**1**	..
0—10 ..	102	51	51	14	11	3	88	40	48	12	11	1	..	..	..
10—15 ..	20	14	6	14	9	5	6	5	1	8	6	2	..	..	..
15—20 ..	94	82	12	47	45	2	47	37	10	20	18	2	..	..	..
20 & over ..	763	703	60	358	344	14	405	359	46	100	92	8	1	1	..
Arya ..	**42**	**27**	**15**	**22**	**17**	**5**	**20**	**10**	**10**	**9**	**6**	**3**	..	..	..
0—10 ..	18	9	9	3	1	2	15	8	7	3	1	2	..	..	..
10—15 ..	4	4	..	3	3	..	1	1	..	2	2	..	..	..	..
15—20 ..	1	1	..	1	1	..	..	..	..	..	..	..	..	..	..
20 & over ..	19	13	6	15	12	3	4	1	3	4	3	1	..	..	..
Sikh ..	**117**	**76**	**41**	**69**	**52**	**17**	**48**	**24**	**24**	**19**	**17**	**2**	..	..	..
0—10 ..	25	7	18	..	..	..	25	7	18	..	..	..	..	..	..
10—15 ..	15	11	4	8	7	1	7	4	3	6	6	..	..	..	..
15—20 ..	12	6	6	10	4	6	2	2	..	4	4	..	..	..	..
20 & over ..	65	52	13	51	41	10	14	11	3	9	7	2	..	..	..
Buddhist ..	**37,241**	**18,610**	**18,631**	**1,193**	**1,159**	**34**	**36,048**	**17,451**	**18,597**	**14**	**13**	**1**	**5**	**5**	..
0—10 ..	7,231	3,503	3,728	2	2	..	7,229	3,501	3,728	..	..	..	..	..	..
10—15 ..	3,410	1,705	1,705	35	35	..	3,375	1,670	1,705	1	1	..	..	..	..
15—20 ..	3,581	1,965	1,616	54	51	3	3,527	1,914	1,613	3	3	..	..	..	..
20 & over ..	23,019	11,437	11,582	1,102	1,071	31	21,917	10,366	11,551	10	9	1	5	5	..
Musalman ..	**173,718**	**87,529**	**86,189**	**1,658**	**1,626**	**32**	**172,060**	**85,903**	**86,157**	**684**	**682**	**2**	**671**	**657**	**14**
0—10 ..	49,987	25,153	24,834	5	5	..	49,982	25,148	24,834	5	5	..	..	..	..
10—15 ..	19,465	10,243	9,222	78	75	3	19,387	10,168	9,219	53	53	..	8	8	..
15—20 ..	15,834	8,633	7,201	169	164	5	15,665	8,469	7,196	98	98	..	33	33	..
20 & over ..	88,432	43,500	44,932	1,406	1,382	24	87,026	42,118	44,908	528	526	2	630	616	14
Christian ..	**85**	**46**	**39**	**45**	**30**	**15**	**40**	**16**	**24**	**3**	**3**	..	..	..	..
0—10 ..	22	10	12	1	1	..	21	9	12	1	1	..	..	..	..
10—15 ..	8	3	5	4	3	1	4	..	4	1	1	..	..	..	..
15—20 ..	5	2	3	4	2	2	1	..	1	1	1	..	..	..	..
20 & over ..	50	31	19	36	24	12	14	7	7	..	..	..	..	..	..

VIII.

Religion and Age.

State Census 1921.

vincial Tables.

ATE IN.

Arabic.			Dogri.			Hindi.			Bodhi.			Gurmukhi.			Others			English.		
Persons.	Males.	Females.	Persons.	Males.	Females.	Persons.	Males.	Females.	Persons.	Males.	Females.	Persons.	Males.	Females.	Persons.	Males.	Females.	Persons	Males.	Females.
17	18	19	20	21	22	23	24	25	26	27	28	29	30	31	32	33	34	35	36	37
DISTRICTS.																				
145	**130**	**15**	**30**	**30**	..	**35**	**28**	**7**	**1,238**	**1,209**	**29**	**46**	**32**	**14**	**118**	**105**	**13**	**262**	**248**	**14**
..	..	..	..	..	..	1	..	1	2	2	..	..	..	..	..	..	..	1	..	1
3	..	3	1	1	..	3	1	2	32	31	1	2	1	1	..	..	..	22	21	1
16	11	5	..	..	..	1	1	.	52	48	4	5	1	4	12	9	3	40	40	..
126	119	7	29	29	..	30	26	4	1,152	1,128	24	39	30	9	10[illegible]	98	10	199	187	12
..	..	..	**27**	**27**	..	**31**	**26**	**5**	..	..	..	**8**	**5**	**3**	**104**	**104**	..	**122**	**119**	**3**
..	..	..	..	..	..	1	..	1	..	..	..	..	..	..	..	..	..	1	..	1
..	..	..	1	1	..	2	..	2	..	..	..	1	1	..	..	..	..	2	1	1
..	..	..	..	..	..	1	1	..	..	..	..	1	1	..	9	9	..	16	16	..
..	..	..	26	25	..	27	25	2	..	..	..	6	3	3	95	95	..	103	102	1
..	..	..	..	..	..	**2**	**1**	**1**	..	..	..	..	..	..	..	..	..	**11**	**10**	**1**
..	..	..	..	..	..	..	..	..	..	..	..	..	..	..	..	..	..	..	..	..
..	..	..	..	..	..	..	..	..	..	..	..	..	..	..	..	..	..	1	1	..
..	..	..	..	..	..	..	..	..	..	..	..	..	..	..	..	..	..	1	1	..
..	..	..	..	..	..	2	1	1	..	..	..	..	..	..	..	..	..	9	8	1
..	..	..	..	..	..	**2**	**1**	**1**	..	..	..	**37**	**26**	**11**	**3**	..	**3**	**8**	**8**	..
..	..	..	..	..	..	..	..	..	..	..	..	..	..	..	..	..	..	..	..	..
..	..	..	..	..	..	1	1	..	..	..	..	1	..	1	..	..	..	..	..	..
..	..	..	..	..	..	..	..	..	..	..	..	4	..	4	2	..	2	..	..	..
..	..	..	..	..	..	1	..	1	..	..	..	32	26	6	1	..	1	8	8	..
..	..	..	..	..	..	..	..	..	**1,160**	**1,137**	**23**	—	..	..	**10**	..	**10**	**4**	**4**	..
..	..	..	..	..	..	..	..	..	2	2	..	..	..	..	..	..	..	..	..	..
..	..	..	..	..	..	..	..	..	31	31	..	..	..	..	..	..	..	3	3	..
..	..	..	..	..	..	..	..	..	49	47	2	..	..	..	1	..	1	1	1	..
..	..	..	..	..	..	..	..	..	1,078	1,057	21	..	..	..	9	..	9	..	—	..
145	**130**	**15**	**3**	**3**	..	..	..	..	**66**	**65**	**1**	**1**	**1**	..	**1**	**1**	..	**87**	**87**	..
..	..	..	..	..	..	..	..	..	..	..	..	..	..	..	..	..	..	..	..	..
3	..	3	..	..	..	..	..	..	..	..	..	..	..	..	..	..	..	14	14	..
16	11	5	..	..	..	..	..	..	1	1	..	..	..	..	..	..	..	21	21	..
123	119	7	3	3	..	..	..	..	65	64	1	1	1	..	1	1	..	52	52	..
..	..	..	..	..	..	..	..	..	**12**	**7**	**5**	..	..	..	..	..	..	**30**	**20**	**10**
..	..	..	..	..	..	..	..	..	..	..	..	..	..	..	..	..	..	..	..	..
..	..	..	..	..	..	..	..	..	1	..	1	..	..	..	..	..	..	2	2	..
..	..	..	..	..	..	..	..	..	2	..	2	..	..	..	..	..	..	1	1	..
..	..	..	..	..	..	..	..	..	9	7	2	..	..	..	..	..	..	27	17	10

TABLE

EDUCATION BY

Jammu and Kashmir

Part II—Di

Age.	POPULATION. Total. Persons.	Total. Males.	Total. Females.	Literate. Persons.	Literate. Males.	Literate. Females.	Illiterate. Persons.	Illiterate. Males.	Illiterate. Females.	LITER Urdu. Persons.	Urdu. Males.	Urdu. Females.	Persian. Persons.	Persian. Males.	Persian. Females.
1	2	3	4	5	6	7	8	9	10	11	12	13	14	15	16
													(1) JAMMU		
All Religions	**334,834**	**183,681**	**152,153**	**13,834**	**12,667**	**1,167**	**321,000**	**170,014**	**150,986**	**6,913**	**6,670**	**243**	**202**	**196**	**6**
0—10 ..	91,459	46,889	44,570	852	742	110	90,607	46,147	44,460	649	616	33	..	..	..
10—15 ..	38,593	21,773	16,820	1,703	1,500	203	36,880	20,273	16,617	1,186	1,150	36	5	5	..
15—20 ..	27,320	14,586	12,734	2,187	1,967	220	25,133	12,619	12,514	1,232	1,195	37	16	13	3
20 & over ..	177,482	99,433	78,029	9,092	8,458	634	168,370	90,975	70,395	3,846	3,709	137	181	178	3
Hindu ..	**191,782**	**104,553**	**87,229**	**9,813**	**9,083**	**730**	**181,969**	**95,470**	**86,499**	**4,455**	**4,393**	**62**	**162**	**161**	**1**
0—10 ..	49,640	25,488	24,152	546	487	59	49,094	25,001	24,093	402	398	4	..	..	..
10—15 ..	20,824	11,820	9,004	1,182	1,052	130	19,642	10,768	8,874	813	801	12	5	5	..
15—20 ..	15,661	8,330	7,331	1,545	1,409	136	14,116	6,921	7,195	831	855	6	12	12	..
20 & over ..	105,657	58,915	46,742	6,540	6,135	405	99,117	52,780	46,337	2,379	2,339	40	145	144	1
Arya ..	**5,595**	**3,242**	**2,353**	**346**	**257**	**89**	**5,249**	**2,985**	**2,264**	**69**	**56**	**13**	..	..	..
0—10 ..	1,655	936	719	23	12	11	1,632	924	708	10	10	..	..	..	..
10—15 ..	668	391	277	38	21	17	630	370	260	11	6	5	..	..	..
15—20 ..	465	273	192	64	49	15	401	224	177	8	8	..	..	..	..
20 & over ..	2,807	1,642	1,165	221	175	46	2,586	1,467	1,119	40	32	8	..	..	..
Brahmo ..	**15**	**7**	**8**	**6**	**3**	**3**	**9**	**4**	**5**	**1**	**1**	..	..	..	..
0—10 ..	4	3	1	1	..	1	3	3	..	..	..	..	..	..	..
10—15 ..	2	..	2	..	..	..	2	..	2	..	..	..	..	..	..
15—20 ..	..	..	..	..	..	..	..	..	..	..	..	..	..	..	..
20 & over ..	9	4	5	5	3	2	4	1	3	1	1	..	..	..	..
Sikh ..	**4,932**	**2,651**	**2,281**	**431**	**347**	**84**	**4,501**	**2,304**	**2,197**	**114**	**104**	**10**	..	..	..
0—10 ..	1,474	751	723	18	18	..	1,456	733	723	8	8	..	..	..	..
10—15 ..	652	322	290	51	32	19	601	330	271	22	20	2	..	..	..
15—20 ..	397	219	178	53	39	14	344	180	164	16	15	1	..	..	..
20 & over ..	2,409	1,319	1,090	309	258	51	2,100	1,061	1,039	68	61	7	..	..	..
Jain ..	**521**	**290**	**231**	**180**	**157**	**23**	**341**	**133**	**208**	**27**	**25**	**2**	..	..	..
0—10 ..	140	61	79	3	2	1	137	59	78	1	1	..	..	..	..
10—15 ..	70	42	28	22	16	6	48	26	22	10	9	1	..	..	..
15—20 ..	38	24	14	25	17	8	13	7	6	5	4	1	..	..	..
20 & over ..	273	163	110	130	122	8	143	41	102	11	11	..	..	..	..
Buddhist ..	**4**	**4**	..	**3**	**3**	..	**1**	**1**	..	..	..	..	..	..	..
0—10 ..	..	..	..	..	..	..	..	..	..	..	..	..	..	..	..
10—15 ..	..	..	..	..	..	..	..	..	..	..	..	..	..	..	..
15—20 ..	..	..	..	..	..	..	..	..	..	..	..	..	..	..	..
20 & over ..	4	4	..	3	3	..	1	1	..	..	..	..	..	..	..
Zoroastrian ..	**5**	**3**	**2**	**5**	**3**	**2**	..	..	..	..	..	..	..	..	..
0—10 ..	..	..	..	..	..	..	..	..	..	..	..	..	..	..	..
10—15 ..	..	..	..	..	..	..	..	..	..	..	..	..	..	..	..
15—20 ..	1	..	1	1	..	1	..	..	..	..	..	..	..	..	..
20 & over ..	4	3	1	4	3	1	..	..	..	..	..	..	..	..	..
Musalman ...	**130,721**	**71,242**	**59,479**	**2,995**	**2,781**	**214**	**127,726**	**68,461**	**59,265**	**2,225**	**2,078**	**147**	**40**	**35**	**5**
0—10 ..	38,176	19,437	18,719	235	208	27	37,941	19,249	18,692	216	192	24	..	..	..
10—15 ..	16,227	9,082	7,145	398	371	27	15,829	8,711	7,118	324	309	15	..	..	..
15—20 ..	10,038	5,674	4,964	488	448	40	10,150	5,226	4,924	338	312	26	4	1	3
20 & over ...	65,680	37,029	28,651	1,874	1,754	120	63,806	35,275	28,531	1,347	1,265	82	36	34	2
Christian ..	**1,040**	**573**	**467**	**55**	**33**	**22**	**985**	**540**	**445**	**22**	**13**	**9**	..	..	..
0—10 ..	280	134	146	26	15	11	254	119	135	12	7	5	..	..	..
10—15 ..	120	60	60	12	8	4	108	52	56	6	5	1	..	..	..
15—20 ..	103	55	48	11	5	6	92	50	42	4	1	3	..	..	..
20 & over ..	537	324	213	6	5	1	531	319	212	..	..	..	..	..	..
Others ..	**219**	**116**	**103**	..	..	..	**219**	**116**	**103**	..	..	..	..	..	..
0—10 ..	90	59	31	..	..	..	90	59	31	..	..	..	..	..	..
10—15 ..	30	16	14	..	..	..	30	16	14	..	..	..	..	..	..
15—20 ..	17	11	6	..	..	..	17	11	6	..	..	..	..	..	..
20 & over ..	82	30	52	..	..	..	82	30	52	..	..	..	..	..	..

VIII. | VIII Education.

RELIGION AND AGE.

State Census 1921.

trict Tables.

ATE IN.

Arabic.			Dogri.			Hindi.			Bodhi.			Gurmukhi.			Others.			English.		
Persons.	Males.	Females.	Persons.	Males.	Females.	Persons.	Males.	Females.	Persons.	Males.	Females.	Persons.	Males.	Females.	Persons.	Males.	Females.	Persons.	Males.	Females.
17	18	19	20	21	22	23	24	25	26	27	28	29	30	31	32	33	34	35	36	37
DISTRICT.																				
265	**217**	**48**	**1,186**	**1,158**	**28**	**2,511**	**1,895**	**616**	..	..	..	**489**	**339**	**150**	**30**	**28**	**2**	**2,238**	**2,164**	**74**
13	10	3	16	14	2	110	60	50	..	..	..	21	7	14	1	..	1	42	35	7
29	18	11	22	20	2	198	84	114	..	..	..	37	7	30	..	..	..	226	216	10
26	19	7	57	56	1	269	138	131	..	..	..	44	21	23	..	..	..	543	525	18
197	170	27	1,091	1,068	23	1,934	1,613	321	..	..	..	387	304	83	29	28	1	1,427	1,388	39
..	..	..	**1,159**	**1,132**	**27**	**2,140**	**1,659**	**481**	..	..	..	**364**	**243**	**121**	**21**	**20**	**1**	**1,512**	**1,475**	**37**
..	..	..	15	14	1	91	53	38	..	..	..	14	3	11	1	..	1	23	19	4
..	..	..	21	19	2	157	71	86	..	..	..	27	2	25	..	..	..	159	154	5
..	..	..	57	56	1	222	120	102	..	..	..	36	15	21	..	..	..	357	351	6
..	..	..	1,066	1,043	23	1,670	1,415	255	..	..	..	287	223	64	20	20	..	973	951	22
..	..	..	**2**	**2**	..	**71**	**11**	**60**	..	..	..	**21**	**14**	**7**	..	..	..	**183**	**174**	**9**
..	..	..	..	..	..	11	1	10	..	..	..	1	..	1	..	..	..	1	1	..
..	..	..	..	..	..	12	1	11	..	..	..	1	1	..	..	..	..	14	13	1
..	..	..	..	..	..	13	1	12	..	..	..	1	..	1	..	..	..	42	40	2
..	..	..	2	2	..	35	8	27	..	..	..	18	13	5	..	..	..	126	120	6
..	..	..	..	..	..	**3**	..	**3**	..	..	..	..	..	..	..	..	..	**2**	**2**	..
..	..	..	..	..	..	1	..	1	..	..	..	..	..	..	..	..	..	..	..	..
..	..	..	..	..	..	..	..	..	..	..	..	..	..	..	..	..	..	..	..	..
..	..	..	..	..	..	..	..	..	..	..	..	..	..	..	..	..	..	..	..	..
..	..	..	..	..	..	2	..	2	..	..	..	..	..	..	..	..	..	2	2	..
..	..	..	**5**	**5**	..	**144**	**91**	**53**	..	..	..	**99**	**81**	**18**	..	..	..	**69**	**66**	**3**
..	..	..	..	..	..	5	5	..	..	..	..	4	4	..	..	..	..	1	1	..
..	..	..	..	..	..	19	5	14	..	..	..	7	4	3	..	..	..	3	3	..
..	..	..	..	..	..	17	6	11	..	..	..	6	5	1	..	..	..	14	13	1
..	..	..	5	5	..	103	75	28	..	..	..	82	68	14	..	..	..	51	49	2
..	..	..	..	..	..	**126**	**108**	**18**	..	..	..	**2**	..	**2**	..	..	..	**25**	**24**	**1**
..	..	..	..	..	..	2	1	1	..	..	..	..	..	..	..	..	..	..	..	..
..	..	..	..	..	..	9	6	3	..	..	..	2	..	2	..	..	..	1	1	..
..	..	..	..	..	..	16	10	6	..	..	..	..	..	..	..	..	..	4	3	1
..	..	..	..	..	..	99	91	8	..	..	..	..	..	..	..	..	..	20	20	..
..	..	..	..	..	..	..	..	..	..	..	..	..	..	..	3	3	..	..	..	—
..	..	..	..	..	..	..	..	..	..	..	..	..	..	..	..	..	..	..	..	..
..	..	..	..	..	..	..	..	..	..	..	..	..	..	..	..	..	..	..	..	..
..	..	..	..	..	..	..	..	..	..	..	..	..	..	..	..	..	..	..	..	..
..	..	..	..	..	..	..	..	..	..	..	..	..	..	..	3	3	..	..	..	..
..	..	..	..	..	..	..	..	..	..	..	..	..	..	..	..	..	..	**5**	**3**	**2**
..	..	..	..	..	..	..	..	..	..	..	..	..	..	..	..	..	..	..	..	..
..	..	..	..	..	..	..	..	..	..	..	..	..	..	..	..	..	..	..	..	..
..	..	..	..	..	..	..	..	..	..	..	..	..	..	..	..	..	..	1	..	1
..	..	..	..	..	..	..	..	..	..	..	..	..	..	..	..	..	..	4	3	1
265	**217**	**48**	**19**	**19**	..	**27**	**26**	**1**	..	..	..	**1**	**1**	..	**6**	**5**	**1**	**412**	**400**	**12**
13	10	3	..	..	..	..	..	..	..	..	..	..	..	..	..	..	..	6	6	—
29	18	11	1	1	..	1	1	..	..	..	..	..	..	..	..	..	..	43	42	1
26	19	7	..	..	..	1	1	..	..	..	..	1	1	..	..	..	..	118	114	4
197	170	27	18	18	..	25	24	1	..	..	..	..	..	..	6	5	1	245	238	7
..	..	..	**1**	..	**1**	..	..	..	..	..	..	**2**	..	**2**	..	..	..	**30**	**20**	**10**
..	..	..	1	..	1	..	..	..	..	..	..	2	..	2	..	..	..	11	8	3
..	..	..	..	..	..	..	..	..	..	..	..	..	..	..	..	..	..	6	3	3
..	..	..	..	..	..	..	..	..	..	..	..	..	..	..	..	..	..	7	4	3
..	..	..	..	..	..	..	..	..	..	..	..	..	..	..	..	..	..	6	5	1
..	..	..	..	..	..	..	..	..	..	..	..	..	..	..	..	..	..	..	..	..
..	..	..	..	..	..	..	..	..	..	..	..	..	..	..	..	..	..	..	..	..
..	..	..	..	..	..	..	..	..	..	..	..	..	..	..	..	..	..	..	..	..
..	..	..	..	..	..	..	..	..	..	..	..	..	..	..	..	..	..	..	..	..
..	..	..	..	..	..	..	..	..	..	..	..	..	..	..	..	..	..	..	..	..

VIII
Education.

TABLE

Education by

Jammu and Ka·hmir

Part II—Dis

Age.	Population.												Liter		
	Total.			Literate.			Illiterate.			Urdu.			Persian.		
	Persons.	Males.	Females.	Persons.	Males.	Females.	Persons.	Males.	Females.	Persons.	Males.	Females.	Persons.	Males.	Females.
1	2	3	4	5	6	7	8	9	10	11	12	13	14	15	16
													(2.	KAT	HUA
All Religions	**154,209**	**82,467**	**71,742**	**4,447**	**4,351**	**96**	**149,762**	**78,116**	**71,646**	**1,284**	**1,240**	**44**	**11**	**7**	**4**
0—10 ..	41,729	21,198	20,531	34	22	12	41,695	21,176	20,519	22	16	6	2	..	2
10—15 ..	17,171	9,783	7,388	292	274	18	16,879	9,509	7,370	191	183	8	1	..	1
15—20 ..	13,540	7,079	6,461	443	439	4	13,097	6,640	6,457	233	230	3	1	1	..
20 & over ..	81,769	44,407	37,362	3,678	3,616	62	78,091	40,791	37,300	838	811	27	7	6	1
Hindu ..	**109,572**	**57,696**	**51,876**	**3,905**	**3,854**	**51**	**105,687**	**53,842**	**51,825**	**942**	**927**	**15**	**6**	**6**	..
0—10 ..	28,146	14,043	14,103	14	13	1	28,132	14,030	14,102	8	8	..	..	..	..
10—15 ..	11,694	6,630	5,064	225	218	7	11,469	6,412	5,057	146	146	..	..	..	..
15—20 ..	9,558	4,848	4,740	382	380	2	9,206	4,468	4,738	190	189	1	1	1	..
20 & over ..	60,144	32,175	27,969	3,284	3,243	41	56,860	28,932	27,928	598	584	14	5	5	..
Arya ..	**7,930**	**4,444**	**3,486**	**83**	**79**	**4**	**7,847**	**4,365**	**3,432**	**31**	**31**	..	..	..	..
0—10 ..	2,422	1,285	1,137	4	2	2	2,418	1,283	1,135	2	2	..	..	..	..
10—15 ..	1,057	610	447	8	8	..	1,049	602	447	3	3	..	..	..	..
15—20 ..	603	365	238	4	4	..	599	361	238	2	2	..	..	..	..
20 & over ..	3,848	2,184	1,664	67	65	2	3,781	2,119	1,662	24	24	..	..	..	..
Sikh ..	**257**	**148**	**109**	**46**	**45**	**1**	**211**	**103**	**108**	**23**	**23**	..	..	..	..
0—10 ..	71	38	33	2	2	..	69	36	33	2	2	..	..	..	..
10—15 ..	27	16	11	6	6	..	21	10	11	4	4	..	..	..	..
15—20 ..	26	16	10	6	6	..	20	10	10	3	3	..	..	..	..
20 & over ..	133	78	55	32	31	1	101	47	54	14	14	..	..	..	..
Jain ...	**1**	**1**	—	**1**	**1**	..	..	..	..	**1**	**1**	..	..	..	..
0—10 ..	..	—	—	..	..	..	..	..	..	..	..	..	..	..	..
10—15 ..	..	..	..	..	..	..	..	..	..	..	..	..	..	..	..
15—20 ..	..	—	..	..	..	..	..	..	..	..	..	..	..	..	..
20 & over ..	1	1	..	1	1	..	..	..	..	1	1	..	..	..	..
Musalman ...	**36,303**	**20,099**	**16,204**	**407**	**367**	**40**	**35,896**	**19,732**	**16,164**	**282**	**253**	**29**	**5**	**1**	**4**
0—10 ..	11,051	5,817	5,234	14	5	9	11,037	5,812	5,225	10	4	6	2	..	2
10—15 ..	4,376	2,516	1,860	53	42	11	4,323	2,474	1,849	38	30	8	1	..	1
15—20 ..	3,309	1,843	1,466	50	48	2	3,259	1,795	1,464	37	35	2	..	..	..
20 & over ..	17,567	9,923	7,644	290	272	18	17,277	9,651	7,626	197	184	13	2	1	1
Christian ...	**146**	**79**	**67**	**5**	**5**	..	**141**	**74**	**67**	**5**	**5**	..	..	..	..
0—10 ..	39	15	24	..	..	..	39	15	24	..	..	..	..	..	..
10—15 ..	17	11	6	..	..	..	17	11	6	..	..	..	..	..	..
15—20 ..	14	7	7	1	1	..	13	6	7	1	1	..	..	..	..
20 & over ..	76	46	30	4	4	..	72	42	30	4	4	..	..	..	..
												(3)	UDH	AM P	UR
All Religions	**218,261**	**115,135**	**103,126**	**4,317**	**4,173**	**144**	**213,944**	**110,962**	**102,982**	**1,165**	**1,141**	**24**	**105**	**97**	**8**
0—10 ..	58,884	29,872	29,012	46	39	7	58,838	29,833	29,005	31	30	1	..	..	..
10—15 ..	22,654	12,285	10,369	321	300	21	22,333	11,985	10,348	170	167	3	8	6	2
15—20 ..	18,519	9,441	9,078	310	294	16	18,209	9,147	9,062	170	167	3	4	3	1
20 & over ..	118,204	63,537	54,667	3,640	3,540	100	114,564	59,997	54,567	794	777	17	93	88	5
Hindu ..	**132,214**	**68,935**	**63,279**	**3,658**	**3,550**	**108**	**128,556**	**65,385**	**63,171**	**812**	**796**	**16**	**13**	**13**	—
0—10 ..	32,738	16,265	16,473	29	24	5	32,709	16,241	16,468	17	16	1	..	..	..
10—15 ..	12,848	6,971	5,877	257	242	15	12,591	6,729	5,862	124	122	2	1	1	..
15—20 ..	10,980	5,470	5,510	251	238	13	10,729	5,232	5,497	122	121	1	2	2	..
20 & over ..	75,648	40,229	35,419	3,121	3,046	75	72,527	37,183	35,344	549	537	12	10	10	..
Arya ..	**21**	**10**	**11**	**10**	**5**	**5**	**11**	**5**	**6**	**2**	**2**	..	..	..	—
0—10 ..	7	3	4	1	—	1	6	3	3	..	..	..	..	..	..
10—15 ..	3	1	2	1	..	1	2	1	1	..	..	..	..	..	..
15—20 ..	1	1	—	..	..	..	1	1	..	..	..	..	..	..	..
20 & over ..	10	5	5	8	5	3	2	..	2	2	2	..	..	..	..
Sikh ..	**332**	**175**	**157**	**48**	**39**	**9**	**284**	**136**	**148**	**17**	**17**	..	..	..	..
0—10 ..	84	38	46	2	1	1	82	37	45	1	1	..	—	..	..
10—15 ..	36	20	16	5	3	2	31	17	14	2	2	..	..	..	..
15—20 ..	27	12	15	4	4	..	23	8	15	2	2	..	..	..	..
20 & over ..	185	105	80	37	31	6	148	74	74	12	12	..	..	..	..

VIII.

RELIGION AND AGE.

State Census 1921.

ict Tables.

VIII
Education.

ATE IN.

Arabic.			*Dogri*			*Hindi.*			*Bodhi.*			*Gurmukhi.*			*Others.*			*English.*		
Persons.	Males.	Females.	Persons.	Males.	Females.	Persons.	Males.	Females.	Persons.	Males.	Females.	Persons.	Males.	Females.	Persons.	Males.	Females.	Persons.	Males.	Females.
17	18	10	20	21	22	23	24	25	26	27	28	29	30	31	32	33	34	35	36	37
DIST	RICT.																			
63	**56**	**7**	**1,467**	**1,465**	**2**	**1,378**	**1,344**	**34**	**1**	**1**	..	**66**	**63**	**3**	**5**	**5**	..	**172**	**170**	**2**
1	..	1	3	3	..	6	3	3	..	..	..	..	..	..	..	..	..	..	..	..
11	9	2	22	22	..	46	40	6	..	..	..	..	..	..	..	..	..	21	20	1
4	4	..	118	118	..	43	42	1	..	..	..	2	2	..	2	2	..	40	40	..
47	43	4	1,324	1,322	2	1,283	1,259	24	1	1	..	64	61	3	3	3	..	111	110	1
..	..	..	**1,436**	**1,434**	**2**	**1,358**	**1,329**	**29**	..	..	..	**45**	**42**	**3**	**4**	**4**	..	**114**	**112**	**2**
..	..	..	3	3	..	3	2	1	..	..	..	..	..	..	..	..	..	..	..	..
..	..	..	22	22	..	46	40	6	..	..	..	..	..	..	..	..	..	11	10	1
..	..	..	117	117	..	42	41	1	..	..	..	1	1	..	2	2	..	29	29	..
..	..	..	1,294	1,292	2	1,267	1,246	21	..	..	..	44	41	3	2	2	..	74	73	1
..	..	..	**18**	**18**	..	**12**	**8**	**4**	**1**	**1**	..	**6**	**6**	..	**1**	**1**	..	**14**	**14**	..
..	..	..	..	..	..	2	..	2	..	..	..	..	..	..	..	..	..	..	..	..
..	..	..	..	..	..	..	..	..	..	..	..	..	..	..	..	..	..	5	5	..
..	..	..	..	..	..	1	1	..	..	..	..	..	..	..	..	..	..	1	1	..
..	..	..	18	18	..	9	7	2	1	1	..	6	6	..	1	1	..	8	8	..
..	..	..	..	..	..	**1**	..	**1**	..	..	..	**11**	**11**	..	..	..	..	**11**	**11**	..
..	..	..	..	..	..	..	..	..	..	..	..	..	..	..	..	..	..	..	..	..
..	..	..	..	..	..	..	..	..	..	..	..	..	..	..	..	..	..	2	2	..
..	..	..	..	..	..	..	..	..	..	..	..	1	1	..	..	..	..	2	2	..
..	..	..	..	..	..	1	..	1	..	..	..	10	10	..	..	..	..	7	7	..
..	..	..	..	..	..	..	..	..	..	..	..	..	..	..	..	..	..	..	..	..
..	..	..	..	..	..	..	..	..	..	..	..	..	..	..	..	..	..	..	..	..
..	..	..	..	..	..	..	..	..	..	..	..	..	..	..	..	..	..	..	..	..
..	..	..	..	..	..	..	..	..	..	..	..	..	..	..	..	..	..	..	..	..
..	..	..	..	..	..	..	..	..	..	..	..	..	..	..	..	..	..	..	..	..
63	**56**	**7**	**13**	**13**	..	**7**	**7**	..	..	..	..	**4**	**4**	..	..	..	..	**33**	**33**	..
1	..	1	..	..	..	1	1	..	..	..	..	..	..	..	..	..	..	..	..	..
11	9	2	..	..	..	..	..	..	..	..	..	..	..	..	..	..	..	3	3	..
4	4	..	1	1	..	..	..	..	..	..	..	..	..	..	..	..	..	8	8	..
47	43	4	12	12	..	6	6	..	..	..	..	4	4	..	..	..	..	22	22	..
..	..	..	..	..	..	..	..	..	..	..	..	..	..	..	..	..	..	..	..	..
..	..	..	..	..	..	..	..	..	..	..	..	..	..	..	..	..	..	..	..	..
..	..	..	..	..	..	..	..	..	..	..	..	..	..	..	..	..	..	..	..	..
..	..	..	..	..	..	..	..	..	..	..	..	..	..	..	..	..	..	..	..	..
..	..	..	..	..	..	..	..	..	..	..	..	..	..	..	..	..	..	..	..	..
DIST	RICT																			
83	**82**	**1**	**1,841**	**1,814**	**27**	**800**	**733**	**67**	**4**	**4**	..	**39**	**26**	**13**	..	..	..	**280**	**276**	**4**
1	1	..	3	2	1	9	5	4	..	..	..	1	..	1	..	..	..	1	1	..
5	5	..	81	80	1	46	32	14	..	..	..	1	..	1	..	..	..	10	10	..
..	..	..	52	51	1	52	42	10	..	..	..	4	3	1	..	..	..	28	28	..
77	76	1	1,705	1,681	24	693	654	39	4	4	..	33	23	10	..	..	..	241	237	4
..	..	..	**1,788**	**1,764**	**24**	**791**	**729**	**62**	..	..	..	**23**	**19**	**4**	..	..	..	**231**	**229**	**2**
..	..	..	3	2	1	8	5	3	..	..	..	..	..	..	..	..	..	1	1	..
..	..	..	80	79	1	43	31	12	..	..	..	..	..	..	..	..	..	9	9	..
..	..	..	51	50	1	51	41	10	..	..	..	3	2	1	..	..	..	22	22	..
..	..	..	1,654	1,633	21	689	652	37	..	..	..	20	17	3	..	..	..	199	197	2
..	..	..	**1**	**1**	..	**3**	..	**3**	..	..	..	**2**	..	**2**	..	..	..	**2**	**2**	..
..	..	..	..	..	..	1	..	1	..	..	..	..	..	..	..	..	..	..	..	..
..	..	..	..	..	..	1	..	1	..	..	..	..	..	..	..	..	..	..	..	..
..	..	..	..	..	..	..	..	..	..	..	..	..	..	..	..	..	..	..	..	..
..	..	..	1	1	..	1	..	1	..	..	..	2	..	2	..	..	..	2	2	..
..	..	..	**1**	**1**	..	**5**	**3**	**2**	..	..	..	**14**	**7**	**7**	..	..	..	**11**	**11**	..
..	..	..	..	..	..	..	..	..	..	..	..	1	..	1	..	..	..	..	..	..
..	..	..	..	..	..	2	1	1	..	..	..	1	..	1	..	..	..	..	..	..
..	..	..	..	..	..	1	1	..	..	..	..	1	1	..	..	..	..	..	..	..
..	..	..	1	1	..	2	1	1	..	..	..	11	6	5	..	..	..	11	11	..

VIII
Education.

TABLE

EDUCATION BY

Jammu and Kashmir

Part II—Sh

Age.	POPULATION. Total. Persons.	Total. Males.	Total. Females.	Literate. Persons.	Literate. Males	Literate. Females.	Illiterate. Persons.	Illiterate. Males.	Illiterate. Females.	LITER Urdu. Persons.	Urdu. Males.	Urdu. Females	Persian. Persons.	Persian. Males.	Persian. Females.
1	2	3	4	5	6	7	8	9	10	11	12	13	14	15	16
Buddhist ..	**438**	**222**	**216**	**5**	**5**	..	**433**	**217**	**216**	..	..	..	..	..	..
0—10 ..	82	43	39	..	..	..	82	43	39	..	..	..	..	..	..
10—15 ..	34	18	16	..	..	..	34	18	16	..	..	..	..	..	..
15—20 ..	52	26	26	..	..	..	52	26	26	..	..	..	..	..	..
20 & over ..	270	135	135	5	5	..	265	130	135	..	..	..	..	..	..
Musalman ...	**85,254**	**45,792**	**39,462**	**594**	**573**	**21**	**84,660**	**45,219**	**39,441**	**333**	**325**	**8**	**92**	**84**	**8**
0—10	25,973	13,523	12,450	14	14	..	25,959	13,509	12,450	13	13	..	..	..	..
10—15	9,733	5,275	4,458	58	55	3	9,675	5,220	4,455	44	43	1	7	5	2
15—20	7,459	3,932	3,527	55	52	3	7,404	3,880	3,524	46	44	2	2	1	1
20 & over ..	42,089	23,062	19,027	467	452	15	41,622	22,610	19,012	230	225	5	83	78	5
Christian ..	**2**	**1**	**1**	**2**	**1**	**1**	..	..	..	**1**	**1**	..	..	..	..
0—10 ..	..	..	..	..	..	..	..	..	..	..	..	..	..	..	..
10—15 ..	..	..	..	..	..	..	..	..	..	..	..	..	..	..	..
15—20 ..	..	..	..	..	..	..	..	..	..	..	..	..	..	..	..
20 & over ..	2	1	1	2	1	1	..	..	..	1	1	..	..	..	..
														(4) RIASI	
All religions	**224,589**	**118,575**	**106,014**	**3,282**	**2,644**	**638**	**221,307**	**115,931**	**105,376**	**1,068**	**1,033**	**35**	**52**	**52**	..
0—10 ..	65,287	33,444	31,843	43	32	11	65,244	33,412	31,832	25	24	1	..	..	..
10—15 ..	25,861	14,224	11,637	160	131	29	25,701	14,093	11,608	107	101	6	1	1	..
15—20 ..	18,516	9,370	9,146	232	183	49	18,284	9,187	9,097	105	97	8	1	1	..
20 & over ..	114,925	61,537	53,388	2,847	2,298	549	112,078	59,239	52,839	831	811	20	50	50	..
Hindu ..	**74,065**	**39,122**	**34,943**	**1,803**	**1,721**	**82**	**72,262**	**37,401**	**34,861**	**566**	**541**	**25**	**6**	**6**	..
0—10 ..	17,112	8,555	8,557	26	15	11	17,086	8,540	8,546	12	11	1	..	..	..
10—15 ..	7,285	4,029	3,256	84	67	17	7,201	3,962	3,239	53	49	4	..	..	..
15—20 ..	5,747	2,914	2,833	121	104	17	5,626	2,810	2,816	62	55	7	..	..	..
20 & over	43,921	23,624	20,297	1,572	1,535	37	42,349	22,089	20,260	439	426	13	6	6	..
Arya ..	**5,515**	**2,672**	**2,843**	**65**	**56**	**9**	**5,450**	**2,616**	**2,834**	**35**	**29**	**6**	..	..	..
0—10 ..	1,288	613	675	2	2	..	1,286	611	675	2	2	..	..	..	..
10—15 ..	526	250	276	7	6	1	519	244	275	6	5	1	..	..	..
15—20 ..	447	183	264	5	4	1	442	179	263	5	4	1	..	..	..
20 & over ..	3,254	1,626	1,628	51	44	7	3,203	1,582	1,621	22	18	4	..	..	..
Sikh ..	**814**	**401**	**413**	**100**	**99**	**1**	**714**	**302**	**412**	**29**	**29**	..	..	..	..
0—10 ..	223	105	118	1	1	..	222	104	118	..	..	..	..	..	..
10—15 ..	76	34	42	6	6	..	70	28	42	4	4	..	..	..	..
15—20 ..	77	30	47	11	11	..	66	19	47	5	5	..	..	..	..
20 & over ..	438	232	206	82	81	1	356	151	205	20	20	..	..	..	..
Musalman ..	**144,195**	**76,380**	**67,815**	**1,314**	**768**	**546**	**142,881**	**75,612**	**67,269**	**438**	**434**	**4**	**46**	**46**	..
0—10 ..	46,664	24,171	22,493	14	14	..	46,650	24,157	22,493	11	11	..	..	..	..
10—15 ..	17,974	9,911	8,063	63	52	11	17,911	9,859	8,052	44	43	1	1	1	..
15—20 ..	12,245	6,243	6,002	95	64	31	12,150	6,179	5,971	33	33	..	1	1	..
20 & over ..	67,312	36,055	31,257	1,142	638	504	66,170	35,417	30,753	350	347	3	44	44	..
														MIRPUR	
All Religions ..	**318,971**	**160,186**	**158,785**	**6,155**	**5,761**	**394**	**312,816**	**154,425**	**158,391**	**3,744**	**3,708**	**36**	**45**	**45**	..
0—10 ..	97,539	50,648	46,921	105	65	40	97,464	50,583	46,881	52	49	3	1	1	..
10—15 ..	37,274	20,449	16,825	549	490	59	33,725	19,959	16,766	417	416	1	..	...	..
15—20 ...	23,768	11,251	12,517	603	535	68	23,165	10,716	12,449	377	370	7	2	2	..
20 & over ..	160,360	77,838	82,522	4,898	4,671	227	155,462	73,167	82,295	2,898	2,873	25	42	42	..
Hindu ..	**52,591**	**27,319**	**23,272**	**2,625**	**2,495**	**130**	**49,966**	**24,824**	**25,142**	**1,187**	**1,180**	**7**	**10**	**10**	..
0—10 ..	15,232	7,929	7,303	37	27	10	15,195	7,902	7,293	21	20	1	..	..	..
10—15 ..	5,932	3,301	2,631	230	211	19	5,702	3,090	2,612	174	174	..	..	..	..
15—20 ..	4,234	2,234	2,000	238	207	31	3,996	2,027	1,969	115	113	2	..	..	..
20 & over ..	27,193	13,855	13,338	2,120	2,050	70	25,073	11,805	13,268	877	873	4	10	10	..
Arya ..	**3,930**	**2,159**	**1,771**	**343**	**290**	**58**	**3,582**	**1,889**	**1,713**	**160**	**157**	**3**	..	..	..
0—10 ..	930	465	465	12	4	8	918	461	457	3	3	..	..	..	..
0—15 ...	341	195	143	42	27	15	299	168	131	20	20	..	..	..	..
5—20 ..	321	146	175	39	32	7	282	114	168	24	23	1	..	..	..
20 & over ..	2,338	1,353	985	25[illegible]	227	28	2,0[illegible]3	1,126	957	113	111	2	..	..	..

VIII.

VIII
Education.

Religion and Age.

State Census 1921.

trict Tables.

ATE IN.

Arabic.			Dogri.			Hindi.			Bodhi			Gurmukhi.			Others.			English.		
Persons.	Males.	Females.	Persons.	Males.	Females.	Persons.	Males.	Females.	Persons.	Males.	Females.	Persons.	Males.	Females.	Persons.	Males.	Females.	Persons.	Males.	Females.
17	18	19	20	21	22	23	24	25	26	27	28	29	30	31	32	33	34	35	36	37
..	..	..	**1**	**1**	..	..	..	..	**4**	**4**	..	..	..	..	..	..	..	..	..	..
..	..	..	..	..	..	..	..	..	..	..	..	..	..	..	..	..	..	..	..	..
..	..	..	..	..	..	..	..	..	..	..	..	..	..	..	..	..	..	..	..	..
..	..	..	..	..	..	..	..	..	..	..	..	..	..	..	..	..	..	..	..	..
..	..	..	1	1	..	..	..	..	4	4	..	..	..	..	..	..	..	..	..	..
83	**82**	**1**	**50**	**47**	**3**	**1**	**1**	..	..	..	..	..	..	..	..	..	..	**35**	**34**	**1**
1	1	..	..	..	..	..	..	..	..	..	..	..	..	..	..	..	..	..	..	..
5	5	..	1	1	..	..	..	..	..	..	..	..	..	..	..	..	..	1	1	..
..	..	..	1	1	..	..	..	..	..	..	..	..	..	..	..	..	..	6	6	..
77	76	1	48	45	3	1	1	..	..	..	..	..	..	..	..	..	..	28	27	1
..	..	..	..	..	..	..	..	..	..	..	..	..	..	..	..	..	..	**1**	..	**1**
..	..	..	..	..	..	..	..	..		..	..	..	..	..	..	..	..	..	..	..
..	..	..	..	..	..	..	..	..		..	..	..	..	..	..	..	..	..	..	..
..	..	..	..	..	..	..	..	..		..	..	..	..	..	..	..	..	..	..	..
..	..	..	..	..	..	..	..	..		..	..	..	..	..	..	..	..	1	..	1
DIST	RICT.																			
287	**249**	**38**	**665**	**512**	**153**	**1,071**	**687**	**384**	..	..	..	**41**	**25**	**16**	**17**	**8**	**9**	**81**	**78**	**3**
2	2	..	6	4	2	9	1	8	..	..	..	..	..	..	..	..	..	1	1	..
11	8	3	10	6	4	22	8	14	..	..	..	2	..	2	1	1	..	8	6	..
35	30	5	32	22	10	48	25	23	..	..	..	2	1	1	2	..	2	7	7	..
239	209	30	617	480	137	992	653	339	..	..	..	37	24	13	14	7	7	67	64	3
..	..	..	**494**	**487**	**7**	**644**	**603**	**41**	..	..	..	**19**	**14**	**5**	**9**	**7**	**2**	**65**	**63**	**2**
..	..	..	4	2	2	9	1	8	..	..	..	..	..	..	..	..	..	1	1	..
..	..	..	7	6	1	17	7	10	..	..	..	2	..	2	..	..	..	5	5	..
..	..	..	23	22	1	27	21	6	..	..	..	1	..	1	2	..	2	6	6	..
..	..	..	460	457	3	591	574	17	..	..	..	16	14	2	7	7	..	53	51	2
..	..	..	**7**	**7**	..	**19**	**18**	**1**	..	..	..	**1**	..	**1**	..	..	..	**3**	**2**	**1**
..	..	..	..	..	..	..	..	..	..	..	..	..	..	..	..	..	..	..	..	..
..	..	..	..	..	..	1	1	..	..	..	..	..	..	..	..	..	..	..	..	..
..	..	..	..	..	..	..	..	..	..	..	..	..	..	..	..	..	..	..	..	..
..	..	..	7	7	..	18	17	1	..	..	..	1	..	1	..	..	..	3	2	1
..	..	..	**3**	**3**	..	**50**	**49**	**1**	..	..	..	**10**	**10**	..	**1**	**1**	..	**7**	**7**	..
..	..	..	1	1	..	..	..	..	..	..	..	..	..	..	..	..	..	..	..	..
..	..	..	..	..	..	..	..	..	..	..	..	..	..	..	1	1	..	1	1	..
..	..	..	..	..	..	4	4	..	..	..	..	1	1	..	..	..	..	1	1	..
..	..	..	2	2	..	46	45	1	..	..	..	9	9	..	..	..	..	5	5	..
287	**249**	**38**	**161**	**15**	**146**	**358**	**17**	**341**	..	..	..	**11**	**1**	**10**	**7**	..	**7**	**6**	**6**	..
2	2	..	1	1	..	..	..	..	..	..	..	..	..	..	..	..	..	..	..	..
11	8	3	3	..	3	4	..	4	..	..	..	..	..	..	..	..	..	..	..	..
35	30	5	9	..	9	17	..	17	..	..	..	..	..	..	..	..	..	..	..	..
239	209	30	148	14	134	337	17	320	..	..	..	11	1	10	7	..	7	6	6	..
DIST	RICT.																			
100	**88**	**12**	**92**	**91**	**1**	**1,297**	**1,143**	**154**	..	..	..	**510**	**325**	**185**	**21**	**21**	..	**346**	**340**	**6**
1	1	..	..	..	..	25	8	17	..	..		25	6	19	..	..	..	1	..	1
3	3	..	1	1	..	56	23	33	..	..		34	9	25	3	3	..	35	35	..
9	8	1	20	20	..	68	38	30	..	..		50	20	30	2	2	..	75	75	..
87	76	11	71	70	1	1,148	1,074	74	..	..		401	290	111	16	16	..	235	230	5
..	..	..	**62**	**61**	**1**	**1,026**	**930**	**96**	..	..	..	**134**	**110**	**24**	**11**	**11**	..	**195**	**193**	**2**
..	..	..	..	..	..	15	6	9	..	..	..	1	1	..	..	..	..	..	..	..
..	..	..	1	1	..	31	13	18	..	..	..	1	..	1	2	2	..	21	21	..
..	..	..	20	20	..	51	27	24	..	..	..	5	..	5	2	2	..	45	45	..
..	..	..	41	40	1	929	884	45	...	..	..	127	109	18	7	7	..	129	127	2
..	..	..	**23**	**23**	..	**118**	**66**	**52**	..	..	..	**4**	**1**	**3**	..	..	..	**43**	**43**	
..	..	..	..	..	..	9	1	8	..	..	..	..	..	..	..	..	..	..	..	..
..	..	..	..	..	..	20	5	15	..	..	..	..	..	..	..	..	..	2	2	..
..	..	..	..	..	..	8	3	5	..	..	..	2	1	1	..	..	..	5	5	..
..	..	..	23	23	..	81	57	24	..	..	..	2	..	2	..	..	..	26	36	..

VIII
Education.

TABLE

EDUCATION BY

Jammu and Kashmir

Part II—Dis

Age.	POPULATION. Total. Persons.	Males.	Females.	Literate. Persons.	Males.	Females.	Illiterate. Persons.	Males.	Females.	LITER... Urdu. Persons.	Males.	Females.	Persian. Persons.	Males.	Females.
1	2	3	4	5	6	7	8	9	10	11	12	13	14	15	16
													(5)	MIR	PUR
Sikh ..	**4,698**	**2,481**	**2,217**	**845**	**676**	**169**	**3,853**	**1,805**	**2,048**	**285**	**280**	**5**	..	..	..
9—10 ...	1,366	756	610	32	12	20	1,334	744	590	8	7	1	..	..	..
10—15 ...	467	313	254	108	84	24	459	229	230	68	68	..	..	..	..
15—20 ...	374	169	205	95	70	25	279	99	180	38	38	..	..	..	..
20 & over ...	2,391	1,243	1,148	610	510	100	1,781	733	1,048	138	167	4	..	..	..
Jain ...	**5**	**2**	**3**	**2**	**1**	**1**	**3**	**1**	**2**	..	..	..	..	..	..
0—10 ..	2	1	1	..	..	..	2	1	1	..	..	..	..	..	..
10—15 ..	..	..	..	..	..	..	..	..	..	..	..	..	..	..	..
15—20 ..	1	..	1	..	..	..	1	..	1	..	..	..	..	..	..
20 & over ..	2	1	1	2	1	1	..	..	..	..	..	..	..	..	..
Musalman ..	**257,741**	**128,222**	**129,519**	**2,330**	**2,297**	**33**	**255,411**	**125,925**	**129,486**	**2,112**	**2,091**	**21**	**35**	**35**	..
0—10 ..	80,037	41,496	38,541	23	22	1	80,014	41,474	38,540	20	19	1	1	1	..
10—15 ..	30,434	16,640	13,794	169	168	1	30,265	16,472	13,793	155	154	1	..	..	..
15—20 ..	18,838	8,702	10,136	231	226	5	18,607	8,476	10,131	200	196	4	2	2	..
20 & over ..	128,432	61,384	67,048	1,907	1,881	26	126,525	59,503	67,022	1,737	1,722	15	32	32	..
Christian ..	**6**	**3**	**3**	**5**	**2**	**3**	**1**	**1**	..	..	...	..	..	..	..
0—10 ..	2	1	1	1	..	1	1	1	..	..	..	..	..	..	..
10—15 ..	..	..	..	..	..	..	..	..	..	..	..	..	..	..	..
15—20 ..	..	..	..	..	..	..	..	..	..	..	..	..	..	..	..
20 & over ..	4	2	2	4	2	2	..	..	..	..	..	..	..	..	..
													(6) BH	ADAR	WAH
All Religions	**37,614**	**19,227**	**18,387**	**1,184**	**1,176**	**8**	**36,430**	**18,051**	**18,379**	**508**	**505**	**3**	**6**	**6**	..
0—10 ..	10,100	5,118	4,982	71	70	1	10,029	5,048	4,981	69	68	1	..	..	..
10—15 ..	4,282	2,393	1,889	133	133	..	4,149	2,260	1,889	114	114	..	..	..	..
15—20 ..	3,457	1,511	1,946	117	117	..	3,340	1,394	1,946	78	78	..	..	..	..
20 & over ..	19,775	10,205	9,570	863	856	7	18,912	9,349	9,563	247	245	2	6	6	..
Hindu ..	**22,561**	**11,384**	**11,177**	**863**	**859**	**4**	**21,698**	**10,525**	**11,173**	**315**	**313**	**2**	..	..	..
0—10 ..	5,528	2,806	2,722	35	34	1	5,493	2,772	2,721	33	32	1	..	..	..
10—15 ..	2,459	1,385	1,074	92	92	..	2,367	1,293	1,074	75	75	..	..	..	..
15—20 ..	2,035	810	1,225	85	85	..	1,950	725	1,225	51	51	..	..	..	..
20 & over ..	12,539	6,383	6,156	651	648	3	11,888	5,735	6,153	156	155	1	..	..	..
Arya ..	**3**	**1**	**2**	..	..	..	**3**	**1**	**2**	..	..	..	..	..	..
0—10 ..	..	..	..	..	..	..	..	..	..	..	..	..	..	..	..
10—15 ..	1	..	1	..	..	..	1	..	1	..	..	..	..	..	..
15—20 ..	..	..	..	..	..	..	..	..	..	..	..	..	..	..	..
20 & over ..	2	1	1	..	..	..	2	1	1	..	..	..	..	..	..
Sikh ..	**9**	**5**	**4**	**5**	**4**	**1**	**4**	**1**	**3**	**2**	**2**	..	..	..	..
0—10 ..	3	1	2	1	1	..	2	..	2	1	1	..	..	..	..
10—15 ..	1	1	..	1	1	..	..	..	..	1	1	..	..	..	..
15—20 ..	..	..	..	..	..	..	..	..	..	..	..	..	..	..	..
20 & over ..	5	3	2	3	2	1	2	1	1	..	..	..	..	..	..
Musalman ..	**150,040**	**7,836**	**7,204**	**315**	**312**	**3**	**14,725**	**7,524**	**7,201**	**191**	**190**	**1**	**6**	**6**	..
0—10 ..	4,569	2,311	2,258	35	35	..	4,534	2,276	2,258	35	35	..	..	..	..
10—15 ..	1,821	1,007	814	40	40	..	1,781	967	814	38	38	..	..	..	..
15—20 ..	1,422	701	721	32	32	..	1,390	669	721	27	27	..	..	..	..
20 & over ..	7,228	3,817	3,411	208	205	3	7,020	3,612	3,408	91	90	1	6	6	..
Christian ..	**1**	**1**	..	**1**	**1**	..	..	..	..	..	..	..	..	..	..
0—10 ..	..	..	..	..	..	..	..	..	..	..	..	..	..	..	..
10—15 ..	..	..	..	..	..	..	..	..	..	..	..	..	..	..	..
15—20 ..	..	..	..	..	..	..	..	..	..	..	..	..	..	..	..
20 & over ..	1	1	..	1	1	..	..	..	..	..	..	..	..	..	..
														P	UNCH
All Religions	**351,781**	**181,348**	**170,433**	**4,242**	**3,984**	**258**	**347,539**	**177,364**	**170,175**	**2,624**	**2,563**	**61**	**73**	**73**	..
0—10 ..	112,326	57,822	54,504	159	134	25	112,167	57,688	54,479	108	99	9	5	5	..
10—15 ..	42,686	23,722	18,964	374	340	34	42,312	23,382	18,930	278	273	5	2	2	..
15—20 ..	30,131	15,335	14,796	512	464	48	29,619	14,871	14,748	354	344	10	19	19	..
20 & over ..	166,638	84,469	82,169	3,197	3,046	151	163,441	81,423	82,018	1,884	1,847	37	47	47	..

VIII. VIII Education.

RELIGION AND AGE.

States Census 1921.

trict Tables.

ATE IN

Arabic.			Dogri.			Hindi.			Bodhi.			Gurmukhi.			Others.			English.		
Persons.	Males.	Females.	Persons.	Males.	Females.	Persons.	Males.	Females.	Persons.	Males.	Females.	Persons.	Males.	Females.	Persons.	Males.	Females.	Persons.	Males.	Females.
17	18	19	20	21	22	23	24	25	26	27	28	29	30	31	32	33	34	35	36	37
DIST	RICT.																			
..	..	..	**2**	**2**	..	**142**	**137**	**5**	..	..	..	**370**	**212**	**158**	**9**	**9**	..	**37**	**36**	**1**
...	..	..	..	...	..	..	..	..	..	..	..	24	5	19	..	..	..	..	..	..
..	...	...	..	..	..	3	3	..	..	..	..	33	9	24	1	1	..	3	3	..
..	...	...	..	...	..	7	6	1	..	..	..	43	19	24	..	..	..	7	7	..
..	..	..	2	2	..	132	128	4	..	..	..	270	179	91	8	8	..	27	26	1
...	..	...	..	..	..	**1**	...	**1**	..	...	..	..	...	..	..	...	..	**1**	**1**	..
..	..	..	..	..	..	..	..	..	..	..	..	..	..	..	..	..	..	..	..	..
..	..	..	..	..	..	..	..	..	..	..	..	..	..	..	..	..	..	..	..	..
..	..	..	..	..	..	..	..	..	..	..	..	..	..	..	..	..	..	..	..	..
..	..	..	..	..	..	1	..	1	..	..	..	..	..	..	..	..	..	1	1	1
100	**88**	**12**	**5**	**5**	..	**10**	**10**	...	...	..	...	**2**	**2**	..	**1**	**1**	...	**65**	**65**	..
1	1	..	..	..	..	1	1	..	..	..	..	..	..	..	..	..	..	..	..	..
3	3	..	..	..	..	2	2	..	..	..	..	..	..	..	..	..	..	9	9	..
9	8	1	..	..	..	2	2	..	..	..	..	..	..	..	..	..	..	18	18	..
87	76	11	5	5	..	5	5	..	..	..	..	2	2	..	1	1	..	38	38	..
..	..	...	..	...	..	..	..	..	..	..	..	..	..	..	...	..	..	**5**	**2**	**3**
..	..	..	..	..	..	..	..	..	..	..	..	..	..	..	..	..	..	1	..	1
..	..	..	..	..	..	..	..	..	..	..	..	..	..	..	..	..	..	..	..	..
..	..	..	..	..	..	..	..	..	..	..	..	..	..	..	..	..	..	..	..	..
..	..	..	..	..	..	..	..	..	..	..	..	..	..	..	..	..	..	4	2	2
JAGI	R.																			
38	**37**	**1**	**388**	**388**	..	**141**	**139**	**2**	..	..	..	**8**	**6**	**2**	**27**	**27**	..	**68**	**68**	..
..	..	..	..	..	..	2	2	..	..	..	..	..	..	..	..	..	..	..	..	..
1	1	..	3	3	..	8	8	..	..	..	..	..	..	..	..	..	..	7	7	..
4	4	..	10	10	..	9	9	..	..	..	..	..	..	..	..	..	..	16	16	..
33	32	1	375	375	..	122	120	2	..	..	..	8	6	2	27	27	..	45	45	..
..	..	..	**319**	**319**	..	**139**	**137**	**2**	..	..	..	**5**	**5**	..	**27**	**27**	..	**58**	**58**	..
..	..	..	..	..	..	2	2	..	..	..	..	..	..	..	..	..	..	..	..	..
..	..	..	2	2	..	8	8	..	..	..	..	..	..	..	..	..	..	7	7	..
..	..	..	10	10	..	9	9	..	..	..	..	..	..	..	..	..	..	15	15	..
..	..	..	307	307	..	120	118	2	..	..	..	5	5	..	27	27	..	36	36	..
..	..	..	..	..	..	..	..	..	..	..	..	..	..	..	..	..	..	..	..	..
..	..	..	..	..	..	..	..	..	..	..	..	..	..	..	..	..	..	..	..	..
..	..	..	..	..	..	..	..	..	..	..	..	..	..	..	..	..	..	..	..	..
..	..	..	..	..	..	..	..	..	..	..	..	..	..	..	..	..	..	..	..	..
..	..	..	..	..	..	..	..	..	..	..	..	..	..	..	..	..	..	..	..	..
..	..	..	..	..	..	..	..	..	..	..	..	**2**	**1**	**1**	..	..	..	**1**	**1**	..
..	..	..	..	..	..	..	..	..	..	..	..	..	..	..	..	..	..	..	..	..
..	..	..	..	..	..	..	..	..	..	..	..	..	..	..	..	..	..	..	..	..
..	..	..	..	..	..	..	..	..	..	..	..	..	..	..	..	..	..	..	..	..
..	..	..	..	..	..	..	..	..	..	..	..	2	1	1	..	..	..	1	1	..
38	**37**	**1**	**69**	**69**	..	**2**	**2**	..	..	..	..	**1**	..	**1**	..	..	..	**8**	**8**	..
..	..	..	..	..	..	..	..	..	..	..	..	..	..	..	..	..	..	..	..	..
1	1	..	1	1	..	..	..	..	..	..	..	..	..	..	..	..	..	..	..	..
4	4	..	..	..	..	..	..	..	..	..	..	..	..	..	..	..	..	1	1	..
33	32	1	68	68	..	2	2	..	..	..	..	1	..	1	..	..	..	7	7	..
..	..	..	..	..	..	..	..	..	..	..	..	..	..	..	..	..	..	**1**	**1**	..
...	..	..	..	..	..	..	..	..	..	..	..	..	..	..	..	..	..	..	..	..
..	..	..	..	..	..	..	..	..	..	..	..	..	..	..	..	..	..	..	..	..
..	..	..	..	..	..	..	..	..	..	..	..	..	..	..	..	..	..	..	..	..
..	..	..	..	..	..	..	..	..	..	..	..	..	..	..	..	..	..	1	1	..
ILAQ	A.																			
515	**448**	**67**	**33**	**32**	**1**	**366**	**296**	**70**	..	..	..	**439**	**390**	**49**	..	..	..	**192**	**182**	**10**
13	6	7	..	..	..	15	9	6	..	..	..	13	10	3	..	..	..	5	5	..
51	36	15	..	..	..	15	5	10	..	..	..	15	13	2	..	..	..	13	11	2
42	31	11	..	..	..	31	16	15	..	..	..	39	29	10	..	..	..	27	25	2
409	375	34	33	32	1	305	266	39	..	..	..	372	338	34	..	..	..	147	114	6

VIII
Education.

TABLE

EDUCATION BY

Jammu and Kashmir

Part II.—Di

Age.	Population.									Liter					
	Total.			*Literate.*			*Illiterate.*			*Urdu.*			*Persian.*		
	Persons.	Males.	Females.	Persons.	Males.	Females.	Persons.	Males.	Females.	Persons.	Males.	Females.	Persons.	Males.	Females.
1	2	3	4	5	6	7	8	9	10	11	12	13	14	15	16
Hindu ..	**20,764**	**10,919**	**9,845**	**1,164**	**1,074**	**90**	**19,600**	**9,845**	**9,755**	**612**	**598**	**14**	**4**	**4**	..
0—10 ..	6,266	3,273	2,993	58	53	5	6.208	3,220	2,988	42	41	1	1	1	..
10—15 ..	2,484	1,411	1,073	72	62	10	2,412	1,349	1,063	55	53	2	..	..	..
15—20 ..	1,662	840	822	156	138	18	1,506	702	804	108	105	3	..	..	..
20 & over ..	10,352	5,395	4,957	878	821	57	9,474	4,574	4,900	407	399	8	3	3	..
Arya ..	**51**	**32**	**19**	**17**	**14**	**3**	**34**	**18**	**16**	**6**	**6**	..	..	..	..
0—10 ..	11	7	4	..	..	..	11	7	4	..	..	..	..	..	..
10—15 ..	5	5	—	3	3	..	2	2	..	2	2	..	..	..	..
15—20 ..	7	2	5	2	1	1	5	1	4	..	..	..	..	..	..
20 & over ..	28	18	10	12	10	2	16	8	8	4	4	..	..	..	..
Sikh ..	**10,585**	**5,520**	**5,065**	**561**	**516**	**45**	**10,024**	**5,004**	**5,020**	**183**	**180**	**3**	..	..	..
0—10 ..	3,409	1,718	1,691	17	11	6	3,392	1,707	1,685	9	8	1	..	..	..
10—15 ..	1,293	736	557	51	47	4	1,242	689	553	31	31	..	..	..	..
15—20 ..	970	485	485	66	57	9	904	428	476	31	31	..	..	..	..
20 & over ..	4,913	2,581	2,332	427	401	26	4,486	2,180	2,306	112	110	2	..	..	..
Jain ..	**1**	**1**	..	**1**	**1**	..	—	..	..	..	..	..	..	..	..
0—10 ..	..	..	..	..	..	..	..	..	..	..	..	..	..	..	..
10—15 ..	..	..	..	..	..	..	..	..	..	..	..	..	..	..	..
15—20 ..	..	..	..	..	..	..	..	..	..	..	..	..	..	..	..
20 & over ..	1	1	..	1	1	..	..	..	..	..	..	..	..	..	..
Musalman ..	**320,368**	**164,871**	**155,497**	**2,487**	**2,374**	**113**	**317,881**	**162,497**	**155,384**	**1,820**	**1,778**	**42**	**69**	**69**	..
0—10 ..	102,637	52,823	49,814	81	69	12	102 556	52,754	49,802	54	49	5	4	4	..
10—15 ..	38,903	21,570	17,333	247	228	19	38,656	21,342	17,314	190	187	3	2	2	..
15—20 ..	27,490	14,008	13,482	286	268	18	27,204	13,740	13,464	215	208	7	19	19	..
20 & over ..	151,338	76,470	74,868	1,873	1,809	64	149,465	74,661	74,804	1,361	1 334	27	44	44	..
Christian ..	**12**	**5**	**7**	**12**	**5**	**7**	..	..	..	**3**	**1**	**2**	..	..	..
0—10 ..	3	1	2	3	1	2	..	..	..	3	1	2	..	..	..
10—15 ..	1	..	1	1	..	1	..	..	..	..	..	..	..	..	..
15—20 ..	2	..	2	2	..	2	..	..	..	..	..	..	..	..	..
20 & over ..	6	4	2	6	4	2	..	..	..	..	..	..	..	..	..
													(8)	KAS	HMIR
All Religions	**502,490**	**269,685**	**232,805**	**6,463**	**6,246**	**217**	**496,027**	**263,439**	**232,588**	**2,088**	**2,040**	**48**	**2,397**	**2,375**	**22**
0—10 ..	158,636	82,086	76,550	102	77	25	158,534	82,009	76,525	41	38	3	18	17	1
10—15 ..	57,732	32,212	25,520	397	376	21	57,335	31,836	25,499	204	202	2	73	70	3
15—20 ..	43,290	23,100	20,190	633	604	29	42,657	22,496	20,161	296	291	5	141	139	2
20 & over ..	242,832	132,287	110,545	5,331	5,189	142	237,501	127,098	110,403	1,547	1,509	38	2,165	2,149	16
Hindu ..	**10,371**	**6,242**	**4,129**	**2,549**	**2,485**	**64**	**7,822**	**3,757**	**4,065**	**1,174**	**1,152**	**22**	**636**	**631**	**5**
0—10 ..	2,471	1,272	1,199	34	25	9	2,437	1,247	1,190	21	18	3	4	4	..
10—15 ..	1,112	637	475	171	167	4	941	470	471	119	119	..	11	11	..
15—20 ..	807	486	321	236	228	8	571	258	313	134	131	3	25	24	1
20 & over ..	5,981	3,847	2,134	2,108	2,065	43	3,873	1,782	2,091	900	884	16	596	592	4
Sikh ..	**5,332**	**2,779**	**2,553**	**556**	**513**	**43**	**4,776**	**2,266**	**2,510**	**130**	**128**	**2**	**4**	**4**	..
0—10 ..	1,778	940	838	23	15	8	1,755	925	830	7	7	..	..	..	..
10—15 ..	546	283	263	55	46	9	491	237	254	12	12	..	..	..	..
15—20 ..	441	212	229	54	48	6	387	164	223	21	20	1	..	..	..
20 & over ..	2,567	1,344	1,223	424	404	20	2,143	940	1,203	90	89	1	4	4	..
Jain ..	**1**	**1**	..	**1**	**1**	..	..	..	..	..	..	..	..	..	..
0—10 ..	..	..	..	..	..	..	..	..	..	..	..	..	..	..	..
10—15 ..	..	..	..	..	..	..	..	..	..	..	..	..	..	..	..
15—20 ..	..	..	..	..	..	..	..	..	..	..	..	..	..	..	..
20 & over ..	1	1	..	1	1	..	..	..	..	..	..	..	..	..	..
Musalman ..	**486,680**	**260,608**	**226,072**	**3,334**	**3,233**	**101**	**483,346**	**257,375**	**225,971**	**784**	**760**	**24**	**1,757**	**1,740**	**17**
0—10 ..	154,366	79,867	74,499	44	37	7	154,322	79,830	74,492	13	13	..	14	13	1
10—15 ..	56,059	31,285	24,774	171	163	8	55,888	31,122	24,766	73	71	2	62	59	3
15—20 ..	42,038	22,400	19,638	343	328	15	41,695	22,072	19,623	141	140	1	116	115	1
20 & over ..	234,217	127,056	107,161	2,776	2,705	71	231,441	124,351	107,090	557	536	21	1,565	1,553	12

VIII.

Religion and Age.

State Census 1921.

rict Tables.

ate in

Arabic.			Dogri.			Hindi.			Bodhi.			Gurmukhi.			Others.			English.		
Persons.	Males.	Females.	Persons.	Males.	Females.	Persons.	Males.	Females.	Persons.	Males.	Females.	Persons.	Males.	Females.	Persons.	Males.	Females.	Persons.	Males.	Females.
17	18	19	20	21	22	23	24	25	26	27	28	29	30	31	32	33	34	35	36	37
..	..	..	**29**	**28**	**1**	**299**	**242**	**57**	..	..	..	**109**	**93**	**16**	..	..	..	**111**	**109**	**2**
..	..	..	..	..	..	10	6	4	..	..	..	2	2	..	..	..	..	3	3	..
..	..	..	..	..	..	12	5	7	..	..	..	2	1	1	..	..	..	3	3	..
..	..	..	..	..	..	24	11	13	..	..	..	10	8	2	..	..	..	14	14	..
..	..	..	29	28	1	253	220	33	..	..	..	95	82	13	..	..	..	91	89	2
..	..	..	..	..	..	**7**	**4**	**3**	..	..	..	..	..	..	..	..	..	**4**	**4**	..
..	..	..	..	..	..	..	..	..	..	..	..	..	..	..	..	..	..	..	..	..
..	..	..	..	..	..	..	..	..	..	..	..	..	..	..	..	..	..	1	1	..
..	..	..	..	..	..	2	1	1	..	..	..	..	..	..	..	..	..	..	..	..
..	..	..	..	..	..	5	3	2	..	..	..	..	..	..	..	..	..	3	3	..
..	..	..	**4**	**4**	..	**37**	**28**	**9**	..	..	..	**323**	**290**	**33**	..	..	..	**14**	**14**	..
..	..	..	..	..	..	2	..	2	..	..	..	6	3	3	..	..	..	..	..	..
..	..	..	..	..	..	3	..	3	..	..	..	13	12	1	..	..	..	4	4	..
..	..	..	..	..	..	4	3	1	..	..	..	28	20	8	..	..	..	3	3	..
..	..	..	4	4	..	28	25	3	..	..	..	276	255	21	..	..	..	7	7	..
..	..	..	..	..	..	..	..	..	..	..	..	..	..	..	..	..	..	**1**	**1**	..
..	..	..	..	..	..	..	..	..	..	..	..	..	..	..	..	..	..	..	..	..
..	..	..	..	..	..	..	..	..	..	..	..	..	..	..	..	..	..	..	..	..
..	..	..	..	..	..	..	..	..	..	..	..	..	..	..	..	..	..	..	..	..
..	..	..	..	..	..	..	..	..	..	..	..	..	..	..	..	..	..	1	1	..
515	**448**	**67**	..	..	..	**23**	**22**	**1**	..	..	..	**7**	**7**	..	..	..	..	**53**	**50**	**3**
13	6	7	..	..	..	3	3	..	..	..	..	5	5	..	..	..	..	2	2	..
51	36	15	..	..	..	..	..	..	..	..	..	..	..	..	..	..	..	4	3	1
42	31	11	..	..	..	1	1	..	..	..	..	1	1	..	..	..	..	8	8	..
409	375	34	..	..	..	19	18	1	..	..	..	1	1	..	..	..	..	39	37	2
..	..	..	..	..	..	..	..	..	..	..	..	..	..	..	..	..	..	**9**	**4**	**5**
..	..	..	..	..	..	..	..	..	..	..	..	..	..	..	..	..	..	..	..	..
..	..	..	..	..	..	..	..	..	..	..	..	..	..	..	..	..	..	1	..	1
..	..	..	..	..	..	..	..	..	..	..	..	..	..	..	..	..	..	2	..	2
..	..	..	..	..	..	..	..	..	..	..	..	..	..	..	..	..	..	6	4	2
NORTH.																				
679	**622**	**57**	**14**	**12**	**2**	**61**	**48**	**13**	..	..	..	**377**	**328**	**49**	**98**	**91**	**7**	**749**	**730**	**19**
16	10	6	..	..	..	2	..	2	...	..	..	16	7	9	3	1	2	6	4	2
31	28	3	..	..	..	4	2	2	...	..	..	38	29	9	2	..	2	45	45	..
62	49	13	1	1	..	7	5	2	...	..	..	22	15	7	1	1	..	103	103	..
570	535	35	13	11	2	48	41	7	...	..	..	301	277	24	92	89	3	595	578	17
..	..	..	**9**	**8**	**1**	**47**	**34**	**13**	..	..	..	**21**	**12**	**9**	**94**	**89**	**5**	**568**	**559**	**9**
..	..	..	..	..	..	2	..	2	..	..	..	1	..	1	2	1	1	4	2	2
..	..	..	..	..	..	2	..	2	..	..	..	..	..	..	2	..	2	37	37	..
..	..	..	..	..	..	6	4	2	..	..	..	2	..	2	1	1	..	68	68	..
..	..	..	9	8	1	37	30	7	..	..	..	18	12	6	89	87	2	59	452	7
..	..	..	**5**	**4**	**1**	**13**	**13**	..	..	..	..	**355**	**315**	**40**	**1**	**1**	..	**48**	**48**	..
..	..	..	..	..	..	..	..	..	..	..	..	15	7	8	..	..	..	1	1	..
..	..	..	..	..	..	2	2	..	..	..	..	38	29	9	..	..	..	3	3	..
..	..	..	1	1	..	1	1	..	..	..	..	20	15	5	..	..	..	11	11	..
..	..	..	4	3	1	10	10	..	..	..	..	282	264	18	1	1	..	33	33	..
..	..	..	..	..	..	..	..	..	..	..	..	..	..	..	..	..	..	**1**	**1**	..
..	..	..	..	..	..	..	..	..	..	..	..	..	..	..	..	..	..	..	..	..
..	..	..	..	..	..	..	..	..	..	..	..	..	..	..	..	..	..	..	..	..
..	..	..	..	..	..	..	..	..	..	..	..	..	..	..	..	..	..	..	..	..
..	..	..	..	..	..	..	..	..	..	..	..	..	..	..	..	..	..	1	1	..
679	**622**	**57**	..	..	..	**1**	**1**	..	..	..	..	**1**	**1**	..	**2**	**1**	**1**	**110**	**108**	**2**
16	10	6	..	..	..	..	..	..	..	..	..	..	..	..	..	..	..	1	1	..
31	28	3	..	..	..	..	..	..	..	..	..	..	..	..	..	..	..	5	5	..
62	49	13	..	..	..	..	..	..	..	..	..	..	..	..	..	..	..	24	24	..
570	535	35	..	..	..	1	1	..	..	..	..	1	1	..	2	1	1	80	78	2

TABLE

EDUCATION BY

Jammu and Kashmir

Part II.—Dis

Age.	POPULATION.									LITER					
	Total.			*Literate.*			*Illiterate.*			*Urdu.*			*Persian.*		
	Persons.	Males.	Females.	Persons.	Males.	Females.	Persons.	Males.	Females.	Persons.	Males.	Females.	Persons.	Males.	Females.
1	2	3	4	5	6	7	8	9	10	11	12	13	14	15	16
Christian ..	**33**	**19**	**14**	**21**	**13**	**8**	**12**	**6**	**6**	..	..	..	..	..	..
0—10 ..	5	3	2	..	..	..	5	3	2	..	..	..	..	..	..
10—15 ..	2	1	1	..	..	..	2	1	1	..	..	..	..	..	..
15—20 ..	..	..	..	..	..	..	..	..	..	..	..	..	..	..	..
20 and over..	26	15	11	21	13	8	5	2	3	..	..	..	..	..	..
Others ..	**73**	**36**	**37**	**2**	**1**	**1**	**71**	**35**	**36**	..	..	..	..	..	..
0—10 ..	16	4	12	1	..	1	15	4	11	..	..	..	..	..	..
10—15 ..	13	6	7	..	..	..	13	6	7	..	..	..	..	..	..
15—20 ..	4	2	2	..	..	..	4	2	2	..	..	..	..	..	..
20 and over..	40	24	16	1	1	..	39	23	16	..	..	..	..	..	..
													(9)	KAS	HMIR
All Religions	**688,487**	**372,459**	**316,028**	**21,040**	**20,354**	**686**	**667,447**	**352,105**	**315,342**	**6,205**	**6,020**	**185**	**5,842**	**5,777**	**65**
0—10 ..	207,193	106,822	100,311	562	488	63	206,631	106,383	100,248	351	334	17	34	28	6
10—15 ..	40,459	45,499	34,960	2,087	1,986	101	78,372	43,513	34,859	957	924	33	120	119	1
15—20 ..	58,483	31,558	26,925	2,565	2,477	88	55,918	29,081	26,837	738	713	25	286	280	6
20 and over ..	342,352	188,520	153,832	15,826	15,392	434	326,526	173,128	153,398	4,159	4,049	110	5,402	5,350	52
Hindu ..	**49,692**	**27,638**	**22,054**	**13,472**	**13,217**	**255**	**36,220**	**14,421**	**21,799**	**4,292**	**4,206**	**86**	**2,722**	**2,701**	**21**
0—10 ..	11,892	5,959	5,933	342	307	35	11,550	5,652	5,898	210	199	11	19	15	4
10—15 ..	5,893	3,472	2,421	1,417	1,372	45	4,476	2,100	2,376	629	616	13	30	30	..
15—20 ..	4,335	2,669	1,666	1,692	1,664	28	2,643	1,005	1,638	479	467	12	60	60	
20 and over ..	27,572	15,538	12,034	10,021	9,874	147	17,551	5,664	11,887	2,974	2,924	50	2,613	2,596	17
Arya ..	**29**	**21**	**8**	**13**	**13**	**1**	**16**	**9**	**7**	**6**	**6**	..	..	..	..
0—10 ..	11	9	2	5	5	..	6	4	2	5	5	..	..	..	..
10—15 ..	4	3	1	1	1	..	3	2	1	1	1	..	..	..	..
15—20 ..	1	1	..	..	..	..	1	1	..	..	..	..	..	..	..
20 and over ..	13	8	5	7	6	1	6	2	4	..	..	..	..	..	..
Sikh ..	**3,202**	**1,778**	**1,424**	**377**	**353**	**24**	**2,825**	**1,425**	**1,400**	**80**	**75**	**5**	**5**	**5**	..
0—10 ..	1,093	553	540	9	5	4	1,184	548	536	4	3	1	..	..	..
10—15 ..	356	210	146	31	27	4	325	183	142	8	8	..	..	..	..
15—20 ..	273	140	133	41	34	7	232	106	126	16	14	2	..	..	..
20 and over ..	1,480	875	605	296	287	9	1,184	588	596	52	50	2	5	5	..
Budh ..	**2**	**2**	..	**2**	**2**	..	..	..	..	..	..	..	..	..	..
0—10 ..	..	..	..	..	..	..	..	..	..	..	..	..	..	..	..
10—15 ..	..	..	..	..	..	..	..	..	..	..	..	..	..	..	..
15—20 ..	..	..	..	..	..	..	..	..	..	..	..	..	..	..	..
20 and over ..	2	2	..	2	2	..	..	..	..	..	..	..	..	..	..
Zoroastrian ..	**2**	**2**	..	**2**	**2**	..	..	..	..	..	..	..	..	—	—
0—10 ..	..	..	..	..	..	..	..	..	..	..	..	..	—	..	—
10—15 ..	..	..	..	..	..	..	..	..	..	..	..	..	..	..	—
15—20 ..	1	1	..	1	1	..	..	..	..	..	..	..	..	..	—
20 and over ..	1	1	..	1	1	..	..	..	..	..	..	..	..	..	—
Musalman ..	**635,225**	**342,841**	**292,384**	**6,925**	**6,643**	**282**	**628,300**	**336,198**	**292,102**	**1,825**	**1,731**	**94**	**3,113**	**3,069**	**44**
0—10 ..	194,141	100,328	93,813	192	179	13	193,949	100,149	93,800	131	126	5	14	12	2
10—15 ..	74,200	41,810	32,390	635	584	51	73,565	41,226	32,339	319	299	20	89	88	1
15—20 ..	53,859	28,737	25,1[illegible]2	818	768	50	53,041	27,969	25,072	243	232	11	226	220	6
20 and over ..	313,025	171,936	141,059	5,280	5,112	168	307,745	166,854	140,891	1,132	1,074	58	2,784	2,749	35
Christian ..	**302**	**156**	**146**	**247**	**124**	**123**	**55**	**32**	**23**	**2**	**2**	..	**2**	**2**	—
0—10 ..	44	23	21	14	3	11	30	20	10	1	1	..	1	1	—
10—15 ..	4	2	2	3	2	1	1	..	1	..	..	..	1	1	—
15—20 ..	13	10	3	13	10	3	..	..	..	..	..	..	..	..	—
20 and over ..	241	121	120	217	109	108	24	12	12	1	1	..	..	—	..
Others ..	**33**	**21**	**12**	**2**	**1**	**1**	**31**	**20**	**11**	..	..	..	..	..	..
0—10 ..	12	10	2	..	..	..	12	10	2	..	..	..	..	..	..
10—15 ..	2	2	..	..	..	..	2	2	..	..	..	..	..	..	..
15—20 ..	1	..	1	..	..	..	1	..	1	..	..	..	..	..	..
20 and over ..	18	9	9	2	1	1	16	8	8	..	..	..	..	—	..

VIII.

VIII Education.

RELIGION AND AGE.

State Census 1921.

trict Tables.

ATE IN.

Arabic. Persons.	Arabic. Males.	Arabic. Females.	Dogri. Persons.	Dogri. Males.	Dogri. Females.	Hindi. Persons.	Hindi. Males.	Hindi. Females.	Bodhi. Persons.	Bodhi. Males.	Bodhi. Females.	Gurmukhi. Persons.	Gurmukhi. Males.	Gurmukhi. Females.	Others. Persons.	Others. Males.	Others. Females.	English. Persons.	English. Males.	English. Females.
17	18	19	20	21	22	23	24	25	26	27	28	29	30	31	32	33	34	35	36	37
..	..	..	..	..	..	..	..	..	..	..	..	..	..	..	..	..	..	21	13	8
..	..	..	..	..	..	..	..	..	..	..	..	..	..	..	..	..	..	..	..	..
..	..	..	..	..	..	..	..	..	..	..	..	..	..	..	..	..	..	..	..	..
..	..	..	..	..	..	..	..	..	..	..	..	..	..	..	..	..	..	..	..	..
..	..	..	..	..	..	..	..	..	..	..	..	..	..	..	..	..	..	21	13	8
..	..	..	..	..	..	..	..	..	..	..	..	..	..	..	1	..	1	1	1	..
..	..	..	..	..	..	..	..	..	..	..	..	..	..	..	1	..	1	..	..	..
..	..	..	..	..	..	..	..	..	..	..	..	..	..	..	..	..	..	..	..	..
..	..	..	..	..	..	..	..	..	..	..	..	..	..	..	..	..	..	..	..	..
..	..	..	..	..	..	..	..	..	..	..	..	..	..	..	..	..	..	1	1	..
SOUTH.																				
1,154	1,026	128	86	86	–	231	177	54	5	5	..	248	222	26	1,433	1,394	39	5,836	5,647	189
31	25	6	1	1	..	16	6	10	..	..	..	5	2	3	12	8	4	112	95	17
115	86	29	1	1	..	27	8	19	..	..	..	9	6	3	104	95	9	754	747	7
119	92	27	2	2	..	20	18	2	2	2	..	23	15	8	93	91	2	1,282	1,264	18
889	823	66	82	82	..	168	145	23	3	3	..	211	199	12	1,224	1,200	24	3,688	3,541	147
..	..	..	83	83	..	215	167	48	2	2	..	41	29	12	1,415	1,377	38	4,702	4,652	50
..	..	..	1	1	..	25	5	10	..	..	..	2	1	1	12	8	4	83	78	5
..	..	..	1	1	..	26	8	18	..	..	..	3	3	..	103	94	9	625	620	5
..	..	..	2	2	..	20	18	2	1	1	..	5	3	2	93	91	2	1,032	1,022	10
..	..	..	79	79	..	154	136	18	1	1	..	31	22	9	1,207	1,184	23	2,962	2,932	30
..	–	–	–	–	..	2	1	1	..	..	..	..	..	..	..	..	..	5	5	..
..	..	..	..	..	..	..	..	..	..	..	..	..	..	..	..	..	..	..	..	..
..	..	..	..	..	..	..	..	..	..	..	..	..	..	..	..	..	..	..	..	..
..	..	..	..	..	..	..	..	..	..	..	..	..	..	..	..	..	..	..	..	..
..	..	..	..	..	..	2	1	1	..	..	..	..	..	..	..	..	..	5	5	..
..	..	..	1	1	..	11	7	4	..	..	..	205	192	13	16	16	..	59	57	2
..	..	..	..	..	..	1	1	–	..	..	..	2	..	2	..	..	..	2	1	1
..	..	..	..	..	..	1	..	1	..	..	..	6	3	3	..	..	..	16	16	..
..	..	..	..	..	..	..	..	..	..	..	..	17	12	5	..	..	..	8	8	..
..	..	..	1	1	..	9	6	3	..	..	..	180	177	3	16	16	..	33	32	1
..	..	..	..	..	..	..	..	..	1	1	..	..	..	..	..	..	..	1	1	..
..	..	..	..	..	..	..	..	..	..	..	..	..	..	..	..	..	..	..	..	..
..	..	..	..	..	..	..	..	..	..	..	..	..	..	..	..	..	..	..	..	..
..	..	..	..	..	..	..	..	..	..	..	..	..	..	..	..	..	..	..	..	..
..	..	..	..	..	..	..	..	..	1	1	..	..	..	..	..	..	..	1	1	..
..	..	..	..	..	..	..	..	..	..	..	..	..	..	..	..	..	..	2	2	..
..	..	..	..	..	..	..	..	..	..	..	..	..	..	..	..	..	..	..	..	..
..	..	..	..	..	..	..	..	..	..	..	..	..	..	..	..	..	..	..	..	..
..	..	..	..	..	..	..	..	..	..	..	..	..	..	..	..	..	..	1	1	..
..	..	..	..	..	..	..	..	..	–	..	..	..	..	..	..	..	..	1	1	..
1,154	1,026	128	2	2	..	3	2	1	1	1	..	2	1	1	2	1	1	823	810	13
31	25	6	–	..		..	..	..	..	..	..	1	1	..	..	..	..	15	15	..
115	86	29	..	..		..	..	..	..	..	..	..	..	..	1	1	..	111	110	1
119	92	27	..	..		..	..	..	1	1	..	1	..	1	..	..	..	228	223	5
889	823	66	2	2		3	2	1	..	..	..	..	..	..	1	..	1	469	462	7
..	..	..	..	..	..	..	..	–	..	..	..	..	..	..	..	..	..	243	120	123
..	..	..	..	..	..	..	..	..	..	..	..	..	..	..	..	..	..	12	1	11
..	..	..	..	..	..	..	..	..	..	..	..	..	..	..	..	..	..	2	1	1
..	..	–	..	..	..	..	..	..	..	..	..	..	..	..	..	..	..	13	10	3
..	..	..	–	..	..	..	..	..	..	..	..	..	..	..	..	..	..	216	108	108
..	..	..	..	..	..	..	..	..	1	1	..	..	..	..	..	..	..	1	..	1
–	..	..	..	..	–	..	..	..	..	..	..	..	..	..	..	..	..	..	..	..
..	..	..	..	..	..	..	..	..	..	..	..	..	..	..	..	..	..	..	..	..
..	..	..	..	..	..	..	..	..	..	..	..	..	..	..	..	..	..	..	..	..
–	..	..	..	..	..	..	..	..	1	1	..	..	..	..	..	..	..	1	..	1

TABLE
EDUCATION BY
Jammu and Kashmir

Part II—Dis

Age.	POPULATION. Total. Persons.	Total. Males.	Total. Females.	Literate. Persons.	Literate. Males.	Literate. Females.	Illiterate. Persons.	Illiterate. Males.	Illiterate. Females.	LITER[ATE] Urdu. Persons.	Urdu. Males.	Urdu. Females.	Persian. Persons.	Persian. Males.	Persian. Females.
1	2	3	4	5	6	7	8	9	10	11	12	13	14	15	16
													(10)	MUZA	FFAR
All Religions	**216,109**	**115,680**	**100,429**	**3,844**	**3,572**	**272**	**212,265**	**112,108**	**100,157**	**1,734**	**1,696**	**38**	**206**	**197**	**9**
0—10 ..	68,717	35,626	33,091	76	63	13	68,641	35,563	33,078	3	33	4	3	3	..
10—15 ..	24,252	14,245	10,007	277	256	21	23,975	13,989	9,986	161	157	4	7	7	..
15—20 ..	19,439	9,733	9,706	334	313	21	19,105	9,420	9,685	193	190	3	12	12	..
20 and over..	103,701	56,076	47,625	3,157	2,940	217	100,544	53,136	47,408	1,343	1,316	27	184	175	9
Hindu ..	**4,397**	**2,702**	**1,695**	**1,039**	**990**	**49**	**3,358**	**1,712**	**1,646**	**375**	**368**	**7**	**20**	**17**	**3**
0—10 ..	990	475	515	22	12	10	968	463	505	7	5	2	..	..	..
10—15 ..	437	244	193	75	66	9	362	178	184	50	47	3	1	1	..
15—20 ..	439	290	149	99	88	11	340	202	138	31	31	..	..	..	..
20 and over..	2,531	1,693	838	843	824	19	1,688	869	819	287	285	2	19	16	3
Sikh ..	**9,208**	**4,759**	**4,449**	**830**	**689**	**141**	**8,378**	**4,070**	**4,308**	**89**	**81**	**8**	**3**	**2**	**1**
0—10 ..	3,230	1,649	1,581	26	26	..	3,204	1,623	1,581	9	9	..	..	..	..
10—15 ..	1,052	593	459	79	77	2	973	516	457	20	19	1	..	..	..
15—20 ..	621	198	423	35	30	5	586	168	418	6	5	1	..	..	..
20 and over..	4,305	2,319	1,986	690	566	134	3,615	1,763	1,852	54	48	6	3	2	1
Musalman ..	**202,498**	**108,215**	**94,283**	**1,969**	**1,889**	**80**	**200,529**	**106,326**	**94,203**	**1,270**	**1,247**	**23**	**183**	**178**	**5**
0—10 ..	64,497	33,502	30,995	28	25	3	64,469	33,477	30,992	21	19	2	3	3	..
10—15 ..	22,763	13,408	9,355	123	113	10	22,640	13,295	9,345	91	91	..	6	6	..
15—20 ..	18,379	9,245	9,134	200	195	5	18,179	9,050	9,129	156	154	2	12	12	..
20 and over..	96,859	52,060	44,799	1,618	1,556	62	95,241	50,504	44,737	1,002	983	19	162	157	5
Christian ..	**6**	**4**	**2**	**6**	**4**	**2**	..	..	..	..	..	..	..	..	..
0—10 ..	..	..	..	..	..	..	..	..	..	..	..	..	..	..	..
10—15 ..	..	..	..	..	..	..	..	..	..	..	..	..	..	..	..
15—20 ..	..	..	..	..	..	..	..	..	..	..	..	..	..	..	..
20 and over..	6	4	2	6	4	2	..	..	..	..	..	..	..	..	..
													(11)	LAD	AKH
All Religions	**183,476**	**91,258**	**92,218**	**2,462**	**2,385**	**77**	**181,014**	**88,873**	**92,141**	**424**	**416**	**8**	**579**	**567**	**12**
0—10 ..	48,087	24,164	23,923	12	9	3	48,075	24,155	23,920	10	7	3	..	..	..
10—15 ..	19,972	10,454	9,518	97	95	2	19,875	10,359	9,516	48	48	..	8	8	..
15—20 ..	17,038	9,120	7,918	175	165	10	16,863	8,955	7,908	66	65	1	26	26	..
20 and over..	93,379	47,520	50,859	2,178	2,116	62	96,201	45,404	50,797	300	296	4	545	533	12
Hindu ...	**268**	**185**	**83**	**119**	**114**	**5**	**149**	**71**	**78**	**41**	**38**	**3**	**1**	**1**	..
0—10 ..	62	27	35	5	4	1	57	23	34	5	4	1	..	..	..
10—15 ..	8	7	1	5	5	..	3	2	1	4	4	..	..	..	..
15—20 ..	18	10	8	8	7	1	10	3	7	3	2	1	..	..	..
20 and over..	180	141	39	101	98	3	79	43	36	29	28	1	1	1	..
Arya ...	**25**	**16**	**9**	**14**	**11**	**3**	**11**	**5**	**6**	**7**	**5**	**2**	..	..	..
0—10 ..	11	6	5	3	1	2	8	5	3	3	1	2	..	..	..
10—15 ..	2	2	..	2	2	..	..	..	..	1	1	..	..	..	..
15—20 ..	1	1	..	1	1	..	..	..	..	..	..	..	..	..	..
20 and over..	11	7	4	8	7	1	3	..	3	3	3	..	..	..	..
Sikh ..	**48**	**30**	**18**	**32**	**22**	**10**	**16**	**8**	**8**	**9**	**8**	**1**	..	..	..
0—10 ..	10	3	7	..	..	..	10	3	7	..	..	..	..	..	..
10—15 ..	3	2	1	2	1	1	1	1	..	1	1	..	..	..	..
15—20 ..	8	4	4	6	2	4	2	2	..	2	2	..	..	..	..
20 and over..	27	21	6	24	19	5	3	2	1	6	5	1	..	..	..
Buddhst ...	**37,241**	**18,610**	**18,631**	**1,193**	**1,159**	**34**	**36,048**	**17,451**	**18,597**	**14**	**13**	**1**	**5**	**5**	..
0—10 ..	7,231	3,503	3,728	2	2	..	7,229	3,501	3,728	..	..	..	..	..	..
10—15 ..	3,410	1,705	1,705	35	35	..	3,375	1,670	1,705	1	1	..	..	..	..
15—20 ..	3,581	1,935	1,616	54	51	3	3,527	1,914	1,613	3	3	..	..	..	..
20 and over..	23,019	11,437	11,582	1,102	1,071	31	21,917	10,366	11,551	10	9	1	5	5	..
Musalman ...	**145,824**	**72,380**	**73,444**	**1,072**	**1,058**	**14**	**44,752**	**71,322**	**73,430**	**350**	**349**	**1**	**573**	**561**	**12**
0—10 ..	40,753	20,615	20,138	1	1	..	40,752	20,614	20,138	1	1	..	..	..	..
10—15 ..	16,541	8,735	7,806	49	49	..	16,492	8,686	7,806	40	40	..	8	8	..
15—20 ..	13,425	7,138	6,287	102	102	..	13,323	7,036	6,287	57	57	..	26	26	..
20 and over..	75,105	35,892	39,213	920	906	14	74,185	34,986	39,199	252	251	1	539	527	12

VIII.
VIII
Education.

Religion and Age.

State Census 1921.

rict Tables.

ATE IN.

Arabic.			Dogri.			Hindi.			Bodhi.			Gurmukhi.			Others.			English.		
Persons.	Males.	Females.	Persons.	Males.	Females.	Persons.	Males.	Females.	Persons.	Males.	Females.	Persons.	Males.	Females.	Persons.	Males.	Females.	Persons.	Males.	Females.
17	18	19	20	21	22	23	24	25	26	27	28	29	30	31	32	33	34	35	36	37
ABAD	DIST	RICT.																		
467	**416**	**51**	**19**	**12**	**7**	**425**	**414**	**11**	..	..	..	**720**	**575**	**145**	..	..	..	**273**	**262**	**11**
4	3	1	..	..	..	5	3	2	..	..	..	27	21	6	..	..	..	..	..	..
25	15	10	..	..	..	15	14	1	..	..	..	60	55	5	..	..	..	9	8	1
23	20	3	..	..	..	29	24	5	..	..	..	33	23	10	..	..	..	44	44	..
415	378	37	19	12	7	376	373	3	..	..	..	600	476	124	..	..	..	220	210	10
..	..	..	**17**	**10**	**7**	**368**	**359**	**9**	..	..	..	**53**	**31**	**22**	..	..	..	**206**	**205**	**1**
..	..	..	..	..	..	4	2	2	..	..	..	11	5	6	..	..	..	..	..	..
..	..	..	..	..	..	11	10	1	..	..	..	6	2	5	..	..	..	7	6	1
..	..	..	..	..	..	26	21	5	..	..	..	8	2	6	..	..	..	34	34	..
..	..	..	17	10	7	327	326	1	..	..	..	28	22	6	..	..	..	165	165	..
..	..	..	..	..	..	**56**	**54**	**2**	..	—	..	**662**	**539**	**123**	..	..	..	**20**	**13**	**7**
..	..	..	..	..	..	1	1	..	..	..	..	16	16	..	..	..	..	..	..	..
..	..	..	..	..	..	4	4	..	..	..	..	54	53	1	..	..	..	1	1	..
..	..	..	..	..	..	3	3	..	..	..	..	25	21	4	..	..	..	1	1	..
..	..	..	..	..	..	48	46	2	..	..	..	567	449	118	..	..	..	18	11	7
467	**416**	**51**	**2**	**2**	..	**1**	**1**	..	..	..	..	**5**	**5**	..	..	..	..	**41**	**40**	**1**
4	3	1	..	..	..	..	..	..	..	..	..	..	..	..	..	..	..	..	..	..
25	15	10	..	..	..	..	..	..	..	..	..	..	..	..	..	..	..	1	1	..
23	20	3	..	..	..	..	..	..	..	..	..	..	..	..	..	..	..	9	9	..
415	378	37	2	2	..	1	1	..	..	..	..	5	5	..	..	..	..	31	30	1
..	..	..	..	..	..	..	..	..	..	..	..	..	..	..	..	..	..	**6**	**4**	**2**
..	..	..	..	..	..	..	..	..	..	..	..	..	..	..	..	..	..	..	..	..
..	..	..	..	..	..	..	..	..	..	..	..	..	..	..	..	..	..	..	..	..
..	..	..	..	..	..	..	..	..	..	..	..	..	..	..	..	..	..	..	..	..
..	..	..	..	..	..	..	..	..	..	..	..	..	..	..	..	..	..	6	4	2
DIST	RICT.																			
44	**44**	..	**8**	**8**	..	**20**	**20**	..	**1,238**	**1,209**	**29**	**23**	**12**	**11**	**11**	**1**	**10**	**115**	**108**	**7**
..	..	..	..	..	..	..	..	..	2	2	..	..	..	..	..	..	..	..	..	..
..	..	..	..	..	..	..	..	..	32	31	1	1	..	1	..	..	..	8	8	..
..	..	..	..	..	..	1	1	..	52	48	4	5	1	4	1	..	1	24	21	..
44	44	..	8	8	..	19	19	..	1,152	1,128	24	17	11	6	10	1	9	83	76	7
..	..	..	**7**	**7**	..	**19**	**19**	..	..	..	..	**3**	**1**	**2**	..	..	..	**48**	**48**	—
..	..	..	..	..	..	..	..	..	..	..	..	..	..	..	..	..	..	..	..	..
..	..	..	..	..	..	..	..	..	..	..	..	..	..	..	..	..	..	1	1	..
..	..	..	..	..	..	1	1	..	..	..	..	1	1	..	..	..	..	3	3	..
..	..	..	7	7	..	18	18	..	..	..	..	2	..	2	..	..	..	44	44	..
..	..	..	..	..	..	**1**	**1**	..	..	..	..	..	..	..	..	..	..	**6**	**5**	**1**
..	..	..	..	..	..	..	..	..	..	..	..	..	..	..	..	..	..	..	..	..
..	..	..	..	..	..	..	..	..	..	..	..	..	..	..	..	..	..	1	1	..
..	..	..	..	..	..	..	..	..	..	..	..	..	..	..	..	..	..	1	1	..
..	..	..	..	..	..	1	1	..	..	..	..	..	..	..	..	..	..	4	3	1
..	..	..	..	..	..	..	..	..	..	..	..	**20**	**11**	**9**	..	..	..	**3**	**3**	..
..	..	..	..	..	..	..	..	..	..	..	..	..	..	..	..	..	..	..	..	..
..	..	..	..	..	..	..	..	..	..	..	..	1	..	1	..	..	..	..	..	..
..	..	..	..	..	..	..	..	..	..	..	..	4	..	4	..	..	..	..	..	..
..	..	..	..	..	..	..	..	..	..	..	..	15	11	4	..	..	..	3	3	..
..	..	..	..	..	..	..	..	..	**1,160**	**1,137**	**23**	..	..	..	**10**	..	**10**	**4**	**4**	..
..	..	..	..	..	..	..	..	..	2	2	..	..	..	..	..	..	..	..	..	..
..	..	..	..	..	..	..	..	..	31	31	..	..	..	..	..	..	..	3	3	..
..	..	..	..	..	..	..	..	..	49	47	2	..	..	..	1	..	1	1	1	..
..	..	..	..	..	..	..	..	..	1,078	1,057	21	..	..	..	9	..	9	..	..	..
44	**44**	..	**1**	**1**	..	..	..	..	**66**	**65**	**1**	..	..	..	**1**	**1**	..	**37**	**37**	..
..	..	..	..	..	..	..	..	..	..	..	..	..	..	..	..	..	..	..	..	..
..	..	..	..	..	..	..	..	..	..	..	..	..	..	..	..	..	..	1	1	..
..	..	..	..	..	..	..	..	..	1	1	..	..	..	..	..	..	..	13	18	..
44	44	..	1	1	..	..	..	..	65	64	1	..	..	..	1	1	..	18	18	..

TABLE

EDUCATION BY

Jammu and Kashmir

Part II—Di

Age.	Population. Total. Persons.	Population. Total. Males.	Population. Total. Females.	Literate. Persons.	Literate. Males.	Literate. Females.	Illiterate. Persons.	Illiterate. Males.	Illiterate. Females.	Literate in Urdu. Persons.	Urdu. Males.	Urdu. Females.	Persian. Persons.	Persian. Males.	Persian. Females.
1	2	3	4	5	6	7	8	9	10	11	12	13	14	15	16
Christian ..	**70**	**37**	**33**	**32**	**21**	**11**	**38**	**16**	**22**	**3**	**3**	..	..	..	..
0—10 ..	20	10	10	1	1	..	19	9	10	1	1	..	..	..	..
10—15 ..	8	3	5	4	3	1	4	..	4	1	1	..	..	..	..
15—20 ..	5	2	3	4	2	2	1	..	1	1	1	..	..	..	..
20 and over..	37	22	15	23	15	8	14	7	7	..	..	..	..	..	..
														(12) GILGIT	
All Religions	**28,706**	**15,880**	**12,826**	**958**	**908**	**50**	**27,748**	**14,972**	**12,776**	**445**	**43[illegible]**	**13**	**98**	**96**	**2**
0—10 ..	9,298	4,569	4,729	13	11	2	9,285	4,558	4,727	11	1[illegible]	..	..	..	..
10—15 ..	2,950	1,526	1,424	45	37	8	2,905	1,489	1,416	23	2[illegible]	2	..	..	..
15—20 ..	2,489	1,569	920	110	102	8	2,379	1,467	912	60	5[illegible]	1	7	7	..
20 and over..	13,969	8,216	5,753	790	758	32	13,179	7,458	5,721	351	34[illegible]	10	91	89	2
Hindu ..	**711**	**665**	**46**	**314**	**295**	**19**	**397**	**370**	**27**	**99**	**89**	**10**	..	..	..
0—10 ..	40	24	16	9	7	2	31	17	14	7	7	..	..	..	..
10—15 ..	12	7	5	9	4	5	3	3	..	4	2	2	..	..	..
15—20 ..	76	72	4	39	38	1	37	34	3	17	16	1	..	..	..
20 and over..	583	562	21	257	246	11	326	316	10	71	64	7	..	..	..
Arya ..	**17**	**11**	**6**	**8**	**6**	**2**	**9**	**5**	**4**	**2**	**1**	**1**	..	..	..
0—10 ..	7	3	4	..	..	..	7	3	4	..	..	..	..	..	..
10—15 ..	2	2	..	1	1	..	1	1	..	1	1	..	..	..	..
15—20 ..	..	..	..	..	..	..	..	..	..	..	..	..	..	..	..
20 and over..	8	6	2	7	5	2	1	1	..	1	..	1	..	..	..
Sikh ..	**69**	**46**	**23**	**37**	**30**	**7**	**32**	**16**	**16**	**10**	**9**	**1**	..	..	..
0—10 ..	15	4	11	..	..	..	15	4	11	..	..	..	..	..	..
10—15 ..	12	9	3	6	6	..	6	3	3	5	5	..	..	..	..
15—20 ..	4	2	2	4	2	2	..	..	..	2	2	..	..	..	..
20 and over ..	38	31	7	27	22	5	11	9	2	3	2	1	..	..	..
Musalman ..	**27,894**	**15,149**	**12,745**	**586**	**568**	**18**	**27,308**	**14,581**	**12,727**	**334**	**333**	**1**	**98**	**96**	**2**
0—10 ..	9,234	4,538	4,696	4	4	..	9,230	4,534	4,696	4	4	..	..	..	..
10—15 ..	2,924	1,508	1,416	29	26	3	2,895	1,482	1,413	13	13	..	..	..	..
15—20 ..	2,409	1,495	914	67	62	5	2,342	1,433	909	41	41	..	7	7	..
20 and over ..	13,327	7,608	5,719	486	476	10	12,841	7,132	5,709	276	275	1	91	89	2
Christian ..	**15**	**9**	**6**	**13**	**9**	**4**	**2**	..	**2**	..	..	..	..	..	..
0—10 ..	2	..	2	..	..	..	2	..	2	..	..	..	..	..	..
10—15 ..	..	..	..	..	..	..	..	..	..	..	..	..	..	..	..
15—20 ..	..	..	..	..	..	..	..	..	..	..	..	..	..	..	..
20 and over ..	13	9	4	13	9	4	..	..	..	..	..	..	..	..	..

VIII.

RELIGION AND AGE.

State Census 1921.

trict Tables.

ATE IN.

Arabic.			*Dogri.*			*Hindi.*			*Bodhi.*			*Gurmukhi.*			*Others.*			*English.*		
Persons.	Males.	Females.	Persons.	Males.	Females.	Persons.	Males.	Females.	Persons.	Males.	Females.	Persons.	Males.	Females	Persons.	Males.	Females.	Persons.	Males.	Females.
17	18	19	20	21	22	23	24	25	26	27	28	29	30	31	32	33	34	35	36	37
..	..	..	..	..	..	..	..	..	12	7	5	..	..	..	..	..	..	17	11	6
..	..	..	..	..	..	..	..	..	..	..	..	..	..	..	..	..	..	..	..	..
..	..	..	..	..	..	..	..	..	1	..	1	..	..	..	..	..	..	2	2	..
..	..	..	..	..	..	..	..	..	2	..	2	..	..	..	..	..	..	1	1	..
..	..	..	..	..	..	..	..	..	9	7	2	..	..	..	..	..	..	14	8	6
DIST	RICT.																			
101	**86**	**15**	**22**	**22**	..	**15**	**8**	**7**	..	..	..	**23**	**20**	**3**	**107**	**104**	**3**	**147**	**140**	
..	..	..	..	..	..	1	..	1	..	..	..	..	..	..	..	..	..	1	..	1
3	..	3	1	1	..	3	1	2	..	..	..	1	1	..	..	..	..	14	13	1
16	11	5	..	..	..	..	..	..	..	..	..	..	..	..	11	9	2	16	16	..
82	75	7	21	21	..	11	7	4	..	..	..	22	19	3	96	95	1	116	111	5
..	..	..	**20**	**20**	..	**12**	**7**	**5**	..	..	..	**5**	**4**	**1**	**104**	**104**	..	**74**	**71**	**3**
..	..	..	..	..	..	1	..	1	..	..	..	..	..	..	..	..	..	1	..	1
..	..	..	1	1	..	2	..	2	..	..	..	1	1	..	..	..	..	1	..	1
..	..	..	..	..	..	..	..	..	..	..	..	..	..	..	9	9	..	13	13	..
..	..	..	19	19	..	9	7	2	..	..	..	4	3	1	95	95	..	59	58	
..	..	..	..	..	..	**1**	..	**1**	..	..	..	..	..	..	..	..	..	**5**	**5**	..
..	..	..	..	..	..	..	..	..	..	..	..	..	..	..	..	..	..	..	..	..
..	..	..	..	..	..	..	..	..	..	..	..	..	..	..	..	..	..	..	..	..
..	..	..	..	..	..	..	..	..	..	..	..	..	..	..	..	..	..	..	..	..
..	..	..	..	..	..	1	..	1	..	..	..	..	..	..	..	..	..	5	5	..
..	..	..	..	..	..	**2**	**1**	**1**	..	..	..	**17**	**15**	**2**	**3**	..	**3**	**5**	**5**	..
..	..	..	..	..	..	..	..	..	..	..	..	..	..	..	..	..	..	..	..	..
..	..	..	..	..	..	1	1	..	..	..	..	..	..	..	..	..	..	..	..	..
..	..	..	..	..	..	..	..	..	..	..	..	..	..	..	2	..	2	..	..	..
..	..	..	..	..	..	1	..	1	..	..	..	17	15	2	1	..	1	5	5	..
101	**86**	**15**	**2**	**2**	..	..	..	..	..	..	..	**1**	**1**	..	..	..	..	**50**	**50**	..
..	..	..	..	..	..	..	..	..	..	..	..	..	..	..	..	..	..	..	..	..
3	..	3	..	..	..	..	..	..	..	..	..	..	..	..	..	..	..	13	13	..
16	11	5	..	..	..	..	..	..	..	..	..	..	..	..	..	..	..	3	3	..
82	75	7	2	2	..	..	..	..	..	..	..	1	1	..	..	..	..	34	34	..
..	..	..	..	..	..	..	..	..	..	..	..	..	..	..	..	..	..	**13**	**9**	**4**
..	..	..	..	..	..	..	..	..	..	..	..	..	..	..	..	..	..	..	..	
..	..	..	..	..	..	..	..	..	..	..	..	..	..	..	..	..	..	..	..	
..	..	..	..	..	..	..	..	..	..	..	..	..	..	..	..	..	..	..	..	
..	..	..	..	..	..	..	..	..	..	..	..	..	..	..	..	..	..	13	9	

TABLE

EDUCATION BY

Jammu and Kashmir

Part III—

Age.	Population.														
										Lite[rate]					
	Total.			*Literate.*			*Illiterate.*			*Urdu.*			*Persian.*		
	Persons.	Males.	Females.	Persons.	Males.	Females.	Persons.	Males.	Females.	Persons.	Males.	Females.	Persons.	Males.	Females.
1	2	3	4	5	6	7	8	9	10	11	12	13	14	15	16
													(a) JAMMU		
All Religions	**31,506**	**19,121**	**12,385**	**6,170**	**5,169**	**1,001**	**25,336**	**13,952**	**11,384**	**2,355**	**2,165**	**190**	**161**	**155**	**6**
0—10 ..	5,833	2,964	2,869	369	267	102	5,464	2,697	2,767	216	188	28	..	..	..
10—15 ..	2,928	1,750	1,178	747	574	173	2,181	1,176	1,005	385	358	27	4	4	..
15—20 ..	3,219	1,986	1,233	965	769	196	2,254	1,217	1,037	287	255	32	14	11	2
20 and over..	19,526	12,421	7,105	4,089	3,559	530	15,437	8,862	6,575	1,467	1,364	103	143	140	3
Hindu ..	**20,220**	**12,380**	**7,840**	**4,304**	**3,638**	**666**	**15,916**	**8,742**	**7,174**	**1,520**	**1,471**	**49**	**137**	**136**	**1**
0—10 ..	3,386	1,696	1,690	240	185	55	3,146	1,511	1,635	132	129	3	..	..	..
10—15 ..	1,799	1,116	683	525	403	122	1,274	713	581	262	252	10	4	4	..
15—20 ..	2,095	1,307	788	685	561	124	1,410	746	664	221	217	4	10	10	..
20 and ove ..	12,940	8,261	4,679	2,854	2,489	365	10,086	5,772	4,314	905	873	32	123	122	1
Arya ..	**560**	**319**	**241**	**290**	**208**	**82**	**270**	**111**	**159**	**54**	**42**	**12**	..	..	..
0—10 ..	140	75	65	22	11	11	118	64	54	9	9	..	..	..	..
10—15 ..	51	23	28	34	18	16	17	5	12	10	5	5	..	..	..
15—20 ..	75	48	27	56	42	14	19	6	13	5	5	..	..	..	..
20 and over..	294	173	121	178	137	41	116	36	80	30	23	7	..	..	..
Brahmo ..	**15**	**7**	**8**	**6**	**3**	**3**	**9**	**4**	**5**	**1**	**1**	..	..	..	..
0—10 ..	4	3	1	1	..	1	3	3	..	..	..	..	..	..	..
10—15 ..	2	..	2	..	..	..	2	..	2	..	..	..	..	..	..
15—20 ..	..	..	..	..	..	..	..	..	..	..	..	..	..	..	..
20 and over..	9	4	5	5	3	2	4	1	3	1	1	..	..	..	..
Sikh ..	**708**	**400**	**308**	**234**	**177**	**57**	**474**	**223**	**251**	**64**	**57**	**7**	..	..	..
0—10 ..	192	98	94	10	10	..	182	88	94	4	4	..	..	..	..
10—15 ..	75	41	34	30	17	13	45	24	21	11	10	1	..	..	..
15—20 ..	51	30	21	30	19	11	21	11	10	4	4	..	..	..	..
20 and over..	390	231	159	164	131	33	226	100	126	45	39	6	..	..	..
Jain ..	**520**	**289**	**231**	**180**	**157**	**23**	**340**	**132**	**208**	**27**	**25**	**2**	..	..	..
0—10 ..	140	61	79	3	2	1	137	59	78	1	1	..	..	..	..
10—15 ..	70	42	28	22	16	6	48	26	22	10	9	1	..	..	..
15—20 ..	38	24	14	25	17	8	13	7	6	5	4	1	..	..	..
20 and over..	272	162	110	130	122	8	142	40	102	11	11	..	..	..	..
Buddhist ..	**4**	**4**	..	**3**	**3**	..	**1**	**1**	..	..	..	..	..	..	..
0—10 ..	..	..	..	..	..	..	..	..	..	..	..	..	..	..	..
10—15 ..	..	..	..	..	..	..	..	..	..	..	..	..	..	..	..
15—20 ..	..	..	..	..	..	..	..	..	..	..	..	..	..	..	..
20 and over..		4	..	3	3	..	1	1	..	..	..	..	..	..	..
Musalman ..	**9,001**	**5,463**	**3,538**	**1,104**	**955**	**149**	**7,897**	**4,508**	**3,389**	**667**	**556**	**111**	**24**	**19**	**5**
0—10 ..	1,851	968	883	67	44	23	1,784	924	860	58	38	20	..	..	..
10—15 ..	878	502	376	124	112	12	754	390	364	86	77	9	..	..	..
15—20 ..	901	544	357	158	125	33	743	419	324	48	24	24	4	1	2
20 and over..	5,371	3,449	1,922	755	674	81	4,616	2,775	1,841	475	417	58	20	18	2
Christian ..	**478**	**259**	**219**	**49**	**28**	**21**	**429**	**231**	**198**	**22**	**13**	**9**	..	..	..
0—10 ..	120	63	57	26	15	11	94	48	46	12	7	5	..	..	..
10—15 ..	53	26	27	12	8	4	41	18	23	6	5	1	..	..	..
15—20 ..	59	33	26	11	5	6	48	28	20	4	1	3	..	..	..
20 and over..	246	137	109	..	..	..	246	137	109	..	..	..	..	..	..
												(b)	SRINAGAR		
All Religions	**141,735**	**76,604**	**65,131**	**12,354**	**11,933**	**421**	**129,381**	**64,671**	**64,710**	**3,731**	**3,613**	**118**	**1,764**	**1,747**	**17**
0—10 ..	36,827	18,074	18,753	380	338	42	36,447	17,736	18,711	221	200	12	19	17	2
10—15 ..	17,864	10,384	7,480	1,400	1,335	65	16,464	9,049	7,415	557	537	20	21	21	..
15—20 ..	12,492	6,895	5,597	1,639	1,595	44	10,853	5,300	5,553	339	328	11	31	31	..
20 and over..	74,552	41,251	33,301	8,935	8,665	270	65,617	32,586	33,031	2,614	2,539	75	1,693	1,678	15
Hindu ..	**30,004**	**16,515**	**13,489**	**9,432**	**9,230**	**202**	**20,572**	**7,285**	**13,287**	**2,828**	**2,766**	**62**	**1,137**	**1,127**	**10**
0—10 ..	6,905	3,394	3,514	283	254	29	6,622	3,137	3,485	171	161	19	12	10	2
10—15 ..	3,500	2,154	1,346	1,064	1,027	37	2,436	1,127	1,309	394	386	8	..	..	..
15—20 ..	2,850	1,769	1,081	1,270	1,246	24	1,580	523	1,057	24[illegible]	235	8	..	..	..
20 and over ..	16,749	9,201	7,548	6,815	6,703	112	9,934	2,498	7,436	2,02[illegible]	1,984	36	1,125	1,117	8

VIII.

Religion and Age.

State Census 1921.

City Tables.

ATE IN

Arabic. Persons.	Arabic. Males.	Arabic. Females.	Dogri. Persons.	Dogri. Males.	Dogri. Females.	Hindi. Persons.	Hindi. Males.	Hindi. Females.	Bodhi. Persons.	Bodhi. Males.	Bodhi. Females.	Gurmukhi. Persons.	Gurmukhi. Males.	Gurmukhi. Females.	Others. Persons.	Others. Males.	Others. Females.	English. Persons.	English. Males.	English. Females.
17	18	19	20	21	22	23	24	25	26	27	28	29	30	31	32	33	34	35	36	37
CITY.																				
41	**22**	**19**	**359**	**336**	**23**	**1,157**	**589**	**568**	..	..	..	**273**	**149**	**124**	**29**	**28**	**1**	**1,795**	**1,725**	**70**
3	..	3	5	3	2	89	41	48	..	..	..	16	2	14	..	..	..	40	33	7
2	..	2	5	4	1	160	53	107	..	..	..	27	1	26	..	..	..	164	154	10
4	2	2	17	16	1	188	68	120	..	..	..	23	2	21	..	..	..	432	415	17
32	20	12	332	313	19	720	427	293	..	..	..	207	144	63	29	28	1	1,159	1,123	36
..	..	..	**353**	**331**	**22**	**832**	**388**	**444**	..	..	..	**258**	**145**	**113**	**20**	**20**	..	**1,184**	**1,147**	**37**
..	..	..	4	3	1	70	34	36	..	..	..	13	2	11	..	..	..	21	17	4
..	..	..	5	4	1	124	42	82	..	..	..	24	..	24	..	..	..	106	101	5
..	..	..	17	16	1	145	52	93	..	..	..	22	2	20	..	..	..	270	264	6
..	..	..	327	308	19	493	260	233	..	..	..	199	141	58	20	20	..	787	765	22
..	..	..	**1**	**1**	..	**63**	**9**	**54**	..	..	..	**11**	**4**	**7**	..	..	..	**161**	**152**	**9**
..	..	..	..	..	..	11	1	10	..	..	..	1	..	1	..	..	..	1	1	..
..	..	..	..	..	..	10	..	10	..	..	..	1	1	..	..	..	..	13	12	1
..	..	..	..	..	..	12	1	11	..	..	..	1	..	1	..	..	..	38	36	2
..	..	..	1	1	..	30	7	23	..	..	..	8	3	5	..	..	..	109	103	6
..	..	..	..	..	..	**3**	..	**3**	..	..	..	..	..	..	..	..	..	**2**	**2**	..
..	..	..	..	..	..	1	..	1	..	..	..	..	..	..	..	..	..	..	..	..
..	..	..	..	..	..	..	..	..	..	..	..	..	..	..	..	..	..	..	..	..
..	..	..	..	..	..	..	..	..	..	..	..	..	..	..	..	..	..	..	..	..
..	..	..	..	..	..	2	..	2	..	..	..	..	..	..	..	..	..	2	2	..
..	..	..	..	..	..	**124**	**76**	**48**	..	..	..	..	..	..	..	..	..	**46**	**44**	**2**
..	..	..	..	..	..	5	5	..	..	..	..	..	..	..	..	..	..	1	1	..
..	..	..	..	..	..	17	5	12	..	..	..	..	..	..	..	..	..	2	2	..
..	..	..	..	..	..	15	5	10	..	..	..	..	..	..	..	..	..	11	10	1
..	..	..	..	..	..	87	61	26	..	..	..	..	..	..	..	..	..	32	31	1
..	..	..	..	..	..	**126**	**108**	**18**	..	..	..	**2**	..	**2**	..	..	..	**25**	**24**	**1**
..	..	..	..	..	..	2	1	1	..	..	..	..	..	..	..	..	..	..	..	..
..	..	..	..	..	..	9	6	3	..	..	..	2	..	2	..	..	..	1	1	..
..	..	..	..	..	..	16	10	6	..	..	..	..	..	..	..	..	..	4	3	1
..	..	..	..	..	..	99	91	8	..	..	..	..	..	..	..	..	..	20	20	..
..	..	..	..	..	..	..	..	..	..	..	..	..	..	..	**3**	**3**	..	..	..	..
..	..	..	..	..	..	..	..	..	..	..	..	..	..	..	..	..	..	..	..	..
..	..	..	..	..	..	..	..	..	..	..	..	..	..	..	..	..	..	..	..	..
..	..	..	..	..	..	..	..	..	..	..	..	..	..	..	..	..	..	..	..	..
..	..	..	..	..	..	..	..	..	..	..	..	..	..	..	3	3	..	..	..	..
41	**22**	**19**	**4**	**4**	..	**9**	**8**	**1**	..	..	..	..	..	..	**6**	**5**	**1**	**353**	**341**	**12**
3	..	3	..	..	..	..	..	..	..	..	..	..	..	..	..	..	..	6	6	..
2	..	2	..	..	..	..	..	..	..	..	..	..	..	..	..	..	..	36	35	1
4	2	2	..	..	..	..	..	..	..	..	..	..	..	..	..	..	..	102	98	4
32	20	12	4	4	..	9	8	1	..	..	..	..	..	..	6	5	1	209	202	7
..	..	..	**1**	..	**1**	..	..	..	..	..	..	**2**	..	**2**	..	..	..	**24**	**15**	**9**
..	..	..	1	..	1	..	..	..	..	..	..	2	..	2	..	..	..	11	8	3
..	..	..	..	..	..	..	..	..	..	..	..	..	..	..	..	..	..	6	3	3
..	..	..	..	..	..	..	..	..	..	..	..	..	..	..	..	..	..	7	4	3
..	..	..	..	..	..	..	..	..	..	..	..	..	..	..	..	..	..	..	..	..
CITY.																				
362	**326**	**36**	**49**	**48**	..	**182**	**137**	**45**	..	..	..	**125**	**102**	**23**	**1,087**	**1,054**	**33**	**5,054**	**4,905**	**149**
13	12	1	1	1	..	14	5	9	..	..	..	5	2	3	2	..	2	105	92	13
40	28	12	1	1	..	27	8	19	..	..	..	6	4	2	80	73	7	668	663	5
28	23	5	1	1	..	19	17	2	..	..	..	15	7	8	71	69	2	1,135	1,119	16
281	263	18	46	46	..	122	107	15	..	..	..	99	89	10	934	912	22	3,146	3,031	115
..	..	..	**48**	**48**	..	**169**	**128**	**41**	..	..	..	**38**	**27**	**11**	**1,083**	**1,052**	**32**	**4,129**	**4,083**	**46**
..	..	..	1	1	..	13	4	9	..	..	..	2	1	1	2	..	2	[illegible]	[illegible]	5
..	..	..	1	1	..	26	8	18	..	..	..	3	3	..	79	72	7	[illegible]	[illegible]	4
..	..	..	1	1	..	19	17	2	..	..	..	5	3	2	71	69	2	[illegible]	[illegible]	10
..	..	..	45	45	..	111	99	12	..	..	..	28	20	8	931	910	21	2,6[illegible]	[illegible]28	27

VIII
Education.

TABLE

EDUCATION BY

Jammu and Kashmir

Part III—

Age.	POPULATION. Total.			Literate.			Illiterate.			LITERATE. Urdu.			Persian.		
	Persons.	Males.	Females.	Persons.	Males.	Females.	Persons.	Males.	Females.	Persons.	Males.	Females.	Persons.	Males.	Females.
1	2	3	4	5	6	7	8	9	10	11	12	13	14	15	16
													(b)	SRIN	AGAR
Arya ..	**13**	**13**	..	**6**	**6**	..	**7**	**7**	..	**3**	**3**	..	..	..	..
0—10 ..	6	6	..	3	3	..	3	3	..	3	3	..	..	..	..
10—15 ..	2	2	..	..	..	..	2	2	..	..	..	..	..	..	..
15—20 ..	1	1	..	..	..	..	1	1	..	..	..	..	..	..	..
20 and over ..	4	4	..	3	3	..	1	1	..	..	..	..	..	..	..
Sikh ..	**541**	**361**	**180**	**182**	**163**	**19**	**359**	**198**	**161**	**34**	**31**	**3**	**1**	**1**	..
0—10 ..	107	54	53	8	4	4	99	50	49	3	2	1	..	..	..
10—15 ..	61	45	16	22	19	3	39	26	12	4	4	..	..	..	..
15—20 ..	54	27	27	21	16	5	33	11	22	6	6	..	..	..	..
20 and over ..	319	235	84	131	124	7	188	111	77	21	19	2	1	1	..
Buddhist ..	**1**	**1**	..	**1**	**1**	..	..	..	..	..	..	..	..	..	..
0—10 ..	..	..	..	..	..	..	..	..	..	..	..	..	..	..	..
10—15 ..	..	..	..	..	..	..	..	..	..	..	..	..	..	..	..
15—20 ..	..	..	..	..	..	..	..	..	..	..	..	..	..	..	..
20 and over ..	1	1	..	1	1	..	..	..	..	..	..	..	..	..	..
Zoroastrian ..	**2**	**2**	..	**2**	**2**	..	..	..	..	..	..	..	..	..	..
0—10 ..	..	..	..	..	..	..	..	..	..	..	..	..	..	..	..
10—15 ..	..	..	..	..	..	..	..	..	..	..	..	..	..	..	..
15—20 ..	1	1	..	1	1	..	..	..	..	..	..	..	..	..	..
20 and over ..	1	1	..	1	1	..	..	..	..	..	..	..	..	..	..
Musalman ..	**110,935**	**59,579**	**51,356**	**2,536**	**2,425**	**111**	**108,399**	**57,154**	**51,245**	**865**	**812**	**53**	**624**	**617**	**7**
0—10 ..	29,778	14,605	15,173	76	74	2	29,702	14,531	[illegible]	43	42	1	6	6	..
10—15 ..	14,298	8,181	6,117	312	287	25	13,986	7,894	[illegible]	159	147	12	20	20	..
15—20 ..	9,576	5,088	4,488	337	323	14	9,239	4,765	[illegible]	90	87	3	31	31	..
20 and over ..	57,283	31,705	25,578	1,811	1,741	70	55,472	29,964	[illegible]	573	536	37	567	560	7
Christian ..	**238**	**133**	**105**	**194**	**106**	**88**	**44**	**27**	[illegible]	**1**	**1**	..	**2**	**2**	..
0—10 ..	31	18	13	10	3	7	21	15	[illegible]	1	1	..	1	1	..
10—15 ..	3	2	1	2	2	..	1	..	[illegible]	..	..	..	1	1	..
15—20 ..	10	9	1	10	9	1	..	..	..	..	..	..	..	..	..
20 and over ..	194	104	90	172	92	80	22	12	[illegible]	..	..	..	..	..	..
Others ..	**1**	..	**1**	**1**	..	**1**	..	..	..	..	..	..	..	..	..
0—10 ..	..	..	..	..	..	..	..	..	..	..	..	..	..	..	..
10—15 ..	..	..	..	..	..	..	..	..	..	..	..	..	..	..	..
15—20 ..	..	..	..	..	..	..	..	..	..	..	..	..	..	..	..
20 and over ..	1	..	1	1	..	1	..	..	..	..	..	..	..	..	..

VIII.

RELIGION AND AGE.

State Census 1921.

City Tables.

VIII
Education.

ATE IN.

Arabic.			Dogri.			Hindi.			Budhi.			Gurmukhi.			Others.			English.		
Persons.	Males.	Females.	Persons.	Males.	Females.	Persons.	Males.	Females.	Persons.	Males.	Females.	Persons.	Males.	Females.	Persons.	Males.	Females.	Persons.	Males.	Females.
17	18	19	20	21	22	23	24	25	26	27	28	29	30	31	32	33	34	35	36	37
CITY,																				
..	..	..	..	..	..	..	..	..	..	..	..	..	..	..	..	..	..	**3**	**3**	..
..	..	..	..	..	..	..	..	..	..	..	..	..	..	..	..	..	..	..	..	..
..	..	..	..	..	..	..	..	..	..	..	..	..	..	..	..	..	..	..	..	..
..	..	..	..	..	..	..	..	..	..	..	..	..	..	..	..	..	..	..	..	..
..	..	..	..	..	..	..	..	..	..	..	..	..	..	..	..	..	..	3	3	..
..	..	..	..	..	..	**10**	**7**	**3**	..	..	..	**85**	**74**	**11**	**2**	**2**	..	**50**	**48**	**2**
..	..	..	..	..	..	1	1	..	..	..	..	2	..	2	..	..	..	2	1	1
..	..	..	..	..	..	1	..	1	..	..	..	3	1	2	..	..	..	14	14	..
..	..	..	..	..	..	..	..	..	..	..	..	9	4	5	..	..	..	6	6	..
..	..	..	..	..	..	8	6	2	..	..	..	71	69	2	2	2	..	28	27	1
..	..	..	..	..	..	..	..	..	..	..	..	..	..	..	..	..	..	**1**	**1**	..
..	..	..	..	..	..	..	..	..	..	..	..	..	..	..	..	..	..	..	..	..
..	..	..	..	..	..	..	..	..	..	..	..	..	..	..	..	..	..	..	..	..
..	..	..	..	..	..	..	..	..	..	..	..	..	..	..	..	..	..	..	..	..
..	..	..	..	..	..	..	..	..	..	..	..	..	..	..	..	..	..	1	1	..
..	..	..	..	..	..	..	..	..	..	..	..	..	..	..	..	..	..	**2**	**2**	..
..	..	..	..	..	..	..	..	..	..	..	..	..	..	..	..	..	..	..	..	..
..	..	..	..	..	..	..	..	..	..	..	..	..	..	..	..	..	..	..	..	..
..	..	..	..	..	..	..	..	..	..	..	..	..	..	..	..	..	..	1	1	..
..	..	..	..	..	..	..	..	..	..	..	..	..	..	..	..	..	..	1	1	..
362	**326**	**36**	**1**	**1**	..	**3**	**2**	**1**	..	..	..	**2**	**1**	**1**	**2**	**1**	**1**	**677**	**665**	**12**
13	12	1	..	..	..	..	..	..	..	..	..	1	1	..	..	..	..	13	13	..
40	28	12	..	..	..	..	..	..	..	..	..	..	..	..	1	1	..	92	91	1
28	23	5	..	..	..	..	..	..	..	..	..	1	..	1	..	..	..	187	182	5
281	263	18	1	1	..	3	2	1	..	..	..	..	..	..	1	..	1	385	379	6
..	..	..	..	..	..	..	..	..	..	..	..	..	..	..	..	..	..	**191**	**103**	**88**
..	..	..	..	..	..	..	..	..	..	..	..	..	..	..	..	..	..	8	1	7
..	..	..	..	..	..	..	..	..	..	..	..	..	..	..	..	..	..	1	1	..
..	..	..	..	..	..	..	..	..	..	..	..	..	..	..	..	..	..	10	9	1
..	..	..	..	..	..	..	..	..	..	..	..	..	..	..	..	..	..	172	92	80
..	..	..	..	..	..	..	..	..	..	..	..	..	..	..	..	..	..	**1**	..	**1**
..	..	..	..	..	..	..	..	..	..	..	..	..	..	..	..	..	..	..	..	..
..	..	..	..	..	..	..	..	..	..	..	..	..	..	..	..	..	..	..	..	..
..	..	..	..	..	..	..	..	..	..	..	..	..	..	..	..	..	..	..	..	..
..	..	..	..	..	..	..	..	..	..	..	..	..	..	..	..	..	..	1	..	1

TABLE IX.

EDUCATION BY SELECTED CASTES, TRIBES OR RACES.

Jammu and Kashmir State Census 1921.

1. This Table and Tables XIV and XXI deal only with a few typical castes among Hindus (including Aryas and Brahmos) and Musalmans, selected with reference to their suitability to the subject of the tables concerned. The present selection differs in some respects from that of the last Census.

2. The figures for Christians and Sikhs do not appear in Tables IX and XIV, as their literacy and civil condition have been dealt with in Tables VIII and VII respectively.

3. The totals of certain castes in this Table and in Table XII A, XIV and XXI will correspond to the totals for those castes in Table XIII by adding the caste totals of Frontier *Ilaqas*.

TABLE IX.

Education by Selected Castes, Tribes or Races.

Jammu and Kashmir State Census 1921.

Caste, Tribe or Race.	Population.									Literate in English.		
	Total.			*Literate.*			*Illiterate.*					
	Persons.	Males.	Females.	Persons.	Males.	Females.	Persons.	Males.	Females.	Persons.	Males.	Females.
1	2	3	4	5	6	7	8	9	10	11	12	13
					HINDU.							
Brahman ..	172,051	89,205	82,846	8,032	7,797	235	164,019	81,408	82,611	531	522	9
Jat	25,861	13,342	12,519	333	329	4	25,528	13,013	12,515	11	11	..
Kashmiri Pandit ..	55,052	30,944	24,108	14,749	14,465	284	40,303	16,479	23,824	5,154	5,104	50
Khatri ..	18,758	11,061	7,697	4,534	3,934	600	14,224	7,127	7,097	1,052	1,023	29
Mahajan ..	19,888	11,199	8,689	3,860	3,734	126	16,028	7,465	8,563	243	237	6
Megh	78,808	41,080	37,728	265	257	8	78,543	40,823	37,720	4	4	..
Mohyal ..	2,494	1,312	1,182	503	437	66	1,991	875	1,116	106	102	4
Rajput.. ..	48,994	28,331	20,663	3,416	3,336	80	45,578	24,995	20,583	309	303	6
Thakkar ..	92,025	48,951	43,074	1,602	1,576	26	90,423	47,375	43,048	70	66	4
					MUSALMAN.							
Arain	26,370	15,644	10,726	404	390	14	25,966	15,254	10,712	19	17	2
Balti	124,727	61,762	62,965	568	557	11	124,159	61,205	62,954	6	6	..
Gujjar	359,076	189,349	169,727	1,159	1,110	49	357,917	188,239	169,678	17	17	..
Jat	102,649	52,514	50,135	524	513	11	102,125	52,001	50,124	21	20	1
Kashmiri ..	796,392	428,452	367,940	5,231	5,031	200	791,158	423,418	367,740	340	335	5
Mughal ..	34,281	17,845	16,436	484	459	25	33,797	17,386	16,411	54	53	1
Pathan ..	31,775	17,282	14,493	573	542	31	31,202	16,740	14,462	57	55	2
Rajput ..	172,584	84,713	87,871	2,343	2,249	94	170,241	82,464	8,777	130	128	2
Sheikh ..	102,846	56,959	45,887	1,870	1,747	123	100,976	55,212	45,764	204	199	5
Yashkun ..	16,596	8,841	7,755	155	152	3	16,441	8,869	7,752	..	..	..
					BUDDHIST.							
Mangriks (Bhots) ..	33,183	16,193	16,990	1,095	1,061	34	32,088	15,132	16,956	4	4	..

TABLE X.

LANGUAGE.

Jammu and Kashmir State Census 1921.

1. This table which gives the territorial and philological presentation of languages, arranged according to their family affinity, is composed of the following parts :—

Part I—Languages of the State.
,, II— ,, India.
,, III— ,, Asia.
,, IV— ,, Europe.

2. Contrary to local instructions dialects were also returned here and there and those important among them have been shown in this table under the main languages to which they appear to belong.

3. Sansi and Bazigari were the only gipsy languages returned, which have been shown under the head "Unclassified" at the end of Part IV. Labhani was also treated as such at the last Census; but this time, it has, on the authority of Dr. Grierson's Linguistic Survey of India, been shown under Rajasthani of which it is a dialect.

4. The population dealt with in this Table falls short of that in Kashmir Table I by 60,991 persons, who were enumerated in the Frontier Ilaqas where language was not recorded.

TABLE X.

LANGUAGE.

Jammu and Kashmir State Census 1921.

Part I—Languages of the State.

District Jagir or Ilaqa.	Population.			Tibeto Chinese Family. Tibeto-Burman Sub-Family. Tibeto-Himalayan Branch. Tibetan Group. Bhotia.																		Indo-European Family. Aryan Sub-Family. Dardic Branch. Khowar Group.		
				Total.			Balti.			Bhotia.			Ladakhi.			Tibetan.			Chitrali.		
	Persons.	Males.	Females.	Persons.	Males.	Females.	Persons.	Males.	Females.	Persons.	Males.	Females.	Persons.	Males.	Females.	Persons.	Males.	Females.	Persons.	Males.	Females.
1	2	3	4	5	6	7	8	9	10	11	12	13	14	15	16	17	18	19	20	21	22
Kashmir State	**3,259,527**	**1,724,581**	**1,534,946**	**181,739**	**91,023**	**90,716**	**148,356**	**74,116**	**74,240**	**3**	**3**	..	**33,174**	**16 701**	**16,473**	**206**	**203**	**3**	**111**	**111**	..
I—Jammu Province (including *Jagirs*) ..	**1,640,259**	**859,619**	**780,640**	**700**	**467**	**233**	**44**	**33**	**11**	**3**	**3**	..	**442**	**223**	**219**	**206**	**203**	**3**	..	..	..
1. Jammu District (including City) ..	334,834	182,681	152,153	23	18	5	20	15	5	3	3	..	..	..	..	..	..	..	..	..	..
2. Kathua District	154,209	82,467	71,742	4	3	1	4	3	1	..	..	..	..	..	..	..	..	..	..	..	..
3. Udhampur (including Chaneni *Jagir*) ..	218,261	115,135	103,126	478	255	223	1	..	1	..	..	..	446	227	219	31	28	3	..	..	..
4. Riasi District	224,589	118,576	106,014	10	6	4	10	6	4	..	..	..	..	..	..	..	..	..	..	..	..
5. Mirpur „	318,971	160,186	158,785	..	..	..	..	..	..	..	..	..	..	..	..	..	..	..	..	..	..
6. Bhadarwah *Jagir*	37,614	19,227	18,387	1	1	..	..	..	..	..	..	..	1	1	..	..	..	..	..	..	..
7. Punch *Ilaqa*	351,781	181,348	170,433	184	184	..	9	9	..	..	..	..	..	..	..	175	175	..	..	..	..
II—Kashmir Province (including *Jagirs*) ..	**1,407,086**	**757,824**	**649,262**	**556**	**384**	**172**	**488**	**335**	**153**	..	..	..	**68**	**49**	**19**	..	..	..	**1**	**1**	..
8. Kashmir North (including Langet *Jagir*) ..	502,490	269,685	232,805	59	42	17	58	41	17	..	..	..	1	1	..	..	..	..	..	..	..
9. Kashmir South (including City) ..	688,487	372,459	316,028	434	280	154	367	232	135	..	..	..	67	48	19	..	..	..	1	1	..
10. Muzaffarabad District	216,109	115,680	100,429	63	62	1	63	62	1	..	..	..	..	..	..	..	..	..	..	..	..
III—Frontier Districts	**212,182**	**107,138**	**105,044**	**180,483**	**90,172**	**90,311**	**147,824**	**73,748**	**74,076**	..	..	..	**32,659**	**16,424**	**16,235**	..	..	..	**110**	**110**	..
11. Ladakh District (including Mansar) ..	183,476	91,258	92,218	178,890	88,726	90,164	146,382	72,453	73,929	..	..	..	32,508	16,273	16,235	..	..	..	..	..	..
12. Gilgit District	28,706	15,880	12,826	1,593	1,446	147	1,442	1,295	147	..	..	..	151	151	..	..	..	..	110	110	..

TABLE X.

LANGUAGE.

Jammu and Kashmir State Census 1921.

Part I—Languages of the State.—*continued.*

District, Jagir or Ilaqa.	Indo-European Family. Aryan Sub-Family. Dardic Branch. Dard Group.																	
	DARDISTANI.			KOHISTANI.									KASHMIRI.					
				Total.			*Bambagi.*			*Kaghani.*			*Total.*			*Banjwahi.*		
	Persons.	Males.	Females.	Persons.	Males.	Females.	Persons.	Males.	Females.	Persons.	Males.	Females.	Persons.	Males.	Females.	Persons.	Males.	Females.
	23	24	25	26	27	28	29	30	31	32	33	34	35	36	37	38	39	40
Kashmir State	**5,891**	**2,944**	**2,947**	**6,640**	**3,371**	**3,269**	**694**	**80**	**614**	**5,946**	**3,291**	**2,655**	**1,256,986**	**679,391**	**577,595**	**230**	**115**	**115**
I—Jammu Province (including *Jagirs*)	..	..	..	**5,601**	**2,819**	**2,782**	**692**	**78**	**614**	**4,909**	**2,741**	**2,168**	**135,229**	**75,793**	**59,436**	**230**	**115**	**115**
1. Jammu District (including City)	..	..	..	118	109	9	..	..	..	118	109	9	1,426	1,188	238	..	..	..
2. Kathua "	..	..	..	371	215	156	..	..	..	371	215	156	2,099	961	1,138	..	..	..
3. Udhampur (including Chanoni *Jagir*)	..	..	..	341	175	166	10	..	10	331	175	156	88,403	46,678	41,725	230	115	115
4. Riasi District	..	..	..	3,991	1,929	2,062	682	78	604	3,309	1,851	1,458	12,559	10,416	2,143	..	..	..
5. Mirpur "	..	..	..	306	136	170	..	..	..	306	136	170	86	75	11	..	..	..
6. Bhadarwah *Jagir*	..	..	..	4	2	2	..	..	..	4	2	2	11,438	5,947	5,541	..	..	..
7. Punch *Ilaqa*	..	..	..	470	253	217	..	..	..	470	253	217	19,168	10,528	8,640	..	..	..
II—Kashmir Province (including *Jagirs*)	**5,891**	**2,944**	**2,947**	**1,039**	**552**	**487**	**2**	**2**	..	**1,037**	**550**	**487**	**1,120,561**	**602,825**	**517,736**	..	..	..
8. Kashmir North (including Langet *Jagir*)	5,773	2,867	2,906	139	80	59	..	..	..	139	80	59	452,387	242,796	209,591	..	..	..
9. Kashmir South (including City)	118	77	41	894	468	426	2	2	..	892	466	426	648,970	350,839	298,131	..	..	..
10. Muzaffarabad District	..	..	..	6	4	2	..	..	..	6	4	2	19,204	9,190	10,014	..	..	..
III—Frontier Districts	..	..	..	..	..	..	..	..	..	..	..	..	**1,196**	**773**	**423**	..	..	..
11. Ladakh District (including Mansar)	..	..	..	..	..	..	..	..	..	..	..	..	995	577	418	..	..	..
12. Gilgit "	..	..	..	..	..	..	..	..	..	..	..	..	201	196	5	..	..	..

TABLE X.

LANGUAGE.

Jammu and Kashmir State Census 1921.

Part I—Languages of the State—*continued.*

District, Jagir or Ilaqa.	Indo-European Family. Aryan Sub-Family. Dardic Branch. Dard Group. Kashmiri.														
	Kashmiri.			*Kashtawari.*			*Poguli.*			*Rambani.*			*Siraji.*		
	Persons.	Males.	Females.	Persons.	Males.	Females.	Persons.	Males.	Females.	Persons.	Males.	Females.	Persons.	Males.	Females.
	41	42	43	44	45	46	47	48	49	50	51	52	53	54	55
Kashmir State	**1,221,110**	**661,122**	**559,988**	**10,722**	**5,499**	**5,223**	**10,233**	**5,265**	**4,968**	**139**	**79**	**60**	**14,552**	**7,311**	**7,241**
I—Jammu Province (including *Jagirs*) ..	**99,358**	**57,529**	**41,829**	**10,717**	**5,494**	**5,223**	**10,233**	**5,265**	**4,968**	**139**	**79**	**60**	**14,552**	**7,311**	**7,241**
1. Jammu District (including City) ..	1,411	1,176	235	15	12	3	..	..	..	..	..	..	..	..	..
2. Kathua "	2,098	960	1,138	1	1	..	..	..	..	..	..	..	..	..	..
3. Udampur (including Chaneni *Jagir*)	52,610	28,474	24,136	10,695	5,475	5,220	10,218	5,250	4,968	134	79	55	14,516	7,285	7,231
4. Riasi District..	12,512	10,382	2,130	..	..	..	15	15	..	5	..	5	27	19	8
5. Mirpur "	86	75	11	..	..	..	..	..	..	..	..	..	..	..	..
6. Bhadarwah *Jagir*	11,473	5,934	5,539	6	6	..	..	..	..	..	..	..	9	7	2
7. Punch *Ilaqa*	19,168	10,528	8,640	..	..	..	..	..	..	..	..	..	..	..	..
II—Kashmir Province (including *Jagirs*) ..	**1,120,558**	**602,822**	**517,736**	**3**	**3**	..	..	..	..	..	..	..	..	..	..
8. Kashmir North (including Langet *Jagir*).	452,387	242,796	209,591	..	..	..	..	..	..	..	..	..	..	..	..
9. Kashmir South (including City) ..	648,967	350,836	298,131	3	3	..	..	..	..	..	..	..	..	..	..
10. Muzaffarabad District	19,204	9,190	10,014	..	..	..	..	..	..	..	..	..	..	..	..
III—Frontier Districts	**1,194**	**771**	**423**	**2**	**2**	..	..	..	..	..	..	..	..	..	..
11. Laddakh District (including Mansar)	994	576	418	1	1	..	..	..	..	..	..	..	..	..	..
12. Gilgit "	200	195	5	1	1	..	..	..	..	..	..	..	..	..	..

TABLE X.

LANGUAGE.

Jammu and Kashmir State Census 1921.

Part I.—Languages of the State—*continued.*

District, Jagir or Ilaqa.	Indo-European Family. *Aryan Sub-Family.* Dardic Branch. *Dard Group.* Shina.			Outer Sub-Branch. (Sanskrit) *North Western Group.* Lahnda (Chibhali).			Inner Sub-Branch. *Central Group.* Punjabi. *Dogri.*			Rajasthani. *Gojari.*			*Pahari Group.* Western Pahari. *Total.*			*Bahadarwahi.*		
	Persons.	Males.	Females.	Persons.	Males.	Females.	Persons.	Males.	Females.	Persons.	Males.	Females.	Persons.	Males.	Females.	Persons.	Males.	Females.
	56	57	58	59	60	61	62	63	64	65	66	67	68	69	70	71	72	73
Kashmir State	28,478	14,351	14,127	86,050	44,622	41,428	524,850	282,254	242,596	289,485	154,680	134,805	536,059	273,141	262,918	21,650	10,876	10,774
I—Jammu Province (including *Jagirs*) ..	..	..	..	86,043	44,615	41,428	522,982	280,737	242,245	198,611	104,124	94,487	370,184	185,379	184,805	21,628	10,864	10,764
1. Jammu District (including City) ..	..	..	..	23	23	..	227,967	123,010	104,957	21,640	12,116	9,524	1,230	624	606	34	34	..
2. Kathua "	..	..	..	1	1	..	120,679	64,857	55,822	13,880	7,255	6,625	13,786	7,178	6,608	172	157	15
3. Udhampur (including Chaneni *Jagir*)	..	..	..	218	6	212	86,804	45,984	40,820	17,415	9,208	8,207	22,241	11,377	10,864	142	111	31
4. Riasi District	..	..	..	14,711	7,515	7,196	55,067	29,855	25,212	69,149	33,885	35,264	65,154	32,661	32,493	424	38	386
5. Mirpur "	..	..	..	71,086	37,070	34,016	28,880	15,172	13,708	9,789	5,161	4,628	2,618	1,437	1,181	..	..	..
6. Bhadarwah *Jagir*	..	..	..	..	..	..	2,611	1,369	1,242	2,002	1,028	974	21,350	10,769	10,581	20,856	10,524	10,332
7. Punch *Ilaqa*..	..	..	..	4	..	4	974	490	484	64,736	35,471	29,265	243,805	121,333	122,472	..	..	..
II—Kashmir Province (including *Jagirs*)	5	5	..	..	..	..	1,505	1,158	347	90,644	50,326	40,318	165,832	87,732	78,100	2	2	..
8. Kashmir North (including Langet *Jagir*).	1	1	..	..	..	..	40	12	28	24,272	13,141	11,131	8,633	4,849	3,784	..	..	..
9. Kashmir South (including City) ..	4	4	..	..	..	..	1,317	999	318	25,857	13,826	12,031	2,932	1,406	1,526	2	2	..
10 Muzaffarabad District	..	..	..	..	..	..	148	147	1	40,515	23,359	17,156	154,267	81,477	72,790	..	..	..
III—Frontier Districts	28,473	14,346	14,127	7	7	..	363	359	4	230	230	..	43	30	13	20	10	10
11. Laddakh District (including Mansar)	3,171	1,639	1,532	..	..	..	30	26	4	..	..	..	36	26	10	20	10	10
12. Gilgit "	25,302	12,707	12,595	7	7	..	333	333	..	230	230	..	7	4	3	..	..	..

TABLE X.

LANGUAGE.

Jammu and Kashmir State Census 1921.

Part I.—Languages of the State—*concluded.*

Indo-European Family. — Inner Sub-Branch. — *Aryan Sub-Family.* — Pahari Group. — WESTERN PAHARI.

District, Jagir or Ilaqa.	*Bhujwali.*			*Budhali.*			*Gadi.*			*Padari.*			*Pahari.*			*Sarori.*		
	Persons.	Males.	Females.	Persons.	Males.	Females.	Persons.	Males.	Females.	Persons.	Males.	Females.	Persons.	Males.	Females.	Persons.	Males.	Females.
	74	75	76	77	78	79	80	81	82	83	84	85	86	87	88	89	90	91
Kashmir State	2	..	2	506	257	249	11,050	5,468	5,582	5,252	2,654	2,598	496,590	253,314	243,276	1,009	572	437
I.—Jammu Province (including *Jagirs*)	2	..	2	506	257	249	11,050	5,468	5,582	5,252	2,654	2,598	330,737	165,564	165,173	1,009	572	437
1. Jammu District (including City)	..	..	..	..	..	..	21	21	..	..	..	..	1,175	569	606	..	..	..
2. Kathua ,, ...	..	..	..	..	..	..	5,759	2,937	2,822	..	..	..	7,855	4,084	3,771	..	..	..
3. Udhampur ,, (including Chaneni *Jagir*).	..	..	..	..	..	..	4,743	2,250	2,493	5,251	2,654	2,597	11,096	5,790	5,306	1,009	572	437
4. Riasi District	2	..	2	506	257	249	34	15	19	..	..	..	64,188	32,351	31,837	..	..	..
5. Mirpur ,, ...	..	..	..	..	..	..	..	..	..	..	..	..	2,618	1,437	1,181	..	..	..
6. Bhadarwah *Jagir* ..	..	..	..	..	..	..	493	245	24	1	..	1	..	..	..	..	..	..
7. Punch *Ilaqa*	..	..	..	..	..	..	..	..	..	..	..	..	243,805	121,333	122,472	..	..	..
II—Kashmir Province (including *Jagirs.*)	..	..	..	..	..	..	..	..	..	..	..	..	165,830	87,730	78,100	..	..	..
8. Kashmir North (including Langet *Jagir*).	..	..	..	..	..	..	..	..	..	..	..	..	8,633	4,849	3,784	..	..	..
9. Kashmir South (including City)	..	..	..	..	..	..	..	..	..	..	..	..	2,930	1,404	1,526	..	..	..
10. Muzaffarabad District ..	..	..	..	..	..	..	..	..	..	..	..	..	154,267	81,477	72,790	..	..	..
III—Frontier Districts ..	..	..	..	..	..	..	..	..	..	..	..	..	23	20	3	..	..	..
11. Ladakh District (including Mansar.)	..	..	..	..	..	..	..	..	..	..	..	..	16	16	..	..	..	..
12. Gilgit	..	..	..	..	..	..	..	..	..	..	..	..	7	4	3	..	..	..

TABLE X.

LANGUAGE.

Jammu and Kashmir State Census 1921.

Part II.—Languages of India.

District, Jagir or Ilaqa.	Dravidian Family — Dravida Group — *Tamil.* Persons.	Males.	Females.	Indo-European Family — Aryan Sub-Family — Indo-Aryan Branch — Outer Sub-Branch — North Western Group — Lahnda — *Pothwari.* Persons.	Males.	Females.	Sindhi — *Total.* Persons.	Males.	Females.	*Kachchi.* Persons.	Males.	Females.	*Sindhi.* Persons.	Males.	Females.	Southern Group — Marathi — *Kulvadi.* Persons.	Males.	Females.	Eastern Group — *Bengali.* Persons.	Males.	Females.
1	2	3	4	5	6	7	8	9	10	11	12	13	14	15	16	17	18	19	20	21	22
Kashmir State	7	4	3	92,724	44,411	48,313	9	8	1	2	1	1	7	7	..	19	12	7	45	24	21
I—Jammu Province (including *Jagirs*) ..	3	3	..	92,721	44,408	48,313	9	8	1	2	1	1	7	7	..	19	12	7	37	24	13
1. Jammu District (including City) ..	..	..	..	160	34	126	5	5	..	..	..	..	5	5	..	..	..	..	37	24	13
2. Kathua "	..	..	..	62	5	57	2	1	1	2	1	1	..	..	..	17	10	7	..	..	..
3. Udhampur " (including Chaneni *Jagir*)	3	3	..	70	60	10	..	..	..	..	..	..	..	..	..	2	2	..	..	..	..
4. Riasi "	..	..	..	13	..	13	..	..	..	..	..	..	..	..	..	..	..	..	..	..	..
5. Mirpur "	..	..	..	89,404	42,702	46,702	..	..	..	..	..	..	..	..	..	..	..	..	..	..	..
6. Bhadarwah *Jagir*	..	..	..	..	..	..	..	..	..	..	..	..	..	..	..	..	..	..	..	..	..
7. Punch *Ilaqa*	..	..	..	3,012	1,607	1,405	2	2	..	..	..	..	2	2	..	..	..	..	..	..	..
II—Kashmir Province (including *Jagirs*)	3	..	3	1	1	..	..	..	..	..	..	..	..	..	..	..	..	..	8	..	8
8. Kashmir North (including Langet *Jagir*).	..	..	..	..	..	..	..	..	..	..	..	..	..	..	..	..	..	..	..	..	..
9. Kashmir South (including City) ..	3	..	3	1	1	..	..	..	..	..	..	..	..	..	..	..	..	..	8	..	..
10. Muzaffarabad District ..	..	..	..	..	..	..	..	..	..	..	..	..	..	..	..	..	..	..	..	..	..
III—Frontier Districts	1	1	..	2	2	..	..	..	..	..	..	..	..	..	..	..	..	..	..	..	..
11. Ladakh District (including Mansar)	..	..	..	..	..	..	..	..	..	..	..	..	..	..	..	..	..	..	..	..	..
12. Gilgit "	1	1	..	2	2	..	..	..	..	..	..	..	..	..	..	..	..	..	..	..	..

TABLE X.

LANGUAGE.

Jammu and Kashmir State Census 1921.

Part II.—Languages of India—*continued.*

District, Ilaqa or Jagir.	*Indo-European Family.* Aryan Sub-Family. *Indo-Aryan Branch.* Mediate Sub-Branch. MEDIATE GROUP. Eastern Hindi.			*Indo-European Family.* Aryan Sub-Family. *Indo Aryan Branch.* Inner Sub-Branch. CENTRAL GROUP. Gujrati.												Punjabi.		
	Purbi.			*Total.*			*Gujrati.*			*Khatri (Patnuli).*			*Malvi.*			*Total.*		
	Persons.	Males.	Females.	Persons.	Males.	Females.	Persons.	Males.	Females.	Persons.	Males.	Females.	Persons.	Males.	Females.	Persons.	Males.	Females.
	23	24	25	26	27	28	29	30	31	32	33	34	35	36	37	38	39	40
Total of State ...	**16**	**7**	**9**	**423**	**115**	**308**	**13**	**7**	**6**	**409**	**107**	**302**	**1**	**1**	..	**241,439**	**128,232**	**113,207**
I—Jammu Province (including *Jagirs*).	**16**	**7**	**9**	**422**	**114**	**308**	**12**	**6**	**6**	**409**	**107**	**302**	**1**	**1**	..	**221,399**	**116,993**	**105,006**
1. Jammu District (including City)	16	7	9	..	..	..	..	..	..	..	..	..	..	..	..	78,200	42,609	35,591
2. Kathua "	..	..	..	1	1	..	..	..	..	..	..	..	1	1	..	2,812	1,656	1,156
3. Udhampur " (including Chaneni *Jagir*).	..	..	..	409	107	302	..	..	..	409	107	302	..	..	..	1,524	1,030	494
4. Riasi "	..	..	..	..	..	..	..	..	..	..	..	..	..	..	..	3,785	2,211	1,574
5. Mirpur "	..	..	..	..	..	..	..	..	..	..	..	..	..	..	..	116,704	58,371	58,333
6. Bhadarwah *Jagir*	..	..	..	..	..	..	..	..	..	..	..	..	..	..	..	90	75	15
7. Punch *Ilaqa*	..	..	..	12	6	6	12	6	6	..	..	..	..	..	..	18,884	11,041	7,843
II—Kashmir Province (including *Jagirs*).	..	..	..	1	1	..	1	1	..	..	..	..	..	..	..	**18,592**	**10,510**	**8,082**
8. Kashmir North (including Langet *Jagir*).	..	..	..	..	..	..	..	..	..	..	..	..	..	..	..	10,779	5,668	5,111
9. Kashmir South (including City)	..	..	..	1	1	..	1	1	..	..	..	..	..	..	..	6,237	3,646	2,591
10. Muzaffarabad District ..	..	..	..	..	..	..	..	..	..	..	..	..	..	..	..	1,576	1,196	380
III—Frontier Districts	..	..	..	..	..	..	..	..	..	..	..	..	..	..	..	**848**	**729**	**119**
11. Ladakh District (including Mansar).	..	..	..	..	..	..	..	..	..	..	..	..	..	..	..	237	178	59
12. Gilgit "	..	..	..	..	..	..	..	..	..	..	..	..	..	..	..	611	551	60

TABLE X.

LANGUAGE.

Jammu and Kashmir State Census 1921.

Part II.—Languages of India—*continued.*

District, Jagir or Ilaqa.	Indo-European Family. — Aryan Sub-Family. — Indo Aryan Branch. — Inner Sub-Branch. — CENTRAL GROUP.																	
	Punjabi.												Rajasthani.					
	Kangri.			*Powadhi.*			*Punjabi.*			*Bathi.*			*Total.*			*Jodhpuri.*		
	Persons.	Males.	Females.	Persons.	Males.	Females.	Persons.	Males.	Females.	Persons.	Males.	Females.	Persons.	Males.	Females.	Persons.	Males.	Females.
	41	42	43	44	45	46	47	48	49	50	51	52	53	54	55	56	57	58
Kashmir State ..	745	200	545	22	4	18	240,669	128,025	112,644	3	3	..	2,117	1,553	564	6	3	3
I.—Jammu Province (including *Jagirs*).	687	145	542	22	4	18	221,287	116,841	104,446	3	3	..	2,116	1,552	564	6	3	3
1. Jammu District (including City)	532	2	530	..	..	..	77,668	42,607	35,061	..	..	..	1.907	1,433	474	6	3	3
2. Kathua „	7	7	..	22	4	18	2,780	1,642	1,138	3	3	..	160	88	72	..	..	..
3. Udhampur „ (including Chanani *Jagir*).	133	133	..	..	..	..	1,391	897	494	..	..	..	..	..	..	..	..	..
4. Riasi District	7	..	7	..	..	..	3,778	2,211	1,567	..	..	..	49	31	18	..	..	..
5. Mirpur District	8	3	5	..	..	..	116,696	58,368	58,328	..	..	..	..	..	..	..	..	..
6. Bhadarwah *Jagir*	..	..	..	..	..	..	90	75	15	..	..	..	..	..	..	..	..	..
7. Punch *Ilaqa*	..	..	..	..	..	..	18,884	11,041	7,843	..	..	..	..	..	..	..	..	..
II.—Kashmir Province (including *Jagirs*).	56	54	2	..	..	..	18,536	10,456	8,080	..	..	..	..	..	..	..	..	..
8. Kashmir North (including Langet *Jagir*.)	..	..	..	..	..	..	10,779	5,668	5,111	..	..	..	..	..	..	..	..	..
9. Kashmir South (including City)	3	1	2	..	..	..	6,234	3,645	2,589	..	..	..	..	..	..	..	..	..
10. Muzaffarabad District ..	53	53	..	..	..	..	1,523	1,143	380	..	..	..	..	..	..	..	..	..
III.—Frontier Districts.. ..	2	1	1	..	..	..	846	728	118	..	..	..	1	1	..	..	..	..
11. Ladakh District (including Manvar).	2	1	1	..	..	..	235	177	58	..	..	..	1	1	..	..	..	..
12. Gilgit „	..	..	..	..	..	..	611	551	60	..	..	..	..	..	..	..	..	..

TABLE X.

Language.

Jammu and Kashmir State Census 1921.

Part II.—Languages of India.—*continued.*

District, Jagir or Ilaqa.	Indo-European Family. Aryan Sub-Family. Indo-Aryan Branch. Inner Sub-Branch. Central Group.																	
	Rajasthani.						Western Hindi.											
	Lubhani.			*Marwari.*			*Total.*			*Bundhelkhandi.*			*Hindi.*			*Hindustani.*		
	Persons.	Males.	Females.	Persons.	Males.	Females.	Persons.	Males.	Females.	Persons.	Males.	Females.	Persons.	Males.	Females.	Persons.	Males.	Females.
	59	60	61	62	63	64	65	66	67	68	69	70	71	72	73	74	75	76
Kashmir State ..	**1,957**	**1,484**	**473**	**154**	**66**	**88**	**2,071**	**1,420**	**651**	**1**	**1**	..	**265**	**158**	**107**	**749**	**599**	**150**
I.—Jammu Province (including *Jagirs*).	**1,957**	**1,484**	**473**	**153**	**65**	**88**	**1,388**	**969**	**429**	**1**	**1**	..	**186**	**98**	**88**	**749**	**599**	**150**
1. Jammu District (including City)	1,748	1,365	383	153	65	88	1,099	772	327	..	..	..	171	92	79	564	480	84
2. Kathua "	160	88	72	..	..	..	43	40	3	..	..	..	..	..	..	43	40	3
3. Udampur " (including Chaneni *Jagir*).	..	..	..	..	..	..	52	42	10	1	1	..	3	3	..	14	14	..
4. Riasi District	49	31	18	..	..	..	35	23	12	..	..	..	8	..	8	12	12	..
5. Mirpur "	..	..	..	..	..	..	82	51	31	..	..	..	..	..	..	72	45	27
6. Bhadarwah *Jagir*	..	..	..	..	..	..	2	2	..	..	..	..	..	..	..	..	..	..
7. Punch *Ilaqa*	..	..	..	..	..	..	85	39	46	..	..	..	4	3	1	44	8	36
II.—Kashmir Province (including *Jagirs*).	..	..	..	..	..	..	**485**	**277**	**208**	..	..	..	**57**	**49**	**8**	..	..	..
8. Kashmir North (including Langet *Jagir*).	..	..	..	..	..	..	170	84	86	..	..	..	..	..	..	..	..	..
9. Kashmir South (including City)	..	..	..	..	..	..	289	174	115	..	..	..	57	49	8	..	..	..
10. Muzaffarabad District ..	..	..	..	..	..	..	26	19	7	..	..	..	..	..	..	..	..	..
III.—Frontier Districts ..	..	..	..	**1**	**1**	..	**188**	**174**	**14**	..	..	..	**22**	**11**	**11**	..	..	..
11. Ladakh District (including Mansar).	..	..	..	1	1	..	43	39	4	..	..	..	3	1	2	..	..	..
12. Gilgit "	..	..	..	..	..	..	145	135	10	..	..	..	19	10	9	..	..	..

TABLE X.

LANGUAGE.

Jammu and Kashmir State Census 1921.

Part II.—Languages of India—*concluded.*

District, Jagir or Ilaqa.	Indo-European Family. Aryan Sub-Family. Indo Aryan Branch. Inner Sub-Branch.						Indo-European Family. Aryan Sub-Family. Indo Aryan Branch. Inner Sub-Branch. Pahari Group.																		Eranian Branch. Eastern Group.					
	Central Group.																													
	WESTERN HINDI.									WESTERN PAHARI.															AFGHANISTAN-BALOCHISTAN SUB-GROUP.					
	Kanauji (Bangrahi.)			*Urdu.*			*Naipali (Gorkhali.)*			*Total.*			*Chambiali (Chameali.)*			*Mandeali.*			*Fangwali.*			*Balochi.*			*Pashto.*				
	Persons.	Males.	Females.	Persons.	Males.	Females.	Persons.	Males.	Females.	Persons.	Males.	Females.	Persons.	Males.	Females.	Persons.	Males.	Females.	Persons.	Males.	Females.	Persons.	Males.	Females.	Persons.	Males.	Females.			
	77	78	79	80	81	82	83	84	85	86	87	88	89	90	91	92	93	94	95	96	97	98	99	100	101	102	103			
Kashmir State ..	7	7	..	1,049	655	394	1,220	849	371	309	195	114	190	91	99	101	100	1	18	4	14	15	15	..	2,159	1,435	724			
I.—Jammu Province (including *Jagirs*).	7	7	..	455	264	191	1,009	747	262	309	195	114	190	91	99	101	100	1	18	4	14	15	15	..	685	552	133			
1. Jammu District (including City)	..	..	..	364	200	164	799	604	195	..	..	..	..	..	..	..	..	..	..	..	..	..	..	..	114	67	47			
2. Kathua „	..	..	..	..	..	..	161	106	55	89	57	32	67	35	32	21	21	..	1	1	..	..	..	..	14	13	1			
3. Udhampur „ (including Chaneni *Jagir.*)	..	..	..	34	24	10	34	31	3	164	110	54	67	28	39	80	79	1	17	3	14	..	..	..	69	52	17			
4. Riasi District	..	..	..	15	11	4	4	1	3	..	..	..	..	..	..	..	..	..	..	..	..	15	15	..	47	27	20			
5. Mirpur „	..	..	..	10	6	4	1	1	..	..	..	..	..	..	..	..	..	..	..	..	..	..	..	..	8	7	1			
6. Bhadarwah *Jagir*.. ..	..	..	..	2	2	..	6	2	4	56	28	28	56	28	28	..	..	..	..	..	..	..	..	..	1	1	..			
7. Punch *Ilaqa*	7	7	..	30	21	9	4	2	2	..	..	..	..	..	..	..	..	..	..	..	..	..	..	..	423	385	47			
II.—Kashmir Province (including *Jagirs*).	..	..	..	428	228	200	208	99	109	..	..	..	..	..	..	..	..	..	..	..	..	..	..	..	1,350	759	591			
8. Kashmir North (including Langet *Jagir.*)	..	..	..	170	84	86	42	22	20	..	..	..	..	..	..	..	..	..	..	..	..	..	..	..	172	109	63			
9. Kashmir South (including City.)	..	..	..	232	125	107	166	77	89	..	..	..	..	..	..	..	..	..	..	..	..	..	..	..	988	534	454			
10. Muzaffarabad District ..	..	..	..	26	19	7	..	..	..	..	..	..	..	..	..	..	..	..	..	..	..	..	..	..	190	116	74			
III.—Frontier Districts.. ..	..	..	..	166	163	3	3	3	..	..	..	..	..	..	..	..	..	..	..	..	..	..	..	..	124	124	..			
11. Ladakh District (including Mansar).	..	..	..	40	38	2	..	..	..	..	..	..	..	..	..	..	..	..	..	..	..	..	..	..	4	4	..			
12. Gilgit „	..	..	..	126	125	1	..	..	..	..	..	..	..	..	..	..	..	..	..	..	..	..	..	..	120	120	..			

TABLE X.

LANGUAGE.

Jammu and Kashmir State Census 1921.

Part III—Asiatic Languages.

District, Jagir or Ilaqa.	*Tibeto-Chinese Family.* Tibeto-Burman Sub-Family. *Tibeto-Himalayan Branch.* TIBETAN GROUP. *Lhassi.*			*Assam-Burmese Branch.* BARA OR BUDO GROUP. *Kebrat (Bara).*			*Mongolian Family.* URAL ALTAIC GROUP. *Yarkandi (Turkistani)*			MONOSYLLABIC GROUP. *Chinese.*			*Semitic Family.* *Arabic.*			*Indo-European Family.* ERANIAN GROUP. *Persian.*		
	Persons.	Males.	Females.	Persons.	Males.	Females.	Persons.	Males.	Females.	Persons.	Males.	Females.	Persons.	Males.	Females.	Persons.	Males.	Females.
1	2	3	4	5	6	7	8	9	10	11	12	13	14	15	16	17	18	19
Kashmir State	43	21	22	1	1	..	11	9	2	1	1	..	2	1	1	181	168	13
I—Jammu Province (including *Jagirs*) ..	..	..	..	1	1	..	1	1	..	1	1	..	1	..	1	12	10	2
1. Jammu District (including City) ..	..	..	..	..	..	..	..	..	..	..	..	..	..	..	..	6	5	1
2. Kathua „ ..	..	..	..	..	..	..	..	..	..	..	..	..	..	..	..	..	..	..
3. Udhampur (including Chaneni *Jagir*.)	..	..	..	1	1	..	..	..	..	1	1	..	..	..	..	..	..	..
4. Riasi District ..	..	..	..	..	..	..	..	..	..	..	..	..	..	..	..	..	..	..
5. Mirpur ..	..	..	..	..	..	..	..	..	..	..	..	..	..	..	..	1	..	1
6. Bahadarwah *Jagir* ..	..	..	..	..	..	..	1	1	..	..	..	..	..	..	..	1	1	..
7. Punch *Ilaqa* ..	..	..	..	..	..	..	..	..	..	..	..	..	1	..	1	4	4	..
II—Kashmir Province (including *Jagirs*)	1	1	..	..	..	..	10	8	2	..	..	..	..	..	..	123	113	10
8. Kashmir North (including Langet *Jagir*).	..	..	..	..	..	..	..	..	..	..	..	..	..	..	..	1	1	..
9. Kashmir South (including City) ..	1	1	..	..	..	..	10	8	2	..	..	..	..	..	..	14	6	8
10. Muzaffarabad District ..	..	..	..	..	..	..	..	..	..	..	..	..	..	..	..	108	106	2
III—Frontier Districts ..	42	20	22	..	..	..	..	..	..	..	..	..	1	1	..	46	45	1
11. Laddakh District (including *Mansar*).	42	20	22	..	..	..	..	..	..	..	..	..	1	1	..	20	19	1
12. Gilgit ..	..	..	..	..	..	..	..	..	..	..	..	..	..	..	..	26	26	..

TABLE X.

LANGUAGE.

Jammu and Kashmir State Census 1921.

Part IV—European Languages.

District, Jagir or Ilaqa.	Indo-European Family. Tutonic Group. English. Persons.	English. Males.	English. Females.	Gaelic. Persons.	Gaelic. Males.	Gaelic. Females.	Romanic Group. French. Persons.	French. Males.	French. Females.
1	2	3	4	5	6	7	8	9	10
Kashmir State ..	329	163	166	1	1	..	3	2	1
I—Jammu Province (including *Jagirs*) ..	42	27	15	..	..	..	..	..	..
1. Jammu District (including City) ..	30	20	10	..	..	..	..	..	..
2. Kathua " ..	..	..	..	..	..	..	..	..	..
3. Udhampur (including Chaneni *Jagir*)	1	..	1	..	..	..	..	..	..
4. Riasi District ..	..	..	..	..	..	..	..	..	..
5. Mirpur ..	6	3	3	..	..	..	..	..	..
6. Bhadarwah *Jagir* ..	1	1	..	..	..	..	..	..	..
7. Punch *Ilaqa* ..	4	3	1	..	..	..	..	..	..
II—Kashmir Province (including *Jagirs*) ..	267	126	141	..	..	..	3	2	1
8. Kashmir North (including Langet *Jagir*).	22	13	9	..	..	..	..	..	..
9. Kashmir South (including City) ..	239	109	130	..	..	..	3	2	1
10. Muzaffarabad District ..	6	4	2	..	..	..	..	..	..
III—Frontier Districts ..	20	10	10	1	1	..	..	..	..
11. Ladakh District (including *Mansar*)	6	2	4	..	..	..	..	..	..
12. Gilgit " ..	14	8	6	1	1	..	..	..	..

Unclassified Languages.

District, Jagir or Ilaqa.	*Bazigari.* Persons.	*Bazigari.* Males.	*Bazigari.* Females.	*Sansi.* Persons.	*Sansi.* Males.	*Sansi.* Females.
1	2	3	4	5	6	7
Kashmir State ..	87	41	46	6	5	1
I—Jammu Province (including *Jagirs*) ..	87	41	46	6	5	1
1. Jammu District (including City) ...	28	8	20	6	5	1
2. Kathua ..	28	20	8	..	..	..
3. Udhampur (including Chaneni *Jagir*) ..	31	13	18	..	..	..
4. Riasi ..	..	..	..	..	..	..
5. Mirpur ..	..	..	..	..	..	..
6. Bhadarwah *Jagir* ..	..	..	..	..	..	..
7. Punch *Ilaqa* ..	..	..	..	..	..	..
II—Kashmir Province (including *Jagirs*) ..	..	..	..	..	..	..
8. Kashmir North (including Langet *Jagir*) ..	..	..	..	..	..	..
9. Kashmir South (including City) ..	..	..	..	..	..	..
10. Muzaffarabad District ..	..	..	..	..	..	..
III—Frontier Districts ..	..	..	..	..	..	..
11. Ladakh District (including *Mansar*) ..	..	..	..	..	..	..
12. Gilgit " ..	..	..	..	..	..	..

TABLE XI.

BIRTH-PLACE.

Jammu and Kashmir State Census 1921.

1. This Table is exclusive of the population of Frontier *Ilaqas* (Males 32,541, Females 28,450) as birth-place was not recorded in the special Schedule adopted for these *Ilaqas*.

2. The arrangement of the countries, Provinces and Districts of birth of immigrants is in accordance with the lists circulated with the Census Commissioner's letter No. 722, dated 29th August, 1921.

XI
Birth-Place.

TABLE

BIRTH-

Jammu and Kashmir

District, State, Province or Country where born.	District, Jagir, Ilaqa or								
	Population of the State.			*Jammu District.*			*Kathua District.*		
	Persons.	Males.	Females.	Persons.	Males.	Females.	Persons.	Males.	Females.
1	2	3	4	5	6	7	8	9	10
Kashmir State ..	**3,259,527**	**1,724,581**	**1,534,946**	**334,834**	**182,681**	**152,153**	**154,209**	**82,467**	**71,742**
A.—Born in District, Ilaqa or Jagir within the State Territories.	**3,196,107**	**1,694,131**	**1,501,976**	**306,290**	**169,916**	**136,374**	**142,981**	**77,307**	**65,674**
Jammu Province ..	**1,586,064**	**834,375**	**751,689**	**304,440**	**168,456**	**135,984**	**142,781**	**77,157**	**65,624**
Jammu District ..	313,311	173,106	140,205	293,033	162,744	130,289	4,079	2,106	1,973
Kathua " ..	139,499	74,928	64,571	2,166	788	1,378	136,010	73,530	62,480
Udhampur " ..	221,331	116,813	104,518	2,685	1,359	1,326	1,549	724	825
Riasi " ..	206,240	107,532	98,708	3,308	1,630	1,678	92	56	36
Mirpur " ..	314,432	161,057	153,375	2,841	1,641	1,200	73	47	26
Bhadarwah *Jagir* ..	37,832	19,663	18,169	214	167	47	897	651	246
Punch *Ilaqa* ..	353,419	181,276	172,143	193	127	66	81	43	38
Kashmir Province ..	**1,399,257**	**753,948**	**645,309**	**1,770**	**1,396**	**374**	**185**	**137**	**48**
Kashmir (North) ..	498,307	267,260	231,047	54	45	9	43	28	15
Kashmir (South) ..	687,678	373,079	314,599	1,646	1,317	329	128	98	30
Muzaffarabad District ..	213,272	113,609	99,663	70	34	36	14	11	2
Frontier Districts ..	**210,786**	**105,808**	**104,978**	**80**	**64**	**16**	**15**	**13**	**2**
Ladakh District ..	183,853	91,553	92,300	50	43	7	15	13	2
Gilgit " ..	26,933	14,255	12,678	30	21	9	..	..	..
B.—Born in Provinces, Districts or States in India Beyond the State.	**61,561**	**29,071**	**32,490**	**27,707**	**12,102**	**15,605**	**11,119**	**5,073**	**6,046**
N. W. F. Province ..	**3,738**	**4,677**	**3,061**	**166**	**101**	**65**	**16**	**11**	**5**
Districts ..	7,332	4,415	2,917	162	97	65	15	11	4
Conterminous ..	6,619	3,875	2,744	39	20	19	12	9	3
Hazara ..	6,619	3,875	2,744	39	20	19	12	9	3
Remote ..	713	540	173	123	77	46	3	2	1
Dera Ismail Khan ..	21	15	6	7	5	2	..	..	..
Peshawar ..	645	483	162	101	59	42	3	2	1
Bannu ..	24	20	4	15	13	2	..	..	..
Kohat ..	23	22	1	..	..	..	..	..	..
Punjab Province ..	**52,463**	**23,450**	**29,013**	**26,960**	**11,564**	**15,396**	**11,051**	**5,015**	**6,036**
Districts ..	51,863	23,079	28,724	26,873	11,511	15,362	10,728	4,854	5,874
Conterminous ..	46,096	19,562	26,534	23,888	9,788	14,100	10,341	4,590	5,751
Gujrat ..	7,368	2,890	4,478	1,930	1,071	859	21	16	5
Gurdaspur ..	13,448	5,868	7,580	3,949	1,499	2,450	9,052	4,106	4,946
Jhelum ..	1,965	1,022	943	319	203	116	35	30	5
Kangra ..	1,923	791	1,132	682	154	528	660	152	508
Rawalpindi ..	2,011	1,218	793	273	169	104	34	20	14
Sialkot ..	19,381	7,773	11,608	16,735	6,692	10,043	539	266	273
Remote ..	5,707	3,517	2,190	2,985	1,723	1,262	387	264	123
Ambala ..	63	46	17	34	21	13	4	4	..
Amritsar ..	990	627	363	494	270	224	59	43	16
Campbellpur (Attock) ..	360	198	162	12	9	3	1	1	..
Dera Ghazi Khan ..	1	1	..	..	..	..	..	..	..
Ferozepore ..	40	23	17	23	9	14	3	3	..
Gujranwala ..	1,263	736	527	838	467	371	38	30	8
Gurgaon ..	36	17	19	35	16	19	1	1	..
Hissar ..	3	3	..	1	1	..	2	2	..
Hoshiarpur ..	590	353	237	262	149	113	149	81	68
Jhang ..	71	48	23	47	34	13	..	..	..
Jullundur ..	522	336	186	275	172	103	50	37	13
Karnal ..	26	10	16	11	9	2	..	..	..
Lahore ..	896	575	321	532	301	231	28	22	6
Lyallpur ..	133	75	58	94	51	43	9	8	1
Ludhiana ..	103	79	24	30	25	5	6	3	3
Mianwali ..	12	12	..	9	9	..	..	..	..
Montgomery ..	16	9	7	9	5	4	5	3	2
Multan ..	62	45	17	33	26	7	1	1	..
Muzaffargarh ..	22	18	4	16	14	2	2	2	..
Rohtak ..	4	3	1	3	2	1	1	1	..
Shahpur ..	384	223	161	189	99	90	19	13	6
Sheikhupura ..	9	9	..	9	9	..	..	..	..
Simla ..	101	71	30	29	25	4	9	9	..
States ..	631	354	277	87	53	34	323	161	162
Conterminous ..	433	203	230	26	19	7	286	128	158
Chamba ..	433	203	230	26	19	7	286	128	158
Remote ..	198	151	47	61	34	27	37	33	4
Bahawalpur ..	5	2	3	4	1	3	1	1	..
Bilaspur ..	3	3	..	..	..	..	..	..	..
Jind ..	2	2	..	..	..	..	..	..	..
Kapurthala ..	48	28	20	24	15	9	4	2	2
Maler Kotla ..	4	3	1	1	..	1	..	..	..
Mandi ..	55	51	4	2	..	2	24	23	1
Nabha ..	8	6	2	2	..	2	..	..	..
Patiala ..	66	49	17	28	18	10	7	6	1
Nahan ..	1	1	..	..	..	..	1	1	..
Suket ..	6	6	..	..	..	..	..	..	..
Punjab unspecified ..	29	17	12	..	..	..	..	..	..
Delhi Province ..	**144**	**91**	**53**	**84**	**59**	**25**	**6**	**6**	..

XI. | XI Birth-Place.

PLACE.

State Census 1921.

CITY WHERE ENUMERATED.

Udhampur District.			*Riasi District.*			*Mirpur District.*			*Bhadarwah Jagir.*		
Persons.	Males.	Females.	Persons.	Males.	Females.	Persons.	Males.	Females.	Persons.	Males.	Females.
11	12	13	14	15	16	17	18	19	20	21	22
218,261	**115,135**	**103,126**	**224,589**	**118,575**	**106,014**	**318,971**	**160,186**	**158,785**	**37,614**	**19,227**	**18,387**
216,833	**114,152**	**102,681**	**222,884**	**117,471**	**105,413**	**310,639**	**157,506**	**153,133**	**37,426**	**19,112**	**18,314**
215,053	**112,870**	**102,183**	**220,238**	**115,865**	**104,373**	**310,177**	**157,199**	**152,978**	**37,274**	**19,008**	**18,226**
2,045	1,052	993	10,179	5,129	5,050	1,713	463	1,250	110	67	43
1,048	429	619	44	30	14	18	12	6	62	34	28
209,857	10,395	99,462	4,429	2,803	1,626	31	17	14	894	430	464
1,421	509	912	198,969	104,117	94,852	1,116	334	782	55	35	20
99	74	25	3,808	2,272	1,536	306,235	156,041	150,094	4	4	..
429	301	128	66	54	12	..	..	..	36,145	18,435	17,710
154	110	44	2,743	1,460	1,283	1,064	332	732	4	3	1
1,685	**1,213**	**472**	**2,637**	**1,598**	**1,039**	**458**	**304**	**154**	**147**	**102**	**45**
45	30	15	121	100	21	87	70	17	2	2	..
1,553	1,131	422	1,954	1,176	778	246	171	75	139	95	44
87	52	35	562	322	240	125	63	62	6	5	1
95	**69**	**26**	**9**	**8**	**1**	**4**	**3**	**1**	**5**	**2**	**3**
86	63	23	..	..	..	1	..	1	5	2	3
9	6	3	9	8	1	3	3	..	..	..	..
1,382	**944**	**438**	**1,674**	**1,083**	**591**	**8,314**	**2,668**	**5,646**	**180**	**107**	**73**
86	**51**	**35**	**753**	**505**	**248**	**94**	**52**	**42**	**8**	**6**	**2**
67	42	25	663	450	213	91	50	41	8	6	2
40	19	21	603	414	189	57	31	26	6	4	2
40	19	21	603	414	189	57	31	26	6	4	2
27	23	4	60	36	24	34	19	15	2	2	..
..	..	..	4	4	..	4	3	1	..	..	..
23	19	4	53	31	22	27	14	13	2	2	..
4	4	..	2	..	2	1	1	..	..	..	..
..	..	..	1	1	..	2	1	1	..	..	..
1,228	**836**	**392**	**792**	**527**	**265**	**8,121**	**2,555**	**5,566**	**162**	**92**	**70**
1,130	762	368	774	518	256	8,104	2,544	5,560	102	68	34
817	555	262	597	398	199	7,721	2,310	5,411	57	34	23
73	52	21	260	198	62	4,750	1,353	3,397	5	5	..
157	93	64	62	34	28	91	41	50	15	12	3
26	22	4	59	32	27	964	360	604	1	..	1
223	188	35	26	17	9	23	13	10	23	6	17
61	44	17	48	27	21	617	256	361	3	3	..
277	156	121	142	90	52	1,276	287	989	10	8	2
313	207	106	177	120	57	383	234	149	45	34	11
3	3	..	1	..	1	12	10	2	1	1	..
29	18	11	17	12	5	21	14	7	7	6	1
4	4	..	..	..	..	21	11	10	..	..	..
1	1	..	..	..	..	..	..	..	..	..	..
2	2	..	2	..	2	4	3	1	..	..	..
58	34	24	49	37	12	103	60	43	5	4	1
..	..	..	..	..	..	..	..	..	..	..	..
..	..	..	..	..	..	..	..	..	..	..	..
33	16	17	17	13	4	29	20	9	5	5	..
18	11	7	1	1	..	2	2	..	..	..	..
45	33	12	21	13	8	36	20	16	4	3	1
1	1	..	..	..	..	..	..	..	..	..	..
40	33	7	37	24	13	44	25	19	9	8	1
5	3	2	4	2	2	20	11	9	..	..	..
31	23	8	1	1	..	13	8	5	..	..	..
..	..	1	..	..	..	1	1	..	..	..	..
..	..	..	..	..	..	2	1	1	..	..	..
3	1	2	7	3	4	8	6	2	4	3	1
1	..	1	..	..	..	1	1	..	..	..	..
..	..	..	..	..	..	..	..	..	..	..	..
14	6	8	19	13	6	64	39	25	2	2	..
..	..	..	..	..	..	..	..	..	..	..	..
25	18	7	1	1	..	2	2	..	8	2	5
98	74	24	18	9	9	17	11	6	60	24	35
47	24	23	12	5	7	1	1	..	57	22	31
47	24	23	12	5	7	1	1	..	57	22	36
5[illegible]	58	1	6	4	2	1[illegible]	10	6	3	2	6
3	3	..	..	..	..	..	..	..	..	..	..
..	..	..	..	..	..	..	..	..	..	..	..
..	..	..	4	3	1	10	5	5	1	1	..
3	3	..	..	..	..	..	..	..	..	..	1
28	28	..	..	..	..	..	..	..	1	..	..
1	1	..	..	..	..	1	1	..	1	1	..
10	9	1	2	1	1	5	4	1	..	..	..
6	6	..	..	..	..	..	..	..	..	..	..
6	**5**	**1**	**1**	**1**	..	9	**3**	**6**	..	..	..

TABLE
BIRTH
Jammu and Kashmir

District, State, Province or Country where born.	DISTRICT, JAGIR, ILAQA OR								
	Punch Ilaqa.			*Kashmir North.*			*Kashmir South.*		
	Persons.	Males.	Females.	Persons.	Males.	Females.	Persons.	Males.	Females.
	23	24	25	26	27	28	29	30	31
Kashmir State ..	**351,781**	**181,348**	**170,433**	**502,490**	**269,685**	**232,805**	**688,487**	**372,459**	**316,028**
A.—Born in District, Ilaqa or Jagir within the State Territories.	**350,287**	**180,193**	**170,094**	**499,480**	**267,930**	**231,550**	**684,792**	**370,326**	**314,466**
Jammu Province ..	**349,249**	**179,410**	**169,839**	**829**	**494**	**335**	**4,103**	**2,498**	**1,605**
Jammu District ..	808	465	343	80	54	26	939	738	201
Kathua ,, ..	14	6	8	7	5	2	96	60	36
Udhampur ,, ..	17	9	8	25	25	..	1,690	910	780
Riasi ,, ..	182	77	105	58	31	27	696	405	291
Mirpur ,, ..	921	624	297	53	35	18	158	98	60
Bhadarwah *Jagir* ..	6	4	2	15	6	9	39	31	8
Punch *Ilaqa* ..	347,301	178,225	169,076	591	338	253	485	256	229
Kashmir Province ..	**918**	**666**	**252**	**498,563**	**267,393**	**231,170**	**680,232**	**367,524**	**312,708**
Kashmir (North) ..	197	175	22	494,738	264,998	229,740	2,040	1,085	955
Kashmir (South) ..	431	323	108	2,875	1,873	1,002	677,944	366,291	311,653
Muzaffarabad District ..	290	168	122	950	522	428	248	148	100
Frontier Districts ..	**120**	**117**	**3**	**88**	**43**	**45**	**457**	**304**	**153**
Ladakh District ..	120	117	3	88	43	45	457	304	153
Gilgit ,, ..	..	..	..	49	19	30	92	69	23
B.—Born in Provinces, Districts or States in India beyond the State.	**1,412**	**1,079**	**333**	**2,893**	**1,686**	**1,207**	**3,416**	**2,008**	**1,408**
N.-W. F. Province ..	**491**	**444**	**47**	**2,220**	**1,236**	**984**	**2,052**	**1,088**	**964**
Districts ..	491	444	47	2,204	1,223	981	1,995	1,057	938
Conterminous ..	204	164	40	2,176	1,202	974	1,961	1,033	928
Hazara ..	204	164	40	2,176	1,202	974	1,961	1,033	928
Remote ..	287	280	7	28	21	7	34	24	10
Dera Ismail Khan ..	..	..	..	1	1	..	..	..	..
Peshawar ..	268	261	7	27	20	7	31	21	10
Bannu ..	..	..	..	..	..	..	2	2	..
Kohat ..	19	19	..	..	..	..	1	1	..
Punjab Province ..	**864**	**593**	**271**	**619**	**424**	**195**	**1,127**	**759**	**368**
Districts ..	853	584	269	619	424	195	1,087	733	354
Conterminous ..	761	515	246	416	289	127	504	329	175
Gujrat ..	64	42	22	38	26	12	87	57	30
Gurdaspur ..	23	12	11	14	8	6	24	22	2
Jhelum ..	307	206	101	112	78	34	57	35	22
Kangra ..	28	22	6	16	10	6	17	13	4
Rawalpindi ..	274	194	80	178	127	51	159	98	61
Sialkot ..	65	39	26	58	40	18	160	104	56
Remote ..	92	69	23	203	135	68	583	404	179
Ambala ..	2	1	1	..	..	..	3	3	..
Amritsar ..	11	10	1	30	21	9	296	212	84
Campbellpur (Attock) ..	7	4	3	77	57	18	9	8	1
Dera Ghazi Khan ..	..	..	..	..	..	..	..	..	..
Ferozepur ..	6	6	..	..	..	..	..	..	..
Gujranwala ..	17	13	4	38	24	14	60	44	16
Gurgaon ..	..	..	..	..	..	..	..	..	..
Hissar ..	..	..	..	..	..	..	..	..	..
Hoshiarpur ..	15	11	4	10	4	6	41	30	11
Jhang ..	..	..	..	..	..	..	..	..	..
Jullundur ..	7	7	..	26	15	11	43	24	19
Karnal ..	..	..	..	..	..	..	13	..	13
Lahore ..	14	7	7	5	2	3	65	43	22
Lyallpur ..	..	..	..	..	..	..	1	..	1
Ludhiana ..	3	3	..	1	1	..	9	8	1
Mianwali ..	..	..	..	..	..	..	..	..	..
Montgomery ..	..	..	..	..	..	..	..	..	..
Multan ..	1	1	..	1	1	..	3	2	1
Muzaffargarh ..	..	..	..	..	..	..	..	..	..
Rohtak ..	..	..	..	..	..	..	..	..	..
Shahpur ..	6	5	1	17	10	7	35	28	7
Sheikhupura ..	..	..	..	..	..	..	..	..	..
Simla ..	3	1	2	..	..	..	5	2	3
States ..	11	9	2	..	..	..	11	9	2
Conterminous ..	4	4	..	..	..	..	..	..	..
Chamba ..	4	4	..	..	..	..	..	..	..
Remote ..	7	5	2	..	..	..	11	9	2
Bahawalpur ..	..	..	..	..	..	..	..	..	..
Bilaspur ..	..	..	..	..	..	..	..	..	..
Jind ..	2	2	..	..	..	..	..	..	..
Kapurthala ..	1	..	1	..	..	..	1	1	..
Maler Kotla ..	..	..	..	..	..	..	..	..	..
Mandi ..	..	..	..	..	..	..	..	..	..
Nabha ..	1	1	..	..	..	..	2	2	..
Patiala ..	3	2	1	..	..	..	8	6	2
Nahan ..	..	..	..	..	..	..	..	..	..
Suket ..	..	..	..	..	..	..	..	..	..
Punjab unspecified ..	..	..	..	..	..	..	29	17	12
Delhi Province ..	**1**	**1**	..	**6**	**2**	**4**	**23**	**12**	**11**

CITY WHERE ENUMERATED.

Muzaffarabad District.			*Ladakh District.*			*Gilgit District.*			*Jammu City.*			*Srinagar City.*		
Persons.	Males.	Females.	Persons.	Males.	Females.	Persons	Males.	Females.	Persons.	Males.	Females.	Persons.	Males.	Females.
32	33	34	35	36	37	38	39	40	41	42	43	44	45	46
216,109	**115,680**	**100,429**	**183,476**	**91,258**	**92,218**	**28,706**	**15,880**	**12,826**	**31,506**	**19,121**	**12,385**	**141,735**	**76,604**	**65,131**
213,171	**113,753**	**99,418**	**183,169**	**91,048**	**92,121**	**28,155**	**15,417**	**12,738**	**25,340**	**15,346**	**9,994**	**140,388**	**75,717**	**64,671**
928	**470**	**458**	**179**	**152**	**27**	**813**	**796**	**17**	**24,148**	**14,380**	**9,768**	**1,297**	**1,101**	**196**
72	56	16	55	42	13	198	190	8	20,912	11,865	9,047	663	558	105
6	6	..	1	1	..	27	27	..	369	274	95	23	23	..
21	15	6	26	19	7	107	107	..	1,018	758	260	209	197	12
20	15	5	43	43	..	280	280	..	900	701	199	201	176	25
35	23	12	28	28	..	177	170	7	710	600	110	74	58	16
..	..	..	21	14	7	..	..	..	142	123	19	30	26	4
774	355	419	5	5	..	24	22	2	97	59	38	97	63	34
212,155	**113,198**	**98,957**	**193**	**158**	**35**	**314**	**259**	**55**	**1,127**	**913**	**214**	**138,918**	**74,479**	**64,439**
801	555	246	21	19	2	158	153	5	34	34	..	134	84	50
435	360	75	171	138	33	156	106	50	1,074	871	203	138,758	74,375	64,383
210,919	112,283	98,636	1	1	..	..	..	..	19	8	11	26	20	6
88	**85**	**3**	**182,797**	**90,738**	**92,059**	**27,028**	**14,362**	**12,666**	**65**	**53**	**12**	**173**	**137**	**36**
59	58	1	182,792	90,735	92,057	321	263	58	49	43	6	123	95	28
29	27	2	5	3	2	26,707	14,099	12,608	16	10	6	50	42	8
2,800	**1,889**	**1,001**	**193**	**136**	**57**	**381**	**206**	**85**	**5,942**	**3,590**	**2,352**	**1,139**	**796**	**343**
1,657	1,023	634	13	11	2	182	149	33	118	80	38	85	67	18
1,556	967	589	12	10	2	68	58	10	114	76	38	83	65	18
1,488	952	536	4	4	..	29	23	6	18	11	7	57	45	12
1,488	952	536	4	4	..	29	23	6	18	11	7	57	45	12
68	15	53	8	6	2	39	35	4	96	65	31	26	20	6
..	..	..	4	2	2	1	..	1	5	3	2	..	..	..
68	15	53	4	4	..	38	35	3	77	49	28	23	17	6
..	..	..	..	..	..	..	..	..	14	13	1	2	2	..
..	..	..	..	..	..	..	..	..	..	..	..	1	1	..
1,209	855	354	148	96	52	182	134	48	5,393	3,188	2,205	852	590	262
1,207	853	354	147	96	51	179	132	47	5,321	3,141	2,180	815	567	248
791	591	200	91	68	23	112	95	17	3,466	2,116	1,350	343	227	116
127	57	70	7	7	..	6	6	..	506	336	170	61	46	15
54	37	17	1	1	..	6	3	3	445	309	136	20	18	2
51	35	16	13	6	7	21	15	6	230	158	72	20	11	9
192	189	3	19	13	6	14	14	..	138	100	38	12	8	4
304	232	72	49	39	10	11	9	2	194	118	76	140	87	53
63	41	22	2	2	..	54	48	6	1,953	1,095	858	90	57	33
416	262	154	56	28	28	67	37	30	1,855	1,025	830	472	340	132
..	..	..	3	3	..	..	..	..	25	15	10	3	3	..
18	14	4	..	..	..	8	7	1	333	168	165	270	196	74
229	104	125	..	..	..	2	..	2	5	4	1	4	3	1
..	..	..	..	..	..	..	..	..	..	..	..	..	..	..
..	..	..	..	..	..	..	..	..	3	1	2	..	..	..
11	2	9	32	12	20	14	9	5	592	323	269	42	34	8
..	..	..	..	..	..	..	..	..	12	2	10	..	..	..
..	..	..	..	..	..	..	..	..	1	1	..	..	..	..
23	19	4	5	5	..	1	..	1	132	80	52	33	24	9
..	..	..	..	..	..	3	..	3	38	27	11	..	..	..
8	5	3	2	2	..	5	5	..	180	114	66	32	20	12
..	..	..	..	..	..	1	..	1	1	1	..	8	..	8
115	108	7	..	..	..	7	2	5	301	156	145	53	35	8
..	..	..	..	..	..	..	..	..	22	16	6	1	..	1
5	4	1	..	..	..	4	3	1	21	17	4	7	6	1
2	2	..	..	..	..	..	..	..	2	2	..	..	..	..
..	..	..	..	..	..	..	..	..	7	5	2	..	..	..
..	..	..	1	1	..	..	..	..	6	2	4	1	1	..
..	..	..	..	..	..	2	1	1	1	..	1	..	..	..
..	..	..	..	..	..	..	..	..	1	..	1	..	..	..
2	1	1	..	..	..	17	7	10	143	66	77	16	16	..
..	..	..	..	..	..	..	..	..	3	3	..	..	..	..
3	3	..	13		8	3	3	..	26	22	4	2	2	..
2	2	..	1	..	1	3	2	1	72	47	25	8	6	2
..	..	..	..	..	..	..	..	..	23	19	4	..	..	..
..	..	..	..	..	..	..	..	..	23	19	4	..	..	..
2	2	..	1	..	1	3	2	1	49	28	21	8	6	2
..	..	..	..	..	..	..	..	..	4	1	3	..	..	..
..	..	..	..	..	..	..	..	..	..	..	..	..	..	..
..	..	..	..	..	..	..	..	..	..	..	..	..	..	..
..	..	..	1	..	1	2	1	1	20	12	8	1	1	..
..	..	..	..	..	..	..	..	..	..	..	..	..	..	..
..	..	..	..	..	..	..	..	..	2	..	2	..	..	..
..	..	..	..	..	..	..	..	..	2	..	2	..	..	..
2	2	..	..	..	..	1	1	..	21	15	6	7	5	2
..	..	..	..	..	..	..	..	..	..	..	..	..	..	..
..	..	..	..	..	..	..	..	..	..	..	..	29	17	12
8	2	6	..	..	..	..	..	..	71	49	22	21	10	11

XI
Birth-Place.

TABLE

BIRTH

Jammu and Kashmir

District, State, Province or Country where born.	DISTRICT JAGIR, ILAQA OR CITY								
	Population of State.			*Jammu District.*			*Kathua District.*		
	Persons.	Males.	Females.	Persons.	Males.	Females.	Persons.	Males.	Females.
1	2	3	4	5	6	7	8	9	10
United Provinces of Agra and Oudh ..	**557**	**404**	**153**	**281**	**213**	**68**	**21**	**20**	**1**
Districts	551	400	151	278	211	67	21	20	1
States	6	4	2	3	2	1	..	..	..
Bengal	**105**	**77**	**28**	**51**	**35**	**16**	**2**	**2**	..
Bihar and Orissa	**32**	**30**	**2**	**15**	**14**	**1**	**1**	**1**	..
Assam	**2**	**2**	..	..	..	..	..	..	..
Ajmere Merwara	**11**	**1**	**10**	**9**	..	**9**	..	..	..
Bombay Presidency	**150**	**115**	**35**	**61**	**51**	**10**	**8**	**6**	**2**
Districts	140	111	29	59	51	8	6	4	2
States	10	4	6	2	..	2	2	2	..
Madras Presidency	**34**	**22**	**12**	**1**	..	**1**	..	..	..
Central Provinces	**30**	**24**	**6**	**1**	**1**	..	..	..	..
Baluchistan	**94**	**20**	**74**	**5**	**5**		**3**	**1**	**2**
Burma	**8**	**4**	**4**	**2**	**2**	..	**1**	**1**	..
Hyderabad (Deccan)	**7**	**5**	**2**	**3**	**1**	**2**	..	..	..
Central India Agency	**11**	**8**	**3**	**1**	**1**	..	**1**	**1**	..
Mysore	**2**	**2**	..	..	..	..	..	..	..
Baroda	**6**	**4**	**2**	..	..	..	**1**	**1**	..
Rajputana Agency	**113**	**92**	**21**	**52**	**43**	**9**	**3**	**3**	..
Gawalior	**23**	**20**	**3**	**11**	**9**	**2**	**4**	**4**	..
Portuguese Settlements (Goa) ..	**16**	**16**	..	..	..	..	..	..	..
India unspecified	**15**	**7**	**8**	**4**	**3**	**1**	**1**	**1**	..
C.—Born in countries in Asia beyond India.	**1,681**	**1,292**	**389**	**820**	**653**	**167**	**109**	**87**	**22**
Conterminous	139	101	38	..	..	..	..	..	..
Tibet	139	101	38	..	..	..	..	..	..
Remote	1,542	1,191	351	820	653	167	109	87	22
Afghanistan	329	267	62	64	61	3	4	4	..
Arabia	5	2	3	2	1	1	..	..	..
Ceylon	7	2	5	..	..	..	..	..	..
China	8	8	..	..	..	..	..	..	..
Chinese Turkistan	19	18	1	..	..	..	..	..	..
St.—Settlements and Malaya States ..	2	1	1	..	..	..	..	..	..
Nepal	1,157	885	272	749	586	161	105	83	22
Persia	13	7	6	2	..	2	..	..	..
Siam	1	..	1	..	..	..	..	..	..
Turkey	1	1	..	..	..	..	..	..	..
D.—Born in Countries in Europe ..	**158**	**75**	**83**	**9**	**6**	**3**	..	..	..
United Kingdom	148	68	80	9	6	3	..	..	..
England and Wales	111	49	62	8	5	3	..	..	..
Scotland	18	13	5	1	1	..	..	..	..
Ireland	19	6	13	..	..	..	..	..	..
France	6	3	3	..	..	..	..	..	..
Holland	1	1	..	..	..	..	..	..	..
Italy	1	1	..	..	..	..	..	..	..
Europe unspecified	2	2	..	..	..	..	..	..	..
E.—Born in Countries in Africa ..	**8**	**3**	**5**	**5**	**2**	**3**	..	..	..
Africa unspecified	8	3	5	5	2	3	..	..	..
F.—Born in Countries in America ..	**8**	**5**	**3**	**3**	**2**	**1**	..	..	..
North America	8	5	3	3	2	1	..	..	..
South America	..	..	..	..	..	..	..	..	..
G.—Born in Australasia	**4**	**4**	..	**3**	**3**	..	..	..	..
Australia	1	1	..	..	..	..	..	..	..
Java	3	3	..	3	3	..	..	..	..

XI.

XI
Birth-Place.

PLACE.

State Census 1921.

WHERE ENUMERATED.

Udhampur District.			*Riasi District.*			*Mirpur District.*			*Bhadarwah Jagir.*		
Persons.	Males.	Females.	Persons.	Males.	Females.	Persons.	Males.	Females.	Persons.	Males.	Females.
11	12	13	14	15	16	17	18	19	20	21	22
27	24	3	19	12	7	57	37	20	6	5	1
27	24	3	19	12	7	57	37	20	3	3	...
...	...	...	...	...	...	...	...	...	3	2	1
...	...	..	4	4	...	3	2	1	1	1	...
12	12	..	...	...	...	2	2	...	...	...	...
...	...	..	...	...	...	...	...	...	...	...	...
1	...	1	...	...	...	...	...	...	...	...	...
...	...	...	34	22	12	...	...	...	1	1	...
...	...	..	34	22	12	...	...	...	1	1	...
...	...	...	...	...	..	...	...	...	...	...	...
2	2	...	...	...	...	2	2	...	...	...	...
1	1	...	2	...	2	...	...	...	...	...	...
2	1	1	64	7	57	2	...	2	...	...	...
...	...	...	...	...	...	1	...	1	...	...	...
1	1	...	...	...	...	1	1	...	...	...	...
4	2	2	...	...	...	3	3	...	1	1	...
...	...	...	2	2	...	...	...	...	...	...	...
...	...	...	...	...	...	5	3	2	...	...	...
11	8	3	1	1	...	13	7	6	1	1	...
1	1	...	2	2	...	1	1	...	...	...	...
...	...	...	...	...	...	...	...	...	...	...	...
...	...	...	...	...	...	...	...	...	...	...	..
45	39	6	31	21	10	15	11	4	8	8	...
1	...	1	...	...	...	...	..	...	...	...	...
1	...	1	...	...	...	...	...	...	...	...	...
44	39	5	31	21	10	15	11	4	8	8	...
26	24	2	21	14	7	6	6	...	3	3	...
1	...	1	...	...	...	...	...	...	...	...	...
...	...	...	...	...	...	..	...	...	...	...	...
5	5	...	...	...	...	...	...	...	...	...	...
...	...	...	...	...	...	...	...	...	...	...	...
...	...	...	..	...	...	...	...	...	...	...	...
12	10	2	10	7	3	7	5	2	5	5	...
...	...	...	...	...	...	1	...	1	...	...	...
...	...	...	...	...	...	1	...	1	...	...	...
...	...	...	...	...	...	...	...	...	...	...	...
1	...	1	...	...	...	1	1	...	...	...	...
1	...	1	...	...	...	1	1	...	...	...	...
1	...	1	...	...	...	1	1	...	...	...	...
...	...	...	...	...	...	...	...	...	...	...	...
...	...	...	...	...	...	...	...	...	...	...	...
...	...	...	...	...	...	...	...	...	...	...	...
...	...	...	...	..	...	...	...	...	...	...	...
...	...	...	...	...	...	...	...	...	...	...	...
...	...	...	..	...	...	...	...	...	...	...	...
...	...	...	...	...	...	1	...	1	...	...	...
...	...	...	...	...	...	1	...	1	...	...	...
...	...	...	...	...	...	1	...	1	...	...	...
...	...	...	...	...	...	1	...	1	...	...	...
...	...	...	...	...	...	...	...	...	...	...	...
...	...	...	...	...	...	...	...	...	...	...	...
...	...	...	...	...	...	...	...	...	...	...	...
...	...	...	...	...	...	...	...	...	...	...	...

TABLE

BIRTH-

Jammu and Kashmir

District, State, Province or Country where born.	District, Jagir, Ilaqa or								
	Punch Ilaqa.			*Kashmir North.*			*Kashmir South.*		
	Persons.	Males.	Females.	Persons.	Males.	Females.	Persons.	Males.	Females.
	23	24	25	26	27	28	29	30	31
U. P. of Agra and Oudh	**22**	**14**	**8**	**36**	**17**	**19**	**56**	**34**	**22**
Districts	22	14	8	36	17	19	56	34	22
States	..	..	..	..	..	..	..	..	..
Bengal	..	..	..	..	..	..	**37**	**26**	**1**
Bihar and Orissa	**1**	**1**	..	..	..	..	**1**	..	**11**
Assam	..	..	..	..	..	..	..	..	..
Ajmere (Merwara)	..	..	..	..	..	..	**1**	**1**	..
Bombay Presidency	**10**	**8**	**2**	**11**	**6**	**5**	**17**	**15**	**2**
Districts	10	8	2	5	4	1	17	15	2
State	..	..	..	6	2	4	..	..	..
Madras Presidency	**8**	**8**	..	..	..	..	**18**	**9**	**9**
General Provinces	..	..	..	..	..	..	**24**	**20**	**4**
Baluchistan	**3**	**1**	**2**	..	..	..	**5**	**1**	**4**
Burma	..	..	..	..	..	..	**3**	..	**3**
Hyderabad (Deccan)	..	..	..	**1**	**1**	..	**1**	**1**	..
Central India Agency	..	..	..	..	..	..	**1**	..	**1**
Mysore	..	..	..	..	..	..	..	..	..
Baroda	..	..	..	..	..	..	..	..	..
Rajputana Agency	**12**	**9**	**3**	..	..	..	**20**	**20**	..
Gawalior	..	..	..	..	..	..	**4**	**3**	**1**
Portuguese Settlements (Goa) ..	..	..	..	..	..	..	**16**	**16**	..
India unspecified	..	..	..	..	..	..	**10**	**3**	**7**
C.—Born in countries in Asia beyond India.	**81**	**76**	**5**	**104**	**61**	**43**	**160**	**72**	**88**
Conterminous	43	43	..	1	1	..	11	8	3
Tibet	43	43	..	1	1	..	11	8	3
Remote	38	33	5	103	60	43	149	64	85
Afghanistan	22	18	4	64	35	29	29	20	9
Arabia	1	..	1	..	..	..	..	..	..
Ceylon	..	..	..	..	..	..	7	2	5
China	..	..	..	..	..	..	..	..	..
Chinese Turkistan	..	..	..	1	1	..	[illegible]	8	1
St :—Settlements and Malaya States ..	..	..	..	2	1	1	..	..	..
Nepal	15	15	..	36	[illegible]	13	101	33	68
Persia	..	..	..	..	..	..	[illegible]	..	..
Siam	..	..	..	..	..	..	..	..	..
Turkey	..	..	..	..	..	..	1	1	..
D.—Born in Countries in Europe ..	**1**	..	**1**	**10**	**7**	**3**	**116**	**50**	**66**
United Kingdom	1	..	1	8	5	3	108	45	63
England and Wales	1	..	1	3	2	1	85	36	49
Scotland	..	..	..	3	1	2	7	5	2
Ireland	..	..	..	2	2	..	16	4	12
France	..	..	..	..	..	..	6	3	3
Holland	..	..	..	1	1	..	..	..	..
Italy	..	..	..	1	1	..	..	..	..
Europe Unspecified	..	..	..	..	..	..	2	2	..
E.—Born in Countries in Africa ..	..	..	..	**1**	..	**1**	..	..	..
Africa unspecified	..	..	..	1	..	1	..	..	..
F.—Born in Countries in America ..	..	..	..	**2**	**1**	**1**	**2**	**2**	..
North America	..	..	..	2	1	1	2	2	..
South America	..	..	..	..	..	..	..	..	..
G.—Born in Australaia	..	..	..	..	..	..	**1**	**1**	..
Australia	..	..	..	..	..	..	1	1	..
Java	..	..	..	..	..	..	..	..	..

CITY WHERE ENUMERATED.

Muzaffarabad District.			*Laddakh District.*			*Gilgit District.*			*Jammu City.*			*Srinagar City.*		
Persons.	Males.	Females.	Persons.	Males.	Females.	Persons.	Males.	Females.	Persons.	Males.	Females.	Persons.	Males.	Females.
32	33	34	35	36	37	38	39	40	41	42	43	44	45	46
3	**2**	**1**	**27**	**24**	**3**	**2**	**2**	..	**201**	**153**	**48**	**42**	**25**	**17**
3	2	1	27	24	3	2	2	..	199	152	47	42	25	17
..	..	..	..	..	..	..	..	..	2	1	1	..	..	..
3	**3**	..	..	..	..	**4**	**4**	..	**49**	**35**	**14**	**32**	**24**	**8**
...	...	..	...	..	..	..	..	..	**13**	**12**	**1**	..	...	...
..	..	..	**2**	**2**	..	..	..	..	...	...	...	...	...	...
..	..	..	..	..	..	..	..	..	**5**	..	**5**	**1**	**1**	..
..	..	..	**1**	**1**	..	**7**	**5**	**2**	**44**	**38**	**6**	**13**	**11**	**2**
..	..	..	1	1	..	7	5	2	42	38	4	13	11	2
..	..	..	..	..	..	..	..	..	2	..	2	..	..	..
..	..	..	..	..	..	**3**	**1**	**2**	..	..	..	**15**	**7**	**8**
..	..	..	**2**	**2**	..	..	..	..	**1**	**1**	..	**23**	**19**	**4**
10	**4**	**6**	..	..	..	..	..	..	**4**	**4**	..	**5**	**1**	**4**
..	..	..	..	..	..	**1**	**1**	..	..	..	..	**1**	..	**1**
..	..	..	..	..	..	..	..	..	**3**	**1**	**2**	**1**	**1**	..
..	..	..	..	..	..	..	..	..	..	..	..	**1**	..	**1**
..	..	..	..	..	..	..	..	..	..	..	..	..	..	..
..	..	..	..	..	..	..	..	..	..	..	..	..	..	..
..	..	..	..	..	..	..	..	..	**27**	**19**	**8**	**20**	**20**	...
..	..	..	..	...	..	..	..	..	**11**	**9**	**2**	**2**	**2**	...
..	..	..	..	...	..	..	..	..	...	...	...	**15**	**15**	..
..	..	..	..	...	..	..	...	..	...	...	...	**10**	**3**	**7**
42	**34**	**8**	**103**	**72**	**30**	**161**	**161**	..	**218**	**180**	**36**	**115**	**45**	**70**
3	3	..	80	46	34	..	..	..	..	..	..	1	..	1
3	3	..	80	46	34	..	..	..	..	..	..	1	...	1
39	31	8	28	26	2	161	161	..	216	180	36	114	45	69
37	29	8	6	6	..	47	47	..	60	57	3	20	14	6
..	..	..	1	1	..	..	..	..	2	1	1	..	..	..
..	..	..	..	..	..	..	..	..	..	..	..	2	2	..
..	..	..	3	3	..	..	..	..	..	..	..	..	..	..
..	..	..	7	7	..	2	2	..	..	..	..	9	8	1
..	..	..	..	..	..	..	..	..	..	..	..	..	..	..
2	2	..	3	2	1	112	112	..	149	119	30	83	21	6
..	..	..	8	7	1	..	..	..	2	..	2	..	..	..
..	..	..	..	..	..	..	..	..	..	..	..	..	..	..
..	..	..	..	..	..	..	..	..	..	..	..	..	..	..
5	**3**	**2**		**2**	**4**	**9**	**6**	**3**	**5**	**3**	**2**	**92**	**45**	**47**
5	3	2	6	2	4	9	6	3	5	3	2	89	45	44
3	2	1	4	..	4	5	3	2	4	2	2	72	36	36
2	1	1	2	2	..	3	3	..	1	1	..	6	5	1
..	..	..	..	..	..	1	..	1	..	..	..	11	4	7
..	..	..	..	..	..	..	..	..	..	..	..	3	..	3
..	..	..	..	..	..	..	..	..	..	..	..	..	..	..
..	..	..	..	..	..	..	..	..	..	..	..	..	..	..
..	..	..	..	..	..	..	..	..	..	..	..	..	..	..
1	**1**	..	..	..	..	..	..	..	..	..	..	..	..	..
1	1	..	..	..	..	..	..	..	..	..	..	..	..	..
..	..	..	..	..	..	..	..	..	**3**	**2**	**1**	**1**	**1**	..
..	..	..	..	..	..	..	..	..	3	2	1	1	1	..
..	..	..	..	..	..	..	..	..	..	..	..	..	..	..
..	..	..	..	..	..	..	..	..	..	..	..	..	..	..
..	..	..	..	..	..	..	..	..	..	..	..	..	..	..
..	..	..	..	..	..	..	..	..	..	..	..	..	..	..

TABLE XII.

INFIRMITIES.

Jammu and Kashmir State Census, 1921.

1. This Table is divided into two parts. Part I exhibits the distribution by age of the entire afflicted population, and Part II its distr bution according to locality. Table XII-A deals with the infirmities of a few typical castes.

2. Cases of double infirmities were almost negligible.

3. The Census of Political Ilaqas having been conducted on special lines, they do not appear in this Table.

XII
Infirmities.

TABLE XII—INFIRMITIES.

PART I—DISTRIBUTION BY AGE.

Jammu and Kashmir State Census, 1921.

Entire State.

Age.	Population Afflicted.			Insane.			Deaf-Mutes.			Blind.			Lepers.		
	Persons.	Males.	Females.	Persons.	Males.	Females.	Persons.	Males.	Females.	Persons.	Males.	Females.	Persons.	Males.	Females.
1	2	3	4	5	6	7	8	9	10	11	12	13	14	15	16
All Ages ..	**11,931**	**6,989**	**4,942**	**1,284**	**874**	**410**	**4,513**	**2,644**	**1,869**	**4,649**	**2,442**	**2,207**	**1,485**	**1,029**	**456**
0—1	34	23	11	...	...	...	18	14	4	13	7	6	3	2	1
1—2	33	18	15	...	...	...	14	7	7	14	8	6	5	3	2
2—3	89	44	45	2	...	2	56	27	29	22	13	9	9	4	5
3—4	144	70	74	12	5	7	82	47	39	36	14	22	10	4	6
4—5	165	97	68	14	8	6	116	17	54	27	21	51	8	6	2
Total 0—5	**465**	**252**	**213**	**28**	**13**	**15**	**290**	**166**	**124**	**112**	**54**	**58**	**35**	**19**	**16**
5—10	1,124	641	483	112	67	45	723	394	329	225	139	86	64	41	23
10—15	1,160	687	473	138	88	50	726	418	308	217	134	83	79	47	32
15—20	1,064	587	477	151	90	61	604	332	272	216	115	101	93	50	43
20—25	984	550	434	117	86	35	481	271	210	274	128	146	112	69	43
25—30	825	543	282	118	86	32	334	212	122	254	154	100	119	91	28
30—35	980	621	359	152	114	38	384	239	145	298	159	139	146	109	33
35—40	699	452	247	108	82	26	224	147	77	245	134	111	122	89	33
40—45	836	507	329	105	76	29	243	149	94	319	170	149	169	112	57
45—50	490	285	205	53	43	10	97	67	30	248	108	140	92	67	25
50—55	701	406	295	78	49	29	133	80	53	336	159	177	154	118	36
55—60	223	140	40	13	12	1	44	33	15	111	50	52	51	36	15
60—65	885	478	83	58	36	22	100	65	35	576	268	308	151	109	42
65—70	163	101	62	9	4	5	21	15	6	111	64	47	22	18	4
70 and over	1,332	739	593	44	32	12	105	52	49	1,107	597	510	76	54	22

PART II—DISTRIBUTION BY DISTRICTS.

District, Jagir or Ilaqa.	Population Afflicted.			Insane.			Deaf-Mutes.			Blind.			Lepers.		
	Persons.	Males.	Females.	Persons.	Males.	Females.	Persons.	Males.	Females.	Persons.	Males.	Females.	Persons.	Males.	Females.
1	2	3	4	5	6	7	8	9	10	11	12	13	14	15	16
Kashmir State	**11,931**	**6,988**	**4,942**	**1,284**	**374**	**410**	**4,513**	**2,644**	**1,869**	**4,649**	**2,442**	**2,207**	**1,485**	**1,029**	**456**
I.—Jammu Province ..	**5,767**	**3,404**	**2,363**	**473**	**278**	**195**	**2,335**	**1,368**	**967**	**2,112**	**1,157**	**955**	**847**	**601**	**246**
1. Jammu District ..	978	382	396	57	36	21	421	924	172	464	268	196	36	29	7
2. Kathua " ..	625	582	243	40	27	13	255	156	99	265	147	118	65	52	13
3. Udhampur " ..	1,134	665	469	88	57	31	284	270	214	336	186	150	226	152	74
4. Riasi " ..	746	471	275	60	42	18	216	137	9	291	163	128	179	129	50
5. Mirpur " ..	1,236	687	549	84	39	45	588	338	250	484	254	230	80	56	24
6. Bhadarwah *Jagir* ..	294	147	147	25	12	13	113	71	42	104	33	71	52	31	21
7. Punch *Ilaqa*	754	470	284	119	65	54	258	147	111	168	106	62	209	152	57
II.—Kashimr Province ..	**4,182**	**2,689**	**1,493**	**721**	**527**	**194**	**1,263**	**808**	**455**	**1,66 8**	**989**	**679**	**530**	**365**	**165**
8. Kashmir North ..	1,365	886	479	196	138	58	390	258	132	622	374	248	157	116	41
9. Kashmir South ..	2,063	1,336	727	392	305	87	645	422	223	832	497	335	194	112	82
10. Muzaffarabad ..	754	467	287	133	84	49	228	178	100	214	118	96	179	137	42
III.—Frontier Districts ..	**1,982**	**896**	**1,086**	**90**	**69**	**21**	**915**	**468**	**447**	**869**	**296**	**573**	**108**	**63**	**45**
11. Ladakh District ..	1,706	746	960	76	59	17	703	353	350	825	276	549	102	58	44
12. Gilgit " ..	276	150	126	14	10	4	212	115	97	44	20	24	6	5	1

TABLE XII-A.

INFIRMITIES BY SELECTED CASTES, TRIBES OR RACES.

Jammu and Kashmir State Census, 1921.

Caste, Tribe or Race.	Population dealt with.			Insane.			Deaf-Mutes.			Blind.			Lepers.		
	Persons.	Males.	Females.	Persons.	Males.	Females.	Persons.	Males.	Females.	Persons.	Males.	Females.	Persons.	Males.	Females.
1	2	3	4	5	6	7	8	9	10	11	12	13	14	15	16
Total ..	**3,217,547**	**1,702,448**	**1,515,099**	**1,284**	**874**	**410**	**4,513**	**2,644**	**1,869**	**4,649**	**2,442**	**2,207**	**1,485**	**1,029**	**456**
HINDU.															
Brahman ..	172,051	89,205	82,846	84	60	24	270	181	89	344	214	130	73	66	7
Chamiar ..	39,088	20,607	18,413	10	8	2	94	60	34	62	35	27	9	9	..
Dum ..	30,617	15,870	14,747	5	4	1	73	51	22	47	26	21	46	31	15
Jat ..	102,649	52,514	50,135	..	..	..	12	4	8	9	7	2	..	..	..
Jhiwar ..	10,938	5,802	5,136	..	..	..	11	7	4	10	5	5	1	1	..
Khatri ..	18,758	11,061	7,697	3	3	..	27	18	9	46	20	26	14	12	2
Megh ..	78,808	41,080	37,728	17	13	4	136	78	58	171	79	92	76	49	27
Sadhu ..	2,237	1,474	763	..	..	..	..	..	..	..	..	..	1	..	1
Thakkar ..	92,025	48,951	43,074	34	23	11	179	101	78	170	86	84	115	81	34
MUSALMAN.															
Arain ..	26,370	15,644	10,726	1	1	..	73	58	15	36	31	5	6	6	..
Bafinda ..	28,162	14,813	13,349	7	5	2	49	34	15	33	25	8	7	6	1
Balti ..	124,727	61,762	62,962	61	47	14	599	299	300	683	218	470	78	44	34
Chuhra ..	5,619	2,763	2,856	1	1	..	12	11	1	32	31	1	1	1	..
Dhund ..	15,436	7,837	7,599	10	6	4	14	9	5	9	4	5	6	5	1
Gujjar ..	359,076	189,349	169,727	81	40	41	213	120	93	249	129	120	190	146	44
Hanji ..	6,035	3,414	2,621	2	1	1	5	4	1	11	8	3	..	..	..
Kashmiri ..	796,392	428,452	367,940	22	13	9	143	88	55	73	37	36	28	22	6
Lohar ..	24,483	12,852	11,631	11	5	6	52	35	17	43	32	11	17	15	2
Sayed ..	88,310	47,220	41,090	17	15	2	26	6	20	33	18	15	10	8	2
Sheikh ..	102,846	56,959	45,887	54	38	16	145	82	63	113	75	38	46	26	20
Shin ..	4,576	2,205	2,371	1	1	..	13	5	8	5	2	3	..	..	..
Tarkhan ..	26,424	14,087	12,337	9	7	2	38	23	15	27	20	7	17	12	5
Yashkun ..	16,596	8,841	7,755	7	4	3	163	90	73	22	10	12	5	4	1
BUDH.															
Mangriks ..	3,183	16,193	16,990	[illegible]	5	2	31	14	17	71	26	45	11	5	6
COMBINED.															
Rajput ..	221,5[illegible]8	113,044	108,534	2[illegible]	14	11	142	85	57	105	67	38	37	27	10
Others ..	790,563	420,386	370,177	813	560	255	1,993	1,181	812	2,240	1,237	1,003	691	453	238

TABLE XIII.

CASTE, TRIBE, RACE OR NATIONALITY.

Jammu and Kashmir State Census 1921.

1. The present arrangement of this Table is different from that of the last Census in-as-much as it is not divided into three parts and instead of exhibiting a detailed classification of Castes, only such Castes, Tribes or Races were selected as were sufficiently numerous or important to represent the main composition of the population in its various social or economic grades.

2. Some castes profess more than one religion. In such cases separate figures have been given for each religion, with a caste strength exceeding 20, figures for castes below that number being thrown into the total of the main religion for that caste. Such additions have been explained by foot-notes.

3. Sub-Castes have as far as possible been added to the main castes concerned, and figures for minor and unspecified castes, etc., have been grouped under the head "Others."

4. Europeans and Anglo-Indians, having been separately dealt with in Table XV, have been omitted from this Table.

5. One European female falling under the category of "Indefinite Beliefs" has been shown under the head "Others."

6. Aryas and Brahmos are included in the Hindus for the purposes of this Table.

TABLE XIII.

Caste, Tribe or Nationality.

Jammu and Kashmir State Census 1921.

District, Jagir or Ilaqa.	Total.			Arain.		Arghun.		Arora.				Bafinda		Balti.		Barwala.	
	Musalman.							*Hindu.*		*Sikh.*		*Musalman.*				*Hindu.*	
	Persons.	Males.	Females.	Males.	Females.	Males.	Females.	Males.	Females.	Males.	Females.	Males.	Females.	Males.	Females.	Males.	Females.
State ..	3,320,201	1,756,964	1,563,237	15,644	10,726	566	702	1,023	773	994	874	14,813	13,349	61,786	62,974	*3,105	*5,315
I.—Jammu Province (including *Jagirs*).	1,640,222	859,595	780,627	15,641	10,724	6	127	913	711	934	828	13,952	12,468	373	191	3,090	5,306
1. Jammu District (including City).	334,809	182,664	152,145	10,016	6,747	6	127	622	489	148	124	506	613	36	167	2,079	4,693
2. Kathua District ..	154,209	82,467	71,742	1,081	831	..	..	12	13	5	3	3,228	2,609	..	..	114	158
3. Udhampur District ..	218,260	115,135	103,125	203	156	..	..	26	11	21	10	258	236	33	..	299	265
4. Riasi District ...	224,589	118,575	106,014	221	217	..	..	113	68	124	117	1,047	1,017	..	9	60	85
5. Mirpur District ..	318,965	160,183	158,782	3,922	2,607	..	..	101	87	619	557	5,412	5,197	14	11	436	13
6. Bhadarwah *Jagir* ..	37,613	19,226	18,387	1	3	..	..	..	..	..	..	4	1	..	..	102	94
7. Punch *Ilaqa* ..	351,777	181,345	170,432	197	163	..	..	29	43	17	17	3,497	2,795	290	4	..	..
II.—Kashmir Province (including *Jagirs*).	1,406,827	757,701	649,126	3	2	..	2	88	46	46	37	861	881	204	128	15	7
8. Kashmir North (including Langet *Jagir*).	502,468	269,672	232,796	3	2	..	2	30	20	28	26	18	16	19	24	..	..
9. Kashmir South (including City).	688,256	372,353	315,903	..	..	..	..	27	4	13	6	94	58	124	103	..	..
10. Muzaffarabad District..	216,103	115,676	100,427	..	..	..	..	31	22	5	5	749	807	61	1	15	7
III.—Frontier Districts ..	273,152	139,668	133,484	..	..	560	573	22	16	14	9	..	..	61,209	62,655	..	..
11. Ladakh District (including Mansar).	183,470	91,256	92,214	..	..	560	573	3	1	14	9	..	..	60,847	62,442	..	..
12. Gilgit District ..	28,692	15,872	12,820	..	..	..	..	16	13	..	..	..	..	338	204	..	..
13. Frontier *Ilaqas* ..	60,990	32,540	28,450	..	..	..	..	3	2	..	..	..	..	24	9	..	..

* Includes 7 Males and 3 Females (Sikh).

TABLE XIII.

CASTE, TRIBE OR NATIONALITY.

Jammu and Kashmir State Census 1921.

District, Jagir or Ilaqa.	BASITH.				BHATI.		BRAHMAN.				BRUKPA.		BUDHAN.		CHAMAR.	
	Hindu.		*Sikh.*		*Musalman.*		*Hindu.*		*Sikh.*		*Musalman.*				*Hindu.*	
	Males.	Females.	Males.	Females.	Males.	Females.	Males.	Females.	Males.	Females.	Males.	Females.	Males.	Females.	Males.	Females.
State ..	**2,718**	**2,702**	**394**	**409**	**3,320**	**2,928**	**89,230**	**82,848**	**9,549**	**6,560**	**5,935**	**6,120**	**971**	**3,021**	***20,673**	**18,418**
I.—Jammu Province (including *Jagirs*)	**2,716**	**2,702**	**394**	**409**	**2,676**	**2,440**	**87,650**	**81,729**	**5,042**	**4,675**	**2**	**96**	**776**	**2,745**	**20,650**	**18,407**
1 Jammu District (including City) ..	2	..	3	..	579	624	27,262	24,274	6	2	..	96	7	10	7,476	6,511
2. Kathua District	..	..	..	..	37	28	16,421	15,575	9	9	..	..	..	..	4,203	3,878
3. Udhampur ,, (including Chaneni *Jagir*).	..	..	..	..	..		14,420	14,257	31	35	..	..	8	..	2,978	2,558
4. Riasi District	1,250	1,257	141	138	1,226	918	13,374	12,484	8	7	..	..	235	136	2,452	2,471
5. Mirpur ,, ...	1,464	1,445	250	271	288	176	6,070	5,682	62	54	..	..	23	237	3,187	2,637
6 Bhadarwah *Jagir*	..	..	..	..	..	..	1,042	938	..	..	..	..	..	..	273	265
7. Punch *Ilaqa*	..	..	..	..	546	690	9,061	8,519	4,926	4,568	2	..	503	2,362	81	87
II.—Kashmir Province (including *Jagirs*)	..	..	..	..	**638**	**488**	**1,505**	**1,097**	**4,502**	**3,881**	**1**	..	**194**	**276**	**18**	**11**
8. Kashmir North (including Langet *Jagir*).	..	..	..	..	97	62	683	466	1,091	1,054	..	..	..	1	..	..
9. Kashmir South (including City) ..	..	..	..	..	8	2	260	178	1,327	1,143	1	..	..	..	16	11
10 Muzaffarabad District ..	..	..	..	..	533	424	562	453	2,084	1,684	..	..	194	275	2	..
III.—Frontier Districts	**2**	..	..	..	**6**	..	**75**	**22**	**5**	**4**	**5,932**	**6,024**	**1**	..	**5**	..
11. Ladakh District (including Mansar)	..	..	..	..	..	..	38	4	..	..	5,932	6,024	..	..	..	..
12. Gilgit District	..	..	..	..	6	..	12	16	5	4	..	..	..	..	3	..
13. Frontier *Ilaqas* ..	2	..	..	..	..	..	25	2	..	..	..	..	1	..	2	..

*Includes one Sikh male.

TABLE XIII

Caste, Tribe or Nationality.

Jammu and Kashmir State Census 1921.

District, Jagir or Ilaqa.	Chuhra.				Darwesh.		Darzi		Dhobi.		Dhund.		Domal.		Dum.	
	Musalman		*Christian.*		*Musalman.*										*Hindu.*	
	Males.	Females.	Males.	Females.	Males.	Females.	Males.	Females.	Males.	Females.	Males.	Females.	Males.	Females.	Males.	Females.
State ..	2,763	2,856	632	525	7,279	5,611	2,463	2,086	3,699	3,331	7,837	7,599	3,892	3,778	15,870	14,747
I.—Jammu Province (including *Jagirs*)	2,544	2,707	652	525	4,592	3,264	1,859	1,684	2,871	2,399	5,016	4,991	3,885	3,778	15,857	14,744
1. Jammu District (including City) ..	168	325	552	4 58	2,441	1,593	226	158	1,532	1,118	..	96	12	2	7,441	5,155
2. Kathua District	6	8	79	67	505	131	47	26	554	396	..	..	..	..	3,213	2,674
3. Udhampur District (including Chaneni *Jagir.*)	93	94	1	..	384	273	10	7	38	73	..	..	..	..	2,909	5,036
4. Riasi District	568	748	..	..	391	314	77	72	199	184	..	..	1,362	1,320	1,650	1,377
5. Mirpur District	702	859	..	..	709	824	1,340	1,337	469	286	6	9	158	152	106	86
6. Bhadarwah *Jagir*	11	9	..	..	38	9	..	..	9	2	..	..	..	..	501	392
7. Punch *Ilaqa*	996	664	..	..	124	120	159	84	70	240	5,010	4,886	2,353	2,304	35	24
II.—Kashmir Province (including *Jagirs*)	219	129	..	..	2,616	2,266	601	402	827	831	2,821	2,559	3	..	11	2
8. Kashmir North (including Langet *Jagir*).	102	71	..	..	1,435	1,381	60	41	361	355	108	92	..	..	..	..
9. Kashmir South (including City) ..	98	15	..	..	1,159	879	452	296	400	514	..	..	3	..	5	2
10. Muzaffarabad District ..	19	43	..	..	22	6	89	65	66	62	2,713	2,467	..	..	6	..
III.—Frontier Districts	..	20	..	..	71	81	3	..	1	1	..	49	4	..	2	1
11. Ladakh District (including Mansar)	..	..	..	..	71	81	1	..	1	1	..	49	4	..	..	..
12. Gilgit District	..	20	..	..	..	..	2	..	..	..	..	..	..	..	2	1
13. Frontier *Ilaqas*	..	..	..	..	..	..	..	..	..	..	..	..	..	..	..	..

TABLE XIII.

Caste, Tribe or Nationality.

Jammu and Kashmir State Census 1921.

District, Jagir or Ilaqa.	Gaddi.				Gujjar.		Hajjam.				Hanji.		Harni.		Jat.	
	Hindu.		*Musalman.*		*Musalman.*		*Hindu.*		*Musalman.*		*Musalman.*				*Hindu.*	
	Males.	Females.	Males.	Females.	Males.	Females.	Males.	Females.	Males.	Females.	Males.	Females.	Males.	Females.	Males.	Females.
State ..	**5,585**	***5,399**	**89**	**55**	**191,004**	**171,103**	**‡2,358**	**‡2,430**	**16,529**	**14,287**	**3,414**	**2,621**	**492**	**127**	**13,342**	**12,519**
I.—Jammu Province (including *Jagirs*)	**5,578**	**5,399**	**51**	**15**	**126,868**	**116,424**	**2,351**	**2,426**	**7,224**	**6,535**	**132**	**187**	**492**	**127**	**13,256**	**12,511**
1. Jammu District (including city) ..	18	1	4	5	24,295	25,328	899	927	1,231	651	118	174	492	127	3,820	2,897
2. Kathua District ..	1,884	2,010	8	..	8,663	7,106	593	537	134	110	2	..	..	..	782	652
3. Udhampur District (including Chaneni *Jagir*).	3,368	3,097	20	10	9,561	8,705	407	294	720	715	..	..	..	..	379	220
4. Riasi District ..	32	8	16	..	37,164	30,369	367	298	967	1,190	..	..	..	..	79	18
5. Mirpur „ ..	..		..	..	13,270	14,319	79	368	1,966	1,880	12	2	..	..	8,181	8,718
6. Bhadarwah *Jagir* ..	276	283	..	..	1,106	1,029	..	..	105	77	..	..	..	..	2	..
7. Punch *Ilaqa* ..	..	..	3	..	32,809	29,068	6	2	2,101	1,912	..	1	..	..	13	6
II—Kashmir Province (including *Jagirs*)	**7**	..	**38**	**40**	**82,207**	**53,103**	**7**	**4**	**9,189**	**7,651**	**3,282**	**2,434**	..	..	**29**	**8**
8. Kashmir North (including Langet *Jagir*).	..	..	..	1	16,279	13,559	..	..	3,982	3,367	1,516	1,276	..	..	..	..
9. Kashmir South (including city) ..	7	..	24	30	17,026	15,004	6	4	4,533	3,738	1,761	1,158	..	..	26	5
10. Muzaffarabad District ..	..	..	14	9	28,902	24,540	1	..	674	546	5	..	..	..	3	3
III—Frontier Districts ..	..	..	..	..	**1,929**	**1,576**	..	..	**116**	**101**	..	..	..	..	**57**	..
11 Ladakh District (including Mansar)	..	..	..	..	3	..	..	..	59	47	..	..	..	..	..	..
12. Gilgit District ..	..	..	..	..	271	200	..	..	57	54	..	..	..	..	57	..
13. Frontier *Ilaqas* ..	..	..	..	..	1,655	1,370	..	..	..	..	..	..	..	..	..	..

* Includes one Sikh female.
‡ Includes 1 male and 1 female (Sikh).

TABLE XIII.

CASTE, TRIBE OR NATIONALITY.

Jammu and Kashmir Census 1921.

District, Jagir or Ilaqa.	JAT.				JHIWAR.		JOGI.		KASHMIRI.				KHATRI.			
	Musalman.		*Sikh.*		*Hindu.*				*Hindu Pandit.*		*Musalman.*		*Hindu.*		*Sikh.*	
	Males.	Females.	Males.	Females.	Males.	Females.	Males.	Females.	Males.	Females.	Males.	Females.	Males.	Females.	Males.	Females.
State ..	† 52,516	† 50,140	768	648	* 5,817	* 5,149	1,584	1,458	30,947	24,108	428,675	368,129	11,098	7,697	2,124	1,763
I.—Jammu Province (including *Jagirs*)	52,335	49,983	685	586	5,780	5,144	1,567	1,443	994	391	52,322	44,267	8,959	6,296	1,192	1,080
1. Jammu District (including city) ..	4,816	1,975	116	150	3,546	3,147	545	587	339	115	1,853	1,374	3,699	2,346	97	86
2. Kathua District ..	116	35	26	17	1,180	1,144	514	457	..	5	1,043	1,278	339	400	28	15
3. Udhampur „ (including Chaneni *Jagir*).	50	22	9	1	418	282	104	101	514	134	23,421	17,459	1,399	1,323	23	44
4. Riasi District ..	1,297	1,101	..	..	103	106	132	106	37	48	9,570	7,298	1,035	820	32	27
5. Mirpur „ ..	42,973	44,285	534	418	477	414	121	43	7	..	3,999	4,388	1,654	945	819	751
6. Bhadarwah *Jagir* ..	1	..	..	..		2	149	149	75	72	4,118	3,804	139	27	1	1
7. Punch *Ilaqa* ..	3,082	2,565	..	..	52	49	2	..	22	17	8,318	8,666	694	435	192	156
II.—Kashmir Province (including *Jagirs*)	178	157	83	62	9	5	15	15	29,703	23,685	374,558	321,650	2,067	1,369	897	659
8. Kashmir North (including Langet Jagir).	..	5	20	2	2	2	5	..	4,592	2,845	175,127	152,449	668	434	562	511
9. Kashmir South (including city) ..	120	80	14	15	..	..	3	11	24,962	20,797	186,325	157,412	635	369	190	110
10. Muzaffarabad District ..	58	72	49	45	7	3	7	4	239	43	13,106	11,789	764	566	145	38
III.—Frontier Districts ..	3	..	..	..	28	..	2	..	160	34	1,795	2,212	72	32	35	24
11. Ladakh District (including *Mansar*)	..	..	..	..	..		..	..	65	34	949	854	21	21	6	5
12. Gilgit District ..	3	..	..	..	20	..	2	..	92	..	623	1,169	14	11	29	19
13. Frontier *Ilaqas* ..	..	..	..	..	8	..	..	..	3	..	223	189	37	..	..	..

* Includes 8 males and 13 females (Sikh).
† Includes 2 males and 5 females (Indian Christian.)

TABLE XIII.

CASTE, TRIBE OR NATIONALITY.

Jammu and Kashmir State Census 1921.

District, Jagir or Ilaqa.	KHOJA.		KUMHIAR.				LABANA.				LOHAR.					
	Musalman.		*Hindu.*		*Musalman.*		*Hindu.*		*Sikh.*		*Hindu.*		*Musalman.*		*Sikh.*	
	Males.	Females.	Males.	Females.	Males.	Females.	Males.	Females.	Males.	Females.	Males.	Females.	Males.	Females.	Males.	Females.
State ..	**2,536**	**1,705**	* **2,693**	* **2,313**	**11,540**	**10,046**	**963**	**823**	**2,245**	**1,897**	**5,635**	**5,119**	* **12,856**	* **11,632**	**93**	**94**
I.—Jammu Province (including *Jagirs*)	**2,447**	**1,584**	**2,676**	**2,313**	**7,270**	**6,063**	**730**	**614**	**1,920**	**1,571**	**5,599**	**5,119**	**7,390**	**7,291**	**90**	**93**
1. Jammu District (including city) ..	262	159	1,180	1,142	1,003	362	275	324	1,712	1,368	1,641	1,321	850	548	86	91
2. Kathua District ..	67	43	992	786	144	101	150	116	57	38	1,014	854	24	18	..	..
3. Udhampur „ (including Chaneni *Jagir*).	493	413	116	77	1,090	962	..	..	..	..	1,093	1,063	731	656	..	..
4. Riasi District ..	142	106	247	177	571	518	222	170	49	63	1,436	1,372	1,184	1,246	..	..
5. Mirpur „ ..	102	90	131	122	2,245	2,126	63	..	3	..	26	125	1,799	2,444	2	..
6. Bhadarwah *Jagir* ..	21	15	1	..	305	264	..	..	..	..	337	331	17	13	..	..
7. Punch *Ilaqa* ..	1,360	758	9	9	1,912	1,730	20	4	99	102	52	53	2,785	2,366	2	2
II.—Kashmir Province (including *Jagirs*)	**89**	**121**	**13**	..	**4,109**	**3,858**	**233**	**209**	**325**	**326**	**19**	..	**5,137**	**4,093**	**3**	**1**
8. Kashmir North (including Langet *Jagir*).	8	2	..	..	1,980	1,634	1	..	4	12	..	..	1,517	1,146	..	..
9. Kashmir South (including city) ..	18	11	13	..	1,947	1,940	..	..	..	..	13	..	2,187	1,797	..	
10. Muzaffarabad District ..	63	108	..	..	182	284	232	209	321	314	6	..	1,433	1,150	3	1
III.—Frontier Districts ..	..	..	**4**	..	**161**	**125**	..	..	..	..	**17**	..	**329**	**248**	..	..
11. Ladakh District (including Mansar)	..	..	1	..	80	54	..	..	..	..	1	..	174	128	..	..
12. Gilgit District ..	..	..	3	..	81	71	..	..	..	..	16	..	83	75	..	..
13. Frontier *Ilaqas* ..	..	..	..	..	..	..	..	..	..	..	..	..	72	45	..	..

* Includes 10 males and 19 females (Sikh).

* Includes 4 males and 1 female (Indian Christian).

TABLE XIII.

Caste, Tribe or Nationality.

Jammu and Kashmir State Census 1921.

District, Jagir or Ilaqa.	Mahajan.				Mangriks.		Megh.				Mirasi.		Mochi.		Mohyal.	
	Hindu.		*Sikh.*		*Budh.*		*Hindu.*		*Sikh.*		*Musalman.*				*Hindu.*	
	Males.	Females.	Males.	Females.	Males.	Females.	Males.	Females.	Males.	Females.	Males.	Females.	Males.	Females.	Males.	Females.
State ..	**11,199**	**8,689**	**62**	**33**	**16,193**	**16,990**	**41,081**	**37,728**	**86**	**87**	**4,269**	**3,503**	**12,890**	**10,261**	**1,312**	**1,182**
I.—Jammu Province (including *Jagirs*)	**11,114**	**8,647**	**60**	**33**	**2**	**94**	**41,044**	**37,698**	**86**	**87**	**3,680**	**3,019**	**6,015**	**4,659**	**1,261**	**1,150**
1. Jammu District (including city) ...	4,405	3,520	28	16	..	..	17,774	15,459	10	14	1,104	782	506	134	331	278
2. Kathua District	2,187	1,529	5	2	..	..	6,117	5,389	11	12	163	102	4	..	...	3
3. Udhampur District (including Chaneni *Jagir.*)	2,154	1,551	..	..	2	94	9,928	10,013	65	61	70	69	375	335	29	37
4. Riasi District	661	571	..	..	..	..	3,418	2,916	..	..	407	406	525	437	286	248
5. Mirpur "	1,376	1,252	13	4	..	..	738	635	...	...	468	576	2,332	2,068	561	518
6. Bhadarwah *Jagir*	161	97	..	...	..	..	3,065	3,285	..	..	5	4	54	46	2	..
7. Punch *Ilaqa*	170	127	14	11	..	..	4	1	..	..	1,463	1,080	2,319	1,619	52	66
II.—Kashmir Province (including *Jagirs*)	**85**	**42**	**2**	..	..	..	**36**	**30**	..	..	**550**	**482**	**6,796**	**5,485**	**51**	**32**
8. Kashmir North (including Langet *Jagir.*)	2	4	..	..	..	..	3	...	..	..	...	..	1,902	1,574	20	13
9. Kashmir South (including city) ...	40	8	..	..	..	..	16	8	..	...	7	5	4,231	3,434	16	7
10. Muzaffarabad District ..	43	30	2	..	...	..	17	22	..	..	543	477	663	477	15	12
III.—Frontier Districts ..	..	..	..	..	**16,191**	**16,896**	**1**	..	...	..	**39**	**2**	**79**	**117**	..	..
11. Ladakh District (including Mansar)..	..	..	..	...	16,191	16,896	..	..	..	..	37	2	65	105	..	..
12. Gilgit District ..	..	..	..	..	..	..	..	..	..	..	2	..	..	..	..	..
13. Frontier *Ilaqas* ..	..	...	..	..	..	..	1	..	..	..	..	...	14	12	..	..

TABLE XIII.

CASTE, TRIBE OR NATIONALITY.

Jammu and Kashmir State Census 1921.

District, Jagir or Ilaqa.			Mughal.		Pathan.				Rajput.				Rigzang.		Sadhu.	
	Sikh.		*Musalman.*		*Musalman.*		*Hindu.*		*Mussalman.*		*Sikh.*		*Budh.*		*Hindu.*	
	Males.	Females.	Males.	Females.	Males.	Females.	Males.	Females.	Males.	Females.	Males.	Females.	Males.	Females.	Males.	Females.
State ..	659	540	18,489	17,020	17,515	14,664	28,331	20,663	84,910	88,034	191	146	27	17	*1,478	763
I.—**Jammu Province** (including *Jagirs.*)	51	36	5,605	6,046	5,478	4,374	27,392	20,406	68,589	72,833	159	140	4	..	1,438	763
1. Jammu District (including City) ..	2	..	482	575	1,056	353	11,974	8,165	6,799	4,957	129	113	..	..	645	284
2. Kathua District	..	..	33	20	143	97	5,181	4,162	162	147	..	..	..	..	236	142
3. Udhampur District (including Chaneni *Jagir*).	..	..	204	249	617	463	4,269	3,599	1,650	1,507	1	..	4	..	259	186
4. Riasi District	2	2	1,266	1,659	423	393	1,721	1,439	7,724	7,869	..	..	..	..	158	94
5. Mirpur ,, ...	23	23	1,436	1,474	429	414	3,650	2,538	24,191	27,249	14	11	..	..	68	4
6. Bhadarwah *Jagir*	..	..	69	50	335	341	385	378	18	19	..	..	..	..	59	51
7. Punch *Ilaqa*	24	11	2,115	2,019	2,475	2,313	212	125	28,045	31,085	15	16	..	..	13	2
II.—**Kashmir Province** (including *Jagir*)s.	608	504	12,019	10,230	11,560	9,969	756	251	15,782	14,961	20	6	..	..	40	..
8. Kashmir North (including Langet *Jagir*).	464	409	2,505	2,058	3,540	3,147	49	24	1,041	961	5	2	..	..	2	..
9. Kashmir South (including City) ..	58	23	3,420	2,807	5,490	4,723	450	217	456	553	5	3	..	..	32	..
10. Muzaffarabad District.. ..	86	72	6,094	5,365	2,530	2,099	257	10	14,285	13,447	10	1	..	..	6	..
III.—**Frontier Districts**	..	..	865	744	477	321	183	6	539	240	12	..	23	17	..	..
11. Ladakh District (including Mansar).	..	..	64	36	57	29	21	2	124	17	..	..	23	17	..	..
12. Gilgit District	..	..	157	124	187	121	162	4	218	60	12	..	..	..	..	..
13. Frontier *Ilaqas*	..	..	644	584	233	171	..	..	197	163	..	..	..	..	..	..

* Includes 4 Sikh Males.

TABLE XIII.

CASTE, TRIBE OR NATIONALITY.

Jammu and Kashmir State Census 1921.

District, Jagir or Ilaqa.	Sayed.		Sheikh.		Shin.		Sudhan.		Tarkhan.						Teli.	
			Musalman.						*Hindu.*		*Musalman.*		*Sikh.*		*Musalman.*	
	Males.	Females.	Males.	Females.	Males.	Females.	Males.	Females.	Males.	Females.	Males.	Females.	Males.	Females.	Males.	Females.
State ..	**47,772**	**41,581**	**57,043**	**45,950**	**7,665**	**7,441**	**31,801**	**32,191**	**5,401**	**4,498**	**14,101**	**12,344**	**70**	**59**	**13,423**	**10,711**
I.—Jammu Province (including *Jagirs*)	**11,242**	**9,983**	**15,182**	**13,300**	**54**	**432**	**31,482**	**31,971**	**5,394**	**4,498**	**7,337**	**6,698**	**67**	**47**	**8,127**	**6252**
1. Jammu District (including City) ..	1,792	917	1,251	782	16	2	13	5	2,591	2,122	987	767	36	29	3,107	2,334
2. Kathua District	54	11	154	184	..	..	..	4	1,670	1,421	41	27	6	8	1,574	864
3. Udhampur District (including Chaneni *Jagir*).	485	510	3,061	2,593	..	..	..	..	648	444	200	61	6	5	285	255
4. Riasi District	1,187	1,119	1,611	1,382	..	..	18	70	264	348	1,128	1,135	1	..	578	553
5. Mirpur District	2,238	2,237	1,644	1,602	29	430	103	1,223	203	161	3,305	3,382	18	5	1,972	1,702
6. Bhadarwah *Jagir*	69	55	947	806	..	..	..	..	18	2	14	16	..	..	8	2
7. Punch *Ilaqa*	5,417	5,134	6,514	5,951	9	..	31,348	30,669	..	..	1,662	1,310	..	..	603	542
II.—Kashmir Province (including *Jagirs*)	**34,326**	**29,555**	**41,487**	**32,357**	**29**	**6**	**316**	**220**	**5**	..	**6,653**	**5,552**	**3**	**12**	**5,295**	**4,459**
8. Kashmir North (including Langet *Jagir*).	13,505	11,645	14,958	12,378	8	4	..	..	1	..	3,290	2,832	..	..	2,145	1,791
9. Kashmir South (including City) ..	14,394	10,841	19,870	14,151	15	2	..	..	3	..	2,797	2,428	3	12	2,940	2,450
10. Muzaffarabad District	6,427	7,069	6,659	5,828	6	..	316	220	1	..	566	292	..	..	210	218
III.—Frontier Districts	**2,204**	**2,043**	**374**	**293**	**7,582**	**7,003**	**3**	..	**2**	..	**111**	**94**	..	..	**1**	..
11. Ladakh District (including Mansar).	1,443	1,383	226	176	83	62	..	..	..	..	54	42	..	..	..	..
12. Gilgit District	209	169	64	54	2,039	1,871	..	..	2	..	43	45	..	..	1	..
13. Frontier *Ilaqas*	552	491	84	63	5,460	5,070	3	..	..	..	14	7	..	..	..	..

TABLE XIII.

CASTE, TRIBE OR NATIONALITY.

Jammu and Kashmir State Census 1921.

District, Jagir, or Ilaqa.	Thakkar.		Watal.		Yashkun.		Zargar.				Others (Minor and unspecified castes, etc.)					
	Hindu.		Musalman.				Hindu.		Sikh.		Hindu.		Musalman.		Sikh.	
	Males.	Females.	Males.	Females.	Males.	Females.	Males.	Females.	Males.	Females.	Males.	Females.	Males.	Females.	Males.	Females.
State ..	**48,996**	***43,075**	**1,598**	**1,739**	**23,373**	**20,714**	**2,255**	**2,027**	**199**	**176**	**17,528**	**11,743**	**160,484**	**141,473**	**3,321**	**3,397**
I.—Jammu Province (including *Jagirs*)	**48,641**	**43,022**	**556**	**507**	..	**2**	**2,249**	**2,027**	**176**	**155**	**15,820**	**10,684**	**40,377**	**35,020**	**501**	**468**
1. Jammu District (including City) ..	3,711	2,759	40	15	..	..	800	700	7	3	4,732	2,382	3,640	5,478	266	277
2. Kathua District	12,435	10,722	26	7	..	..	293	330	1	1	2,610	2,405	2,086	2,021	..	4
3. Udhampur (including Chaneni *Jagir*)	18,969	17,337	248	257	..	2	397	376	..	..	3,862	1,030	1,484	3,376	19	..
4. Riasi District	8,853	7,519	42	39	..	..	272	250	..	..	3,572	3,536	5,234	5,490	41	59
5. Mirpur	59	..	..	..	..	..	445	347	82	82	291	932	10,666	5,903	24	12
6. Bhadarwah *Jagir*	4,557	4,646	134	130	..	..	2	1	..	..	235	166	447	509	4	3
7. Punch Ilaqa	57	39	66	59	..	..	40	23	86	69	318	233	16,820	12,243	144	113
II.—Kashmir Province (including *Jagirs*)	**293**	**53**	**1,042**	**1,232**	**1**	**1**	**6**	..	**23**	**21**	**1,508**	**1,022**	**108,033**	**97,059**	**2,798**	**2,917**
8. Kashmir North (including Langet *Jagir*).	23	2	124	399	..	..	..	..	..	..	161	321	14,978	13,797	605	537
9. Kashmir South (including City) ..	258	47	918	833	1	1	2	..	3	..	869	394	72,022	67,119	165	112
10. Muzaffarabad District ..	1	4	..	..	..	..	4	..	20	21	478	307	21,033	16,143	2,028	2,268
III.—Frontier Districts	**62**	..	..	..	**23,372**	**20,711**	..	..	..	..	**400**	**37**	**12,074**	**9,394**	**22**	**12**
11. Ladakh District (including Mansar)	10	..	..	..	40	3	..	..	..	..	41	30	1,506	1,336	10	4
12. Gilgit District	7	..	..	..	8,800	7,749	..	..	..	..	268	7	1,965	759	..	..
13. Frontier *Ilaqas*	45	..	..	..	14,532	12,959	..	..	..	..	91	..	8,603	7 2	12	8

* Includes 1 Sikh female.

TABLE XIII.

Caste, Tribe or Nationality.

Jammu and Kashmir State Census 1921.

District, Jagir or Ilaqa.	Others (Minor and unspecified castes, &c.													
	Jain.		*Buddhist.*		*Zoroastrian.*		*Indian Christian.*		*Sansi.*		*Sapiada.*		*Others.*	
	Males.	Females.	Males.	Females.	Males.	Females.	Males.	Females.	Males.	Females.	Males.	Females.	Males.	Females.
State ..	**296**	**234**	**2,618**	**1,840**	**5**	**2**	**92**	**56**	**162**	**140**	**11**	**11**	..	**1**
I—Jammu Province (including *Jagirs*) ..	**296**	**234**	**220**	**122**	**3**	**2**	..	**1**	**105**	**92**	**11**	**11**	..	..
1. Jammu District (including City) ..	290	231	4	..	3	2	..	..	105	92	11	11	..	..
2. Kathua District	1	..	..	..	..	..	..	..	..	..	..	..	..	..
3. Udhampur District (including Chaneni *Jagir*).	..	..	216	122	..	..	..	..	..	..	..	..	..	..
4. Riasi District	..	..	..	..	..	..	..	..	..	..	..	..	..	..
5. Mirpur District	2	3	..	..	..	..	..	..	..	..	..	..	..	..
6. Bhadarwah *Jagir*	..	..	..	..	..	..	..	..	..	..	..	..	..	..
7. Punch *Ilaqa*	1	..	..	..	..	..	..	1	..	..	..	..	..	..
II—Kashmir Province (including *Jagirs*)	**1**	..	**2**	..	**2**	..	**56**	**26**	**57**	**48**	..	..	..	**1**
8. Kashmir North (including Langet *Jagir*).	1	..	..	..	..	..	6	5	36	37	..	..	..	..
9. Kashmir South (including City) ..	..	..	2	..	2	..	50	21	21	11	..	..	..	1
10. Muzaffarabad District ..	..	..	..	..	..	..	..	..	..	..	..	..	..	..
III—Frontier Districts	..	..	**2,396**	**1,718**	..	..	**36**	**29**	..	..	..	..	..	..
11. Ladakh District (including Mansar)	..	..	2,396	1,718	..	..	35	29	..	..	..	..	..	..
12. Gilgit District	..	..	..	..	..	..	1	..	..	..	..	..	..	..
13. Frontier *Ilaqas*	..	..	..	..	..	..	..	..	..	..	..	..	..	..

TABLE XIV.

CIVIL CONDITION BY AGE FOR SELECTED CASTES.

Jammu and Kashmir State Census 1921.

TABLE XIV.

Civil condition by age for selected cases.

Caste, Tribe and Race.	Total.	Sexes.	Population dealt with.	Unmarried.							Married.							Widowed.						
				Total	0–5	5–12	12–15	15–20	20–40	40 & over.	Total.	0–5	5–12	12–15	15–20	20–40	40 & over.	Total.	0–5	5–12	12–15	15–20	20–40	40 & over.
1	2	3	4	5	6	7	8	9	10	11	12	13	14	15	16	17	18	19	20	21	22	23	24	25
Hindu.																								
1 Arora	1,791	Males ..	1,020	476	99	76	38	70	168	25	427	..	5	6	40	193	183	117	..	..	..	..	57	60
		Females ..	771	273	86	131	39	16	1	..	344	..	6	16	60	188	74	154	..	..	..	1	48	105
2. Brahman ..	172,051	Males ..	89,205	46,522	10,420	13,717	7,470	5,379	7,250	2,286	34,778	9	231	393	1,619	15,668	16,858	7,905	2	9	21	60	1,786	6,027
		Females ..	82,846	26,650	10,827	12,338	2,910	392	159	24	38,232	56	2,535	3,326	7,041	17,598	7,676	17,964	3	122	132	347	5,010	12,350
3. Chamiar ..	39,088	Males ..	20,670	9,755	2,816	3,312	1,404	939	980	304	9,129	4	130	218	721	4,153	3,903	1,786	1	8	16	21	481	1,259
		Females ..	18,418	6,012	2,359	2,860	649	98	33	13	9,500	9	625	1,077	1,747	4,360	1,682	2,906	..	13	16	107	699	2,071
4. Jat	25,861	Males ..	13,342	6,976	1,776	2,522	863	741	896	178	5,340	2	48	78	226	2,196	2,790	1,026	..	3	8	5	232	778
		Females ..	12,519	5,325	2,297	2,491	442	63	22	10	5,384	6	332	471	780	2,648	1,147	1,810	..	1	4	35	292	1,478
5. Kashmiri Pandit ..	55,052	Males ..	30,944	17,707	2,981	4,830	2,369	2,261	4,086	1,180	11,108	..	33	97	467	6,164	4,347	2,129	..	2	..	10	432	1,685
		Females ..	24,108	8,662	2,746	4,831	977	78	29	1	10,901	..	103	550	1,558	6,858	1,832	4,545	..	6	54	53	1,145	3,287
6. Khatri.. ..	18,758	Males ..	11,061	6,115	1,202	1,846	875	779	1,112	301	3,709	1	31	57	289	1,766	1,565	1,237	..	4	2	5	394	832
		Females ..	7,697	2,787	1,060	1,298	326	77	24	2	3,602	3	105	215	858	1,713	708	1,308	..	1	4	37	377	889
7. Megh	78,808	Males ..	41,080	19,758	4,503	7,424	2,768	2,012	2,392	659	18,017	4	274	402	1,054	8,193	8,090	3,305	..	5	9	31	782	2,478
		Females ..	37,728	11,992	5,750	4,854	1,038	239	72	39	18,415	42	1,285	1,610	2,864	8,917	3,697	7,321	..	22	49	223	2,030	4,997
8. Rajput ..	48,994	Males ..	28,331	15,854	4,203	3,896	1,814	2,160	3,114	667	10,140	4	35	113	691	5,172	4,125	2,337	..	5	5	24	647	1,656
		Females ..	20,663	5,567	2,479	2,424	464	151	34	15	9,940	8	361	751	1,590	5,063	2,167	5,156	3	23	19	90	1,323	3,698
9. Thakkar ..	92,025	Males ..	48,951	24,412	4,978	7,257	2,514	3,105	4,653	1,905	20,172	4	192	325	880	10,114	8,657	4,367	..	3	8	35	1,125	3,196
		Females ..	43,074	12,168	5,174	5,616	986	237	110	45	21,737	28	1,431	1,140	2,857	12,781	3,500	9,169	1	42	53	178	2,318	6,577
Musalman.																								
1. Arain	26,370	Males ..	15,644	7,372	1,884	2,304	1,108	921	982	173	6,894	8	115	160	324	3,053	3,234	1,378	2	37	26	35	393	885
		Females ..	10,726	4,263	1,827	1,674	616	94	41	11	5,244	3	263	539	825	2,228	1,386	1,219	..	..	1	26	286	906
2. Bafinda ..	28,162	Males ..	14,813	7,751	2,191	2,641	1,019	869	833	198	5,931	12	145	229	399	2,791	2,355	1,131	..	6	2	29	287	807
		Females ..	13,349	5,581	2,222	2,478	495	270	96	20	6,258	12	294	469	1,138	2,946	1,399	1,510	..	7	7	40	291	1,165
3. Balti	124,727	Males ..	61,762	31,766	9,338	10,760	4,627	4,068	2,735	238	27,383	4	143	427	1,777	13,436	11,596	2,613	..	6	16	75	643	1,873
		Females ..	62,965	25,819	9,621	9,792	3,129	2,155	983	139	30,010	..	229	1,014	3,063	17,872	7,832	7,136	..	9	25	90	1,213	5,799
4. Brukpa ..	12,055	Males ..	5,935	2,729	963	1,007	287	287	168	17	2,951	..	12	112	200	1,521	1,106	255	..	..	1	4	64	186
		Females ..	6,120	2,505	1,153	948	273	74	48	9	3,023	..	35	148	353	1,835	652	592	..	..	1	7	133	451
5. Gujjar.. ..	359,076	Males ..	189,349	99,918	27,982	36,986	14,712	10,527	8,439	1,272	78,898	112	1,081	1,915	4,777	39,339	31,674	10,533	5	46	96	173	3,151	7,062
		Females ..	169,727	67,679	25,947	29,337	7,177	3,853	1,415	150	86,262	111	4,293	5,280	12,925	45,788	17,865	15,786	..	79	95	266	3,171	12,175
6. Hanji	6,035	Males ..	3,414	1,700	392	613	191	258	236	10	1,240	1	4	13	45	752	425	474	..	2	1	9	46	416
		Females ..	2,621	1,121	388	551	112	45	20	5	1,192	..	17	95	192	690	198	308	..	5	3	13	66	221
7. Jat	102,649	Males ..	52,514	29,669	7,948	10,771	3,728	3,468	3,263	491	18,889	10	173	269	805	8,805	8,827	3,956	1	25	20	59	933	2,927
		Females ..	50,135	19,638	5,945	10,453	1,975	824	352	89	23,220	46	416	820	2,907	11,468	7,563	7,277	5	19	14	81	1,133	6,025
8. Kashmiri ..	796,392	Males ..	428,452	222,604	63,807	79,920	28,207	25,930	22,190	2,550	183,016	32	1,911	3,344	13,534	104,360	59,835	22,832	2	27	34	245	7,142	15,382
		Females ..	367,940	148,316	63,082	64,663	13,595	4,335	1,965	676	184,598	8	4,003	12,351	27,376	106,088	34,772	35,026	1	67	182	696	6,787	27,293
9. Mughal ..	34,281	Males ..	17,845	9,431	2,729	3,422	1,125	1,046	963	146	7,440	1	61	185	562	3,613	3,018	974	..	1	7	17	303	646
		Females ..	16,436	7,230	2,870	3,132	878	246	84	20	7,524	4	280	403	1,204	3,981	1,652	1,682	..	1	13	32	402	1,234
10. Pathan ..	31,775	Males ..	17,282	9,072	2,357	3,179	1,104	1,004	1,119	309	7,064	2	56	214	577	3,730	2,485	1,146	..	5	18	80	325	718
		Females ..	14,493	5,919	2,323	2,701	560	207	96	32	7,076	3	152	400	1,036	4,119	1,366	1,498	..	4	10	36	269	1,179
11. Rajput ..	172,584	Males ..	84,713	46,576	14,829	15,710	5,826	5,268	4,374	569	33,360	24	215	511	1,779	15,457	15,374	4,777	..	28	25	46	1,423	3,255
		Females ..	87,871	38,796	14,313	16,765	5,360	1,612	621	125	37,933	31	1,225	1,833	5,253	21,488	8,103	11,142	..	19	37	116	1,761	9,209
12. Sayed	88,310	Males ..	47,220	25,264	7,118	9,082	3,056	2,960	2,486	562	19,046	6	225	480	1,500	10,383	6,452	2,910	2	23	30	70	841	1,944
		Females ..	41,090	17,616	6,449	7,797	1,942	855	447	126	19,253	5	325	1,221	2,770	10,872	4,060	4,221	1	7	27	140	1,022	3,024
13. Shin	4,576	Males ..	2,205	1,128	350	447	86	118	115	12	1,007	..	2	2	56	628	319	70	..	2	1	2	24	41
		Females ..	2,371	1,084	319	462	192	80	22	9	1,110	..	21	243	135	510	201	177	..	..	1	5	49	122
14. Tarkhan ..	26,424	Males ..	14,087	7,370	2,129	2,694	953	740	716	138	5,904	6	69	148	404	3,139	2,138	813	5	7	15	19	226	541
		Females ..	12,337	4,905	2,004	2,082	541	169	103	6	5,949	2	164	364	931	3,088	1,400	1,483	..	1	22	31	284	1,145

TABLE XV.

TERRITORIAL DISTRIBUTION OF THE CHRISTIAN POPULATION BY SECT AND RACE.

Jammu and Kashmir State Census, 1921.

1. Riasi is the only administrative division which has not returned any Christian population.

2. One European female falling under the category of "Indefinite Beliefs" has been excluded from this table.

TABLE XV.

Territorial Distribution of the Christian Population by Sect and Race.

Jammu and Kashmir State Census, 1921.

District, Jagir or Ilaqa.	All Denominations.									Anglican Communion.									Lutheran.								
	Total.			Distribution by Race.						Total.			Distribution by Race.						Total.			Distribution by Race.					
				European and Allied races.		Anglo-Indian.		Indian.					European and Allied races.		Anglo-Indian.		Indian.					Europeans and Allied races.		Anglo-Indian.		Indian.	
	Persons.	Males.	Females.	Males.	Females.	Males.	Females.	Males.	Females.	Persons.	Males.	Females.	Males.	Females.	Males.	Females.	Males.	Females.	Persons.	Males.	Females.	Males.	Females.	Males.	Females.	Males.	Females.
1	2	3	4	5	6	7	8	9	10	11	12	13	14	15	16	17	18	19	20	21	22	23	24	25	26	27	28
KASHMIR STATE.	1,634	888	746	128	141	30	18	730	587	508	244	264	88	116	11	10	145	138	1	1	..	..	..	1	..	..	..
I. Jammu Province (including *Jagirs*).	1,207	662	545	8	5	16	8	638	532	272	143	129	1	3	7	3	135	123	..	..	..	..	..	..	..	..	..
1. Jammu District (including city).	1,040	573	467	7	3	10	5	556	459	259	137	122	1	2	4	3	132	117	..	..	..	..	..	..	..	..	..
2. Kathua District ..	146	79	67	..	..	..	..	79	67	..	..	..	..	..	..	..	..	..	..	..	..	..	..	..	..	..	..
3. Udhampur " ..	2	1	1	..	1	..	..	1	..	1	1	..	..	..	..	..	1	..	..	..	..	..	..	..	..	..	..
4. Riasi " ..	..	..	..	..	..	..	..	..	..	..	..	..	..	..	..	..	..	..	..	..	..	..	..	..	..	..	..
5. Mirpur " ..	6	3	3	1	..	2	3	..	..	..	..	..	..	..	..	..	..	..	..	..	..	..	..	..	..	..	..
6. Bhadarwah *Jagir* ..	1	1	..	..	..	1	..	..	..	..	..	..	..	..	..	..	..	..	..	..	..	..	..	..	..	..	..
7. Punch *Ilaqa* ..	12	5	7	..	1	3	..	2	6	12	5	7	..	1	3	..	2	6	..	..	..	..	..	..	..	..	..
II. Kashmir Province (including *Jagirs*).	341	179	162	111	128	12	10	56	26	227	97	130	84	108	3	7	10	15	1	1	..	..	..	1	..	..	..
8. Kashmir North (including Langet *Jagir*).	33	19	14	13	9	..	..	6	5	14	8	6	8	6	..	..	..	..	..	..	..	..	..	..	..	..	..
9. Kashmir South (including city).	302	156	146	94	115	12	10	50	21	207	85	122	72	100	3	7	10	15	1	1	..	..	..	1	..	..	..
10. Muzaffarbad District ..	6	4	2	4	2	..	..	..	..	6	4	2	4	2	..	..	..	..	..	..	..	..	..	..	..	..	..
III. Frontier Districts ..	86	47	39	9	10	2	..	36	29	9	4	5	3	5	1	..	..	..	..	..	..	..	..	..	..	..	..
11. Ladakh " ..	70	37	33	2	4	..	..	35	29	2	..	2	..	2	..	..	..	..	..	..	..	..	..	..	..	..	..
12. Gilgit " ..	15	9	6	6	6	2	..	1	..	6	3	3	2	3	1	..	..	..	..	..	..	..	..	..	..	..	..
13. Frontier *Ilaqas* ..	1	1	..	1	..	..	..	..	..	1	1	..	1	..	..	..	..	..	..	..	..	..	..	..	..	..	..

TABLE XV.

TERRITORIAL DISTRIBUTION OF THE CHRISTIAN POPULATION BY SECT AND RACE.

Jammu and Kashmir State Census, 1921.

DISTRICT, JAGIR OR ILAQA.	METHODIST.									MINOR PROTESTANT DENOMINATIONS.									PRESBYTERIAN.								
	TOTAL.			DISTRIBUTION BY RACE.						TOTAL.			DISTRIBUTION BY RACE.						TOTAL.			DISTRIBUTION BY RACE.					
				European and Allied races.		Anglo-Indian.		Indian.					European and Allied races.		Anglo-Indian.		Indian.					European and Allied races.		Anglo-Indian.		Indian.	
	Persons.	Males.	Females.	Males.	Females.	Males.	Females.	Males.	Females.	Persons.	Males.	Females.	Males.	Females.	Males.	Females.	Males.	Females.	Persons.	Males.	Females.	Males.	Females.	Males.	Females.	Males.	Females.
	29	30	31	32	33	34	35	36	37	38	39	40	41	42	43	44	45	46	47	48	49	50	51	52	53	54	55
KASHMIR STATE ..	1	..	1	..	..	..	..	..	1	66	37	29	1	..	..	..	36	29	815	457	358	9	4	5	..	443	354
I. Jammu Province (including *Jagirs*).	..	..	..	..	..	..	..	..	..	8	8	..	1	..	..	..	7	..	803	449	354	1	..	5	..	443	354
1. Jammu District (including city).	..	..	..	..	..	..	..	..	..	8	8	..	1	..	..	..	7	..	658	370	288	..	..	4	..	366	288
2. Kathu District ..	..	..	..	..	..	..	..	..	..	..	..	..	..	..	..	..	..	..	143	77	66	..	..	..	..	77	66
3. Udhampur " ..	..	..	..	..	..	..	..	..	..	..	..	..	..	..	..	..	..	..	..	..	..	..	..	..	..	..	..
4. Riasi " ..	..	..	..	..	..	..	..	..	..	..	..	..	..	..	..	..	..	..	..	..	..	..	..	..	..	..	..
5. Mirpur " ..	..	..	..	..	..	..	..	..	..	..	..	..	..	..	..	..	..	..	1	1	..	1	..	..	..	..	..
6. Bhadarwah *Jagir* ..	..	..	..	..	..	..	..	..	..	..	..	..	..	..	..	..	..	..	1	1	..	..	..	1	..	..	..
7. Punch *Ilaqa* ..	..	..	..	..	..	..	..	..	..	..	..	..	..	..	..	..	..	..	..	..	..	..	..	..	..	..	..
II. Kashmir Province (including *Jagirs*).	1	..	1	..	..	..	..	..	1	..	..	..	..	..	..	..	..	..	8	6	2	6	2	..	..	..	..
8. Kashmir North (including Langet *Jagir*).	..	..	..	..	..	..	..	..	..	..	..	..	..	..	..	..	..	..	2	1	1	1	1	..	..	..	..
9. Kashmir South (including city).	1	..	1	..	..	..	..	..	1	..	..	..	..	..	..	..	..	..	6	5	1	5	1	..	..	..	..
10. Muzaffarabad District ..	..	..	..	..	..	..	..	..	..	..	..	..	..	..	..	..	..	..	..	..	..	..	..	..	..	..	..
III. Frontier Districts ..	..	..	..	..	..	..	..	..	..	58	29	29	..	..	..	..	29	29	4	2	2	2	2	..	..	..	..
11. Ladakh " ..	..	..	..	..	..	..	..	..	..	58	29	29	..	..	..	..	29	29	..	..	..	..	..	..	..	..	..
12. Gilgit " ..	..	..	..	..	..	..	..	..	..	..	..	..	..	..	..	..	..	..	4	2	2	2	2	..	..	..	..
13. Frontier *Ilaqas* ..	..	..	..	..	..	..	..	..	..	..	..	..	..	..	..	..	..	..	..	..	..	..	..	..	..	..	..

TABLE XV.

Territorial Distribution of the Christian Population by Sect and Race.

Jammu and Kashmir State Census, 1921.

DISTRICT, JAGIR OR ILAQA.	PROTESTANT (UNSECTARIAN AND UNSPECIFIED).								
	Total.			Distribution by Race.					
				European and Allied races.		Anglo-Indian.		Indian.	
	Persons.	Males.	Females.	Males.	Females.	Males	Females.	Males.	Females.
	56	57	58	59	60	61	62	63	64
KASHMIR STATE ..	123	64	59	8	3	4	5	52	51
I. Jammu Province (including *Jagirs.*)	110	53	57	5	1	4	5	44	51
1. Jammu District (including city.)	105	51	54	5	1	2	2	44	51
2. Kathua District ..	..	..	..	..	..	..	..	..	..
3. Udhampur " ..	..	..	..	..	..	..	..	..	..
4. Riasi " ..	..	..	..	..	..	..	..	..	..
5. Mirpur " ..	5	2	3	..	..	2	3	..	..
6. Bhadarwah *Jagir* ..	..	..	..	..	..	..	..	..	..
7. Punch *Ilaqa* ..	..	..	..	..	..	..	..	..	..
II. Kashmir Province (including *Jagirs*).	12	10	2	3	2	..	..	7	..
8. Kashmir North (including Langet *Jagir*).	1	1	..	1	..	..	..	..	..
9. Kashmir South (including city.)	11	9	2	2	2	..	..	7	..
10. Muzaffarabad District ..	..	..	..	..	..	..	..	..	..
III. Frontier Districts ..	1	1	..	..	..	..	..	1	..
11. Ladakh " ..	..	..	..	..	..	..	..	..	..
12. Gilgit " ..	1	1	..	..	..	..	..	1	..
13. Frontier *Ilaqas* ..	..	..	..	..	..	..	..	..	..

DISTRICT, JAGIR OR ILAQA.	ROMAN CATHOLIC.								
	Total.			Distribution by Race.					
				European and Allied races.		Anglo-Indian.		Indian.	
	Persons.	Males.	Females.	Males.	Females.	Males.	Females.	Males.	Females.
	65	66	67	68	69	70	71	72	73
KASHMIR STATE ..	70	49	21	14	12	9	3	26	6
I. Jammu Province (including *Jagirs.*)	14	9	5	..	1	..	..	9	4
1. Jammu District (including city.)	10	7	3	..	..	..	..	7	3
2. Kathua District ..	3	2	1	..	..	..	..	2	1
3. Udhampur " ..	1	..	1	..	1	..	..	..	..
4. Riasi " ..	..	..	..	..	..	..	..	..	..
5. Mirpur " ..	..	..	..	..	..	..	..	..	..
6. Bhadarwah *Jagir* ..	..	..	..	..	..	..	..	..	..
7. Punch *Ilaqa* ..	..	..	..	..	..	..	..	..	..
II. Kashmir Province (including *Jagirs*).	53	38	15	13	10	8	3	17	2
8. Kashmir North (including Langet *Jagir*).	5	3	2	3	2	..	..	..	..
9. Kashmir South (including city.)	48	35	13	10	8	8	3	17	2
10. Muzaffarabad District ..	..	..	..	..	..	..	..	..	..
III. Frontier Districts ..	3	2	1	1	1	1	..	..	..
11. Ladakh " ..	..	..	..	..	..	..	..	..	..
12. Gilgit " ..	3	2	1	1	1	1	..	..	..
13. Frontier *Ilaqas* ..	..	..	..	..	..	..	..	..	..

DISTRICT, JAGIR OR ILAQA.	SECT NOT RETURNED.								
	Total.			Distribution by Race.					
				European and Allied races.		Anglo-Indian.		Indian.	
	Persons.	Males.	Females.	Males.	Females.	Males.	Females.	Males.	Females.
	74	75	76	77	78	79	80	81	82
KASHMIR STATE ..	50	36	14	8	6	..	..	28	8
I. Jammu Province (including *Jagirs.*)	..	..	..	..	..	..	..	..	..
1. Jammu District (including city.)	..	..	..	..	..	..	..	..	..
2. Kathua District ..	..	..	..	..	..	..	..	..	..
3. Udhampur " ..	..	..	..	..	..	..	..	..	..
4. Riasi " ..	..	..	..	..	..	..	..	..	..
5. Mirpur " ..	..	..	..	..	..	..	..	..	..
6. Bhadarwah *Jagir* ..	..	..	..	..	..	..	..	..	..
7. Punch *Ilaqa* ..	..	..	..	..	..	..	..	..	..
II. Kashmir Province (including *Jagirs*).	39	27	12	5	4	..	..	22	8
8. Kashmir North (including Langet *Jagir*).	11	6	5	..	..	..	..	6	5
9. Kashmir South (including city.)	28	21	7	5	4	..	..	16	3
10. Muzaffarabad District ..	..	..	..	..	..	..	..	..	..
III. Frontier Districts ..	11	9	2	3	2	..	..	6	..
11. Ladakh " ..	10	8	2	2	2	..	..	6	..
12. Gilgit " ..	1	1	..	1	..	..	..	..	..
13. Frontier *Ilaqas* ..	..	..	..	..	..	..	..	..	..

IMPERIAL TABLE XVI.

EUROPEAN AND ALLIED RACES AND ANGLO-INDIANS BY RACE AND AGE.

Jammu and Kashmir State Census, 1921.

1. This table has been split up into two parts. Part (*a*) deals with European and Allied Races, and Part (*b*) relates to Anglo-Indians. No Armenians were returned at this Census.

2. There are no entries against the districts of Kathua and Riasi in either part of the Table, for no European or Anglo-Indian was enumerated there. Similarly there are no entries for Bhadarwah *Jagir* in Part (*a*) and for the districts of Udhampur, Kashmir North, Muzaffarabad, and Ladakh, and Frontier *Ilaqas* in Part (*b*).

3. One European female belonging to the category of Indefinite Beliefs has been included in the figures of this table.

IMPERIAL TABLE XVI.

European and Allied Races and Anglo Indians by Race and Age.

Jammu and Kashmir State Census, 1921.

(*a*) European and Allied Races.

District, Jagir or Ilaqa.	Total.			European and Allied Races.																																	
				British Subjects.																	Others.																
				All ages.			0—10		10—16		16—18		18—30		30—40		40—50		50 and over		*All ages.*			0—10		10—16		16—18		18—30		30—40		40—50		50 and over.	
	Total.	Males.	Females	Total.	Males.	Females	Males.	Females.	Males.	Females.	Males.	Females.	Males.	Females.	Males.	Females.	Males.	Females.	Males.	Females.	Total.	Males.	Females.	Males.	Females.	Males.	Females.	Males.	Females.	Males.	Females.	Males.	Females.	Males.	Females.	Males.	Females.
1	2	3	4	5	6	7	8	9	10	11	12	13	14	15	16	17	18	19	20	21	22	23	24	25	26	27	28	29	30	31	32	33	34	35	36	37	38
Kashmir State ..	**270**	**128**	**142**	**263**	**123**	**140**	**14**	**17**	..	**6**	..	..	**19**	**21**	**26**	**27**	**24**	**24**	**40**	**45**	**7**	..	..	..	..	..	..	..	..	**1**	..	**2**	..	**1**	..	**1**	**2**
I.—Jammu Province (including *Jagirs.*)	**13**	..	**5**	**12**	**7**	**5**	..	..	..	..	..	..	..	**1**	..	**2**	**2**	**2**	**2**	..	**1**	**1**	..	..	..	..	..	..	..	..	..	..	..	**1**	..	..	..
1. Jammu District (including city).	10	7	3	9	6	3	..	..	..	..	..	..	..	1	..	1	..	..	2	..	1	1	..	..	..	..	..	..	..	..	..	..	..	1	..	..	..
2. Kathua District ..	..	..	..	..	..	...	..	..	..	..	..	..	..	..	..	..	..	..	..	..	..	..	..	..	..	..	..	..	..	..	..	..	..	..	..	..	..
3. Udhampur „ ..	1	..	1	1	..	1	..	..	..	..	..	..	..	..	..	1	..	..	..	..	..	..	..	..	..	..	..	..	..	..	..	..	..	..	..	..	..
4. Riasi „ ..	..	..	..	..		..	..	..	..	..	..	..	..	..	..	..	..	..	..	..	..	..	..	..	..	..	..	..	..	..	..	..	..	..	..	..	..
5. Mirpur „ ..	1	1	..	1	1	1	..	..	..	..	..	..	1	..	..	..	..	..	..	..	..	..	..	..	..	..	..	..	..	..	..	..	..	..	..	..	..
6. Bhadarwah Jagir ..	..	..	..	..	..	..	..	..	..	..	..	..	..	..	..	..	..	..	..	..	..	..	..	..	..	..	..	..	..	..	..	..	..	..	..	..	..
7. Punch Ilaqa ..	1	..	1	1	..	1	..	..	..	..	..	..	..	..	..	..	..	1	..	..	..	..	..	..	..	..	..	..	..	..	..	..	..	..	..	..	..
II.—Kashmir Province (including *Jagirs.*)	**238**	**111**	**127**	**232**	**107**	**125**	**14**	**15**	..	**4**	..	..	**16**	**20**	**21**	**23**	**18**	**18**	**38**	**45**	**6**	**4**	**2**	..	..	..	..	..	..	**1**	..	**2**	..	..	..	**1**	**2**
8. Kashmir North (including Langet *Jagir.*)	22	13	9	20	11	9	1	1	..	..	..	..	1	1	2	3	4	3	3	1	2	2	..	..	..	..	..	..	..	..	..	2	..	..	..	..	..
9. Kashmir South (including city).	210	94	116	206	92	114	13	14	..	4	..	..	13	18	18	20	13	15	35	43	4	2	2	..	..	..	..	..	..	1	..	..	..	..	..	1	2
10. Muzaffarabad District ..	6	4	2	6	4	2	..	..	..	..	..	..	2	1	1	..	1	..	..	1	..	..	..	..	..	..	..	..	..	..	..	..	..	..	..	..	..
III.— Frontier Districts ..	**19**	**9**	**10**	**19**	**9**	**10**	..	**2**	..	**2**	..	..	..	..	**5**	**2**	**4**	**4**	..	..	..	..	..	..	..	..	..	..	..	..	..	..	..	..	..	..	..
11. Ladakh District ..	6	2	4	6	2	4	..	..	..	..	..	..	..	..	..	..	2	4	..	..	..	..	..	..	..	—	..	..	..	..	..	..	..	..	..	..	..
12. Gilgit „ ..	12	6	6	12	6	6	..	2	..	2	..	..	..	..	5	2	1	..	..	..	..	..	..	..	..	..	..	..	..	..	..	..	..	..	..	..	..
13. Frontier Ilaqas ..	1	1	..	1	1	..	..	..	..	..	..	..	..	..	..	..	1	..	..	..	..	..	..	..	..	..	..	..	..	..	..	..	..	..	..	..	..

(b) Anglo Indians.

District, *Jagir* or *Ilaqa*.	ANGLO INDIANS.																										
	ALL AGES.			0—1		1—5		5—10		10—15		16—18		18—20		15—20		20—30		30—40		40—50		50—60		60 and over.	
	Total.	Males.	Females.	Males.	Females.	Males.	Females.	Males.	Females.	Males.	Females.	Males.	Females.	Males.	Females.	Males.	Females.	Males.	Females.	Males.	Females.	Males.	Females.	Males.	Females.	Males.	Females.
1	2	3	4	5	6	7	8	9	10	11	12	13	14	15	16	17	18	19	20	21	22	23	24	25	26	27	28
Kashmir State ..	48	30	18	..	..	4	2	1	1	..	1	1	..	..	..	1	..	6	4	5	4	10	2	1	2	2	2
I.—Jammu Province (including *Jagirs.*)	24	16	8	..	..	2	..	..	1	..	1	1	..	..	..	1	..	3	2	1	1	6	1	1	1	2	1
1. Jammu District (including city).	15	10	5	..	..	1	..	..	..	..	1	1	..	..	..	1	..	2	1	..	..	3	1	1	1	2	1
2. Kathua District ..	..	..	..	..	..	..	..	..	..	..	..	..	..	..	..	..	..	..	..	..	..	..	..	..	..	..	..
3. Udhampur ,, ..	..	..	..	..	..	..	..	..	..	..	..	..	..	..	..	..	..	..	..	..	..	..	..	..	..	..	..
4. Riasi ,, ..	..	..	..	..	..	..	..	..	..	..	..	..	..	..	..	..	..	..	..	..	..	..	..	..	..	..	..
5. Mirpur ,, ..	5	2	3	..	..	1	..	..	1	..	..	..	..	..	..	..	..	..	1	..	1	1	..	..	..	..	..
6. Bhadarwah *Jagir* ..	1	1	..	..	..	..	..	..	..	..	..	..	..	..	..	..	..	1	..	..	..	..	..	..	..	..	..
7. Punch *Ilaqa* ..	3	3	..	..	..	..	..	..	..	..	..	..	..	..	..	..	..	..	..	1	..	2	..	..	..	..	..
II.—Kashmir Province (including *Jagirs*).	22	12	10	..	..	2	2	1	..	..	..	..	..	..	..	..	..	3	2	3	3	3	1	..	1	..	1
8. Kashmir North (including Langet *Jagir*).	..	..	..	..	..	..	..	..	..	..	..	..	..	..	..	..	..	..	..	..	..	..	..	..	..	..	..
9. Kashmir South (including city.)	22	12	10	..	..	2	2	1	..	..	..	..	..	..	..	..	..	3	2	3	3	3	1	..	1	..	1
10. Muzaffarbad District ..	..	..	..	..	..	..	..	..	..	..	..	..	..	..	..	..	..	..	..	..	..	..	..	..	..	..	..
III.—Frontier Districts ..	2	2	..	..	..	..	..	..	..	..	..	..	..	..	..	..	..	..	..	1	..	1	..	..	..	..	..
11. Ladakh District ..	..	..	..	..	..	..	..	..	..	..	..	..	..	..	..	..	..	..	..	..	..	..	..	..	..	..	..
12. Gilgit ,, ..	2	2	..	..	..	..	..	..	..	..	..	..	..	..	..	..	..	..	..	1	..	1	..	..	..	..	..
13. Frontier *Ilaqas* ..	..	..	..	..	..	..	..	..	..	..	..	..	..	..	..	..	..	..	..	..	..	..	..	..	..	..	..

TABLE XVII.

OCCUPATION OR MEANS OF LIVELIHOOD.

JAMMU AND KASHMIR STATE CENSUS, 1921.

No entries having been returned under the following Orders and Groups, they have been omitted from the Table. Orders :—19 and 43.

Groups :—6, 10, 20, 24, 28, 57, 71, 73, 74, 82, 90, 91, 102, 104, 106, 117, 144, 145, 158.

TABLE XVII.

Occupation or Means of Livelihood.

Jammu and Kashmir State Census, 1921.

DISTRICT, JAGIR, ILAQA OR CITY.	Entire State.						Class A.—Production of raw materials.						Sub-Class I.—Exploitation of animals and vegetation.					
	Total workers and dependents.	Actual Workers.				Dependents.	Total workers and dependents.	Actual Workers.				Dependents.	Total workers and dependents.	Actual Workers.				Dependents.
		Total.		Partially Agriculturists.				Total.		Partially Agriculturists.				Total.		Partially Agriculturists.		
		Males.	Females.	Males.	Females.			Males.	Females.	Males.	Females.			Males.	Females.	Males.	Females.	
1	2	3	4	5	6	7	8	9	10	11	12	13	14	15	16	17	18	19
State	**3,259,527**	**928,341**	**287,554**	**24,546**	**1,681**	**2,033,632**	**2,664,120**	**723,834**	**263,058**	**2,260**	**289**	**1,677,228**	**2,664,036**	**723,787**	**263,057**	**2,254**	**289**	**1,677,192**
I.—Jammu Province (including *Jagirs*).	**1,640,259**	**447,251**	**82,872**	**14,419**	**1,316**	**1,110,136**	**1,363,901**	**348,003**	**66,107**	**948**	**251**	**949,791**	**1,363,897**	**348,002**	**66,106**	**948**	**251**	**949,789**
1. Jammu District (including City)	334,834	97,657	9,233	5,291	222	227,944	213,871	55,021	4,540	122	1	154,310	213,871	55,021	4,540	122	1	154,310
2. Kathua District	154,[illegible]09	51,606	19,212	2,166	283	83,391	111,891	37,555	15,295	209	12	59,041	111,891	37,555	15,295	209	12	59,041
3. Udhampur District (including Chaneni *Jagir*).	218,261	68,468	22,860	1,950	253	126,933	194,276	58,390	20,548	303	67	115,338	194,272	58,389	20,547	303	67	115,336
4. Riasi District	224,[illegible]89	55,547	12,976	1,227	221	156,066	205,014	48,522	11,336	157	11	145,156	205,014	48,522	11,336	157	11	145,156
5. Mirpur District	318,971	91,956	9,028	2,032	98	217,987	267,581	75,024	5,702	57	2	186,855	267,581	75,024	5,702	57	2	186,855
6. Bhadarwah *Jagir* ..	37,614	12,714	5,795	312	202	19,105	34,011	11,079	5,400	21	155	17,532	34,011	11,079	5,400	21	155	17,532
7. Punch *Ilaqa*	351,781	69,303	3,768	1,441	37	278,710	337,257	62,412	3,286	79	3	271,559	337,257	62,412	3,286	79	3	271,559
II.—Kashmir Province (including *Jagirs*).	**1,407,086**	**412,968**	**153,931**	**9,193**	**334**	**840,187**	**1,099,342**	**314,029**	**138,268**	**1,290**	**38**	**647,045**	**1,099,342**	**314,029**	**38,268**	**1,290**	**38**	**647,045**
8. Kashmir North (including Langet *Jagir*).	502,490	143,524	23,769	2,885	81	335,197	439,440	122,162	22,046	347	8	295,232	439,440	122,162	22,046	347	8	295,232
9. Kashmir South (including City)	688,487	212,646	95,779	5,658	236	380,062	455,954	139,534	82,299	916	30	234,121	455,954	139,534	82,299	916	30	234,121
10. Muzaffarabad District ..	216,109	56,798	34,383	650	17	124,928	203,948	52,333	33,923	27	..	117,692	203,948	52,333	33,923	27	..	117,692
III.—Frontier Districts	**212,182**	**68,122**	**60,751**	**934**	**31**	**83,309**	**200,877**	**61,802**	**58,683**	**22**	..	**80,392**	**200,797**	**61,756**	**58,683**	**16**	..	**80,358**
11. Ladakh District (including Mansar).	183,476	59,558	56,598	800	30	67,320	174,466	55,001	54,636	3	..	64,829	174,428	54,984	54,636	3	..	64,808
12. Gilgit ,, ...	28,706	8,564	4,153	134	1	15,989	26,411	6,801	4,017	19	..	15,563	26,369	6,772	4,047	13	..	15,550
Cities.																		
13. Jammu	31,506	14,147	1,282	231	94	16,077	1,130	526	15	7	..	589	1,130	526	15	7	..	589
14. Srinagar	141,735	42,113	7,776	464	9	91,846	7,109	2,307	209	118	..	4,593	7,109	2,307	209	118	..	4,593

TABLE XVII.

Occupation or Means of Livelihood.

Jammu and Kashmir State Census, 1921.

DISTRICT, JAGIR, ILAQA OR CITY.	Order (I).—Pasture and Agriculture.						Order I (a)—Ordinary Cultivation.						Group (I).—Income from rent of agricultural land.					
	Total workers and dependents.	Actual Workers.				Dependents.	Total workers and dependents.	Actual Workers.				Dependents.	Total workers and dependents.	Actual Workers.				Dependents.
		Total.		Partially Agriculturists.				Total.		Partially Agriculturists.				Total.		Partially Agriculturists.		
		Males.	Females.	Males.	Females.			Males.	Females.	Males.	Females.			Males.	Females.	Males.	Females.	
	20	21	22	23	24	25	26	27	28	29	30	31	32	33	34	35	36	37
State ..	**2,660,650**	**722 773**	**262,870**	**2,173**	**273**	**1,674,996**	**2,612,740**	**707,491**	**259,745**	**64**	**6**	**1,645,504**	**125,684**	**20,130**	**9,336**	..	..	**96,218**
I—Jammu Province (including *Jagirs.*)	**1,363,801**	**347,833**	**66,105**	**947**	**251**	**949,768**	**1,337,638**	**339,763**	**64,306**	**37**	**6**	**933,569**	**104,928**	**14,330**	**7,212**	..	..	**83,386**
1. Jammu District (including City)	213,854	55,014	4,540	122	1	154,300	205,466	53,878	4,318	36	1	147,270	10,491	2,953	726	..	..	6,812
2. Kathua "	111,887	37,553	15,295	208	12	59,039	108,493	35,649	15,019	..	..	57,825	6,405	2,072	691	..	..	3,642
3. Udhampur District (including Chaneni *Jagir.*)	194,272	58,389	20,547	303	67	115,336	190,698	56,999	20,004	1	5	113,695	18,383	4,177	1,830	..	..	12,376
4. Riasi District	2,05,013	48,522	11,335	157	11	145,156	197,869	46,555	10,948	..	..	140,366	17,989	3,056	2,465	..	..	12,468
5. Mirpur	267,575	75,023	5,702	57	2	186,850	266,239	74,266	5,653	..	..	186,320	9,384	737	616	..	..	8,031
6. Bhadarwah *Jagir*	34,009	11,078	5,400	21	155	17,531	33,373	10,889	5,125	..	..	17,359	211	43	30	..	..	138
7. Punch *Ilaqa*	337,251	62,409	3,286	79	3	271,556	335,500	61,527	3,239	..	..	270,734	42,065	1,292	854	..	..	39,919
II—Kashmir Province (including *Jagirs.*)	**1,095,993**	**313,035**	**138,088**	**1,210**	**22**	**844,870**	**1,075,150**	**306,280**	**137,026**	**24**	..	**631,844**	**19,980**	**5,540**	**1,833**	..	..	**12,607**
8. Kashmir North (including Langet *Jagir.*)	437,871	121,704	21,997	336	7	294,170	431,620	119,726	21,861	19	..	290,033	5,774	1,540	408	..	..	3,826
9. Kashmir South (including City)	454,174	138,998	82,168	847	15	233,008	440,239	134,548	81,251	5	..	224,440	11,589	3,209	1,384	..	..	6,996
10. Muzaffarabad District ..	203,948	52,333	33,923	27	..	117,692	203,291	52,006	33,914	..	..	117,371	2,617	791	41	..	..	1,785
III—Frontier Districts	**200,796**	**61,755**	**58,683**	**16**	..	**80,358**	**19 9,952**	**61,448**	**58,413**	**3**	..	**80,091**	**776**	**260**	**291**	..	..	**225**
11. Ladakh District (including Mansar.)	174,428	54,984	54,636	3	..	64,808	173,709	54,708	54,376	1	..	64,625	683	203	288	..	..	192
12. Gilgit District	26,368	6,771	4,047	13	..	15,550	26,243	6,740	4,037	2	..	15,466	93	57	3	..	..	33
Cities																		
13. Jammu	1,124	523	15	7	..	586	1,001	478	15	..	..	508	754	346	9	..	..	399
14. Srinagar	6,822	2,219	204	118	..	4,399	3,497	1,343	79	..	..	2,075	776	250	6	..	..	520

TABLE XVII.

Occupation or Means of Livelihood.

Jammu and Kashmir State Census, 1921.

DISTRICT, JAGIR, ILAQA OR CITY.	Group (2).—*Ordinary Cultivators.*						Group (3).—*Agents, Managers of landed estates (not Planters), Clerks, Rent Collectors, etc.*						Group (4).—*Farm Servants.*					
	Total workers and dependents.	Actual Workers. Total. Males.	Actual Workers. Total. Females.	Actual Workers. Partially Agriculturists. Males.	Actual Workers. Partially Agriculturists. Females.	Dependents.	Total workers and dependents.	Actual Workers. Total. Males.	Actual Workers. Total. Females.	Actual Workers. Partially Agriculturists. Males.	Actual Workers. Partially Agriculturists. Females.	Dependents.	Total workers and dependents.	Actual Workers. Total. Males.	Actual Workers. Total. Females.	Actual Workers. Partially Agriculturists. Males.	Actual Workers. Partially Agriculturists. Females.	Dependents.
	38	39	40	41	42	43	44	45	46	47	48	49	50	51	52	53	54	55
State ..	**2,465,329**	**683,381**	**248,659**	..	..	**1,533,289**	**682**	**190**	**48**	**11**	..	**444**	**3,986**	**1,408**	**222**	**40**	**1**	**2,356**
I.—Jammu Province (including ***Jagirs*****)**	**1,213,651**	**322,476**	**55,696**	..	..	**835,479**	..	..	..	..	..	..	**3,613**	**1,315**	**166**	**32**	**1**	**2,132**
1. Jammu District (including City.)	188,780	49,498	2,996	..	..	136,286	..	..	..	..	..	..	3,065	1,040	122	32	..	1,903
2. Kathua ,, ...	100,049	32,833	13,975	..	..	53,241	..	..	..	..	..	..	397	194	30	..	..	173
3. Udhampur,, (including Chaneni *Jagir*).	171,720	52,549	18,095	..	..	101,076	..	..	..	..	..	..	96	60	9	..	1	27
4. Riasi District	179,731	43,400	8,477	..	..	127,854	..	..	..	..	..	..	20	..	4	..	..	16
5. Mirpur District	246,923	73,209	4,676	..	..	169,038	..	..	..	..	..	..	2	1	1	..	..	..
6. Bhadarwah *Jagir*	33,162	10,846	5,096	..	..	17,221	..	..	..	..	..	..	..	..	..	..	..	..
7. Punch *Ilaqa*	293,286	60,141	2,382	..	..	230,763	..	..	..	..	..	..	33	20	..	..	..	13
II.—Kashmir Province (including ***Jagirs.*****)**	**1,053,131**	**299,960**	**135,094**	..	..	**618,077**	**653**	**189**	**20**	**10**	..	**444**	**373**	**93**	**58**	**8**	..	**224**
8. Kashmir North (including Langet *Jagir*).	425,105	117,955	21,434	..	..	285,716	242	95	...	10	..	147	193	60	13	3	..	120
9. Kashmir South (including City) ..	427,617	130,927	79,789	..	..	216,901	411	94	20	..	..	297	180	33	43	5	..	104
10. Muzaffarabad District ..	200,409	51,078	33,871	..	..	115,460	..	..	..	..	..	..	..	..	..	..	..	..
III.—Frontier Districts	**198,547**	**60,945**	**57,869**	..	..	**79,733**	**29**	**1**	**28**	**1**	..	..	..	..	..	..	..	..
11. Ladakh District (including Mansar.)	172,546	54,345	53,868	..	..	64,333	29	1	28	1	..	..	..	..	..	..	..	..
12. Gilgit ,, ...	26,001	6,600	4,001	..	..	15,400	..	..	..	..	..	..	..	..	..	..	..	..
Cities																		
13. Jammu	243	128	6	..	..	109	..	...	..	..	..	..	..	..	..	..	..	..
14. Srinagar	2,676	1,063	73	..	..	1,540	45	30	..	..	..	15	..	..	..	..	..	..

TABLE XVII.

Occupation or Means of Livelihood.

Jammu and Kashmir State Census, 1921.

DISTRICT, JAGIR, ILAQA OR CITY.	Group (5)—*Field labourers.*						Order I (b).—Growers of special products and market gardening						Group (7).—*Fruit, flower, vegetable, betel, vine, areca nut, etc., growers.*					
	Total workers and dependents.	Actual Workers.				Dependents.	Total workers and dependents.	Actual Workers.				Dependents.	Total workers and dependents.	Actual Workers.				Dependents.
		Total.		*Partially Agriculturists.*				*Total.*		*Partially Agriculturists.*				*Total.*		*Partially Agriculturists.*		
		Males.	Females.	Males.	Females.			Males.	Females.	Males.	Females.			Males.	Females.	Males.	Females.	
	56	57	58	59	60	61	62	63	64	65	66	67	68	69	70	71	72	73
State ..	**17,059**	**2,382**	**1,480**	**13**	**5**	**13,197**	**5,164**	**1,242**	**229**	**153**	..	**3,693**	**5,164**	**1,242**	**229**	**153**	..	**3,693**
I.—Jammu Province (including *Jagirs*).	**15,446**	**1,642**	**1,232**	**5**	**5**	**12,572**	**462**	**96**	**56**	**1**	..	**310**	**462**	**96**	**56**	**1**	..	**310**
1. Jammu District (including City)	3,130	387	474	4	1	2,269	278	24	20	..	..	234	278	24	20	..	..	234
2. Kathua "	1,642	550	323	..	..	769	134	58	14	..	..	62	134	58	14	..	..	62
3. Udhampur " (including Chaneni *Jagir*).	499	213	70	1	4	216	5	1	..	..	..	4	5	1	..	..	..	4
4. Riasi "	129	99	2	..	..	28	3	2	..	..	..	1	3	2	..	..	..	1
5. Mirpur "	9,930	319	360	..	..	9,251	36	8	22	..	..	6	36	8	22	..	..	6
6. Bhadarwah *Jagir*	..	..	..	..	..	..	..	..	..	..	..	..	..	..	..	..	..	..
7. Punch *Ilaqa*	116	74	3	..	..	39	6	3	..	1	..	3	6	3	..	1	..	3
II.—Kashmir Province (including *Jagir*).	**1,013**	**498**	**23**	**6**	..	**492**	**4,702**	**1,146**	**173**	**152**	..	**3,383**	**4,702**	**1,146**	**173**	**152**	..	**3,383**
8. Kashmir North (including Langet *Jagir*).	306	76	6	6	..	224	1,105	332	15	49	..	758	1,105	332	15	49	..	758
9. Kashmir South (including City.)	442	285	15	..	..	142	3,597	814	158	103	..	2,625	3,597	814	158	103	..	2,625
10. Muzaffarabad District ..	265	137	2	..	..	126	..	..	..	..	..	..	..	..	..	..	..	..
III—Frontier Districts	**600**	**242**	**225**	**2**	..	**133**	..	..	..	..	..	..	..	..	..	..	..	..
11. Ladakh District (including *Mansar*).	451	159	192	..	..	100	..	..	..	..	..	..	..	..	..	..	..	..
12. Gilgit "	149	83	33	2	..	33	..	..	..	..	..	..	..	..	..	..	..	..
Cities.																		
13. Jammu	4	4	..	..	..	..	..	4	..	..	..	4	8	4	..	..	..	4
14. Srinagar	..	..	..	..	..	..	1,899	283	125	..	..	1,491	1,899	283	125	..	..	1,491

TABLE XVII.

OCCUPATION OR MEANS OF LIVELIHOOD.

Jammu and Kashmir State Census, 1921.

DISTRICT, JAGIR, ILAQA OR CITY.	Order 1 (c).—Forestry.						Group (8) *Forest Officers, Rangers, Guards, etc.*						Group (9).—*Wood-Cutters; firewood, Catechu, rubber, etc., collectors, and charcoal burners.*					
	Total workers and dependents.	Actual Workers. Total.		Actual Workers. Partially Agriculturists.		Dependents.	Total workers and dependents.	Actual Workers. Total.		Actual Workers. Partially Agriculturists.		Dependents.	Total workers and dependents.	Actual Workers. Total.		Actual Workers. Partially Agriculturists.		Dependents.
		Males.	Females.	Males.	Females.			Males.	Females.	Males.	Females.			Males.	Females.	Males.	Females.	
	74	75	76	77	78	79	80	81	82	83	84	85	86	87	88	89	90	91
State ..	**5,241**	**2,103**	**128**	**222**	..	**3,010**	**2,560**	**1,234**	**2**	**103**	..	**1,324**	**2,681**	**869**	**126**	**119**	..	**1,686**
I.—Jammu Province (including *Jagirs.*)	**2,310**	**897**	**76**	**144**	..	**1,337**	**1,141**	**564**	**1**	**70**	..	**576**	**1,189**	**333**	**75**	**74**	..	**761**
1. Jammu District (including City	1,366	396	71	52	..	899	447	185	..	15	..	262	919	211	71	37	..	637
2. Kathua „	188	107	..	14	..	81	188	107	..	14	..	81	..	..	..	..	..	..
3. Udhampur „ (including Chaneni *Jagir.*)	149	74	..	9	..	75	149	74	..	9	..	75	..	..	..	..	..	..
4. Riasi „	22	16	..	2	..	6	22	16	..	2	..	6	..	..	..	..	..	..
5. Mirpur „	363	164	5	38	..	194	209	106	1	14	..	102	154	58	4	24	..	92
6. Bhadarwah *Jagir* ..	140	94	..	16	..	46	57	40	..	5	..	17	83	54	..	11	..	29
7. Punch *Ilaqa* ..	82	46	..	13	..	36	69	36	..	11	..	33	13	10	..	2	..	3
II.—Kashmir Province (including *Jagirs*).	**2,914**	**1,196**	**49**	**76**	..	**1,669**	**1,408**	**660**	**1**	**31**	..	**747**	**1,506**	**536**	**48**	**45**	..	**922**
8. Kashmir North (including Langet *Jagir.*)	784	348	24	18	..	412	349	217	..	10	..	132	435	131	24	8	..	280
9. Kashmir South (including City)	1,910	711	24	47	..	1,176	928	363	1	10	..	564	982	348	23	37	..	611
10. Muzaffarabad District ..	220	137	1	11	..	82	131	80	..	11	..	51	89	57	1	..	..	31
III.—Frontier Districts	**17**	**10**	**3**	**2**	..	**4**	**11**	**10**	..	**2**	..	**1**	**6**	..	**3**	..	..	**3**
11. Ladakh District (including *Mansar*).	9	9	..	2	..	..	9	9	..	2	..	..	..	..	..	..	..	..
12. Gilgit District	8	1	3	..	..	4	2	1	..	..	..	1	6	..	3	..	..	3
Cities.																		
13. Jammu	98	30	..	7	..	68	98	30		7	..	421	..	..	..	..	..	..
14. Srinagar	781	261	..	3	..	520	630	209	..	3	..	68	151	52	..	..	..	99

TABLE XVII.

Occupation or Means of Livelihood.

Jammu and Kashmir State Census, 1921.

DISTRICT, JAGIR, ILAQA OR CITY.	Order I,(d).—Raising of farm Stock.						Group (11) *Cattle and buffalo breeders and keepers.*						Group (12) *Sheep, goat and pig breeders.*					
	Total workers and dependents.	Actual Workers.				Dependents.	Total workers and dependents.	Actual Workers.				Dependents.	Total workers and dependents.	Actual Workers.				Dependents.
		Total.		*Partially Agriculturists.*				*Total.*		*Partially Agriculturists.*				*Total.*		*Partially Agriculturists.*		
		Males.	Females.	Males.	Females.			Males.	Females.	Males.	Females.			Males.	Females.	Males.	Females.	
	92	93	94	95	96	97	98	99	100	101	102	103	104	105	106	107	108	109
State ...	**37,369**	**11,873**	**2,770**	**1,723**	**266**	**22,726**	**21,279**	**7,824**	**2,005**	**1,194**	**231**	**11,450**	**10,021**	**1,593**	**333**	**370**	**18**	**8,095**
I—Total Jammu Province (including *Jagirs*).	**23,433**	**7,216**	**1,666**	**765**	**245**	**14,551**	**10,819**	**4,402**	**1,075**	**550**	**217**	**5,342**	**8,308**	**1,003**	**249**	**132**	**17**	**7,056**
1. Jammu District (including City)	6,744	716	131	34	..	5,897	711	429	14	14	..	268	4,967	38	18	1	..	4,911
2. Kathua „	3,072	1,739	262	194	12	1,071	1,321	509	179	57	4	633	1,221	894	45	124	6	282
3. Udhampur „ (including Chaneni)	3,420	1,315	543	293	62	1,562	2,974	1,208	396	269	48	1,370	271	36	116	4	o	119
4. Riasi „	7,102	1,933	387	155	11	4,782	4,591	1,918	194	155	8	2,479	1,733	..	53	..		1,680
5. Mirpur „	936	685	21	19	2	330	428	149	4	9	..	275	56	..	10	..	..	46
6. Bhadarwah *Jagir* ..	496	95	275	5	155	126	479	79	271	2	155	126	17	16	1	3	..	..
7. Punch *Ilaqa*	1,663	833	47	65	3	783	315	110	14	44	2	191	43	19	6	..	..	18
II.—Kashmir Province (including *Jagirs*).	**13,109**	**4,360**	**837**	**947**	**21**	**7,912**	**9,696**	**3,130**	**705**	**633**	**14**	**5,861**	**1,713**	**590**	**84**	**233**	**1**	**1,039**
8. Kashmir North (including Langet *Jagir*).	4,293	1,279	95	247	6	2,919	2,743	793	68	196	6	1,832	603	143	20	10	..	440
9. Kashmir South (including City)	8,379	2,891	734	684	15	4,754	6,912	2,315	335	437	8	3,962	1,110	447	64	228	1	599
10. Muzaffarbad District ..	437	190	8	16	..	239	41	22	2	..	..	17	..	..	..	..	..	..
III.—Frontier Districts	**827**	**297**	**267**	**11**	..	**263**	**764**	**292**	**225**	**11**	..	**247**	..	..	..	..	..	..
11. Ladakh District (including Mansar).	710	267	260	..	..	183	647	262	218	..	..	167	..	..	..	..	..	..
12. Gilgit „	117	30	7	11	..	80	117	30	7	11	..	80	..	..	..	..	..	..
Cities.																		
13. Jammu	17	11	..	..	..	6	..	..	..	..	..	..	..	..	..	..	..	..
14. Srinagar	645	332	..	115	..	313	110	..	..	..	..	113	422	222	..	115	..	200

TABLE XVII.

Occupation or Means of Livelihood.

Jammu and Kashmir State Census, 1921

DISTRICT, JAGIR, ILAQA OR CITY.	Group (13).—*Breeders of other animals (horses, mules, camels, asses, etc.)*						Group (14).—*Herdsmen, Shepherds, goat-herds, etc.*						Order I (e).—Raising of small animals.					
	Total workers and dependents.	Actual Workers. Total. Males.	Actual Workers. Total. Females.	Actual Workers. Partially Agriculturists. Males.	Actual Workers. Partially Agriculturists. Females.	Dependents	Total workers and dependents.	Actual Workers. Total. Males.	Actual Workers. Total. Females.	Actual Workers. Partially Agriculturists. Males.	Actual Workers. Partially Agriculturists. Females.	Dependents.	Total workers and dependents.	Actual Workers. Total. Males.	Actual Workers. Total. Females.	Actual Workers. Partially Agriculturists. Males.	Actual Workers. Partially Agriculturists. Females.	Dependents.
	110	111	112	113	114	115	116	117	118	119	120	121	122	123	124	125	126	127
State ...	**15**	**6**	**6**	..	..	..	**6,054**	**2,450**	**426**	**159**	**17**	**3,178**	**136**	**69**	**4**	**11**	**1**	**63**
I.—Jammu Province (including *Jagirs*).	**1**	**1**	..	..	..	..	**4,305**	**1,810**	**342**	**83**	**11**	**2,153**	**18**	**16**	**1**	..	..	**1**
1. Jammu District (including City)	..	..	..	..	..	..	1,066	249	99	19	..	718	..	..	..	..	..	..
2. Kathua „	..	..	..	..	..	..	530	336	38	13	2	156	..	..	..	..	..	..
3. Udhampur „ (including Chaneni *Jagir*).	..	..	..	..	..	..	175	71	31	20	6	73	..	..	..	..	..	..
4. Riasi „	..	..	..	..	..	..	778	15	140	..	...	623	17	16	..	..	..	1
5. Mirpur „	1	1	..	..	..	..	451	435	7	10	2	9	1	..	1	..	..	..
6. Bhadarwah *Jagir* ..	..	..	..	..	..	..	..	..	..	..	...	..	..	..	..	..	..	..
7. Punch *Ilaqa* ..	..	..	..	..	..	..	1,305	704	27	21	1	574	..	..	..	..	..	..
II.—Kashmir Province (including *Jagirs*).	..	..	..	..	..	..	**1,700**	**640**	**48**	**76**	**6**	**1,012**	**118**	**53**	**3**	**11**	**1**	**62**
8. Kashmir North (including Langet *Jagir*).	..	..	..	..	..	..	947	343	7	41	..	597	69	19	2	3	1	48
9. Kashmir South (including City)	..	..	..	..	..	..	357	129	35	19	6	193	49	34	1	8	..	14
10. Muzaffarabad District ..	..	..	..	..	..	..	396	168	6	16	..	222	...	..	..	..	..	..
III.—Frontier Districts	**14**	**5**	**6**	..	..	**3**	**49**	..	**36**	...	...	**13**	..	..	..	..	..	..
11. Ladakh District (including Mansar).	14	5	6	..	..	3	49	..	36	..	..	13	..	..	..	..	..	..
12. Gilgit „	..	..	...	..	..	..	..	..	..	..	..	...	..	..	..	..	..	..
Cities.																		
13. Jammu District	..	..	..	..	..	..	17	11	..	..	..	6	..	..	..	..	..	..
14. Srinagar „	..	..	..	..	..	..	..	..	..	..	..	..	..	..	..	..	..	..

TABLE XVII.

Occupation or Means of Livelihood.

Jammu and Kashmir State Census, 1921.

District, Jagir, Ilaqa or City.	Group (15).—*Birds, bees, etc.*						Group (16).—*Silkworms.*						Order 2.—Fishing and hunting.					
	Total workers and dependents.	Actual Workers. Total. Males.	Actual Workers. Total. Females.	Actual Workers. Partially Agriculturists. Males.	Actual Workers. Partially Agriculturists. Females.	Dependents.	Total workers and dependents.	Actual Workers. Total. Males.	Actual Workers. Total. Females.	Actual Workers. Partially Agriculturists. Males.	Actual Workers. Partially Agriculturists. Females.	Dependents.	Total workers and dependents.	Actual Workers. Total. Males.	Actual Workers. Total. Females.	Actual Workers. Partially Agriculturists. Males.	Actual Workers. Partially Agriculturists. Females.	Dependents.
	128	129	130	131	132	133	134	135	136	137	138	139	140	141	142	143	144	145
State ..	**47**	**19**	**1**	..	**1**	**27**	**89**	**50**	**3**	**11**	..	**36**	**3,388**	**1,009**	**181**	**81**	**16**	**2,196**
I.—Jammu Province (including *Jagirs*).	17	16	..	..	..	1	1	..	1	..	..	..	36	14	1	1	..	21
1. Jammu District (including City)	..	..	..	..	..	..	..	..	..	..	..	..	17	7	..	..	..	10
2. Kathua „	..	..	..	..	..	..	..	..	..	..	..	..	4	2	..	1	..	2
3. Udhampur „ (including Chaneni *Jagir*).	..	..	..	..	..	..	..	..	..	..	..	..	..	..	..	..	..	..
4. Riasi „ ..	17	16	..	..	..	1	..	..	..	..	..	..	1	..	1	..	..	..
5. Mirpur „ ..	..	..	..	..	..	..	1	..	1	..	..	..	6	1	..	..	..	5
6. Bhadarwah *Jagir* ..	..	..	..	..	..	..	..	..	..	..	..	..	2	1	..	..	..	1
7. Punch *Ilaqa* ..	..	..	..	..	..	..	..	..	..	..	..	..	6	3	..	..	..	3
II.—Kashmir Province (including *Jagirs*).	**30**	**3**	**1**	..	**1**	**26**	**88**	**50**	**2**	**11**	..	**36**	**3,349**	**994**	**180**	**80**	**16**	**2,175**
8. Kashmir North (including Langet *Jagir*).	30	3	1	..	1	26	39	16	1	3	..	22	1,569	458	49	11	1	1,062
9. Kashmir South (including City)	..	..	..	..	..	..	49	34	1	8	..	14	1,780	536	131	69	15	1,113
10. Muzaffarabad District ..	..	..	..	..	..	..	..	..	..	..	..	..	..	..	..	..	..	..
III.—Frontier Districts	..	..	..	..	..	..	..	..	..	..	..	..	**1**	**1**	..	..	..	..
11. Ladakh District (including Mansar).	..	..	..	..	..	..	..	..	..	..	..	..	..	..	..	..	..	..
12. Gilgit	..	..	..	..	..	..	..	..	..	..	..	..	1	1	..	..	..	..
Cities.																		
13. Jammu	..	..	..	..	..	..	..	..	..	..	..	..	6	3	..	..	..	3
14. Srinagar	..	..	..	..	..	..	..	..	..	..	..	..	287	88	5	..	..	194

TABLE XVII.

OCCUPATION OR MEANS OF LIVELIHOOD.

Jammu and Kashmir State Census, 1921.

DISTRICT, JAGIR, ILAQA OR CITY.	Group (17).—Fishing.						Group (18).—Hunting.						Sub-class II.—Exploitation of Minerals.					
	Total workers and dependents.	ACTUAL WORKERS.				Dependents.	Total workers and dependents.	ACTUAL WORKERS.				Dependents.	Total workers and dependents	ACTUAL WORKERS.				Dependents.
		Total		Partially Agriculturists.				Total.		Partially Agriculturists.				Total.		Partially Agriculturists.		
		Males.	Females.	Males.	Females.			Males.	Females.	Males.	Females.			Males.	Females	Males.	Females.	
	146	147	148	149	150	151	152	153	154	155	156	157	158	159	160	161	162	163
State ..	**3,325**	**988**	**181**	**80**	**16**	**2,156**	**61**	**21**	...	**1**	...	**40**	**84**	**47**	**1**	**6**	...	**38**
I.—Jammu Province (including *Jagirs*).	**28**	**13**	**1**	..	..	**14**	**8**	**1**	...	**1**	...	**7**	**4**	**1**	**1**	...	...	**2**
1. Jammu District (including City	17	7	..	..	..	10	..	..	...	..	..	..	..	..	..	..	..	..
2. Kathua	1	1	..	..	..	..	3	1	..	1	..	2	..	..	..	..	..	..
3. Udhampur " (including Chaneni *Jagir*).	..	..	..	..	..	..	..	..	..	...	..	..	4	1	1	..	..	2
4. Riasi "	1	..	1	..	..	..	..	..	..	..	...	..	..	..	..	..	..	..
5. Mirpur "	1	1	..	..	...	..	5	..	..	..	..	5	..	..	..	..	..	..
6. Bhadarwah *Jagir* ..	2	1	..	..	..	1	..	..	...	..	..	..	..	..	..	..	..	..
7. Punch *Ilaqa* ..	6	3	...	..	..	3	..	..	..	..	..	..	..	..	..	..	..	..
II.—Kashmir Province (including *Jagirs*).	**3,297**	**975**	**180**	**80**	**16**	**2,142**	**52**	**19**	..	..	..	**33**	..	..	..	..	..	..
8. Kashmir North (including Langet *Jagir*).	1,569	458	49	11	1	1,062	..	..	..	..	..	..	..	..	..	..	..	..
9. Kashmir South (including City)	1,728	517	131	69	15	1,080	52	19	..	..	..	33	..	..	..	..	..	..
10. Muzaffarabad District ..	..	..	...	..	..	..	..	..	..	..	..	..	..	..	..	...	..	..
III.—Frontier Districts	..	..	..	..	..	...	**1**	**1**	..	..	..	..	**80**	**46**	...	**6**	...	**34**
11. Ladakh District (including Mansar).	..	..	...	..	..	..	..	..	..	..	..	..	38	17	..	..	..	21
12. Gilgit "	..	..	..	..	..	..	1	1	..	..	...	..	42	29	..	6	..	13
Cities.																		
13. Jammu	6	3	..	..	..	3	..	..	..	..	..	..	..	..	..	..	..	..
14. Srinagar	287	88	5	..	...	194	..	..	..	..	..	..	..	...	...	...	..	..

TABLE XVII.

OCCUPATION OR MEANS OF LIVELIHOOD.

Jammu and Kashmir State Census, 1921.

DISTRICT, JAGIR, ILAQA OR CITY.	Order 3.—Mines.						*Group* (19).—*Coal mines.*						*Group* (21).—*Mines and metallic minerals* (*Gold, iron, manganese, etc*).					
	Total workers and dependents.	ACTUAL WORKERS.				Dependents.	Total workers and dependents	ACTUAL WORKERS.				Dependents.	Total workers and dependents.	ACTUAL WORKERS.				Dependents.
		Total.		*Partially Agriculturists.*				*Total.*		*Partially Agriculturists.*				*Total.*		*Partially Agriculturists.*		
		Males.	Females.	Males.	Females.			Males.	Females.	Males.	Females.			Males.	Females.	Males	Females.	
	164	165	166	167	168	169	170	171	172	173	174	175	176	177	178	179	180	181
State ..	46	30	1	6	...	15	4	1	1	..	..	2	42	29	..	6	..	13
I.—Jammu Province (including *Jagirs*).	4	1	1	...	...	2	4	1	1	..	..	2	..	..	..	..	..	..
1. Jammu District (including City)	..	..	..	..	..	..	..	..	..	..	..	..	..	..	...	...	..	..
2. Kathua ,, ...	..	..	..	..	..	..	..	..	..	..	..	..	..	..	..	..	..	..
3. Udhampur ,, (including Chaneni *Jagir*).	4	1	1	..	..	2	4	1	1	..	..	2	...	..	..	...	..	..
4. Riasi ,, ...	..	..	..	..	..	..	..	..	..	..	..	..	..	..	..	..	..	..
5. Mirpur ,, ...	..	..	..	..	..	..	..	..	..	..	..	..	...	..	..	..	..	..
6. Bhadarwah *Jagir* ..	..	..	..	..	..	..	..	..	..	..	..	..	..	..	..	..	..	..
7. Punch *Ilaqa*	..	..	..	..	..	..	..	..	..	..	..	..	..	..	..	..	..	..
II.—Kashmir Province (including *Jagirs*).	..	..	..	..	..	..	..	...	..	..	..	..	..	..	..	..	..	..
8. Kashmir North (including Langet *Jagir*).	..	..	..	..	..	..	..	..	..	..	..	..	..	..	..	..	..	..
9. Kashmir South (including City)	..	..	..	..	..	..	..	..	..	..	..	..	..	..	..	..	..	..
10. Muzaffarabad District ..	..	..	..	..	..	..	..	..	..	..	..	..	..	..	..	..	..	..
III.—Frontier Districts	42	29	...	6	...	13	..	..	..	..	..	..	42	29	..	6	..	13
11. Ladakh District (including Mansar).	..	..	..	..	..	..	..	..	..	..	..	..	..	..	..	..	..	..
12. Gilgit ,, ...	42	29	..	6	..	13	..	..	..	..	..	..	42	29	..	6	..	13
Cities.																		
13. Jammu	..	..	..	..	..	..	..	..	..	..	..	..	..	..	..	..	..	..
14. Srinagar	..	..	..	..	..	..	..	..	..	..	..	..	..	..	..	..	..	..

TABLE XVII.

Occupation or Means of Livelihood.

Jammu and Kashmir State Census, 1921.

DISTRICT, JAGIR, ILAQA OR CITY.	Order 4.—Quarries of hard rocks.						Group (22)—*Other minerals (Jade, diamonds, limestone, etc.)*						Order 5—Salt, etc.					
	Total workers and dependents.	Actual Workers. Total. Males.	Actual Workers. Total. Females.	Actual Workers. Partially Agriculturists. Males.	Actual Workers. Partially Agriculturists. Females.	Dependents	Total workers and dependents.	Actual Workers. Total. Males.	Actual Workers. Total. Females.	Actual Workers. Partially Agriculturists. Males.	Actual Workers. Partially Agriculturists. Females.	Dependents.	Total workers and dependents.	Actual Workers. Total. Males.	Actual Workers. Total. Females.	Actual Workers. Partially Agriculturists. Males.	Actual Workers. Partially Agriculturists. Females.	Dependents.
	182	183	184	185	186	187	188	189	190	191	192	193	194	195	196	197	198	199
State ..	2	2	..	..	..	..	2	2	..	..	..	..	36	15	..	..	..	21
I—Jammu Province (including *Jagirs*)	..	..	..	..	..	..	..	..	..	..	..	..	..	..	..	..	..	..
1. Jammu District (including City)	..	..	..	..	..	..	..	..	..	..	..	..	..	..	..	..	..	..
2. Kathua „ ..	..	..	..	..	..	..	..	..	..	..	..	..	..	..	..	..	..	..
3. Udhampur „ (including Chaneni *Jagir.*)	..	..	..	..	..	..	..	..	..	..	..	..	..	..	..	..	..	..
4. Riasi „ ..	..	..	..	..	..	..	..	..	..	..	..	..	..	..	..	..	..	..
5. Mirpur „ ..	..	..	..	..	..	..	..	..	..	..	..	..	..	..	..	..	..	..
6. Bhadarwah *Jagir* ..	..	..	..	..	..	..	..	..	..	..	..	..	..	..	..	..	..	..
7. Punch *Ilaqa*	..	..	..	..	..	..	..	..										
II—Kashmir Province (including *Jagirs.*)	..	..	..	..	..	..	...	..	..	..	..	..	..	..	..	..	..	..
8. Kashmir North (including Langet *Jagir.*)	..	..	..	..	..	..	..	..	..	..	..	..	..	..	..	..	..	..
9. Kashmir South (including City)	..	..	..	..	..	..	..	..	..	..	..	..	..	..	..	..	..	..
10. Muzaffarabad District ..	..	..	..	..	..	..	..	..	..	..	..	..	..	..	..	..	..	..
III.—Frontier Districts ..	2	2	...	..	..	..	2	2	..	..	..	..	36	15	..	..	..	21
11. Ladakh District (including Mansar).	2	2	..	..	..	..	2	2	..	..	..	..	36	15	..	..	..	21
12. Gilgit „ ..	..	..	..	..	..	..	..	..	..	..	...	..	..	..	..	..	..	..
Cities																		
13. Jammu ..	..	..	..	..	..	..	..	..		..	..	..	..	..	..	..	..	..
14. Srinagar ..	..	..	..	..	..	..	..	..	..	..	..	..		..	..	..	..	..

TABLE XVII.

Occupation or Means of Livelihood.

Jammu and Kashmir State Census, 1921.

DISTRICT, JAGIR, ILAQA OR CITY.	Group (23)—Rock, sea and marsh salt.						Class B.—Preparation and supply of material substances.						Sub-Class III.—Industry.					
	Total workers and dependents.	Actual Workers.				Dependents.	Total workers and dependents.	Actual Workers.				Dependents.	Total workers and dependents.	Actual Workers.				Dependents.
		Total.		Partially Agriculturists.				Total.		Partially Agriculturists.				Total.		Partially Agriculturists.		
		Males.	Females.	Males.	Females.			Males.	Females.	Males.	Females.			Males.	Females.	Males.	Females.	
	200	201	202	203	204	205	206	207	208	209	210	211	212	213	214	215	216	217
State ..	36	15	..	..	..	21	377,961	122,492	23,199	13,694	948	232,270	240,900	76,471	17,442	9,317	673	146,987
I.—Jammu Province (including *Jagirs*).	..	..	..	..	..	..	165,134	54,154	9,707	7,898	706	101,273	105,329	33,708	7,715	5,558	524	63,906
1. Jammu District (including City) ..	...	..	..	..	..	..	66,078	20,804	2,222	2,473	71	43,052	49,896	12,999	1,565	1,716	59	26,332
2. Kathua " ..	..	..	..	..	..	..	28,899	9,301	2,857	1,351	233	16,741	18,250	5,147	2,363	1,056	185	10,740
3. Udhampur " (including Chaneni *Jagir*).	..	..	..	..	..	..	12,882	4,815	1,246	870	127	6,821	6,993	2,570	1,020	556	104	3,403
4. Riasi " ..	..	..	..	..	..	..	11,123	3,421	790	769	157	6,912	5,396	1,682	515	431	92	3,199
5. Mirpur " ..	..	..	..	..	..	..	36,133	11,620	2,236	1,492	63	22,277	26,516	8,244	2,003	1,063	57	16,269
6. Bhadarwah *Jagir* ..	..	..	..	..	..	..	2,086	746	215	163	45	1,125	1,252	464	148	101	21	640
7. Punch *Ilaqa* ..	..	..	..	..	..	..	7,933	3,447	141	780	10	4,345	6,026	2,602	101	635	6	3,323
II.—Kashmir Province (including *Jagirs*).	..	..	..	..	..	..	208,888	66,614	12,892	5,259	236	129,382	134,479	42,302	9,429	3,669	143	32,688
8. Kashmir North (including Langet *Jagir*).	..	..	..	..	..	..	41,362	13,560	1,058	1,612	48	26,744	24,884	8,157	575	1,231	46	16,152
9. Kashmir South (including City) ..	..	..	..	..	..	..	159,561	5,022	211,694	3,226	172	97,645	106,108	33,013	8,778	2,232	83	64,317
10. Muzaffarabad District ..	..	..	..	..	...	..	7,965	2,832	140	421	16	4,993	3,487	1,192	76	206	14	2,219
III.—Frontier Districts ..	36	15	..	..	..	21	3,939	1714	600	537	6	1,615	1,092	401	298	90	6	393
11. Ladakh District (including Mansar).	36	15	..	..	..	21	3,447	1,428	553	509	6	1,466	849	271	254	78	6	324
12. Gilgit " ..	..	..	..	..	..	..	492	296	47	28	..	149	243	130	44	12	..	69
Cities.																		
13. Jammu ..	..	..	..	...	..	..	9,616	3,572	251	49	5	5,793	4,993	1,906	234	6	4	2,853
14. Srinagar ..	..	..	..	..	..	..	92,127	18,115	6,792	221	1	67,210	59,606	17,839	5,721	106	1	36,046

TABLE XVII.

Occupation or Means of Livelihood.

Jammu and Kashmir State Census, 1921.

DISTRICT, JAGIR, ILAQA OR CITY.	Order (6).—Textiles.						Group (25).—Cotton ginning, cleaning and pressing.						Group (26).—Cotton spinning.					
	Total workers and dependents.	Actual Workers. Total. Males.	Actual Workers. Total. Females.	Actual Workers. Partially Agriculturists. Males.	Actual Workers. Partially Agriculturists. Females.	Dependents.	Total workers and dependents.	Actual Workers. Total. Males.	Actual Workers. Total. Females.	Actual Workers. Partially Agriculturists. Males.	Actual Workers. Partially Agriculturists. Females.	Dependents.	Total workers and dependents.	Actual Workers. Total. Males.	Actual Workers. Total. Females.	Actual Workers. Partially Agriculturists. Males.	Actual Workers. Partially Agriculturists. Females.	Dependents.
	218	219	220	221	222	223	224	225	226	227	228	229	230	231	232	233	234	235
State ..	**55,825**	**16,793**	**7,529**	**1,843**	**208**	**31,503**	**2,042**	**711**	**140**	**65**	**4**	**1,191**	**5,328**	**624**	**2,107**	**57**	**60**	**2,597**
I.—Jammu Province (including *Jagirs*)	**28,534**	**8,515**	**3,741**	**1,433**	**146**	**16,278**	**1,177**	**450**	**64**	**31**	**2**	**663**	**2,532**	**28**	**1,738**	**2**	**58**	**766**
1. Jammu District (including City)...	11,079	3,074	799	568	30	7,206	483	169	10	2	..	304	660	23	361	..	11	276
2. Kathua „ ..	4,353	1,061	985	159	26	2,307	34	14	3	..	..	17	590	2	464	..	9	124
3. Udhampur „ (including Chaneni *Jagir*).	1,502	309	569	72	32	624	45	18	4	2	..	23	747	..	493	..	21	254
4. Riasi „ ...	1,064	321	195	87	29	548	40	17	3	2	..	20	146	..	122	..	7	24
5. Mirpur „ ..	8,516	2,876	1,115	426	23	4,525	513	193	44	21	2	276	314	2	250	2	4	62
6. Bhadarwah *Jagir* ...	163	34	54	4	6	75	..	..	..	..	..	..	58	..	41	..	6	14
7. Punch *Ilaqa* ...	1,857	840	24	117	..	993	62	39	..	4	..	23	17	1	4	..	..	12
II.—Kashmir Province (including *Jagirs*).	**28,749**	**8,159**	**3,530**	**382**	**56**	**15,060**	**865**	**261**	**76**	**34**	**2**	**528**	**2,796**	**596**	**369**	**55**	**2**	**1,831**
8. Kashmir North (including Langet *Jagir*).	3,714	1,585	177	93	13	1,952	191	64	24	17	...	103	1,063	263	40	13	1	760
9. Kashmir South (including City)..	22,459	6,371	3,348	265	41	12,740	615	173	48	15	..	394	1,727	328	329	42	1	1,070
10. Muzaffarabad District ..	576	203	5	24	2	368	59	24	4	2	2	31	6	5	..	..	..	1
III.—Frontier Districts ..	**542**	119	**258**	**28**	**6**	**165**	..	..	..	...	..	..	..	..	...	..	..	..
11. Ladakh District (including Mansar)	485	108	229	28	6	148	..	..	..	..	..	..	..	..	..	..	..	...
12. Gilgit „ ..	57	11	29	..	..	17	..	..	...	..	..	..	..	...	..	..	..	..
Cities.																		
13. Jammu ..	170	65	..	..	..	105	..	..	..	..	..	..	..	..	..	..	..	..
14. Srinagar ...	15,534	4,504	1,910	42	1	9,030	208	62	35	..	..	106	1,076	51	327	..	1	734

TABLE XVII.

Occupation or Means of Livelihood.

Jammu and Kashmir State Census, 1921.

District, Jagir, Ilaqa or City.	Group (27).—*Cotton sizing and weaving.*					
	Total workers and dependents.	Actual Workers.				Dependents.
		Total.		*Partially Agriculturists.*		
		Males.	Females.	Males.	Females.	
	236	237	238	239	240	241
State ..	**28,662**	**8,621**	**3,331**	**1,445**	**130**	**16,710**
I.—Jammu Province (including *Jagirs*).	**24,399**	**7,949**	**1,828**	**1,396**	**82**	**14,622**
1. Jammu District (including City)	9,846	2,844	428	566	19	6,574
2. Kathua „	3,622	1,042	442	159	16	2,138
3. Udhampur „ (including Chaneni *Jagir*).	651	285	45	70	8	321
4. Riasi „	870	304	70	85	22	496
5. Mirpur „	7,684	2,681	821	403	17	4,182
6. Bhadarwah *Jagir*	96	28	7	4	..	61
7. Punch *Ilaqa*	1,630	765	15	109	..	850
II.—Kashmir Province (including *Jagirs*).	**4,250**	**661**	**1,503**	**49**	**48**	**2,088**
8. Kashmir North (including Langet *Jagir*).	668	211	91	15	12	366
9. Kashmir South (including City)	3,582	450	1,412	34	36	1,720
10. Muzaffarabad District ..	..	..	..	..	..	..
III.—Frontier Districts	**13**	**11**	..	..	..	**2**
11. Ladakh District (including Mansar).	..	..	..	..	..	..
12. Gilgit „	13	11	..	..	..	2
Cities.						
13. Jammu	86	30	..	..	..	56
14. Srinagar	556	136	70	..	..	350

District, Jagir, Ilaqa or City.	Group (29).—*Rope, twine and string.*					
	Total workers and dependents.	Actual Workers.				Dependents.
		Total.		*Partially Agriculturists.*		
		Males.	Females.	Males.	Females.	
	242	243	244	245	246	247
State ..	**769**	**312**	**8**	**16**	..	**449**
I.—Jammu Province (including *Jagirs*).	**2**	..	..	..	..	**2**
1. Jammu District (including City)	..	..	..	..	..	..
2. Kathua „	..	..	..	..	..	..
3. Udhampur „ (including Chaneni *Jagir*).	..	..	..	..	..	..
4. Riasi „	..	..	..	..	..	..
5. Mirpur „	2	..	..	..	..	2
6. Bhadarwah *Jagir*	..	..	..	..	..	..
7. Punch *Ilaqa*	..	..	..	..	..	..
II.—Kashmir Province (including *Jagirs*).	**767**	**312**	**8**	**16**	..	**447**
8. Kashmir North (including Langet *Jagir*).	47	21	..	..	..	26
9. Kashmir South (including City)	720	291	8	16	..	421
10. Muzaffarabad District ..	..	..	..	..	..	..
III.—Frontier Districts	..	..	..	..	..	..
11. Ladakh District (including Mansar).	..	..	..	..	..	..
12. Gilgit „	..	..	..	..	..	..
Cities.						
13. Jammu	..	..	..	..	..	..
14. Srinagar	82	36	7	..	..	39

District, Jagir, Ilaqa or City.	Group (30).—*Other fibres* (*Cocoanut, aloes, flax, hemp, straw, etc.*)					
	Total workers and dependents.	Actual Workers.				Dependents.
		Total.		*Partially Agriculturists.*		
		Males.	Females.	Males.	Females.	
	248	249	250	251	252	253
State ..	**80**	**13**	**10**	..	..	**57**
I.—Jammu Province (including *Jagirs*).	**62**	**13**	..	..	..	**49**
1. Jammu District (including City)	..	..	..	..	..	..
2. Kathua „	6	1	..	..	..	5
3. Udhampur „ (including Chaneni *Jagir*).	..	..	..	..	..	..
4. Riasi „	..	..	..	..	..	..
5. Mirpur „	2	..	..	..	..	..
6. Bhadarwah *Jagir*	..	..	..	..	..	..
7. Punch *Ilaqa*	56	12	..	..	..	44
II.—Kashmir Province (including *Jagirs*).	**18**	..	**10**	..	..	**8**
8. Kashmir North (including Langet *Jagir*).	18	..	10	..	..	8
9. Kashmir South (including City)	...	..	..	..	..	..
10. Muzaffarabad District ..	..	..	..	..	..	..
III.—Frontier Districts	..	..	..	..	..	..
11. Ladakh District (including Mansar).	..	..	..	..	..	..
12. Gilgit „	...	..	..	..	..	..
Cities.						
13. Jammu	..	..	..	..	..	..
14. Srinagar	..	..	..	..	..	..

TABLE XVII.

Occupation or Means of Livelihood.

Jammu and Kashmir State Census, 1921.

DISTRICT, JAGIR, ILAQA OR CITY.	*Group* (31).—*Wool carding and spinning.*						*Group* (32).—*Weaving of woollen blankets.*						*Group* (33).—*Weaving of woollen carpets.*					
	Total workers and dependents.	Actual Workers.				Dependents.	Total workers and dependents.	Actual Workers.				Dependents.	Total workers and dependents.	Actual Workers.				Dependents.
		Total.		*Partially Agriculturists.*				*Total.*		*Partially Agriculturists.*				*Total.*		*Partially Agriculturists.*		
		Males.	Females.	Males.	Females.			Males.	Females.	Males.	Females.			Males.	Females.	Males.	Females.	
	254	255	256	257	258	259	260	261	262	263	264	265	266	267	268	269	270	271
State ..	**2,173**	**275**	**985**	**9**	**13**	**913**	**8,253**	**2,693**	**788**	**154**	..	**4,772**	**3,699**	**1,540**	**12**	**2**	..	**2,147**
I.—Jammu Province (including *Jagirs*).	**76**	**6**	**38**	..	**3**	**32**	**97**	**26**	**6**	**4**	..	**65**	..	..	..	..	..	..
1. Jammu District (including City)	..	..	..	..	..	..	..	..	..	..	..	..	..	..	..	..	..	..
2. Kathua „	21	2	9	..	..	10	..	..	..	..	..	..	..	..	..	..	..	..
3. Udhampur „ (including Chaneni *Jagir*).	53	4	27	..	3	22	..	..	..	..	..	..	..	..	..	..	..	..
4. Riasi „	..	..	..	..	..	..	..	..	..	..	..	..	..	..	..	..	..	..
5. Mirpur „	...	..	..	...	..	...	3	..	..	..	..	3	..	..	..	..	..	..
6. Bhadarwah *Jagir*	2	...	2	...	...	...	7	6	1	..	..	..	..	..	..	..	..	..
7. Punch *Ilaqa*	...	...	..	..	...	...	87	20	5	4	...	62	..	..	..	..	..	
II—Kashmir Province (including *Jagirs*).	**1,866**	**263**	**755**	**9**	**4**	**848**	**7,974**	**2,616**	**745**	**143**	..	**4,613**	**3,685**	**1,529**	**12**	..	..	**2,144**
8. Kashmir North (including Langet *Jagir*).	235	143	...	9	...	92	331	118	..	14	..	213	..	...	...	..	..	...
9. Kashmir South (including City)	1,631	120	755	..	4	756	7,165	2,337	744	108	..	4,084	3,685	1,529	12	..	..	2,144
10. Muzaffarabad District ..	...	...	...	..	..	...	478	161	1	21	..	316	..	..	..	..	..	..
III.—Frontier Districts	**231**	**6**	**192**	..	**6**	**33**	**182**	**51**	**37**	**7**	..	**94**	**14**	**11**	..	**2**	..	**3**
11. Ladakh District (including Mansar).	231	6	192	...	6	33	182	51	37	7	..	94	14	11	..	2	..	3
12. Gilgit „	..	..	..	..	...	..	..	..	...	..	..	..	..	..	..	..	..	..
Cities.																		
13. Jammu	..	..	..	..	..	...	..	..	..	..	..	..	..	..	..	..	..	..
14. Srinagar	1,600	120	720	...	..	751	6,382	2,073	722	42	..	3,587	3,685	1,529	12	..	..	2,144

TABLE XVII.

OCCUPATION OR MEANS OF LIVELIHOOD.

Jammu and Kashmir State Census, 1921.

DISTRICT, JAGIR, ILAQA OR CITY.	Group (34).—*Silk spinners.*						Group (35).—*Silk weavers.*						Group (36).—*Hare, camel and horse hair.*					
	Total workers and dependents.	ACTUAL WORKERS. Total. Males.	ACTUAL WORKERS. Total. Females.	ACTUAL WORKERS. Partially Agriculturists. Males.	ACTUAL WORKERS. Partially Agriculturists. Females.	Dependents.	Total workers and dependents.	ACTUAL WORKERS. Total. Males.	ACTUAL WORKERS. Total. Females.	ACTUAL WORKERS. Partially Agriculturists. Males.	ACTUAL WORKERS. Partially Agriculturists. Females.	Dependents.	Total workers and dependents.	ACTUAL WORKERS. Total. Males.	ACTUAL WORKERS. Total. Females.	ACTUAL WORKERS. Partially Agriculturists. Males.	ACTUAL WORKERS. Partially Agriculturists. Females.	Dependents.
	272	273	274	275	276	277	278	279	280	281	282	283	284	285	286	287	288	289
State ..	**2,230**	**1,226**	**27**	**59**	...	**977**	**238**	**50**	**67**	..	**1**	**121**	**3**	**3**	..	..	..	..
I.—Jammu Province (including *Jagirs.*)	**80**	**34**	..	..	..	**46**	**93**	**3**	**67**	..	**1**	**23**	..	..	..	..	..	..
1. Jammu District (including City)	80	34	...	...	..	46	..	..	..	..	...	..	..	..	..	..	..	..
2. Kathua "	...	...	..	...	...	...	80	..	67	..	1	13	..	..	..	..	..	..
3. Udhampur " (including Chaneni *Jagir*).	...	...	...	...	...	...	..	...	..	..	..	..	..	..	..	..	..	..
4. Riasi "	...	..	...	..	...	..	8	..	..	..	..	8	..	..	..	..	..	..
5. Mirpur "	...	...	...	...	...	..	..	..	..	...	..	..	..	..	..	..	..	..
6. Bhadarwah *Jagir*	...	..	...	...	...	..	...	..	..	..	..	...	..	..	..	..	..	..
7. Punch *Ilaqa*	...	..	...	...	...	..	5	3	..	..	..	2	..	..	..	..	..	..
II.—Kashmir Province (including *Jagirs.*)	**2,145**	**1,192**	**27**	**59**	..	**926**	**145**	**47**	..	..	...	**98**	**3**	**3**	..	..	..	..
8. Kashmir North (including Langet *Jagir.*)	783	718	...	22	..	65	...	...	..	...	...	..	..	..	..	...	..	..
9. Kashmir South (including City)	1,343	467	27	37	..	849	145	47	...	..	...	98	3	3	..	..	..	..
10. Muzaffarabad District ...	19	7	...	..	...	12	...	..	..	..	...	...	..	..	...	...	...	..
III.—Frontier Districts	**5**	..	...	...	..	**5**	...	..	...	..	...	...	..	..	..	..	..	..
11. Ladakh District (including Mansar).	...	...	..	...	...	...	...	..	...	...	..	...	..	..	..	..	..	..
12. Gilgit "	5	...	...	..	..	5	...	...	...	..	...	...	..	..	..	..	..	..
Cities.																		
13. Jammu	80	34	...	...	..	46	...	..	...	..	..	..	..	..	..	...	..	...
14. Srinagar	327	10	...	...	...	222	145	47	...	..	..	98	..	...	...	...	..	..

TABLE XVII.

Occupation or Means of Livelihood.

Jammu and Kashmir State Census, 1921.

District, Jagir, Ilaqa or City.	Group 37.—*Dyeing, bleaching, printing, preparation and sponging of textiles.* Total workers and dependents.	Actual Workers. Total. Males.	Total. Females.	Partially Agriculturists. Males	Partially Agriculturists. Females.	Dependents.
	290	291	292	293	294	295
State	**1,193**	**301**	**18**	**1**	..	**874**
I.—Jammu Province (including *Jagirs*).	**4**	...	...	...	...	**4**
1. Jammu District (including City)	..	..	...	...	...	...
2. Kathua "	...	...	..	..	...	..
3. Udhampur " (including Chaneni *Jagir*).	4	...	..	..	...	4
4. Riasi "	...	..	..	...	..	..
5. Mirpur "	..	..	..	..	..	..
6. Bhadarwah *Jagir*	..	..	..	..	..	..
7. Punch *Ilaqa*	..	..	..	..	..	..
II.—Kashmir Province (including *Jagirs*).	**1,189**	**301**	**18**	**1**	..	**870**
8. Kashmir North (including Langet *Jagir*).	279	4	12	..	..	263
9. Kashmir South (including City)	896	291	6	..	..	599
10. Muzaffarabad District ...	14	6	..	1	..	8
III.—Frontier Districts	..	..	..	..	..	..
11. Ladakh District (including Mansar).	..	..	..	..	..	..
12. Gilgit "	..	..	..	..	..	..
Cities.						
13. Jammu	..	..	..	..	..	..
14. Srinagar	889	291	3	..	..	595

District, Jagir, Ilaqa or City.	Group 38.—*Lace, crepe, embroideries, fringes, etc., and insufficiently described textile industries.* Total workers and dependents.	Actual Workers. Total. Males	Total. Females.	Partially Agriculturists. Males.	Partially Agriculturists. Females.	Dependents.
	296	297	298	299	300	301
State	**1,155**	**424**	**36**	**35**	..	**695**
I.—Jammu Province (including *Jagirs*).	**12**	**6**	..	..	..	**6**
1. Jammu District (including City)	10	4	..	...	...	6
2. Kathua "	...	..	..	...	...	..
3. Udhampur " (including Chaneni *Jagir*).	2	2	...	..	...	..
4. Riasi "	..	...	...	...	...	...
5. Mirpur "	..	...	..	...	...	...
6. Bhadarwah *Jagir*	..	...	..	...	...	...
7. Punch *Ilaqa*	..	..	..	...	...	...
II.—Kashmir Province (including *Jagirs*).	**1,046**	**378**	**7**	**16**	..	**661**
8. Kashmir North (including Langet *Jagir*).	99	43	...	3	...	56
9. Kashmir South (including City)	947	335	7	13	...	605
10. Muzaffarabad District ...	..	..	...	...	..	..
III.—Frontier Districts	97	40	29	19	..	28
11. Ladakh District (including Mansar).	58	40	...	19	...	18
12. Gilgit "	39	..	29	...	...	10
Cities.						
13. Jammu	4	1	...	...	...	3
14. Srinagar	589	180	5	...	...	404

District, Jagir, Ilaqa or City.	Order 7.—Hides, skins, and hard materials from the animal kingdom. Total workers and dependents.	Actual Workers. Total. Males	Total. Females	Partially Agriculturists. Males.	Partially Agriculturists. Females.	Dependents.
	302	303	304	305	306	307
State	**2,724**	**680**	**204**	**73**	**30**	**1,840**
I.—Jammu Province (including *Jagirs*).	**1,684**	**414**	**179**	**64**	**30**	**1,091**
1. Jammu District (including City)	513	167	14	..	..	332
2. Kathua "	..	..	..	..	..	..
3. Udhampur " (including Chaneni *Jagir*).	245	12	102	5	26	131
4. Riasi "	460	162	50	59	4	248
5. Mirpur "	436	66	13	..	..	357
6. Bhadarwah *Jagir*	..	..	..	..	..	..
7. Punch *Ilaqa*	30	7	..	..	..	23
II.—Kashmir Province (including *Jagirs*).	**1,037**	**263**	**25**	**9**	..	**749**
8. Kashmir North (including Langet *Jagir*).	171	52	2	9	..	117
9. Kashmir South (including City)	840	209	23	..	..	608
10. Muzaffarabad District ...	26	2	..	..	..	24
III.—Frontier Districts	3	3	..	..	..	..
11. Ladakh District (including Mansar).	..	..	..	..	..	..
12. Gilgit "	3	3	..	..	..	..
Cities.						
13. Jammu	488	166	11	..	..	311
14. Srinagar	770	185	23	..	..	562

TABLE XVII.

Occupation or Means of Livelihood.

Jammu and Kashmir State Census, 1921.

DISTRICT, JAGIR, ILAQA OR CITY.	Group (39).—Tanners, curriers, leather dressers and leather dyers, etc.						Group (40).—Makers of leather articles, such as trunks, water bags, saddlery or harness, etc., etc., excluding articles of dress.						Group (41).—Furriers and persons occupied with feathers and bristles, brush makers.					
	Total workers and dependents.	Actual Workers.				Dependents.	Total workers and dependents.	Actual Workers.				Dependents.	Total workers and dependents.	Actual Workers.				Dependents.
		Total		Partially Agriculturists				Total.		Partially Agriculturists				Total.		Partially Agriculturists.		
		Males.	Females.	Males.	Females.			Males.	Females.	Males.	Females.			Males.	Females.	Males.	Females.	
	308	309	310	311	312	313	314	315	316	317	318	319	320	321	322	323	324	325
State ..	**525**	**139**	**20**	..	..	**366**	**2,042**	**508**	**181**	**73**	**30**	**1,353**	**30**	**1**	..	..	..	**29**
I.—Jammu Province (including *Jagirs*).	**168**	**71**	**3**	..	..	**94**	**1,516**	**343**	**176**	**64**	**30**	**997**	..	..	..	..	..	..
1. Jammu District (including City)..	49	11	3	..	..	35	464	156	11	..	..	297	..	..	..	..	..	..
2. Kathua „	..	..	..	..	..	..	..	..	..	..	..	..	..	..	..	..	..	..
3. Udhampur „ (including Chaneni *Jagir*).	..	..	..	..	..	..	245	12	102	5	26	131	..	..	..	..	..	..
4. Riasi „	..	..	..	..	..	..	460	162	50	59	4	248	..	..	..	..	..	..
5. Mirpur „	119	60	..	..	..	59	317	6	13	..	..	298	..	..	..	..	..	..
6. Bhadarwah *Jagir*	..	..	..	..	..	..	..	..	..	..	..	..	..	..	..	..	..	..
7. Punch *Ilaqa*	..	..	..	..	..	..	30	7	..	..	..	23	..	..	..	..	..	..
II.—Kashmir Province (including *Jagirs*).	**356**	**67**	**17**	..	..	**272**	**524**	**163**	**5**	**9**	..	**356**	**30**	**1**	..	..	..	**29**
8. Kashmir North (including Langet *Jagir*).	102	13	2	..	..	87	53	34	..	9	..	19	..	..	..	..	..	..
9. Kashmir South (including City)..	228	52	15	..	..	161	471	129	5	..	..	337	30	1	..	..	..	29
10. Muzaffarabad District ..	26	2	..	..	..	24	..	..	..	..	..	..	..	..	..	..	..	..
III.—Frontier Districts.. ..	**1**	**1**	..	..	..	..	**2**	**2**	..	..	..	..	..	..	..	..	..	..
11. Ladakh District (including Mansar.)	..	..	..	..	..	..	..	..	..	..	..	..	..	..	..	..	..	..
12. Gilgit „	1	1	..	..	..	..	2	2	..	..	..	..	..	..	..	..	..	..
Cities																		
13. Jammu	24	10	..	..	..	14	464	156	11	..	..	297	..	..	..	..	..	..
14. Srinagar	196	40	15	..	..	141	433	117	5	..	..	311	30	1	..	..	..	29

TABLE XVII.

Occupation or Means of Livelihood.

Jammu and Kashmir State Census, 1921.

DISTRICT, JAGIR, ILAQA OR CITY.	Group (42).—Bone, ivory, horn, shell, etc., workers (except button)						Order 8.—Wood.						Group (43).—Sawyers.					
	Total workers and dependents.	Actual Workers. Total. Males.	Actual Workers. Total. Females.	Actual Workers. Partially Agriculturists. Males.	Actual Workers. Partially Agriculturists. Females.	Dependents.	Total workers and dependents.	Actual Workers. Total. Males.	Actual Workers. Total. Females.	Actual Workers. Partially Agriculturists. Males.	Actual Workers. Partially Agriculturists. Females.	Dependents.	Total workers and dependents.	Actual Workers. Total. Males.	Actual Workers. Total. Females.	Actual Workers. Partially Agriculturists. Males.	Actual Workers. Partially Agriculturists. Females.	Dependents.
	326	327	328	329	330	331	332	333	334	335	336	337	338	339	340	341	342	343
State ..	**127**	**32**	**3**	..	..	**92**	**2,309**	**8,546**	**2,658**	**1,385**	**58**	**18,105**	**6,660**	**2,008**	**67**	**374**	**3**	**4,585**
I.—Jammu Province (including *Jagirs*).	..	..	..	..	..	..	**11,414**	**3,720**	**301**	**724**	**54**	**7,393**	**1,264**	**519**	**46**	**127**	**3**	**699**
1. Jammu District (including City) ..	..	..	..	..	..	..	4,389	1,300	70	145	..	3,019	265	155	..	37	..	110
2. Kathua ,, ...	..	..	..	..	..	..	2,651	880	69	224	15	1,702	58	31	6	5	1	21
3. Udhampur ,, (including Chaneni *Jagir*).	..	..	..	..	..	..	857	397	80	82	22	380	169	99	3	25	1	67
4. Riasi ,, ...	..	..	..	..	..	..	980	285	43	47	16	652	65	44	8	2	..	13
5. Mirpur ,, ...	..	..	..	..	..	..	1,804	460	9	104	..	1,335	490	50	..	36	..	440
6. Bhadarwah *Jagir*	..	..	..	..	..	..	170	97	30	7	1	43	166	94	29	7	1	43
7. Punch *Ilaqa*	..	..	..	..	..	..	563	301	..	115	..	262	51	46	..	4	..	5
II.—Kashmir Province (including *Jagirs*).	**127**	**32**	**3**	..	..	**92**	**17,847**	**4,797**	**2,356**	**651**	**2**	**10,694**	**5,392**	**1,488**	**21**	**247**	..	**3,883**
8. Kashmir North (including Langet *Jagir*).	16	5	..	..	..	11	4,519	1,368	58	203	..	3,093	2,036	584	17	173	..	1,435
9. Kashmir South (including City)	111	27	3	..	..	81	12,961	3,262	2,298	400	2	7,401	3,192	824	4	51	..	2,364
10. Muzaffarabad District ..	..	..	..	..	..	..	367	167	..	48	..	200	164	80	..	23	..	84
III.—Frontier Districts ..	..	..	..	..	..	..	**48**	**29**	**1**	**10**	..	**18**	**4**	**1**	..	..	..	**3**
11. Ladakh District (including Mansar).	..	..	..	..	..	..	38	20	1	8	..	17	4	1	..	..	..	3
12. Gilgit ,, ...	..	..	..	..	..	..	10	9	..	2	..	1	..	..	..	..	..	..
Cities ...																		
13. Jammu	..	..	..	..	..	..	587	151	..	2	..	436	..	..	..	..	..	..
14. Srinagar	111	27	3	..	..	81	6,577	1,200	2,128	1	..	3,249	1,960	515	2	1	..	1,443

TABLE XVII.

Occupation or Means of Livelihood.

Jammu and Kashmir State Census, 1921.

DISTRICT, JAGIR, ILAQA OR CITY.	Group (44).—Carpenters, turners and joiners, etc.						Group (45).—Basket makers and other industries of woody material, including leaves and thatchers and builders working with bamboo reeds or similar materials.						Order 8.—Metals.					
	Total workers and dependents.	Actual Workers. Total.		Actual Workers. Partially Agriculturists.		Dependents.	Total workers and dependents.	Actual Workers. Total.		Actual Workers. Partially Agriculturists.		Dependents.	Total workers and dependents.	Actual Workers. Total.		Actual Workers. Partially Agriculturists.		Dependents.
		Males.	Females.	Males.	Females.			Males.	Females.	Males.	Females.			Males.	Females.	Males.	Females.	
	344	345	346	347	348	349	350	351	352	353	354	355	356	357	358	359	360	361
State ..	**13,130**	**4,654**	**126**	**734**	**13**	**8,350**	**9,519**	**1,884**	**2,465**	**277**	**40**	**5,170**	**15,199**	**5,269**	**113**	**925**	**10**	**9,817**
I.—Jammu Province (including *Jagirs*).	**6,780**	**2,386**	**82**	**440**	**12**	**4,312**	**3,370**	**815**	**173**	**157**	**39**	**2,382**	**8,295**	**2,839**	**74**	**597**	**9**	**5,382**
1. Jammu District (including City)	3,340	976	34	74	..	2,330	784	169	36	34	..	579	4,402	1,595	26	217	1	2,781
2. Kathua District	1,270	529	..	160	..	741	1,323	320	63	59	14	940	1,146	332	4	109	1	810
3. Udhampur District (including Chaneni *Jagir*).	357	184	15	32	3	158	331	114	62	14	18	155	537	232	8	65	1	297
4. Riasi District	383	178	24	27	9	181	532	63	11	18	7	458	595	156	17	55	1	422
5. Mirpur „	988	307	9	62	..	672	326	103	..	6	..	223	1,268	356	15	89	..	897
6. Bhadarwah *Jagir*	..	..	..	..	..	..	4	3	1	..	..	..	49	28	1	7	..	20
7. Punch *Ilaqa*	442	212	..	85	..	230	70	43	..	26	..	27	298	140	3	55	1	155
II.—Kashmir Province (including *Jagirs*).	**6,306**	**2,240**	**43**	**284**	**1**	**4,023**	**6,149**	**1,063**	**2,292**	**120**	**1**	**2,788**	**6,829**	**2,380**	**38**	**313**	**1**	**4,411**
8. Kashmir North (including Langet *Jagir*).	1,287	500	2	..	..	785	1,196	284	39	30	..	873	1,525	441	11	125	..	1,073
9. Kashmir South (including City)	4,829	1,654	41	259	1	3,134	4,940	784	2,253	90	1	1,903	4,982	1,824	26	173	..	3,132
10. Muzaffarabad District ..	190	86	..	25	..	104	13	1	..	..	..	12	322	115	1	15	1	206
III.—Frontier Districts	**44**	**28**	**1**	**10**	..	**15**	..	..	..	..	..	..	**75**	**50**	**1**	**15**	..	**24**
11. Ladakh District (including Mansar).	34	19	1	8	..	14	..	..	..	..	..	..	60	38	1	15	..	21
12. Gilgit „	10	9	..	2	..	1	..	..	..	..	..	..	15	12	..	..	..	3
Cities																		
13. Jammu	565	145	..	2	..	420	22	6	..	..	..	16	278	100	..	..	..	178
14. Srinagar	1,826	593	2	..	..	1,231	2,791	92	2,124	..	..	575	2,589	985	10	...	..	1,594

TABLE XVII.

OCCUPATION OR MEANS OF LIVELIHOOD.

Jammu and Kashmir State Census, 1921.

DISTRICT, JAGIR, ILAQA OR CITY.	Group (46)—*Forging and rolling of iron and other metals.*						Group (47).—*Makers of Arms, Guns, etc.*						Group (48).—*Other workers in iron and makers of implements and tools, principally or exclusively of iron.*					
	Total workers and dependents.	Actual Workers.					Total workers and dependents.	Actual Workers.					Total workers and dependents.	Actual Workers.				
		Total.		*Partially Agriculturists.*				*Total.*		*Partially Agriculturists.*				*Total.*		*Partially Agriculturists.*		
		Males.	Females.	Males.	Females.	Dependents.		Males.	Females.	Males.	Females.	Dependents.		Males.	Females.	Males.	Females.	Dependents.
	362	363	364	365	366	367	368	369	370	371	372	373	374	375	376	377	378	379
State ..	**4,511**	**1,472**	**47**	**308**	**8**	**2,992**	**483**	**148**	**5**	**40**	...	**330**	**8,194**	**3,035**	**56**	**561**	**2**	**5,103**
I.—Jammu Province (including *Jagirs*).	**4,511**	**1,472**	**47**	**308**	**8**	**2,992**	**333**	**108**	**5**	**40**	..	**220**	**3,268**	**1,181**	**20**	**246**	**1**	**2,067**
1. Jammu District (including City.)	2,519	814	26	107	1	1,679	39	16	..	3	..	23	1,747	732	..	107	..	1,015
2. Kathua ,, ...	974	281	..	84	..	693	3	..	..	..	..	3	163	51	4	25	1	108
3. Udhampur ,, (including Chaneni *Jagir*).	472	188	8	58	1	276	5	3	..	1	..	2	22	16	..	5	..	6
4. Riasi District	294	56	12	12	5	226	286	89	5	36	..	192	13	9	..	7	..	4
5. Mirpur ,, ...	6	2	..	..	..	4	..	..	..	..	..	..	1,256	351	15	89	..	890
6. Bhadarwah *Jagir*	34	18	..	6	..	16	..	..	..	..	..	..	..	..	..	..	..	..
7. Punch *Ilaqa*	212	113	1	41	1	98	..	..	..	..	..	..	67	22	1	13	..	44
II.—Kashmir Province (including *Jagirs*).	..	..	..	..	..	..	**150**	**40**	..	..	..	**110**	**4,851**	**1,804**	**35**	**300**	**1**	**3,012**
8. Kashmir North (including Langet *Jagir*).	..	..	..	..	..	..	..	..	..	..	..	..	1,412	426	11	125	..	975
9. Kashmir South (including City)	..	..	..	..	..	..	150	40	..	..	..	110	3,122	1,264	23	160	..	1,835
10. Muzaffarabad District ...	..	..	..	..	..	..	..	..	..	..	..	..	317	114	1	15	1	202
III.—Frontier Districts	..	..	..	..	..	..	..	..	..	..	..	..	**75**	**50**	**1**	**15**	..	**24**
11. Ladakh District (including Mansar).	..	..	..	..	..	..	..	..	..	..	..	..	60	38	1	15	..	21
12. Gilgit ,, ...	..	..	..	..	..	..	..	..	..	..	..	..	15	12	..	...	..	3
Cities.																		
13. Jammu	218	72	..	..	..	146	..	..	..	..	..	..	..	..	..	..	..	..
14. Srinagar	..	..	..	..	..	..	150	40	..	..	..	110	1,081	563	7	..	..	511

TABLE XVII.

Occupation or Means of Livelihood.

Jammu and Kashmir State Census, 1921.

District, Jagir, Ilaqa or City.	Group (49).—Workers in brass, copper, and bell metal.						Group (50).—Workers in other metals (tin, zinc, lead, quick-silver, etc., except precious metals.)						Group (51).—Workers in mints, die-sinkers, etc.					
	Total workers and dependents.	Actual Workers. Total.		Actual Workers. Partially Agriculturists.		Dependents.	Total workers and dependents.	Actual Workers. Total.		Actual Workers. Partially Agriculturists.		Dependents.	Total workers and dependents.	Actual Workers. Total.		Actual Workers. Partially Agriculturists.		Dependents.
		Males.	Females.	Males.	Females.			Males.	Females.	Males.	Females.			Males.	Females.	Males.	Females.	
	380	381	382	383	384	385	386	387	388	389	390	391	392	393	394	395	396	397
State ..	**1,326**	**394**	**3**	**10**	..	**923**	**371**	**129**	**1**	..	..	**241**	**314**	**91**	**1**	**6**	..	**222**
I.—Jammu Province (including *Jagirs*).	**88**	**33**	**1**	**3**	..	**54**	**95**	**45**	**1**	..	...	**49**	..	..	..	..	..	..
1. Jammu District (including City.)	31	1	..	..	..	30	66	32	..	..	..	34	..	..	..	..	..	..
2. Kathua "	6	..	..	..	..	5	..	..	..	..	..	..	..	..	..	..	..	..
3. Udhampur " (including Chaneni *Jagir*).	32	19	..	1	..	13	6	6	..	..	..	..	..	..	..	..	..	..
4. Riasi District	..	..	..	..	..	..	2	2	..	..	..	..	..	..	..	..	..	..
5. Mirpur "	2	2	..	..	..	..	4	1	..	..	..	3	..	..	..	..	...	..
6. Bhadarwah *Jagir*	15	10	1	1	..	4	..	..	..	..	..	..	..	..	..	..	..	..
7. Punch *Ilaqa*	2	1	..	1	..	1	17	4	1	..	..	12	..	..	..	..	..	..
II.—Kashmir Province (including *Jagirs*).	**1,238**	**361**	**2**	**7**	...	**875**	**276**	**84**	..	..	..	**1**	**314**	**91**	**1**	**6**	..	**222**
8. Kashmir North (including Langet *Jagir*).	20	7	..	..	..	13	93	8	..	..	..	85	..	..	..	..	..	..
9. Kashmir South (including City)..	1,215	353	2	7	..	860	181	76	..	..	..	105	314	91	1	6	..	222
10. Muzaffarabad District ..	3	1	..	..	..	2	2	..	..	..	..	2	..	..	..	..	..	..
III.—Frontier Districts	..	..	..	..	..	..	..	..	..	..	..	..	..	..	..	..	..	..
11. Ladakh District (including Mansar).	..	..	..	..	..	..	..	..	..	..	..	..	..	..	..	..	..	..
12. Gilgit "	..	..	..	..	..	..	..	..	..	..	..	..	..	..	..	..	..	..
Cities.																		
13. Jammu	..	..	..	..	..	..	60	28	..	..	..	32	..	..	..	..	..	..
14. Srinagar	910	238	2	..	..	670	159	71	..	..	..	88	239	73	1	..	..	215

TABLE XVII.

OCCUPATION OR MEANS OF LIVELIHOOD.

Jammu and Kashmir State Census, 1921.

DISTRICT, JAGIR, ILAQA OR CITY.	Order 10.—Ceramics.						Group (52)—Makers of glass and crystal ware.						Group (53).—Makers of glass bangles, glass beads necklaces and glass ear studs, etc.					
	Total workers and dependents.	Actual Workers. Total.		Actual Workers. Partially Agriculturists.		Dependents.	Total workers and dependents.	Actual Workers. Total.		Actual Workers. Partially Agriculturists.		Dependents.	Total workers and dependents.	Actual Workers. Total.		Actual Workers. Partially Agriculturists.		Dependents.
		Males.	Females.	Males.	Females.			Males.	Females.	Males.	Females.			Males.	Females.	Males.	Females.	
	398	399	400	401	402	403	404	405	406	407	408	409	410	411	412	413	414	415
State ...	**14,744**	**4,697**	**1,131**	**817**	**50**	**8,916**	**95**	**30**	..	..	..	**65**	**4**	**3**	..	..	..	**1**
I.—Jammu Province (including *Jagirs*).	**6,385**	**2,111**	**269**	**289**	**25**	**4,005**	..	..	..	..	..	..	**4**	**3**	..	..	..	**1**
1. Jammu District (including City.)	2,042	743	31	78	1	1,268	..	..	..	..	..	..	..	..	..	..	..	..
2. Kathua "	790	236	38	38	7	516	..	..	..	..	..	..	..	..	..	..	..	..
3. Udhampur District (including Chaneni *Jagir*).	465	175	42	45	4	248	..	..	..	..	..	..	..	..	..	..	..	..
4. Riasi District	428	153	46	44	8	229	..	..	..	..	..	..	4	3	..	..	..	1
5. Mirpur "	2,141	607	91	56	1	1,443	..	..	..	..	..	..	..	..	..	..	..	..
6. Bhadarwah *Jagir*	101	31	7	5	2	63	..	..	..	..	..	..	..	..	..	..	..	..
7. Punch *Ilaqa*	418	166	14	23	2	238	..	..	..	..	..	..	..	..	..	..	..	..
II.—Kashmir Province (including *Jagirs*).	**8,314**	**2,566**	**861**	**524**	**25**	**4,887**	**95**	**30**	..	..	..	**65**	..	..	..	..	..	..
8. Kashmir North (including Langet *Jagir*).	2,359	753	86	200	14	1,520	..	..	..	..	..	..	..	..	..	..	..	..
9. Kashmir South (including City)	5,791	1,750	752	302	11	3,289	95	30	..	..	..	65	..	..	..	..	..	..
10. Muzaffarabad District ..	164	63	23	22	..	78	..	..	..	..	..	..	..	..	..	..	..	..
III.—Frontier Districts	**45**	**20**	**1**	**4**	..	**24**	..	..	..	..	..	..	..	..	..	..	..	..
11. Ladakh District (including Mansar)	39	14	1	4	..	24	..	..	..	..	..	..	..	..	..	..	..	..
12. Gilgit "	6	6	..	..	..	..	..	..	..	..	..	..	..	..	..	..	..	..
Cities.																		
13. Jammu	230	154	4	1	1	72	..	..	..	..	..	..	..	..	..	..	..	..
14. Srinagar	1,715	517	200	..	..	998	95	30	..	..	..	65	..	..	..	..	..	..

TABLE XVII.

OCCUPATION OR MEANS OF LIVELIHOOD.

Jammu and Kashmir State Census, 1921.

DISTRICT, JAGIR, ILAQA OR CITY.	Group (54).—*Makers of porcelain and crockery.*						Group (55).—*Potters and earthen pipe and bowl makers.*						Group (56).—*Brick and tile makers.*					
	Total workers and dependents.	ACTUAL WORKERS. Total. Males.	ACTUAL WORKERS. Total. Females.	ACTUAL WORKERS. *Partially Agriculturists.* Males.	ACTUAL WORKERS. *Partially Agriculturists.* Females.	Dependents.	Total workers and dependents.	ACTUAL WORKERS. Total. Males.	ACTUAL WORKERS. Total. Females.	ACTUAL WORKERS. *Partially Agriculturists.* Males.	ACTUAL WORKERS. *Partially Agriculturists.* Females.	Dependents.	Total workers and dependents.	ACTUAL WORKERS. Total. Males.	ACTUAL WORKERS. Total. Females.	ACTUAL WORKERS. *Partially Agriculturists.* Males.	ACTUAL WORKERS. *Partially Agriculturists.* Females.	Dependents.
	416	417	418	419	420	421	422	423	424	425	426	427	428	429	430	431	432	433
State ..	**970**	**342**	**114**	**49**	**10**	**514**	**13,453**	**4,202**	**1,014**	**767**	**40**	**8,237**	**222**	**120**	**3**	**1**	..	**99**
I.—Jammu Province (including *Jagirs*).	**525**	**181**	**53**	**49**	**10**	**291**	**5,823**	**1,915**	**213**	**240**	**15**	**3,695**	**33**	**12**	**3**	..	..	**18**
1. Jammu District (including City).	..	..	..	..	..	..	2,028	738	28	78	1	1,262	14	5	3	..	..	6
2. Kathua "	..	..	..	..	..	..	778	229	38	38	7	511	12	7	..	..	..	5
3. Udhampur " (including Chaneni *Jagir*).	..	..	..	..	..	..	464	175	42	45	4	247	1	..	..	..	..	1
4. Riasi District	424	150	46	44	8	228	..	..	..	...	..	..	..	..	..	..	..	..
5. Mirpur "	..	..	..	..	..	..	2,135	607	91	56	1	1,437	6	..	..	..	..	6
6. Bhadarwah *Jagir* ..	101	31	7	5	2	63	..	..	..	..	..	..	..	..	..	..	...	..
7. Punch *Ilaqa*	..	..	..	..	..	..	418	166	14	23	2	238	..	..	..	..	..	..
II.—Kashmir Province (including *Jagirs*).	**445**	**161**	**61**	..	..	**223**	**7,585**	**2,267**	**800**	**523**	**25**	**4,518**	**189**	**108**	..	**1**	..	**81**
8. Kashmir North (including Langet *Jagir*).	..	..	..	..	..	..	2,359	753	86	200	14	1,520	..	..	..	..	..	..
9. Kashmir South (including City)	445	161	61	..	..	223	5,062	1,451	691	301	11	2,920	189	108	..	1	..	81
10. Muzaffarabad District.. ...	..	..	..	..	..	..	164	63	23	22	..	78	..	..	..	..	..	..
III.—Frontier Districts	..	..	..	..	..	..	**45**	**20**	**1**	**4**	..	**24**	...	..	..	..	..	..
11. Ladakh District (including Mansar).	..	..	..	..	..	..	39	14	1	4	..	24	..	..	..	..	..	..
12. Gilgit "	..	..	..	..	..	..	6	6	..	...	..	..	..	..	..	..	..	..
Cities.																		
13. Jammu	..	..	..	..	..	..	221	154	1	1	1	66	9	..	3	..	..	6
14. Srinagar	445	161	..	..	..	223	1,006	231	139	..	..	636	169	95	..	..	..	74

TABLE XVII.

Occupation or Means of Livelihood.

Jammu and Kashmir State Census, 1921.

DISTRICT, JAGIR, ILAQA OR CITY.	Order II.—Chemical products properly so called and analogous.						*Group* (58).—*Manufacture of matches and explosive materials.*						*Group* (59).—*Manufacture of aerated and mineral waters and ice.*					
	Total workers and dependents.	Actual Workers.				Dependents.	Total workers and dependents.	Actual Workers.				Dependents.	Total workers and dependents.	Actual Workers.				Dependents.
		Total.		*Partially Agriculturists.*				*Total.*		*Partially Agriculturists.*				*Total.*		*Partially Agriculturists.*		
		Males.	Females.	Males.	Females.			Males.	Females.	Males.	Females.			Males.	Females.	Males.	Females.	
	434	435	436	437	438	439	440	441	442	443	444	445	446	447	448	449	450	451
State ...	**10,777**	**3,736**	**526**	**569**	**37**	**6,515**	**217**	**85**	**2**	**1**	..	**130**	**49**	**19**	..	..	..	**30**
I. Jammu Province (including *Jagirs*).	**3,017**	**1,244**	**122**	**117**	**16**	**1,651**	**190**	**73**	**2**	**1**	..	**115**	..	..	..	..	..	..
1. Jammu District (including City.)	1,189	536	16	51	2	637	94	35	..	..	..	59	..	..	..	..	..	..
2. Kathua " ..	418	193	31	19	6	194	10	3	..	..	..	7	..	..	..	..	..	..
3. Udhampur " (including Chaneni *Jagir*.)	248	83	46	25	7	119	3	2	..	1	..	1	..	..	..	..	..	..
4. Riasi District	77	34	5	5	1	38	11	1	1	..	..	9	..	..	..	..	..	..
5. Mirpur "	966	344	21	7	..	601	67	29	1	..	..	37	..	..	..	..	..	...
6. Bhadarwah *Jagir*	1	...	1	...	..	..	..	..	..	..	..	..	..	..	..	..	..	..
7. Puncha *Ilaqa*	118	54	2	10	..	62	5	3	..	..	..	2	..	..	...	..	...	..
II.—Kashmir Province (including *Jagirs*.)	**7,760**	**2,492**	**404**	**452**	**21**	**4,864**	**27**	**12**	..	..	..	**15**	**49**	**19**	..	..	..	**30**
8. Kashmir North (including Langet *Jagir*).	2,162	685	18	145	..	1,459	..	..	..	..	..	..	..	..	..	..	..	..
9. Kashmir South (including City.)	5,478	1,778	383	298	21	3,317	27	12	..	..	..	15	48	18	..	..	..	30
10. Muzaffarabad District ..	120	29	3	9	..	88	...	..	..	..	..	..	1	1	..	..	..	..
III.—Frontier Districts ..	..	..	...	...	..	..	..	..	..	..	..	..	..	..	..	..	..	..
11. Ladakh District (including Mansar).	...	..	...	..	..	..	..	..	..	..	...	..	..	..	..	..	..	..
12. Gilgit " .	...	...	..	..	..	...	..	..	..	..	...	..	..	...	..	..	..	..
Cities.																		
13. Jammu	122	48	...	...	..	74	86	30	..	..	..	56	..	..	..	..	..	..
14. Srinagar	1,587	585	32	40	..	970	27	12	..	..	...	15	48	18	..	..	..	30

TABLE XVII.

Occupation or Means of Livelihood.

Jammu and Kashmir State Census, 1921.

DISTRICT, JAGIR, ILAQA OR CITY.	Group (60).—*Manufacture of dyes, paint and ink.*						Group (61).—*Manufacture and refining of vegetable oils*						Group (62)—*Manufacture and refining of mineral oils.*					
	Total workers and dependents.	Actual Workers. Total. Males.	Actual Workers. Total. Females.	Actual Workers. Partially Agriculturists. Males.	Actual Workers. Partially Agriculturists. Females.	Dependents.	Total workers and dependents.	Actual Workers. Total. Males.	Actual Workers. Total. Females.	Actual Workers. Partially Agriculturists. Males.	Actual Workers. Partially Agriculturists. Females	Dependents.	Total workers and dependents.	Actual Workers. Total. Males.	Actual Workers. Total. Females.	Actual Workers. Partially Agriculturists. Males.	Actual Workers. Partially Agriculturists. Females.	Dependents.
	452	453	454	455	456	457	458	459	460	461	462	463	464	465	466	467	468	469
State ..	**135**	**31**	**18**	**1**	**6**	**86**	**9,376**	**3,198**	**495**	**525**	**31**	**5,683**	**9**	**6**	..	**1**	..	**3**
I.—Jammu Province (including *Jagirs.*)	..	..	..	..	..	..	**2,821**	**1,167**	**120**	**116**	**16**	**1,534**	..	..	..	..	..	..
1. Jammu District (including City.)	..	..	..	..	..	..	1,090	498	16	51	2	576	..	..	..	..	..	..
2. Kathua „	..	..	..	..	..	..	407	189	31	19	6	187	..	..	..	..	..	..
3. Udhampur „ (including Chaneni *Jagir.*)	..	..	..	..	..	..	245	81	46	24	7	118	..	..	..	..	..	..
4. Riasi District	..	..	..	..	..	..	66	33	4	5	1	29	..	..	..	..	..	..
5. Mirpur „	..	..	..	..	..	..	899	315	20	7	..	564	..	..	..	..	..	..
6. Bhadarwah *Jagir* ..	..	..	..	..	..	..	1	..	1	..	..	..	..	..	..	..	..	..
7. Punch *Ilaqa*	..	..	..	..	..	..	113	51	2	10	..	60	..	..	..	..	..	..
II.—Kashmir Province (including *Jagirs*).	**135**	**31**	**18**	**1**	**6**	**86**	**6,555**	**2,031**	**375**	**409**	**15**	**4,149**	**9**	**6**	..	**1**	..	**3**
8. Kashmir North (including Langet *Jagir*).	29	7	..	1	..	22	2,077	667	15	144	..	1,395	..	..	..	..	..	..
9. Kashmir South (including City.)	105	23	18	..	6	64	4,360	1,337	357	256	15	2,666	9	6	..	1	..	3
10. Muzaffarabad District ..	1	1	..	..	..	..	118	27	3	9	..	88	..	..	..	..	..	..
III—Frontier Districts	..	..	..	..	..	..	..	..	..	..	..	..	..	..	..	..	..	..
11. Ladakh District (including Mansar.)	..	..	..	..	..	..	..	..	..	..	..	..	..	..	..	..	..	..
12. Gilgit „	..	..	..	..	..	..	..	..	..	..	..	..	..	..	..	..	..	..
Cities.																		
13. Jammu ..	..	..	..	..	..	..	32	16	..	..	..	16	..	..	..	..	..	..
14. Srinagar	74	22	..	..	..	52	680	219	25	1	..	436	..	..	..	..	..	..

TABLE XVII.

Occupation or Means of Livelihood.

Jammu and Kashmir State Census, 1921.

DISTRICT, JAGIR, ILAQA OR CITY.	Group (63).—*Manufacture of paper, card-board and papier machie.*						Group (64).—*Others (soap, candles, lac, cutch, perfumes and miscellaneous drugs.*						Order 12.— Food Industries.					
	Total workers and dependents.	Actual Workers.				Dependents.	Total workers and dependents.	Actual Workers.				Dependents.	Total workers and dependents.	Actual Workers.				Dependents.
		Total.		Partially Agriculturists.				Total.		Partially Agriculturists.				Total.		Partially Agriculturists.		
		Males.	Females.	Males.	Females.			Males.	Females.	Males.	Females.			Males.	Females.	Males.	Females.	
	470	471	472	473	474	475	476	477	478	479	480	481	482	483	484	485	486	487
State ...	**432**	**192**	..	1	..	**240**	**559**	**205**	**11**	**40**	..	**343**	**19,178**	**5,886**	**1,594**	**314**	**80**	**11,698**
I.—Jammu Province (including *Jagirs*).	..	..	..	..	..	..	**6**	**4**	..	..	..	**2**	**7,167**	**2,219**	**1,164**	**201**	**79**	**3,784**
1. Jammu District (including City.)	..	..	..	..	..	..	5	3	..	..	..	2	1,991	764	133	43	2	1,094
2. Kathua „ ..	..	..	..	..	..	..	1	1	..	..	..	..	2,759	516	868	51	66	1,375
3. Udhampur „ (including Chaneni *Jagir.*)	..	..	..	..	..	..	..	..	..	..	..	..	606	314	58	59	2	234
4. Riasi District ..	..	..	..	..	..	..	..	..	..	..	..	..	366	126	41	16	4	199
5. Mirpur „ ..	..	..	..	..	..	..	..	..	..	..	..	..	1,083	370	55	37	5	678
6. Bhadarwah *Jagir* ..	..	..	..	..	..	..	..	..	..	..	..	..	42	23	4	4	..	15
7. Punch *Ilaqa*	..	..	..	..	..	..	..	..	..	..	..	..	320	126	5	11	..	189
II.—Kashmir Province (including *Jagirs*).	**432**	**192**	..	1	..	**240**	**553**	**201**	**11**	**40**	..	**341**	**11,938**	**3,638**	**423**	**108**	**1**	**7,877**
8. Kashmir North (including Langet *Jagir*).	..	..	..	..	..	..	56	11	..	..		42	2,380	650	84	26	..	1,646
9. Kashmir South (including City.)	432	192	..	1	..	240	497	190	3	40	..	299	9,177	2,845	331	74	1	6,001
10. Muzaffarabad District ..	..	..	..	..	..	..	..	..	8	..	..	..	381	143	8	8	..	230
III.—Frontier Districts ..	..	..	...	..	..	..	..	..	..	..	..	..	**73**	**29**	**7**	**5**	..	**37**
11. Ladakh District (including Mansar.)	..	..	...	..	..	..	..	..	..	..	..	..	61	23	7	5	..	31
12. Gilgit „	..	..	..	..	..	..	..	..	..	..	..	..	12	6	..	..	..	6
Cities.																		
13. Jammu	..	..	..	..	..	..	4	2	..	..	..	2	384	157	1	1	1	226
14. Srinagar	306	135	..	..	..	171	452	179	7	38	..	266	5,478	1,668	163	..	..	3,647

TABLE XVII.

Occupation or Means of Livelihood.

Jammu and Kashmir State Census, 1921.

DISTRICT, JAGIR, ILAQA OR CITY.	Group (65).—*Rice pounders and huskers and flour grinders.*						Group (66).—*Bakers and biscuit makers.*						Group (67).—*Grain parchers, etc.*					
	Total workers and dependents.	Actual Workers. Total.		Actual Workers. *Partially Agriculturists.*		Dependents.	Total workers and dependents.	Actual Workers. Total.		Actual Workers. *Partially Agiculturists.*		Dependents.	Total workers and dependents.	Actual Workers. Total.		Actual Workers. *Partially Agriculturists.*		Dependents.
		Males.	Females.	Males.	Females.			Males.	Females.	Males.	Females.			Males.	Females.	Males.	Females.	
	488	489	490	491	492	493	494	495	496	497	498	499	500	501	502	503	504	505
State	**5,568**	**1,996**	**603**	**201**	**14**	**2,969**	**5,538**	**1,822**	**246**	**44**	**2**	**3,476**	**592**	**41**	**19**	**3**	..	**532**
I.—Jammu Province (including *Jagirs*).	**4,470**	**1,679**	**457**	**172**	**14**	**2,334**	**323**	**148**	**8**	**4**	**1**	**167**	**46**	**33**	**3**	**3**	..	**10**
1. Jammu District (including City.)	1,351	493	129	32	1	729	229	107	4	2	1	118	3	3	..	..	..	..
2. Kathua „	1,222	445	174	50	2	603	..	..	..	...	..	..	..	..	..	..	..	..
3. Udhampur „ (including Chaneni *Jagir*).	472	247	56	29	2	169	34	15	2	2	..	17	[illegible]0	25	..	1	..	5
4. Riasi „	347	118	38	14	4	191	7	4	..	..	..	3	12	4	3	2	..	5
5. Mirpur „	901	294	54	36	5	553	..	..	..	..	..	..	..	..	..	..	..	..
6. Bhadarwah *Jagir*	22	15	4	2	..	3	..	..	..	..	..	..	..	..	..	..	..	..
7. Punch *Ilaqa*	155	67	2	9	..	86	53	22	2	..	..	29	1	1	..	..	..	..
II.—Kashmir Province (including *Jagirs*).	**1,078**	**308**	**144**	**26**	..	**626**	**5,194**	**1,663**	**227**	**40**	**1**	**3,304**	**546**	**8**	**16**	..	..	**522**
8. Kashmir North (including Langet *Jagir*).	195	43	23	2	..	129	1,287	358	44	18	..	885	..	..	..	..	..	..
9. Kashmir South (including City)	772	193	118	24	..	461	3,784	1,263	180	16	1	2,341	546	8	16	..	..	522
10. Muzaffarabad District ..	111	72	3	..	..	36	123	42	3	6	..	78	..	..	..	..	..	..
III.—Frontier Districts ..	**20**	**9**	**2**	**3**	..	**9**	**21**	**11**	**5**	..	..	**5**	..	..	..	..	..	..
11. Ladakh District (including Mansar).	20	9	2	3	..	9	15	5	5	..	..	5	..	..	..	..	..	..
12. Gilgit District ..	..	..	..	..	..	..	6	6	..	..	..	..	..	..	..	...	..	..
Cities.																		
13. Jammu	..	..	..	..	..	..	173	79	1	1	1	93	..	..	..	..	..	..
14. Srinagar	491	121	90	..	..	280	1,582	535	50	..	..	997	50	8	7	..	..	35

TABLE XVII.

Occupation or Means of Livelihood.

Jammu and Kashmir State Census, 1921.

District, Jagir, Ilaqa or City.	Group (68).—*Butchers.*						Group (69).—*Fish curers.*						Group (70).—*Butter, cheese and ghee makers.*					
	Total workers and dependents.	Actual Workers.				Dependents.	Total workers and dependents.	Actual Workers.				Dependents.	Total workers and dependents.	Actual Workers.				Dependents.
		Total.		*Partially Agriculturists.*				*Total.*		*Partially Agriculturists.*				*Total.*		*Partially. Agriculturists.*		
		Males.	Females.	Males.	Females.			Males.	Females.	Males.	Females.			Males.	Females.	Males.	Females.	
	506	507	508	509	510	511	512	513	514	515	516	517	518	519	520	521	522	523
State. ..	**4,503**	**1,478**	**6**	**52**	..	**3,019**	**136**	**31**	**3**	..	..	**102**	**1,238**	**25**	**694**	**8**	**64**	**519**
I—Jammu Province (including *Jagirs.*)	**679**	**230**	**2**	**8**	..	**447**	..	..	..	..	..	..	**1,236**	**25**	**693**	**8**	**64**	**518**
1. Jammu District (including City)	297	104	..	3	..	193	..	..	..	..	..	..	32	15	..	1	..	17
2. Kathua " ..	53	27	..	..	..	26	..	..	..	..	..	..	1,189	..	693	..	64	496
3. Udhampur " (including Chaneni *Jagir*).	55	17	..	..	..	38	..	..	..	..	..	..	15	10	..	7	..	5
4. Riasi " ..	..	..	..	..	..	..	..	..	..	..	..	..	..	..	..	..	..	..
5. Mirpur " ..	148	42	1	1	..	105	..	..	..	..	..	..	..	..	..	..	..	..
6. Bhadarwah *Jagir* ..	20	8	..	2	..	12	..	..	..	..	..	..	..	..	..	..	..	..
7. Punch *Ilaqa* ..	106	32	1	2	..	73	..	..	..	..	..	..	..	..	..	..	..	..
II.—Kashmir Province (including *Jagirs*).	**3,792**	**1,239**	**4**	**42**	..	**2,549**	**136**	**31**	**3**	..	..	**102**	**2**	..	**1**	..	..	**1**
8. Kashmir North (including Langet *Jagir*).	794	224	4	6	..	566	29	8	3	..	..	18	..	..	..	..	..	..
9. Kashmir South (including City)	2,889	999	..	34	..	1,890	107	23	..	..	..	84	..	..	..	..	..	..
10. Muzaffarabad District ..	109	16	..	2	..	93	..	..	..	..	..	..	2	..	1	..	..	1
III.—Frontier Districts ..	**32**	**9**	..	**2**	..	**23**	..	..	..	..	..	..	..	..	..	..	..	..
11. Ladakh District	26	9	..	2	..	17	..	..	..	..	..	..	..	..	..	..	..	..
12. Gilgit "	6	..	..	..	..	6	..	..	..	..	..	..	..	..	..	..	..	..
Cities.																		
13. Jammu	162	61	..	..	..	101	..	..	..	..	..	..	..	..	..	..	..	..
14. Srinagar	2,275	646	..	..	..	1,629	107	23	..	..	..	84	..	..	..	..	..	..

TABLE XVII.

Occupation or Means of Livelihood.

Jammu and Kashmir State Census, 1921.

District, Jagir, Ilaqa or City.	Group (72).—*Sweetmeat makers, preparers of jam and condiments, etc.*						Group (75).—*Manufacturers of tobacco, opium, and ganja.*						Order 13.—Industries of dress and the toilet.					
	Total workers and dependents.	Actual Workers. Total.		Actual Workers. *Partially Agriculturists.*		Dependents.	Total workers and dependents.	Actual Workers. Total.		Actual Workers. *Partially Agriculturists.*		Dependents.	Total workers and dependents.	Actual Workers. Total.		Actual Workers. *Partially Agriculturists.*		Dependents.
		Males.	Females.	Males.	Females.			Males.	Females.	Males.	Females.			Males.	Females.	Males.	Females.	
	524	525	526	527	528	529	530	531	532	533	534	535	536	537	538	539	540	541
State ..	**1,254**	**375**	**20**	**1**	...	**859**	**349**	**118**	**9**	**5**	..	**222**	**73,449**	**24,188**	**3,144**	**3,050**	**184**	**46,117**
I.—Jammu Province (including *Jagirs*).	**383**	**78**	**1**	**1**	...	**304**	**30**	**26**	...	**5**	..	**4**	**30,836**	**10,052**	**1,457**	**1,879**	**147**	**19,327**
1. Jammu District (including City).	53	19	...	...	...	34	26	23	..	5	..	3	12,034	3,828	262	588	20	7,944
2. Kathua " ..	295	44	1	1	..	250	..	..	..	..	..	..	4,999	1,597	271	421	59	3,126
3. Udhampur " (including Chaneni *Jagir*).	...	..	...	...	...	..	..	..	..	..	..	..	1,701	735	72	175	6	894
4. Riasi " ..	..	.	...	...	...	..	..	..	...	..	..	..	1,165	358	113	101	25	694
5. Mirpur " ..	34	14	..	..	...	20	..	..	..	..	..	..	8,350	2,514	654	279	21	5,182
6. Bhadarwah *Jagir* ..	..	..	..	...	...	..	..	...	..	..	..	..	510	178	49	44	10	283
7. Punch *Ilaqa* ..	1	1	...	..	...	..	4	3	..	..	..	1	2,082	842	36	271	3	1,204
II.—Kashmir Province (including *Jagirs*).	**871**	**297**	**19**	...	..	**555**	**319**	**92**	**9**	..	..	**218**	**42,417**	**14,035**	**1,671**	**1,152**	**37**	**26,711**
8. Kashmir North (including Langet *Jagir*).	64	15	7	...	..	42	11	2	3	..	..	6	7,074	2,201	103	396	19	4,770
9. Kashmir South (including City)..	772	269	12	..	..	491	307	90	5	..	..	212	34,166	11,449	1,541	684	7	21,176
10. Muzaffarabad District ..	35	13	..	..	...	22	1	..	1	..	..	..	1,177	385	27	72	11	765
III.—Frontier Districts ..	..	...	..	..	..	..	..	..	..	..	..	..	**196**	**101**	**16**	**19**	..	**79**
11. Ladakh District ..	..	...	...	..	..	...	..	..	..	..	..	..	112	46	15	11	..	51
12. Gilgit " ..	..	..	...	...	..	..	..	..	...	..	..	..	84	55	1	8	..	28
Cities.																		
13. Jammu ..	49	17	..	..	..	32	..	..	..	..	..	..	1,504	604	70	2	2	830
14. Srinagar ..	704	257	12	..	...	435	269	78	4	..	..	187	17,422	5,341	1,219	19	..	10,862

TABLE XVII.

OCCUPATION OR MEANS OF LIVELIHOOD.

Jammu and Kashmir State Census, 1921.

DISTRICT, JAGIR, ILAQA OR CITY.	Group (76)—*Hat, cap and turban makers.*						Group (77)—*Tailors, milliners, dress makers, darners and embroiderers on linen.*						Group (78).—*Shoe, boot and sandal makers.*					
	Total workers and dependents.	Actual Workers.				Dependents.	Total workers and dependents.	Actual Workers.				Dependents.	Total workers and dependents.	Actual Workers.				Dependents.
		Total.		*Partially Agriculturists.*				*Total.*		*Partially Agriculturists.*				*Total.*		*Partially Agriculturists.*		
		Males.	Females.	Males.	Females.			Males	Females.	Males.	Females.			Males.	Females.	Males.	Females.	
	542	543	544	545	546	547	548	549	550	551	552	553	554	555	556	557	558	559
State ..	**88**	**21**	**6**	..	..	**61**	**26,587**	**9,434**	**1,359**	**490**	**27**	**15,794**	**27,155**	**8,321**	**1,114**	**1,539**	**126**	**17,720**
I.—Jammu Province (including *Jagirs.*)	**8**	**3**	**2**	..	..	**3**	**4,311**	**1,534**	**355**	**197**	**24**	**2,422**	**17,156**	**5,244**	**917**	**1,234**	**112**	**10,995**
1. Jammu District (including City)	4	3	..	..	..	1	1,410	608	91	9	3	711	6,481	1,739	110	423	14	4,632
2. Kathua " ..	..	..	..	..	..	..	353	149	37	6	6	167	2,861	860	204	3[illegible]4	48	1,797
3. Udhampur " (including Chaneni *Jagir.*)	2	..	..	..	..	2	371	124	17	15	2	230	908	410	4[illegible]	113	3	453
4. Riasi " ..	..	..	..	..	..	..	378	86	21	9	5	270	457	145	75	51	20	237
5. Mirpur " ..	2	..	2	..	..	..	1,229	374	174	41	8	681	5,026	1,504	422	205	14	3,100
6. Bhadarwah *Jagir* ..	..	..	..	..	..	..	167	67	4	22	..	96	307	101	44	16	10	162
7. Punch *Ilaqa* ..	..	..	..	..	..	..	403	126	11	95	..	266	1,116	483	17	132	3	614
II—Kashmir Province (including *Jagirs.*)	**76**	**18**	..	..	..	**58**	**22,150**	**7,830**	**1,000**	**282**	**3**	**13,320**	**9,978**	**3,065**	**195**	**272**	**14**	**6,718**
8. Kashmir North (including Langet *Jagir.*)	5	1	...	..	..	4	2,158	715	17	97	2	1,426	2,212	613	18	64	1	1,581
9. Kashmir South (including City) ..	71	17	..	..	..	54	19,008	6,971	980	168	1	11,657	7,264	2,310	158	177	2	4,796
10. Muzaffarabad District ..	..	..	..	..	..	..	384	144	3	17	..	237	502	142	19	31	11	341
III.—Frontier Districts ..	**4**	..	**4**	..	..	..	**126**	**70**	**4**	**11**	..	**52**	**21**	**12**	**2**	**3**	..	**7**
11. Ladakh District (including Mansar). "	4	..	4	..	..	..	61	26	4	3	..	31	21	12	2	3	..	7
12. Gilgit	..	..	..	..	..	..	65	44	..	8	..	21	..	..	..	..	..	..
Cities.																		
13. Jammu ..	..	7	..	..	..	..	910	386	62	2	2	462	..	..	..	..	..	..
14. Srinagar ..	20	..	..	..	..	13	12,276	3,827	937	19	..	7,512	2,246	800	2	..	..	1,444

TABLE XVII.

Occupation or Means of Livelihood.

Jammu and Kashmir State Census, 1921.

DISTRICT, JAGIR ILAQA OR CITY.	Group (79).—Other industries pertaining to dress, gloves, socks, gaiters, belts, buttons, umbrellas, canes, etc.						Group (80).—Washing, cleaning and dyeing.						Group (81).—Barbers, hair-dressers, and wig makers.					
	Total workers and dependents.	Actual Workers. Total.		Actual Workers. Partially Agriculturists.		Dependents.	Total workers and dependents.	Actual Workers. Total.		Actual Workers. Partially Agriculturists.		Dependents.	Total workers and dependents.	Actual Workers. Total.		Actual Workers. Partially Agriculturists.		Dependents.
		Males.	Females.	Males.	Females.			Males.	Females.	Males.	Females.			Males.	Females.	Males.	Females.	
	560	561	562	563	564	565	566	567	568	569	570	571	572	573	574	575	576	577
State ...	**270**	**98**	**4**	..	..	**168**	**6,893**	**2,246**	**605**	**170**	**23**	**4,042**	**12,456**	**4,068**	**56**	**851**	**8**	**8,332**
I.—Jammu Province (including *Jagirs*).	**11**	**2**	..	...	..	**9**	**3,664**	**1,351**	**136**	**89**	**5**	**2,177**	**5,686**	**1,918**	**47**	**329**	**6**	**3,721**
1. Jammu District (including City)	..	..	..	..	..	..	1,697	668	39	51	..	990	2,442	810	22	105	3	1,610
2. Kathua „ ..	..	..	..	..	..	..	737	263	22	11	3	452	1,043	325	8	80	2	710
3. Udhampur „ (including Chaneni *Jagir*)	..	..	..	..	..	..	91	34	9	5	..	48	329	167	1	42	1	161
4. Riasi „	..	..	..	..	..	..	90	39	10	7	..	41	240	88	7	34	..	145
5. Mirpur „	10	1	..	..	..	9	888	316	52	11	2	520	1,195	319	4	22	..	872
6. Bhadarwah *Jagir*	..	..	..	..	..	..	14	6	1	2	..	7	22	4	..	4	..	18
7. Punch *Ilaqa*	1	1	..	..	..	..	147	25	3	2	..	119	415	205	5	42	..	205
II.—Kashmir Province (including *Jagirs*).	**255**	**96**	**1**	..	..	**158**	**3,206**	**885**	**466**	**78**	**18**	**1,855**	**6,752**	**2,141**	**9**	**520**	**2**	**4,602**
8. Kashmir North (including Langet *Jagir*).	23	8	..	..	..	15	647	210	63	26	15	374	2,029	654	5	209	1	1,370
9. Kashmir South (including City)..	232	88	1	..	..	143	2,499	653	398	48	3	1,448	4,492	1,410	4	291	1	3,078
10. Muzaffarabad District ..	..	..	..	..	..	..	60	22	5	4	..	33	231	77	..	20	..	154
III—Frontier Districts	**4**	..	**3**	..	..	**1**	**23**	**10**	**3**	**3**	..	**10**	**18**	**9**	..	**2**	..	**9**
11. Ladakh District (including Mansar).	4	..	3	..	..	1	15	4	2	3	..	9	7	4	..	2	..	3
12. Gilgit „	..	..	..	..	..	..	8	6	1	..	..	1	11	5	..	..	..	6
Cities.																		
13. Jammu	..	..	..	..	..	..	396	112	8	..	..	246	198	76	..	..	..	122
14. Srinagar	223	86	..	..		137	1,391	280	280	..	..	831	1,266	341	..	..	..	925

TABLE XVII.

Occupation or Means of Livelihood.

Jammu and Kashmir State Census, 1921.

DISTRICT, JAGIR, ILAQA OR CITY.	Order 14.—Furniture industries.						Group (83).—Cabinet makers, carriage painters, etc.						Group (84).—Upholsterers, tent makers, etc.					
	Total workers and dependents	Actual Workers.				Dependents.	Total workers and dependents.	Actual Workers.				Dependents.	Total workers and dependents.	Actual Workers.				Dependents.
		Total.		Partially Agriculturists.				Total.		Partially Agriculturists.				Total.		Partially Agriculturists.		
		Males.	Females.	Males.	Females.			Males.	Females.	Males.	Females.			Males.	Females.	Males.	Females.	
	578	579	580	581	582	583	584	585	586	587	588	589	590	591	592	593	594	595
State ..	**26[illegible]**	**87**	..	..	..	**182**	**185**	**59**	..	..	..	**126**	**84**	**28**	..	..	..	**56**
I.—Jammu Province (including *Jagirs*).	**11**	**5**	..	..	..	**6**	**11**	**5**	..	..	..	**6**	..	..	..	..	..	..
1. Jammu District (including City)	10	4	..	..	..	6	10	4	..	..	..	6	..	..	..	..	..	..
2. Kathua " ..	1	1	..	..	..	..	1	1	..	..	..	..	..	..	..	..	..	..
3. Udhampur " (including Chaneni *Jagir*). ..	..	..	..	..	..	..	..	..	..	..	..	..	..	..	..	..	..	..
4. Riasi " ..	..	..	..	..	..	..	..	..	..	..	..	..	..	..	..	..	..	..
5. Mirpur " ..	..	..	..	..	..	..	..	..	..	..	..	..	..	..	..	..	..	..
6. Bhadarwah *Jagir* ..	..	..	..	..	..	..	..	..	..	..	..	..	..	..	..	..	..	..
7. Punch *Ilaqa* ..	..	..	..	..	..	..	..	..	..	..	..	..	..	..	..	..	..	..
II—Kashmir Province (including *Jagirs*).	**258**	**82**	..	..	..	**6**	**174**	**54**	..	..	..	**120**	**84**	**28**	..	..	..	**56**
8. Kashmir North (including Langet *Jagir*).	..	..	..	..	..	..	..	..	..	..	..	..	..	..	..	..	..	..
9. Kashmir South (including City)..	258	82	..	..	..	176	174	54	..	..	..	120	84	28	..	..	..	56
10. Muzaffarabad District ..	..	..	..	..	..	..	..	..	..	..	..	..	..	..	..	..	..	..
III—Frontier Districts ...	..	..	..	..	..	..	..	..	..	..	..	..	..	..	..	..	..	..
11. Ladakh District (including Mansar).	..	..	..	..	..	..	..	..	..	..	..	..	..	..	..	..	..	..
12. Gilgit " ..	..	..	..	..	..	..	..	..	..	..	..	..	..	..	..	..	..	..
Cities.																		
13. Jammu ..	10	4	..	..	..	6	10	4	..	..	..	6	..	..	..	..	..	..
14. Srinagar ..	258	82	..	..	..	176	174	54	..	..	..	120	84	28	..	..	..	56

TABLE XVII.

Occupation or Means of Livelihood.

Jammu and Kashmir State Census, 1921.

DISTRICT, JAGIR, ILAQA OR CITY.	Order 15.—Building Industries.						Group (85).—*Lime burners, cement workers.*						Group (86)—*Excavators and well sinkers.*					
	Total workers and dependents.	Actual Workers.				Dependents.	Total workers and dependents.	Actual Workers.				Dependents.	Total workers and dependents.	Actual Workers.				Dependents.
		Total.		*Partially Agriculturists.*				*Total.*		*Partially Agriculturists.*				*Total.*		*Partially Agriculturists.*		
		Males.	Females.	Males.	Females.			Males.	Females.	Males.	Females.			Males.	Females.	Males.	Females.	
	596	597	598	599	600	601	602	603	604	605	606	607	608	609	610	611	612	613
State ..	**4,730**	**1,459**	**35**	**95**	**4**	**3,236**	**157**	**67**	..	..	..	**90**	**460**	**83**	**4**	..	..	**373**
I.—Jammu Province (including *Jagirs*)	**1,670**	**513**	**22**	**77**	**4**	**1,135**	**15**	..	..	..	..	**15**	**277**	**16**	..	..	..	**261**
1. Jammu District (including City).	980	253	..	9	..	727	..	..	..	..	..	..	193	..	..	..	..	193
2. Kathua " ..	174	32	1	..	..	141	15	..	..	..	..	15	84	16	..	..	..	68
3. Udhampur " (including Chaneni *Jagir*)	106	44	21	3	4	41	..	..	..	..	..	..	..	..	..	..	..	..
4. Riasi " ..	17	..	..	..	..	17	..	..	..	..	..	..	..	..	..	..	..	..
5. Mirpur " ..	304	141	..	5[illegible]	..	163	..	..	..	..	..	..	..	..	..	..	..	..
6. Bhadarwah *Jagir* ..	35	18	..	5	..	17	..	..	..	..	..	..	..	..	..	..	..	..
7. Punch *Ilaqa* ..	54	25	..	10	..	29	..	..	..	..	..	..	..	..	..	..	..	..
II.—Kashmir Province including *Jagirs*).	**3,057**	**946**	**13**	**18**	..	**2,093**	**142**	**67**	..	..	..	**75**	**183**	**67**	**4**	..	..	**112**
8. Kashmir North (including Langet *Jagir*).	298	81	7	6	..	210	..	..	..	..	..	..	45	11	..	..	..	34
9. Kashmir South (including City).	2,696	842	5	10	..	1,849	142	67	..	..	..	75	138	56	4	..	..	78
10. Muzaffarabad District ..	63	23	1	2	..	39	..	..	..	..	..	..	..	..	..	..	..	..
III.—Frontier Districts	**3**	..	..	..	..	**3**	..	..	..	..	..	..	..	..	..	..	..	..
11. Ladakh District (including Mansar.	..	..	..	..	..	..	..	..	..	..	..	..	..	..	..	..	..	..
12. Gilgit "	3	..	..	..	..	3	..	..	..	..	..	..	..	..	..	..	..	..
Cities.																		
13 Jammu	419	161	..	..	..	258	..	..	..	..	..	..	..	..	..	..	..	..
14 Srinagar	2,139	682	1	3	..	1,456	136	96	..	..	..	70	..	..	..	..	..	..

TABLE XVII.

OCCUPATIONS OR MEANS OF LIVELIHOOD.

Jammu and Kashmir State Census, 1921.

DISTRICT, JAGIR, ILAQA OR CITY.	Group (87).—*Stone cutters and dressers.*						Group (88).—*Brick layers and masons.*						Group (89).—*Builders (other than buildings made of bamboo or similar materials), decorators of houses, painters, tilers, plumbers, etc.*					
	Total workers and dependents.	ACTUAL WORKERS.				Dependents.	Total workers and dependents.	ACTUAL WORKERS.				Dependents.	Total workers and dependents.	ACTUAL WORKERS.				Dependents.
		Total.		*Partially Agriculturists.*				*Total.*		*Partially Agriculturists.*				*Total.*		*Partially Agriculturists.*		
		Males.	Females.	Males.	Females.			Males.	Females.	Males.	Females.			Males.	Females.	Males.	Females.	
	614	615	616	617	618	619	620	621	622	623	624	625	626	627	628	629	630	631
State ..	**450**	**142**	**4**	**13**	..	**304**	**1,867**	**632**	**26**	**59**	**4**	**1,209**	**1,796**	**535**	**1**	**23**	..	**1,260**
I.—Jammu Province (including *Jagirs*).	**203**	**69**	..	**11**	..	**134**	**999**	**366**	**21**	**58**	**4**	**612**	**176**	**62**	**1**	**8**	..	**113**
1. Jammu District (including City).	63	35	..	..	..	28	634	206	..	8	..	428	90	12	..	1	..	78
2. Kathua ,, ...	..	..	..	..	..	..	70	16	..	..	..	54	5	..	1	..	..	4
3. Udhampur ,, (including Chanani *Jagir*).	19	18	..	2	..	1	65	17	21	1	4	27	22	9	..	..	..	13
4. Riasi ,, ...	17	..	..	..	..	17	..	..	..	..	..	..	..	..	..	..	..	..
5. Mirpur ,, ...	62	..	..	..	..	62	210	122	..	48	..	88	32	19	..	2	..	13
6. Bhadarwah *Jagir*	..	..	..	..	..	..	20	5	..	1	..	15	15	13	..	4	..	2
7. Punch *Ilaqa*	42	16	..	9	..	26	..	..	..	..	..	..	12	9	..	1	..	3
II.—Kashmir Province (including *Jagirs*).	**247**	**73**	**4**	**2**	..	**170**	**868**	**266**	**5**	**1**	..	**597**	**1,617**	**473**	..	**15**	..	**1,144**
8. Kashmir North (including Langet *Jagir*).	67	20	2	..	..	45	107	25	5	1	..	77	79	25	..	5	..	54
9. Kashmir South (including City).	140	37	1	..	..	102	742	234	..	..	..	508	1,534	448	..	10	..	1,086
10. Muzaffarabad District ..	40	16	1	2	..	23	19	7	..	..	..	12	4	..	..	..	..	4
III.—Frontier Districts	..	..	..	..	..	..	..	..	..	..	..	..	**3**	..	..	..	..	**3**
11. Ladakh District (including Mansar).	..	..	..	..	..	..	..	..	..	..	..	..	..	..	..	..	..	..
12. Gilgit ,, ...	..	..	..	..	..	..	..	..	..	..	..	..	3	..	..	..	..	3
Cities.																		
13. Jammu	..	..	..	..	..	..	419	161	..	..	..	258	..	..	..	..	..	..
14. Srinagar	117	22	1	..	..	94	600	203	..	..	..	397	1,286	391	..	3	..	895

TABLE XVII.

OCCUPATION OR MEANS OF LIVELIHOOD.

Jammu and Kashmir State Census, 1921.

DISTRICT, JAGIR, ILAQA OR CITY.	Order 16—Construction of means of transport.						*Group (92).—Ship, boat, aeroplane builders.*						Order 17.—Production and transmission of physical forces (heat, light, electricity, motive power, etc.)					
	Total workers and dependents.	Actual Workers. Total. Males.	Actual Workers. Total. Females.	Actual Workers. Partially Agriculturists. Males.	Actual Workers. Partially Agriculturists. Females.	Dependents.	Total workers and dependents.	Actual Workers. Total. Males.	Actual Workers. Total. Females.	Actual Workers. Partially Agriculturists. Males.	Actual Workers. Partially Agriculturists. Females.	Dependents.	Total workers and dependents.	Actual Workers. Total. Males.	Actual Workers. Total. Females.	Actual Workers. Partially Agriculturists. Males.	Actual Workers. Partially Agriculturists. Females.	Dependents.
	632	633	634	635	636	637	638	639	640	641	642	643	644	645	646	647	648	649
State ..	376	158	..	1	..	218	376	158	..	1	..	218	53	36	..	..	..	17
I—Jammu Province (including *Jagirs*).	...	..	..	..	..	..	..	..	..	..	..	..	..	..	..	..	..	..
1. Jammu District (including City)	..	..	..	..	..	..							..	..	..	..	..	..
2. Kathua „	..	..	..	..	..	..	..	..	..	..	..	...	..	..	..	..	..	..
3. Udhampur „ (including Chaneni *Jagir*).	..	..	..	..	..	..	..	..	..	..	..	..	..	..	..	..	..	..
4. Riasi „	..	..	..	..	..	..	..	..	..	..	..	..	..	..	..	..	..	..
5. Mirpur „	..	..	..	..	..	..	..	..	..	..	..	..	..	..	..	..	..	..
6. Bhadarwah *Jagir*	..	..	..	..	..	..	..	..	..	..	..	..	..	..	..	..	..	..
7. Punch *Ilaqa*	..	..	..	..	..	..	..	..	..	..	..	..	..	..	..	..	..	..
II—Kashmir Province (including *Jagirs*).	376	158	..	1	..	218	376	158	..	1	1	218	53	36	...	..	..	17
8. Kashmir North (including Langet *Jagir*).	37	13	..	..	..	24	37	13	..	..	..	24	50	36	..	..	..	14
9. Kashmir South (including City)	339	145	..	1	..	194	339	145	..	1	1	194	3	..	..	..	..	3
10. Muzaffarabad District ..	..	..	..	..	..	..	..	..	..	..	..	..	..	..	..	..	..	..
III—Frontier Districts	..	..	..	..	..	..	..	..	..	..	..	..	..	..	..	..	..	..
11. Laddakh District (including Mansar).	..	..	..	..	..	..	..	..	..	..	..	..	..	..	..	..	..	..
12. Gilgit „	..	..	..	..	..	..	..	..	..	..	..	..	..	..	..	..	..	..
Cities.																		
13. Jammu	..	..	..	..	..	..	..	..	..	..	..	..	..	..	..	..	..	..
14. Srinagar	293	126	..	..	..	167	293	126	..	..	..	167	..	..	..	..	..	..

TABLE XVII.

Occupation or Means of Livelihood.

Jammu and Kashmir State Census, 1921.

DISTRICT, JAGIR, ILAQA OR CITY.	Group (93).—Gas works and electric light and power.						Order 18.—Other miscellaneous and undefined industries.						Group (94).—Printers, lithographers, engravers, etc.					
	Total workers and dependents.	Actual Workers. Total. Males.	Actual Workers. Total. Females.	Actual Workers. Partially Agriculturists. Males.	Actual Workers. Partially Agriculturists. Females.	Dependents.	Total workers and dependents.	Actual Workers. Total. Males.	Actual Workers. Total. Females.	Actual Workers. Partially Agriculturists. Males.	Actual Workers. Partially Agriculturists. Females.	Dependents.	Total workers and dependents.	Actual Workers. Total. Males.	Actual Workers. Total. Females.	Actual Workers. Partially Agriculturists. Males.	Actual Workers. Partially Agriculturists. Females.	Dependents.
	650	651	652	653	654	655	656	657	658	659	660	661	662	663	664	665	666	667
State	53	36	..	..	..	17	14,267	4,936	508	245	14	8,823	86	30	..	..	..	56
I.—Jammu Province (including *Jagirs*).	..	..	..	..	..	..	6,316	2,076	386	177	14	3,854	..	..	..	..	..	..
1. Jammu District (including City)	..	..	..	..	..	..	2,267	735	214	17	3	1,318	..	..	..	..	..	..
2. Kathua ,,	..	..	..	..	..	..	964	299	96	35	5	569	..	..	..	..	..	..
3. Udhampur ,, (including Chaneni *Jagir*).	..	..	..	..	..	..	726	269	22	45	..	435	..	..	..	..	..	..
4. Riasi ,,	..	..	..	..	..	..	244	87	5	17	–	152	..	..	..	..	..	..
5. Mirpur ,,	..	..	..	..	..	..	1,648	530	30	15	4	1,088	..	..	..	..	..	..
6. Bhadarwah *Jagir*	..	..	..	..	..	..	181	55	2	25	2	124	..	..	..	..	..	..
7. Punch *Ilaqa*	..	..	..	..	..	..	286	101	17	23	..	168	..	..	..	..	..	..
II.—Kashmir Province (including *Jagirs*).	53	36	..	..	..	17	7,844	2,810	108	59	..	4,926	86	30	..	..	..	56
8. Kashmir North (including Langet *Jagir*).	50	36	..	..	..	14	595	292	29	28	..	274	60	21	..	..	..	39
9. Kashmir South (including City)	3	..	..	..	..	3	6,958	2,456	71	25	..	4,431	26	9	..	..	..	17
10. Muzaffarabad District	..	..	..	..	..	..	291	62	8	6	..	221	..	..	..	..	..	..
III.—Frontier Districts	..	..	..	..	..	..	107	50	14	9	..	43	..	..	..	..	..	..
11. Ladakh District (including Manser).	..	..	..	..	..	..	54	22	..	7	..	32	..	..	..	..	..	..
12. Gilgit ,,	7	..	..	..	..	..	53	28	14	2	..	11	..	..	..	..	..	..
Cities																		
13. Jammu	..	..	..	..	..	..	801	206	148	..	..	357	..	..	..	..	..	..
14. Srinagar	..	..	..	..	..	..	5,244	1,874	85	1	..	3,335	26	9	..	..	..	17

TABLE XVII.

OCCUPATION OR MEANS OF LIVELIHOOD.

Jammu and Kashmir State Census, 1921.

DISTRICT, JAGIR, ILAQA OR CITY.	Group (95).—Book binders and stitchers, envelope makers, etc.						Group (96).—Makers of musical instruments						Group (97)—Makers of watches and clocks and optical, photograpic, mathematical and surgical instruments.					
	Total workers and dependents.	ACTUAL WORKERS.				Dependents.	Total workers and dependents.	ACTUAL WORKERS.				Dependents.	Total workers and dependents.	ACTUAL WORKERS.				Dependents.
		Total		Partially Agriculturists.				Total.		Partially Agriculturists.				Total.		Partially Agriculturists.		
		Males.	Females.	Males.	Females.			Males.	Females.	Males.	Females.			Males.	Females.	Males.	Females.	
	668	669	670	671	672	673	674	675	676	677	678	679	680	681	682	683	684	685
Kashmir State ..	150	55	..	3	..	95	36	15	..	4	..	21	158	58	..	..	..	100
I.—Jammu Province (including *Jagirs.*)	30	12	..	3	..	18	1	1	..	..	..	..	6	3	..	..	..	
1. Jammu District (including City)	18	6	..	..	..	12	..	..	..	..	..	..	2	2	..	..	..	..
2. Kathua " ..	2	2	..	2	..	..	..	..	..	..	..	..		..	..	..	..	..
3. Udhampur " (including Chaneni *Jagir.*)	1	1	..	1	..	..	..	..	..	..	..	..	..	..	..	..	..	..
4. Riasi "	..	..	..	..	..	..	..	..	..	..	..	..	..	..	..	..	..	..
5. Mirpur "	5	2	..	..	..	3	..	..	..	..	..	..	..	..	..	..	..	..
6. Bhadarwah *Jagir*	..	..	..	..	..	..	1	1	..	..	..	..	..	..	..	..	..	..
7. Punch *Ilaqa*	4	1	..	..	..	3	..	..	..	..	..	..	4	1	..	..	..	3
II—Kashmir Province (including *Jagirs.*)	120	43	..	..	..	77	35	14	..	4	..	21	152	55	..	..	..	97
8. Kashmir North (including Langet *Jagir.*)	6	2	..	..	..	4	..	..	..	..	..	..	11	7	..	..	..	4
9. Kashmir South (including City)..	114	41	..	..	..	73	35	14	..	4	..	21	141	48	..	..	..	93
10. Muzaffarabad District ..	..	..	..	..	..	..	..	..	..	..	..	..	..	..	..	..	..	..
III—Frontier Districts	..	..	..	..	..	..	..	..	..	..	..	..	..	..	..	..	..	..
11. Ladakh District (including Mansar).	..	..	..	..	..	..	..	..	..	..	..	..	..	..	..	..	..	..
12. Gilgit .. " ..	..	..	..	..	..	..	..	..	..	..	..	..	..	..	..	..	..	..
13. Jammu	18	6	..	..	..	12	..	..	..	..	..	..	..	..	..	..	..	..
14. Srinagar	102	36	..	..	..	66	21	7	..	..	..	14	141	48	..	..	..	93

TABLE XVII.

OCCUPATION OR MEANS OF LIVELIHOOD.

Jammu and Kashmir State Census, 1921.

DISTRICT, JAGIR, ILAQA OR CITY.	Group (98)—*Workers in precious stones, metals, enamellers imitation jewellery makers, gilders, etc.*						Group (99).—*Makers of bangles or beads or necklaces of other material than glass and makers of spangles, rosaries, lingams and sacred threads.*						Group (100).—*Toy, kite, cage, fishing tackle, etc., makers, taxidermists, etc.*					
	Total workers and dependents.	ACTUAL WORKERS. Total. Males.	ACTUAL WORKERS. Total. Females.	ACTUAL WORKERS. Partially Agriculturists. Males.	ACTUAL WORKERS. Partially Agriculturists. Females.	Dependents.	Total workers and dependents.	ACTUAL WORKERS. Total. Males.	ACTUAL WORKERS. Total. Females.	ACTUAL WORKERS. Partially Agriculturists. Males.	ACTUAL WORKERS. Partially Agriculturists. Females.	Dependents.	Total workers and dependents.	ACTUAL WORKERS. Total. Males.	ACTUAL WORKERS. Total. Females.	ACTUAL WORKERS. Partially Agriculturists. Males.	ACTUAL WORKERS. Partially Agriculturists. Females.	Total workers and dependents.
	686	687	688	689	690	691	692	693	694	695	696	697	698	619	700	701	702	703
State ..	**8,644**	**3,049**	**66**	**217**	**7**	**5,529**	**1,473**	**628**	**2**	**7**	..	**843**	**115**	**45**	..	..	..	**70**
I.—Jammu Province (including *Jagirs*)	**4,112**	**1,459**	**37**	**158**	**7**	**2,616**	**86**	**47**	...	**7**	...	**39**	**2**	**2**	..	..	..	..
1. Jammu District (including City)...	1,102	387	16	11	1	699	70	41	..	6	..	29	2	2	..	..	..	..
2. Kathua ,, ...	716	234	8	31	..	474	16	6	..	1	..	10	..	..	..	..	..	..
3. Udhampur ,, (including Chaneni *Jagir*.)	617	221	4	39	..	392	..	..	..	...	..	...	..	..	..	..	..	..
4. Riasi ,, ...	180	73	1	17	..	106	..	..	..	..	..	...	..	..	..	..	..	..
5. Mirpur ,, ...	1,137	409	6	13	4	722	..	..	..	..	..	..	..	..	...	..	..	..
6. Bhadarwah *Jagir*	180	54	2	25	2	124	..	..	..	..	..	..	..	..	..	..	..	..
7. Punch *Ilaqa*	180	81	..	22	..	99	..	..	...	..	..	..	..	..	...	..	..	..
II.—Kashmir Province (including *Jagirs*)	**4,499**	**1:575**	**29**	**52**	..	**2,895**	**1,387**	**581**	**2**	...	..	**804**	**113**	**43**	..	...	..	**70**
8. Kashmir North (including Langet *Jagir*).	361	184	10	25	..	167	..	...	..	..	..	..	..	..	..	...	..	...
9. Kashmir South (including City)	3,942	1,349	17	21	..	2,576	1,387	581	2	..	..	804	113	43	..	..	...	70
10. Muzaffarabad District ..	196	42	2	6	..	152	..	...	...	..	..	..	..	..	...	..	..	..
III.—Frontier Districts ..	**33**	**15**	..	**7**	..	**18**	..	..	...	..	...	..	..	—	..	..	..	..
11. Ladakh District (including Mansr).	33	15	..	7	..	18	...	..	..	..	..	..	..	..	..	..	..	..
12. Gilgit ,, ...	..	..	..	..	...	..	..	..	..	..	..	..	..	..	..	..	..	..
Cities.																		
13. Jammu	2,197	86	...	..	..	111	35	508	..	..	..	615	..	...	..	..	..	..
14. Srinagar	774	949	.	1	...	1,825	1,134	20	..	..	..	29	118	43	..	..	..	70

TABLE XVII

Occupation or Means of Livelihood.

Jammu and Kashmir State Census, 1921.

DISTRICT, JAGIR, ILAQA OR CITY.	Group (101).—Others, including managers, persons (other than performers) employed in theatres and other places of public entertainment, employés of public societies, race course service, huntsmen, etc.						Group (103).—Sweepers, scavengers, etc.						Sub-class IV.—Transport.					
		Actual Workers.						Actual Workers.						Actual Workers.				
		Total.		Partially Agriculturists.				Total.		Partially Agriculturists.				Total.		Partially Agriculturists.		
	Dependents.	Males.	Females.	Males.	Females.	Dependents.	Total workers and dependents.	Males.	Females.	Males.	Females.	Dependants.	Total workers and dependents.	Males.	Females.	Males.	Females.	Dependents.
	704	705	706	707	708	709	710	711	712	713	714	715	716	717	718	719	720	721
State ..	**8**	**5**	..	..	..	**3**	**3,597**	**1,051**	**440**	**14**	**7**	**2,106**	**27,815**	**10,070**	**1,981**	**1,216**	**13**	**15,764**
I.—Jammu Province (including *Jagirs*).	**1**	**1**	..	..	..	..	**2,078**	**551**	**349**	**9**	**7**	**1,178**	**8,753**	**3,306**	**289**	**592**	**5**	5,158
1. Jammu District (including City)	..	..	..	..	..	..	1,073	297	198	..	2	578	4,136	1,383	218	206	2	2,535
2. Kathua "	..	..	..	..	..	..	230	57	88	1	5	85	2,105	973	37	34	1	1,095
3. Udhampur " (including Chaneni *Jagir*).	..	..	..	..	..	..	108	47	18	5	..	43	285	123	13	33	...	149
4. Riasi " ..	...	..	..	..	..	..	64	14	4	..	..	46	720	131	16	63	..	573
5. Mirpur "	1	1	..	..	..	..	505	118	24	2	..	363	1,345	604	5	163	2	736
6. Bhadarwah *Jagir*	..	..	..	..	..	..	..	...	..	..	..	..	15	11	..	2	...	4
7. Punch *Ilaqa*	..	..	..	..	..	..	98	18	17	1	...	63	147	81	..	31	..	66
II.—Kashmir Province (including *Jagirs*.	**7**	**4**	..	..	..	**3**	**1,445**	**465**	**77**	**3**	..	**903**	**18,156**	**6,280**	**1,686**	**353**	**8**	**10,190**
8. Kashmir North (including Langet *Jagir*).	..	..	..	..	..	..	157	78	19	3	..	60	3,637	1,209	236	61	..	2,192
9. Kashmir South (including City)	7	4	..	..	..	3	1,193	367	52	..	..	774	13,841	4,631	1,441	229	8	7,769
10. Muzaffarabad District ..	...	..	..	..	...	..	95	20	6	..	..	69	678	440	9	63	..	229
III.—Frontier Districts ..	..	...	..	..	..	..	**74**	**35**	**14**	**2**	..	**25**	**906**	**484**	**6**	**331**	..	**416**
11. Ladakh District (including Mansar).	..	..	..	...	..	..	21	7	..	..	..	14	856	453	6	331	..	397
12. Gilgit "	..	..	..	..	..	..	53	28	14	2	..	11	50	31	..	..	..	19
Cities.																		
13. Jammu	..	..	..	..	..	..	551	184	148	..	..	219	493	229	1	13	1	263
14. Srinagar	..	..	..	..	..	3	926	873	35	..	..	618	6,807	2,150	615	7	..	4,042

TABLE XVII.

OCCUPATION OR MEANS OF LIVELIHOOD.

Jammu and Kashmir State Census, 1921.

DISTRICT, JAGIR, ILAQA OR CITY.	Order 20.—Transport by water.						Group (105).—Persons (other than labourers) employed in harbours and docks including pilots.						Group (107).—Ship owners and their employés, ship brokers, Ships' officers, Engineers, mariners and firemen.					
	Total workers and dependents.	Actual Workers. Total.		Actual Workers. Partially Agriculturists.		Dependents.	Total workers and dependents.	Actual Workers. Total.		Actual Workers. Partially Agriculturists.		Dependents.	Total workers and dependents.	Actual Workers. Total.		Actual Workers. Partially Agriculturists.		Dependents.
		Males.	Females.	Males.	Females.			Males.	Females.	Males.	Females.			Males.	Females.	Males.	Females.	
	722	723	724	725	726	727	728	729	730	731	732	733	734	735	736	737	738	739
State ..	**14,308**	**4,642**	**1,677**	**247**	**6**	**7,989**	**163**	..	..	..	..	**163**	**82**	**29**	..	**5**	..	**53**
I.—Jammu Province (including *Jagirs*).	**2,192**	**856**	**35**	**123**	**1**	**1,301**	**151**	..	..	..	..	**151**	**82**	**29**	..	**5**	..	**53**
1. Jammu District (including City)	1,064	272	14	4	..	778	..	..	..	..	..	..	..	..	..	..	..	..
2. Kathua „	415	217	21	11	1	177	..	..	..	..	..	..	..	..	..	..	..	..
3. Udhampur „ (including Chaneni *Jagir*).	17	4	..	1	..	13	..	..	..	..	..	..	..	..	..	..	..	..
4. Riasi „	5	5	..	..	..	..	..	..	..	..	..	..	..	..	..	..	..	..
5. Mirpur „	687	355	..	107	..	332	151	..	..	..	..	151	82	29	..	5	..	53
6. Bhadarwah *Jagir*	..	..	..	..	..	..	..	..	..	..	..	..	..	..	..	..	..	..
7. Punch *Ilaqa*	4	3	..	..	..	1	..	..	..	..	..	..	..	..	..	..	..	..
II.—Kashmir Province (including *Jagirs*)	**12,110**	**3,780**	**1,642**	**124**	**5**	**6,688**	**12**	..	..	..	..	**12**	..	..	..	..	..	..
8. Kashmir North (including Langet *Jagir*).	2,544	778	235	9	..	1,531	12	..	..	..	..	12	..	..	..	..	..	..
9. Kashmir South (including City)	9,537	2,991	1,407	114	5	5,139	..	..	..	..	..	..	..	..	..	..	..	..
10. Muzaffarabad District ..	29	11	..	1	..	18	..	..	..	..	..	..	..	..	..	..	..	..
III.—Frontier Districts	**6**	**6**	..	..	..	..	..	..	..	..	..	..	..	..	..	..	..	..
11. Ladakh District (including Mansar).	1	1	..	..	..	..	..	..	..	..	..	..	..	..	..	..	..	..
12. Gilgit „	5	5	..	..	..	..	..	..	..	..	..	..	..	..	..	..	..	..
Cities.																		
13. Jammu	9	4	..	..	..	5	..	..	..	..	..	..	..	..	..	..	..	..
14. Srinagar	5,142	1,516	615	7	..	3,011	..	..	..	..	..	..	..	..	..	..	..	..

TABLE XVII.

OCCUPATION OR MEANS OF LIVELIHOOD;

Jammu and Kashmir State Census, 1921.

DISTRICT, JAGIR, ILAQA OR CITY.	Group (108).—*Persons (other than labourers) employed on the maintenance of harbours, docks, streams, rivers and canals (including construction).*						Group (109).—*Labourers employed on the construction and maintenance of harbours, docks, streams, rivers and canals.*						Group (110).—*Boat owners, boat men and tow men.*					
	Total workers and dependents.	ACTUAL WORKERS.				Dependents.	Total workers and dependents.	ACTUAL WORKERS.				Dependents.	Total workers and dependents.	ACTUAL WORKERS.				Dependents.
		Total.		*Partially Agriculturists.*				*Total.*		*Partially Agriculturists.*				*Total.*		*Partially Agriculturists.*		
		Males.	Females.	Males.	Females.			Males.	Females.	Males.	Females.			Males.	Females.	Males.	Females.	
	740	741	742	743	744	745	746	747	748	749	750	751	752	753	754	755	756	757
State ..	**966**	**285**	**3**	**22**	..	**678**	**1,804**	**329**	**256**	**91**	**1**	**1,219**	**11,293**	**3,999**	**1,418**	**129**	**5**	**5,876**
I.—Jammu Province (including *Jagirs*).	**909**	**265**	**3**	**22**	..	**641**	**543**	**318**	**21**	**90**	**1**	**204**	**507**	**244**	**11**	**6**	..	**252**
1. Jammu District (including City)	603	49	3	..	..	551		..	..	..	..	..	461	223	11	4	..	227
2. Kathua "	127	80	..	3	..	38	285	127	21	7	1	137	3	1	..	1	..	2
3. Udhampur ", Chaneni (including *Jagir*).	4	3	..	1	..	1	..	..	—	—	..	..	13	1	..	..	..	12
4. Riasi "	..	..	..	..	..	—	..	..	..	..	..	..	5	5	..	..	..	..
5. Mirpur "	173	123	..	18	..	50	258	191	..	83	..	67	23	12	..	1	..	11
6. Bhadarwah *Jagir*	..	..	..	..	..	..		..	..	..	—	..	..	..	..	..	..	..
7. Punch *Ilaqa* — ..	2	1	—	..	..	1		..	..	—	..	..	2	2	..	..	..	..
II.—Kashmir Province (including *Jagirs*).	**57**	**20**	..	..	..	**37**	**1,261**	**11**	**235**	**1**	..	**1,016**	**10,780**	**3,749**	**1,487**	**123**	**5**	**5,624**
8. Kashmir North (including Langet *Jagir*).	..	..	..	—	..	..	1,232	..	235	..	..	997	1,300	778	..	9	..	522
9. Kashmir South (including City).	57	20	—	..	..	37	..	..	..	..	..	..	9,480	2,971	1,407	114	5	5,102
10. Muzaffarabad District.. ..	..	..	..	..	..	—	29	11	..	1	..	18	..	..	..	..	..	..
III.—Frontier Districts	..	..	..	..	..	..	..	—	..	..	..	..	**6**	**6**	..	..	..	—
11. Ladakh District (including Mansar).	..	—	..	..	..	..	—	..	..	..	..	..	1	1	..	..	..	..
12. Gilgit "	..	..	..	..	..	..	..	..	..	—	..	..	5	5	..	..	—	..
Cities.																		
13. Jammu	..	..	..	..	..	..	..	..	..	..	..	..	9	4	..	..	..	5
14. Srinagar	57	20	..	..	..	37	..	..	..	..	..	..	5,085	1,496	615	7	..	2,974

TABLE XVII.

Occupation or Means of Livelihood.

Jammu and Kashmir State Census, 1921.

District, Jagir, Ilaqa or City.	Order 21.—Transport by Road.						Group (111).—Persons (other than labourers) employed on the construction and maintenance of roads and bridges.						Group (112).—Labourers employed on roads and bridges.					
	Total workers and dependents	Actual Workers. Total. Males.	Actual Workers. Total. Females.	Actual Workers. Partially Agriculturists. Males.	Actual Workers. Partially Agriculturists. Females.	Dependents.	Total workers and dependents.	Actual Workers. Total. Males.	Actual Workers. Total. Females.	Actual Workers. Partially Agriculturists. Males.	Actual Workers. Partially Agriculturists. Females.	Dependents.	Total workers and dependents.	Actual Workers. Total. Males.	Actual Workers. Total. Females.	Actual Workers. Partially Agriculturists. Males.	Actual Workers. Partially Agriculturists. Females.	Dependents.
	758	759	760	761	762	763	764	765	766	767	768	769	770	771	772	773	774	775
State ..	**11,652**	**4,654**	**295**	**859**	**4**	**6,703**	**1,639**	**737**	**39**	**101**	**2**	**863**	**887**	**221**	**194**	**53**	..	**472**
I.—Jammu Province (including *Jagirs*).	**5,690**	**2,072**	**245**	**344**	**1**	**3,373**	**608**	**326**	**4**	**89**	..	**278**	**708**	**126**	**191**	**48**	..	**391**
1. Jammu District (including City)	2,733	935	200	190	1	1,598	74	269	3	84	..	202	464	..	182	..	..	282
2. Kathua "	1,586	718	16	22	..	852	12	6	..	..	..	6	17	2	1	1	..	14
3. Udhampur " (including Chaneni *Jagir*).	208	93	13	24	..	102	43	20	1	3	..	22	86	22	8	9	..	56
4. Riasi "	689	1(5	16	53	..	568	..	..	..	..	..	..	80	50	..	15	..	30
5. Mirpur "	369	163	..	38	..	206	3	1	..	..	..	2	34	25	..	8	..	9
6. Bhadarwah *Jagir*	5	5	..	..	..	..	..	..	..	..	..	..	5	5	..	..	..	..
7. Punch *Ilaqa*	100	53	..	17	..	47	76	30	..	2	..	46	22	22	..	15	..	..
II.—Kashmir Province (including *Jagirs*).	**5,175**	**2,171**	**44**	**198**	**3**	**2,960**	**1,012**	**404**	**34**	**12**	**2**	**574**	**174**	**90**	**3**	**5**	..	**81**
8. Kashmir North (including Langet *Jagir*).	913	368	1	50	..	544	224	112	..	2	..	112	..	..	..	..	..	..
9. Kashmir South (including City)	3,644	1,396	34	88	3	2,214	664	234	30	4	2	400	..	..	..	..	..	..
10. Muzaffarabad District ..	618	407	9	60	..	202	124	58	4	6	..	62	174	90	3	5	..	81
III.—Frontier Districts	**787**	**411**	**6**	**317**	..	**370**	**19**	**7**	**1**	..	..	**11**	**5**	**8**	..	..	..	..
11. Ladakh District (including Mensar).	756	396	6	317	..	354	6	2	1	..	..	3	5	5	..	..	..	..
12. Gilgit "	31	15	..	..	..	16	13	5	..	..	..	8	..	..	..	..	..	..
Cities.																		
13. Jammu	330	134	..	10	..	196	..	..	..	..	..	..	..	..	..	..	..	..
14. Srinagar	1,165	473	..	..	..	692	59	21	..	..	..	38	..	..	..	..	..	..

TABLE XVII.

Occupation or Means of Livelihood.

Jammu and Kashmir State Census, 1921.

District, Jagir, Ilaqa or City.	Group (113).—Owners, managers, and employès (excluding personal servants) connected with Mechanically driven vehicles including trams.)						Group (114).—Owners, managers and employès (excluding personal servants) connected with other vehicles.						Group (115).—Palki, etc., bearers and owners.					
	Total workers and dependents.	Actual Workers. Total.		Actual Workers. Partially Agriculturists.		Dedendents.	Total workers and dependents.	Actual Workers. Total.		Actual Workers. Partially Agriculturists.		Dependents.	Total workers and dependents.	Actual Workers. Total.		Actual Workers. Partially Agriculturists.		Dependents.
		Males.	Females.	Males.	Females.			Males.	Females.	Males.	Females.			Males.	Females.	Males.	Females.	
	776	777	778	779	780	781	782	783	784	785	786	787	788	789	790	791	792	793
State ..	146	83	..	..	..	63	1,513	711	3	70	..	799	12	2	1	..	..	.. 9
I.—Jammu Province (including *Jagirs*).	6	1	..	..	..	5	470	167	..	13	..	303	12	2	1	..	..	.. 9
1. Jammu District (including City)	..	..	..	..	..	..	450	147	..	10	..	303	..	..	..	..	..	..
2. Kathua " ..	..	..	..	..	..	..	..	..	..	..	..	..	2	2	..	..	..	..
3. Udhampur " including Chaneni *Jagir*).	4	..	..	..	..	4	20	20	..	3	..	..	..	..	..	..	..	..
4. Riasi "	..	..	..	..	..	..	..	..	..	..	..	..	10	..	1	..	..	9
5. Mirpur "	..	..	..	..	..	..	..	..	..	..	..	..	..	..	..	..	..	..
6. Bhadarwah *Jagir*	..	..	..	..	..	..	..	..	..	..	..	..	..	..	..	..	..	..
7. Punch *Ilaqa*	2	1	..	..	..	1	..	..	..	..	..	..	..	..	..	..	..	..
II.—Kashmir Province (including *Jagirs*).	140	82	..	..	..	58	1,043	544	3	57	..	496	..	..	..	..	..	..
8. Kashmir North (including Langet *Jagir*).	1	1	..	..	..	..	62	15	1	2	..	46	..	..	..	..	..	..
9. Kashmir South (including City)	126	73	..	..	..	53	674	278	..	6	..	396	..	..	..	..	..	..
10. Muzaffarabad District ..	13	8	..	..	..	5	307	251	2	49	..	54	..	..	..	..	..	..
III.—Frontier Districts	..	..			..	..	..	..	..	..	..	..	..	..	..	..	..	..
11. Ladakh District (including Mansar).	..	..	..	..	..	..	..	..	..	..	..	..	..	..	..	..	..	..
12. Gilgit "	..	..	..	..	..	..	..	..	..	..	..	..	..	..	..	..	..	..
Cities.																		
13. Jammu	..	..	..	..	..	..	327	132	..	10	..	195	..	..	..	..	..	..
14. Srinagar	126	73	..	..	..	53	422	150	..	..	..	272	..	..	..	..	..	..

TABLE XVII.

Occupation or Means of Livelihood.

Jammu and Kashmir State Census, 1921.

DISTRICT, JAGIR, ILAQA OR CITY.	Group (116)—*Pack elephant, camel, mule, ass and bullock owners and drivers.*						Order 22.—Transport by Rail.						Group (118)—*Railway employès of all kinds other than coolies.*					
	Total workers and dependents.	Actual Workers. *Total.* Males.	Actual Workers. *Total.* Females.	Actual Workers. *Partially Agriculturists.* Males.	Actual Workers. *Partially Agriculturists.* Females.	Dependents.	Total workers and dependents.	Actual Workers. *Total.* Males.	Actual Workers. *Total.* Females.	Actual Workers. *Partially Agriculturists.* Males.	Actual Workers. *Partially Agriculturists.* Females.	Dependents.	Total workers and dependents.	Actual Workers. *Total.* Males.	Actual Workers. *Total.* Females.	Actual Workers. *Partially Agriculturists.* Males.	Actual Workers. *Partially Agriculturists.* Females.	Dependents.
	794	795	796	797	798	799	800	801	802	803	804	805	806	807	808	809	810	811
State ..	**7,455**	**2,900**	**58**	**635**	**2**	**4,497**	**295**	**96**	**5**	**25**	**2**	**194**	**249**	**91**	**5**	**25**	**2**	**153**
I.—Jammu Province (**including** *Jagirs*).	**3,886**	**1,450**	**49**	**194**	**1**	**2,387**	**288**	**95**	**5**	**25**	**2**	**188**	**242**	**90**	**5**	**25**	**2**	**147**
1. Jammu District (including City	1,345	519	15	96	1	811	83	40	..	4	..	43	80	37	..	4	..	43
2. Kathua „ ..	1,555	708	15	21	..	832	33	7	..	1	..	26	31	6	..	1	..	25
3. Udhampur (including Chaneni *Jagir*).	55	31	4	9	..	20	9	1	..	..	..	8	9	1	..	..	..	8
4. Riasi „	599	55	15	38	..	529	13	13	..	8	..	..	13	13	..	8	..	..
5. Mirpur „	332	137	..	30	..	195	148	32	5	12	2	111	107	31	5	12	2	71
6. Bhadarwah *Jagir*	..	..	..	..	..	..	1	1	..	..	..	..	1	1	..	...	..	..
7. Punch *Ilaqa*	..	..	..	..	..	..	1	1	..	..	..	..	1	1	..	..	..	..
II.—Kashmir Province (**including** *Jagirs*).	**2,806**	**1,051**	**4**	**124**	**1**	**1,751**	**7**	**1**	..	..	..	**6**	**7**	**1**	..	..	..	**6**
8. Kashmir North (including Langet *Jagir*).	626	240	..	46	..	386	..	..	..	..	..	..	..	..	..	..	..	..
9. Kashmir South (including City)	2,180	811	4	78	1	1,365	7	1	..	..	..	6	7	1	..	..	..	6
10. Muzaffarabad District ..	..	..	..	..	..	..	..	..	..	..	..	..	..	..	..	..	..	..
III.—Frontier Districts	**763**	**399**	**5**	**317**	..	**359**	..	..	..	..	..	..	..	..	..	..	..	..
11. Ladakh District (including Mansar).	745	389	5	317	..	351	..	..	..	..	..	..	..	..	..	..	..	..
12. Gilgit „	18	10	..	..	..	8	..	..	..	..	..	..	..	..	..	..	..	..
Cities.																		
13. Jammu	3	2	..	..	..	1	19	7	..	..	..	12	19	7	..	..	..	12
14. Srinagar	558	229	..	..	..	329	7	1	..	..	..	6	7	1	..	..	..	6

TABLE XVII.

Occupation or Means of Livelihood.

Jammu and Kashmir State Census, 1921.

DISTRICT, JAGIR, ILAQA OR CITY.	Group (119)—Labourers employed on Railway construction and maintenance and coolies or porters employed on Railway premises.						Order 23—Post-Office, Telegraph and Telephone services.						Group (120).—Post office, Telegraph and Telephone services.					
	Total workers and dependents.	Actual Workers. Total. Males.	Actual Workers. Total. Females.	Actual Workers. Partially Agriculturists. Males.	Actual Workers. Partially Agriculturists. Females.	Dependents.	Total workers and dependents.	Actual Workers. Total. Males.	Actual Workers. Total. Females.	Actual Workers. Partially Agriculturists. Males.	Actual Workers. Partially Agriculturists. Females.	Dependents.	Total workers and dependents.	Actual Workers. Total. Males.	Actual Workers. Total. Females.	Actual Workers. Partially Agriculturists. Males.	Actual Workers. Partially Agriculturists. Females.	Dependents.
	812	813	814	815	816	817	818	819	820	821	822	823	824	825	826	827	828	829
State ..	**46**	**5**	..	..	..	**41**	**1,560**	**678**	**4**	**85**	**1**	**878**	**1,560**	**678**	**4**	**85**	**1**	**878**
I.—Jammu Province (including *Jagirs*).	**46**	**5**	..	..	..	**41**	**583**	**283**	**4**	**40**	**1**	**296**	**583**	**283**	**4**	**40**	**1**	**296**
1. Jammu District (including City)	3	3	..	..	..	..	256	136	4	8	1	116	256	136	4	8	1	116
2. Kathua "	2	1	..	..	..	1	71	31	..	..	..	40	71	31	..	..	..	40
3. Udhampur " (including Chaneni *Jagir*).	..	..	..	..	..	..	51	25	..	8	..	20	51	25	..	8	..	26
4. Riasi "	..	..	..	..	..	..	13	8	..	2	..	5	13	8	..	2	..	5
5. Mirpur "	41	1	..	..	..	40	141	54	..	6	..	87	141	54	..	6	..	87
6. Bhadarwah *Jagir*	..	..	..	..	..	..	9	5	..	2	..	4	9	5	..	2	..	4
7. Punch *Ilaqa*	..	..	..	..	..	..	42	24	..	14	..	18	42	24	..	14	..	18
II.—Kashmir Province (including *Jagirs*).	..	..	..	..	..	..	**864**	**328**	..	**31**	..	**536**	**864**	**328**	..	**31**	..	**536**
8. Kashmir North (including Langet *Jagir*)	..	..	..	..	..	..	180	63	..	2	..	117	180	63	..	2	..	117
9. Kashmir South (including City)..	..	..	..	..	..	..	653	243	..	27	..	410	653	243	..	27	..	410
10. Muzaffarabad District ..	..	..	..	..	..	..	31	22	..	2	..	9	31	22	..	2	..	9
III.—Frontier Districts	..	..	..	..	..	..	**113**	**67**	..	**14**	..	**46**	**113**	**67**	..	**14**	..	**46**
11. Ladakh District (including Mansar).	..	..	..	..	..	..	99	56	..	14	..	43	99	56	..	14	..	43
12. Gilgit "	..	..	..	..	..	..	14	11	..	..	..	3	14	11	..	..	..	3
Cities																		
13. Jammu	..	..	..	..	..	..	135	84	1	3	1	50	135	84	1	3	1	50
14. Srinagar	..	..	..	..	..	..	493	160	..	..	..	333	493	160	..	..	..	333

TABLE XVII.

OCCUPATION OR MEANS OF LIVELIHOOD.

Jammu and Kashmir State Census, 1921.

DISTRICT, JAGIR, ILAQA OR CITY.	Sub-class V—Trade.						Order 24.—Banks, establishments of credit, exchange and insurance.						Group (121).—Bank managers, money lenders, exchange and insurance agents, money changers and brokers and their employes.					
	Total workers and dependents.	ACTUAL WORKERS.				Dependents.	Total workers and dependents.	ACTUAL WORKERS.				Dependents.	Total workers and dependents.	ACTUAL WORKERS.				Dependents.
		Total.		Partially Agriculturists.				Total.		Partially Agriculturists.				Total.		Partially Agriculturists.		
		Males.	Females.	Males.	Females.			Males.	Females.	Males.	Females.			Males.	Females.	Males.	Females.	
	830	831	832	833	834	835	836	837	838	839	840	841	842	843	844	845	846	847
State ..	**109,246**	**35,951**	**3,776**	**3,161**	**262**	**69,519**	**2,890**	**654**	**45**	**77**	**6**	**2,191**	**2,890**	**654**	**45**	**77**	**6**	**2,191**
I.—Jammu Province (including *Jagirs*).	**51,052**	**17,140**	**1,703**	**1,808**	**177**	**32,209**	**2,425**	**497**	**44**	**76**	**5**	**1,884**	**2,425**	**497**	**44**	**76**	**5**	**1,884**
1. Jammu District (including City)	21,046	6,422	439	551	10	14,185	2,014	301	44	25	5	1,669	2,014	301	44	25	5	1,669
2. Kathua "	8,544	3,181	457	261	47	4,906	1	..	..	..	..	1	1	..	..	..	..	1
3. Udhampur " (including Chaneni *Jagir*.)	5,604	2,122	213	281	23	3,269	348	167	..	33	..	181	348	167	..	33	..	181
4. Riasi "	5,007	1,608	259	275	65	3,140	..	..	..	..	..	..	..	..	..	..	..	..
5. Mirpur "	8,272	2,772	228	266	4	5,272	..	..	..	..	..	..	..	..	..	..	..	..
6. Bhadarwah *Jagir*	819	271	67	60	24	481	1	1	..	..	..	..	1	1	..	..	..	..
7. Punch *Ilaqa*	1,760	764	40	114	4	956	61	28	..	18	..	33	61	28	..	18	..	33
II.—Kashmir Province (including *Jagirs*).	**56,253**	**17,972**	**1,777**	**1,237**	**85**	**36,504**	**465**	**157**	**1**	**1**	**1**	**307**	**465**	**157**	**1**	**1**	**1**	**307**
8. Kashmir North (including Langet *Jagir*.	12,841	4,194	247	320	2	8,400	48	14	1	..	1	33	48	14	1	..	1	33
9. Kashmir South (including City)..	39,612	12,578	1,475	765	81	25,559	398	138	..	..	..	260	398	138	..	..	..	260
10. Muzaffarabad District ..	3,800	1,200	55	152	2	2,645	19	5	..	1	..	14	19	5	..	1	..	14
Frontier Districts	**1,941**	**839**	**296**	**116**	..	**806**	..	..	..	..	..	..	..	..	..	..	..	..
11. Ladakh District (including Mansar).	1,742	704	293	100	..	745	..	..	..	..	..	..	..	..	..	..	..	..
12. Gilgit "	199	135	3	16	..	61	..	..	..	..	..	..	..	..	..	..	..	..
Cities																		
13. Jammu	4,130	1,437	16	30	..	2,677	10	2	..	..	..	8	10	2	..	..	..	8
14. Srinagar	25,704	8,126	456	108	..	17,122	355	128	..	..	..	227	355	128	..	..	..	227

TABLE XVII.

OCCUPATION OR MEANS OF LIVELIHOOD.

Jammu and Kashmir State Census, 1921.

DISTRICT, JAGIR, ILAQA OR CITY.	Order 25—Brokerage, Commission and Export.						Group (122).—Brokers, commission agents, commercial travellers, ware-house owners and employés.						Order 26.—Trade in textiles.					
	Total workers and dependents.	Actual Workers.				Dependents.	Total workers and dependents.	Actual Workers.				Dependents.	Total workers and dependents.	Actual Workers.				Dependents.
		Total.		Partially Agriculturists.				Total.		Partially Agriculturists.				Total.		Partially Agriculturists.		
		Males.	Females.	Males.	Females.			Males.	Females.	Males.	Females.			Males.	Females.	Males.	Females.	
	848	849	850	851	852	853	854	855	856	857	858	859	860	861	862	863	864	865
State ..	**262**	**72**	**2**	**2**	..	**188**	**262**	**72**	**2**	**2**	..	**1**	**6,464**	**2,072**	**32**	**173**	..	**4,360**
I.—Jammu Province (including *Jagirs*).	**16**	**1**	**1**	**1**	..	**14**	**16**	**1**	**1**	**1**	..	**14**	**1,663**	**602**	**16**	**62**	..	**1,645**
1. Jammu District (including City)	15	..	1	..	..	14	15	..	1	..	..	14	332	96	4	9	..	232
2. Kathua „	..	..	..	..	..	..	..	..	..	..	..	..	559	206	5	16	..	348
3. Udhampur „ (including Chaneri *Jagir*).	1	1	..	1	..	..	1	1	..	1	..	..	457	180	7	6	..	270
4. Riasi „	..	..	..	..	..	..	..	..	..	..	..	..	..	..	..	..	..	..
5. Mirpur „	..	..	..	..	..	..	..	..	..	..	..	..	148	49	..	3	..	99
6. Bhadarwah *Jagir*	..	..	..	..	..	..	..	..	..	..	..	..	137	57	..	26	..	80
7. Punch *Ilaqa*	..	..	..	..	..	..	..	..	..	..	..	..	30	14	..	2	..	16
II.—Kashmir Province (including *Jagirs*).	**242**	**67**	**1**	..	..	**174**	**242**	**67**	**1**	..	..	**174**	**4,628**	**1,410**	**13**	**93**	..	**3,205**
8. Kashmir North (including Langet *Jagir*).	14	3	..	..	..	11	14	3	..	..	..	11	176	26	..	..	..	150
9. Kashmir South (including City)	228	64	1	..	..	163	228	64	1	..	..	162	4,231	1,331	1	91	..	2,887
10. Muzaffarabad District ...	..	..	..	..	..	..	..	..	..	..	..	..	221	53	..	2	..	168
III.—Frontier Districts ..	**4**	**4**	..	**1**	..	..	**4**	**4**	..	**1**	..	..	**173**	**60**	**3**	**18**	..	**110**
11. Ladakh District (including Mansar).	4	4	..	1	..	..	4	4	..	1	..	..	173	60	3	18	..	110
12. Gilgit „	..	..	..	..	..	..	..	..	..	..	..	..	..	..	..	..	..	..
Cities.																		
13. Jammu	..	..	..	..	..	..	..	..	..	..	..	..	106	35	4	..	..	67
14. Srinagar	228	64	1	..	..	163	228	64	1	..	..	163	2,624	800	2	..	..	1,822

TABLE XVII.

Occupation or Means of Livelihood.

Jammu and Kashmir State Census, 1921.

DISTRICT, JAGIR, ILAQA OR CITY.	Group (122).—*Trade in piece-goods, wool, cotton, silk, hair and other textiles.*						Order 27.—Trade in skins, leather and furs.						Group (124).—*Trade in skins, leather, furs, feathers, horn, etc., and articles made from these.*					
	Total workers and dependents.	Actual Workers. Total.		Actual Workers. *Partially Agriculturists.*		Dependents.	Total workers and dependents.	Actual Workers. Total.		Actual Workers. *Partially Agriculturists.*		Dependents.	Total workers and dependents.	Actual Workers. Total.		Actual Workers. *Partially Agriculturists.*		Dependents.
		Males.	Females.	Males.	Females.			Males.	Females.	Males.	Females.			Males.	Females.	Males.	Females.	
	866	867	868	869	870	871	872	873	874	875	876	877	878	879	880	881	882	883
State	**6,464**	**2,072**	**32**	**173**	..	**4,360**	**2,065**	**1,102**	**1**	**179**	..	**962**	**2,065**	**1,102**	**1**	**179**	..	**962**
I.—Jammu Province (including *Jagirs*).	**1,663**	**602**	**16**	**62**	..	**1,045**	**1,484**	**926**	**1**	**172**	..	**557**	**1,484**	**926**	**1**	**172**	..	**557**
1. Jammu District (including City).	332	96	4	9	..	232	1,308	865	..	162	.	443	1,308	865	..	162	..	443
2. Kathua „	559	206	5	16	..	348	120	31	1	..	..	88	120	31	1	..	..	88
3. Udhampur „ (including Chaneni *Jagir*).	457	180	7	6	..	270	9	7	..	..	..	2	9	7	..	..	..	2
4. Riasi „	..	..	..	..	..	..	..	..	..	..	..	..	..	..	..	..	..	..
5. Mirpur „	148	49	..	3	..	99	33	14	..	9	..	19	33	14	..	9	..	19
6. Bhadarwah *Jagir*	137	57	..	26	..	80	..	..	..	..	..	..	..	..	..	..	..	..
7. Punch *Ilaqa*	30	14	..	2	..	16	14	9	..	1	..	5	14	9	..	1	..	5
II.—Kashmir Province (including *Jagirs*).	**4,628**	**1,410**	**13**	**93**	..	**3,205**	**581**	**176**	..	**7**	..	**405**	**581**	**176**	..	**7**	..	**405**
8. Kashmir North (including Langet *Jagir*).	176	26	..	..	..	150	308	85	..	7	..	223	308	85	..	7	..	223
9. Kashmir South (including City).	4,231	1,331	13	91	..	2,887	272	90	..	..	..	182	272	90	..	..	..	182
10. Muzaffarabad District ..	221	53	..	2	..	168	1	1	..	..	..	..	1	1	..	..	..	..
III.—Frontier Districts ..	**173**	**60**	**3**	**18**	..	**110**	..	..	..	..	..	..	..	..	..	..	..	..
11. Ladakh District (including Mansar).	173	60	3	18	..	110	..	..	..	..	..	..	..	..	..	..	..	..
12. Gilgit „	..	..	..	..	..	..	..	..	..	..	..	..	..	..	..	..	..	..
Cities.																		
13. Jammu	106	35	4	..	..	67	..	..	..	..	..	..	..	..	..	..	..	..
14. Srinagar	2,624	800	2	..	..	1,822	253	80	..	..	..	173	253	80	..	..	..	173

TABLE XVII.

Occupation or Means of Livelihood.

Jammu and Kashmir State Census, 1921.

DISTRICT, JAGIR, ILAQA OR CITY.	Order 28.—Trade in wood.						Group (126).—*Trade in wood (not firewood) cork, bark, bamboo, thatch, etc., and articles made from these.*						Order 29.—Trade in metals.					
	Total workers and dependents	Actual Workers. Total. Males.	Actual Workers. Total. Females.	Actual Workers. Partially Agriculturists. Males.	Actual Workers. Partially Agriculturists. Females.	Dependents.	Total workers and dependents	Actual Workers. Total. Males.	Actual Workers. Total. Females.	Actual Workers. Partially Agriculturists. Males.	Actual Workers. Partially Agriculturists. Females.	Dependents.	Total workers and dependents	Actual Workers. Total. Males.	Actual Workers. Total. Females.	Actual Workers. Partially Agriculturists. Males.	Actual Workers. Partially Agriculturists. Females.	Dependents.
	884	885	886	887	888	889	890	891	892	893	894	895	896	897	898	899	900	901
State	**1,418**	**444**	**29**	**24**	**3**	**945**	**1,418**	**444**	**29**	**24**	**3**	**945**	**189**	**1**	..	..	..	**188**
I.—Jammu Province (including *Jagirs*).	**288**	**78**	**12**	**20**	**3**	**198**	**288**	**78**	**12**	**20**	**3**	**198**	**189**	**1**	..	..	..	**188**
1. Jammu District (including City)	164	52	..	15	..	112	164	52	..	15	..	112	188	..	..	..	..	188
2. Kathua "	9	7	..	..	..	2	9	7	..	..	..	2	..	..	..	..	..	..
3. Udhampur " (including Chaneni *Jagir*).	21	3	5	3	..	13	21	3	5	3	..	13	..	..	..	..	..	..
4. Riasi "	..	..	..	..	..	..	..	..	..	..	..	..	..	..	..	..	..	..
5. Mirpur "	24	10	..	1	..	14	24	10	..	1	..	14	..	..	..	..	..	..
6. Bhadarwah *Jagir*	..	..	..	..	..	..	..	..	..	..	..	..	..	..	..	..	..	..
7. Punch *Ilaqa*	70	6	7	1	3	57	70	6	7	1	3	57	1	1	..	..	..	..
II.—Kashmir Province (including *Jagirs*).	**1,097**	**338**	**17**	**4**	..	**742**	**1,097**	**338**	**17**	**4**	..	**742**	..	..	..	..	..	..
8. Kashmir North (including Langet *Jagir*).	52	20	..	..	..	38	52	20	..	..	..	32	..	..	..	..	..	..
9. Kashmir South (including City)	1,018	298	17	4	..	703	1,018	298	17	4	..	703	..	..	..	..	..	..
10. Muzaffarabad District ..	27	20	..	..	...	7	27	20	..	..	..	7	..	..	..	..	..	..
III.—Frontier Districts	**33**	**28**	..	..	..	**5**	**33**	**28**	..	..	..	**5**	..	..	..	..	..	..
11. Ladakh District (including Mansar).	..	..	..	..	..	..	..	..	..	..	..	..	..	..	..	..	..	..
12. Gilgit "	33	28	..	..	..	5	33	28	..	..	..	5	..	..	..	..	...	..
Cities.																		
13. Jammu	6	22	..	12	..	74	96	22	..	10	..	74	14	3		..	..	11
14. Srinagar	811	228	6	..	..	577	811	228	6	..	..	577	..	..	..	..	..	..

TABLE XVII.

Occupation or Means of Livelihood.

Jammu and Kashmir State Census, 1921.

DISTRICT, JAGIR, ILAQA OR CITY.	*Group* (126).—*Trade in metals, machinery, knives, tools, etc.*						**Order 30.—Trade in pottery.**						*Group* (127).—*Trade in pottery, bricks and tiles.*					
	Total workers and dependents	Actual Workers.				Dependents.	Total workers and dependents	Actual Workers.				Dependents.	Total workers and dependents	Actual Workers.				Dependents.
		Total.		*Partially Agriculturists.*				*Total.*		*Partially Agriculturists.*				*Total.*		*Partially Agriculturists.*		
		Males.	Females.	Males.	Females.			Males.	Females.	Males.	Females.			Males.	Females.	Males.	Females.	
	902	903	904	905	906	907	908	909	910	911	912	913	914	915	916	917	918	919
State ..	**189**	**1**	..	..	..	**188**	**752**	**204**	**18**	**35**	**1**	**530**	**752**	**204**	**18**	**35**	**1**	**530**
I.—Jammu Province (including *Jagirs*).	**189**	**1**	..	..	..	**188**	**8**	**4**	..	..	..	**4**	**8**	**4**	..	..	..	**4**
1. Jammu District (including City)	188	..	..	..	..	188	..	..	..	..	..	..	..	..	..	..	..	..
2. Kathua "	..	..	..	..	..	..	5	3	..	..	..	2	5	3	..	..	..	2
3. Udhampur " (including Chaneni *Jagir*).	..	..	..	..	..	..	..	..	..	..	..	...	..	..	..	..	..	..
4. Riasi "	..	..	..	..	..	..	..	..	..	..	..	...	..	..	..	..	..	..
5. Mirpur "	..	..	...	..	..	..	..	..	..	...	..	..	..	..	..	..	..	..
6. Bhadarwah *Jagir*	...	..	..	..	..	..	..	..	..	..	..	..	..	..	..	..	..	..
7. Punch *Ilaqa*	1	1	..	...	..	..	3	1	..	..	..	2	3	1	..	..	..	2
II.—Kashmir Province (including *Jagirs*).	..	..	..	..	..	..	**744**	**200**	**18**	**35**	**1**	**526**	**744**	**200**	**18**	**35**	**1**	**526**
8. Kashmir North (including Langet *Jagir*).	..	..	..	..	..	..	145	36	5	..	..	104	145	36	5	..	..	104
9. Kashmir South (including City)..	..	..	..	..	..	..	599	164	13	35	1	422	599	164	13	35	1	422
10. Muzaffarabad District ...	..	..	..	..	..	..	..	..	..	..	..	..	..	..	..	..	..	..
III.—Frontier Districts	..	...	..	..	..	..	..	..	..	..	...	..	..	..	..	..	..	..
11. Ladakh District (including Mansar).	..	..	..	..	..	..	..	..	..	..	..	..	..	..	..	..	..	..
12. Gilgit "	..	..	..	..	..	..	..	..	..	..	..	..	..	..	..	..	..	..
Cities.																		
13. Jammu ..	14	3	..	..	..	11	..	..	..	..	..	..	..	..	..	..	..	..
14. Srinagar ...	..	..	..	..	..	..	480	139	6	30	..	344	480	139	6	30	..	344

TABLE XVII.

Occupation or Means of Livelihood.

Jammu and Kashmir State Census, 1921.

DISTRICT, JAGIR, ILAQA OR CITY.	Order 31.—Trade in chemical products.						*Group* (128).—*Trade in chemical products (drugs, dyes, paints, petroleum, explosives, etc.)*						Order 32.—Hotels, Cafes, restaurants, etc.					
	Total workers and dependents.	Actual Workers. Total.		Actual Workers. *Partially Agriculturists.*		Dependents.	Total workers and dependents.	Actual Workers. Total.		Actual Workers. *Partially Agriculturists.*		Dependents.	Total workers and dependents.	Actual Workers. Total.		Actual Workers. *Partially Agriculturists.*		Dependents.
		Males.	Females.	Males.	Females.			Males.	Females.	Males.	Females.			Males.	Females.	Males.	Females.	
	920	921	922	923	924	925	926	927	928	929	930	931	932	933	934	935	936	937
State ..	**822**	**23**	**16**	**1**	..	**783**	**822**	**23**	**16**	**1**	..	**783**	**301**	**142**	..	**1**	..	**159**
I.—Jammu Province (including *Jagirs*).	**770**	**9**	**16**	**1**	..	**745**	**770**	**9**	**16**	**1**	..	**745**	**62**	**35**	..	**1**	..	**27**
1. Jammu District (including City).	763	5	16	..	..	742	763	5	16	..	..	742	11	2	..	..	..	9
2. Kathua ,, ...	1	1	..	..	..	..	1	1	..	..	..	..	8	3	..	..	..	5
3. Udhampur ,, (including Chaneni *Jagir*).	..	..	..	..	..	..	..	...	..	..	..	..	16	12	..	..	:	4
4. Riasi ,, ...	..	..	..	..	..	..	..	..	..	..	..	..	..	..	..	..	..	..
5. Mirpur ,, ...	6	3	..	1	..	3	6	3	..	1	..	3	3	2	..	..	..	1
6. Bhadarwah *Jagir*	..	..	..	..	..	..	..	..	..	..	..	..	4	4	..	1	..	..
7. Punch *Ilaqa*	..	..	..	..	..	..	..	..	..	..	..	..	20	12	..	...	..	8
II.—Jammu Province (including *Jagirs*.)	**50**	**12**	..	..	..	**38**	**50**	**12**	..	..	..	**38**	**239**	**107**	..	..	..	**132**
8. Kashmir North (including Langet *Jagir*.)	..	..	..	..	..	..	..	..	..	..	..	..	42	19	..	..	..	23
9. Kashmir South (including City)..	4	2	..	..	..	2	4	2	..	..	...	2	192	84	..	..	..	108
10. Muzaffarabad District ...	46	10	..	..	..	36	46	10	..	..	..	36	5	4	..	..	..	1
III.—Frontier Districts ..	**2**	**2**	..	..	..	..	**2**	**2**	..	..	..	..	..	..	..	..	..	..
11. Ladakh District (including Mansar).	2	2	..	..	..	..	2	2	..	..	..	..	..	..	..	..	..	..
12. Gilgit ,, ...	..	..	..	..	..	..	..	..	..	..	..	..	..	..	..	..	..	..
Cities.																		
13. Jammu	21	2	..	..	..	19	21	2	...		..	91	..	..	..	..	..	..
14. Srinagar	4	2	..	..	..	2	4	2	..	..	..	2	152	72	..	..	..	80

TABLE XVII.

OCCUPATION OR MEANS OF LIVELIHOOD.

Jammu and Kashmir State Census, 1921.

DISTRICT, JAGIR, ILAQA OR CITY.	Group (129).—Vendors of wine, liquors, ærated waters and ice. Total workers and dependents.	Actual Workers. Total. Males.	Actual Workers. Total. Females.	Actual Workers. Partially Agriculturists. Males.	Actual Workers. Partially Agriculturists. Females.	Dependents.	Group (130).—Owners and managers of hotels, cookshops, sarais, etc., and their employés. Total workers and dependents.	Actual Workers. Total. Males.	Actual Workers. Total. Females.	Actual Workers. Partially Agriculturists. Males.	Actual Workers. Partially Agriculturists. Females.	Dependents.	Order 33.—Other trade in foodstuffs. Total workers and dependents.	Actual Workers. Total. Males.	Actual Workers. Total. Females.	Actual Workers. Partially Agriculturists. Males.	Actual Workers. Partially Agriculturists. Females.	Dependents.
	938	939	940	941	942	943	944	945	946	947	948	949	950	951	952	953	954	955
State ..	**259**	**105**	..	**1**	..	**154**	**42**	**37**	..	..	..	**5**	**40,887**	**13,959**	**2,674**	**1,172**	**170**	**24,254**
I.—Jammu Province (including *Jagirs*).	**48**	**25**	..	**1**	..	**23**	**14**	**10**	..	...	..	**4**	**14,963**	**5,568**	**850**	**472**	**89**	**8,545**
1. Jammu District (including City)...	11	2	..	..	..	9	..	..	..	..	..	..	5,621	1,797	248	153	..	3,576
2. Kathua "	8	3	..	..	..	5	..	..	..	..	..	..	4,454	1,952	226	140	45	2,276
3. Udhampur (including Chaneni *Jagir*).	16	12	..	..	..	4	..	..	..	..	..	..	1,420	524	144	85	20	752
4. Riasi "	..	..	..	..	..	..	..	..	..	..	..	..	463	154	68	22	..	241
5. Mirpur "	3	2	..	..	..	1	..	..	..	..	..	..	2,404	877	105	45	..	1,422
6. Bhadarwah *Jagir*	4	4	..	1	..	..	..	..	..	..	..	..	214	75	58	3	24	81
7. Punch *Ilaqa*	6	2	..	..	..	4	14	10		..	..	4	387	189	1	24	..	197
II.—Kashmir Province (including *Jagirs*).	**211**	**80**	..	..	..	**131**	**28**	**27**	..	..	..	**1**	**24,918**	**7,984**	**1,555**	**666**	**81**	**15,379**
8. Kashmir North (including Langet *Jagir*)	42	19	..	..	..	23	..	..	..	..	..	..	4,910	1,861	187	162	1	3,062
9. Kashmir South (including City)...	165	57	..	..	..	108	27	27	..	..	..	..	19,351	6,148	1,340	493	80	11,863
10. Muzaffarabad District ..	4	4	..	..	..	..	1	..	..	..	..	1	657	175	28	11	..	454
III.—Frontier Districts	..	..	..	..	..	..	..	..	..	..	..	..	1,006	407	269	34	..	330
11. Ladakh District (including Mansar.)	..	..	..	..	..	..	..	..	..	..	..	..	983	398	268	34	..	317
12. Gilgit "	..	..	..	..	..	..	..	..	..	..	..	..	23	9	1	..	..	13
Cities.																		
13. Jammu	..	..	..	..	..	..	..	..	..	..	..	..	89	24	..	..	..	65
14. Srinagar	125	45	..	..	..	80	27	27	..	..	..	..	10,057	3,444	371	76	..	6,242

TABLE XVII.

Occupation or Means of Livelihood.

Jammu and Kashmir State Census, 1921.

DISTRICT, JAGIR, ILAQA OR CITY.	Group (131).—*Fish dealers.*						Group (132).—*Grocers and sellers of vegetable oil, salt and other condiments.*						Group (133)—*Sellers of milk, butter, Ghee, poultry, eggs, etc.*					
	Total workers and dependents	Actual Workers.				Dependents.	Total workers and dependents	Actual Workers.				Dependents.	Total workers and dependents.	Actual Workers.				Dependents.
		Total.		*Partially Agriculturists.*				*Total.*		*Partially Agriculturists.*				*Total.*		*Partially Agriculturists.*		
		Males.	Females.	Males.	Females.			Males.	Females.	Males.	Females.			Males.	Females.	Males.	Females.	
	956	957	958	959	960	961	962	963	964	965	966	967	968	969	970	971	972	973
State ..	**105**	**38**	**6**	**1**	..	**61**	**10,428**	**3,885**	**317**	**236**	**1**	**6,226**	**7,771**	**2,643**	**918**	**482**	**106**	**4,210**
I.—Jammu Province (including *Jagirs*).	..	..	..	..	..	..	**610**	**322**	**3**	**25**	..	**285**	**3,598**	**1,513**	**403**	**156**	**70**	**1,682**
1. Jammu District (including City)	..	..	..	..	..	..	590	312	3	22	..	275	695	211	151	54	..	333
2. Kathua "	..	..	..	..	..	..	1	1	..	1	..	..	1,629	776	103	30	36	750
3. Udhampur " (including Chaneni *Jagir*).	..	..	..	..	..	..	16	7	..	2	..	9	754	255	72	61	10	427
4. Riasi "	..	..	..	..	..	..	..	..	..	..	..	..	229	93	23	2	..	113
5. Mirpur "	..	..	..	..	..	..	..	..	..	..	..	..	125	104	1	7	..	20
6. Bhadarwah *Jagir*	..	..	..	..	..	..	..	..	..	..	..	..	159	68	52	2	24	39
7. Punch *Ilaqa*	..	..	..	..	..	..	3	2	..	..	..	1	7	6	1	..	..	..
II.—Kashmir Province (including *Jagirs*).	**105**	**38**	**6**	**1**	..	**61**	**9,058**	**3,256**	**117**	**180**	1	**5,685**	**4,166**	**1,123**	**515**	**326**	**36**	**2,528**
8. Kashmir North (including Langet *Jagir*).	105	38	6	1	..	61	2,432	873	26	25	..	1,533	1,117	321	138	105	1	658
9. Kashmir South (including City)..	..	..	..	..	..	..	6,112	2,252	64	144	1	3,796	3,024	795	376	218	35	1,853
10. Muzaffarabad District ..	..	..	..	..	..	..	514	131	27	11	..	356	25	7	1	..	..	17
III.—Frontier Districts	..	..	..	..	..	..	**760**	**307**	**197**	**31**	..	**256**	**7**	**7**	..	..	..	..
11. Ladakh District (including Mansar).	..	..	..	..	..	..	737	298	196	31	..	243	7	7	..	..	..	..
12. Gilgit "	..	..	..	..	..	..	23	9	1	..	..	13	..	..	..	..	..	..
Cities.																		
13. Jammu	..	..	..	..	..	..	36	3	..	..	..	30	53	21	..	..	..	32
14. Srinagar	..	..	..	..	..	..	2,239	879	..	..	..	1,363	1,940	534	222	58	..	1,184

TABLE XVII.

OCCUPATION OR MEANS OF LIVELIHOOD.

Jammu and Kashmir State Census, 1921.

DISTRICT, JAGIR, ILAQA OR CITY.	Group (134)—*Sellers of sweetmeats, sugar, gur and molasses.*						Group (135).—*Cardamom, betel leaf, vegetables, fruit and areca nut sellers.*						Group (136)—*Grain and pulse dealers.*					
	Total workers and dependents.	ACTUAL WORKERS.				Dependents.	Total workers and dependents.	ACTUAL WORKERS.				Dependents.	Total workers and dependents.	ACTUAL WORKERS.				Dependents.
		Total.		*Partially Agriculturists.*				*Total.*		*Partially Agriculturists.*				*Total.*		*Partially Agriculturists.*		
		Males.	Females.	Males.	Females.			Males.	Females.	Males.	Females.			Males.	Females.	Males.	Females.	
	974	975	976	977	978	979	980	981	982	983	984	985	986	987	988	989	990	991
State	**1,078**	**455**	**9**	**19**	..	**614**	**4,008**	**1,452**	**166**	**105**	**2**	**2,390**	**13,739**	**4,556**	**419**	**6**	**1**	**8,764**
I.—Jammu Province (including *Jagirs.*)	**686**	**329**	**2**	**19**	..	**355**	**522**	**160**	**134**	**19**	**1**	**228**	**7,564**	**2,693**	**103**	**207**	**1**	**4,768**
1. Jammu District (including City)	279	72	1	7	..	206	212	87	35	11	..	90	2,737	815	34	51	..	1,888
2. Kathua „	119	78	..	4	..	41	107	32	9	6	..	66	2,180	913	47	86	..	1,220
3. Udhampur „ (including Chaneni *Jagir.*)	95	59	1	1	..	35	4	..	1	..	1	3	389	189	5	18	1	195
4. Riasi „ ..	..	..	..	..	..	..	..	..	..	..	..	..	..	..	..	..	..	..
5. Mirpur „ ..	20	9	..	..	..	11	197	39	89	1	..	69	2,038	710	15	35	..	1,313
6. Bhadarwah *Jagir* ..	7	5	..	1	..	2	1	1	..	..	..	..	3	..	2	..	..	31
7. Punch *Ilaqa*	166	106	..	6	..	60	1	1	..	1	..	..	187	66	..	17	..	121
II.—Kashmir Province (including *Jagirs.*)	**392**	**126**	**7**	...	...	**259**	**3,486**	**1,292**	**32**	**86**	**1**	**2,162**	**5,936**	**1,770**	**244**	**56**	..	**3,922**
8. Kashmir North (including Langet *Jagir.*)	39	14	2	..	..	23	454	195	11	5	..	248	573	161	3	14	..	409
9. Kashmir South (including City.)	338	107	5	..	..	226	3,032	1,097	21	81	1	1,914	5,261	1,578	241	42	..	3,442
10. Muzaffarabad District ..	15	5	..	..	..	10	..	..	..	..	..	..	102	31	..	..	..	71
III.—Frontier Districts ..	..	..	..	..	..	..	..	..	..	..	..	..	**239**	**93**	**72**	**3**	..	**74**
11. Ladakh District (including Mansar.)	..	..	..	..	..	..	..	..	..	..	..	..	239	93	72	3	..	74
12. Gilgit „ ..	..	..	..	..	..	..	..	..	..	..	..	..	..	..	..	..	..	..
Cities.																		
13. Jammu	..	..	..	..	..	..	..	..	..	..	..	..	..	..	..	..	..	..
14. Srinagar	283	86	5	..	..	192	1,103	548	..	15	..	555	3,789	1,199	113	1	..	2,477

TABLE XVII.

Occupation or Means of Livelihood.

Jammu and Kashmir State Census, 1921.

DISTRICT, JAGIR, ILAQA OR CITY.	Group (137).—Tabacco, opium, ganja, etc., sellers.						Group (138).—Dealers in sheep, goats and pigs.						Group (139).—Dealers in hay, grass and fodder.					
	Total workers and dependents.	Actual Workers. Total.		Actual Workers. Partially Agriculturists.		Dependents.	Total workers and dependents.	Actual Workers. Total.		Actual Workers. Partially, Agriculturists.		Dependents.	Total workers and dependents.	Actual Workers. Total.		Actual Workers. Partially Agriculturists.		Dependents.
		Males.	Females.	Males.	Females.			Males.	Females.	Males.	Females.			Males.	Females.	Males.	Females.	
	992	993	994	995	996	997	998	999	1000	1001	1002	1003	1004	1005	1006	1007	1008	1009
State ..	**108**	**15**	..	**1**	..	**93**	**314**	**97**	**14**	**20**	..	**203**	**3,336**	**818**	**825**	**42**	**60**	**1,693**
I.—Jammu Province (**including** *Jagirs.*)	**107**	**14**	..	**1**	..	**93**	**295**	**87**	**14**	**15**	..	**194**	**1,581**	**450**	**191**	**30**	**17**	**940**
1. Jammu District (including City)	34	6	..	1	..	28	78	33	..	3	..	45	996	261	24	4	..	711
2. Kathua "	13	4	..	..	..	9	94	40	1	10	..	53	311	108	66	3	9	137
3. Udhampur " (including Chaneni *Jagir.*)	60	4	..	..	..	56	8	3	1	2	..	4	94	7	64	1	8	23
4. Riasi "	..	..	..	..	..	..	90	..	12	..	..	78	144	61	33	20	..	50
5. Mirpur "	..	..	..	..	..	..	5	5	..	..	..	..	19	10	..	2	..	1
6. Bhadarwah *Jagir*	..	..	..	..	..	..	..	..	..	..	..	..	14	1	4	..	..	9
7. Punch *Ilaqa*	..	..	..	..	..	..	20	6	..	..	..	14	3	2	..	..	..	1
II.—Kashmir Province (**including** *Jagirs*).	**1**	**1**	..	..	..	..	**19**	**10**	..	**5**	..	**9**	**1,755**	**368**	**634**	**12**	**43**	**774**
8. Kashmir North (including Langet *Jagir*).	..	..	..	..	..	..	19	10	..	5	..	9	171	49	1	4	..	121
9. Kashmir South (including City)	..	..	..	..	..	..	..	..	..	..	..	..	1,584	319	633	8	43	632
10. Muzaffarabad District ..	1	1	..	..	..	..	..	..	..	..	..	..	..	..	..	..	..	..
III.—Frontier Districts	..	..	..	..	..	..	..	..	..	..	..	..	..	..	..	..	..	..
11. Ladakh District (including Mansar). "	..	..	..	..	..	..	..	..	..	..	..	..	..	..	..	..	..	..
12. Gilgit "	..	..	..	..	..	..	..	..	..	..	..	..	..	..	..	..	..	..
Cities.																		
13. Jammu ..	..	..	..	..	..	..	..	..	..	..	..	..	..	..	..	..	..	..
14. Srinagar ..	..	..	..	..	..	..	..	..	..	..	..	..	703	198	31	2	..	474

TABLE XVII.

Occupation or Means of Livelihood.

Jammu and Kashmir State Census, 1921.

District, Jagir, Ilaqa or City.	Order 34.—Trade in Clothing and toilet articles. Total workers and dependents.	Actual Workers. Total. Males.	Total. Females.	Partially Agriculturists. Males.	Partially Agriculturists. Females.	Dependents.	Group (140).—Trade in ready-made clothing and other articles of dress and the toilet (hats, umbrellas, socks, ready-made shoes, perfumes, etc.) Total workers and dependents.	Actual Workers. Total. Males.	Total. Females.	Partially Agriculturists. Males.	Partially Agriculturists. Females.	Dependents.	Order 35.—Trade in furniture. Total workers and dependents.	Actual Workers. Total. Males.	Total. Females.	Partially Agriculturists. Males.	Partially Agriculturists. Females.	Dependents.
	1010	1011	1012	1013	1014	1015	1016	1017	1018	1019	1020	1021	1022	1023	1024	1025	1026	1027
State ..	**497**	**1**	**4**	**13**	..	**299**	**497**	**194**	**4**	**13**	..	**299**	**1,022**	**422**	**9**	**1**	..	**591**
I.—Jammu Province (including *Jagirs.*)	**79**	**57**	..	**13**	..	**22**	**79**	**57**	..	**13**	..	**22**	**317**	**121**	**9**	..	..	**187**
1. Jammu District (including City)	63	51	..	13	..	12	63	51	..	13	..	12	259	104	..	..	..	155
2. Kathua "	7	4	..	..	..	3	7	4	..	..	..	3	49	17	..	..	..	32
3. Udhampur " (including Chaneni *Jagirs.*)	..	..	..	..	..	..	..	..	..	..	..	..	..	..	..	..	..	..
4. Riasi "	1	..	..	..	..	1	1	..	..	..	..	1	9	..	9	..	..	..
5. Mirpur "	..	..	..	..	..	..	..	..	..	..	..	..	..	..	..	..	..	..
6. Bhadarwah *Jagir*	..	..	..	..	..	..	..	..	..	..	..	..	..	..	..	..	..	..
7. Punch *Ilaqa*	8	2	..	..	..	6	8	2	..	..	..	6	..	..	..	..	..	..
II.—Kashmir Province (including *Jagirs.*)	**418**	**137**	**4**	..	..	**277**	**418**	**137**	**4**	..	..	**277**	**697**	**298**	..	..	..	**399**
8. Kashmir North (including Langet *Jagir.*)	13	..	1	..	..	12	13	..	1	..	..	12	..	..	..	..	..	..
9. Kashmir South (including City)	405	137	3	..	..	265	405	137	3	..	..	265	697	298	..	..	..	390
10. Muzaffarabad District ..	..	..	..	..	..	..	..	..	..	..	..	..	..	..	..	..	..	..
III.—Frontier Districts	..	..	..	..	..	..	..	..	..	..	..	..	**8**	**3**	..	**1**	..	**5**
11. Ladakh District (including Mansar.)	..	..	..	..	..	..	..	..	..	..	..	..	8	3	..	1	..	5
12. Gilgit "	..	..	..	..	..	..	..	..	..	..	..	..	..	..	..	..	..	..
Cities																		
13. Jammu	..	..	..	..	..	..	..	..	..	..	..	..	259	104	..	..	..	155
14. Srinagar	391	133	2	..	..	256	391	133	2	..	..	256	697	298	..	..	..	399

TABLE XVII.

Occupation or Means of Livelihood.

Jammu and Kashmir State Census, 1921.

DISTRICT, JAGIR, ILAQA OR CITY.	Group (141).—*Trade in furniture, carpets, curtains and bedding.*						Group (142).—*Hardware, cooking utensils, Porcelain, crockery, glassware, bottles, articles for gardening, etc.*						Order 36—Trade in building materials.					
	Total workers and dependents.	Actual Workers.				Dependents.	Total workers and dependents.	Actual Workers.				Dependents.	Total workers and dependents.	Actual Workers.				Dependents.
		Total.		*Partially Agriculturists.*				*Total.*		*Partially Agriculturists.*				*Total.*		*Partially Agriculturists.*		
		Males.	Females.	Males.	Females.			Males.	Females	Males.	Females.			Males.	Females.	Males.	Females.	
	1028	1029	1030	1031	1032	1033	1034	1035	1036	1037	1038	1039	1040	1041	1042	1043	1044	1045
State ..	**699**	**296**	**9**	**1**	..	**394**	**323**	**126**	...	...	...	**197**	**7**	**6**	..	..	..	**1**
I.—Jammu Province (including *Jagirs*).	**9**	..	**9**	..	..	..	**308**	**121**	..	..	..	**187**	**7**	**6**	..	..	...	**1**
1. Jammu District (including City.)	..	..	..	..	..	..	259	104	..	..	..	155	..	..	..	..	..	..
2. Kathua „ ..	..	..	..	..	..	..	49	17	..	..	..	32	..	..	..	..	..	..
3. Udhampur „ (including Chaneni *Jagir*).	..	..	..	..	..	..	..	..	..	..	..	..	7	6	..	..	..	1
4. Riasi „ ..	9	..	9	..	..	..	..	..	..	..	..	..	..	..	..	..	..	..
5. Mirpur „ ..	..	..	..	..	..	..	..	..	..	..	..	..	..	..	..	..	..	..
6 Bhadarwah *Jagir* ..	..	..	..	..	..	..	..	..	..	..	..	..	..	..	..	..	..	...
7 Punch *Ilaqa* ..	..	..	..	..	..	..	..	..	..	..	..	..	..	..	..	..	..	...
II.—Kashmir Province (including *Jagirs*).	**682**	**293**	..	..	..	**389**	**15**	**5**	..	..	..	**10**	..	..	..	..	..	..
8. Kashmir North (including Langet *Jagir*).	..	..	..	..	..	..	...	..	..	..	...	..	..	..	..	..	..	..
9. Kashmir South (including City)	682	293	..	..	..	389	15	5	..	..	..	10	..	..	..	..	..	..
10. Muzaffarabad District ..	..	..	..	..	..	..	..	..	..	..	..	..	..	..	..	..	..	..
III.—Frontier Districts ..	**8**	**3**	..	**1**	..	**5**	..	..	...	..	...	...	..	..	..	..	..	..
11. Ladakh District (including Mansar).	8	3	..	1	..	5	..	..	..	..	..	..	..	..	..	..	..	..
12. Gilgit „	..	..	..	..	..	..	..	..	..	..	..	..		..	..	..	..	..
Cities.																		
13. Jammu	..	..	..	..	..	..	259	104	..	..	..	155		..	..	..	..	..
14. Srinagar	682	293	..	..	..	389	15	5	..	..	..	10		..	...	..	..	..

TABLE XVII.

Occupation or Means of Livelihood.

Jammu and Kashmir State Census, 1921.

DISTRICT, JAGIR, ILAQA OR CITY.	*Group* (143)—*Trade in building materials other than bricks, tiles, and woody materials.*						Order 37—Trade in means of transport.						*Group* (146)—*Dealers and hirers of elephants, camels, horses, cattle, asses mules, etc.*					
	Total workers and dependents.	Actual Workers.				Dependents.	Total workers and dependents.	Actual Workers.				Dependents.	Total workers and dependents.	Actual Workers.				Dependents.
		Total.		*Partially Agriculturists.*				*Total.*		*Partially Agriculturists.*				*Total.*		*Partially Agriculturists.*		
		Males.	Females.	Males.	Females.			Males.	Females.	Males.	Females.			Males.	Females.	Males.	Females.	
	1016	1047	1048	1049	1050	1051	1052	1053	1054	1055	1056	1057	1058	1059	1060	1061	1062	1063
State	7	6	..	..	..	1	1,792	815	4	46	..	973	1,792	815	4	46	..	973
I.—Jammu Province (including *Jagirs.*)	7	6	..	..	..	1	1,668	765	4	44	..	899	1,668	765	4	44	..	899
1. Jammu District (including City)	..	..	..	..	..	..	393	285	..	5	..	108	393	285	..	5	..	108
2. Kathua "	..	..	..	..	..	..	654	197	4	5	..	453	654	197	4	5	..	453
3. Udhampur " (including Chaneni *Jagir*).	7	6	..	..	..	1	106	53	..	12	..	53	106	53	..	12	..	53
4. Riasi "	..	..	..	..	..	..	..	..	..	..	..	..	..	..	..	..	..	..
5. Mirpur "	..	..	..	..	..	..	487	205	..	18	..	282	487	205	..	18	..	282
6. Bahadarwah *Jagir*	..	..	..	..	..	..	1	1	..	..	..	..	1	1	..	..	..	..
7. Punch *Ilaqa*	..	..	..	..	..	..	27	24	..	4	..	3	27	24	..	4	..	3
II.—Kashmir Province (including *Jagirs,*)	..	..	..	..	..	..	124	50	..	2	..	74	124	50	..	2	..	74
8. KashmirNorth (including Langet *Jagir*).	..	..	..	..	..	..	124	50	..	2	..	74	124	50	..	2	..	74
9. Kashmir South (including City)	..	..	..	..	..	..	..	..	..	..	..	..	..	..	..	..	..	..
10. Muzaffarabad District ..	..	..	..	..	..	..	..	..	..	..	..	..	..	..	..	..	..	..
III.—Frontier Districts	..	..	..	..	..	..	..	..	..	..	..	..	..	..	..	..	..	..
11. Ladakh District (including Mansar).	..	..	..	..	..	..	..	..	..	..	..	..	..	..	..	..	..	..
12. Gilgit "	..	..	..	..	..	..	..	..	..	..	..	..	..	..	..	..	..	..
Cities.																		
13. Jammu	..	..	..	..	..	..	..	..	..	..	..	..	..	..	..	..	..	..
14. Srinagar	..	..	..	..	..	..	..	..	..	..	..	..	..	..	..	..	..	..

TABLE XVII.

Occupation or Means of Livelihood.

Jammu and Kashmir State Census, 1921.

District, Jagir, Ilaqa or City.	Order 38.—Trade in Fuel.						Group (147).—Dealers in firewood, charcoal, coal, cowdung, etc						Order 39.—Trade in articles of luxury and those pertaining to letter and the arts and sciences.					
	Total workers and dependents.	Actual Workers. Total.		Actual Workers. Partially Agriculturists.		Dependents.	Total workers and dependents.	Actual Workers. Total.		Actual Workers. Partially Agriculturists.		Dependents.	Total workers and dependents.	Actual Workers. Total.		Actual Workers. Partially Agriculturists.		Dependents.
		Males.	Females.	Males.	Females.			Males.	Females.	Males.	Females.			Males.	Females.	Males.	Females.	
	1064	1065	1066	1067	1068	1069	1070	1071	1072	1073	1074	1075	1076	1077	1078	1079	1080	1081
State ..	**4,373**	**1,176**	**188**	**69**	**3**	**3,009**	**4,373**	**1,176**	**188**	**69**	**3**	**3,009**	**3,242**	**1,004**	**64**	**26**	..	**2,174**
I.—Jammu Province (including *Jagirs*).	**2,732**	**668**	**139**	**69**	**3**	**1,925**	**2,732**	**668**	**139**	**69**	**3**	**1,925**	**11,00**	**338**	**56**	**6**	..	**706**
1. Jammu District (including City).	2,324	574	79	65	1	1,671	2,324	574	79	65	1	1,671	679	212	..	3	..	467
2. Kathua ,, ..	116	28	53	2	..	35	116	28	53	2	..	35	101	47	1	..	..	53
3. Udhampur ,, (including Chaneni *Jagir*).	58	36	5	2	2	17	58	36	5	2	2	17	54	19	..	3	..	35
4. Riasi District	2	..	..	..	..	2	2	..	..	..	..	2	..	..	..	..	..	..
5. Mirpur ,, ...	225	27	..	..	..	198	225	27	..	..	..	198	266	60	55	..	..	151
6. Bhadarwah *Jagir*	5	2	2	..	..	1	5	2	2	..	..	1	..	..	..	..	..	..
7. Punch *Ilaqa*	2	1	..	..	..	1	2	1	..	..	..	1	..	..	..	..	..	..
II.—Kashmir Province (including *Jagirs*).	**1,641**	**508**	**49**	..	..	**1,084**	**1,641**	**508**	**49**	..	..	**1,084**	**2,137**	**666**	**8**	**20**	..	**1,463**
8. Kashmir North (including Langet *Jagir*).	400	147	7	..	..	306	460	147	7	..	..	306	489	124	6	19	..	329
9. Kashmir South (including City) ..	1,178	360	42	..	..	776	1,178	360	42	..	..	776	1,678	542	2	1	..	1,134
10. Muzaffarabad District ..	3	1	..	..	..	2	3	1	..	..	..	2	..	..	..	..	..	..
III.—Frontier Districts	..	..	..	..	..	..	..	..	..	..	..	..	**5**	..	..	..	..	**5**
11. Ladakh District (including Mansar).	..	..	..	..	..	..	..	..	..	..	..	..	2	..	..	..	..	2
12. Gilgit ,, ...	..	..	..	..	..	..	..	..	..	..	..	..	3	..	..	..	..	3
Cities.																		
13. Jammu	..	..	..	..	..	..	..	..	..	..	..	..	255	82	..	..	..	173
14. Srinagar	641	182	31	..	..	428	641	182	31	..	..	428	1,377	462	1	..	..	914

TABLE XVII.

Occupation or Means of Livelihood.

Jammu and Kashmir State Census, 1921.

DISTRICT, JAGIR, ILAQA OR CITY.	Group (148).—*Dealers in precious stones, jewellery (real and imitation) clocks, optical instruments, etc.*						Group (149).—*Dealers in common bangles, bead necklaces, fans, small articles, toys, hunting and fishing tackles, flowers, etc.*						Group (150).—*Publishers, booksellers, stationers, dealers in music, pictures, musical instruments and curiosities.*					
	Total workers and dependents.	Actual Workers. Total.		Actual Workers. Partially Agriculturists.		Dependents.	Total workers and dependent.	Actual Workers. Total.		Actual Workers. Partially Agriculturists.		Dependents.	Total workers and dependents.	Actual Workers. Total.		Actual Workers. Partially Agriculturists.		Dependents.
		Males.	Females.	Males.	Females.			Males.	Females.	Males.	Females.			Males.	Females.	Males.	Females.	
	1082	1083	1084	1085	1086	1087	1088	1089	1090	1091	1092	1093	1094	1095	1096	1097	1098	1099
State ..	2,390	732	2	21	..	1,356	698	207	62	5	..	429	154	65	..	..	..	89
I.—Jammu Province (including *Jagirs*).	512	130	..	3	..	382	460	155	56	3	..	249	128	53	..	..	..	75
1. Jammu District (including City)	494	126	..	3	..	368	59	35	..	..	..	24	126	51	..	..	..	75
2. Kathua " ..	..	..	..	..	..	..	101	47	1	..	..	53	..	..	..	..	..	..
3. Udhampur " (including Cheneni *Jagir*.)	..	..	..	..	..	..	54	19	..	3	..	35	..	..	..	..	..	..
4. Riasi District ..	..	..	..	..	..	..	..	..	..	..	..	...	..	..	..	..	..	..
5. Mirpur " ..	18	4	..	..	..	14	246	54	55	..	..	137	2	2	..	..	..	..
6. Bhadarwah *Jagir* ..	..	..	..	..	..	..	..	..	..	..	..	..	..	..	..	..	..	..
7. Punch *Ilaqa* ..	..	..	..	..	..	..	..	..	..	..	..	..	..	..	..	..	..	..
II.—Kashmir Province (including *Jagirs*).	1,873	602	2	18	..	1,269	238	52	6	2	..	180	26	12	..	..	..	14
8. Kashmir North (including Lenget *Jagir*).	329	98	..	18	..	231	130	26	6	1	..	98	..	..	..	..	..	..
9. Kashmir South (including City).	1,544	504	2	..	..	1,038	108	26	..	1	..	82	26	12	..	..	..	14
10. Muzaffarabad District ..	..	..	..	..	..	..	..	..	..	...	..	..	..	..	..	..	..	..
III.—Frontier Districts ..	5	..	..	..	..	5	..	..	..	..	..	..	..	..	..	..	..	..
11. Ladakh District (including Mansar).	2	..	..	..	..	2	..	..	..	..	..	..	..	..	..	..	..	..
12. Gilgit " ..	3	..	..	..	..	3	..	..	..	..	..	..	..	..	..	..	..	..
Cities																		
13. Jammu	129	31	..	..	..	98	..	..	..	..	..	..	126	51	..	..	..	75
14. Kashmir	1,351	450	1	..	..	900	..	..	..	..	..	..	26	12	..	..	..	14

TABLE XVII.

Occupation or Means of Livelihood.

Jammu and Kashmir State Census, 1921.

DISTRICT, JAGIR, ILAQA OR CITY.	Order. 40.—Trade of other sorts.						Group (151).—Dealers in rags, stable refuse, etc.						Group (152).—General-Storekeepers and shopkeepers otherwise unspecified.					
	Total workers and dependents.	Actual Workers. Total. Males.	Actual Workers. Total. Females.	Actual Workers. Partially Agriculturists. Males.	Actual Workers. Partially Agriculturists. Females.	Dependents.	Total workers and dependents.	Actual Workers. Total. Males.	Actual Workers. Total. Females.	Actual Workers. Partially Agriculturists. Males.	Actual Workers. Partially Agriculturists. Females.	Dependents.	Total workers and dependents.	Actual Workers. Total. Males.	Actual Workers. Total. Females.	Actual Workers. Partially Agriculturists. Males.	Actual Workers. Partially Agriculturists. Females.	Dependents.
	1100	1101	1102	1103	1104	1105	1106	1107	1108	1109	1110	1111	1112	1113	1114	1115	1116	1117
State ..	**42,263**	**13,661**	**690**	**1,342**	**79**	**27,912**	**336**	**79**	**2**	..	..	**255**	**39,271**	**12,852**	**662**	**1,321**	**79**	**25,757**
I.—Jammu Province (including *Jagirs*).	**23,281**	**7,464**	**555**	**8.71**	**77**	**15,262**	..	..	..	..	..	..	**22,859**	**7,360**	**542**	**858**	**77**	**14,957**
1. Jammu District (including city) ..	6,912	2,078	47	101	4	4,787	..	..	..	..	..	..	6,568	1,985	35	89	4	4,548
2. Kathua District ..	2,460	685	167	98	2	1,608	..	..	..	..	..	..	2,409	680	166	97	2	1,563
3. Udhampur " (including Chaneni *Jagir*).	3,107	1,114	52	136	1	1,941	..	..	..	..	..	..	3,100	1,111	52	136	1	1,937
4. Riasi District ..	4,532	1,454	182	253	65	2,896	..	..	..	..	..	..	45,23	1,454	182	253	65	2,887
5. Mirpur " ..	4,676	1,525	68	189	4	3,083	..	..	..	..	..	..	4,665	1,522	68	189	4	3,075
6. Bhadarwah *Jagir* ..	457	131	7	30	...	319	..	..	..	..	...	..	457	131	7	30	..	319
7. Punch *Ilaqa* ..	1,137	477	32	64	1	628	..	..	..	..	..	..	1,137	477	32	64	1	628
II.—Kashmir Province (including *Jagirs*).	**18,272**	**5,862**	**111**	**409**	**2**	**12,299**	**336**	**79**	**2**	..	..	**255**	**15,710**	**5,162**	**98**	**401**	**2**	**10,450**
8. Kashmir North (including Langet *Jagir*).	6,090	2,009	40	130	..	4,041	2	2	..	..	..	..	5,611	1,869	38	124	..	3,704
9. Kashmir South (including City) ..	9,361	2,922	44	141	..	6,395	334	77	2	..	..	255	7,281	2,365	33	139	..	4,883
10. Muzaffarabad District ..	2,821	931	27	138	2	1,863	..	..	..	..	..	..	2,818	928	27	138	2	1,862
III.—Frontier Districts ..	**710**	**335**	**24**	**62**	..	**351**	..	..	..	..	..	..	**702**	**330**	**22**	**62**	..	**350**
11. Ladakh District (including Mansar).	570	237	22	46	..	311	..	..	..	...	..	..	566	236	20	46	..	310
12. Gilgit " ..	140	98	2	16	..	40	..	...	..	..	..	..	136	94	2	16	..	40
Cities.																		
13. Jammu	3,280	1,163	12	18	..	2,105	..	..	..	..	..	..	3,280	1,163	12	18	..	2,105
14. Srinagar	7,625	2,094	36	2		5,493	329	72	2	..	...	255	6,076	1,703	26	2	..	4,347

TABLE XVII.

Occupation or Means of Livelihood:

Jammu and Kashmir State Census, 1921.

DISTRICT, JAGIR, ILAQA, OR CITY.	Group (153).—*Itinerant traders, pedlars hawkers, etc.*						Group (154)—*Other trades (including farmers of pounds, tolls and markets.)*						Class C.—Public administration and liberal arts.					
	Total workers and dependents.	Actual Workers. Total. Males.	Actual Workers. Total. Females.	Actual Workers. Partially Agriculturists. Males.	Actual Workers. Partially Agriculturists. Females.	Dependents.	Total workers and dependents.	Actual Workers. Total. Males.	Actual Workers. Total. Females.	Actual Workers. Partially Agriculturists. Males.	Actual Workers. Partially Agriculturists. Females.	Dependents.	Total workers and dependents.	Actual Workers. Total. Males.	Actual Workers. Total. Females.	Actual Workers. Partially Agriculturists. Males.	Actual Workers. Partially Agriculturists. Females.	Dependents.
	1118	1119	1120	1121	1122	1123	1124	1125	1126	1127	1128	1129	1130	1131	1132	1133	1134	1135
State	**1,730**	**441**	**25**	**1**	..	**1,264**	**926**	**289**	**1**	**20**	..	**636**	**113,792**	**43,729**	**2,801**	**5,901**	**223**	**67,262**
I.—Jammu Province (including *Jagirs*).	**227**	**24**	**13**	**1**	..	**190**	**155**	**80**	..	**12**	..	**115**	**48,711**	**21,053**	**1,387**	**3,586**	**153**	**26,271**
1. Jammu District (including City).	156	15	12	..	..	129	188	78	..	12	..	110	27,271	11,965	686	2,125	89	14,620
2. Kathua " ..	51	5	1	1	..	45	..	..	..	..	..	..	5,841	2,327	135	320	17	3,379
3. Udhampur " (including Chaneni *Jagir*).	5	2	..	..	..	3	2	1	..	..	..	1	3,852	1,808	99	356	9	1,915
4. Riasi " ..	9	..	..	..	..	9	..	..	..	..	..	..	2,909	1,057	184	115	18	1,668
5. Mirpur " ..	6	2	..	..	..	4	5	1	..	..	..	4	6,594	2,539	247	311	14	3,808
6. Bahadarwah *Jagir* ..	..	..	..	..	..	..	..	..	..	..	..	..	461	230	6	65	1	225
7. Punch *Ilaqa* ..	..	..	..	..	..	..	..	..	..	..	..	..	1,783	1,127	30	294	5	626
II.—Kashmir Province (including *Jagirs*).	**1,499**	**416**	**10**	..	..	**1,073**	**727**	**205**	**1**	**8**	..	**521**	**60,[illegible]01**	**19,528**	**890**	**1,979**	**48**	**40,083**
8. Kashmir North (including Langet *Jagir*).	401	111	1	..	..	289	76	27	1	6	..	48	11,723	4,244	202	629	23	7,277
9. Kashmir South (including City) ..	1,097	304	9	..	..	784	649	176	..	2	..	473	45,699	13,933	590	1,158	24	31,176
10. Muzaffarabad District ..	1	1	..	..	..	..	2	2	..	..	..	..	3,079	1,351	98	192	1	1,630
III.—Frontier Districts ..	**4**	1	**2**	..	..	**1**	**4**	**4**	..	..	..	..	**4,580**	**3,148**	**524**	**336**	**22**	**908**
11. Laddakh District (including Mansar).	4	1	2	..	..	1	..	..	..	..	..	..	3,206	2,000	501	262	21	705
12. Gilgit " ..	..	..	..	..	..	..	4	4	..	..	..	..	1,374	1,148	23	74	1	203
Cities.																		
13. Jammu	..	..	..	..	..	..	..	..	..	..	..	..	11,377	6,239	352	87	75	4,786
14. Srinagar	603	156	8	..	..	439	617	163	..	..	..	454	26,927	7,192	131	111	..	19,604

TABLE XVII.

Occupation or Means of Livelihood.

Jammu and Kashmir State Census, 1921.

District, Jagir, Ilaqa or City.	Sub-Class VI.—Public force.						Order 41.—Army.						Group (155).—Army (Imperial.)					
	Total workers and dependents.	Actual Workers. Total.		Actual Workers. Partially Agriculturists.		Dependents.	Total workers and dependents.	Actual Workers. Total.		Actual Workers. Partially Agriculturists.		Dependents.	Total workers and dependents.	Actual Workers. Total.		Actual Workers. Partially Agriculturists.		Dependants.
		Males.	Females.	Males.	Females.			Males.	Females.	Males.	Females.			Males.	Females.	Males.	Females.	
	1136	1137	1138	1139	1140	1141	1142	1143	1144	1145	1146	1147	1148	1149	1150	1151	1152	1153
State ..	**21,372**	**10,099**	**127**	**2,525**	**57**	**11,146**	**12,554**	**6,422**	**94**	**2,021**	**41**	**6,038**	**419**	**284**	..	**19**	..	**135**
I.—Jammu Province (including *Jagirs*).	**14,884**	**6,920**	**126**	**2,193**	**57**	**7,838**	**10,712**	**4,918**	**94**	**1,872**	**41**	**5,700**	**241**	**154**	..	**15**	..	**87**
1. Jammu District (including City)	9,741	4,575	96	1,741	52	5,070	7,625	3,492	75	1,655	36	4,058	63	13	..	1	..	50
2. Kathua " ..	1,325	479	5	113	5	841	741	251	5	63	5	485	90	73	..	14	..	17
3. Udhampur " (including, Chaneni *Jagir*).	787	450	2	90	..	385	409	276	1	38	..	132	68	64	..	..	..	4
4. Riasi District ..	560	286	17	35	..	257	355	181	7	14	...	167	..	..	..	..	..	..
5. Mirpur " ..	1,826	652	6	98	..	1,168	1,258	444	6	64	..	808	16	..	..	...	..	16
6. Bhadarwah *Jagir* ..	89	52	..	17	..	37	11	10	..	..	..	1	..	..	..	..	...	..
7. Punch *Ilaqa* ..	556	426	..	99	..	130	313	264	..	38	..	49	4	4	..	..	..	..
II.—Kashmir Province (including *Jagirs*).	**5,551**	**2,300**	**1**	**206**	–	**3,250**	**932**	**644**	–	**28**	..	**288**	**135**	**96**	..	**2**	..	**39**
8. Kashmir North (including Langet *Jagir*).	918	459	..	55	..	459	95	60	..	2	..	35	10	6	–	1	..	4
9. Kashmir South (including City)	4,287	1,631	..	118	..	2,656	724	505	..	24	..	219	73	40	..	..	..	33
10. Muzaffarabad District ..	346	210	1	33	..	135	113	79	..	2	..	34	52	50	..	1	..	2
III.—Frontier Districts ..	**937**	**879**	..	**126**	...	**58**	**910**	**860**	..	**121**	..	**50**	**43**	**34**	..	**2**	..	**9**
11. Ladakh District (including Mansar).	203	182	..	124	..	21	184	171	..	119	...	13	..	..	..	..	..	..
12. Gilgit " ..	734	697	..	2	..	37	726	689	..	2	..	37	43	34	..	2	..	9
Cities.																		
13. Jammu	2,863	1,647	45	52	45	1,171	1,839	1,017	29	28	29	793	..	..	..	..	..	..
14. Srinagar	3,113	1,171	..	34	..	1,942	618	455	..	18	..	163	44	30	..	..	..	14

TABLE XVII.

Occupation or Means of Livelihood.

Jammu and Kashmir State Census, 1921.

DISTRICT, JAGIR, ILAQA OR CITY.	*Group (156).—Army (Indian States).*						**Order 42.—Navy.**						*Group (157).—Navy.*					
	Total workers and dependents.	Actual Workers.				Dependents.	Total workers and dependents.	Actual Workers.				Dependents.	Total workers and dependents.	Actual Workers.				Dependents.
		Total.		*Partially Agriculturists.*				*Total.*		*Partially Agriculturists.*				*Total.*		*Partially Agriculturists.*		
		Males.	Females.	Males.	Females.			Males.	Females.	Males.	Females.			Males.	Females.	Males.	Females.	
	1154	1155	1156	1157	1158	1159	1160	1161	1162	1163	1164	1165	1166	1167	1168	1169	1170	1171
State ..	**12,135**	**6,138**	**94**	**2,002**	**41**	**5,903**	**7**	**3**	..	..	..	**4**	**7**	**3**	..	..	..	**4**
I.—Jammu Province (Including *Jagirs*).	**10,471**	**4,764**	**94**	**1,857**	**41**	**5,613**	..	..	..	..	..	..	..	..	..	..	..	..
1. Jammu District (including City)	7,562	3,479	75	1,654	36	4,008	..	..	..	..	..	..	..	..	..	..	..	..
2. Kathua " ..	651	178	5	49	5	468	..	..	..	..	..	..	..	..	..	..	..	..
3. Udhampur " (including Chaneni *Jagir.*)	341	212	1	38	..	128	..	..	..	..	..	..	..	..	..	..	..	..
4. Riasi District ..	355	181	7	14	..	167	..	..	..	..	..	..	..	..	..	..	..	..
5. Mirpur " ..	1,242	444	6	64	..	792	..	..	..	..	..	..	..	..	..	..	..	..
6. Bhadarwah *Jagir* ..	11	10	..	..	..	1	..	..	..	..	..	..	..	..	..	..	..	..
7. Punch *Ilaqa* ..	309	260	..	38	..	49	..	..	..	..	..	..	..	..	..	..	..	...
II.—Kashmir Province (Including *Jagirs*).	**797**	**548**	..	**26**	..	**249**	**7**	**3**	...	..	..	**4**	**7**	**3**	..	..	..	**4**
8. Kashmir North (including Langet *Jagir*).	85	54	..	1	..	31	..	..	..	..	..	..	..	..	..	..	..	..
9. Kashmir South (including City).	651	465	..	24	..	186	7	3	..	..	..	4	7	3	..	..	..	4
10. Muzaffarabad District ..	61	29	..	1	..	32	..	..	..	..	..	..	..	..	..	..	..	..
III.—Frontier Districts ..	**867**	**826**	..	**119**	..	**41**	..	..	..	..	..	..	..	..	..	..	..	..
11. Ladakh District (including Mansar).	184	171	..	119	..	13	..	..	..	..	..	..	..	..	..	..	..	..
12. Gilgit " ..	683	655	..	..	..	28	..	...	..	..	..	..	..	..	..	..	..	..
Cities.																		
13. Jammu	**1,839**	**1,017**	**29**	**28**	**29**	**793**	..	..	..	..	..	..	..	..	..	..	..	..
14. Srinagar	**574**	**425**	..	**18**	..	**149**	..	..	..	..	..	..	..	..	..	..	..	..

TABLE XVII.

Occupation or Means of Livelihood.

Jammu and Kashmir State Census, 1921.

DISTRICT, JAGIR, ILAQA OR CITY.	Order 44.—Police.						Group (159).—Police.						Group (160).—Village Watchmen.					
	Total workers and dependents.	Actual Workers. Total.		Partially Agriculturists.		Dependents.	Total workers and dependents.	Actual Workers. Total.		Partially Agriculturists.		Dependents.	Total workers and dependents.	Actual Workers. Total.		Partially Agriculturists.		Dependents.
		Males.	Females.	Males.	Females.			Males.	Females.	Males.	Females.			Males.	Females.	Males.	Females.	
	1172	1173	1174	1175	1176	1177	1178	1179	1180	1181	1182	1183	1184	1185	1186	1187	1188	1189
State ..	**8,811**	**3,674**	**33**	**504**	**16**	**5,104**	**5,570**	**2,347**	**29**	**199**	**16**	**3,194**	**3,241**	**1,327**	**4**	**305**	..	**1,910**
I.—Jammu Province (including *Jagirs*).	**4,172**	**2,002**	**32**	**321**	**16**	**2,138**	**2,415**	**1,257**	**29**	**141**	**16**	**1,129**	**1,757**	**745**	**3**	**180**	..	**1,009**
1. Jammu District (including City)..	2,116	1,083	21	86	16	1,012	1,366	763	19	40	16	534	750	320	2	46	..	428
2. Kathua „	584	228	..	50	..	356	240	105	..	9	..	135	344	123	..	41	..	221
3. Udhampur „ (including Chaneni *Jagir*.)	378	174	1	32	..	203	137	67	..	12	..	70	241	107	1	40	..	133
4. Riasi „	205	105	10	21	..	90	135	59	10	6	..	66	70	46	..	15	..	24
5. Mirpur „	568	208	..	34	..	360	293	105	..	23	..	188	275	103	..	11	..	172
6. Bhadarwah *Jagir*	78	42	..	17	..	36	58	29	..	9	..	29	20	13	..	8	..	7
7. Punch *Ilaqa*	243	162	..	61	..	81	186	129	..	42	..	57	57	33	..	19	..	24
II.—Kashmir Province (including *Jagirs*.)	**4,612**	**1,653**	**1**	**178**	..	**2,558**	**3,132**	**1,074**	..	**53**	..	**2,058**	**1,480**	**579**	**1**	**125**	..	**900**
8. Kashmir North (including Langet *Jagir*).	823	399	..	53	..	424	244	134	..	7	..	110	579	265	..	46	..	314
9. Kashmir South (including City).	3,556	1,123	..	94	..	2,433	2,741	841	..	29	..	1,900	815	282	..	65	..	533
10. Muzaffarabad District ..	233	131	1	31	..	101	147	99	..	17	..	48	86	32	1	14	..	53
III.—Frontier Districts	**27**	**19**	..	**5**	..	**8**	**23**	**16**	..	**5**	..	**7**	**4**	**3**	..	..	..	**1**
11. Ladakh District (including Mansar.)	19	11	..	5	..	8	15	8	..	5	..	7	4	3	..	...	..	1
12. Gilgit „	8	8	..	..	..	..	8	8	..	..	..	..	..	..	..	..	..	..
Cities.																		
13. Jammu	1,024	630	16	24	16	378	1,024	630	16	24	16	378	.	..	..	..	..	..
14. Srinagar	2,495	716	..	16	..	1,779	2,495	716	..	16	..	11,779	..	..	..	..	..	..

TABLE XVII.

Occupation or Means of Livelihood.

Jammu and Kashmir State Census, 1921.

District, Jagir, Ilaqa or City.	Sub-class VII.—Public administration.						Order 45.—Public administration.						Group (161).—Service of the State.					
	Total workers and dependents.	Actual Workers. Total.		Actual Workers. Partially Agriculturists.		Dependents.	Total workers and dependents.	Actual Workers. Total.		Actual Workers. Partially Agriculturists.		Dependents.	Total workers and dependents.	Actual Workers. Total.		Actual Workers. Partially Agriculturists.		Dependants.
		Males.	Females.	Males.	Females.			Males.	Females.	Males.	Females.			Males.	Females.	Males.	Females.	
	1190	1191	1192	1193	1194	1195	1196	1197	1198	1199	1200	1201	1202	1203	1204	1205	1206	1207
State ..	**35,324**	**12,575**	**229**	**1,064**	**39**	**22,520**	**35,324**	**12,575**	**229**	**1,064**	**39**	**22,520**	**31,713**	**11,154**	**214**	**841**	**38**	**20,345**
I.—Jammu Province (including *Jagirs*.)	**13,175**	**6,050**	**206**	**605**	**39**	**6,919**	**13,175**	**6,050**	**206**	**605**	**39**	**6,919**	**12,192**	**5 692**	**201**	**501**	**38**	**6,299**
1. Jammu District (including City).	6,843	3,012	77	107	31	3,754	6,843	3,012	77	107	31	3,754	6,544	2,926	73	95	30	3,545
2. Kathua " ..	910	402	4	41	..	504	910	402	4	41	..	504	700	736	4	28	..	360
3. Udhampur " (including Chaneni *Jagir*.)	1,574	900	1	180	..	673	1,574	900	1	180	..	673	1,405	828	..	155	..	677
4. Riasi " ..	1,262	470	92	39	4	700	1,262	470		39	4	700	1,256	464	92	35	4	700
5. Mirpur " ..	1,766	757	22	70	3	987	1,766	757	92	70	3	987	1,577	706	22	61	3	849
6. Bhadarwah *Jagir* ..	148	71	1	21	1	76	148	71	1	21	1	76	138	68	1	21	1	69
7. Punch *Ilaqa* ..	672	438	9	147	..	225	672	438		147	..	225	572	364	9	106	..	199
II.—Kashmir Province (including *Jagirs*.)	**21,326**	**6,007**	**21**	**343**	..	**15,298**	**21,326**	**6,007**	**21**	**343**	..	**15 298**	**18,850**	**5,016**	**11**	**253**	..	**13,783**
8. Kashmir North (including Langet *Jagir*).	2,340	1,155	8	123	..	1,177	2,310	1,155	8	123	..	1,177	1,686	873	1	56	..	812
9. Kashmir South (including City).	18,212	4,401	11	146	..	13,800	18,212	4,401	11	146	..	13,800	16,139	3,765	9	131	..	12,665
10. Muzaffarabad District ..	774	451	2	74	..	321	774	451	2	74	..	321	725	418	1	66	..	306
III.—Frontier Districts ..	**823**	**518**	**2**	**116**	..	**303**	**823**	**18**	**2**	**116**	..	**303**	**671**	**406**	**2**	**87**	..	**263**
11. Ladakh District (including Mansurs)	439	201	..	47	..	238	439	201	..	47	..	238	287	89	..	18	..	198
12. Gilgit " ..	384	317	2	69	..	65	384	317	2	69	..	65	384	317	2	69	..	65
Cities.																		
13. Jammu	3,656	2,144	31	25	30	1,481	3,656	2,144	31	25	30	1,481	..	..	..	..	..	..
14. Srinagar	15,139	3,251	2	45	..	11,886	15,139	3,251	2	45	..	11,886	14,602	3,002	..	44	..	11,600

TABLE XVII.

Occupation or Means of Livelihood.

Jammu and Kashmir State Census, 1921.

District, Jagir, Ilaqa or City.	Group (162).—*Service of Indian and Foreign states.*						Group (163).—*Municipal and other local (not village) Service*						Group (164).—*Village officials and servants other than watchmen.*					
	Total workers and dependents.	Actual Workers. Total. Males.	Actual Workers. Total. Females.	Actual Workers. Partially Agriculturists. Males.	Actual Workers. Partially Agriculturists. Females.	Dependents.	Total workers and dependents.	Actual Workers. Total. Males.	Actual Workers. Total. Females.	Actual Workers. Partially Agriculturists. Males.	Actual Workers. Partially Agriculturists. Females.	Dependents.	Total workers and dependents.	Actual Workers. Total. Males.	Actual Workers. Total. Females.	Actual Workers. Partially Agriculturists. Males.	Actual Workers. Partially Agriculturists. Females.	Dependents.
	1208	1209	1210	1211	1212	1213	1214	1215	1216	1217	1218	1219	1220	1221	1222	1223	1224	1225
State ..	57	45	..	5	..	12	691	251	12	2	..	428	2,863	1,125	3	216	1	1,735
I.—Jammu Province (including *Jagirs*).	..	..	..	..	..	..	35	9	3	1	..	23	948	349	2	103	1	597
1. Jammu District (including City).	..	..	..	..	..	..	11	..	3	..	..	8	288	86	1	12	1	501
2. Kathua "	..	..	..	..	..	..	22	7	..	1	..	15	188	59	..	12	..	129
3. Udhampur " (including Chaneni *Jagir*).	..	..	..	..	..	..	..	..	..	..	..	..	169	72	1	25	..	96
4. Riasi District	..	..	..	..	..	..	..	..	..	..	..	..	6	6	..	4	..	..
5. Mirpur "	..	..	..	..	..	..	2	2	..	..	..	..	187	49	..	9	..	138
6. Bhadarwah *Jagir*	..	..	..	..	..	..	..	..	..	..	..	..	10	3	..	..	..	7
7. Punch *Ilaqa*	..	..	..	..	..	..	..	..	..	..	..	..	100	74	..	41	..	26
II.—Kashmir Province (including *Jagirs*).	31	24	..	..	..	7	656	242	9	1	..	405	1,789	685	1	89	..	1,103
8. Kashmir North (including Langet *Jagir*).	6	6	..	..	..	..	116	23	7	..	..	86	532	253	..	67	..	279
9. Kashmir South (including City).	25	18	..	..	..	7	540	219	2	1	..	319	1,208	399	..	14	..	809
10. Muzaffarabad District ..	..	..	..	..	..	..	..	..	..	..	..	..	49	33	1	8	..	15
III.—Frontier Districts	26	21	..	5	..	5	..	..	..	..	..	..	126	91	..	24	..	35
11. Ladakh District (including Mansar).	26	21	..	5	..	5	..	..	..	..	..	..	126	91	..	24	..	35
12. Gilgit "	..	..	..	..	..	..	..	..	..	..	..	..	..	..	..	..	..	..
Cities.																		
13. Jammu	..	..	..	..	..	..	..	..	..	..	..	..	..	..	..	..	..	..
14. Srinagar	25	18	..	..	..	7	492	211	2	1	..	..	20	20	..	..	..	..

TABLE XVII.

Occupation or Means of Livelihood.

Jammu and Kashmir State Census, 1921.

DISTRICT, JAGIR, ILAQA OR CITY.	Sub-class VIII.—Professions and liberal arts.						Order 46.—Religion.						Group (165).—*Priests, Ministers, etc.*					
	Total workers and dependents.	Actual Workers. Total.		Actual Workers. *Partially Agriculturists.*		Dependents.	Total workers and dependents.	Actual Workers. Total.		Actual Workers. *Partially Agriculturists.*		Dependents.	Total workers and dependents.	Actual Workers. Total.		Actual Workers. *Partially Agriculturists.*		Dependents.
		Males.	Females.	Males.	Females.			Males.	Females.	Males.	Females.			Males.	Females.	Males.	Females.	
	1226	1227	1228	1229	1230	1231	1232	1233	1234	1235	1236	1237	1238	1239	1240	1241	1242	1243
State ..	**57,096**	**21,055**	**2,445**	**2,312**	**127**	**33,596**	**44,513**	**16,659**	**2,013**	**2,017**	**108**	**25,841**	**31,905**	**12,061**	**961**	**1,446**	**71**	**18,883**
I.—Jammu Province (including *Jagirs*).	**20,652**	**8,083**	**1,055**	**788**	**57**	**11,514**	**15,968**	**6,355**	**851**	**685**	**54**	**8,762**	**14,762**	**5,819**	**827**	**639**	**54**	**8,116**
1. Jammu District (including City).	10,687	4,378	513	277	6	5,796	8,471	3,555	382	243	6	4,534	7,851	3,256	380	223	56	4,215
2. Kathua „	3,606	1,446	126	166	12	2,034	2,807	1,187	101	155	11	1,519	2,339	1,013	80	141	11	1,246
3. Udhampur „ (including Chaneni *Jagir*).	1,491	458	96	86	9	937	1,051	301	68	67	7	682	1,050	301	68	67	7	681
4. Riasi District	1,087	301	75	41	14	711	1,003	272	74	37	14	657	993	272	73	37	1	648
5. Mirpur „	3,002	1,130	219	143	11	1,653	2,230	840	212	134	11	1,178	2,136	785	212	122	11	1,139
6. Bhadarwah *Jagir*	224	107	5	27	..	112	130	63	3	18	..	64	130	63	3	18	..	64
7. Punch *Ilaqa*	555	263	21	48	5	271	276	137	11	31	5	128	263	129	11	31	5	123
II.—Kashmir Province (including *Jagirs*).	**33,624**	**11,221**	**868**	**1,430**	**48**	**21,535**	**25,995**	**8,678**	**653**	**1,254**	**32**	**16,659**	**15,734**	**5,039**	**77**	**764**	**14**	**10,618**
8. Kashmir North (including Langet *Jagir*).	8,465	2,630	194	451	23	5,641	6,673	2,011	145	376	14	4,517	3,366	992	23	248	6	2,351
9. Kashmir South (including City).	23,200	7,901	579	894	24	14,720	17,594	6,058	422	799	17	11,114	11,781	3,813	50	460	8	7,918
10. Muzaffarabad District ..	1,959	690	95	85	1	1,174	1,728	609	91	79	1	1,028	587	234	4	56	..	349
III.—Frontier Districts ..	**2,820**	**1,751**	**522**	**94**	**22**	**547**	**2,550**	**1,626**	**504**	78	22	420	1,409	1,203	57	43	3	**149**
11. Ladakh District (includi.. Mansar.	2,564	1,617	501	91	21	446	2,367	1,533	485	75	21	349	1,340	1,166	53	41	3	121
12. Gilgit „ ..	256	134	21	3	1	101	183	93	19	3	1	71	69	37	4	2	..	28
Cities.																		
13. Jammu	4,868	2,448	276	10	..	12,43	3,611	1,996	221	2	..	1,394	3,517	1,967	221	2	..	1,329
14. Srinagar	8,675	2,770	120	32	..	5,776	4,960	1,645	28	9	..	3,287	4,350	1,382	..	..	..	2,977

TABLE XVII.

Occupation or Means of Livelihood.

Jammu and Kashmir State Census, 1921.

DISTRICT, JAGIR, ILAQA OR CITY.	*Group* (166).—*Religious Mendicants, inmates of monasteries.*						*Group* (167).—*Catechists, Readers, Church and Mission Service.*						*Group* (168).—*Temple, Burial or Burning Ground service, Pilgrim Conductors, Circumcisers.*					
	Total workers and dependents.	Actual Workers.				Dependents.	Total workers and dependents.	Actual Workers.				Dependents.	Total workers and dependents.	Actual Workers.				Dependents.
		Total.		*Partially Agriculturists.*				*Total.*		*Partially Agriculturists.*				*Total.*		*Partially Agriculturists.*		
		Males.	Females.	Males.	Females.			Males.	Females.	Males.	Females.			Males.	Females.	Males.	Females.	
	1244	1245	1246	1247	1248	1249	1250	1251	1252	1253	1254	1255	1256	1257	1258	1259	1260	1261
State	**12,201**	**4,483**	**1,051**	**556**	**37**	**6,667**	**309**	**86**	**1**	**14**	..	**222**	**98**	**29**	..	**1**	..	**69**
I.—Jammu Province (including *Jagirs*).	**1,071**	**486**	**23**	**43**	..	**562**	**129**	**49**	**1**	**3**	..	**79**	**6**	**1**	..	..	..	**5**
1. Jammu District (including City	523	270	[illegible]	2[illegible]	..	[illegible]51	94	28	..	..	..	66	3	1	..	..	..	2
2. Kathua "	467	174	11	14	..	272	1	..	..	..	..	1	..	..	..	..	..	..
3. Udhampur " (including Chaneni *Jagir*).	1	..	..	..	..	1	..	..	..	..	..	..	..	..	..	..	..	..
4. Riasi District	6	..	..	..	..	6	4	..	1	..	..	3	..	..	..	..	..	..
5. Mirpur "	74	42	..	9	..	32	20	13	..	3	..	7	..	..	..	..	..	..
6. Bhadarwah *Jagir*	..	..	..	..	..	..	..	..	..	..	..	..	..	..	..	..	..	..
7. Punch *Ilaqa*	..	..	..	..	..	..	10	8	..	..	..	2	3	..	..	..	..	3
II.—Kashmir Province (including *Jagirs*).	**9,990**	**3,575**	**581**	**478**	**18**	**5,834**	**180**	**37**	..	**11**	..	**143**	**91**	**27**	..	**1**	..	**64**
8. Kashmir North (including Langet *Jagir*)	3,126	983	122	117	8	2,021	179	36	..	11	..	143	2	..	..	..	..	2
9. Kashmir South (including City).	5,[illegible]23	2,217	372	338	9	3,134	1	1	..	..	..	..	89	27	..	1	..	62
10. Muzaffarabad District ..	1,141	375	8[illegible]	23	1	6[illegible]9	..	..	..	..	..	..	..	..	..	..	..	..
III.—Frontier Districts ..	**1,140**	**422**	**447**	**35**	**19**	**2[illegible]1**	..	..	..	..	..	..	1	1	..	..	..	..
11. Ladakh District (including Mansar).	1,026	366	452	34	18	2[illegible]8	..	..	..	..	..	..	1	1	..	..	..	..
12. Gilgit "	114	56	15	1	1	43	..	..	..	..	..	..	..	..	..	..	..	..
Cities.																		
13. Jammu	..	..	..	..	..	..	91	28	..	..	..	63	3	1	..	..	..	2
14. Srinagar	601	263	28	9	..	310	..	..	..	..	..	..	..	..	..	..	..	..

TABLE XVII.

Occupation or Means of Livelihood.

Jammu and Kashmir State Census, 1921.

Order 47.—Law.

DISTRICT, JAGIR, ILAQA OR CITY.	Total workers and dependents.	Actual Workers. Total. Males.	Actual Workers. Total. Females.	Actual Workers. Partially Agriculturists. Males.	Actual Workers. Partially Agriculturists. Females.	Dependents.
	1262	1263	1264	1265	1266	1267
State	**2,022**	**686**	..	**22**	..	**1,336**
I.—Jammu Province (including *Jagirs.*)	**768**	**297**	..	**13**	..	**471**
1. Jammu District (including City)	310	150	..	1	..	160
2. Kathua "	73	22	..	5	..	51
3. Udhampur " (including Chaneni *Jagir.*)	68	17	..	1	..	51
4. Riasi District	25	10	..	2	..	15
5. Mirpur "	223	70	..	2	..	153
6. Bhadarwah *Jagir*	14	5	..	1	..	9
7. Punch *Ilaqa*	55	23	..	1	..	32
II.—Kashmir Province (including *Jagirs*).	**1,226**	**381**	..	**8**	..	**845**
8. Kashmir North (including Langet *Jagir.*)	120	28	..	4	..	92
9. Kashmir South (including City.)	1,009	325	..	2	..	684
10. Muzaffarabad District ..	97	28	..	2	..	69
III.—Frontier Districts ..	**28**	**8**	..	**1**	..	**20**
11. Ladakh District (including Mansar).	24	4	..	1	..	20
12. Gilgit "	4	4	..	..	..	..
Cities.						
13. Jammu	259	130	..	1	..	129
14. Srinagar	804	263	..	1	..	541

Group (169).—Lawyers of all kinds including Kazis, Law Agents and Mukhtars.

DISTRICT, JAGIR, ILAQA OR CITY.	Total workers and dependents.	Actual Workers. Total. Males.	Actual Workers. Total. Females.	Actual Workers. Partially Agriculturists. Males.	Actual Workers. Partially Agriculturists. Females.	Dependents.
	1268	1269	1270	1271	1272	1273
State	**949**	**336**	..	**11**	..	**613**
I.—Jammu Province (including *Jagirs.*)	**318**	**126**	..	**7**	..	**192**
1. Jammu District (including City)	138	76	..	1	..	62
2. Kathua "	11	4	..	1	..	7
3. Udhampur " (including Chaneni *Jagir.*)	29	6	..	..	..	23
4. Riasi District	24	10	..	2	..	14
5. Mirpur "	104	25	..	2	..	79
6. Bhadarwah *Jagir*	12	5	..	1	..	7
7. Punch *Ilaqa*	..	..	..	..	..	..
II.—Kashmir Province (including *Jagirs*).	**631**	**210**	..	**4**	..	**421**
8. Kashmir North (including Langet *Jagir.*)	48	12	..	2	..	36
9. Kashmir South (including City.)	540	188	..	2	..	352
10. Muzaffarabad District ..	43	10	..	..	..	33
III.—Frontier Districts ..	..	..	..	..	..	..
11. Ladakh District (including Mansar).	..	..	..	..	..	..
12. Gilgit "	..	..	..	..	..	..
Cities.						
13. Jammu	123	70	..	1	..	53
14. Srinagar	459	159	..	1	..	300

Group (170).—Lawyer's Clerks, Petition-writers, etc.

DISTRICT, JAGIR, ILAQA OR CITY.	Total workers and dependents.	Actual Workers. Total. Males.	Actual Workers. Total. Females.	Actual Workers. Partially Agriculturists. Males.	Actual Workers. Partially Agriculturists. Females.	Dependents.
	1274	1275	1276	1277	1278	1279
State	**1,073**	**350**	..	**11**	..	**723**
I.—Jammu Province (including *Jagirs.*)	**450**	**171**	..	**6**	..	**279**
1. Jammu District (including City)	172	74	..	..	..	98
2. Kathua "	62	18	..	4	..	44
3. Udhampur " (including Chaneni *Jagir.*)	39	11	..	1	..	28
4. Riasi District	1	..	..	..	..	1
5. Mirpur "	119	45	..	..	..	74
6. Bhadarwah *Jagir*	2	..	..	..	..	2
7. Punch *Ilaqa*	55	23	..	1	..	32
II.—Kashmir Province (including *Jagirs*).	**595**	**171**	..	**4**	..	**424**
8. Kashmir North (including Langet *Jagir.*)	72	16	..	2	..	56
9. Kashmir South (including City.)	469	137	..	..	..	332
10. Muzaffarabad District ..	54	18	..	2	..	36
III.—Frontier Districts ..	**28**	**8**	..	**1**	..	**20**
11. Ladakh District (including Mansar).	24	4	..	1	..	20
12. Gilgit "	4	4	..	..	..	..
Cities.						
13. Jammu	136	60	..	..	..	76
14. Srinagar	345	104	..	..	..	241

TABLE XVII.

Occupation or Means of Livelihood.

Jammu and Kashmir State Census, 1921.

Order 48.—Medicine.

District, Jagir, Ilaqa or City.	Total workers and dependents.	Actual Workers. Total. Males.	Actual Workers. Total. Females.	Actual Workers. Partially Agriculturists. Males.	Actual Workers. Partially Agriculturists. Females.	Dependents.
	1280	1281	1282	1283	1284	1285
State ...	**3,261**	**910**	**283**	**88**	**5**	**2,068**
I.—Jammu Province (including *Jagirs*).	**1,384**	**374**	**149**	**34**	**3**	**861**
1. Jammu District (including City.)	847	224	102	18	..	521
2. Kathua „	223	46	14	4	1	163
3. Udhampur „ (including Chaneni *Jagir*).	109	26	23	4	2	60
4. Riasi „	27	7	1	1	..	19
5 Mirpur „	99	39	5	2	..	55
6. Bhaderwah *Jagir*	32	15	1	2	..	16
7. Punch *Ilaqa*	47	17	3	3	..	27
II.—Kashmir Province (including *Jagirs*).	**1,804**	**510**	**131**	**51**	**2**	**1,163**
8. Kashmir North (including Langet *Jagir*).	256	71	34	13	2	151
9. Kashmir South (including City.)	1,499	419	96	38	..	984
10. Muzaffarabad District ..	49	20	1	..	..	28
III.—Frontier Districts	**73**	**26**	**3**	**3**	..	**44**
11. Ladakh District (including Mansar).	51	21	1	3	..	29
12. Gilgit „	22	5	2	..	..	15
Cities.						
13. Jammu	456	69	33	5	..	354
14. Srinagar	979	260	62	5	..	657

Group (171).—Medical practitioners of all kinds including dentists, Occulists and veterinary surgeons.

District, Jagir, Ilaqa or City.	Total workers and dependents.	Actual Workers. Total. Males.	Actual Workers. Total. Females.	Actual Workers. Partially Agriculturists. Males.	Actual Workers. Partially Agriculturists. Females.	Dependents.
	1286	1287	1288	1289	1290	1291
State ...	**2,056**	**622**	**23**	**70**	**2**	**1,411**
I.—Jammu Province (including *Jagirs*).	**924**	**256**	**11**	**25**	..	**657**
1. Jammu District (including City.)	537	161	3	14	..	373
2. Kathua „	181	36	2	3	..	143
3. Udhampur „ (including Chaneni *Jagir*).	69	18	3	3	..	48
4. Riasi „	27	7	1	1	..	19
5 Mirpur „	66	23	2	2	..	41
6. Bhaderwah *Jagir*	9	..	..	..	..	9
7. Punch *Ilaqa*	35	11	..	2	..	24
II.—Kashmir Province (including *Jagirs*).	**1,092**	**346**	**12**	**42**	**2**	**734**
8. Kashmir North (including Langet *Jagir*).	203	65	2	12	2	136
9. Kashmir South (including City.)	841	262	9	30	..	570
10. Muzaffarabad District ..	48	19	1	..	..	28
III.—Frontier Districts	**40**	**20**	..	**3**	..	**20**
11. Ladakh District (including Mansar).	35	18	..	3	..	17
12. Gilgit „	5	2	..	..	..	3
Cities.						
13. Jammu	264	28	2	2	..	234
14. Srinagar	449	128	2	..	..	319

Group (172)—Midwives, Vaccinators, compounders, nurses, masseurs, etc.

District, Jagir, Ilaqa or City.	Total workers and dependents.	Actual Workers. Total. Males.	Actual Workers. Total. Females.	Actual Workers. Partially Agriculturists. Males.	Actual Workers. Partially Agriculturists. Females.	Dependents.
	1292	1293	1294	1295	1296	1297
State ...	**1,205**	**288**	**260**	**18**	**3**	**657**
I.—Jammu Province (including *Jagirs*).	**460**	**118**	**138**	**9**	**3**	**204**
1. Jammu District (including City.)	310	63	99	4	..	148
2. Kathua „	42	10	12	1	1	20
3. Udhampur „ (including Chaneni *Jagir*).	40	8	20	1	2	12
4. Riasi „	..	..	..	..	..	..
5 Mirpur „	33	16	3	..	..	14
6. Bhaderwah *Jagir*	23	15	1	2	..	7
7. Punch *Ilaqa*	12	6	3	1	..	3
II.—Kashmir Province (including *Jagirs*).	**712**	**164**	**119**	**9**	..	**429**
8. Kashmir North (including Langet *Jagir*).	53	6	32	1	..	15
9. Kashmir South (including City.)	658	157	87	8	..	414
10. Muzaffarabad District ..	1	1	..	..	..	..
III.—Frontier Districts	**33**	**6**	**3**	..	..	**24**
11. Ladakh District (including Mansar).	16	3	1	..	..	12
12. Gilgit „	17	3	2	..	..	12
Cities.						
13. Jammu	192	41	31	3	..	120
14. Srinagar	530	132	60	5	..	338

TABLE XVII.

Occupation or Means of Livelihood.

Jammu and Kashmir State Census, 1921.

DISTRICT, JAGIR, ILAQA OR CITY.	Order 49.—Instruction.						(*Group* 173).—*Professors and teachers of all kinds.*						*Group* (174).—*Clerks and servants connected with education.*					
	Total workers and dependents.	Actual Workers.				Dependents.	Total workers and dependents.	Actual Workers.				Dependents.	Total workers and dependents.	Actual Workers.				Dependents.
		Total.		*Partially Agriculturists.*				*Total.*		*Partially Agriculturists.*				*Total.*		*Partially Agriculturists.*		
		Males.	Females.	Males.	Females.			Males.	Females.	Males.	Females.			Males.	Females.	Males.	Females.	
	1298	1299	1300	1301	1302	1303	1304	1305	1306	1307	1308	1309	1310	1311	1312	1313	1314	1315
State ..	**1,337**	**1,337**	**52**	**89**	..	**2,185**	**3,125**	**1,125**	**43**	**71**	..	**1,957**	**449**	**212**	**9**	**18**	..	**228**
I.—Jammu Province (including *Jagirs.*)	**1,238**	**525**	**26**	**36**	..	**687**	**894**	**365**	**23**	**18**	..	**506**	**344**	**160**	**3**	**18**	..	**181**
1. Jammu District (including City)..	682	263	22	13	..	397	496	190	20	5	..	286	186	73	2	8	..	111
2. Kathua "	154	71	..	..	..	83	127	62	..	..	..	65	27	9	..	..	..	18
3. Udhampur " (including Chaneni *Jagir.*)	122	50	2	8	..	70	122	50	2	8	..	70	..	..	..	..	..	..
4. Riasi "	12	6	..	1	..	6	..	..	..	..	..	..	12	6	..	1	..	6
5. Mirpur "	179	79	1	3	..	99	115	40	1	2	..	74	64	39	..	1	..	25
6. Bhadarwah *Jagir*	30	17	1	5	..	12	..	..	..	..	..	..	30	17	1	5	..	12
7. Punch *Ilaqa*	59	39	..	6	..	20	34	23	..	3	..	11	25	16	..	3	..	9
II.—Kashmir Province (including *Jagirs*)	**2,231**	**746**	**24**	**47**	..	**1,461**	**2,146**	**714**	**18**	**47**	..	**1,414**	**85**	**32**	**6**	..	..	**47**
8. Kashmir North (including Langet *Jagir*).	398	137	4	19	..	257	391	133	4	19	..	254	7	4	..	..	..	3
9. Kashmir South (including City)..	1,770	576	19	24	..	1,175	1,704	555	13	24	..	1,136	66	21	6	..	..	39
10. Muzaffarabad District ..	63	33	1	4	..	29	51	26	1	4	..	24	12	7	..	..	..	5
III.—Frontier Districts	**105**	**66**	**2**	**6**	..	**37**	**85**	**46**	**2**	**6**	..	**37**	**20**	**20**	..	..	..	..
11. Ladakh District (including Mansar).	60	34	2	6	..	24	60	34	2	6	..	24	..	..	..	..	..	..
12. Gilgit "	45	32	..	..	..	13	25	12	..	..	..	13	20	20	..	..	..	..
Cities.																		
13. Jammu	288	127	15	2	..	146	285	125	15	2	..	145	3	2	..	..	..	1
14. Srinagar	1,397	441	19	14	..	937	1,331	420	13	14	..	898	66	21	6	..	..	39

TABLE XVII.

Occupation or Means of Livelihood.

Jammu and Kashmir State Census, 1921.

DISTRICT, JAGIR, ILAQA OR CITY.	Order 50—Letters and arts and sciences.						*Group* (175).—*Public scribes, stenographers, etc.*						*Group*(176)—*Architects, surveyors, engineers & their employés.*					
	Total workers and dependents.	Actual Workers. Total.		Actual Workers. Partially Agriculturists.		Dependents.	Total workers and dependents.	Actual Workers. Total.		Actual Workers. Partially Agriculturists.		Dependents.	Total workers and dependents.	Actual Workers. Total.		Actual Workers. Partially Agriculturists.		Dependents.
		Males.	Females.	Males.	Females.			Males.	Females.	Males.	Females.			Males.	Females.	Males.	Females.	
	1316	1317	1318	1319	1320	1321	1322	1323	1324	1325	1326	1327	1328	1329	1330	1331	1332	1333
State	**3,726**	**1,463**	**97**	**96**	**14**	**2,166**	**64**	**19**	—	**3**	—	**45**	**1,047**	**502**	..	**9**	..	**545**
I.—Jammu Province (**including** *Jagirs*).	**1,294**	**532**	**29**	**20**	..	**733**	**62**	**19**	..	**3**	..	**43**	**41**	**24**	..	**6**	..	**17**
1. Jammu District (including City)	377	186	7	2	..	184	41	6	..	..	..	35	1	1	..	..	..	..
2. Kathua „	349	120	11	2	..	218	1	1	..	..	..	..	15	10	..	1	..	5
3. Udhampur „ (including Chanebi *Jagir*).	141	64	3	6	..	74	18	11	..	3	..	7	2	1	..	..	..	1
4. Riasi „	20	6	..	..	..	14	..	..	..	..	..	..	..	..	..	..	..	..
5. Mirpur „	271	102	1	2	..	168	..	..	..	..	..	..	..	..	..	..	..	..
6. Bhadarwah *Jagir*	18	7	..	1	..	11	..	..	..	..	..	..	..	..	..	..	..	..
7. Punch *Ilaqa*	118	47	7	7	..	64	2	1	..	..	..	1	23	12	..	5	..	11
II.—Kashmir Province (**including** *Jagirs*).	**2,368**	**906**	**55**	**70**	**14**	**1,407**	..	..	..	..	..	..	**1,006**	**478**	..	**3**	..	**528**
8. Kashmir North (including Langet *Jagir*.)	1,018	383	11	39	7	624	..	..	..	..	..	..	394	199	..	..	..	195
9. Kashmir South (including City)	1,328	523	42	31	7	763	..	..	..	..	..	..	612	279	..	3	..	333
10. Muzaffarabad District ..	22	..	2	..	..	20	—	..	..	..	..	..	..	..	..	..	..	..
III.—Frontier Districts ..	**64**	**25**	**13**	**6**	..	**23**	**2**	..	..	..	..	**2**	..	..	..	..	..	..
11. Ladakh District (including Mansar).	62	25	13	6	..	24	..	..	..	..	..	..	..	..	..	..	..	..
12. Gilgit „	2	..	..	..	..	2	2	..	..	..	..	2	..	..	..	..	..	..
13. Jammu	244	126	7	..	..	111	..	..	..	..	..	..	..	..	..	..	..	..
14. Srinagar	535	161	20	3	..	354	..	..	..	..	..	..	151	31	..	3	..	120

TABLE XVII.

Occupation or Means of Livelihood.

Jammu and Kashmir State Census, 1921.

DISTRICT, JAGIR, ILAQA OR CITY.	Group (177).—*Authors, editors, journalists, artists, photographers, sculptors, astronomers, meteorologists botanists, astrologers, etc.* Total workers and dependents.	Actual Workers. Total. Males.	Actual Workers. Total. Females.	Actual Workers. Partially Agriculturists. Males.	Actual Workers. Partially Agriculturists. Females.	Dependents.	Group (178).—*Music composers and masters, players on all kinds of musical instruments (not military), singers, actors, and dancers.* Total workers and dependents.	Actual Workers. Total. Males.	Actual Workers. Total. Females.	Actual Workers. Partially Agriculturists. Males.	Actual Workers. Partially Agriculturists. Females.	Dependents.	Group (179).—*Conjurors, acrobats, fortune tellers, reciters, exhibitors of curiosities and wild animals.* Total workers and dependents.	Actual Workers. Total. Males.	Actual Workers. Total. Females.	Actual Workers. Partially Agriculturists. Males.	Actual Workers. Partially Agriculturists. Females.	Dependents.
	1334	1335	1336	1337	1338	1339	1340	1341	1342	1343	1344	1345	1346	1347	1348	1349	1350	1351
State ..	**490**	**219**	**2**	**4**	..	**269**	**1,699**	**590**	**79**	**79**	**14**	**1,030**	**426**	**133**	**16**	**1**	..	**277**
I.—Jammu Province (including *Jagirs*).	265	**142**	**1**	**4**	..	**122**	**502**	**216**	**12**	**6**	..	**274**	**424**	**131**	**16**	**1**	..	**277**
1. Jammu District (including City)	166	104	..	..	..	62	134	75	7	2	..	52	35	..	..	..	..	35
2. Kathua „	28	11	..	1	..	17	39	21	2	..	..	16	266	77	9	..	..	180
3. Udhampur „ (including Chaneni *Jagir*).	60	22	1	2	..	37	6	4	2	1	..	..	55	26	..	..	..	29
4. Riasi „	1	1	..	..	..	..	19	5	..	..	..	14	..	..	..	..	..	..
5. Mirpur „	5	3	..	1	..	2	266	99	1	1	..	166	..	..	..	..	..	..
6. Bhadarwah *Jagir*	5	1	..	..	..	4	13	6	..	1	..	7	..	..	..	..	..	..
7. Punch *Ilaqa*	..	..	..	..	..	..	25	6	..	1	..	19	63	28	7	1	..	33
II—Kashmir Province (including *Jagir*).	**221**	**74**	**1**	..	..	**146**	**1,139**	**352**	**54**	**67**	**14**	**733**	**2**	**2**	..	..	..	..
8. Kashmir North (including Langet *Jagir*).	31	10	..	..	..	21	591	172	11	33	7	408	2	2	..	..	..	..
9. Kashmir South (including City).	190	64	1	..	..	125	526	180	41	28	7	305	..	..	..	..	..	..
10. Muzaffarabad District ..	..	..	..	..	..	..	22	..	2	..	..	20	..	..	..	..	..	..
III.—Frontier Districts	**4**	**3**	..	..	..	**1**	**58**	**22**	**13**	6	..	**23**	..	..	..	..	..	..
11. Laddakh District (including Mansar.) „	4	3	..	..	..	1	58	22	13	**6**	..	23	..	..	..	..	..	..
12. Gilgit „	..	..	..	..	..	..	..	..	..	..	..	..	..	..	..	..	..	..
Cities.																		
13. Jammu	170	108	..	..	..	62	44	18	7	..	..	19	30	..	..	..	..	30
14. **Srinagar**	142	50	..	..	..	92	242	80	20	..	..	142	..	..	..	..	..	..

TABLE XVII.

Occupation or Means of Livelihood.

Jammu and Kashmir State Census, 1921.

DISTRICT, JAGIR, ILAQA OR CITY.	Class D.—Miscellaneous.						Sub-class IX.—Persons living on their income.						Order 51.—Persons living principally on their income.					
	Total workers and dependents.	Actual Workers. Total.		Actual Workers. Partially Agriculturists.		Dependents.	Total workers and dependents.	Actual Workers. Total.		Actual Workers. Partially Agriculturists.		Dependents.	Total workers and dependents.	Actual Workers. Total.		Actual Workers. Partially Agriculturists.		Dependents.
		Males.	Females.	Males.	Females.			Males.	Females.	Males.	Females.			Males.	Females.	Males.	Females.	
	1352	1353	1354	1355	1356	1357	1358	1359	1360	1361	1362	1363	1364	1365	1366	1367	1368	1369
State	**103,654**	**38,286**	**8,496**	**2,691**	**221**	**56,872**	**3,284**	**1,260**	**147**	**284**	**13**	**1,877**	**3,284**	**1,260**	**147**	**284**	**13**	**1,877**
I.—Jammu Province (including *Jagirs*).	**62,513**	**24,041**	**5,671**	**1,987**	**206**	**32,801**	**2,769**	**1,044**	**120**	**276**	**13**	**1,605**	**2,769**	**1,044**	**120**	**276**	**13**	**1,605**
1. Jammu District (including City).	27,614	9,867	1,785	571	61	15,362	1,692	653	85	135	5	1,154	1,892	653	85	135	5	1,154
2. Kathua "	7,578	2,423	925	286	21	4,230	379	134	6	70	..	239	379	134	6	70	..	239
3. Udhampur " (including Chaneni *Jagir*).	7,251	3,455	967	421	50	2,329	91	37	2	14	..	52	91	37	2	14	..	52
4. Riasi "	5,543	2,547	666	186	35	2,330	60	33	5	3	..	22	60	33	5	3	..	22
5. Mirpur "	8,663	2,773	843	172	19	5,047	153	59	21	9	7	73	153	59	21	9	7	73
6. Bhadarwah *Jagir*	1,056	659	174	63	1	223	3	3	..	2	..	..	3	3	..	2	..	..
7. Punch *Ilaqa*	4,808	2,317	311	288	19	2,180	191	125	1	43	1	65	191	125	1	43	1	65
II.—Kashmir Province (including *Jagirs*).	**38,355**	**12,797**	**1,881**	**665**	**12**	**23,877**	**487**	**213**	**27**	**8**	..	**247**	**487**	**213**	**27**	**8**	..	**247**
8. Kashmir North (including Langet *Jagir*).	9,965	3,558	463	297	2	5,944	62	17	1	8	..	44	62	17	1	8	..	44
9. Kashmir South (including City.)	27,273	8,957	1,196	358	10	17,120	420	195	26	..	..	199	420	195	26	..	..	199
10. Muzaffarabad District ..	1,117	282	222	10	..	613	5	1	..	..	..	4	5	1	..	..	..	4
III.—Frontier Districts ..	**2,786**	**1,448**	**944**	**39**	**3**	**394**	**28**	**3**	..	..	..	**25**	**28**	**3**	..	..	..	**25**
11. Ladakh District (including Mansar).	2,357	1,129	908	26	3	320	6	3	..	..	..	3	6	3	..	..	..	3
12. Gilgit " ..	429	319	36	13	..	74	22	..	..	..	..	22	22	..	..	..	..	22
Cities																		
13. Jammu	9,383	3,810	664	88	14	4,909	739	396	61	29	2	282	739	396	61	29	2	282
14. Srinagar	15,582	4,499	644	14	8	10,439	369	178	21	..	..	170	369	178	21	..	..	170

TABLE XVII.

Occupation or Means of Livelihood.

Jammu and Kashmir State Census, 1921.

DISTRICT, JAGIR, ILAQA OR CITY.	Group (150).—*Proprietors (other than of agricultural land) Fund and Scholarship-holders and Pensioners.*						Sub-class X—Domestic Service.						Order 52—Domestic Service.					
	Total workers and dependents.	Actual Workers.				Dependents.	Total workers and dependents.	Actual Workers.				Dependents.	Total workers and dependents.	Actual Workers.				Dependents.
		Total.		*Partially Agriculturists.*				*Total.*		*Partially Agriculturists.*				*Total.*		*Partially Agriculturists.*		
		Males.	Females.	Males.	Females.			Males.	Females.	Males.	Females.			Males.	Females.	Males.	Females.	
	1370	1371	1372	1373	1374	1375	1376	1377	1378	1379	1380	1381	1382	1383	1384	1385	1386	1387
State ..	**3,284**	**1,260**	**147**	**284**	**13**	**1,877**	**38,470**	**16,677**	**3,827**	**698**	**52**	**17,966**	**38,470**	**16,677**	**3,827**	**698**	**52**	**17,966**
I.—Jammu Province (including *Jagirs*).	**2,769**	**1,044**	**120**	**276**	**13**	**1,605**	**19,535**	**8,556**	**2,184**	**433**	**47**	**8,795**	**19,535**	**8,556**	**2,184**	**433**	**47**	**8,795**
1. Jammu District (including City).	1,892	653	85	135	5	1,154	9,461	3,317	652	120	11	5,492	9,461	3,317	652	120	11	5,492
2. Kathua " ..	379	134	6	70	..	239	1,955	712	550	18	1	693	1,955	712	550	18	1	693
3. Udhampur " (including Chaneni *Jagir*). "	91	37	2	14	..	52	2,670	1,195	542	89	22	933	2,670	1,195	542	89	22	933
4. Riasi " ..	60	33	5	3	..	22	1,631	1,256	93	59	4	282	1,631	1,256	93	59	4	282
5. Mirpur " ..	153	49	21	9	7	73	1,642	828	183	28	2	631	1,642	828	183	28	2	631
6. Bhadarwah *Jagir* ..	3	3	..	2	..	..	507	341	103	9	..	63	507	341	103	9	..	63
7. Punch *Ilaqa* ..	191	125	1	43	1	65	1,669	907	61	110	7	701	1,669	907	61	110	7	701
II.—Kashmir Province (including *Jagirs*).	**487**	**213**	**27**	**8**	...	**247**	**16,456**	**6,812**	**774**	**238**	**2**	**8,870**	**16,456**	**6,812**	**774**	**238**	**2**	**8,870**
8. Kashmir North (including Langet *Jagir*.	62	17	1	8	..	44	3,549	1,654	63	116	..	1,832	3,549	1,654	63	116	..	1,832
9. Kashmir South (including City)..	420	195	26	..	..	199	12,320	5,035	543	116	2	6,742	12,320	5,035	543	116	2	6,742
10. Muzaffarabad District ..	5	1	..	..	..	4	587	123	168	6	..	296	587	123	168	6	..	296
III.—Frontier Districts ..	**28**	**3**	..	..	..	**25**	**2,479**	**1,309**	**869**	**27**	**3**	**301**	**2,479**	**1,309**	**869**	**27**	**3**	**301**
11. Ladakh District (including Mansar).	6	3	..	..	..	3	2,185	1,076	839	19	3	270	2,185	1,076	839	19	3	270
12. Gilgit " ..	22	..	..	..	..	22	294	233	30	8	..	31	294	233	30	8	..	31
Cities																		
13. Jammu ..	739	396	61	29	2	282	4,658	1,808	248	47	9	2,602	4,658	1,808	248	47	9	2,602
14. Srinagar ..	369	178	21	—	..	170	6,958	2,078	284	6	..	3,996	6,958	2,678	284	6	..	3,066

TABLE XVII.

Occupation or Means of Livelihood.

Jammu and Kashmir State Census, 1921.

DISTRICT, JAGIR, ILAQA OR CITY.	Group (181) —Cooks, Water-carriers, Door-keepers, Watchmen other indoor Servants.					
	Total workers and dependents.	Actual Workers. Total. Males.	Actual Workers. Total. Females.	Actual Workers. Partially Agriculturists. Males.	Actual Workers. Partially Agriculturists. Females.	Dependents.
	1388	1389	1390	1391	1392	1393
State ..	**37,374**	**16,128**	**3,740**	**685**	**52**	**17,506**
I.—Jammu Province (including *Jagirs*).	**19,355**	**8,445**	**2,184**	**425**	**47**	**8,726**
1. Jammu District (including City).	9,319	3,227	652	116	11	5,440
2. Kathua " ..	1,953	711	550	18	1	692
3. Udhampur " (including Chaneni *Jagir*).	2,670	1,195	542	89	22	933
4. Rias " ..	1,631	1,256	93	59	4	232
5. Mirpur " ..	1,620	816	183	24	2	621
6. Bhadarwah *Jagir* ..	507	341	103	9	–	63
7. Punch *Ilaqa* ..	1,655	899	61	110	7	695
II.—Kashmir Province (including *Jagirs*).	**15,701**	**6,449**	**748**	**233**	**2**	**8,504**
8. Kashmir North (including Langet *Jagir*).	3,378	1,579	62	113	..	1,737
9. Kashmir South (including City).	11,736	4,747	518	114	2	6,471
10. Muzaffarabad District ..	587	123	168	6	..	296
III.—Frontier Districts ..	**2,318**	**1,234**	**808**	**27**	**3**	**276**
11. Ladakh District (including Manser).	2,081	1,058	778	19	3	245
12. Gilgit " ..	237	176	30	8	–	31
Cities						
13. Jammu ..	4,634	1,800	248	47	9	2,886
14. Srinagar ..	6,472	2,438	274	6	..	3,760

DISTRICT, JAGIR, ILAQA OR CITY.	Group (182).—Private Grooms, Coachmen, Dog, Boys, etc.					
	Total workers and dependents.	Actual Workers. Total. Males.	Actual Workers. Total. Females.	Actual Workers. Partially Agriculturists. Males.	Actual Workers. Partially Agriculturists. Females.	Dependents.
	1394	1395	1396	1397	1398	1399
State ..	**963**	**446**	**87**	**12**	...	**433**
I.—Jammu Province (including *Jagirs*).	**145**	**101**	..	**6**	..	**44**
1. Jammu District (including City).	118	82	..	4	..	36
2. Kathua " ..	2	1	..	..	..	1
3. Udhampur " (including Chaneni *Jagir*).	..	..	..	..	..	..
4. Rias " ..	..	..	..	..	..	..
5. Mirpur " ..	11	10	..	4	..	1
6. Bhadarwah *Jagir* ..	..	..	..	..	..	..
7. Punch *Ilaqa* ..	14	8	..	..	..	6
II.—Kashmir Province (including *Jagirs*).	**717**	**327**	**26**	**4**	..	**364**
8. Kashmir North (including Langet *Jagir*).	165	71	1	2	..	93
9. Kashmir South (including City).	552	256	25	2	..	271
10. Muzaffarabad District ..	..	..	..	..	..	..
III.—Frontier Districts ..	**104**	**18**	**61**	..	..	**25**
11. Ladakh District (including Manser).	104	18	61	..	..	25
12. Gilgit " ..	..	..	..	..	..	..
Cities						
13. Jammu ..	..	..	..	..	..	..
14. Srinagar ..	454	208	10	..	..	236

DISTRICT, JAGIR, ILAQA OR CITY.	Group (183).—Private Motor Drivers and Cleaners.					
	Total workers and dependents.	Actual Workers. Total. Males.	Actual Workers. Total. Females.	Actual Workers. Partially Agriculturists. Males.	Actual Workers. Partially Agriculturists. Females.	Dependents.
	1400	1401	1402	1403	1404	1405
State ..	**130**	**103**	..	**1**	..	**27**
I.—Jammu Province (including *Jagirs*).	**35**	**10**	..	..	..	**25**
1. Jammu District (including City).	24	8	..	..	..	16
2. Kathua " ..	..	..	..	..	..	..
3. Udhampur " (including Chaneni *Jagir*).	..	..	..	..	..	..
4. Rias " ..	..	..	..	..	..	..
5. Mirpur " ..	11	2	..	..	..	..
6. Bhadarwah *Jagir* ..	..	..	..	..	..	..
7. Punch *Ilaqa* ..	..	..	..	..	..	..
II.—Kashmir Province (including *Jagirs*).	**38**	**36**	..	**1**	..	**2**
8. Kashmir North (including Langet *Jagir*).	6	4	..	1	..	2
9. Kashmir South (including City).	32	32	..	..	..	..
10. Muzaffarabad District ..	..	..	..	..	..	..
III.—Frontier Districts ..	**57**	**57**	..	..	..	..
11. Ladakh District (including Manser).	..	..	..	..	..	..
12. Gilgit " ..	57	57	..	..	..	..
Cities						
13. Jammu ..	24	8	..	..	..	16
14. Srinagar ..	32	32	..	..	..	..

TABLE XVII.

OCCUPATION OR MEANS OF LIVELIHOOD.

Jammu and Kashmir State Census, 1921.

DISTRICT, JAGIR, ILAQA OR CITY.	Sub-class XI.—Insufficiently described occupations.						Order 53.—General terms which do not indicate a definite occupation.						Group (184).—*Manufacturers, Businessmen and Contractors, otherwise unspecified.*					
	Total workers and dependents.	ACTUAL WORKERS.				Dependents.	Total workers and dependents.	ACTUAL WORKERS.				Dependents.	Total workers and dependents.	ACTUAL WORKERS.				Dependents.
		Total.		*Partially Agriculturists.*				*Total.*		*Partially Agriculturists.*				*Total.*		*Partially Agriculturists.*		
		Males.	Females.	Males.	Females.			Males.	Females.	Males.	Females.			Males.	Females.	Males.	Females.	
	1406	1407	1408	1409	1410	1411	1412	1413	1414	1415	1416	1417	1418	1419	1420	1421	1422	1423
State ..	**41,123**	**12,330**	**2,498**	**1,177**	**110**	**26,295**	**41,123**	**12,330**	**2,433**	**1,177**	**110**	**26,295**	**566**	**230**	**1**	**30**	..	**335**
I.—Jammu Province (including *Jagirs*).	**23,951**	**7,951**	**1,827**	**895**	**101**	**14,173**	**23,951**	**7,951**	**1,827**	**895**	**101**	**14,173**	**465**	**195**	**1**	**29**	..	**269**
1. Jammu District (including City).	10,619	3,419	737	191	44	6,463	10,619	3,419	737	191	44	6,463	91	37	..	1	..	54
2. Kathua " ..	3,010	705	171	100	8	2,134	3,010	705	171	100	8	2,134	42	7	..	..	..	35
3. Udhampur " (including Chaneni *Jagir*). "	3,238	1,649	274	288	24	1,305	3,228	1,649	274	288	24	1,305	138	69	1	9	..	68
4. Riasi " ..	1,847	507	290	71	19	1,050	1,847	507	290	71	19	1,050	65	25	..	2	..	40
5. Mirpur " ..	3,279	780	228	98	3	2,271	3,279	780	228	98	3	2,271	60	8	..	1	..	52
6. Bhadarwah *Jagir* ..	309	195	34	43	1	80	309	195	34	43	1	80	7	5	..	1	..	2
7. Punch *Ilaqa* ..	1,659	696	93	104	2	870	1,659	696	93	104	2	870	62	44	..	15	..	18
II.—Kashmir Province (including *Jagirs*.)	**16,907**	**4,248**	**601**	**272**	**9**	**12,058**	**16,907**	**4,248**	**601**	**272**	**9**	**12,058**	**90**	**28**	..	..	..	**62**
8. Kashmir North (including Langet *Jagir*.)	4,687	1,456	250	101	1	2,981	4,687	1,456	250	101	1	2,981	37	18	..	..	..	19
9. Kashmir South (including City.	11,854	2,662	340	167	8	8,852	11,854	2,662	340	167	8	8,852	13	1	..	..	..	12
10. Muzaffarabad District	366	130	11	4	..	225	366	130	11	4	..	225	40	9	..	..	..	31
III.—Frontier Districts ..	**265**	**131**	**70**	**10**	..	**64**	**265**	**131**	**70**	**10**	..	**64**	**11**	**7**	..	**1**	..	
11. Ladakh District (including Mansar).	154	47	64	5	..	43	154	47	64	5	..	43	11	7	..	1	..	4
12. Gilgit " ..	111	84	6	5	..	21	111	84	6	5	..	21	..	..	..	..	..	..
Cities																		
13. Jammu ..	2,963	1,073	251	10	2	1,639	2,963	1,073	251	10	2	1,639	..	19	..	..	..	36
14. Srinagar ..	7,376	1,229	139	8	8	6,008	7,376	1,229	139	8	8	6,008	55	..	..	..	..	...

TABLE XVII.

Occupation or Means of Livelihood.

Jammu and Kashmir State Census, 1921.

District, Jagir, Ilaqa or City.	Group (185).—*Cashiers, Accountants, Book-keepers, Clerks, and other employés in unspecified Offices, Ware-houses and Shops.*						Group (186).—*Mechanics otherwise unspecified.*						Group (187).—*Labourers and Workmen otherwise unspecified.*					
	Total workers and dependents.	Actual Workers. Total. Males.	Actual Workers. Total. Females.	Actual Workers. Partially Agriculturists. Males.	Actual Workers. Partially Agriculturists. Females.	Dependents.	Total workers and dependents.	Actual Workers. Total. Males.	Actual Workers. Total. Females.	Actual Workers. Partially Agriculturists. Males.	Actual Workers. Partially Agriculturists. Females.	Dependents.	Total workers and dependents.	Actual Workers. Total. Males.	Actual Workers. Total. Females.	Actual Workers. Partially Agriculturists. Males.	Actual Workers. Partially Agriculturists. Females.	Dependents.
	1424	1425	1426	1427	1428	1429	1430	1431	1432	1433	1434	1435	1436	1437	1438	1439	1440	1441
State, ..	**120**	**58**	**3**	**7**	**1**	**59**	**4,887**	**1,563**	**131**	**223**	**13**	**3,193**	**35,550**	**10,479**	**2,363**	**917**	**96**	**22,708**
I.—Jammu Province (including Jagirs)	**91**	**53**	**3**	**7**	**1**	**35**	**4,810**	**1,557**	**126**	**223**	**13**	**3,127**	**18,585**	**6,146**	**1,697**	**636**	**87**	**10,742**
1. Jammu District (including City).	12	7	..	..	..	5	1,086	496	14	36	..	576	9,430	2,879	723	154	44	5,328
2. Kathua „	23	9	3	..	1	11	917	296	13	66	3	608	2,028	393	155	34	4	1,480
3. Udhampur „ (including Chaneni *Jagir*).	26	12	..	4	..	14	885	344	18	47	1	523	2,17[illegible]	1,224	255	228	23	700
4. Riasi District	..	..	..	..	..	..	227	11	43	1	6	173	1,555	471	247	68	13	837
5. Mirpur „	2	1	..	..	..	1	1,296	268	34	45	3	94	1,921	503	194	52	..	1,224
6. Bhadarwah *Jagir*	26	22	..	3	..	4	6	6	..	..	..	..	270	162	34	39	1	74
7. Punch *Ilaqa*	2	2	..	..	..	..	393	136	4	28	..	253	1,202	514	89	61	2	599
II.—Kashmir Province (including Jagirs).	**29**	**5**	..	..	..	**24**	**73**	**2**	**5**	..	..	**66**	**16,715**	**4,213**	**596**	**272**	**9**	**11,906**
8. Kashmir North (including Langet Jagir.)	..	..	..	..	..	..	73	2	5	..	..	66	4,577	1,436	245	101	1	2,896
9. Kashmir South (including City).	24	..	..	..	..	24	..	..	..	..	..	..	11,817	2,661	340	167	8	8,816
10. Muzaffarabad District ..	5	5	..	..	..	..	..	..	..	..	..	..	321	116	11	4	..	194
III.—Frontier Districts	..	..	..	..	..	..	**4**	**4**	..	..	..	..	**250**	**120**	**70**	**9**	..	**60**
11. Ladakh District (including Mansar.)	..	..	..	..	..	..	..	..	..	..	..	..	143	40	64	4	..	39
12. Gilgit „	..	..	..	..	..	..	4	4	..	..	..	..	107	80	6	5	..	21
Cities.																		
13. Jammu	..	..	..	..	..	..	80	43	7	..	..	39	2,819	1,011	244	10	2	1,564
14. Srinagar	..	..	..	..	..	..	..	..	..	..	..	..	7,376	1,229	139	8	8	6,008

TABLE XVII.

Occupation or Means of Livelihood.

Jammu and Kashmir State Census, 1921.

DISTRICT, JAGIR, ILAQA OR CITY.	Sub-class XII.—Unproductive.						Order 54.—Inmates of Jails, Asylums and Alms houses.						Group (188).—Inmates of Jails, Asylums, and Alms houses.						Order 55—Beggars, Vagrants, Prostitutes.					
	Total workers and dependents.	Actual Workers. Total. Males.	Actual Workers. Total. Females.	Actual Workers. Partially Agriculturists. Males.	Actual Workers. Partially Agriculturists. Females.	Dependents.	Total workers and dependents.	Actual Workers. Total. Males.	Actual Workers. Total. Females.	Actual Workers. Partially Agriculturists. Males.	Actual Workers. Partially Agriculturists. Females.	Dependents.	Total workers and dependents.	Actual Workers. Total. Males.	Actual Workers. Total. Females.	Actual Workers. Partially Agriculturists. Males.	Actual Workers. Partially Agriculturists. Females.	Dependents.	Total workers and dependents.	Actual Workers. Total. Males	Actual Workers. Total. Females.	Actual Workers. Partially Agriculturists. Males.	Actual Workers. Partially Agriculturists. Females.	Dependents.
	1442	1443	1444	1445	1446	1447	1448	1449	1450	1451	1452	1453	1454	1455	1456	1457	1458	1459	1460	1461	1462	1463	1464	1465
State ...	**20,777**	**8,019**	**2,024**	**532**	**46**	**10,734**	**246**	**240**	**6**	**2**	...	...	**246**	**240**	**6**	**2**	..	...	**20,529**	**7,779**	**2,018**	**530**	**46**	**10,732**
I.—Jammu Province (including *Jagirs*).	**16,258**	**6,490**	**1,540**	**383**	**45**	**8,228**	**188**	**188**	..	..	..	..	**188**	**188**	..	..	..	...	**16,068**	**6,302**	**1,540**	**383**	**45**	**8,226**
1. Jammu District (including City).	5,642	2,478	311	125	1	2,853	185	185	..	..	..	..	185	185	..	..	..	..	5,457	2,293	311	125	1	2,853
2. Kathua " ..	2,234	872	198	98	12	1,164	..	..	..	..	..	..	..	..	..	..	..	..	2,232	872	198	98	12	1,162
3. Udhampur " (including Chaneni *Jagir*).	1,262	574	149	30	4	539	..	..	..	..	..	..	..	..	..	..	..	..	1,262	574	149	30	4	539
4. Riasi District	2,005	751	278	53	12	976	..	..	..	..	..	..	..	..	..	..	..	..	2,005	751	278	53	12	976
5. Mirpur "	3,589	1,106	411	37	7	2,072	..	..	..	..	..	..	..	..	..	..	..	..	3,589	1,106	411	37	7	2,072
6. Bhadarwah *Jagir*	237	120	37	9	..	80	3	3	..	..	..	..	3	3	..	..	..	..	234	117	37	9	..	80
7. Punch *Ilaqa*	1,289	589	156	31	9	544	..	..	..	..	..	..	..	..	..	..	..	..	1,289	589	156	31	9	544
II.—Kashmir Province (including *Jagirs*),	**4,505**	**1,524**	**479**	**147**	**1**	**2,502**	**55**	**49**	**6**	..	..	..	**55**	**49**	**6**	..	..	..	**4,450**	**1,475**	**473**	**147**	**1**	**2,502**
8. Kashmir North (including Langet *Jagir*).	1,667	431	149	72	1	1,087	39	33	6	..	..	..	39	33	6	..	..	..	1,628	398	143	72	1	1,087
9. Kashmir South (including City).	2,679	1,065	287	75	..	1,327	16	16	..	..	..	..	16	16	..	..	..	..	2,663	1,049	287	75	..	1,327
10. Muzaffarabad District ..	159	28	43	..	..	88	..	..	..	..	..	..	..	..	..	..	..	..	159	28	43	..	..	88
III.—Frontier Districts	**14**	**5**	**5**	**2**	..	**4**	**3**	**3**	..	**2**	..	..	**3**	**3**	..	**2**	..	..	**11**	**2**	**5**	..	..	**4**
11. Ladakh District (including Mansar.)	12	3	5	2	..	4	3	3	..	2	..	..	3	3	..	2	..	..	9	..	5	..	..	4
12. Gilgit " ..	2	2	..	..	..	..	..	..	..	..	..	..	..		..	..	..	..	2	2	..	..	..	..
Cities.																								
13. Jammu.	1,023	533	104	2	1	386	185	185	..	..	..	..	185	185	..	..	..	..	838	348	104	2	1	386
14. Srinagar	879	414	200	..	..	265	1	1	..	..	..	..	1		..	..	..	..	878	413	200	..	..	265

TABLE XVII.

Occupation or Means of Livelihood.

Jammu and Kashmir State Census, 1921.

DISTRICT, JAGIR, ILAQA OR CITY.	Group (189). *Beggars, Vagrants, Witches, Wizards, etc.*						Group (190).—*Procurers and Prostitutes.*					
	Total workers and dependents.	Actual Workers. Total.		Actual Workers. Partially Agriculturists.		Dependents.	Total workers and dependents.	Actual Workers. Total.		Actual Workers. Partially Agriculturists.		Dependents.
		Males.	Females.	Males.	Females.			Males.	Females.	Males	Females.	
	1466	1467	1468	1469	1470	1471	1472	1473	1474	1475	1476	1477
State ...	**19,959**	**7,616**	**1,769**	**530**	**46**	**10,574**	**570**	**163**	**249**	...	...	**158**
I.—Jammu Province (including *Jagirs*).	**16,003**	**6,302**	**1,486**	**383**	**45**	**8,215**	**65**	..	**54**	..	...	**11**
1. Jammu District (including City).	5,420	2,293	285	125	1	2,842	37	..	26	..	..	11
2. Kathua "	2,232	872	198	98	12	1,162	..	..	..	..	..	..
3. Udhampur " (including Chaneni *Jagir*).	1,262	574	149	30	4	539	..	..	..	..	..	..
4. Riasi District	2,005	751	278	53	12	976	..	..	..	..	..	..
5. Mirpur "	3,561	1,106	383	37	7	2,072	28	..	28	..	..	..
6. Bhadarwah *Jagir* ..	234	117	37	9	..	80	..	..	..	..	..	..
7. Punch *Ilaqa*	1,289	589	156	31	9	544	..	..	..	..	..	..
II.—Kashmir Province (including *Jagirs*).	**945**	**1,312**	**278**	**147**	**1**	**2,355**	**505**	**163**	**195**	..	..	**147**
8. Kashmir North (including Langet *Jagir*).	585	386	128	72	1	1,071	43	12	15	..	..	16
9. Kashmir South (including City)	2,201	898	107	75	..	1,196	462	151	180	..	..	131
10. Muzaffarabad District ..	159	28	43	..	..	88	..	..	..	..	..	..
III.—Frontier Districts ..	**11**	**2**	**5**	..	..	**4**	..	..	..	..	..	..
11. Ladakh District (including Mansar).	9	..	5	..	..	4	..	..	..	..	..	..
12. Gilgit District	2	2	..	..	..	..	..	..	..	..	..	..
Cities.												
13. Jammu	801	348	78	2	1	375	37	..	26	..	..	11
14. Srinagar	445	268	30	..	..	147	433	145	170	..	..	118

DISTRICT, JAGIR, ILAQA OR CITY.	**Order 56.—Other unclassified non-productive Industries.**						Group (191).—*Other unclassified non-productive Industries.*					
	Total workers and dependents	Actual Workers. Total.		Actual Workers. Partially Agriculturists.		Dependents.	Total workers and dependents	Actual Workers. Total.		Actual Workers. Partially Agriculturists.		Dependents.
		Males.	Females.	Males.	Females.			Males.	Females.	Males.	Females.	
	1478	1479	1480	1481	1482	1483	1484	1485	1486	1487	1488	1489
State ...	**2**	..	..	..	..	**2**	**2**	..	..	..	..	**2**
I.—Jammu Province (including *Jagirs*).	**2**	..	..	..	..	**2**	**2**	..	..	..	..	**2**
1. Jammu District (including City).	2	..	..	..	..	2	2	..	..	..	..	2
2. Kathua "	..	..	..	..	..	..	..	..	..	..	..	..
3. Udhampur " (including Chaneni *Jagir*).	..	..	..	..	..	..	..	..	..	..	..	..
4. Riasi District	..	..	..	..	..	..	..	..	..	..	..	..
5. Mirpur "	..	..	..	..	..	..	..	..	..	..	..	..
6. Bhadarwah *Jagir* ..	..	..	..	..	..	..	..	..	..	..	..	..
7. Punch *Ilaqa*	..	..	..	..	..	..	..	..	..	..	..	..
II.—Kashmir Province (including *Jagirs*).	..	..	..	..	..	..	..	..	..	..	..	..
8. Kashmir North (including Langet *Jagir*).	..	..	..	..	..	..	..	..	..	..	..	..
9. Kashmir South (including City)	..	..	..	..	..	..	..	..	..	..	..	..
10. Muzaffarabad District ..	..	..	..	..	..	..	..	..	..	..	..	..
III.—Frontier Districts ..	..	..	..	..	...	..	..	..	..	..	..	..
11. Ladakh District (including Mansar).	..	..	..	..	..	..	..	..	..	..	..	..
12. Gilgit District	..	..	..	..	..	..	..	..	..	..	..	..
Cities.												
13. Jammu	..	..	..	..	..	..	..	..	..	..	..	..
14. Srinagar	..	..	..	..	..	..	..	..	..	..	..	..

TABLE XVIII.

SUBSIDIARY OCCUPATIONS OF AGRICULTURISTS.

Jammu and Kashmir State Census, 1921.

This table is divided into three parts :—

(1) Subsidiary Occupations of Rent-Receivers.
(2) " " " Rent-Payers.
(3) " " " Agricultural labourers.

TABLE XVIII.

SUBSIDIARY OCCUPATIONS OF AGRICULTURISTS—ACTUAL WORKERS ONLY.

(1)—Rent Receivers.

Jammu and Kashmir State Census, 1921.

DISTRICT, JAGIR, ILAQA, OR CITY.	Total number of rent receivers (actual workers) — Males.	Total number of rent receivers (actual workers) — Females.	Number of actual workers who returned subsidiary occupations — Agriculturists — Males.	Agriculturists — Females.	Non-Agriculturists — Males.	Non-Agriculturists — Females	Details of subsidiary occupations returned — Rent payers — Males.	Rent payers — Females.	Agricultural Labourers — Males.	Agricultural Labourers — Females.	Government servants of all kinds — Males.	Government servants of all kinds — Females.	Money-lenders and grain-dealers — Males.	Money-lenders and grain-dealers — Females.	Other traders of all kinds — Males.	Other traders of all kinds — Females.	Priests — Males.	Priests — Females.	Clerks of all kinds — Males.	Clerks of all kinds — Females.	School-masters — Males.	School-masters — Females.	Lawyers — Males.	Lawyers — Females.	Estate agents and managers — Males.	Estate agents and managers — Females.	Medical Practitioners — Males.	Medical Practitioners — Females.	Artisans — Males.	Artisans — Females.	Others — Males.	Others — Females.
1	2	3	4	5	6	7	8	9	10	11	12	13	14	15	16	17	18	19	20	21	22	23	24	25	26	27	28	29	30	31	32	33
State ..	**20,130**	**9,336**	**1,490**	**272**	**3,316**	**662**	**1,436**	**266**	**54**	**6**	**328**	**34**	**175**	**6**	**328**	**29**	**218**	**28**	**39**	**1**	**35**	..	**10**	**3**	**1**	..	**10**	**1**	**319**	**28**	**1,349**	**136**
I—Jammu Province (including Jagirs).	**14,330**	**7,212**	**1,023**	**189**	**2,229**	**217**	**970**	**186**	**53**	**3**	**659**	**34**	**151**	**6**	**195**	**21**	**133**	**26**	**14**	..	**28**	..	**10**	**2**	..	..	**5**	..	**249**	**26**	**785**	**102**
1 Jammu District	2,953	726	171	25	404	82	168	24	3	1	154	28	21	1	32	10	23	14	..	..	7	..	..	..	..	..	2	..	114	5	51	24
2. Kathua „	2,072	691	336	48	183	26	385	48	1	..	21	1	8	1	12	..	22	3	..	..	..	..	..	..	...	..	2	..	18	12	100	9
3. Udhampur „	4,177	1,830	194	83	508	29	171	81	23	2	104	1	15	1	29	..	25	1	..	..	2	..	..	..	..	..	..	..	37	1	296	25
4. Riasi „	3,956	2,465	191	18	740	47	188	18	3	..	267	1	29	..	84	8	45	2	4	..	18	..	9	2	..	..	1	..	52	8	231	26
5. Mirpur „	737	616	44	14	177	26	39	14	5	..	65	2	9	3	27	3	6	2	5	..	1	..	1	..	..	..	..	..	10	..	53	16
6. Bhadarwah Jagir	43	30	7	1	19	..	7	1	..	..	9	..	..	..	1	..	2	..	1	..	..	..	..	..	..	—	..	...	1	..	5	..
7. Punch Ilaqa	1,292	854	30	..	198	7	12	..	18	..	39	1	69	..	10	..	10	4	4	..	..	..	..	—	..	..	..	..	17	..	49	2
II—Kashmir Province (including Jagirs.)	**5,540**	**1,833**	**441**	**68**	**1,060**	**42**	**449**	**65**	**1**	**3**	**164**	..	**24**	..	**133**	**8**	**77**	**2**	**24**	**1**	**7**	..	..	**1**	**1**	..	**5**	**1**	**67**	**2**	**558**	**27**
8. Kashmir North	1,540	408	79	13	249	14	79	12	..	1	31	..	8	..	23	8	8	1	14	..	2	..	..	..	..	..	1	1	8	...	154	4
9. Kashmir South	3,209	1,384	360	47	696	24	359	47	1	..	127	..	12	..	109	..	66	1	10	..	2	..	..	..	..	..	3	..	58	1	309	22
10. Muzaffarabad District ..	791	41	2	8	115	4	2	6	..	2	6	..	4	—	1	..	3	..	..	1	3	..	..	1	1	..	1	..	1	1	95	1
III—Frontier Districts	**260**	**291**	**26**	**15**	**27**	**7**	**26**	**15**	..	..	**9**	..	..	..	..	..	**8**	..	**1**	..	..	...	..	..	..	..	..	..	**3**	..	**6**	**7**
11. Ladakh District	203	288	26	15	24	7	26	15	..	..	6	..	..	..	..	..	8	...	1	..	..	..	..	..	..	..	..	..	3	..	6	7
12. Gilgit „	57	3	..	..	3	..	..	..	..	..	3	..	..	..	...	..	..	..	..	..	..	..	..	..	...	..	..	..	..	..	..	..
Cities																																
14. Jammu	346	9	3	..	37	4	2	..	1	..	11	..	2	..	7	..	3	..	..	..	4	..	..	..	..	..	..	..	1	..	9	4
13. Srinagar	250	6	2	2	63	..	2	2	..	..	46	..	..	..	2	..	4	..	..	..	..	..	..	..	..	..	..	..	..	..	11	..

TABLE XVIII.

SUBSIDIARY OCCUPATIONS OF AGRICULTURISTS—ACTUAL WORKERS ONLY.

(2) Rent-payers.

Jammu and Kashmir State Census, 1921.

DISTRICT, JAGIR, ILAQA, OR CITY.	TOTAL NUMBER OF RENT-PAYERS, (ACTUAL WORKERS.)		NUMBER OF ACTUAL WORKERS WHO RETURNED SUBSIDIARY OCCUPATIONS.				DETAILS OF SUBSIDIARY OCCUPATIONS RETURNED.											
			Agriculturists.		*Non-Agriculturists.*		*Rent receivers.*		*Agricultural labourers.*		*General labourers.*		*Government servants of all kinds.*		*Money lenders and grain dealers.*		*Other traders of all kinds.*	
	Males.	Females.	Males.	Females.	Males.	Females.	Males.	Females.	Males.	Females.	Males.	Females.	Males.	Females.	Males.	Females.	Males.	Females.
1	2	3	4	5	6	7	8	9	10	11	12	13	14	15	16	17	18	19
State ..	**683,381**	**248,659**	**4,365**	**524**	**81,148**	**3,445**	**3,948**	**490**	**417**	**34**	**9,549**	**237**	**5,112**	**123**	**1,068**	**23**	**4,753**	**207**
I—Jammu Province (including Jagirs).	**322,476**	**55,696**	**2,667**	**303**	**37,170**	**1,753**	**2,324**	**269**	**343**	**34**	**6,631**	**165**	**2,989**	**105**	**854**	**20**	**1,351**	**58**
1. Jammu District	49,498	2,996	625	31	5,240	109	490	20	126	11	735	12	541	26	147	2	227	9
2. Kathua "	32,833	13,975	830	41	2,729	130	796	36	34	5	195	6	83	3	31	..	43	2
3. Udhampur "	52,549	18,095	496	179	6,246	633	461	168	35	11	2,007	82	476	17	164	2	166	5
4. Riasi "	43,400	8,477	220	15	4,247	233	210	11	10	4	191	9	264	4	190	10	138	5
5. Mirpur "	73,209	4,676	327	26	9,450	271	239	26	88	..	1,454	31	963	48	229	2	480	6
6. Bhadarwah Jagir ...	10,846	5,095	28	4	1,810	258	28	4	..	..	392	14	230	4	6	..	128	29
7. Punch Ilaqa	60,141	2,382	141	7	7,448	110	91	4	50	3	1,707	11	432	3	87	4	169	2
II—Kashmir Province (including Jagirs).	**299,960**	**135,094**	**1,187**	**109**	**37,154**	**1,405**	**1,136**	**109**	**51**	..	**2,691**	**55**	**1,604**	**18**	**193**	**3**	**3,026**	**145**
8. Kashmir North	117,955	21,434	131	6	13,040	591	115	6	16	..	1,050	19	354	2	28	..	1,387	59
9. Kashmir South	130,927	79,789	955	93	19,795	748	933	93	22	..	1,536	36	1,012	7	161	3	1,406	80
10. Muzaffarabad District ..	51,078	33,871	101	10	4,319	66	88	10	13	..	105	..	238	9	4	..	233	6
III—Frontier Districts	**60,945**	**57,869**	**511**	**112**	**6,824**	**287**	**488**	**112**	**23**	..	**177**	**17**	**519**	..	**21**	..	**376**	**4**
11. Ladakh District	54,345	53,868	508	112	6,221	287	485	112	23	..	127	17	97	...	21	..	358	4
12. Gilgit "	6,600	4,001	3	..	603	..	3	..	..	..	50	..	422	..	..	..	18	..
Cities																		
13. Jammu	128	6	2	..	34	6	1	..	1	..	5	2	9	..	5	..	1	..
14. Srinagar	1,063	73	1	2	422	5	1	2	..	..	62	..	322	..	..	..	1	..

TABLE XVIII.

SUBSIDIARY OCCUPATIONS OF AGRICULTURISTS—ACTUAL WORKERS ONLY.

(2) Rent-payers.

Jammu and Kashmir State Census, 1921.

DETAILS OF SUBSIDIARY OCCUPATIONS RETURNED.

DISTRICT, JAGIR ILAQA OR CITY.	Fishermen and boatmen.		Cattle breeders and milkmen.		Village watchmen.		Weavers.		Barbers.		Oil pressers.		Washermen.		Potters		Blacksmiths and carpenters.		Others.	
	Males.	Females.	Males.	Females.	Males.	Females.	Males.	Females.	Males.	Females.	Males.	Females.	Males.	Females.	Males.	Females.	Males.	Females.	Males.	Females.
	20	21	22	23	24	25	26	27	28	29	30	31	32	33	34	35	36	37	38	39
State ..	393	21	2,719	442	1,067	4	8,704	216	2,869	22	1,648	62	317	22	1,389	67	5,321	73	36,239	1,926
I.—Jammu Province (including Jagirs).	64	..	1,538	398	639	3	4,134	184	1,084	11	436	22	202	7	889	29	2,965	32	13,345	719
1. Jammu District	8	..	169	23	77	2	490	6	96	3	41	1	22	..	18	..	277	1	2,392	24
2. Kathua "	1	..	376	26	24	1	538	43	46	..	60	6	63	5	44	2	334	..	896	36
3. Udhampur "	7	..	612	265	128	..	471	48	155	..	82	2	10	2	130	10	456	16	1,382	190
4. Riasi "	4	..	139	19	90	..	489	13	198	3	55	8	29	..	101	4	371	4	1,988	154
5. Mirpur "	8	..	41	1	137	..	1,380	60	301	8	141	5	10	..	244	4	676	10	3,386	101
6. Bahadarwah Jagir	4	..	83	53	39	..	72	..	11	..	7	..	4	..	53	3	353	3	428	152
7. Punch Ilaqa	32	..	118	11	144	..	699	14	277	2	49	..	64	..	299	6	498	4	2,873	62
II.—Kashmir Province (including Jagir).	313	21	1,179	44	411	1	3,797	22	1,752	11	1,212	40	112	15	446	37	1,969	33	18,448	960
8. Kashmir North	59	7	584	9	199	..	1,044	7	646	7	577	5	57	5	159	2	86	20	6,033	449
9. Kashmir South	252	13	481	35	140	..	2,327	8	826	1	619	35	43	8	175	23	426	8	10,391	491
10. Muzaffarabad District ..	2	1	114	..	72	1	426	7	280	3	17	..	12	2	112	12	680	5	2,024	20
III.—Frontier Districts	16	..	2	..	17	..	773	10	33	..	..	..	3	..	54	1	387	8	4,446	247
11. Ladakh District	16	..	2	..	5	..	764	10	27	..	..	..	1	..	54	1	376	8	4,373	247
12. Gilgit "	..	..	..	..	12	..	9	..	6	..	..	..	2	..	..	..	11	..	73	..
Cities																				
13. Jammu	..	..	..	..	2	..	..	..	..	..	..	..	..	..	..	..	...	..	12	4
14. Srinagar	..	...	...	...	..	...	2	..	..	...	...	...	..	..	..	...	2	...	33	5

TABLE XVIII.

SUBSIDIARY OCCUPATIONS OF AGRICULTURAL LABOURERS—ACTUAL WORKERS ONLY.

(3) Agricultural Labourers.

Jammu and Kashmir State Census, 1921.

District, Jagir, Ilaqa or City.	Total number of actual workers: Males.	Total number of actual workers: Females.	Number of actual workers who returned subsidiary occupations: *Agriculturists.* Males.	*Agriculturists.* Females.	*Non-Agriculturists.* Males.	*Non-Agriculturists.* Females.	Details of subsidiary occupations returned: *Rent receivers.* Males.	*Rent receivers.* Females.	*Rent payers.* Males.	*Rent payers.* Females.	*General labourers.* Males.	*General labourers.* Females.	*Village Watchmen.* Males.	*Village Watchmen.* Females.	*Cattle breeders and milkmen.* Males.	*Cattle breeders and milkmen.* Females.	*Mill hands.* Males.	*Mill hands.* Females.	*Fishermen & boatmen.* Males.	*Fishermen & boatmen.* Females.	*Rice pounders.* Males.	*Rice pounders.* Females.	*Traders of all kinds.* Males.	*Traders of all kinds.* Females.	*Oil pressers.* Males.	*Oil pressers.* Females.	*Weavers.* Males.	*Weavers.* Females.	*Potters.* Males.	*Potters.* Females.	*Leather workers.* Males.	*Leather workers.* Females.	*Washermen* Males.	*Washermen* Females.	*Blacksmiths and carpenters.* Males.	*Blacksmiths and carpenters.* Females.	*Others.* Males.	*Others.* Females.
1	2	3	4	5	6	7	8	9	10	11	12	13	14	15	16	17	18	19	20	21	22	23	24	25	26	27	28	29	30	31	32	33	34	35	36	37	38	39
State ..	**3,790**	**1,702**	**107**	**8**	**249**	**50**	**20**	**1**	**87**	**7**	**82**	**9**	**8**	**3**	**17**	**1**	**1**	..	..	..	..	**9**	**2**	..	..	..	**52**	..	**2**	..	**5**	**3**	**2**	**2**	**13**	**1**	**65**	**22**
I.—Jammu Province (including Jagirs).	**2,957**	**1,398**	**83**	**3**	**218**	**42**	**19**	..	**64**	**3**	**82**	**7**	**7**	**2**	**15**	**1**	..	..	..	..	..	**9**	**2**	..	..	..	**47**	..	..	..	**5**	**2**	**2**	..	**12**	**1**	**46**	**20**
1. Jammu District ..	1,427	596	41	1	118	14	4	..	37	1	58	6	5	..	4	1	..	..	..	..	..	..	..	..	..	..	16	..	..	..	5	..	..	..	4	1	26	6
2. Kathua ,, ..	744	353	7	1	6	18	2	..	5	1		1	..	1	..	..	..	..	..	..	..	9	..	..	..	..	3	..	..	..	..	2	..	..	..	..	3	5
3. Udhampur ,, ..	273	79	15	[illegible]	51	1	4	..	11	1	2	..	2	..	8	..	..	..	..	..	..	..	..	..	..	..	25	..	..	..	..	..	..	..	..	..	14	1
4. Riasi ,, ..	99	6	..	..	..	..	..	..	..	..	..	..	..	..	..	..	..	..	..	..	..	..	..	..	..	..	..	..	..	..	..	..	..	..	..	..	..	..
5. Mirpur ,, ..	320	361	15	..	39	9	8	..	7	..	18	..	..	1	3	..	..	..	..	..	..	..	2	..	..	..	3	..	..	..	..	..	2	..	8	..	3	8
6. Bhadarwah *Jagir* ..	..	..	..	..	..	..	..	..	..	..	..	..	..	..	..	..	..	..	..	..	..	..	..	..	..	..	..	..	..	..	..	..	..	..	..	..	..	..
7. Punch *Ilaqa*	94	3	5	..	4	..	1	..	4	..	4	..	..	..	..	..	..	..	..	..	..	..	..	..	..	..	..	..	..	..	..	..	..	..	..	..	..	..
II.—Kashmir Province (including Jagirs).	**591**	**79**	**20**	**1**	**20**	**1**	**1**	**1**	**19**	..	..	..	**1**	..	**2**	..	..	..	..	..	..	..	..	..	..	..	**1**	..	**2**	..	..	..	..	..	..	..	**14**	**1**
8. Kashmir North ..	136	19	1	..	3	..	1	..	..	..	..	..	..	..	1	..	..	..	..	..	..	..	..	..	..	..	..	..	1	..	..	..	..	..	..	..	1	..
9. Kashmir South ..	318	58	19	..	15	1	..	..	19	..	..	..	..	..	1	..	..	..	..	..	..	..	..	..	..	..	1	..	..	..	..	..	..	..	..	..	13	1
10. Muzaffarabad District ..	137	2	..	1	2	..	..	1	..	..	..	..	1	..	..	..	..	..	..	..	..	..	..	..	..	..	..	..	1	..	..	..	..	..	..	..	..	..
III.—Frontier Districts ..	**242**	**225**	**4**	**4**	**11**	**7**	..	..	**4**	**4**	..	**2**	..	**1**	..	..	**1**	..	..	..	..	..	..	..	..	..	**4**	..	..	..	..	**1**	..	**2**	**1**	..	**5**	**1**
11. Ladakh District ..	159	192	3	..	11	3	..	..	3	..	..	2	..	..	..	..	1	..	..	..	..	..	..	..	..	..	4	..	..	..	..	..	..	..	1	..	5	1
12. Gilgit ,, ..	83	33	1	4	..	4	..	..	1	4	..	..	..	1	..	..	..	..	..	..	..	..	..	..	..	..	..	..	..	..	..	1	..	2	..	..	..	..
Cities.																																						
13. Jammu ..	4	..	..	..	3	..	..	..	..	..	3	..	..	..	..	..	..	..	..	..	..	..	..	..	..	..	..	..	..	..	..	..	..	..	..	..	..	..
14. Srinagar ..	30	..	..	..	..	..	..	..	..	..	..	..	..	..	..	..	..	..	..	..	..	..	..	..	..	..	..	..	..	..	..	..	..	..	..	..	..	..

TABLE XXI.

OCCUPATION BY SELECTED CASTES, TRIBES OR RACES.

JAMMU AND KASHMIR STATE CENSUS, 1921.

TABLE XXI.

Occupation by Selected Castes, Tribes or Races.

Jammu and Kashmir State Census.

Caste, Tribe or Race.	Traditional occupation.	Population dealt with. Actual workers. Males.	Population dealt with. Actual workers. Females.	Population dealt with. Dependents. Both sexes.	Number of actual workers whose traditional caste-occupation was returned as their Principal means of livelihood. Males.	Principal means of livelihood. Females.	Subsidiary means of livelihood. Males.	Subsidiary means of livelihood. Females.	Number of actual workers returning their traditional occupation as their principal means of livelihood who had some subsidiary occupation. Males.	Females.	Recorded Principal — I.—Exploitation of the Surface of the Soil. Income from rent of land. Males.	Income from rent of land. Females.	Cultivation of all kinds. Males.	Cultivation of all kinds. Females.	Agents and managers of landed estates, forest officers and their clerks, rent collectors, etc. Males.	Agents, etc. Females.	Field labourers, wood-cutters, etc. Males.	Field labourers, etc. Females.	Raisers of live-stock, milkmen and herdsmen. Males.	Raisers of live-stock, etc. Females.	Fishing and hunting. Males.	Fishing and hunting. Females.	II.—Extraction of Minerals. Owners, managers, clerks, etc. Males.	Owners, etc. Females.	Labourers. Males.	Labourers. Females.
1	2	3	4	5	6	7	8	9	10	11	12	13	14	15	16	17	18	19	20	21	22	23	24	25	26	27
Hindu.																										
Brahman	Priest	49,981	11,302	710,768	3,805	1,024	1,477	35	1,790	121	3,358	1,193	31,584	7,528	91	...	201	31	187	44	1	..	1	..	17	3
Chamiar	Cobbler	11,060	2,854	15,174	2,928	739	1,420	100	2,082	384	199	186	5,793	1,502	1	..	153	68	34	7	..	..	..	20	13	..
Hajjam	Barber	1,455	222	3,109	560	24	200	19	26	2	42	6	517	126	..	..	3	4	2	2	..	..	..	...	..	..
Jat	Agriculture	7,318	465	18,078	6,111	289	640	40	63	1	32	74	8	11	3	..	26	1	30	..	...	..	..	..	1	..
Jhiwar	Water-bearing & Menial Service	3,189	1,053	6,696	1,084	706	178	51	256	10	40	10	338	59	4	..	281	12	1	2	20	..	1	7	2	..
Kashmiri Pandit	State Service	17,919	1,389	35,744	3,844	31	481	1	208	5	1,025	214	4,376	731	294	..	2	..	4	..	..	..	..	..	..	..
Khatri	Trade & State Service	5,932	544	12,282	2,950	241	613	3	160	4	158	34	686	127	41	..	2	..	3	..	..	..	..	..	10	4
Lohar	Black-Smith	3,272	799	6,683	1,040	74	312	2	450	11	149	26	1,508	616	..	..	33	7	27	7	..	..	...	..	1	..
Rajput	State-Service	16,418	2,365	30,211	11,753	1,966	1,681	12	601	26	291	125	863	65	166	..	122	5	55	25	..	..	1	..	4	..
Tarkhan	Carpenter	3,000	591	6,308	1,170	30	428	..	496	4	64	9	1,056	479	..	..	46	1	1	3	...	..	...	...	..	..
Thakkar	Agriculture	29,886	10,948	51,191	23,508	9,567	2,641	636	556	99	522	23	73	6	63	..	313	78	603	127	..	..	..	..	3	3
Zargar	Gold & Silver-smiths	1,248	145	2,889	866	38	99	4	48	2	20	2	117	42	1	..	1	..	..	..	...	..	..	..	..	...
Musalman.																										
Bafinda	Weavers	7,614	1,581	18,967	2,205	859	627	27	1,479	105	34	14	4,141	488	..	..	46	11	73	5	4	..	..	..	1	2
Darzi	Tailors	1,549	273	2,927	619	219	90	1	233	3	9	2	492	27	1	..	9	..	3	..	..	..	..	..	1	..
Chuhra Watal	Scavengers	2,168	1,208	5,580	569	355	90	8	152	12	38	22	749	472	12	1	43	32	65	48	..	1	..	..	1	2
Gaddi	Goat & Sheep breeders	46	4	94	16	1	..	..	2	...	1	..	12	3	..	..	..	..	..	..	..	..	..	..	..	..
Gujjar	Agriculture & Cattle breeding	88,871	16,019	254,186	11,848	2,604	1,907	230	2,583	468	1,105	345	68,633	12,004	50	..	619	55	543	80	..	..	..	..	2	12
Hanji	Boatmen	1,872	464	3,699	760	229	83	3	54	9	..	2	274	79	28	..	30	..	26	3	150	48	41	..	..	..
Jat	Agriculture	27,555	2,806	72,288	23,166	2,414	2,408	48	399	11	9	11	17	17	4	..	96	4	385	4	..	..	..	..	..	2
Kumhiar	Potters & Carriers	6,204	1,341	14,041	2,432	647	565	30	974	30	165	1	2,673	598	..	..	16	2	44	3	6	..	..	..	3	..
Lohar	Black-smiths	6,551	994	16,021	2,018	191	346	12	1,122	14	159	148	3,711	543	4	..	34	11	23	..	..	..	1	..	20	5
Mochi	Cobblers	6,788	1,271	15,066	2,[illegible]67	417	457	30	982	57	105	21	2,429	589	5	..	41	2	222	73	2	..	..	..	7	2
Tarkhan	Carpenters	7,105	1,051	18,268	2,018	200	719	4	1,402	28	73	12	3,655	747	318	..	10	1	29	2	2	..	..	..	5	3
Teli	Oil pressing	7,664	1,388	15,082	2,218	381	524	29	851	56	62	49	3,196	718	..	..	32	7	42	1	..	..	...	..	1	1
Yashkun	Agriculture	4,503	2,780	9,313	3,734	..	171	..	27	..	6	1	2	2,717	8	..	217	17	11	..	12	..	..	..	115	...
Anglo-Indian	Trade	25	5	18	...	...	..	..	..	..	..	..	..	..	..	..	..	..	..	..	...	..	1	..	..	..
European	Service and Mission work.	113	34	122	...	...	..	..	..	..	..	..	..	..	1	..	..	..	..	..	...	..	2	..	..	...

TABLE XXI.

Occupation by Selected Castes, Tribes or Races

Jammu and Kashmir State Census, 1921.

	Caste, Tribe or Race.	Traditional occupation.	OCCUPATION OF ACTUAL WORKERS. III.—Industry. Owners, managers, clerks, etc. Males.	III. Owners, managers, clerks, etc. Females.	III. Artisans, and other workmen. Males	III. Artisans, and other workmen. Females.	IV.—Transport. Owners, managers and ships' officers. Males.	IV. Owners, managers and ships' officers. Females.	IV. Labourers, boatmen and palki bearers. Males.	IV. Labourers, boatmen and palki bearers. Females.	V.—Trade. Males.	V.—Trade. Females.	VI.—Public Force. Commissioned, and gazetted officers. Males.	VI. Commissioned, and gazetted officers. Females.	VI. Others. Males.	VI. Others. Females.	VII.—Public Administration. Gazetted officers. Males.	VII. Gazetted officers. Females.	VII. Others. Males.	VII. Others. Females.	VIII.—Arts and Professions. Religions. Males.	VIII. Religions. Females.	VIII. Lawyers, doctors, and teachers. Males.	VIII. Lawyers, doctors, and teachers. Females.	VIII. Others. Males.	VIII. Others. Females.	IX.—Persons living on their income. Males.	IX. Females.	X.—Domestic service. Males.	X. Females.	XI.—Insufficiently described occupations. Contractors, clerks, cashiers, etc. Males.	XI. Contractors, clerks, cashiers, etc. Females.	XI. Labourers unspecified. Males.	XI. Labourers unspecified. Females.	XII.—Beggars, Criminal and inmates of Jails. Males.	XII. Females.
			28	29	30	31	32	33	34	35	36	37	38	39	40	41	42	43	44	45	46	47	48	49	50	51	52	53	54	55	56	57	58	59	60	61
Hindu.	Brahman ..	Priest ..	..	..	115	413	4	16	207	2	3,570	162	3	..	408	1	20	..	2,277	9	27	3	212	1	50	..	133	213	1,079	258	115	3	610	255	429	108
Hindu.	Chamiar ..	Cobbler ..	..	..	3	24	..	..	13	..	41	..	..	..	17	3	..	..	44	3	1	..	12	..	2	2	15	44	129	10	..	1	212	110	30	35
Hindu.	Hajjam ..	Barber ..	..	..	2	9	..	..	..	..	5	..	..	..	37	..	..	..	42	..	..	..	1	..	..	..	..	3	28	11	1	..	9	13	6	5
Hindu.	Jat ..	Agriculture ..	..	..	6	7	..	..	17	..	20	..	..	..	85	..	..	..	62	..	16	..	..	..	..	..	5	9	141	5	1	1	70	27	44	1
Hindu.	Jhiwar ..	Water bearing & Menial Service	..	..	160	11	..	..	21	1	149	4	..	..	156	..	..	..	259	..	..	..	3	..	4	..	15	7	194	79	11	..	268	102	..	2
Hindu.	Kashmiri Pandit	State Service ..	..	..	272	339	10	..	68	..	2,070	12	1	..	218	..	6	..	2,970	3	74	..	57	..	129	1	98	4	1,742	46	51	..	47	4	80	3
Hindu.	Khatri ..	Trade & State Servic	..	..	160	49	5	..	33	2	686	16	3	..	18	1	3	2	138	..	7	..	101	2	32	..	33	22	134	8	78	..	17	28	21	5
Hindu.	Lohar ..	Black smith ..	..	..	8	30	1	..	2	..	6	..	7	..	49	..	1	..	33	..	..	..	1	..	3	..	3	5	23	9	1	..	60	19	4	4
Hindu.	Rajput ..	State Service ..	..	..	66	77	..	..	46	..	137	11	1	..	194	3	..	..	412	..	1	..	14	1	7	..	193	46	194	17	20	1	155	26	42	5
Hindu.	Tarkhan ..	Carpenter ..	..	..	9	21	..	..	10	..	8	..	..	..	17	..	..	..	14	..	1	..	..	..	..	..	4	6	40	8	2	..	122	33	8	1
Hindu.	Thakkar ..	Agriculture ..	..	..	106	225	..	..	38	4	139	2	4	..	605	..	6	..	493	3	2	1	3	..	3	1	51	48	444	145	15	..	190	51	64	27
Musalman.	Zargar ..	Gold & Silver smiths.	..	..	23	26	..	..	..	..	43	5	..	..	2	..	..	..	5	..	2	1	1	1	1	..	8	5	33	1	2	1	15	18	9	1
Musalman.	Bafinda ..	Weavers ..	..	..	48	35	..	..	13	2	46	5	..	..	24	..	6	..	47	..	33	21	10	2	5	2	2	..	103	19	5	..	82	54	59	36
Musalman.	Darzi ..	Tailors ..	..	..	62	18	..	..	1	..	15	..	..	..	7	1	..	..	2	..	5	1	1	..	1	..	12	1	1	..	1	..	6	3	11	..
Musalman.	Chuhra Watal ..	Scavengers ..	..	..	83	122	..	..	35	2	40	14	..	..	14	2	..	..	113	1	..	2	..	1	3	..	5	..	117	23	13	..	107	32	71	68
Musalman.	Gaddi ..	Goat & sheepbreeders.	..	..	7	..	..	..	..	..	10	..	..	..	..	..	..	..	..	..	..	..	..	..	..	..	..	..	..	..	..	..	..	..	..	..
Musalman.	Gujjar ..	Agriculture & Cattle breeding	2	..	128	61	..	..	242	25	105	31	..	2	239	25	..	..	272	22	60	3	9	..	2	3	55	15	1,983	152	43	2	476	121	548	227
Musalman.	Hanji ..	Boatmen ..	2	..	71	24	..	..	44	9	244	41	..	..	..	..	..	..	16	1	..	3	..	..	1	..	1	..	49	2	..	1	44	14	8	5
Musalman.	Jat ..	Agriculture ..	..	..	43	61	..	..	171	3	87	8	1	..	86	6	..	..	296	..	55	54	17	1	11	1	35	13	293	22	2	1	233	80	140	54
Musalman.	Kumhiar ..	Potters & Carriers ..	..	..	39	29	..	..	86	7	24	1	..	1	5	..	1	..	14	..	3	3	..	..	..	1	9	..	42	2	1	..	41	5	35	11
Musalman.	Lohar ..	Blacksmiths ..	3	..	84	27	..	1	7	1	5	2	..	..	11	1	..	..	15	..	7	2	..	..	3	..	7	1	44	8	3	..	28	22	21	19
Musalman.	Mochi ..	Cobblers ..	1	..	102	39	..	..	8	4	48	11	..	..	8	..	..	..	120	22	..	7	..	..	11	1	9	..	90	13	1	..	55	20	100	29
Musalman.	Tarkhan ..	Carpenters ..	..	3	63	33	..	1	1	..	15	2	..	..	9	..	..	..	10	1	34	8	2	..	3	..	3	3	59	4	5	..	51	12	21	15
Musalman.	Teli ..	Oil pressers ..	..	1	143	41	3	..	982	32	101	5	..	..	30	10	..	..	40	5	4	5	6	..	3	..	41	2	108	7	..	..	79	69	49	25
Musalman.	Yashkun ..	Agriculture ..	..	..	22	12	..	..	5	..	7	..	..	..	12	..	..	..	36	1	8	..	3	..	7	..	..	..	86	26	5	..	19	3	17	3
	Anglo-Indian ..	Trade ..	1	..	..	..	..	..	..	..	2	..	2	..	..	..	5	..	7	..	3	..	1	2	2	..	1	..	..	3	..	..	..	..	..	...
	European ..	Service and mission work.	4	..	4	2	4	..	1	..	9	4	20	..	7	2	9	..	21	..	5	..	6	4	..	..	15	6	5	16	..	..	...	..	..	..

TABLE XXII.

JAMMU AND KASHMIR STATE CENSUS, 1921.

This Table is divided into 7 Parts, but Parts IV and V have not been prepared for this State as they do not present any features of special interest.

Part I.—Gives the summary of industrial statistics for the whole State.

Part II.—Shows the distribution of industries of Districts.

Part III.—Shows industrial establishments classified according to the class of owners and managers.

Part VI.—Is divided into the following three heads :—

(1). Showing details of Power employed for establishments using steam, oil, gas, water, etc.

(2). Showing details of Power employed for establishments using Electric Power generated on the premises.

(3). Showing details of Power employed for Electric Power supplied from outside.

Part VII.—Shows number of looms in use in Textile establishments.

TABLE XXII.

Industrial Statistics—Part I.—Provincial Summary.

Description of Establishment.	Classification of Establishment according to the number of persons employed (including management.)	Number of establishments.	Total of person employed.		Classification of persons employed. — Direction, Supervision and Clerical Staff. — Managers.		Supervising and Technical staff.		Clerical staff.		Skilled workmen. — Europeans and Anglo-Indians.		Indians.		Unskilled Labourers. — Aged 14 and over.		Under 14.	
			Males.	Females.	Europeans and Anglo-Indians.	Indians.	Europeans and Anglo-Indians.	Indians.	Europeans and Anglo-Indians.	Indians.	Males.	Females.	Males.	Females.	Males.	Females.	Males.	Females.
1	2	3	4	5	6	7	8	9	10	11	12	13	14	15	16	17	18	19
Kashmir State	**Total**	**153**	**7,602**	**115**	**8**	**46**	**11**	***424**	..	**167**	..	..	**4,540**	**38**	**927**	**9**	**1,480**	**67**
I.—Growing of special products	**Total**	**9**	**125**	..	..	**2**	..	**9**	..	**1**	..	..	..	..	**113**	..	..	..
1. Resin tapping	10-20	9	125	..	..	2	..	9	..	1	..	..	..	..	113	..	..	..
II.—Textile Industries	**Total.**	**40**	**4,345**	**106**	**3**	**13**	**9**	***252**	..	**61**	..	..	**2,885**	**38**	**58**	..	**1,065**	**67**
2. Khaddi Khana Jail (cotton weaving and carpet making).	Total.	3	96	1	..	1	..	6	..	3	..	..	56	..	31	..	..	..
	10-20	1	18	..	..	..	..	1	..	..	..	..	13	..	4	..	..	..
	20-50	1	24	..	..	..	..	2	..	1	..	..	20	..	1	..	..	..
	50-100	1	54	1	..	1	..	*3	..	2	..	..	23	..	26	..	..	..
3. Woollen carpet factories	Total	6	1,342	..	2	..	3	9	..	8	..	..	1,021	..	7	..	292	..
	10-20	2	29	..	..	..	..	1	..	..	..	..	18	..	..	..	10	..
	50-100	2	119	..	..	..	..	4	..	1	..	..	103	..	..	..	11	..
	400 and over	2	1,194	..	2	..	3	4	..	7	..	..	900	..	7	..	271	..
4. Shawl weaving factories	Total	24	417	..	..	10	..	1	..	1	..	..	331	..	..	..	74	..
	10-20	18	244	..	..	7	..	1	..	1	..	..	201	..	..	..	34	..
	20-50	6	173	..	..	3	..	..	..	..	..	..	130	..	..	..	40	..
5. Pattoo Weaving	Total	1	11	..	..	1	..	..	..	..	..	..	10	..	..	..	..	..
	10-20	1	11	..	..	1	..	..	..	..	..	..	10	..	..	..	..	..
6. Hashiabafi (weaving of shawl fringes)	Total	4	74	..	..	..	..	..	..	2	..	..	44	..	..	..	28	..
	10-20	4	74					..	..	2	..	..	44	..	..	..	28	..
7. Silk factories (using mechanical power).	Total	2	2,405	105	1	1	6	236	..	47	..	..	1,423	38	20	..	671	67
	200-400	1	175	105	..	1	..	7	..	8	..	..	37	38	20	..	102	67
	400 and over	1	2,230	..	1	..	6	220	..	39	..	..	1,386	..	..	..	569	..
III.—Industries of Dress	**Total**	**56**	**884**	..	..	**5**	..	**3**	..	**13**	..	..	669	..	..	..	**194**	..
8. Embroidery factories	Total	12	158	..	..	4	..	3	..	2	..	..	119	..	..	..	30	..
	10-20	11	137	..	..	4	..	2	..	2	..	..	110	..	..	..	19	..
	20-50	1	21	..	..	..	..	1	..	..	..	..	9	..	..	..	11	..
9. Darning factories	Total	43	699	..	..	..	..	..	..	9	..	..	526	..	..	..	164	..
	10-20	36	476	..	..	..	..	..	..	6	..	..	359	..	..	..	111	..
	20-50	6	170	..	..	..	..	..	..	3	..	..	114	..	..	..	53	..
	50-100	1	53	..	..	..	..	..	..	..	..	..	53	..	..	..	..	..
10. Tailoring factory	Total	1	27	..	..	1	..	..	..	2	..	..	24	..	..	..	..	..
	20-50	1	27	..	..	1	..	..	..	2	..	..	24	..	..	..	..	..
IV.—Industries of Food	Total	3	54	..	..	2	..	5	..	2	..	..	16	..	**29**	..	..	..
11. Oil Press, Central Jail	10-20	1	10	..	..	..	..	..	..	..	..	..	1	..	9	..	..	..
12. Rice Mill (using mechanical power).	20-50	1	20	..	..	1	..	3	..	1	..	..	15	..	..	..	..	..
13. Rice Husker, Central Jail	20-50	1	24	..	..	1	..	2	..	1	..	..	..	..	20	..	..	..
V.—Metal Industries	**Total**	**1**	**20**	..	..	**1**	..	**8**	..	..	..	..	**8**	..	**3**	..	..	..
14. Metal Factory (using mechanical power).	20-50	1	20	..			..	8	..	..	..	..	8	..	3	..	..	..

VI.—Wood, etc., Industries..	**Total**	**15**	**1,005**	**3**	**2**	**11**	..	**67**	..	**31**	..	..	**474**	..	**253**	**3**	**167**	..
15. Timber extraction and floating ..	Total	12	960	3	2	8	..	60	..	27	..	..	460	..	236	3	167	..
	10-20	6	99	..	..	5	..	10	..	8	..	..	41	..	35	..	..	..
	20-50	1	34	..	..	1	..	2	..	1	..	..	..	..	30	..	..	..
	50-100	2	161	..	2	..	..	8	..	3	..	..	108	..	..	..	40	..
	100-200	1	141	..	..	1	..	7	..	7	..	..	..	..	..	..	126	..
	200-400	2	525	3	..	1	..	33	..	8	..	..	311	..	171	3		..
16. Timber extraction and steaming and Saw Mill (using mechanical power.)	10-20	3	45	..	..	3	..	7	..	4	..	..	14	..	17	..	..	..
VII.—Furniture Industries..	**Total**	**13**	**169**	..	..	**2**	..	**9**	..	**6**	..	..	**110**	..	**2**	..	**40**	..
17. Wood carving and furniture making factories.	Total	13	169	..	..	2	..	9	..	6	..	..	110	..	2	..	40	..
Using mechanical power ..	10-20	1	12	..	..	1	..	1	..	..	..	..	9	..	..	..	1	..
Using no mechanical power	Total	12	157	..	..	1	..	8	..	6	..	..	101	..	2	..	39	..
	..	10	131	..	..	1	..	6	..	5	..	..	80	..	..	..	39	..
	10-20	9	110	..	..	..	..	3	..	3	..	..	66	..	..	..	38	..
	20-50	1	21	..	..	1	..	3	..	2	..	..	14	..	..	..	1	..
Wood work factory, Central Jail ..	10-20	2	26	..	..	..	..	2	..	1	..	..	21	..	2	..	..	..
VIII.—Industries connected with Building.	**Total**	**4**	**198**	**6**	..	**4**	..	..	..	**3**	..	..	**2**	..	**175**	**6**	**14**	..
18. Brick kilns	..	3	185	6	..	3	..	..	..	3	..	..	..	..	135	6	14	..
	20-50	1	44	..	..	1	..	..	..	1	..	..	..	..	41	..	1	..
	50-100	2	141	6	..	2	..	..	..	2	..	..	..	..	124	6	13	..
19. Surkhi grinding Mill (using mechanical power).	Total	1	13	..	..	1	..	..	..	..	..	..	2	..	10	..	..	..
	10-20	1	13	..	..	1	..	..	..	..	..	..	2	..	10	..	..	..
IX.—Construction of means of Transport.	**Total**	**1**	**113**	..	**1**	..	..	**11**	..	**7**	..	..	**49**	..	**45**	..	..	..
20. Dredging works. ..	Total	1	113	..	1	..	..	11	..	7	..	..	49	..	45	..	..	..
(Using mechanical power.) ..	100-200	1	113	..	1	..	..	11	..	7	..	..	49	..	45	..	..	..
X.—Production and transmission of Physical forces.	**Total**	**7**	**377**	..	**2**	**5**	**2**	**52**	..	**22**	..	..	**149**	..	**145**	..	..	..
21. Electric supply works ..	Total	1	133	..	..	1	..	7	..	9	..	..	75	..	41	..	..	..
	100-200	1	133	..	..	1	..	7	..	9	..	..	75	..	41	..	..	..
22. Hydro-Electric Installation ..	Total	2	111	..	..	2	..	26	..	10	..	..	43	..	30	..	..	..
	20-50	1	38	..	..	1	..	3	..	1	..	..	19	..	14	..	..	..
	50-100	1	73	..	..	1	..	23	..	9	..	..	24	..	16	..	..	..
23. Maintenance of Lines ..	Total	2	50	..	2	..	2	4	..	2	..	..	15	..	25	..	..	..
	20-50	2	50	..	2	..	2	4	..	2	..	..	15	..	25	..	..	..
24. Flume channel and head works ..	Total	1	54	..	..	1	..	3	..	1	..	..	4	..	45	..	..	..
	50-100	1	54	..	..	1	..	3	..	1	..	..	4	..	45	..	..	..
25. City Water Works	Total	1	29	..	..	1	..	12	..	..	..	..	12	..	4	..	..	..
(Using mechanical power) ..	20-50	1	29	..	..	1	..	12	..	..	..	..	12	..	4	..	..	..
XI.—Industries of Luxury ..	**Total**	**4**	**312**	..	..	**1**	..	**8**	..	**21**	..	..	**178**	..	**104**	..	..	..
26. Printing Press	Total	4	312	..	..	1	..	8	..	21	..	..	178	..	104	..	..	..
Using Mechanical Power ..	100-200	1	165	..	..	1	..	1	..	17	..	..	133	..	13	..	..	..
Using no mechanical power ..	Total	3	147	..	..	..	..	7	..	4	..	..	45	..	91	..	..	..
Litho Press, Central Jail ..	20-50	1	31	..	..	..	..	3	..	2	..	..	8	..	18	..	..	..
Printing Press, English ..	50-100	1	66	..	..	..	..	2	..	1	..	..	18	..	45	..	..	..
Central Jail. ..	20-50	1	50	..	..	..	..	2	..	1	..	..	19	..	28	..	..	..

* Includes one female.

TABLE XXII.

INDUSTRIAL STATISTICS—PART II—DISTRIBUTION BY DISTRICTS.

DESCRIPTION OF ESTABLISHMENT.	District.	Number of establishments.	Total of persons employed.		Classification of persons employed. Direction. Managers.		Supervision and Clerical Staff. Supervising and Technical Staff.		Clerical Staff.		Skilled Workmen. Europeans and Anglo-Indians.		Indians.		Unskilled Labourers. Aged 14 and over		Under 14.		REMARKS.
			Males.	Females.	Europeans and Anglo-Indians.	Indians.	Europeans and Anglo-Indians.	Indians.	Europeans and Anglo-Indians	Indians.	Males.	Females.	Males.	Females.	Males.	Females.	Males.	Females.	
1	2	3	4	5	6	7	8	9	10	11	12	13	14	15	16	17	18	19	20
Kashmir State ..	**Total**	**153**	**7,602**	**115**	**8**	**46**	**11**	*24	..	**167**	..	..	**4,540**	**38**	**927**	**9**	**1,480**	**67**	
	Jammu District.	**14**	**787**	**112**	..	**10**	..	*59	..	**41**	..	..	**282**	**38**	**279**	**6**	**117**	**67**	
Weaving Factory (Jail) ..	..	1	54	1	..	1	..	*3	..	2	..	..	23	..	26	..	..	..	
Carpet, etc., Factory (Jail) ..	..	1	18	..	..	..	..	1	..	..	..	..	13	..	4	..	..	..	
Silk Factory ..	..	1	175	105	..	1	..	7	..	8	..	..	37	38	20	..	102	67	
Brick Kilns	..	3	185	6	..	3	..	..	..	3	..	..	..	..	165	6	14	..	Seasonal.
Furniture Factory	..	1	12	..	..	1	..	1	..	..	..	..	9	..	..	..	1	..	
Carpentry work (Jail)	..	1	15	..	..	..	..	..	..	..	..	..	14	..	1	..	..	..	
Oil Press (Kohloo) Jail	..	1	10	..	..	..	..	..	..	..	..	..	1	..	9	..	..	..	
City Water Works	..	1	29	..	..	1	..	12	..	..	..	..	12	..	4	..	..	..	
Metal Factory	..	1	20	..	..	1	..	8	..	..	..	..	8	..	3	..	..	..	
Hydro-Electric Installation ..	..	1	73	..	..	1	..	23	..	9	..	..	24	..	16	..	..	..	
Printing Press	..	1	165	..	..	1	..	1	..	17	..	..	133	..	13	..	..	..	
Printing Press (Jail)	..	1	31	..	..	..	..	3	..	2	..	..	8	..	18	..	..	..	
	Udhampur District.	**8**	310	**3**	..	..	..	32	..	**8**	..	..	**4**	..	**265**	**3**	**1**	..	
Resin Tapping	..	7	102	..	..	..	..	7	..	1	..	..	..	..	94	..	..	..	Seasonal.
Timber extraction and floating ..	..	1	208	3	..	..	..	25	..	7	..	..	4	..	171	3	1	..	

Resin Tapping	Riasi. District.	2	23	..	..	2	..	2	..	..	..	..	..	..	19	..	..	..	Seasonal.
	Kashmir North.	16	942	..	5	10	2	54	..	32	..	..	533	..	140	..	166	..	
Dredging Works		1	113	..	1	..	..	11	..	7	..	..	49	..	45	..	..	..	
Maintenance of Lines		2	50	..	2	..	2	4	..	2	..	..	15	..	25	..	..	..	
Extraction of Timber	..	12	768	..	2	9	..	36	..	21	..	..	469	..	65	..	166	..	Seasonal.
Timber Steaming Factory ..	..	1	11	..	..	1	..	3	..	2	..	..	..	..	5	..	..	..	
	Kashmir South.	110	5,430	..	3	21	9	268	..	83	..	..	3,697	..	153	..	1,196	..	
Cotton Weaving Factory (Jail) ..	..	1	24	..	..	..	..	2	..	1	..	..	20	..	1	..	..	..	
Woollen Carpet Factories	..	6	1,342	..	2	..	3	9	..	8	..	..	1,021	..	7	..	292	..	
Shawl Weaving Factories ..	..	24	417	..	..	10	..	1	..	1	..	..	331	..	..	..	74	..	
Pattoo Weaving Factory	..	1	11	..	..	1	..	..	..	..	..	..	10	..	..	..	..	..	
Hashiabafi (making of Shawl fringes)	..	4	74	..	..	..	..	..	..	2	..	..	44	..	..	..	28	..	
Silk Factory	..	1	2,230	..	1	..	6	229	..	39	..	..	1,386	..	..	..	569	..	
Surkhi grinding Mill	..	1	13	..	..	1	..	..	..	..	..	..	2	..	10	..	..	..	
Yarmadozi and Jalakdozi (Embroidery) Factories.	..	12	158	..	..	4	..	3	..	2	..	..	119	..	..	..	30	..	
Rafugari (Darning) Factories ..	..	43	699	..	..	..	..	..	..	9	..	..	526	..	..	..	164	..	
Tailoring Factory	..	1	27	..	..	1	..	..	..	2	..	..	24	..	..	..	..	..	
Furniture making and wood carving Factories.	..	10	131	..	..	1	..	6	..	5	..	..	80	..	..	..	39	..	
Wood Factory (Jail)	..	1	11	..	..	..	..	2	..	1	..	..	7	..	1	..	..	..	
Electric Supply Works	..	1	133	..	..	1	..	7	..	9	..	..	75	..	41	..	..	..	
Printing Press (Jail)	..	2	116	..	..	..	..	4	..	2	..	..	37	..	73	..	..	..	
Rice Mill	..	1	20	..	..	1	..	3	..	1	..	..	15	..	..	..	..	..	
Rice Husker (Jail)	..	1	24	..	..	1	..	2	..	1	..	..	..	..	20	..	..	..	
	Muzaffarabad District.	3	110	..	..	3	..	9	..	3	..	..	24	..	71	..	..	..	
Saw Mill	..	1	18	..	..	1	..	3	..	1	..	..	1	..	12	..	..	..	
Flume Channel and head works ..	..	1	54	..	..	1	...	3	..	1	..	..	4	..	45	..	..	..	
Hydro-Electric Installation ..	..	1	38	..	..	1	..	3	..	1	..	..	19	..	14	..	..	..	

* Includes one female.

TABLE XXII.

Industrial Statistics.—Part III—Industrial Establishments Classified according to the Class of Owners and Managers.

DESCRIPTION OF ESTABLISHMENT.	Total Number.	Number Owned by.									Number Managed by.					Remarks.
		Government or Local authority.	Registered Companies with Directors who are.			Private persons who are.					Europeans or Anglo-Indians.	Hindus.	Musalmans.	Parsi.	Others.	
			Europeans or Anglo-Indians.	Indians.	Both.	Europeans or Anglo-Indians.	Hindus.	Musalmans.	Parsi.	Others.						
1	2	3	4	5	6	7	8	9	10	11	12	13	14	15	16	17
Kashmir State ..	**153**	**41**	**2**	..	..	**1**	**8**	**98**	..	**3**	**8**	**17**	**26**	..	**3**	
I.—Growing of special products.	**9**	**7**	..	..	..	..	**2**	..	..	..	..	**2**	..	..	..	
1. Resin Tapping ..	9	7	..	..	..	..	2	..	..	..	..	2	..	..	..	
II.—Textile Industries ..	**40**	**5**	**1**	..	..	**1**	**2**	**31**	..	..	**3**	**4**	**12**	..	..	
2. Khaddi Khana Jail (Cotton weaving and carpet making).	3	3	..	..	..	..	..	..	..	..	..	1	..	..	..	
3. Woollen Carpet Factories.	6	..	1	..	..	1	..	4	..	..	2	1	2	..	..	
4. Shawl Weaving Factories.	24	..	..	..	..	..	1	23	..	..	..	..	10	..	..	
5. Pattoo Weaving ..	1	..	..	..	..	..	1	..	..	..	..	1	..	..	..	
6. Hashiabafi (weaving of shawl fringes.	4	..	..	..	..	..	..	4	..	..	..	..	..	..	..	
7. Silk Factories ..	2	2	..	..	..	..	..	..	..	..	1	1	..	..	..	
III.—Industries of Dress ..	**56**	..	..	..	..	..	..	**56**	..	..	..	..	**5**	..	..	
8. Embroidery Factories	12	..	..	..	..	..	..	12	..	..	..	..	4	..	..	
9. Darning Factories ..	43	..	..	..	..	..	..	43	..	..	..	..	..	..	..	
10. Tailoring Factory ..	1	..	..	..	..	..	..	1	..	..	..	..	1	..	..	
IV.—Industries of Food ..	**3**	**2**	..	..	..	..	..	..	..	**1**	..	**1**	..	..	**1**	
11. Oil Press, Central Jail.	1	1	..	..	..	..	..	..	..	..	..	..	..	..	..	
12. Rice Mill ..	1	..	..	..	..	..	..	..	..	1	..	..	..	..	1	
13. Rice Husker, Central Jail.	1	1	..	..	..	..	..	..	..	..	..	1	..	..	..	
V.—Metal industries ..	**1**	**1**	..	..	..	..	..	..	..	..	..	..	..	..	**1**	
14. Metal factory ..	1	1	..	..	..	..	..	..	..	..	..	..	..	..	1	
VI.—Wood, etc. Industries	**15**	**12**	**1**	..	..	..	..	..	..	**2**	**2**	**2**	**8**	..	..	
15. Timber extraction and floating.	13	10	1	..	..	..	..	..	..	2	2	2	6	..	..	
16. Timber steaming ..	1	1	..	..	..	..	..	..	..	..	..	..	1	..	..	
17. Saw Mill ..	1	1	..	..	..	..	..	..	..	..	..	..	1	..	..	
VII.—Furniture Industries	**13**	**2**	..	..	..	..	..	**11**	..	..	..	..	**1**	..	..	
18. Wood carving and furniture making factories.	11	..	..	..	..	..	..	11	..	..	..	..	1	..	..	
19. Wood work factory (Central Jail).	2	2	..	..	..	..	..	..	..	..	..	..	..	..	..	
VIII.—Industries connected with building.	**4**	..	..	..	..	..	**4**	..	..	..	..	**3**	..	..	..	
20. Brick kilns ..	3	..	..	..	..	..	3	..	..	..	..	2	..	..	..	
21. Surkhi grinding Mill	1	..	..	..	..	..	1	..	..	..	..	1	..	..	..	
IX.—Construction of means of Transport.	**1**	**1**	..	..	..	..	..	..	..	..	**1**	..	..	..	..	
22. Dredging Works ..	1	1	..	..	..	..	..	..	..	..	1	..	..	..	..	
X.—Production and transmission of physical forces.	**7**	**7**	..	..	..	..	..	..	..	..	**2**	**4**	..	..	**1**	
23. Electric Supply Works.	1	1	..	..	..	..	..	..	..	..	..	1	..	..	..	
24. Hydro Electric Installation.	2	2	..	..	..	..	..	..	..	..	..	1	..	..	1	
25. Maintenance of Lines	2	2	..	..	..	..	..	..	..	..	2	..	..	..	..	
26. Flume channel and Lead Works.	1	1	..	..	..	..	..	..	..	..	..	1	..	..	..	
27. City Water Works	1	1	..	..	..	..	..	..	..	..	..	1	..	..	..	
XI.—Industries of Luxury	**4**	**4**	..	..	..	..	..	..	..	..	..	**1**	..	..	..	
28. Printing Press ..	1	1	..	..	..	..	..	..	..	..	..	1	..	..	..	
Printing Press (Central Jail).	1	1	..	..	..	..	..	..	..	..	..	..	..	..	..	
Litho Press (Central Jail).	2	2	..	..	..	..	..	..	..	..	..	..	..	..	..	

TABLE XXII.

Industrial Statistics. Part VI—Details of Power employed.

1. *For Establishments using steam, oil, gas, water, etc.*

Description of Establishment.	Number of Establishments employing.				Number of Engines.				Total Horse-power.				Remarks.
	Steam.	Oil.	Water.	Gas.	Steam.	Oil.	Water.	Gas.	Steam.	Oil.	Water.	Gas.	
1	2	3	4	5	6	7	8	9	10	11	12	13	14
Kashmir State ..	1	1	..	..	1	2	..	..	20	32	..	..	
I.—Textile Industries ..	1	..	..	..	1	..	..	..	20	..	..	..	
1. Silk Factory ..	1	..	..	..	1	..	..	..	20	..	..	..	
II.—Wood, etc., Industries	..	1	..	..	..	2	..	..	..	32	..	..	
2. Timber extraction and floating.	..	1	..	..	..	2	..	..	..	32	..	..	

TABLE XXII.

Industrial Statistics. Part VI—Details of Power employed.

2. *For Establishments using Electric Power generated on the premises.*

Description of Establishment.	Number of Establishments.	Prime Movers.						Electric Power.		Remarks.
		Steam.		Oil.		Water.				
		Number of engines.	Horse power.	Number of engines.	Horse power.	Number of engines.	Horse power.	Number of dynamos.	Power in kilowatts.	
1	2	3	4	5	6	7	8	9	10	11
Kashmir State ..	**2**	..	..	..	..	**4. Water turbines 4. A. C. Generators.**	**7,060 H. P. 4,000 K. V. A.**	**3. Alternators.**	**682**	
Hydro-Electric Installation (Jammu) ..	1	..	..	..	..	..	..	3. Alternators.	682	
Hydro-Electric Installation (Muzaffarabad District) Kashmir.	1	..	..	..	..	4. water turbines, 4. A. C. Generators.	7,060 H. P. 4,000 K. V. A.	..	..	

TABLE XXII.

Industrial Statistics, Part VI.—Details of Power employed.

3.—*For Electric Power supplied from outside.*

DESCRIPTION OF ESTABLISHMENTS.	Number of Establishments.	Number of Motors installed.	Total Horse Power.	Remarks.
1	2	3	4	5
Kashmir State ..	**11**	**56**	**2,039**	
I.—Textile Industries ..	**1**	**27**	**247**	
1. Silk Factory ..	1	27	247	
II.—Industries of Food ..	**1**	**1**	**30**	
2. Rice Mill ..	1	1	30	
III.—Metal Industries ..	**1**	**1**	**75**	
3. Metal Factory ..	1	1	75	
IV.—Wood, etc., Industries ..	**2**	**2**	**175**	
4. Timber Steaming Factory ..	1	1	150	
5. Saw Mill ..	1	1	25	
V.—Furniture Industries ..	**1**	**1**	**6**	
6. Furniture Making Factory ..	1	1	6	
VI.—Construction of means of Transport	**1**	**8**	**621**	
7. Dredging Works ..	1	8	621	
VII.—Production and transmission of Physical forces.	**2**	**14**	**755**	
8. Electric Supply Works ..	1	6	481	
9. City Water Works ..	1	8	274	
VIII.—Industries of Luxury ..	**1**	**1**	**30**	
10. Printing Press ..	1	1	30	
IX.—Industries connected with Building ..	**1**	**1**	**100**	
11. Surkhi Grinding Mill ..	1	1	100	

TABLE XXII.

Industrial Statistics, Part VII.—Number of looms in use in Textile Establishments.

District.	Cotton Weaving Establishments.				Silk Factories.				Wool Weaving Establishments.				Remarks.
	Number of Establishments.	Number of looms at work.			Number of Establishments.	Number of reels at work.			Number of Establishments	Number of looms at work.			
		Worked by power.	Worked by hand.			Worked by power.	Worked by hand.			Worked by power.	Worked by hand.		
			With fly shuttle.	Without fly shuttle.			With fly shuttle.	Without fly shuttle.			With fly shuttle.	Without fly shuttle.	
1	2	3	4	5	6	7	8	9	10	11	12	13	14
Kashmir State ..	**3**	..	**18**	**17**	**2**	**1,598**	..	..	**21**	..	**24**	**303**	
Jammu District ..	2	..	8	15	1	98	..	..	..	..	..	..	
	..	..	..	..	1	98	..	..	..	..	..	..	
	2	..	8	15	..	..	..	..	..	..	..	..	
Kashmir South ..	1	..	10	2	1	1,500	..	..	21	..	24	303	
	..	..	..	..	1	1,500	..	..	..	..	..	..	
	..	..	..	..	..	..	..	..	21	..	24	303	
	1	..	10	2	..	..	..	..	..	..	..	..	

PROVINCIAL TABLE I.

AREA AND POPULATION BY TAHSILS

Jammu and Kashmir State Census, 1921.

Provincial—I.
Area and Population by Tehsils.

PROVINCIAL TABLE I.

AREA AND POPULATION BY TEHSILS.

Jammu and Kashmir State Census, 1921.

Tehsils.	Area in square miles.	Number of Towns.	Number of Villages.	Number of occupied houses.	Population 1921 Persons.	Population 1921 Males.	Population 1921 Females.	Population 1911. (Both sexes.)	Percentage of Variation 1911—1921.	Percentage of Variation 1901—1911.	No of persons per square mile in 1921.	Uninhabited Villages.	Remarks.
1	2	3	4	5	6	7	8	9	10	11	12	13	14
Kashmir State ..	84,258	37	8,915	599,287	3,320,518	1,757,122	1,563,396	3,158,126	+5·1	+8·7	39	176	
I—Jammu Province ..	12,165	20	4,549	329,116	1,640,259	859,619	780,640	1,597,865	+2·7	+5	135	90	
Jammu District ..	1,147	6	1,163	74,531	334,834	182,681	152,153	326,691	+2·5	—5	292	44	
Jammu City ..	4	1	..	7,492	31,506	19,121	12,385	31,726	—·7	—11·1	20,592	..	
Jammu Tehsil ..	367	1	321	19,251	85,036	47,233	37,803	85,577	—·6	—2	231	15	
Karlup Ilaqa ..	6	..	3	509	2,111	1,103	1,008	..	..	..	352	..	
General Sir Raja Sahib's Jagir in Jammu.	375	..	4	285	1,222	705	517	2,086	—41·4	..	..	..	
1. **Total Jammu Tehsil** ..		2	328	27,537	119,875	68,162	51,713	119,389	+·4	—7	319	15	
Samba Tehsil ..		1	321	13,938	66,749	34,646	32,103	67,517	—·3	+6	227	9	
General Sir Raja Sahib's Jagir	296	..	1	126	538	275	263						
2. **Total Samba Tehsil** ..		1	322	14,064	67,287	34,921	32,366	67,517	—·3	+6	227	9	
3. Sri Ranbir Singh Pura ..	156	1	295	16,303	76,780	42,012	34,768	68,061	+12·8	—14	492	14	
4. Akhnur ..	320	2	218	16,627	70,892	37,586	33,306	71,724	—1·2	—3	221	6	
Kathua District ..	1,023	3	570	32,810	154,209	82,467	71,742	151,802	+1·6	—2	151	12	
5. Kathua Tehsil ..	232	2	167	8,695	40,841	22,929	17,912	41,933	—2·6	—2	176	8	Parol consists of 6
6. Jasmergarh ,, ..	191	..	265	9,930	47,889	25,630	22,259	44,530	+7·5	+5	251	3	villages
7. Basohli ,, ..	600	1	138	14,185	65,479	33,908	31,571	65,339	+·2	—5	109	1	and Kathua 3.
Udhampur District ..	4,399	3	660	41,151	218,261	115,135	103,126	215,725	+1·2	..	50	12	
Udhampur Tehsil ..	396	1	194	9,795	45,668	24,653	21,015	44,574	+2·5	..	115	8	
Chaneni Jagir ..	93	..	46	2,310	10,620	5,725	4,895	10,589	+·3	..	114	1	
8. **Total Udhampur Tehsil** ..	489	1	240	12,105	56,288	30,378	25,910	55,163	+2·04	..	115	9	
9. Kishtwar Tehsil ..	2,823	1	154	7,512	47,698	25,117	22,581	48,778	+2·2	..	17	1	
10. Ramban ..	585	..	130	10,117	62,020	32,659	29,361	60,236	+2·9	..	106	1	
11. Ramnagar ,, ..	502	1	136	11,417	52,255	26,981	25,274	51,548	+1·4	..	104	1	
Riasi District ..	1,833	2	657	40,606	224,589	118,575	106,014	206,809	+8·6	..	123	4	
12. Riasi Tehsil ..	985	1	332	19,414	101,858	53,786	48,072	94,658	+7·6	..	103	4	
13. Rampur Rajauri ..	848	1	325	21,192	122,731	64,789	57,942	112,151	+9·4	..	145	..	
Mirpur District ..	1,583	4	709	74,047	318,971	160,186	158,785	324,933	—1·8	..	202	13	
14. Kotli Tehsil ..	540	1	225	20,946	94,342	47,297	47,045	96,121	—1·9	..	175	1	
15. Mirpur ,, ..	353	1	292	23,524	93,381	45,934	47,447	98,119	—4·8	..	265	5	
16. Bhimber ,, ..	690	2	192	29,577	131,248	66,955	64,293	130,693	+·4	..	190	7	
Bhadarwah *Jagir* ..	553	1	308	6,913	37,614	19,227	18,387	37,512	+·3	+9	68	2	
Punch Ilaqa ..	1,627	1	482	59,058	351,781	181,348	170,433	334,393	+5·2	+10	216	3	
Haveli Tehsil ..		1	172	13,831	95,544	51,036	44,518	..	..	..	..	..	
Mahendar ,, ..	1,627	..	98	13,753	83,248	43,490	39,758	..	..	..	..	1	
Bagh ,, ..		..	112	15,085	83,883	42,367	41,516	..	..	..	..	1	
Sadhnoti ,, ..		..	100	16,389	89,096	44,455	44,641	..	..	..	..	1	
II.—Kashmir Province ..	8,533	13	3,595	221,941	1,407,086	757,824	649,262	1,295,201	+8·6	+12	165	83	
Kashmir Valley ..	6,131	12	2,778	189,020	1,190,977	672,144	548,833	1,099,996	+8·3	+11	194	77	
Kashmir North ..	3,317	4	1,382	78,353	502,490	269,685	232,805	460,786	+9·1	..	151	39	
Uttarmachipura Tehsil ..	2,326	1	479	30,943	199,244	106,259	92,985	179,744	+10·8	..	86	12	
Langet Jagir ..	172	..	78	3,404	22,581	12,100	10,481	20,865	+8·2	..	131	1	
17. **Total Uttarmachipura** ..	2,498	1	557	34,347	221,825	118,359	103,466	200,609	+10·5	..	89	13	
Baramula Tehsil ..	391	2	349	20,485	132,687	71,753	60,934	..	..	..	..	7	
Jagir Natipura ..		..	2	121	709	375	334	..	..	..	..	..	
18. **Total Baramula Tehsil** ..	391	2	351	20,606	133,396	72,128	61,268	120,399	+10·8	..	341	7	
Sri Partapsinghpura ..	428	1	473	23,153	145,756	78,371	67,385	..	..	..	..	19	
Jagir Naiipura ..		..	1	247	1,513	827	686	..	..	..	..	..	
19. **Total Sri Partapsinghpura**	428	1	474	23,400	147,269	79,198	68,071	139,778	+5·4	..	344	19	
Kashmir South ..	814	8	1,396	110,667	688,487	372,459	316,028	639,210	+7·7	..	245	38	Srinagar
Tehsil Khas ..	2,707	1	224	17,993	100,463	54,146	46,317	87,003	+15·5	..	142	7	City consists of
Srinagar City ..	9 7 128	1	..	25,673	141,735	76,604	65,131	130,201	+8·9	+3	15,653	..	15 villages.
20. **Total Tehsil Khas** ..	716	2	224	43,630	242,198	130,750	111,448	217,204	+11·5	..	338	7	Pampur
21. Awantipura Tehsil ..	456	1	388	19,811	134,644	73,641	61,003	128,170	+5·1	..	296	8	consists
22. Kulgam ,, ..	587	1	456	22,109	136,581	73,508	63,073	132,061	+3·4	..	233	11	of 3
23. Anantnag ,, ..	1,055	4	328	25,117	175,064	94,560	80,504	161,775	+8·2	..	166	12	villages.
Muzaffarabad District ..	2,402	1	817	32,921	216,109	115,680	100,429	195,205	+10·7	+16	90	6	
24. Karnah Tehsil ..	1,179	..	106	6,826	47,437	25,389	22,048	41,492	+14·3	+17	40	..	
25. Muzaffarabad ,, ..	633	1	435	16,706	104,031	55,589	48,442	94,295	+10·3	+14	164	5	
26. Uri ,, ..	590	..	276	9,389	64,641	34,702	29,939	59,418	+8·8	+19	110	1	
III—Frontier Districts ..	63,560	4	771	48,230	273,173	139,679	133,494	265,060	+3·1	+14	4	3	
Ladakh District ..	45,762	2	468	34,692	183,476	91,258	92,218	186,656	—1·7	..	4	3	
Ladakh Tehsil ..	29,793	1	110	7,869	32,892	16,529	16,363	31,934	+3	..	1	..	
Mansar (Village) ..	55	..	1	44	160	87	73	190	—15·8	..	3	..	
27. **Total Ladakh Tehsil** ..	29,848	1	111	7,913	33,052	16,616	16,436	32,124	+2·9	..	1	..	
28. Skardu ,, ..	8,522	1	194	19,819	102,745	51,572	51,173	106,805	—3·8	..	12	3	Skardu consists
29. Kargil ,, ..	7,392	..	163	6,960	47,679	23,070	24,609	47,727	—·1	..	6	..	of 2
Gilgit District ..	3,118	1	82	4,353	28,706	15,880	12,826	23,969	+19·8	..	9	..	villages.
30. Gilgit Tehsil ..	3,118	1	82	4,353	28,706	15,880	12,826	23,969	+19·8	..	9	..	
Frontier *Ilaqas* ..	14,680	1	221	9,185	60,991	32,541	28,450	54,435	+12	..	4	..	
Chilas ..	2,800	..	63	2,329	13,135	7,180	5,955	12,508	+5·01	..	5	..	
Nagar ..	1,600	..	43	2,486	14,188	7,704	6,484	13,347	+6·3	..	9	..	
Hunza ..	3,900	1	37	1,933	12,117	6,473	5,644	10,126	+19·7	..	3	..	
Punial ..	1,600	..	19	701	5,492	2,897	2,595	4,423	+24·2	..	3	..	
Ishkoman ..	1,100	..	12	282	2,753	1,410	1,343	2,020	+36·3	..	2	..	
Yasin ..	1,200	..	23	753	7,065	3,710	3,355	6,310	+11·9	..	6	..	
Kuh ..	480	..	12	288	2,288	1,229	1,059	2,064	+10·9	..	5	..	
Ghizar ..	1,500	..	12	413	3,953	1,938	2,015	3,637	+8·6	..	3	..	
Total Yasin ..	3,180	..	47	1,454	13,306	6,877	6,429	12,011	+10·8	..	4	..	

PROVINCIAL TABLE II.

POPULATION OF TEHSILS BY RELIGION AND EDUCATION.

Jammu and Kashmir State Census, 1921.

PROVINCIAL TABLE II.

Population of Tehsils by Religion and Education.

Jammu and Kashmir State Census, 1921.

Distribution by Religion.

Tehsil.	Hindu. Males.	Hindu. Females.	Arya. Males.	Arya. Females.	Brahmo. Males.	Brahmo. Females.	Sikh. Males.	Sikh. Females.	Jain. Males.	Jain. Females.	Budh. Males.	Budh. Females.	Zoroastrian. Males.	Zoroastrian. Females.
1	2	3	4	5	6	7	8	9	10	11	12	13	14	15
Kashmir State ..	**357,576**	**311,632**	**12,608**	**10,508**	**7**	**8**	**20,786**	**18,721**	**295**	**234**	**18,838**	**18,847**	**5**	**2**
I—Jammu Province	**319,928**	**283,621**	**12,560**	**10,485**	**7**	**8**	**11,381**	**10,246**	**294**	**234**	**226**	**216**	**3**	**2**
Jammu District	**104,553**	**87,229**	**3,242**	**2,353**	**7**	**8**	**2,651**	**2,281**	**290**	**231**	**4**	..	**3**	**2**
Jammu City	12,380	7,840	319	241	7	8	400	308	289	231	4	..	..	..
Jammu Tehsil	29,561	23,810	69	12	..	..	275	217	1	..	..	..	3	2
Karlup Ilaqa	930	898	..	..	..	..	2	1	..	..	..	..	..	..
General Sir Raja Sahib's Jagir in Jammu.	213	144	..	..	..	..	..	..	..	..	..	..	..	..
1. **Total Jammu Tehsil** ..	**43,084**	**32,692**	**388**	**253**	**7**	**8**	**677**	**526**	**290**	**231**	**4**	..	**3**	**2**
Samba Tehsil	20,491	18,924	247	89	..	..	651	638	..	..	..	..	..	..
General Raja Sahib's *Jagir* ..	153	129	..	..	..	..	..	..	..	..	..	..	..	..
2. **Total Samba Tehsil**	**20,644**	**19,053**	**247**	**89**	..	..	**651**	**638**	..	..	..	..	..	..
3. Sri Ranbir Singhpura Tehsil ..	16,673	14,054	2,607	2,011	..	..	1,249	1,054	..	..	..	..	..	..
4. Akhnur Tehsil	24,152	21,430	..	..	..	..	74	63	..	..	..	..	..	..
Kathua District	**57,696**	**51,876**	**4,444**	**3,486**	..	..	**148**	**109**	**1**	..	..	..	..	..
5. Kathua Tehsil	12,715	10,014	2,461	1,968	..	..	46	33	..	..	..	..	..	..
6. Jasmergarh Tehsil	16,468	15,045	1,961	1,509	..	..	91	66	..	..	..	..	..	..
7. Basohli Tehsil	28,513	26,817	22	9	..	..	11	10	..	..	..	..	..	..
Udhampur District	**68,935**	**63,279**	**10**	**11**	..	..	**175**	**157**	..	..	**222**	**216**	..	..
Udhampur Tehsil	19,637	17,400	10	11	..	..	38	38	..	..	1	..	..	..
Chaneni Jagir	4,916	4,324	..	..	..	..	4	3	..	..	..	..	..	..
8. **Total Udhampur Tehsil** ..	**24,553**	**21,724**	**10**	**11**	..	..	**42**	**41**	..	..	**1**	..	..	..
9. Kishtwar Tehsil	10,776	9,776	..	..	..	..	88	89	..	..	215	214	..	..
10. Ramban "	9,658	9,188	..	..	..	..	35	19	..	..	1	..	..	..
11. Ramnagar "	23,948	22,591	..	..	..	..	10	8	..	..	5	2	..	..
Riasi District	**39,122**	**34,943**	**2,672**	**2,843**	..	..	**401**	**413**	..	..	..	..	..	..
12. Riasi Tehsil	26,005	23,066	1,045	1,066	..	..	39	56	..	..	..	..	..	..
13. Rampur Rajauri Tehsil ..	13,117	11,877	1,627	1,777	..	..	362	357	..	..	..	..	..	..
Mirpur District	**27,319**	**25,272**	**2,159**	**1,771**	..	..	**2,481**	**2,217**	**2**	**3**	..	..	..	..
14. Kotli Tehsil	3,690	3,412	180	163	..	..	571	532	..	..	..	..	..	..
15. **Bhimbar Tehsil**	21,023	19,601	1,708	1,328	..	..	1,051	869	..	..	..	..	..	..

Tehsil.	Musalman. Males.	Musalman. Females.	Christian. Males.	Christian. Females.	Others. Males.	Others. Females.	Number of Literate Persons. 0—15 Males.	0—15 Females.	15—20 Males.	15—20 Females.	20 and over Males.	20 and over Females.
1	16	17	18	19	20	21	22	23	24	25	26	27
Kashmir State ..	**1,345,946**	**1,202,546**	**888**	**747**	**173**	**152**	**7,681**	**829**	**7,660**	**561**	**52,880**	**2,617**
I—Jammu Province	**514,442**	**475,180**	**662**	**545**	**116**	**103**	**4,272**	**570**	**3,999**	**405**	**26,485**	**1,730**
Jammu District	**71,242**	**59,479**	**573**	**467**	**116**	**103**	**2,242**	**313**	**1,967**	**220**	**8,458**	**634**
Jammu City	5,463	3,538	259	219	..	..	841	275	769	196	3,559	530
Jammu Tehsil	17,296	13,756	27	6	1	..	201	15	215	9	1,829	45
Karlup Ilaqa	171	109	..	..	..	..	..	..	..	..	..	..
General Sir Raja Sahib's Jagir in Jammu.	492	373	..	..	..	..	..	..	..	..	..	..
1. **Total Jammu Tehsil** ..	**23,422**	**17,776**	**286**	**225**	..	..	**1,042**	**290**	**984**	**205**	**5,388**	**575**
Samba Tehsil	13,242	12,459	1	..	14	13	798	6	668	5	782	8
General Raja Sahib's *Jagir* ..	122	134	..	..	..	..	..	..	..	..	..	..
2. **Total Samba Tehsil**	**13,364**	**12,573**	**1**	..	**14**	**13**	**798**	**6**	**668**	**5**	**782**	**8**
3. Sri Ranbir Singhpura Tehsil ..	21,107	17,328	286	242	90	79	303	5	225	9	1,364	20
4. Akhnur Tehsil	13,349	11,802	..	..	11	11	99	12	90	1	924	31
Kathua District	**20,099**	**16,204**	**79**	**67**	..	..	**296**	**30**	**439**	**4**	**3,616**	**62**
5. Kathua Tehsil	7,627	5,830	79	67	..	..	102	19	128	2	892	26
6. Jasmergarh Tehsil	7,110	5,639	..	..	..	..	69	6	104	1	839	20
7. Basohli Tehsil	5,362	4,735	..	..	..	..	125	5	207	1	1,885	16
Udhampur District	**45,792**	**39,462**	**1**	**1**	..	..	**339**	**28**	**294**	**16**	**3,540**	**100**
Udhampur Tehsil	4,966	3,565	1	1	..	..	153	25	78	7	1,406	58
Chaneni Jagir	805	568	..	..	..	..	9	..	17	..	174	..
8. **Total Udhampur Tehsil** ..	**5,771**	**4,133**	**1**	**1**	..	..	**162**	**25**	**95**	**7**	**1,580**	**58**
9. Kishtwar Tehsil	14,038	12,502	..	..	..	..	54	..	78	..	432	..
10. Ramban "	22,965	20,154	..	..	..	..	34	3	38	5	598	17
11. Ramnagar "	3,018	2,673	..	..	..	..	89	..	82	4	930	25
Riasi District	**76,380**	**67,815**	..	..	..	..	**163**	**40**	**183**	**49**	**2,298**	**549**
12. Riasi Tehsil	26,697	23,884	..	..	..	..	94	15	68	14	1,120	33
13. Rampur Rajauri Tehsil ..	49,683	43,931	..	..	..	..	69	25	115	35	1,178	516
Mirpur District	**128,222**	**129,519**	**3**	**3**	..	..	**555**	**99**	**535**	**68**	**4,671**	**227**
14. Kotli Tehsil	42,856	42,938	..	..	..	..	73	6	106	4	1,000	27
15. **Bhimbar Tehsil**	43,173	42,495	..	..	..	..	237	2	183	4	1,829	27

16. **Mirpur Tehsil**	2,606	2,259	271	280	..	..	859	816	2	3	..	..	..	..	42,193	44,086	3	3	..	..	245	91	246	60	1,842	173
Bahadarwah *Jagir*	11,384	11,177	1	2	..	..	5	4	..	..	..	..	..	..	7,836	7,204	1	..	..	..	203	1	117	..	856	7
Punch Ilaqa	10,919	9,845	32	19	..	..	5,520	5,065	1	..	..	..	..	..	164,871	155,497	5	7	..	..	474	59	464	48	3,046	151
Haveli Tehsil	2,215	1,723	32	19	..	..	1,008	883	1	..	..	..	..	..	47,778	41,887	2	6	..	..	204	41	201	30	1,150	88
Mahendar ,, ...	1,895	1,628	..	..	..	..	12[illegible]	91	..	..	..	..	..	..	41,470	38,039	..	..	..	..	84	7	80	7	464	13
Bagh	936	817	..	..	..	..	2,986	2,851	..	..	..	..	..	..	38,445	37,848	..	..	..	..	62	5	83	6	693	22
Sadhnoti	5,873	5,677	..	..	..	..	1,401	1,840	..	..	..	..	..	..	37,178	37,723	3	1	..	..	124	6	100	5	739	28
II—Kashmir Province	**36,582**	**27,873**	**21**	**8**	..	..	**9,316**	**8,426**	**1**	..	**2**	..	**2**	..	**711,664**	**612,739**	**179**	**162**	**57**	**49**	**3,257**	**244**	**3,394**	**138**	**23,521**	**793**
Kashmir Valley	33,880	26,183	21	8	..	..	4,557	3,977	1	..	2	..	2	..	603,449	518,456	175	160	57	49	2,938	210	3,081	117	20,581	576
Kashmir North	**6,242**	**4,129**	..	..	..	..	**2,779**	**2,553**	1	..	..	..	..	..	**260,608**	**226,072**	**19**	**14**	**36**	**37**	**413**	**46**	**604**	**29**	**5,189**	**142**
Uttarmachipura Tehsil ..	2,245	1,548	..	..	..	..	1,082	1,011	1	..	..	..	..	..	102,929	90,425	2	1	..	..	160	25	230	12	1,961	57
Langet Jagir	321	232	..	..	..	..	9	5	..	..	..	..	..	..	11,770	10,244	..	..	..	..	6	..	14	2	152	4
17. **Total Uttarmachipura Tehsil** ..	**2,566**	**1,780**	..	..	..	..	**1,091**	**1,016**	**1**	..	..	..	..	..	**114,699**	**100,669**	**2**	**1**	..	..	**166**	**25**	**244**	**14**	**2,113**	**61**
Barmula Tehsil	2,542	1,541	..	..	..	..	976	753	..	..	..	..	..	..	68,220	58,629	15	11	..	..	190	18	265	14	2,121	74
Jagir Natipura	2	..	..	..	..	..	..	..	..	..	..	..	..	..	373	334	..	..	..	..	..	..	..	..	..	..
18. **Total Baramula Tehsil** ..	**2,544**	**1,541**	..	..	..	..	**976**	**753**	..	..	..	..	..	..	**68,593**	**58,563**	**15**	**11**	..	..	**190**	**18**	**265**	**14**	**2,121**	**74**
Sri Partapsinghpura Tahsil ..	1,120	800	..	..	..	..	712	784	..	..	..	..	..	..	76,501	65,762	2	2	36	37	97	3	95	1	955	7
Jagir Natipura	12	8	..	..	..	..	..	..	..	..	..	..	..	..	815	678	..	..	..	..	..	..	..	..	..	..
19. **Total Sri Partapsinghpura Tahsil**	**1,132**	**808**	..	..	..	..	**712**	**784**	..	..	..	..	..	..	**77,316**	**66,440**	**2**	**2**	**36**	**37**	**97**	**3**	**95**	**1**	**955**	**7**
Kashmir South	**27,638**	**22,054**	**21**	**8**	..	..	**1,778**	**1,424**	..	..	**2**	..	**2**	..	**342,841**	**292,384**	**156**	**146**	**21**	**12**	**2,485**	**164**	**2,477**	**88**	**15,392**	**434**
Tehsil Khas	1,402	932	2	1	..	..	62	31	..	..	1	..	..	..	52,635	45,305	23	37	21	11	121	12	116	11	809	54
Srinagar City	16,515	12,489	13	..	..	..	361	180	..	..	1	..	2	..	59,579	51,356	133	105	..	1	1,673	107	1,695	44	8,665	270
20. **Total Tahsil Khas**	**17,917**	**14,421**	**15**	**1**	..	..	**423**	**211**	..	..	**2**	..	**2**	..	**112,214**	**96,661**	**156**	**142**	**21**	**12**	**1,794**	**119**	**1,711**	**55**	**9,534**	**324**
21. Awantipura Tehsil	2,193	1,753	6	7	..	..	876	797	..	..	..	..	..	..	70,566	58,446	..	..	..	..	105	9	144	6	1,523	24
22. Kulgam ,, ...	3,001	2,309	..	..	..	..	84	75	..	..	..	..	..	..	70,423	60,689	..	..	..	..	153	10	254	9	1,816	37
23. Ananlnag,, ...	4,527	3,571	..	..	..	..	395	341	..	..	..	..	..	..	89,638	76,588	..	4	..	..	433	26	368	18	2,519	49
Muzaffarabad District ..	**2,702**	**1,695**	..	..	..	..	**4,759**	**4,449**	..	..	..	..	..	..	**108,215**	**94,283**	**4**	**2**	..	..	**319**	**34**	**313**	**21**	**2,940**	**217**
24. Karnah Tehsil ..	109	38	..	..	..	..	181	142	..	..	..	..	..	..	25,098	21,868	1	..	..	..	26	5	32	2	399	10
25. Muzaffarabad ,, ..	1,850	1,193	..	..	..	..	3,269	3,270	..	..	..	..	..	..	50,467	43,978	3	1	..	..	165	13	191	7	1,622	176
26. Uri ,, ,, ..	743	464	..	..	..	..	1,309	1,037	..	..	..	..	..	..	32,650	28,437	..	1	..	..	128	16	90	12	919	31
III—Frontier Districts	**1,066**	**133**	**27**	**15**	..	..	**89**	**49**	..	..	**18,610**	**18,631**	..	..	**119,840**	**118,627**	**47**	**39**	..	..	**152**	**15**	**257**	**18**	**2,874**	**94**
Ladakh District	**185**	**83**	**16**	**9**	..	..	**30**	**18**	..	..	**18,610**	**18,631**	..	..	**72,380**	**73,444**	**37**	**33**	..	..	**104**	**5**	**165**	**10**	**2,116**	**62**
Ladakh Tehsil	40	13	..	..	..	..	1	..	..	..	14,702	14,650	..	..	1,689	1,667	37	33	..	..	48	1	59	4	1,120	39
Man-ar village	..	..	..	..	..	..	..	..	..	..	..	..	..	..	87	73	..	..	..	..	..	..	..	..	..	..
27. **Total Ladakh Tahsil** ..	**40**	**13**	..	..	..	..	**1**	..	..	..	**14,762**	**14,650**	..	..	**1,776**	**1,740**	**37**	**33**	..	..	**48**	**1**	**59**	**4**	**1,120**	**39**
28. Skardu Tahsil	88	32	14	8	..	..	19	9	..	..	57	..	..	..	51,344	51,124	..	..	..	..	28	3	77	3	583	15
29. Kargil ,, ...	57	38	2	1	..	..	10	9	..	..	3,791	3,981	..	..	19,2[illegible]0	20,580	..	..	..	..	28	1	29	3	413	8
Gilgit District	**665**	**46**	**11**	**6**	..	..	**46**	**23**	..	..	..	..	..	..	**15,149**	**12,745**	**9**	**6**	..	..	**48**	**10**	**102**	**8**	**758**	**32**
30. Gilgit Tehsil	665	46	11	6	..	..	46	23	..	..	..	..	..	..	15,149	12,745	9	6	..	..	48	10	102	8	758	32
Frontier Ilaqas	**216**	**4**	..	..	..	..	13	8	..	..	..	..	..	..	32,311	28,438	1	..	..	..	..	..	..	..	..	..
Chilas	113	2	..	..	..	..	11	4	..	..	..	..	..	..	7,055	5,949	1	..	..	..	..	..	..	..	..	..
Nagar	..	..	..	..	..	..	..	..	..	..	..	..	..	..	7,704	6,484	..	..	..	..	..	..	..	..	..	..
Hunza	..	..	..	..	..	..	..	..	..	..	..	..	..	..	6,473	5,644	..	..	..	..	..	..	..	..	..	..
Punial	1	..	..	..	..	..	2	4	..	..	..	..	..	..	2,894	2,591	..	..	..	..	..	..	..	..	..	..
Ishkoman	..	..	..	..	..	..	..	..	..	..	..	..	..	..	1,410	1,343	..	..	..	..	..	..	..	..	..	..
Yasin	..	..	..	..	..	..	..	..	..	..	..	..	..	..	3,710	3,355	..	..	..	..	..	..	..	..	..	..
Kuh	101	2	..	..	..	..	..	..	..	..	..	..	..	..	1,128	1,057	..	..	..	..	..	..	..	..	..	..
Ghizar	1	..	..	..	..	..	..	..	..	..	..	..	..	..	1,957	2,015	..	..	..	..	..	..	..	..	..	..
Total Yasin	102	2	..	..	..	..	..	..	..	..	..	..	..	..	6,775	6,427	..	..	..	..	..	..	..	..	..	..